55⁰⁰

Novels
for Students

for Novels Students

Presenting Analysis, Context and Criticism on Commonly Studied Novels

Volume 3

Diane Telgen and Kevin Hile, Editors

Carol Jago, Santa Monica High School, Advisor
Kathleen Pasquantonio, Novi High School, Advisor

Foreword by Anne Devereaux Jordan, Teaching and Learning Literature

GALE

DETROIT · NEW YORK · LONDON

Novels for Students

Staff

Series Editors: Diane Telgen and Kevin S. Hile.

Contributing Editors: Marilyn Allen, Linda R. Andres, Sheryl Ciccarelli, Alan Hedblad, Melissa Hill, Motoko Fujishiro Huthwaite, Arlene M. Johnson, Paul Loeber, Thomas F. McMahon, Crystal A. Towns, and Stephen Thor Tschirhart.

Managing Editor: Joyce Nakamura.

Research: Victoria B. Cariappa, *Research Team Manager*. Andy Malonis, *Research Specialist*. Julia C. Daniel, Tamara C. Nott, Tracie A. Richardson, and Cheryl L. Warnock, *Research Associates*. Jeffrey Daniels, *Research Assistant*.

Permissions: Susan M. Trosky, *Permissions Manager*. Maria L. Franklin, *Permissions Specialist*. Edna M. Hedblad and Michele M. Lonoconus, *Permissions Associates*.

Production: Mary Beth Trimper, *Production Director*. Evi Seoud, *Assistant Production Manager*. Deborah Milliken, *Production Assistant*.

Graphic Services: Randy Bassett, *Image Database Supervisor*. Robert Duncan and Michael Logusz, *Imaging Specialists*. Pamela A. Reed, *Photography Coordinator*. Gary Leach, *Macintosh Artist*.

Product Design: Cynthia Baldwin, *Product Design Manager*. Cover Design: Michelle DiMercurio, *Art Director*. Page Design: Pamela A. E. Galbreath, *Senior Art Director*.

Table of Contents

The Informed Dialogue: Interacting with Literature

When we pick up a book, we usually do so with the anticipation of pleasure. We hope that by entering the time and place of the novel and sharing the thoughts and actions of the characters, we will find enjoyment. Unfortunately, this is often not the case; we are disappointed. But we should ask, has the author failed us, or have we failed the author?

We establish a dialogue with the author, the book, and with ourselves when we read. Consciously and unconsciously, we ask questions: "Why did the author write this book?" "Why did the author choose that time, place, or character?" "How did the author achieve that effect?" "Why did the character act that way?" "Would I act in the same way?" The answers we receive depend upon how much information about literature in general and about that book specifically we ourselves bring to our reading.

Young children have limited life and literary experiences. Being young, children frequently do not know how to go about exploring a book, nor sometimes, even know the questions to ask of a book. The books they read help them answer questions, the author often coming right out and *telling* young readers the things they are learning or are expected to learn. The perennial classic, *The Little Engine That Could, tells* its readers that, among other things, it is good to help others and bring happiness:

> "Hurray, hurray," cried the funny little clown and all the dolls and toys. "The good little boys and girls in

the city will be happy because you helped us, kind, Little Blue Engine."

In picture books, messages are often blatant and simple, the dialogue between the author and reader one-sided. Young children are concerned with the end result of a book—the enjoyment gained, the lesson learned—rather than with how that result was obtained. As we grow older and read further, however, we question more. We come to expect that the world within the book will closely mirror the concerns of our world, and that the author will *show* these through the events, descriptions, and conversations within the story, rather than *telling* of them. We are now expected to do the interpreting, carry on our share of the dialogue with the book and author, and glean not only the author's message, but comprehend how that message and the overall affect of the book were achieved. Sometimes, however, we need help to do these things. *Novels for Students* provides that help.

A novel is made up of many parts interacting to create a coherent whole. In reading a novel, the more obvious features can be easily spotted—theme, characters, plot—but we may overlook the more subtle elements that greatly influence how the novel is perceived by the reader: viewpoint, mood and tone, symbolism, or the use of humor. By focusing on both the obvious and more subtle literary elements within a novel, *Novels for Students* aids readers in both analyzing for message and in determining how and why that message is communicated. In the discussion on Harper Lee's *To*

Kill a Mockingbird (Vol. 2), for example, the mockingbird as a symbol of innocence is dealt with, among other things, as is the importance of Lee's use of humor which "enlivens a serious plot, adds depth to the characterization, and creates a sense of familiarity and universality." The reader comes to understand the internal elements of each novel discussed—as well as the external influences that help shape it.

"The desire to write greatly," Harold Bloom of Yale University says, "is the desire to be elsewhere, in a time and place of one's own, in an originality that must compound with inheritance, with an anxiety of influence." A writer seeks to create a unique world within a story, but although it is unique, it is not disconnected from our own world. It speaks to us *because* of what the writer brings to the writing from our world: how he or she was raised and educated; his or her likes and dislikes; the events occurring in the real world at the time of the writing, and while the author was growing up. When we know what an author has brought to his or her work, we gain a greater insight into both the "originality" (the world of the book), and the things that "compound" it. This insight enables us to question that created world and find answers more readily. By informing ourselves, we are able to establish a more effective dialogue with both book and author.

Novels for Students, in addition to providing a plot summary and descriptive list of characters—to remind readers of what they have read—also explores the external influences that shaped each book. Each entry includes a discussion of the author's background, and the historical context in which the novel was written. It is vital to know, for instance, that when Ray Bradbury was writing *Fahrenheit 451* (Vol. 1), the threat of Nazi domination had recently ended in Europe, and the McCarthy hearings were taking place in Washington, D.C. This information goes far in answering the question, "Why did he write a story of oppressive government control and book burning?" Similarly, it is important to know that Harper Lee, author of *To Kill a Mockingbird,* was born and raised in Mon-

roeville, Alabama, and that her father was a lawyer. Readers can now see why she chose the south as a setting for her novel—it is the place with which she was most familiar—and start to comprehend her characters and their actions.

Novels for Students helps readers find the answers they seek when they establish a dialogue with a particular novel. It also aids in the posing of questions by providing the opinions and interpretations of various critics and reviewers, broadening that dialogue. Some reviewers of *To Kill A Mockingbird,* for example, "faulted the novel's climax as melodramatic." This statement leads readers to ask, "Is it, indeed, melodramatic?" "If not, why did some reviewers see it as such?" "If it is, why did Lee choose to make it melodramatic?" "Is melodrama ever justified?" By being spurred to ask these questions, readers not only learn more about the book and its writer, but about the nature of writing itself.

The literature included for discussion in *Novels for Students* has been chosen because it has something vital to say to us. *Of Mice and Men, Catch-22, The Joy Luck Club, My Antonia, A Separate Peace* and the other novels here speak of life and modern sensibility. In addition to their individual, specific messages of prejudice, power, love or hate, living and dying, however, they and all great literature also share a common intent. They force us to *think*—about life, literature, and about others, not just about ourselves. They pry us from the narrow confines of our minds and thrust us outward to confront the world of books and the larger, real world we all share. *Novels for Students* helps us in this confrontation by providing the means of enriching our conversation with literature and the world, by creating an *informed* dialogue, one that brings true pleasure to the personal act of reading.

Sources

Harold Bloom, *The Western Canon, The Books and School of the Ages,* Riverhead Books, 1994.

Watty Piper, *The Little Engine That Could,* Platt & Munk, 1930.

Anne Devereaux Jordan
Senior Editor, *TALL*
(*Teaching and Learning Literature*)

Introduction

Purpose of the Book

The purpose of *Novels for Students* (*NfS*) is to provide readers with a guide to understanding, enjoying, and studying novels by giving them easy access to information about the work. Part of Gale's "For Students" Literature line, *NfS* is specifically designed to meet the curricular needs of high school and undergraduate college students and their teachers, as well as the interests of general readers and researchers considering specific novels. While each volume contains entries on "classic" novels frequently studied in classrooms, there are also entries containing hard-to-find information on contemporary novels, including works by multicultural, international, and women novelists.

The information covered in each entry includes an introduction to the novel and the novel's author; a plot summary, to help readers unravel and understand the events in a novel; descriptions of important characters, including explanation of a given character's role in the novel as well as discussion about that character's relationship to other characters in the novel; analysis of important themes in the novel; and an explanation of important literary techniques and movements as they are demonstrated in the novel.

In addition to this material, which helps the readers analyze the novel itself, students are also provided with important information on the literary and historical background informing each work. This includes a historical context essay, a box comparing the time or place the novel was written to modern Western culture, a critical overview essay, and excerpts from critical essays on the novel. A unique feature of *NfS* is a specially commissioned overview essay on each novel by an academic expert, targeted toward the student reader.

To further aid the student in studying and enjoying each novel, information on media adaptations is provided, as well as reading suggestions for works of fiction and nonfiction on similar themes and topics. Classroom aids include ideas for research papers and lists of critical sources that provide additional material on the novel.

Selection Criteria

The titles for each volume of *NfS* were selected by surveying numerous sources on teaching literature and analyzing course curricula for various school districts. Some of the sources surveyed included: literature anthologies; *Reading Lists for College-Bound Students: The Books Most Recommended by America's Top Colleges;* textbooks on teaching the novel; a College Board survey of novels commonly studied in high schools; a National Council of Teachers of English (NCTE) survey of novels commonly studied in high schools; the NCTE's *Teaching Literature in High School: The Novel;* and the Young Adult Library Services Association (YALSA) list of best books for young adults of the past twenty-five years.

Input was also solicited from our expert advisory board, as well as educators from various areas. From these discussions, it was determined that each volume should have a mix of "classic" novels (those works commonly taught in literature classes) and contemporary novels for which information is often hard to find. Because of the interest in expanding the canon of literature, an emphasis was also placed on including works by international, multicultural, and women authors. Our advisory board members—current high school teachers—helped pare down the list for each volume. If a work was not selected for the present volume, it was often noted as a possibility for a future volume. As always, the editor welcomes suggestions for titles to be included in future volumes.

How Each Entry Is Organized

Each entry, or chapter, in *NfS* focuses on one novel. Each entry heading lists the full name of the novel, the author's name, and the date of the novel's publication. The following elements are contained in each entry:

- **Introduction:** a brief overview of the novel which provides information about its first appearance, its literary standing, any controversies surrounding the work, and major conflicts or themes within the work.

- **Author Biography:** this section includes basic facts about the author's life, and focuses on events and times in the author's life that inspired the novel in question.

- **Plot Summary:** a description of the major events in the novel, with interpretation of how these events help articulate the novel's themes. Lengthy summaries are broken down with subheads.

- **Characters:** an alphabetical listing of major characters in the novel. Each character name is followed by a brief to an extensive description of the character's role in the novel, as well as discussion of the character's actions, relationships, and possible motivation.

  Characters are listed alphabetically by last name. If a character is unnamed—for instance, the narrator in *Invisible Man*—the character is listed and alphabetized as "Narrator." If a character's first name is the only one given, the name will appear alphabetically by that name.

  Variant names are also included for each character. Thus, the full name "Jean Louise Finch" would head the listing for the narrator of *To Kill a Mockingbird*, but listed in a separate cross-reference would be the nickname "Scout Finch."

- **Themes:** a thorough overview of how the major topics, themes, and issues are addressed within the novel. Each theme discussed appears in a separate subhead, and is easily accessed through the boldface entries in the Subject/Theme Index.

- **Style:** this section addresses important style elements of the novel, such as setting, point of view, and narration; important literary devices used, such as imagery, foreshadowing, symbolism; and, if applicable, genres to which the work might have belonged, such as Gothicism or Romanticism. Literary terms are explained within the entry, but can also be found in the Glossary.

- **Historical and Cultural Context:** This section outlines the social, political, and cultural climate *in which the author lived and the novel was created.* This section may include descriptions of related historical events, pertinent aspects of daily life in the culture, and the artistic and literary sensibilities of the time in which the work was written. If the novel is a historical work, information regarding the time in which the novel is set is also included. Each section is broken down with helpful subheads.

- **Critical Overview:** this section provides background on the critical reputation of the novel, including bannings or any other public controversies surrounding the work. For older works, this section includes a history of how novel was first received and how perceptions of it may have changed over the years; for more recent novels, direct quotes from early reviews may also be included.

- **Sources:** an alphabetical list of critical material quoted in the entry, with full bibliographical information.

- **For Further Study:** an alphabetical list of other critical sources which may prove useful for the student. Includes full bibliographical information and a brief annotation.

- **Criticism:** an essay commissioned by *NfS* which specifically deals with the novel and is written specifically for the student audience, as well as excerpts from previously published criticism on the work.

In addition, each entry contains the following highlighted sections, set apart from the main text as sidebars:

- **Media Adaptations:** a list of important film and television adaptations of the novel, including source information. The list also includes stage adaptations, audio recordings, musical adaptations, etc.

- **Compare and Contrast Box:** an "at-a-glance" comparison of the cultural and historical differences between the author's time and culture and late twentieth-century Western culture. This box includes pertinent parallels between the major scientific, political, and cultural movements of the time or place the novel was written, the time or place the novel was set (if a historical work), and modern Western culture. Works written after the mid-1970s may not have this box.

- **What Do I Read Next?:** a list of works that might complement the featured novel or serve as a contrast to it. This includes works by the same author and others, works of fiction and nonfiction, and works from various genres, cultures, and eras.

- **Study Questions:** a list of potential study questions or research topics dealing with the novel. This section includes questions related to other disciplines the student may be studying, such as American history, world history, science, math, government, business, geography, economics, psychology, etc.

Other Features

NfS includes "The Informed Dialogue: Interacting with Literature," a foreword by Anne Devereaux Jordan, Senior Editor for *Teaching and Learning Literature (TALL)*, and a founder of the Children's Literature Association. This essay provides an enlightening look at how readers interact with literature and how *Novels for Students* can help teachers show students how to enrich their own reading experiences.

A Cumulative Author/Title Index lists the authors and titles covered in each volume of the *NfS* series.

A Cumulative Nationality/Ethnicity Index breaks down the authors and titles covered in each volume of the *NfS* series by nationality and ethnicity.

A Subject/Theme Index, specific to each volume, provides easy reference for users who may be studying a particular subject or theme rather than a single work. Significant subjects from events to broad themes are included, and the entries pointing to the specific theme discussions in each entry are indicated in **boldface**.

Each entry has several illustrations, including photos of the author, stills from film adaptations (when available), maps, and/or photos of key historical events.

Citing Novels for Students

When writing papers, students who quote directly from any volume of *Novels for Students* may use the following general forms. These examples are based on MLA style; teachers may request that students adhere to a different style, so the following examples may be adapted as needed.

When citing text from *NfS* that is not attributed to a particular author (i.e., the Themes, Style, Historical Context sections, etc.), the following format should be used in the bibliography section:

"The Adventures of Huckleberry Finn." *Novels for Students*. Ed. Diane Telgen. Vol. 1. Detroit: Gale, 1997. 8–9.

When quoting the specially commissioned essay from *NfS* (usually the first piece under the "Criticism" subhead), the following format should be used:

James, Pearl. Essay on "The Adventures of Huckleberry Finn." *Novels for Students*. Ed. Diane Telgen. Vol. 1. Detroit: Gale, 1997. 8–9.

When quoting a journal or newspaper essay that is reprinted in a volume of *NfS*, the following form may be used:

Butler, Robert J. "The Quest for Pure Motion in Richard Wright's *Black Boy*." *MELUS* 10, No. 3 (Fall, 1983), 5–17; excerpted and reprinted in *Novels for Students*, Vol. 1, ed. Diane Telgen (Detroit: Gale, 1997), pp. 61–64.

When quoting material reprinted from a book that appears in a volume of *NfS*, the following form may be used:

Adams, Timothy Dow. "Richard Wright: 'Wearing the Mask,'" in *Telling Lies in Modern American Autobiography* (University of North Carolina Press, 1990), 69–83; excerpted and reprinted in *Novels for Students*, Vol. 1, ed. Diane Telgen (Detroit: Gale, 1997), pp. 59–61.

We Welcome Your Suggestions

The editor of *Novels for Students* welcomes your comments and ideas. Readers who wish to suggest novels to appear in future volumes, or who have other suggestions, are cordially invited to contact the editor. You may contact the editor via e-mail at: **CYA@gale.com**. Or write to the editor at:

Editor, *Novels for Students*
Gale Research
835 Penobscot Bldg.
645 Griswold St.
Detroit, MI 48226-4094

Literary Chronology

1000: The only existing manuscript of *Beowulf,* an old English epic poem composed sometime between c. 675 A.D. and c. 1000 A.D., is transcribed in approximately the year 1000. The poem served as the inspiration for John Gardner's novel *Grendel.*

1821: Fyodor Mikhaylovich Dostoyevsky was born on October 30, 1821, in Moscow, Russia, at a Hospital for the Poor, where his father was a doctor.

1840: Thomas Hardy was born June 2, 1840, at Higher Bockhampton, Dorset, England. His father, Thomas, was a builder and mason, and his mother, Jemima Hand, was a cook and servant-maid.

1850: Kate Chopin was born Catherine O'Flaherty on February 8, 1850 (other sources say July 12, 1850, and February 8, 1851), in St. Louis, Missouri.

1866: Fyodor Dostoyevsky began work on *Prestupleniye i nakazaniye* (*Crime and Punishment*) in 1865, and it was serialized in the *Russky vestnik* (*Russian Herald*) in 1866.

1879: E. M. Forster was born January 1, 1879, in London, England. His father, Edward, died when the boy was a year old, and he wasa raised by his mother, Alice.

1881: Fyodor Dostoyevsky died on January 28, 1881, in St. Petersburg after suffering from a lung hemorrhage.

1891: Thomas Hardy's *Tess of the d'Urbervilles: A Pure Woman Faithfully Presented* was first published serially in *Graphic* in 1891, and published in a three-volume edition that same year by Osgood, McIlvaine Company. Hardy's novel outraged many Victorian critics, because Tess's actions jarred with the Victorian's strict code of morality for women.

1899: Kate Chopin's *The Awakening* was published on April 22, 1899, and generated negative literary and personal criticism toward her.

1903: Zora Neale Hurston was born on January 7, 1903 (other sources range from 1891 to 1902), in Eatonville, Florida. Her father, John, was a carpenter and Baptist preacher and her mother, Lucy Potts, was a former school teacher.

1903: Alan Paton was born on January 11, 1903, in Pietermaritzburg, Natal, South Africa.

1903: George Orwell was born Eric Arthur Blair on June 25, 1903, in Bengal, India, son of a British civil servant. He came to England as a toddler.

1904: Kate Chopin died on August 22, 1904, in St. Louis, Missouri, of a brain hemorrhage.

1919: E. M. Forster did not mention the Amritsar Massacre of 1919 or Mohandas K. Gandhi, who began a long nonviolent campaign against British rule in that year, in his novel *A Passage to India*, but he does discuss in detail the division between India's Hindus and Moslems.

1922: Kurt Vonnegut, Jr., was born on November 11, 1922, to Kurt and Edith Lieber Vonnegut in Indianapolis, Indiana.

1924: E. M. Forster began *A Passage to India* in 1913. The novel was published in 1924 and was received very favorably in both England and America. Although *A Passage to India* was not written during the Edwardian period, it is considered an Edwardian novel, since Forster's outlook was developed during the first decade of the twentieth century.

1925: Mary Flannery O'Connor was born March 25, 1925, in Savannah, Georgia, to Edward Francis and Regina (née Cline) O'Connor.

1928: Thomas Hardy died January 11, 1928, in Dorchester, Dorset, England. His ashes are buried in Poets' Corner of Westminster Abbey, and his heart is buried in the grave of his first wife in Stinsford, Dorset, England.

1933: John (Champlin) Gardner, Jr., was born on July 21, 1933, in Batavia, New York. His parents are John Champlin Gardner, a farmer and lay preacher, and Priscilla (née Jones) Gardner, an English teacher.

1934: Joan Didion was born December 5, 1934, in Sacramento, California, to Frank Reese and Eduene (née Jerrett) Didion.

1935: Joy Kogawa was born in Vancouver, Canada, on June 6, 1935 to Lois (Yao) and Reverend Gordon Goichi Nakayama.

1937: Lois Lowry was born March 20, 1937, in Honolulu, Hawaii, to Robert E. and Katharine (Landis) Hammersberg.

1937: Zora Neale Hurston wrote *Their Eyes Were Watching God* in seven weeks. It was published by Lippincott on September 18, 1937.

1941: After Japan's bombing of Pearl Harbor on December 7, North Americans of Japanese descent are looked upon with suspicion. The Canadian government's internment of its own citizens is related in Joy Kogawa's novel *Obasan*.

1945: Michael Dorris was born January 30, 1945, in Louisville, Kentucky (some sources show Dayton, Washington, as his birthplace), to Jim and Mary Besy (née Burkhardt) Dorris.

1945: Kurt Vonnegut, Jr., was captured by the Germans at the Battle of the Bulge; he witnessed the Allied firebombing of Dresden, Germany, on February 13, 1945.

1945: George Orwell's *Animal Farm* satirized the Union of Soviet Socialist Republics, and since the U.S.S.R. was an ally of Great Britain, the publishing of Orwell's novel was delayed until after World War II ended.

1948: The Afrikaner Nationalists establish an apartheid government in South Africa. Apartheid was a country-wide policy that allowed the legal discrimination on the basis of race. Alan Paton's *Cry, the Beloved Country* addressed this inequality.

1948: Alan Paton began writing *Cry, the Beloved Country* in 1946 while he was in Trondheim, Norway; it was published in New York in 1948.

1949: Alan Paton won the Ainsfield-Wolf Award for *Cry, the Beloved Country*. The award recognizes authors whose books contribute to the betterment of race relations or to a clearer understanding of the problems of racism.

1949: Jamaica Kincaid was born Elaine Potter Richardson on the island of Antigua, May 25, 1949.

1950: George Orwell died of pulmonary tuberculosis on January 21, 1950.

1952: Flannery O'Connor's first novel, *Wise Blood*, was published by Harcourt.

1960: Zora Neale Hurston died of hypertensive heart disease on January 28, 1960, in the St. Lucie County Welfare Home. She was buried in an unmarked grave in the Garden of Heavenly Rest, Fort Pierce, Florida. Author Alice Walker discovered and marked her grave in August, 1973.

1960: Kaye Gibbons was born in 1960 in Nash County, North Carolina.

1964: Flannery O'Connor died August 3, 1964, in Atlanta, Georgia, of lupus-related kidney failure.

1969: Kurt Vonnegut, Jr., gave a complete treatise on the World War II bombing of Dresden in *Slaughterhouse-Five,* published by Delacorte in 1969.

1970: E. M. Forster died of a stroke June 7, 1970, at the home of Bob and May Buckingham in Coventry, England.

1971: John Gardner's *Grendel* was published by Knopf in 1971.

1975: The South Vietnamese capital of Saigon falls to Communist forces. The American evacuation of Saigon serves as a central event in Joan Didion's *Democracy*.

1981: Joy Kogawa's *Obasan*, the first novel to address the problem of Canadian internment of Japanese citizens during and after World War II, was published by Doubleday in 1981. It won both the Books in Canada First Novel Award and the Canadian Authors' Association Book of the Year Award.

1982: John Gardner died on September 14, 1982, of injuries sustained in a motorcycle accident.

1984: Joan Didion's *Democracy* was published by Simon & Schuster in 1984.

1985: Jamaica Kincaid's *Annie John*, a young girl's coming-of-age story set in Antigua, was published in 1985 by Farrar, Straus & Giroux.

1987: North Carolina native Kaye Gibbons had her first novel, *Ellen Foster,* published in 1987.

1987: Michael Dorris's *A Yellow Raft in Blue Water,* published in 1987 by Holt, describes the complex lives of three Native American women from three different perspectives.

1988: Alan Paton died of throat cancer on April 12, 1988, in Botha's Hill, Natal, South Africa.

1993: Lois Lowry's *The Giver* is published by Houghton.

1994: Lois Lowry's *The Giver* wins the Newbery Medal, given annually by the American Library Association for the year's "most distinguished contribution to literature for children."

1997: Michael Dorris died April 11, 1997, in Concord, New Hampshire. His death was an apparent suicide.

Acknowledgments

The editors wish to thank the copyright holders of the excerpted criticism included in this volume and the permissions managers of many book and magazine publishing companies for assisting us in securing reproduction rights. We are also grateful to the staffs of the Detroit Public Library, the Library of Congress, the University of Detroit Mercy Library, Wayne State University Purdy/Kresge Library Complex, and the University of Michigan Libraries for making their resources available to us. Following is a list of the copyright holders who have granted us permission to reproduce material in this volume of *NFS*. Every effort has been made to trace copyright, but if omissions have been made, please let us know.

COPYRIGHTED EXCERPTS IN *NFS*, VOLUME 3, WERE REPRODUCED FROM THE FOLLOWING PERIODICALS:

American Literature, v. 56, May, 1984. Copyright © 1984 Duke University Press, Durham, NC. Reproduced by permission.

The Centennial Review, v. XX, Summer, 1976 for "Time, Uncertainty, and Kurt Vonnegut, Jr.," by Charles B. Harris. © 1976 by *The Centennial Review.* Reproduced by permission of the publisher and the author.

Critique: Studies in Modern Fiction, v. XX, 1978. Copyright © 1978 Helen Dwight Reid Educational Foundation. Reproduced with permission of the Helen Dwight Reid Educational Foundation,

published by Heldref Publications, 119 18th Street, N. W., Washington, DC 20036–1802.

The Horn Book Magazine, v. LXIX, November-December, 1993; v. LXX, July-August, 1994. Copyright, 1993, 1994, by The Horn Book, Inc., 11 Beacon St., Suite 1000, Boston, MA 02108. All rights reserved. Both reproduced by permission.

Los Angeles Times Book Review, July 11, 1982. Copyright, 1982, *Los Angeles Times.* Reproduced by permission.

The Mississippi Quarterly, v. XXIII, Spring, 1970. Copyright 1970 Mississippi State University. Reproduced by permission.

Modern Language Studies, v. XIX, Summer, 1989 for "From Face Value to the Value in Faces: 'Wise Blood,' and the Limits of Literalism" by Gary M. Ciuba. Reproduced by permission of the publisher and the author.

The New York Review of Books, v. XXXI, May 10, 1984. Copyright © 1984 Nyrev, Inc. Reproduced with permission from *The New York Review of Books.*

Prairie Schooner, v. 63, Fall, 1989. © 1989 by University of Nebraska Press. Reproduced from *Prairie Schooner* by permission of the University of Nebraska Press.

Radical Teacher, v. 9, September, 1978. Reproduced by permission.

Research Studies, v. 42, September, 1974 for "Pilgrim's Dilemma: 'Slaughterhouse-Five'" by

David L. Vanderwerken. Reproduced by permission of the author.

South Atlantic Review, v. 48, January, 1983. Copyright © 1983 by the South Atlantic Modern Language Association. Reproduced by permission.

The Southern Literary Journal, v. XVII, Spring, 1985. Copyright 1985 by the Department of English, University of North Carolina at Chapel Hill. Reproduced by permission.

The Southern Quarterly, v. 30, Winter-Spring, 1992. Copyright © 1992 by the University of Southern Mississippi. Reproduced by permission.

VLS, v. 34, April, 1985 for "Up from Eden" by Jacqueline Austin. Copyright © V. V. Publishing Corporation.

Women's Studies: An Interdisciplinary Journal, v. 13, 1986. © Gordon and Breach Science Publishers. Reproduced by permission.

COPYRIGHTED EXCERPTS IN *NFS,* **VOLUME 3, WERE REPRODUCED FROM THE FOLLOWING BOOKS:**

Brander, Laurence. From ***George Orwell.*** Longmans, Green and Co., 1954. Reproduced by permission of Addison Wesley Longman.

Callan, Edward. From ***Alan Paton.*** Revised edition. Twayne Publishers, 1982. Copyright © 1982 by G. K. Hall & Co. All rights reserved. Excerpted with permission of Twayne Publishers, an imprint of Simon & Schuster Macmillan.

Cheung, King-Kok. From "Attentive Silences in Joy Kogawa's 'Obasan'," in ***Articulate Silences: Hisaye Yamamoto, Maxine Hong Kingston, Joy Kogawa.*** Cornell, 1993. Copyright © 1993 by Cornell University. All rights reserved. Reproduced by permission of the publisher, Cornell University Press. All additional uses of this material—including, but not limited to, photocopying and reprinting—are prohibited without the prior written approval of Cornell University Press.

Greenblatt, Stephen. From ***Three Modern Satirists: Waugh, Orwell, and Huxley.*** Yale University Press, 1965. Copyright © 1965 by Yale University. All rights reserved. Reproduced by permission of the author.

Hinde, Thomas. From "Accident and Coincidence in Tess of the D'Urbervilles," in ***The Genius of Thomas Hardy.*** Edited by Margaret Drabble. Knopf, 1976. Copyright © 1976 by George Weidenfeld and Nicolson Ltd. All rights reserved. Reproduced by permission of the author.

Leatherbarrow, William J. From ***Fedor Dostoevsky.*** Twayne Publishers, 1981. Copyright © 1981 by G. K. Hall & Co. All rights reserved. Excerpted with permission of Twayne Publishers, an imprint of Simon & Schuster Macmillan.

Miller, J. Hillis. From ***Fiction and Repetition: Seven English Novels.*** Cambridge, Mass.: Harvard University Press, 1982. Copyright © 1982 by J. Hillis Miller. All rights reserved. Excerpted by permission of the publishers. In the British Commonwealth by Basil Blackwell, Ltd.

Nagel, James. From "Desperate Hopes, Desperate Lives: Depression and Self-Realization in Jamaica Kincaid's 'Annie John' and 'Lucy'," in ***Traditions, Voices, and Dreams: The American Novel Since the 1960s.*** Edited by Melvin J. Friedman and Ben Siegel. University of Delaware Press, 1995. © 1995 by Associated University Presses, Inc. All rights reserved. Reproduced by permission.

Owens, Louis. From ***Other Destinies: Understanding the American Indian Novel.*** University of Oklahoma Press, 1992. Copyright © 1992 by the University of Oklahoma Press. All rights reserved. Reproduced by permission.

Stout, Janis P. From "Joan Didion and the Presence of Absence," in ***Strategies of Reticence: Silence and Meaning in the Works of Jane Austen, Willa Cather, Katherine Anne Porter and Joan Didion.*** Edited by Sharon Felton. University Press of Virginia, 1990. Reproduced with permissions of The University Press of Virginia.

PHOTOGRAPHS AND ILLUSTRATIONS APPEARING IN *NFS,* **VOLUME 3, WERE REPRODUCED FROM THE FOLLOWING SOURCES:**

AP/WIDE WORLD PHOTOS: Antiguan girl carrying water jug, photograph. AP/Wide World Photos, Inc. Reproduced by permission. —Dorris, Michael, photograph. AP/Wide World Photos, Inc. Reproduced by permission. —Hurston, Zora Neale, photograph. AP/Wide World Photos, Inc. Reproduced by permission. —Orwell, George, photograph. AP/Wide World Photos, Inc. Reproduced by permission. —Peter and Paul Fortress, photograph. AP/Wide World Photos, Inc. Reproduced by permission. —Vonnegut, Kurt, photograph. AP/Wide World Photos, Inc. Reproduced by permission.

ARCHIVE PHOTOS: Dostoevsky, Fyodor, photograph. Archive Photos, Inc. Reproduced by permission. —Forster, E. M., photograph. Archive Photos, Inc. Reproduced by permission. —Kevorkian, Jack (with Geoffrey Feiger), photograph. Archive Photos, Inc. Reproduced by permission. —Lorre, Peter, in the film "Crime and Punishment," photograph. Archive Photos, Inc. Reproduced by permission. —Paton, Alan, photograph. Archive Photos, Inc. Reproduced by permission. —Women marching for the right to vote, photograph. Archive Photos, Inc./Hackett Collection. Reproduced by permission.

JERRY BAUER: Didion, Joan, photograph by Jerry Bauer. © Jerry Bauer. Reproduced by permission. —Gibbons, Kaye, photograph by Jerry Bauer. © Jerry Bauer. Reproduced by permission. —Kinkaid, Jamaica, photograph by Jerry Bauer. © Jerry Bauer. Reproduced by permission.

CANAPRESS PHOTO SERVICE: Japanese-Canadians protesting for compensation for World War II internment, photograph. Canapress Photo Service, 1988. Reproduced by permission.

CORBIS-BETTMANN: Hardy, Thomas, photograph. Corbis-Bettmann. Reproduced by permission. —Mondale, Walter, with Ronald Reagan at presidential debate in Louisville, Kentucky, October 7, 1984, photograph. Corbis-Bettmann. Reproduced by permission. —Neoclassical building in the French Quarter, New Orleans, photograph. Corbis-Bettmann. Reproduced by permission. —O'Connor, Flannery, photograph. Corbis-Bettmann. Reproduced by permission. —Stalin, Joseph, photograph. Corbis-Bettmann. Reproduced by permission.

GEORGIA CURRY: Headstone on grave of Zora Neale Hurston, photograph by Georgia Curry.

GALE RESEARCH: Antigua, map. Gale Research.

THE GLOBE AND MAIL, TORONTO: Kogawa, Joy, 1992, photograph by Randy Velocci. The Globe and Mail, Toronto. Reproduced by permission. —Uprooting of Japanese Canadians, Vancouver, 1942 train shot, photograph. The Globe and Mail, Toronto. Reproduced by permission.

HALLMARK HALL OF FAME: Harris, Julie, with Jena Malone, in a scene from "Ellen Foster," photograph. Hallmark Hall of Fame. Reproduced by permission.

HENRY HOLT AND COMPANY: Robbins, Ken, illustrator. From a jacket of *A Yellow Raft in Blue Water*, by Michael Dorris. Henry Holt and company, Inc. Jacket design copyright © 1987 by Henry Holt and Company, Inc. Reproduced by permission of Ken Robbins.

HOUGHTON MIFFLIN COMPANY: Lowry, Lois, photographer. From a cover of *The Giver*, by Lois Lowry. Houghton Mifflin Company, 1993. Jacket photograph © 1993 by Lois Lowry. Reproduced by permission of Houghton Mifflin Company.

THE KOBAL COLLECTION: Davis, Judy, and Nigel Havers in the film "A Passage to India," 1984, photograph. The Kobal Collection. Reproduced by permission. —Harris, Richard, with James Earl Jones in the film "Cry, the Beloved Country," photograph. The Kobal Collection. Reproduced by permission. —Kinski, Nastassia, and Peter Firth in the film "Tess," photograph. The Kobal Collection. Reproduced by permission. —Pig from animated film "Animal Farm," photograph. The Kobal Collection. Reproduced by permission. —Sacks, Michael, in the 1972 motion picture "Slaughterhouse Five," photograph. The Kobal Collection. Reproduced by permission.

MISSOURI HISTORICAL SOCIETY: Chopin, Kate, photograph. Missouri Historical Society. Reproduced by permission.

LUFTI OZKOK: Gardner, John, photograph by Lutfi Ozkok. Reproduced by permission.

AMANDA SMITH: Lowry, Lois, photograph by Amanda Smith. Reproduced by permission of Lois Lowry.

UPI/CORBIS-BETTMANN: 5th Avenue and 135th street, Harlem, New York, 1927, photograph. UPI/Corbis-Bettmann. Reproduced by permission. —Black South Africans outside shacks in slum of Sofiatown, 1954, Johannesburg, South Africa, photograph. UPI/Corbis-Bettmann. Reproduced by permission. —Ceremonies commemorating Battle of Little Big Horn, photograph. UPI/Corbis-Bettmann. Reproduced by permission. —Demonstration at Grant Park, photograph. UPI/Corbis-Bettmann. Reproduced by permission. —Evacuation plane boarding, Nha Traing, S. Vietnam, photograph. UPI/Corbis-Bettmann. Reproduced by permission. —Gandhi, Mahatma, and Shrimah Sorojini Naidu, photograph. UPI/Corbis-Bettmann. Reproduced by permission. —Lafata, Lorraine, writing down "House Rules" at Safe House in Ann Arbor, Michigan, photograph. UPI/Corbis-Bettmann. Reproduced by permission. —Men among the ruins of Dresden, 1946, Germany, photograph. UPI/Corbis-Bettmann. Reproduced by permission. —Presnell, Tom, photograph. UPI/Corbis-Bettmann. Reproduced by permission.

SALLY WEIGAND: Dorset, England, photograph by Sally Weigand. © 1989. Reproduced by permission of Sally Weigand.

Contributors

Betsy Currier Beacom: Freelance writer, North Haven, CT. Entry on *Ellen Foster.*

Robert Bennett: Doctoral candidate in English Literature, University of California at Santa Barbara. Original essay on *Yellow Raft in Blue Water.*

Anne Boyd: Doctoral candidate in American Studies, Purdue University. Entry on *Their Eyes Were Watching God.*

Julian Connolly: Professor of Slavic Languages and Literatures, University of Virginia. Original essay on *Crime and Punishment.*

F. Brett Cox: Assistant professor of English, Gordon College, Barnesville, GA. Entry and original essay on *Slaughterhouse-Five.*

Sharon Cumberland: Assistant professor of English, Seattle University. Original essay on *Cry, the Beloved Country.*

Lynn Domina: Doctoral candidate in English, State University of New York—Stony Brook; instructor, Hofstra University. Original essay on *Their Eyes Were Watching God.*

John Drexel: Freelance writer and editor, Glen Ridge, NJ. Entries on *Crime and Punishment* and *A Passage to India.*

Anthony Dykema-VanderArk: Doctoral candidate in English, Michigan State University. Original essay on *Obasan.*

Darren Felty: Visiting instructor, College of Charleston (SC); Ph.D. in Literature, University of Georgia. Original essay on *Annie John.*

Kathleen Fitzpatrick: Doctoral candidate in English and American Literature, New York University. Original essay on *Animal Farm.*

Scott Gillam: Freelance writer, New York, NY. Entries on *Grendel* and *Yellow Raft in Blue Water.*

Marian Gonsior: Freelance writer, Westland, MI. Entries on *Animal Farm* and *Tess of the d'Urbervilles.*

Suzanne D. Green: Doctoral candidate in English, University of North Texas. Coauthor of *Kate Chopin: An Annotated Bibliography of Critical Works.* Original essay on *The Awakening.*

Diane Andrews Henningfeld: Professor of English, Adrian College (MI). Original essays on *Grendel* and *Ellen Foster.*

Jeremy W. Hubbell: Freelance writer, Minneapolis, MN. Entries on *Annie John, Cry, the Beloved Country,* and *Obasan.*

Jeffrey M. Lilburn: Writer and translator specializing in twentieth-century American and Canadian literature; M.A., University of Western Ontario. Original essays on *A Passage to India* and *Wise Blood.*

Elyse Lord: Doctoral candidate in English, University of Utah; visiting instructor, University of

Utah and Salt Lake City Community College. Original essay on *The Giver*.

Nancy C. McClure: Educational consultant and freelance writer, Clarksburg, WV; Ed.D., West Virginia University. Entries on *The Awakening* and *Wise Blood*.

Wendy Perkins: Assistant Professor of English, Prince George's Community College, Maryland; Ph.D. in English, University of Delaware. Original essay on *Democracy*.

Michael Thorn: Freelance writer, East Sussex, England; author of literary biographies and study guides. Entries on *Democracy* and *The Giver*.

Stan Walker: Doctoral candidate in English, University of Texas at Austin. Original essay on *Tess of the d'Urbervilles*.

Donna Woodford: Doctoral candidate, Washington University, St. Louis, MO. Original essay on *Ellen Foster*.

Animal Farm

George Orwell
1945

When *Animal Farm* was published in 1945, its British author George Orwell (a pseudonym for Eric Arthur Blair) had already waited a year and a half to see his manuscript in print. Because the book criticized the Soviet Union, one of England's allies in World War II, publication was delayed until the war ended. It was an immediate success as the first edition sold out in a month, nine foreign editions had appeared by the next year, and the American Book-of-the-Month Club edition sold more than a half-million copies. Although Orwell was an experienced columnist and essayist as well as the author of nine published books, nothing could have prepared him for the success of this short novel, so brief he had considered self-publishing it as a pamphlet. The novel brought together important themes—politics, truth, and class conflict—that had concerned Orwell for much of his life. Using allegory—the weapon used by political satirists of the past, including Voltaire and Swift—Orwell made his political statement in a twentieth-century fable that could be read as an entertaining story about animals or, on a deeper level, a savage attack on the misuse of political power. While Orwell wrote *Animal Farm* as a pointed criticism of Stalinist Russia, reviews of the book on the fiftieth-anniversary of its publication declared its message to be still relevant. In a play on the famous line from the book, "Some animals are more equal than others," an *Economist* reviewer wrote, "Some classics are more equal than others," and as proof he noted that *Animal Farm* has never been out of

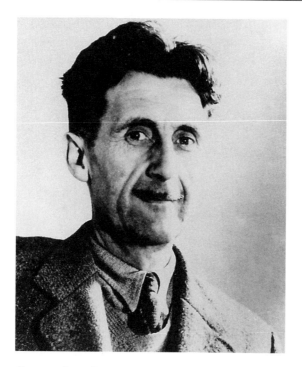

George Orwell

print since it was first published and continues to sell well year after year.

Author Biography

George Orwell was born Eric Arthur Blair in Bengal, India, in 1903, into a family that had to struggle to make ends meet. The son of a British civil servant, Orwell was brought to England as a toddler. The boy became aware of class distinctions while attending St. Cyprian's preparatory school in Sussex, where he received a fine education but felt out of place. He was teased and looked down upon because he was not from a wealthy family. This experience made him sensitive to the cruelty of social snobbery. As a partial-scholarship student whose parents could not afford to pay his entire tuition, Orwell was also regularly reminded of his lowly economic status by school administrators. Conditions improved at Eton, where he studied next, but instead of continuing with university classes, in 1922 he joined the Indian Imperial Police. Stationed in Burma, his class-consciousness intensified as he served as one of the hated policemen enforcing British control of the native population. Sickened by his role as imperialist, he re-

turned to England in 1927 and resigned his position. He planned to become a writer, a profession in which he had not before shown much interest.

In 1928, perhaps to erase guilt from his colonial experiences, he chose to live amongst the poor of London, and later, Paris. In Paris, he published articles in local newspapers, but his fiction was rejected. His own life finally provided the material for his first book, published in 1933. *Down and Out in Paris and London,* which combined fictional narrative based on his time spent in those two cities with social criticism, was his first work published as George Orwell. The pseudonym was used so his parents would not be shocked by the brutal living conditions described in the book. The next year, Orwell published *Burmese Days,* a novel based on his stay in Burma. Subsequent novels, including *A Clergyman's Daughter, Keep the Aspidistra Flying* and *Coming Up for Air,* all contain autobiographical references and served as vehicles for Orwell to explore his growing political convictions.

In 1936, Orwell traveled to Barcelona, Spain, to write about the Spanish Civil War and ended up joining the battle, fighting against Spanish leader Francisco Franco on the side of the Republicans. Wounded, he returned to England. Two nonfiction books, *The Road to Wigan Pier,* a report on deplorable conditions in the mining communities of northern England, and *Homage to Catalonia,* the story of his participation in the Spanish Civil War, allowed Orwell to explicitly defend his political ideas. Dozens of pointed essays also revealed his political viewpoint.

By that time, Orwell clearly saw himself as a political performer whose tool was writing. He wrote in a 1946 essay, "Why I Write," that "every line of serious work that I have written since 1936 has been written, directly or indirectly, *against* totalitarianism and *for* democratic socialism, as I understand it."

Orwell's next book, *Animal Farm,* a fable about the events during and following the Russian Revolution, was well liked by critics and the public. He had had trouble finding a publisher during World War II because the work was a disguised criticism of Russia, England's ally at the time. When it was finally published, just after the war, it was a smashing success.

The money Orwell made from *Animal Farm* allowed him, in 1947, to rent a house on Jura, an island off the coast of Scotland, where he began to work on *1984.* His work was interrupted by treatment for tuberculosis, which he had contracted in the 1930s, and upon his release from the hospital in 1948 Orwell returned to Jura to complete the book. Under doctor's orders to work no more than one hour a day, but unable to find a typist to travel to his home, he typed the manuscript himself and collapsed upon completion of the book. For the next two years he was bedridden. Many critics claim that Orwell's failing health may have influenced him to make *1984* so pessimistic, and Orwell admitted that they were probably right.

Orwell did plan to write other books, according to his friends, and married while in the hospital, but three months later in 1950 he finally died of tuberculosis.

Plot Summary

Chapter I

As *Animal Farm* opens, Mr. Jones, the owner of Manor Farm, is drunkenly heading to bed. The animals gather in the barn as Old Major, the prize boar, tells them that he has thought about the brutal lives that the farm animals lead under human bondage and is convinced that a rebellion must come soon, in which the animals throw off the tyranny of their human oppressors and come to live in perfect freedom and equality. Major teaches the animals *Beasts of England,* a song which will become their revolutionary anthem.

Chapter II

A few days later, Major dies. The animals, under the leadership of the pigs, begin to prepare for the Rebellion. Two of the pigs, Snowball and Napoleon, elaborate Major's ideas into a complete system of thought known as Animalism. The Rebellion comes much sooner than anyone thought, and the animals break free of Jones's tyranny and drive the humans from the farm. Snowball and Napoleon paint over the name "Manor Farm" on the gate, replacing it with "Animal Farm." They also paint the basic principles of Animalism on the wall of the barn:

THE SEVEN COMMANDMENTS

1. *Whatever goes upon two legs is an enemy.*

2. *Whatever goes upon four legs, or has wings, is a friend.*

3. *No animal shall wear clothes.*

4. *No animal shall sleep in a bed.*

5. *No animal shall drink alcohol.*

6. *No animal shall kill any other animal.*

7. *All animals are equal.*

Chapter III

The farm passes through an idyllic time in which the animals work joyously together and make a great success of the harvest. The animals all attend weekly planning meetings at which the decisions for the future of the farm are made. After realizing that some of the other animals cannot read or remember the Seven Commandments, Snowball boils these commandments down to a single maxim: "Four legs good, two legs bad." But all of the milk and apples on the farm, it seems, are now to be reserved for the pigs alone.

Chapter IV

News of the Rebellion at Animal Farm begins to spread, and animals across the countryside are singing *Beasts of England.* The neighboring farmers, led by Mr. Pilkington of Foxwood and Mr. Frederick of Pinchfield Farm, attempt to retake Animal Farm by force. The animals, led by Snowball, successfully fight off the invaders in what comes to be known as the Battle of the Cowshed. Snowball is decorated as an Animal Hero, First Class.

Chapter V

Snowball and Napoleon fight a number of battles over policy, culminating in the controversy over a windmill which Snowball has designed and thinks should be built on the farm. Napoleon argues that the animals need to concentrate on food production. As the debate reaches fever pitch, Napoleon calls in nine dogs which he raised to be loyal only to him. The dogs chase Snowball from the farm. Napoleon declares an end to the planning meetings. Squealer, another pig who serves as Napoleon's functionary, convinces the other animals that Snowball was a criminal. A few days later, Napoleon declares that the windmill will be built after all, and Squealer explains that the idea had belonged to Napoleon from the beginning, but that Snowball had stolen the plans.

Chapter VI

The animals' workload is repeatedly increased throughout the following year as construction begins on the windmill. Napoleon announces that the farm will begin trading with the neighboring farms, which seems to violate one of the early resolutions passed by the animals, but Squealer convinces them otherwise. The pigs, moreover, have moved into the farmhouse, and it is rumored that they are sleeping in the beds. The animals check the barn wall, vaguely remembering an injunction against this—but the commandment says that "No animal shall sleep in a bed *with sheets.*" When the windmill is knocked down during a storm, Napoleon blames its destruction on Snowball and pronounces a death sentence on this traitor. The animals begin the laborious process of rebuilding.

Chapter VII

Rumors begin to fly that Snowball is sneaking into the farm at night, causing small bits of mischief. Moreover, it is asserted that certain of the animals on the farm are in league with Snowball. Napoleon orders a full investigation. A meeting is held in which the animals are invited to confess their connections with Snowball. All the animals that do confess are promptly ripped to pieces by Napoleon's dogs. The others are shocked at such bloodshed and try to comfort themselves by singing *Beasts of England,* only to be told that the song has now been abolished.

Chapter VIII

In the days after the purges, the animals seem to recall a commandment prohibiting the killing of animals, but when they check the barn wall, they discover that it reads "No animal shall kill any other animal *without cause.*" Napoleon bargains to sell Mr. Pilkington a pile of timber. The animals do not trust Pilkington, but they prefer him to Frederick, who, it is whispered, is torturing his animals; in fact, Napoleon declares Frederick to be an enemy of the farm. But several days later it is announced that he has sold the timber to Frederick, and now Pilkington is the enemy. Frederick fools Napoleon by giving him forged banknotes for the timber, and, with a group of men, attacks Animal Farm and destroys the windmill. Squealer, however, informs the animals that the battle was a victory for the animals. Shortly after, the pigs discover a case of whiskey in the basement of the farmhouse, and a raucous celebration is heard throughout the night. The next day, it is announced that Napoleon is near death. When he recovers, the animals discover that the commandment which they thought said that no animal should drink alcohol in fact reads "No animal shall drink alcohol *to excess.*"

Chapter IX

That winter, rations are repeatedly reduced on the farm, for everyone but the pigs. The animals are kept content, however, through an ever-increasing number of formal ceremonies. An old carthorse, Boxer, who has worked tirelessly for Animal Farm, suddenly takes ill. Napoleon announces that arrangements have been made to treat Boxer in a hospital in town. However, the truck that arrives to take Boxer away belongs to a horse slaughterer, and the animals erupt in a great outcry. They are pacified by Squealer, who tells them that, in fact, the truck has been purchased by the veterinarian but has not been repainted.

Chapter X

The years pass, and the animals lead harder and harder lives, though at least no animal is lorded over by a human. Then, one day, Napoleon emerges from the house on two legs. The sheep's traditional chant of "Four legs good, two legs bad" has now, somehow, been changed to "Four legs good, two legs better." And the Seven Commandments have now all been erased from the barn wall and replaced with a single Commandment: "All animals are equal, but some animals are more equal than others." The pigs begin reading newspapers, wearing clothes, and carrying whips in the fields. They call for a meeting between themselves and the human owners of the surrounding farms, at which Napoleon announces that the name of Animal Farm has been changed back to Manor Farm. The other animals peek in the windows of the farmhouse as this meeting progresses and are stunned to discover that they cannot tell the difference between the men and the pigs at all.

Characters

Benjamin

Benjamin, a donkey, is "the oldest animal on the farm, and the worst tempered." He is a sad cynic who believes that whatever the animals do, conditions on the farm will remain equally as bad. Although he usually refuses to read, he is the one who reads the side of the truck that comes to take Boxer away and realizes it belongs to the horse slaughterer. Benjamin is moved to action, but he is too late to save his friend. Benjamin represents the cynical intellectual who refuses to get involved in politics and so fails to affect meaningful change. His cynicism is much like Orwell's own attitude toward life.

Boxer

One of the two cart-horses on the farm, Boxer's biggest triumph is his work on the windmill. Despite his strength, he is sensitive to the feelings of others. During the Battle of the Cowshed, when he accidentally stuns a stable-boy with blows from his hoofs, he is remorseful: "I have no wish to take life, not even human life." Boxer has such blind faith in Napoleon that he refuses to question anything the pig says, reasoning, "If Comrade Napoleon says it, it must be right." He constantly repeats the slogans: "I will work harder" and "Napoleon is always right." In the end, once Boxer's health fails and he is no longer able to work, Napoleon sends him to the horse slaughterer. In Orwell's tale, he represents the common working class who unwittingly accept their base existence, because they believe by hard work they will get ahead and that their leaders will protect them. Boxer's lung trouble seems to refer to Orwell's own bouts with tuberculosis.

Clover

A "stout, motherly mare," Clover is one of the two cart-horses on the farm, and one of Boxer's closest friends. She tries to lead the other animals to see events as they really are but is often frustrated in her attempts. She questions the change in the fourth commandment of Animalism, yet she accepts Squealer's explanation of why it seems different. When Benjamin sounds the alarm that Boxer is being taken to the horse slaughterer, Clover runs after the van but is unable to stop it. Like Boxer, she represents the working class, particularly those who should realize they are being exploited but do not because of their own laziness or apathy.

Mr. Frederick

Mr. Frederick is a neighbor of Mr. Jones who runs the farm called Pinchfield. His farm is better run than Pilkington's, but he is always involved in law suits. In Orwell's allegory, Frederick represents Germany and its leader, Adolf Hitler. Like Hitler, Frederick is treacherous, and after signing an agreement with Napoleon he attacks Animal Farm, destroying the animals' windmill.

Mr. Jones

Mr. Jones, the owner of Manor Farm, gets the animals thinking about revolution when he gets drunk and is unable to perform all of the chores around the farm. When, in his drunkenness, he stays overnight away from the farm, and neither he nor his men feed the farm animals, the animals revolt and chase the humans out of the farm. Jones tries to retake the farm but is unsuccessful. He vanishes "to another part of the country" and dies there in "an inebriates' home." With his common surname Jones could be any farmer, and his farm any farm. In Orwell's political allegory, he represents

Media Adaptations

- *Animal Farm* was adapted as a film by John Halas and Joy Batchelor and released in 1955.

- *Animal Farm* was also adapted by Nelson Slade Bond for a play of the same title, Samuel French, 1964.

Nicholas II, the last tsar of Russia, before the communists took over the government.

Minimus

Described only as "a poet," Minimus composes a poem in honor of Napoleon, and a patriotic song that replaces *Beasts of England*. Minimus represents artists who are used by totalitarian states for propaganda purposes.

Mollie

A vain white mare whose main concerns when Old Major calls for a Rebellion are having sugar lumps to chew and ribbons for her mane. She eventually flees the farm to work for humans. She represents those whose lust for material things blinds them to the importance of freedom.

Moses

A tame raven who belongs to Mr. Jones, Moses represents organized religion. He is tolerated by the pigs because he takes the animals' minds off their troubles by preaching to them about a happy land called the Sugarcandy Mountain.

Muriel

A white goat (named after an actual animal that Orwell kept at his farm), Muriel reads better than most of the other animals and is called on to read the Commandments for them.

Napoleon

A "large, rather fierce-looking Berkshire boar," Napoleon becomes the leader of the animals after Snowball is chased off the farm. He, Snowball, and Squealer are the ones who organize the thoughts proclaimed by Old Major into the principles of An-

A still from the 1955 animated version of Orwell's Animal Farm.

imalism. Soon after the revolt of the animals, Napoleon takes nine puppies from their mothers to "educate" them. The puppies end up being his personal bodyguards and secret police force. He grows increasingly removed from the other animals, dining alone and being addressed as "our Leader, Comrade Napoleon." Like Joseph Stalin, the Soviet leader who had negotiated with England while making a secret deal with Hitler, Napoleon negotiates with one of Jones's neighbors, Mr. Pilkington, while making a secret agreement with Mr. Frederick, another one of Jones's neighbors. Stalin had a reputation for arranging the death of anyone who stood in his way. After Napoleon chases his former friend Snowball off the farm, he has countless animals killed who confess to being Snowball's allies. Near the end of the novel, he stands on two legs, just like the men he had previously denounced, and announces that Animal Farm's name will revert back to Manor Farm. His name is reminiscent of the historical Napoleon, who became the all-powerful, autocratic Emperor of the French. Like his French counterpart, Napoleon seems to embody the idea that with power comes corruption.

Old Major

A "prize Middle White boar," Old Major calls the animals together in the novel's opening scene to explain to them his vision of a world ruled by animals. Although quite old for a pig, he is described as "still a majestic-looking pig." He concludes his speech by teaching of the animals the song, *Beasts of England*. It becomes the rallying cry of the Rebellion. Three nights after the meeting he dies in his sleep. He represents Karl Marx, the German political philosopher who wrote, with Friedrich Engels, the *Communist Manifesto* (1848) that called the workers of the world to unite against the ruling classes.

Mr. Pilkington

Mr. Pilkington is a neighbor of Mr. Jones who runs the farm called Foxwood. His farm is overgrown with woodland, for he enjoys hunting and fishing over farming. In Orwell's allegory, Pilkington represents England.

Sheep

The sheep function as a group and, therefore, have no individual names. They are taught to bleat the latest slogan for hours at a time: first, "four legs good, two legs bad," later, "four legs good, two legs *better*." They are the "yes-men" in every society who blindly repeat party slogans without knowing what they are saying.

Snowball

A "young boar" who, with Napoleon and Squealer, helps to codify Old Major's ideas into the commandments of Animalism. Orwell describes him as "quicker in speech and more inventive" than Napoleon. He is the one who organizes the animals into various committees: "the Egg Production Committee for the hens, the Clean Tails League for the cows, ... the Whiter Wool Movement for the sheep, and various others...." He also plans the defense of the farm against the humans which proves useful when Jones and his friends try to retake the farm. Snowball shows his expert use of military strategy during the attack—which becomes known as the Battle of the Cowshed—and is later awarded a medal. Snowball also comes up with the idea of building a windmill to produce electricity. He represents the historical figure of Leon Trotsky. Like Trotsky, who was exiled from Russia by his former partner Stalin, Snowball is eventually run off the farm by Napoleon. After he is gone, Napoleon uses him as a scapegoat, blaming him for everything that goes wrong on the farm. In an allegory of the bloody purge trials that took place in the Soviet Union during the 1930s, the animals confess to scheming in various ways with Snowball for the downfall of the other pigs. Whoever confesses is slaughtered.

Squealer

"A small, fat pig" known for being a smooth talker, Squealer reportedly "could turn black into white." He is the propaganda chief for the pigs, the equivalent of the Soviet party newspaper *Pravda* (which means "Truth" in Russian) in Orwell's allegory. Squealer has an explanation for everything, including why the pigs need to drink the milk the cows produce, why the commandments of Animalism seem different, and why the "ambulance" called to take Boxer to the hospital has a sign for a horse slaughterer on its side. By the story's end, he is so fat that his eyes are mere slits. Always on the look out for a new slogan, he teaches the sheep a new song to explain why the pigs are suddenly walking on their hind legs. Like any good propaganda boss, he is able to not only explain the present, he is also an expert at rewriting the past. He makes the animals believe, for example, that Snowball never had received the order of "Animal Hero, First Class." But, of course, he had.

Mr. Whymper

An attorney, Mr. Whymper handles negotiations between the pigs and the outside world. He represents an intermediary between warring countries who is only too happy to do what is expedient without thinking about whether it is right.

Themes

Language and Meaning

In *Animal Farm,* his allegory of the Soviet Revolution, Orwell examines the use of language and the subversion of the meaning of words by showing how the powerful manipulate words for their own benefit. As a journalist, Orwell knew the power of words to serve whichever side the writer backed. In the novel, Snowball is a quick talker who can always explain his way out of any situation. When the birds object to the maxim, "Four legs good, two legs bad," that the pig teaches the sheep, he explains that the bird's wing "is an organ of propulsion and not of manipulation. It should therefore be regarded as a leg." The birds do not really understand this explanation, but they accept it. Orwell particularly comments on the abuse of language with his character Squealer, "a brilliant talker," who acts as an unofficial head of propaganda for the pigs. Like Joseph Goebbels, who bore the title of Nazi party minister of propaganda and national enlightenment during World War II, Squealer "could turn black into white." This is also reminiscent of the official newspaper of the Communist Party of the Soviet Union, *Pravda,* which was often used to rewrite the past. (Ironically, its title means "Truth.") When a bad winter forces a reduction in food rations to the animals, Squealer calls it a "readjustment." In a totalitarian state, language can be used to change even the past. Squealer explains to the animals "that Snowball had never—as many of them had believed hitherto—received the order of 'Animal Hero, First Class.'"

God and Religion

In the novel religion is represented by Moses, the tame raven. The clergy is presented as a privileged class tolerated by those in power because of their ability to placate the masses with promises of rewards in the afterlife for suffering endured on Earth. Moses is afforded special treatment not available to the other animals. For example, he is the only animal not present at the meeting called by Old Major as the book opens. Later, the reader is told the other animals hate the raven because he does not do any work; in fact, the pigs give him a

Topics for Further Study

- Research a current political scandal on the state, local, or national level, or one from the past (such as Watergate or Tammany Hall). Develop a brief animal allegory of the main figures involved, using some of the same animals found in Orwell's novel.

- Using examples from classic animal fables, report on how Orwell's novel conforms and/or deviates from features found in those you've investigated.

- Analyze how Squealer manipulates language to get the animals to go along with him, then watch the evening news or read periodicals to find similar uses of language in speeches or press releases from contemporary politicians.

---

daily ration of beer. Like Lenin, who proclaimed religion was the opiate of the people, Orwell sees organized religion as another corruptible institution which serves to keep the masses tranquil. Moses preaches "the existence of a mysterious country called Sugarcandy Mountain, to which all animals went when they died;" in that distant land "it was Sunday seven days a week, clover was in season all the year round, and lump sugar and linseed cake grew on the hedges."

Human Rights

In *Animal Farm,* Orwell comments on those who corrupt the idea of human rights by showing how the animals deal with the issue of equality. In chapter one, Old Major interrupts his speech appealing to the animals for a Rebellion against the humans by asking for a vote on whether "wild creatures, such as rats and rabbits" should be included in the statement "All animals are comrades." Although at this point, the animals vote to accept the rats, later distinctions between different types of animals become so commonplace that the seventh commandment of Animalism is officially changed to read, "All animals are equal, but some are more equal than others." A number of societies have historically "voted" that portions of their populations

were not equal because of their faith, their skin color, or their ancestry.

Class Conflict

Orwell saw firsthand how being a member of a lower class singled him out for abuse at St. Cyprian's, a school which attracted most of its students from the British upper class. He had also seen how the British ruling class in Burma had abused the native population. In *Animal Farm* the animals begin by proclaiming the equality of all animals. The classless society soon becomes divided as preferential treatment is given to the pigs. First, they alone are allowed to consume the milk and the apples which Squealer claims they do not really want to take, but must to preserve their strength. Later, the other animals are told that they must "stand aside" if they meet a pig coming down a path and that all pigs had "the privilege of wearing green ribbons on their tails on Sundays." By this time, not even an explanation from Squealer is necessary; the hierarchy in the society is well-established. A pointed remark by Mr. Pilkington of Foxwood, who represents Great Britain in Orwell's satire, puts the author's distaste for classes in perspective. When Mr. Pilkington and other farmers meet with Napoleon in the novel's last scene, Pilkington chokes with amusement as he says to the pigs, "If you have your lower animals to contend with, ... we have our lower classes." Orwell knew that with power came the abuse of power and only a vigilant citizenry could prevent such abuses.

Politics

Orwell uses *Animal Farm* to express his deeply held political convictions. He stated in his 1946 essay, "Why I Write," "every line of serious work that I have written since 1936 has been written, directly or indirectly, *against* totalitarianism and *for* Democratic socialism." Although the novel is written in direct response to his bitter disappointment that the Russian Revolution, instead of establishing a people's republic, established an essentially totalitarian state, its continued relevance is possible because his criticism stands against any and all totalitarian regimes. The only protection the average citizen has against a similar tyranny developing in his own country is his refusal to blindly follow the crowd (like the sheep), the repudiation of all spurious explanations by propaganda sources (like Squealer), and diligent attention to all government activity, instead of faithfully following those in power (like Boxer).

Truth and Falsehood

In the novel, the animals are often forced to examine the meaning of truth in their society. Again and again, truth becomes simply what Snowball, and later Squealer, tells them. Any questions about past events that do not seem to match the pigs' version of those events are either discounted or explained away. For example, when some of the animals are executed after they confess to various crimes against Napoleon, some of those left alive remember that the Sixth Commandment of Animalism was "No animal shall kill any other animal." When Clover asks Muriel to read the commandment, however, it is discovered that it reads, "No animal shall kill any other animal *without cause.*" "Somehow or other," the narrator comments, "the last two words had slipped out of the animals' memory." Similarly, when the pigs get into a case of whiskey and get drunk, Muriel looks up at the barn wall where the Seven Commandments had been written and sees that the Fifth Commandment reads, "No animal shall drink alcohol *to excess.* " She thinks the animals must have forgotten the last two words of this commandment as well. She comes to believe that the original event of the writing of the commandments on the wall did not happen the way she and other animals remember it. With this theme Orwell challenges the Soviet state's—and any totalitarian state's—method of controlling public opinion by manipulating the truth and, in particular, rewriting history.

Style

Point of View

The third person point of view traditionally used for fables and fairy tales is the one Orwell chooses for *Animal Farm,* his tale of an animal rebellion against humans in which the pigs become the powerful elite. The storyteller in this case, as is also typical of the fable, tells the reader only what is needed to follow the story and the bare minimum about each character, without overt commentary. Orwell focuses on the bewilderment of the simple beasts—the horses, birds, and sheep—in the face of their manipulation by the pigs, eliciting sympathy from the reader.

Setting

Animal Farm takes place at an unspecified time on a British farm near Willingdon, a town that is mentioned only in passing. The farm is first called Manor Farm, later renamed Animal Farm and, finally, Manor Farm once more. Manor—which can mean the land overseen by a lord, the house of a lord, or a mansion—associates the farm with the upper, or ruling, class. Orwell focuses entirely on activities taking place at the farm, except for a brief scene in Willingdon when Jones asks his neighbors to help him. By keeping a narrow focus, Orwell makes the location in England unimportant.

Narrator

The narrator in the novel functions as a storyteller, telling a fable. Orwell gives the fable ironic overtones by using a naive narrator, one who refuses to comment on events in the novel that the reader understands to be false. After Muriel tells Clover that the fourth commandment of Animalism reads, "No animal shall sleep in a bed *with sheets,* " the narrator declares: "Curiously enough, Clover had not remembered that the Fourth Commandment mentioned sheets; but as it was there on the wall, it must have done so." Both the reader and the narrator know the truth of the matter—that the words of the commandment have been changed—but the narrator does not admit it. The tension between what the narrator knows but does not say and what the reader knows is dramatic irony.

Dramatic Irony

With dramatic irony an audience, or reader, understands the difference between the truth of a situation and what the characters know about it, while the characters remain ignorant of the discrepancy. For instance, Squealer explains that the van in which Boxer was taken to the hospital formerly belonged to a horse slaughterer. He further explains that the veterinarian who now uses it did not have the time to paint over the horse slaughterer's sign on its side, so the animals should not worry. The narrator says: "The animals were enormously relieved to hear this." The reader, who assumed the truth when the van originally appeared to carry the horse away, feels doubly outraged by Squealer's explanation.

Fairy Tales

The fairy story, or fairy tale, is a type of folk literature found all over the world. It involves a highly imaginative narrative told in a simple manner easily understood and enjoyed even by children. While they do not have a moral, fairy tales instruct by placing their characters in situations that they have to overcome; children who hear the tales can imagine what they would do in a similar situation. Fairy tales, also, often involve animals that can talk. Orwell gave his work the subtitle "A Fairy Story." The reader can surmise that the story told in *Animal Farm* is universal, with implications for every culture or country, and that it will be easily understood. Using "fairy story" to describe his novel is another bit of irony, because the political story behind the tale is far from the light entertainment the term implies.

Satire

A work that uses humor to criticize a weakness or defect is called a satire. The satirist makes whatever he is criticizing look ridiculous by a variety of methods, often through irony or other types of biting humor. The satirist hopes to change the behavior he is satirizing. Orwell ridicules the so-called achievements of the Russian revolution in a number of ways: by comparing its proponents to animals, by developing irony through the use of the naive narrator, and by allowing each animal or group of animals to stand for one human trait or tendency that he criticizes.

Fable

A fable is a short, imaginative narrative, usually with animal characters, that illustrates a moral. The characters often embody a specific human trait, like jealousy, to make fun of humans who act similarly. Orwell uses details to make his animal characters seem like real animals: the cat vanishes for hours at a time; Molly the mare likes to have her nose stroked. The animals also represent human traits or characteristics: the pigs are selfish power-grabbers, the sheep are dim-witted "yes-men," and the horses are stouthearted workers. *Animal Farm,* like the traditional fable, is told in a simple, straightforward style.

Allegory

In an allegory, characters and events stand for something else. In this case, the characters in the novel stand for significant figures in twentieth-century Russian history. Orwell makes the characters easily identifiable for those who know the historic parallels, because he gives each one a trait, or has them perform certain tasks, that are like that of a historical figure. Old Major is identified with Karl Marx because, just as Old Major develops the teachings that fuel the Animal Rebellion, Marx formulated the ideas that spawned the Russian revolution. Napoleon and Snowball, both pigs, stand for Russian leaders Joseph Stalin and Leon Trotsky. Stalin and Trotsky had a falling out much like

Joseph Stalin, the Soviet leader who was the model for character of Napoleon in George Orwell's satire Animal Farm.

Napoleon and Snowball do. Events from history—the revolution itself and the Moscow purge trials of the 1930s—also appear in allegorical form in the novel.

Historical Context

Ever since Orwell wrote *Animal Farm* readers have enjoyed it as a simple animal story. While it is possible to read the book without being aware of the historical background in which Orwell wrote it, knowing the world's situation during the 1940s adds interest to the novel. The reader understands why the political implications of the book were so important to Orwell, and is encouraged to read the book again, looking for its less obvious political and societal references. As the date of the original publication of the work becomes more remote, the historical events that preceded it lose their immediacy, but Orwell's story remains viable. In fact, Orwell emphasized the universality and timelessness of his message by not setting the story in any particular era, and, while placing the farm in England, not making that fact important.

Compare
&
Contrast

- **1940s:** The first half of the decade is spent dealing with the hardships and turmoil caused by World War II; the second half, adjusting to a post-war economy and the new U.S. role as a world superpower.

  Today: Controversy erupts over a planned $100 million World War II memorial slated to be built on a 7.4 acre site on the National Mall in Washington, DC.

- **1940s:** The truth of rumors of Nazi atrocities during World War II were finally confirmed in 1945 as the Allied Armies liberated the remaining occupants of the Nazi death camps.

  Today: The World Jewish Congress and other organizations demand a full accounting for millions of dollars in gold and other valuables looted from Jews and others killed by the Nazis in World War II that remain in unclaimed Swiss bank accounts.

- **1940s:** President Franklin D. Roosevelt, British Prime Minister Winston Churchill, and Soviet Premier Joseph Stalin met at Tehran, Iran, and other locations to discuss war strategy.

  Today: After the collapse of the Soviet Union in 1991, U. S. presidents regularly meet with the president of Russia to discuss European security and strategic warhead stockpiles in both countries.

World War II

The target of Orwell's satire in *Animal Farm* was the Union of Soviet Socialist Republics (the U.S.S.R., or the Soviet Union), which at the time the work was written was a military ally of Great Britain during World War II. The book's publication was delayed until after fighting had ended on the war's European front in May 1945. When England declared war on Germany in September 1939, it would not have seemed likely that by the war's end England and the U.S.S.R. would be allies. Just a week before, the world community had been stunned by news of a Soviet-German nonaggression pact. Adolf Hitler and Joseph Stalin secretly worked out the agreement, while the Soviet leader publicly pursued an alliance with Great Britain and France against Germany. The pact called for the development of German and Russian spheres of interest in Eastern Europe and the division of Poland between the two countries. The world, which had for several years watched Germany's expansionist moves, was suddenly confronted with the Soviet Union sending troops into eastern Poland and several other bordering countries. In his book, *George Orwell: The Ethical Imagination,* Sant Singh Bal quotes Orwell on the situation: "Suddenly the scum of the earth and the bloodstained butcher of the workers (for so they had described one another) were marching arm in arm, their friendship 'cemented in blood,' as Stalin cheerily expressed it." Orwell portrays the Hitler-Stalin pact in his novel as the agreement between Mr. Frederick and Napoleon.

When the war began, Orwell and his wife were living in a 300-year-old cottage in Wallington, a rural community in southeastern England, where they raised animals and owned a store. When it appeared that Germany was preparing to invade England, the couple moved to London. Disappointed that he was unable to fight in the war against fascism, Orwell wanted to at least be in London where he might still be called on to defend his country. The German Air Force, or *Luftwaffe,* tried in vain to bring about England's surrender with nightly bombing raids over London that continued sporadically for nearly two years. The bombings and shortages of practically every staple made life in London particularly difficult. Orwell felt compelled to stay there. According to Peter Lewis in *George Orwell: The Road to 1984,* Orwell told a friend, "But you can't leave when people are being bombed to hell." The writer, like most of his countrymen, suffered the loss of a family member in the war; his wife's brother, Laurence, an Army surgeon, died during the battle of Dunkirk in 1940.

The war changed when the Soviet Union was unexpectedly invaded by the Germans in June 1941. Still stung by Stalin's betrayal just two years earlier, the Allies (France, England, and—after Pearl Harbor—the United States) were nevertheless forced to join him in order to defeat Hitler. Orwell cringed at photographs of the leaders of England and the United States—Prime Minister Winston Churchill and President Franklin Roosevelt, respectively—and Stalin conferring with each other at the Tehran Conference held November 28 to December 1, 1943. Orwell sat down to write his book at exactly the same moment. In the preface to the Ukrainian edition of the novel, Orwell wrote: "I thought of exposing the Soviet myth in a story that could be easily understood by almost anyone and which could be easily translated into other languages." Orwell knew he would have trouble publishing it because Stalin had become quite popular in England as the one who saved England from an invasion. Orwell couldn't forgive the Soviet leader's complicity with Hitler, or his bloody reshaping of the Soviet Communist Party during the 1930s which resulted in the death or deportation of hundreds of thousands of Russians. Orwell included these so-called purge trials in *Animal Farm* when the animals confess to aiding Snowball in various ways after the pig is exiled from the farm.

Although finished in February 1944, *Animal Farm* wasn't published until 1945, a pivotal year in world history. The war ended, but the year also included such disparate events as the first wartime use of a nuclear bomb and the approval of the charter establishing the United Nations, an international organization promoting peaceful economic cooperation. The cost of the war was staggering: estimates set the monetary cost at one trillion dollars, while an estimated 60 million people lost their lives. Nearly sixty countries were involved in the conflict, with daily life changed dramatically for those in the war zone. The war's end meant the end of rationing, but it also meant an end to the economic machinery that had produced war materials, the return of the soldiers who glutted the suddenly slackened employment market, and a dramatic increase in births in the United States, called the "Baby Boom," that would affect American society until the end of the century. The war had allowed only the United States and the Soviet Union to survive as world powers. So the end of the war brought the beginning of a Cold War, an ideological conflict pitting the Soviet Union and its allies against the United States and its allies, that persisted with varying degrees of intensity until the collapse of the Soviet Union in 1991.

Critical Overview

Although Orwell endured many rejection notices from publishers on both sides of the Atlantic before *Animal Farm* finally appeared in print, ever since it was published in 1945 it has enjoyed widespread critical approval. From the start, reviewers were apt to make a favorable comparison between Orwell's book and the work of the great satirists of the past. In an important early review, influential *New Yorker* critic Edmund Wilson commented that while Orwell's style was reminiscent of that used in the fables of French author Jean de La Fontaine and British author John Gay, he conceded that "'Animal Farm' even seems very creditable if we compare it with Voltaire and [Jonathan] Swift." Arthur M. Schlesinger, Jr., and Adam de Hegedus were among the first critics to attach more significance to the novel beyond that of a political satire. Schlesinger wrote in the *New York Times Book Review* that Orwell's ability to make the reader empathize with the plight of the animals "would compel the attention of persons who never heard of the Russian Revolution." In *Commonweal* de Hegedus stated: "[The novel] has implications—and they are many—which are older and more universal than the past and present of the Union of Soviet Socialist Republics." He, like many critics have since, pointed out the similarity between conclusions drawn from Orwell's text and the famous aphorism of British historian Lord Acton who wrote, "Power tends to corrupt; absolute power corrupts absolutely." Early negative criticism of the novel included *Nation* contributor Isaac Rosenfeld's belief that since the events satirized by Orwell had already passed, it was "a backward work," and *New Republic* critic George Soule's complaint that the book was "on the whole dull."

On Orwell's death in 1950, Arthur Koestler, a friend who shared Orwell's own disillusion with Soviet Communism, again raised comparisons with Swift. "No parable was written since *Gulliver's Travels*," he wrote in the *Observer*, "equal in profundity and mordant satire to 'Animal Farm.'" British journalist Christopher Hollis examined Orwell's ability to craft a fable. "The author of such a fable must have the Swift-like capacity of ascribing with solemn face to the animals idiotic but easily recognized human qualities," Hollis wrote in his *A Study of George Orwell: The Man and His Works,* "decking them out in aptly changed phraseology to suit the animal life—ascribe to them the quality and then pass quickly on before the reader has begun to find the point overlaboured. This Orwell has to perfection." Essayist and novelist C. S. Lewis compared *Animal Farm* to *1984,* Orwell's last novel, and found *Animal Farm* the more powerful of the two. In an essay in *Tide and Time* he wrote, "Wit and humour (absent from the longer work [*1984*]) are employed with devastating effect. The great sentence 'All animals are equal but some are more equal than others' bites deeper than the whole of *1984.*"

In the 1960s and 1970s, critical interest in Orwell continued with scholars such as Jenni Calder, George Woodcock, Stephen J. Greenblatt, and Jeffrey Meyers publishing books that discussed Orwell and his works. Like Lewis, Greenblatt and Woodcock considered both *Animal Farm* and *1984* in their criticism, concluding that *1984* was a thematic continuation of *Animal Farm.* In his *Three Modern Satirists: Waugh, Orwell, & Huxley* Greenblatt wrote: "The horror of both *Animal Farm* and the later *1984* is precisely the cold, orderly, predictable process by which decency, happiness, and hope are systematically and ruthlessly crushed." In his *The Crystal Spirit: A Study of George Orwell,* Woodcock observed: "By transferring the problems of caste division outside a human setting, Orwell was able in *Animal Farm* to avoid the psychological complications inevitable in a novel.... In the process he left out one element which occurs in all his other works of fiction, the individual rebel caught in the machinery of the caste system. Not until he wrote *Nineteen Eighty-Four* did he elaborate the rebel's role in an Animal Farm carried to its monstrously logical conclusion." Calder and Meyers both noted that since Orwell was not adept at creating believable human characters, his use of animals in the book made it more effective than any of his other novels. Calder remarked in her *Chronicles of Conscience: A Study of George Orwell and Arthur Koestler,* "The animals are never mere representations. They have a breathing individuality that is lacking in most of Orwell's human characters."

The 1980s brought a spate of books, articles, and reviews on Orwell's works as the literary community marked the year 1984, the date that Orwell used as the title to his last novel. The literary world also celebrated *Animal Farm*'s fiftieth anniversary in 1995, which saw the publication of a new illustrated edition. While most critiques of the novel remained positive, some reviewers, such as Stephen Sedley, offered negative opinions. In an essay contained in Christopher Norris's *Inside the Myth: Orwell, Views from the Left,* Sedley argued that the book's popularity had as much to do with an atmosphere of anti-communism in England following World War II as it did with Orwell's vision, stating, "Between its covers *Animal Farm* offers little that is creative, little that is original." In the *New York Times Book Review,* however, Arthur C. Danto maintained that "the sustained acceptance of the book is testimony to a human meaning deeper than anti-Soviet polemics." In *Commonweal* Katharine Byrne summarized many critics opinions when she wrote: "Should *Animal Farm* by read during the next fifty years? Of course, but for the right reasons: setting up as it does, with crystal clarity, the price paid when we do not safeguard our freedoms."

Criticism

Kathleen Fitzpatrick

In the following essay, Fitzpatrick, a Ph.D. candidate at New York University, notes that an understanding of the historical setting for Orwell's novel is imperative if the reader is to understand the work as not simply an indictment of Communism in the Soviet Union.

Stephen Sedley, in a 1984 article in *Inside the Myth: Orwell, Views from the Left* attacking George Orwell's *Animal Farm* as both politically and artistically lacking, points to the fact that his thirteen-year-old daughter was "bored stiff" by the novel, because she, like most students today, was "too new to political ideas to have any frame of reference for the story." In this, Sedley has a point: in the early 1980s, I was in high school and was given *Animal Farm* to read for the first time, along with the simple (indeed, simplistic) advice that this novel was an allegory of the Russian Revolution and the decline of subsequent Soviet Communism. The political environment in the United States being what it was in the early 1980s, coupled with the fact of my total lack of awareness of the circumstances of the Russian Revolution and the principles of Marxist-Leninist Socialism which the Revolution at first fought for and then lost sight of, my own interpretation of the novel resembled in both content and complexity the following statement: "George Orwell thought Communism was Bad."

What Do I Read Next?

- Child psychologist Bruno Bettelheim's National Book Award-winning *The Uses of Enchantment* (1976) examines the characteristics of the classic fairy tale and the importance of such stories in society.

- George Orwell's essays, especially "Why I Write" (1947) and "Politics and the English Language" (1946), in which the author explains his dire need to express himself in words and how politicians and others misuse them, ending with a list of six principles for good writing.

- Orwell's 1949 look at a terrifying future world dominated by a totalitarian state, *1984,* which added to the English language such catchwords as "Big Brother," "doublespeak," and "Orwellian."

- Jonathan Swift's satirical *Gulliver's Travels* (1726), especially the fourth voyage which takes Gulliver to Houyhnhnmland, a country inhabited by a race of horses and a human-like inferior race called the Yahoos.

Animal Farm is in fact one of the most studied and most readily misinterpreted novels of the twentieth century. And, given our distance from the events which it allegorizes and from the ideas it counterposes, it has only become easier to misinterpret since the fall of the Berlin Wall. The pigs have at last been vanquished, and Mr. Jones has returned to the farm, as we knew he would all along.

But in 1984, as Stephen Sedley was writing, there was no end to the Cold War in sight. The atmosphere on the Right was one of suspicion of all things Communist—the Soviet Union was, after all, the "Evil Empire," and the anti-Communist forces in the United States government held an unquestionable position of moral superiority. The atmosphere on the Left was no better—anything which looked like a criticism of the Soviet Union was considered a reactionary justification for the oppressions of capitalism.

It is this environment, then, which underscores Mr. Sedley's willful misreading of Orwell's tale. How else could he come to the conclusion that Orwell's argument in the novel is "that socialism in whatever form offers the common people no more hope than capitalism; that it will be first betrayed and then held to ransom by those forces which human beings have in common with beasts; and that the inefficient and occasionally benign rule of capitalism, which at least keeps the beasts in check, is a lesser evil"?

In so far as I believe Orwell to have an argument in *Animal Farm,* I suspect that it was stated much more closely, with less intervening static, by Adam de Hegedus in an early review of the novel in *The Commonweal:*

> Orwell is not angry with Russia, or with any other country, because that country "turned Socialist." On the contrary he is angry with Russia because Russia does not believe in a classless and democratic society.... In short, Orwell is angry with Russia because Russia is *not* socialist.

Contrary to Sedley's claims, *Animal Farm* is not arguing for capitalism as the lesser of two evils, but is rather angrily pointing out the ways in which the Soviet experiment turned its back on its own principles—and is perhaps of the opinion that such descent from idealism to totalitarianism is inevitable in any violent revolution.

In order to read *Animal Farm* as the allegory which Orwell's contemporaries understood it to be, one must first have an outline of the key players. Old Major, the prize boar who first passes on his ideas about animal oppression by the humans and the future Rebellion of the animals, is commonly thought to represent either Karl Marx, one of the authors of the 1848 *Communist Manifesto,* or Vladimir Lenin, who adapted Marx's ideas to the Russian Revolution. Neither Marx's nor Lenin's influence remained long in its original state. Just as with Major's ideas, followers of Marx and Lenin "elaborated" their ideas into a complete system of thought which did not exactly reflect the intent of the original. (Late in his life, Marx insisted that he was certainly not a Marxist.)

Napoleon and Snowball, the pigs who are primarily responsible for this elaboration of ideas into doctrine, represent Joseph Stalin and Leon Trotsky, respectively. Some of the novel's details slip a bit from a strict representation of reality, as Orwell found it necessary to compress some events and change some chronologies in order to make his story work. For instance, Snowball's original plans for building the windmill correspond to Lenin's plans for the electrification of Russia; however, though this plan was not the point on which the Stalin/Trotsky conflict turned, the ultimate result was the same as that between Napoleon and Snowball: Trotsky was driven from the country under a death warrant; he was reported to be hiding in various enemy states; he was held responsible for everything that went wrong under the Stalinist regime; and, ultimately, his supporters were violently purged from the ranks of the Communist Party.

These correspondences between the Russian Revolution and the Rebellion on Animal Farm are generally agreed upon by the critics. Not much has been said, however, about the allegorical roles played by the humans in the story. Mr. Jones, quite clearly, represents the last Czar in Russia, whose dissolution and cruelty laid the groundwork for the workers' rebellion. The neighboring farmers, Mr. Pilkington of Foxwood and Mr. Frederick of Pinchfield, who are described as being "on permanently bad terms," represent the leaders of England and Germany respectively. The closeness of their names seems to imply an essential sameness—quite a shocking notion for a novel written at the end of World War II!—but Pilkington is described as "an easy-going gentleman farmer who spent much of his time in fishing or hunting according to the season," and his farm is "large, neglected, [and] old-fashioned." Frederick, on the other hand, is "a tough, shrewd man, perpetually involved in lawsuits and with a name for driving hard bargains," and his farm is "smaller and better kept." Pilkington is thus representative of the Allies' lackadaisical attitude toward their neighbors, while Frederick carries with him elements of German aggressiveness and bellicosity.

In fact, late in the novel, "terrible stories" begin leaking out of Pinchfield about the cruelties Frederick inflicts on his animals, no doubt corresponding to the horrors of Hitler and the Holocaust. It is thus that much more shocking when Squealer (who, as Napoleon's mouthpiece, might be said to correspond to *Pravda,* the Soviet propagandist press) announces that the deal Napoleon had been working out to sell some timber to Pilkington has instead been changed so that the deal will be made with Frederick. This devastating turn of events corresponds to the revelation in 1939 of the secret Nazi-Soviet anti-aggression pact which, like the peace between Frederick and Animal Farm, did not last long, but was abruptly ended by Hitler's attempted invasion of Russia.

Once Russia entered the European war on the side of the Allies (culminating in victory for the Soviet Union, as Squealer claims for Animal Farm, though the only victory was in gaining back what they had before), increasing attempts were made by Stalin to achieve some level of entente, or agreement, with the other Allied nations. A series of meetings were held between the leaders of the various nations, and one particular conference held in Teheran after the war began the eruption into detente, or discord, which resulted in the protracted Cold War. This conference is represented in the novel by the meeting between the pigs and the humans at the end, at which a quarrel breaks out over cheating at cards.

Despite this discordant note, however, the final lines of the novel reveal the greatest shock of all. As the other animals watch through the windows, they notice:

Twelve voices were shouting in anger, and they were all alike. No question, now, what had happened to the faces of the pigs. The creatures outside looked from pig to man, and from man to pig, and from pig to man again; but already it was impossible to say which was which.

These lines are crucial to a full understanding of the novel. Orwell does not claim here that Napoleon/Stalin is worse than the humans, and thus that the animals would be better off under benign human control. In fact he points to an ultimate identity between the pigs and the humans, between Stalin and the leaders of the "free" nations, an idea which would have been considered heresy by both sides. This conclusion implies not that the Rebellion has been a failure because the animals are worse off than they would have been under the rule of Mr. Jones, but that the Rebellion is a failure because it has completely set aside its own ideals—which may be seen in the corruption of each and every one of Animal Farm's Seven Commandments—and landed everyone back exactly where they started, with the many suffering abuses in order to support the position of an elite few. Or, in the interpretation of George Woodcock in *The Crystal Spirit: A Study of George Orwell:*

> ... old and new tyrannies belong to the same family; authoritarian governments, whether they are based on the codes of old social castes or on the rules of new political elites, are basically similar and present similar dangers to human welfare and liberty.

It seems clear as I reread the novel now, understanding better than I did as a teenager the background against which Orwell wrote his allegory, and paying close attention to the implications of the novel's last few lines, that no part of the novel presents any such simplistic, cut-and-dried message as "Communism is Bad." Even Stephen Sedley's more sophisticated argument about the novel's ideological unsoundness suffers from an apparent—and misguided—belief that Orwell as novelist held any sympathy for Jones, Pilkington, or Frederick.

Other critics, such as Robert A. Lee, writing in *Orwell's Fiction,* hold that it is in fact dangerous to read *Animal Farm* too strictly as an allegory of a specific set of events, as one may in that way miss a broader applicability of its meaning. Lee argues that *Animal Farm* is more than an allegory of twentieth-century Russian politics, and more even than an indictment of revolutions in general: "Orwell is also," claims Lee, "painting a grim picture of the human condition in the political twentieth century, a time which he has come to believe marks the end of the very concepts of human freedom."

This picture of the human condition is what Orwell's allegory has to offer us today, now that the Cold War has been "won" and the humans are back in control of the farm. I do not believe, as Sedley seems to, that Orwell would be relieved that the "benign, inefficient" capitalists are back in charge; I believe he would instead point out that we are deluding ourselves if we think we are closer to those revolutionary ideas of justice, brotherhood, and equality than were the citizens of Stalinist Russia.

Source: Kathleen Fitzpatrick, in an essay for *Novels for Students,* Gale, 1998.

Stephen J. Greenblatt

In the following excerpt, Greenblatt explains how Animal Farm *reveals Orwell's disgust and disillusion with the socialist causes he once expounded.*

Throughout Orwell's early novels, journals, and essays, democratic socialism existed as a sustaining vision that kept the author from total despair of the human condition, but Orwell's bitter experience in the Spanish Civil War and the shock of the Nazi-Soviet pact signaled the breakdown of this last hope and the beginning of the mental and emotional state out of which grew *Animal Farm* and *1984.* The political disappointments of the late '30s and '40s did not in themselves, however, disillusion Orwell—they simply brought to the surface themes and tensions present in his work from the beginning.... [The] socialism Orwell believed

in was not a hardheaded, "realistic" approach to society and politics but a rather sentimental, utopian vision of the world as a "raft sailing through space, with, potentially, plenty of provisions for everybody," provided men, who, after all, are basically decent, would simply use common sense and not be greedy. Such naïve beliefs could only survive while Orwell was preoccupied with his attacks on the British Raj, the artist in society, or the capitalist system. The moment events compelled him to turn his critical eye on the myth of socialism and the "dictatorship of the proletariat," he discerned fundamental lies and corruption. Orwell, in his last years, was a man who experienced daily the disintegration of the beliefs of a lifetime, who watched in horror while his entire life work was robbed of meaning.

The first of his great cries of despair was *Animal Farm,* a satirical beast fable which, curiously enough, has been heralded as Orwell's lightest, gayest work. Laurence Brander, in his biography of Orwell paints a charming but wholly inaccurate picture of *Animal Farm,* presenting it as "one of those apparently chance pieces a prose writer throws off ... a sport out of his usual way," supposedly written by Orwell in a state where "the gaiety in his nature had completely taken charge ... writing about animals, whom he loved." The surface gaiety, the seeming good humor and casualness, the light, bantering tone are, of course, part of the convention of beast fables and *Animal Farm* would be a very bad tale indeed if it did not employ these devices. But it is a remarkable achievement precisely because Orwell uses the apparently frivolous form of the animal tale to convey with immense power his profoundly bitter message. Critics like Laurence Brander and Tom Hopkinson who marvel at Orwell's "admirable good humour and detachment" miss, I think, the whole point of the piece they praise. *Animal Farm* does indeed contain much gaiety and humor, but even in the most comic moments there is a disturbing element of cruelty or fear that taints the reader's hearty laughter. While Snowball, one of the leaders of the revolution of farm animals against their master, is organizing "the Egg Production Committee for the hens, the Clean Tails League for the cows, the Wild Comrades' Re-education Committee..., the Whiter Wool Movement for the sheep," Napoleon, the sinister pig tyrant, is carefully educating the dogs for his own evil purposes. Similarly, the "confessions" forced from the animals in Napoleon's great purges are very funny, but when the dogs tear the throats out of the "guilty" parties and leave a pile of corpses at the tyrant's feet, the scene ceases to amuse. Orwell's technique is similar to [a device used by Evelyn] Waugh, who relates ghastly events in a comic setting.

Another critical mistake in appraising *Animal Farm* is made, I believe, by critics like Christopher Hollis who talk of the overriding importance of the author's love of animals and fail to understand that Orwell in *Animal Farm* loves animals only as much or as little as he loves human beings. To claim that he hates the pigs because they represent human tyrants and sympathizes with the horses because they are dumb animals is absurd. Nor is it necessary, as Hollis believes, that the truly successful animal fable carry with it "a gay and light-hearted message." Indeed, the very idea of representing human traits in animals is rather pessimistic. What is essential to the success of the satirical beast fable, as Ellen Douglass Leyburn observes [in *Satiric Allegory: The Mirror of Man,* 1956], is the author's "power to keep his reader conscious simultaneously of the human traits satirized and of the animals as animals." The storyteller must never allow the animals to be simply beasts, in which case the piece becomes a nonsatirical children's story, or to be merely transparent symbols, in which case the piece becomes a dull sermon. Orwell proved, in *Animal Farm,* his remarkable ability to maintain this delicate, satiric balance.

The beast fable, an ancient satiric technique in which the characteristic poses of human vice and folly are embodied in animals, is, as Kernan points out, "an unrealistic, expressionistic device" [Alvin Kernan, *Modern Satire,* 1962] which stands in bold contrast with Orwell's previous realistic manner. But the seeds for *Animal Farm* are present in the earlier works, not only in the metaphors likening men to beasts but, more important, in Orwell's whole attitude toward society, which he sees as an aggregation of certain classes or types. The types change somewhat in appearance according to the setting—from the snobbish pukka sahibs, corrupt officials, and miserable natives of *Burmese Days* to the obnoxious nouveaux riches, greedy restaurateurs, and overworked plongeurs of *Down and Out in Paris and London,* but there remains the basic notion that men naturally divide themselves into a limited number of groups, which can be isolated and characterized by the astute observer. This notion is given dramatic reality in *Animal Farm,* where societal types are presented in the various kinds of farm animals—pigs for exploiters, horses for laborers, dogs for police, sheep for blind followers, etc. The beast fable need not convey an op-

timistic moral, but it cannot portray complex individuals, and thus it can never sustain the burden of tragedy. The characters of a satirical animal story may be sly, vicious, cynical, pathetic, lovable, or intelligent, but they can only be seen as members of large social groups and not as individuals.

Animal Farm has been interpreted most frequently as a clever satire on the betrayal of the Russian Revolution and the rise of Stalin. Richard Rees comments [in *George Orwell: Fugitive from the Camp of Victory,* 1961] that "the struggle of the farm animals, having driven out their human exploiter, to create a free and equal community takes the form of a most ingeniously worked-out recapitulation of the history of Soviet Russia from 1917 up to the Teheran Conference." And indeed, despite Soviet critics who claim to see only a general satire on bureaucracy in *Animal Farm,* the political allegory is inevitable. Inspired by the prophetic deathbed vision of Old Major, a prize Middle White boar, the maltreated animals of Manor Farm successfully revolt against Mr. Jones, their bad farmer, and found their own utopian community, Animal Farm. The control of the revolution falls naturally upon the pigs, particularly upon Napoleon, "a large, rather fierce-looking Berkshire boar, not much of a talker, but with a reputation for getting his own way," and on Snowball, "a more vivacious pig than Napoleon, quicker in speech and more inventive, but ... not considered to have the same depth of character." Under their clever leadership and with the help of the indefatigable cart horses Boxer and Clover, the animals manage to repulse the attacks of their rapacious human neighbors, Mr. Pilkington and Mr. Frederick. With the farm secured from invasion and the Seven Commandments of Animalism painted on the end wall of the big barn, the revolution seems complete; but as the community develops, it is plain that there are graver dangers than invasion. The pigs at once decide that milk and apples are essential to their well being. Squealer, Napoleon's lieutenant and the ablest talker, explains the appropriation:

> "Comrades!" he cried. "You do not imagine, I hope, that we pigs are doing this in a spirit of selfishness and privilege? Many of us actually dislike milk and apples.... Our sole object in taking these things is to preserve our health. Milk and apples (this has been proven by Science, comrades) contain substances absolutely necessary to the well-being of a pig.... We pigs are brainworkers.... Day and night we are watching over your welfare. It is for *your* sake that we drink that milk and eat those apples. Do you know what would happen if we pigs failed in our duty? Jones would come back!"

A growing rivalry between Snowball and Napoleon is decisively decided by Napoleon's vicious hounds, who drive Snowball off the farm. Laurence Brander sees Snowball as a symbol of "altruism, the essential social virtue" and his expulsion as the defeat of "his altruistic laws for giving warmth, food and comfort to all the animals." This is very touching, but unfortunately there is no indication that Snowball is any less corrupt or power-mad than Napoleon. Indeed, it is remarked, concerning the appropriation of the milk and apples, that "All the pigs were in full agreement on this point, even Snowball and Napoleon." The remainder of *Animal Farm* is a chronicle of the consolidation of Napoleon's power through clever politics, propaganda, and terror. Dissenters are ruthlessly murdered, and when Boxer can no longer work, he is sold to the knacker. One by one, the Commandments of Animalism are perverted or eliminated, until all that is left is:

ALL ANIMALS ARE EQUAL
BUT SOME ANIMALS ARE MORE EQUAL
    THAN OTHERS

After that, it does not seem strange when the pigs live in Jones' house, walk on two legs, carry whips, wear human clothes, take out subscriptions to *John Bull, Tit-Bits,* and the *Daily Mirror,* and invite their human neighbors over for a friendly game of cards. The game ends in a violent argument when Napoleon and Pilkington play an ace of spades simultaneously, but for the animals there is no real quarrel. "The creatures outside looked from pig to man, and from man to pig, and from pig to man again; but already it was impossible to say which was which."

The interpretation of *Animal Farm* in terms of Soviet history (Major, Napoleon, Snowball represent Lenin, Stalin, Trotsky) has been made many times and shall not be pursued further here. It is amusing, however, that many of the Western critics who astutely observe the barbs aimed at Russia fail completely to grasp Orwell's judgment of the West. After all, the pigs do not turn into alien monsters; they come to resemble those bitter rivals Mr. Pilkington and Mr. Frederick, who represent the Nazis and the Capitalists. All three major "powers" are despicable tyrannies, and the failure of the revolution is not seen in terms of ideology at all, but as a realization of Lord Acton's thesis, "Power tends to corrupt; absolute power corrupts absolutely." The initial spark of a revolution, the original intention of a constitution may have been an ideal of the good life, but the result is always the same—tyranny. Communism is no more or less evil

than Fascism or Capitalism—they are all illusions which are inevitably used by the pigs as a means of satisfying their greed and their lust for power. Religion, too, is merely a toy of the oppressors and a device to divert the minds of the sufferers. Moses, the tame raven who is always croaking about the sweet, eternal life in Sugarcandy Mountain, flies after the deposed Farmer Jones, only to return when Napoleon has established his tyranny.

Animal Farm remains powerful satire even as the specific historical events it mocked recede into the past, because the book's major concern is not with these incidents but with the essential horror of the human condition. There have been, are, and always will be pigs in every society, Orwell states, and they will always grab power. Even more cruel is the conclusion that *everyone* in the society, wittingly or unwittingly, contributes to the pigs' tyranny. Boxer, the noblest (though not the wisest) animal on the farm, devotes his unceasing labor to the pigs, who, as has been noted, send him to the knacker when he has outlived his usefulness. There is real pathos as the sound of Boxer's hoofs drumming weakly on the back of the horse slaughterer's van grows fainter and dies away, and the reader senses that in that dying sound is the dying hope of humanity. But Orwell does not allow the mood of oppressive sadness to overwhelm the satire, and Squealer, "lifting his trotter and wiping away a tear," hastens to announce that, after receiving every attention a horse could have, Boxer died in his hospital bed, with the words "Napoleon is always right" on his withered lips. Frederick R. Karl, in *The Contemporary English Novel,* believes that *Animal Farm* fails as successful satire "by virtue of its predictability," but this terrifying predictability of the fate of all revolutions is just the point Orwell is trying to make. The grotesque end of the fable is not meant to shock the reader—indeed, chance and surprise are banished entirely from Orwell's world. The horror of both *Animal Farm* and the later *1984* is precisely the cold, orderly, predictable process by which decency, happiness, and hope are systematically and ruthlessly crushed.

Source: Stephen J. Greenblatt, "George Orwell," in his *Three Modern Satirists: Waugh, Orwell, and Huxley,* Yale University Press, 1965, pp. 35–74.

Laurence Brander

In the following excerpt, Brander applauds Orwell's use of colorful characters and lyrical narrative to balance his bitterly satirical story.

Animal Farm is one of those apparently chance pieces a prose writer throws off, which immediately becomes more popular than his more ambitious writings. A sport, out of his usual way; and yet more effective in the crusade to which he was dedicated than anything else he wrote.

For once, the gaiety in his nature had completely taken charge. He was writing about animals, whom he loved. He had had a rest of nearly three years from serious writing. He wrote with zest, and although humour rarely travels across national boundaries, his enjoyment has been shared everywhere. Humour travels most easily in peasant portraiture, as in *The Good Soldier Schweik* and *Don Camillo;* and in animal stories. Not many books have been translated into so many languages so successfully and so quickly as *Animal Farm....*

The style, like the form, is unique in Orwell's work. He had been a master of the descriptive way of writing from the beginning, from the opening words of *Down and Out,* but he had never before achieved pure narrative. In *Animal Farm,* from the start, we feel the special power of the storyteller. The animals expel the farmer and his men and take over the farm. The farmer tries to come back but is driven away. The other farmers do not interfere because they look forward to taking the farm over cheaply when the animals have ruined it. The animals, led by the pigs, do not make a mess of it, and the farm is well enough run for the authorities to leave it alone. Eventually, the pigs turn out to be harder slave-drivers than men, so in the end the neighbouring farmers make friends with the pigs and admit that they have much to learn from the labour conditions on Animal Farm.

There is no looseness anywhere in the structure. The story is rounded, the end joining the beginning. The opening speech of the old boar, Major, is answered at the end in the words of Mr. Pilkington and Napoleon. The various levels of satire are similarly rounded, so that the story and all its implications form circles each in its own plane.

The convention of writing animal stories is as old as Æsop in European literature and has been used in England from Chaucer's time. Every animal corresponds to a human type, and though there were many animals in the Ark, there are still human types to place against them. Orwell restates the convention right at the beginning, in the meeting of the animals:

At one end of the big barn, on a sort of raised platform, Major was already ensconced on his bed of straw, under a lantern which hung from a beam. He was twelve years old and had lately grown rather stout, but he was still a majestic-looking pig, with a wise and benevolent appearance in spite of the fact that his tushes had never been cut. Before long the other animals began to arrive and make themselves comfortable after their different fashions. First came the three dogs, Bluebell, Jessie, and Pitcher, and then the pigs who settled down in the straw immediately in front of the platform. The hens perched themselves on the window-sills, the pigeons fluttered up to the rafters, the sheep and cows lay down behind the pigs and began to chew the cud. The two cart-horses, Boxer and Clover, came in together, walking very slowly and setting down their vast hairy hoofs with great care lest there should be some small animal concealed in the straw....

The two horses had just laid down when a brood of ducklings, which had lost their mother, filed into the barn, cheeping feebly and wandering from side to side to find some place where they would not be trodden on. Clover made a sort of wall round them with her great foreleg, and the ducklings nestled down inside it and promptly fell asleep.... Last of all came the cat, who looked round, as usual, for the warmest place, and finally squeezed herself in between Boxer and Clover; there she purred contentedly throughout Major's speech without listening to a word of what he was saying.

It is an enchanting description. There is the bustle and excitement of assembly, just as in Chaucer's *Parlement of Foules:*

And that so huge a noyse gan they make
That erthe, and eyr, and tre, and every lake
So full was, that unethe was there space
For me to stonde, so full was all the place.

There is the pleasure of watching each animal comporting itself according to its nature. The animal kingdom at once becomes a reflection of human society.

The scene is a parody of a successful meeting of the political opposition. Get the people together with some bait. Turn on the orator to bemuse them, and send them away feeling happy and satisfied, but with the seeds of revolt planted where you want them. The best thing in the parody is the mockery of the egotistical gravity of political rabble-rousers:

I feel it my duty to pass on to you such political wisdom as I have acquired. I have had a long life. I have had much time for thought as I lay alone in my stall, and I think I may say that I understand the nature of life on this earth as well as any animal now living.

Three days later, Major dies and the spotlight falls upon two younger boars, Napoleon and Snowball, the Stalin and Trotsky of the story. Napoleon was "not much of a talker" but had "a reputation for getting his own way." Snowball was intellectually quicker, but "was not considered to have the same depth of character." (Part of the fun of the animal story is the enormous gravity of the author's approach to his characters.) Snowball obviously has much more brains than Napoleon. It is Snowball who paints the seven commandments against the end wall of the barn, and when it comes to the battle for Manor Farm, and Jones the farmer tries to recover his property, it is Snowball who has prepared and drilled the animals for the expected attack. It is Snowball who leads them and Snowball who is wounded. In the whole episode, Napoleon is never mentioned.

As the community develops, it is observed that Snowball inspired the "Animal Committees," while Napoleon took no interest in such things. Snowball "formed the Egg Production Committee for the hens, the Clean Tails League for the Cows ... the Whiter Wool Movement for the sheep...." This is the sort of exuberant invention of absurd trivialities that Swift enjoyed in Gulliver. Napoleon, meanwhile, said that "the education of the young was more important than anything that could be done for those who were already grown up." Snowball had altruism, the essential social virtue; Napoleon had a lust for power, and intended to get it by making the animals "less conscious," and that was all he meant by educating the young. Eventually Napoleon wins by his education of a litter of young hounds, who attack Snowball after his eloquent exposition of the windmill scheme, and chase him out of the farm. At his best moment, just when his altruistic plans for giving warmth, food and comfort to all the animals are completed and ready to be carried out, Snowball's brutal rival strikes. It is the same sort of dramatic timing that we shall find in *1984,* an ironic twist to the satire.

After that, the Snowball theme is the denigration of the fallen hero. The animals are all greatly upset by the incident, and Napoleon's young lieutenant, Squealer, works hard to make them less conscious of what has happened:

> "He fought bravely at the Battle of the Cowshed," said somebody. "Bravery is not enough," said Squealer.

> "Loyalty and obedience are more important. And as to the Battle of the Cowshed, I believe the time will come when we shall find that Snowball's part in it was much exaggerated. Discipline, comrades, iron discipline! That is the watchword for today. One false step, and our enemies would be upon us. Surely, comrades, you do not want Jones back?"

"Discipline!" the invariable cry of the political gangsters who are destroying freedom and truth.

That is the first step in the legend that Snowball is the source of evil. The legend grows step by step with the building up of Napoleon as the leader who thought of everything and is the father of the farm. The windmill was of course really Napoleon's own idea, and Snowball had stolen the plans from among Napoleon's papers. When the windmill falls down at the first puff with wind, Napoleon himself comes forth and snuffs around till he smells Snowball. " 'Comrades,' he said quietly, 'do you know who is responsible for this? Do you know the enemy who has come in the night and overthrown our windmill? SNOWBALL!' he suddenly roared in a voice of thunder."

Next spring, it was discovered that Snowball "stole the corn, he upset the milk-pails, he broke the eggs, he trampled the seed-beds, he gnawed the bark off the fruit-trees." A typical touch of hypnosis is supplied when "the cows declared unanimously that Snowball crept into their stalls and milked them in their sleep." Napoleon orders a full investigation, and Squealer is able to tell the animals that " 'Snowball was in league with Jones from the very start! He was Jones's secret agent all the time. It has all been proved in documents which he left behind him and which we have only just discovered.' " The authentic note this, and it is heard again when Boxer argues that Snowball was once a good comrade: " 'Our leader, Comrade Napoleon,' announced Squealer, speaking very slowly, and firmly, 'has stated categorically—categorically, comrade—that Snowball was Jones's agent from the very beginning.' "

Boxer was too simple to be safe. So the dogs are set on him, but he kicks them aside and releases the one he traps under his vast hoof only on Napoleon's orders. At the trial, the confessions of the animals are invariably of complicity with Snowball. Later it is discovered that far from being the hero of the Battle of the Cowshed, Snowball was censured for showing cowardice. At all these stages the simple animals are very much perplexed. Eventually it is shown (by the discovery of further documents) that Snowball fought on Jones's side at the Battle of the Cowshed. The animals are perplexed at each stage of this long denigration, but they are tired, overworked and underfed and do not remember clearly and the lies are so persuasively put across that at every stage they believe.

This parable of human perplexity in the face of contemporary propaganda methods is told with great skill. It is one of Orwell's most effective treatments of the problem which had focused his attention since his experiences in Spain.

Squealer is the modern propagandist, the P.R.O. [public relations officer] who explains away the worst with the best of spurious reasons. He is a familiar type, with: "very round cheeks, twinkling eyes, nimble movements, and a shrill voice. He was a brilliant talker, and when he was arguing some difficult point he had a way of skipping from side to side and whisking his tail which was somehow very persuasive. The others said of Squealer that he could turn black into white."

He was the mouthpiece of the pigs, the new class who were elbowing their way into power by the methods Orwell marks in an essay on James Burnham: "All talk about democracy, liberty, equality, fraternity, all revolutionary movements, all visions of Utopia, or 'the classless society,' or 'the Kingdom of Heaven on Earth,' are humbug (not necessarily conscious humbug) covering the ambitions of some new class which is elbowing its way into power."

In contrast to Squealer is Moses, the tame raven, who specialized in the kingdom of heaven, but not on earth. Moses disappeared completely for years when the animals took over. It was only when the pigs were in complete control and had turned themselves into an aristocracy at the expense of the lean and hungry animals that Moses returns. His tales of Sugar Candy Mountain, where "it was Sunday seven days a week, clover was in season all the year round, and lump sugar and linseed oil grew on the hedges," are useful again, and in no way threaten the power of the pigs.

Moses has his allowance of a gill of beer a day from the pigs and he does no work. Squealer works hard all the time. He represents the organized lying practised in totalitarian states, which, Orwell says in "The Prevention of Literature": "is not, as is sometimes claimed, a temporary expedient of the same nature as military deception. It is something integral to totalitarianism, something that would still continue even if concentration camps and secret police forces had ceased to be necessary."

Squealer comes into his own when Snowball is expelled, after making his name on the milk-and-apple question. All supplies had been reserved for the pigs, and there is some grumbling: "Many of us actually dislike milk and apples. I dislike them myself. Our sole object in taking these things is to preserve our health." Needless to say, for the purpose of keeping Jones away.

At the moment of Snowball's expulsion, when Napoleon takes over the leadership, Squealer is at his best: "'Comrades,' he said, 'I trust that every animal here appreciates the sacrifice that Comrade Napoleon has made in taking this extra labour upon himself. Do not imagine, comrades, that leadership is a pleasure!'"

When there is any fighting, Squealer is unaccountably absent. His time comes afterwards, when the victory has to be celebrated.

"What victory?" said Boxer....

"Have we not driven the enemy off our soil? ..."

"Then we have won back what we had before," said Boxer.

"That is our victory," said Squealer.

A few mornings after that conversation, all the pigs are suffering from a dreadful hangover. It is the drollest incident in the book, and like everything else has its satirical implications.

It was nearly nine o'clock when Squealer made his appearance walking slowly and dejectedly, his eyes dull, his tail hanging limply behind him, and with every appearance of being seriously ill. He called the animals together and told them that he had a terrible piece of news to impart. Comrade Napoleon was dying!

A cry of lamentation went up. Straw was laid down outside the doors of the farmhouse, and the animals walked on tiptoe.

The next bulletin was that Comrade Napoleon had pronounced a solemn decree as his last act on earth: "the drinking of alcohol was to be punished by death." Within a couple of days the pigs are busily studying books on brewing and distilling.

Squealer is central. He keeps the animals quiet. He puts their minds at rest. He has the air of a beneficent being, sent to make animals happy. He is the agency by which they become "less conscious."

Napoleon develops in personality. He takes on the character of the legendary Leader more and more. He becomes progressively remote. From the beginning he is quite different from Snowball and Squealer. He has none of their mercurial qualities; he is no talker. In the range of porcine character—which would seem to be as great as the human range—he is at the other extreme: a saturnine, cunning pig. A deep pig, with a persistent way of getting what he wants. He is by far the strongest character on the farm. Just as Benjamin, the donkey, has the clearest idea of things, and Boxer, the carthorse, is the strongest physically.

Boxer's simplicity of character is sentimental comedy of the purest kind. It is the story of the great big good-natured person who thinks harm of nobody, believes all is for the best, so everybody should work as hard as possible and then a little harder still. He is so simple that he does not see his questions are dangerous, and when the pigs make an effort to eliminate him—which is quite hopeless because of his great strength—he never understands what has happened. In the tiny Orwell gallery of pleasant characters, Boxer is the favourite. He is the expression of Orwell's liberal belief in the people: "one sees only the struggle of the gradually awakening common people against the lords of property and their hired liars…". He is the great big gentle peasant, the finest flower of the good earth; and he has the usual reward. When at last he collapses from overwork, the pigs pretend to send him to hospital, and sell him to the knacker. It is the only time that Benjamin, the donkey, forsakes cynicism for action. He attempts a rescue, but too late. With the money they get from the knacker, the pigs buy another case of whisky and hold a Boxer memorial dinner.

Squealer is able to give a complete narrative of Boxer's last moments in hospital and is able to quote his last words: "Long live Animal Farm! Long live Comrade Napoleon! Napoleon is always right." Fortunately, too, he is able to refute the ridiculous rumour that Boxer was sent to the knacker. "The animals were enormously relieved to hear this."

The last stage of the story comes with the legend on the end of the barn which has replaced the seven commandments. None of the animals ever detected that only four of them were commandments and the others were statements of belief. None, except probably Benjamin, who gave no sign, ever quite realized how they were modified. One by one they had been broken down and now they had all disappeared and in their place stood the legend: "All animals are equal but some are more equal than others." The significance of this expunging of the law is explained in Orwell's essay on *Gulliver's Travels,* where he says:

> In a Society in which there is no law, and in theory no compulsion, the only arbiter of behaviour is public opinion. But public opinion, because of the tremendous urge to conformity in gregarious animals, is less tolerant than any system of law.

Squealer arranged public opinion. The pigs were now walking on two legs and wearing clothing. Soon they were indistinguishable from the other farmers, except only in their superior discipline over their workers. Mr. Pilkington, proposing the toast of "Animal Farm" at the dinner which the pigs gave to their neighbours, put it very well: "… a discipline and an orderliness which should be an example to all farmers everywhere. He believed that he was right in saying that the lower animals on Animal Farm did more work and received less food than any animals in the county."

Was it wonderful that when the poor animals gazed in they "looked from pig to man, and from man to pig, and from pig to man again; but already it was impossible to say which was which"?

The question one poses at the end of this fairy story is whether Orwell had given up hope that mankind would ever find decent government. It is very difficult here, as in *1984,* to decide. He had said in his essay on Swift that: "Of course, no honest person claims that happiness is *now* a normal condition among adult human beings; but perhaps it *could* be made normal, and it is upon this question that all serious political controversy really turns."

Essentially, *Animal Farm* is an anatomy of the development of the totalitarian State: "In each great revolutionary struggle the masses are led on by vague dreams of human brotherhood, and then, when the new ruling class is well established in power, they are thrust back into servitude." (*Second Thoughts on James Burnham.*)

It is a comment on all revolution: "History consists of a series of swindles, in which the masses are first lured into revolt by the promise of Utopia, and then, when they have done their job, enslaved over again by new masters." (Same essay.)

Nothing is more obvious than where Orwell's sympathies lay. But whether he hoped that the common man could learn to find rulers is not clear. In *Animal Farm* he is an artist, posing great questions imaginatively; not a preacher, proclaiming a revelation.

Source: Laurence Brander, in his *George Orwell,* Longmans, Green & Co., 1954, pp. 171–82.

Sources

Katharine Byrne, "Not All Books Are Created Equal: Orwell & His Animals at Fifty," in *Commonweal,* Vol. CXXIII, No. 10, May 17, 1996, pp. 14, 16.

Jenni Calder, *Chronicles of Conscience: A Study of George Orwell and Arthur Koestler,* University of Pittsburgh Press, 1968.

Arthur C. Danto, *"Animal Farm* at 50," in *New York Times Book Review,* April 14, 1996, p. 35.

Adam de Hegedus, review of *Animal Farm,* in*Commonweal,* Vol. XLIV, No. 22, September 13, 1946. pp. 528-30.

Stephen J. Greenblatt, *Three Modern Satirists: Waugh, Orwell, and Huxley,* Yale University Press, 1965.

Christopher Hollis, *A Study of George Orwell: The Man and His Works,* Henry Regnery Co., 1956, pp. 140-53.

Arthur Koestler, "A Rebel's Progress: To George Orwell's Death," in *Observer,* January 29, 1950, reprinted in his *The Trail of the Dinosaur and Other Essays,* Macmillan, 1955, pp. 102-5.

C. S. Lewis, "George Orwell," in *Time and Tide,* January 8, 1955.

Jeffrey Meyers, in his *A Reader's Guide to George Orwell,* Thames & Hudson, 1975.

Isaac Rosenfeld, review of *Animal Farm,* in *Nation,* September 7, 1946, p. 373.

Arthur M. Schlesinger, Jr., "Mr. Orwell and the Communists," in *New York Times Book Review,* August 25, 1946, pp. 1, 28.

Stephen Sedley, "An Immodest Proposal: *Animal Farm*" in *Inside the Myth: Orwell, Views from the Left,* edited by Christopher Norris, Lawrence and Wishart, 1984, pp. 155–62.

George Soule, "Orwell's Fables," in *New Republic,* Vol. 115, No. 9, September 2, 1946, pp. 266-67.

Edmund Wilson, review of *Animal Farm,* in *New Yorker,* Vol. XXII, No. 30, September 7, 1946, p. 97.

George Woodcock, in his *The Crystal Spirit: A Study of George Orwell,* Little, Brown, 1966.

For Further Study

Sant Singh Bal, in his *George Orwell: The Ethical Imagination,* Arnold-Heinnemann, 1981.
>   Bal explores the universality of Orwell's novel and compares it to *Darkness at Noon* by Arthur Koestler.

"Beastly," in *Economist,* August 12, 1995, p. 71.
>   Short review praising the novel on the fiftieth anniversary of its publication.

Northrop Frye, "Turning New Leaves," in *The Canadian Forum,* Vol. XXVI, No. 311, December, 1946, pp. 211-12.
>   An early review of *Animal Farm* in which Frye criticizes thenovel for failing to explore the reasons why the principles behind the Soviet revolution failed.

Frederick R. Karl, "George Orwell: The White Man's Burden," in his *A Reader's Guide to the Contemporary English Novel,* revised edition, Farrar, Strauss & Giroux, 1972, pp. 148-66.
>   Karl briefly discusses *Animal Farm* as a failed, predictable satire.

Peter Lewis, *George Orwell: The Road to 1984,* Harcourt, 1981.
>   Mainly a biographical work, profusely illustrated, that gives important background material behind the writing of *Animal Farm.*

George Orwell, "Preface to the Ukrainian Edition of *Animal Farm,*" in his *The Collected Essays, Journalism and Letters of George Orwell: As I Please, 1943-1945, Vol. III,* edited by Sonia Orwell and Ian Angus, Harcourt, 1968, pp. 402-6.
>   Important essay for understanding how Orwell came to write the book.

George Orwell, "Why I Write," in *Orwell's* Nineteen Eighty-Four: *Text, Sources, Criticism,* edited by Irving Howe, 2nd edition, Harcourt, 1982.
>   A significant essay in which Orwell analyzes his need to write.

Edward M. Thomas, "Politics and Literature," in his *Orwell,* Barnes & Noble, 1967, pp. 65-77.
>   Praises *Animal Farm* as a perfect fusion of the political and the artistic.

Annie John

Jamaica Kincaid

1985

Ever since Jamaica Kincaid's work began appearing in *The New Yorker* magazine, it has excited critics and enthralled readers. Kincaid has been praised for her ability to tell the story of a girl attaining womanhood with all the emotion and beauty it deserves. Simultaneously, Kincaid expresses the significance and politics involved in that transition. Her second book, *Annie John* (1985), is comprised of short stories that first appeared in *The New Yorker.* Some critics consider *Annie John* a novel because the compilation of interwoven stories uncover the moral and psychological growth of the title character. This bildungsroman (coming-of-age story) has become Kincaid's best–known work to date.

Through Annie, Kincaid has brilliantly brought girlhood in the West Indies to literature as a masterful work of art. That art is a prose blend of European, American, and Caribbean folk forms of expression. The result is an effective rendering of a girl's struggle to discover her own identity. Annie is a girl growing up in an idyllic garden setting. At first she is the sole figure in that Eden— she has only her parents and Miss Maynard to interact with—and she maintains her sense of singularity when she finally begins mixing with others. Her omnipotent mother keeps the powers of the world and of death at a distance. Gradually, however, her mother introduces death and separation in order to mature Annie and prepare her for the world. The story of the mother creating the daughter is not unlike the works of Mary Shelley

(*Frankenstein*) or John Milton (*Paradise Lost*) in the sense that the created becomes more than the creator intended.

Author Biography

Kincaid once said in an interview that her history began on ships and continues as corruption. By this she meant that the ideal human morality—which the Europeans tried to disseminate with empire—had instead become political, cultural, and moral corruption. That was the gift left behind as independence. Her island of Antigua is a microcosm of all newly independent colonies and the ensuing corruption. And Kincaid, like other West Indian people, is an amalgam of all who arrived at these islands by boat—Carib Indian, African, and Scottish. Kincaid explained this to Allan Vorda, for *The Mississippi Review* by telling how the library (from whence she stole books as a girl) that was ruined by an earthquake in 1974 would have been rebuilt by the colonial administrator. "Antigua used to be a place of standards. There was a sort of decency that it just doesn't have anymore. I think the tragedy of Antigua for me, when I began to see it again, was the loss of the library."

At the time of the earthquake, Kincaid was living in New York and she had recently taken up her name. She was born in Antigua May 25, 1949 as Elaine Potter Richardson, daughter of Annie Richardson and a father of whom she will not speak. When her family's economic situation made a turn for the worse, Kincaid dropped out of the university. At seventeen, she was sent to Westchester, New York, to work as an *au pair,* or nanny. Kincaid continued to pursue her education, however, and studied photography at the New School and later attended Franconia College in New Hampshire. In her early twenties, the desire to write became urgent but she did not think serious writing was being done anymore.

Dreading to be known, should her attempt to write fail, she fished about for a new name. She was not familiar with the black power movement or other African-American political groups and so did not choose an African name. Besides, she has often said, the only thing she has in common with Africa is her skin color. Her consciousness is a construct of the western hemisphere. Reflecting this consciousness, along with her view of her history as a blend of corruption and boats, she chose the name Jamaica. Jamaica is derived from *Xaymaca,*

Jamaica Kincaid

the translation Columbus made of the Carib Indian word for that island, translated again into English. She chose Kincaid because, as she told Allan Vorda, "it just seemed to go together with Jamaica."

Soon after becoming Jamaica Kincaid, her writing came to the attention of William Shawn, editor of the *The New Yorker.* She became a staff writer there in 1976 and married the editor's son, Allen Shawn. In 1983, her collection of stories titled, *At the Bottom of the River* won an American Academy Zabel award. Kincaid followed up *At the Bottom of the River* with *Annie John* in 1985. In addition to writing fiction, Kincaid has published *A Small Place,* about colonialism and tourism in Antigua. She also continues to write a gardening column.

Plot Summary

Jamaica Kincaid's *Annie John* tells the story of a girl's painful growth into young womanhood. Annie Victoria John, the narrator, progresses from a blissful childhood in Antigua, when she is the center of her mother's attention, to a trying adolescence filled with fierce maternal conflict, to her departure from Antigua for England at the age of seventeen.

Figures in the Distance

At ten, Annie does not know that children die until a young girl dies in Annie's mother's arms. Annie's mother (also named Annie John) must prepare the child for burial while Annie's father, Alexander, builds her coffin. Annie begins to see her mother's hands differently after this experience and, for a time, does not want to be touched by or look at them. Soon, after two more of her acquaintances die, Annie secretly begins to sneak to strangers' funerals. Then a humpbacked girl her own age dies. Annie runs to the girl's funeral after school, forgetting to pick up fish for dinner. She is caught lying to her mother about her mistake and must eat dinner alone and go to bed without a kiss. However, when in bed, her mother comes and kisses her anyway.

The Circling Hand

In the chapter's early pages, Annie describes her idyllic holidays when she and her mother bathe together and share her mother's activities. She describes her mother's trunk, in which she has kept all of Annie's possessions since birth. She sometimes tells Annie stories about each of the trunk's objects, delighting Annie, who revels in her mother's love. This life of "paradise" begins to falter, though, when Annie's body begins to change. Annie's mother now forces her to stop wearing dresses made from her mother's fabric and sends Annie to learn both manners and to play the piano, at which Annie fails through misbehavior. Then Annie accidentally catches her parents making love and stares at her mother's hand making circular motions on her father's back. That night, Annie behaves defiantly toward her mother for the first time and is silently sure she will never let her mother touch or kiss her again. The next day, though, she allows her mother to kiss her when she returns from her first day at her new school.

Gwen

When Annie first arrives at her new school, she is friendless and unsure of herself. After her teacher assigns them autobiographical essays to write, however, Annie shows she is the smartest girl in her class. She writes of a day she spent with her mother bathing nude in the sea. She lost sight of her mother and, afraid of the water, could not swim to find her. When her mother returned, she comforted Annie, telling her she would never leave her. Annie later dreamt of this event, only her mother does not return in the dream. She told her mother of the dream and received comfort again. Annie moves many of the girls to tears with this story. She does not tell them, though, that the story's ending is fiction. In actuality, her mother responded to the nightmare by warning Annie against eating unripe fruit before bed. Later that day, Annie makes friends with Gweneth Joseph, and they become inseparable companions. Annie soon becomes the first of her friends to menstruate. At school recess, in a nook of old tombstones, she exhibits her menstruation to them and they comfort her. Annie returns home to her mother, whom she feels she no longer loves.

The Red Girl

In her continuing rebellion against her mother, Annie strikes up a secret friendship with the Red Girl, an unkept girl with red hair who loves to play marbles, a game forbidden by Annie's mother. Annie begins to see the Red Girl secretly, to play marbles, and to steal, hiding her treasures underneath the house. When caught with a marble, Annie lies that she does not play marbles. Her mother, not believing her, searches under the house for Annie's marble collection but cannot find it. After days of futile searching, she tells Annie a terrifying story of her own girlhood. Annie, moved by the story, almost tells the truth until she recognizes her mother's attempt to manipulate her. The Red Girl soon moves away, and Annie dreams of living with her on a deserted island, where they joyfully send misdirected ships crashing into rocks.

Columbus in Chains

During history class, Annie reads ahead to a picture of Columbus chained in the bottom of a ship. Annie loves this picture of the colonizer brought low, and she relates it to a story about her grandfather, Pa Chess, who was rendered immobile by an illness. Annie writes her mother's laughing response to Pa Chess's plight under Columbus's picture: "'The Great Man Can No Longer Just Get Up and Go.'" She is caught by her teacher and must copy Books I and II of John Milton's *Paradise Lost*. At home, Annie's misery is compounded when her mother disguises breadfruit, which Annie hates, as rice and then laughs about it.

Somewhere, Belgium

When fifteen, Annie feels an inexplicable misery that sits inside her like a "thimble that weighed worlds." She and her mother are constantly at odds, though they hide their conflicts from others. Annie has a recurring dream in which she thinks, "'My mother would kill me if she got the chance. I would kill my mother if I had the courage.'" Since she has always been taught that dreams are the same as real life, the dream's words haunt her. Annie daydreams of living alone in Belgium like Charlotte Brontë, the author of *Jane Eyre,* her favorite novel. One day, while studying her reflection in a shop window, Annie is taunted by four boys. She recognizes one of them as a childhood playmate who once almost hanged himself accidentally while she just stood by watching and who made her sit naked on a red ants' nest. When she returns home, her mother scolds her for talking to the boys, saying she acted like a slut. Annie retorts in kind, then goes to her room. She thinks about the trunk under her bed, which makes her both long for her mother and wish her dead. When her father offers to build her some new furniture, Annie requests her own trunk.

The Long Rain

Despite a lack of clear symptoms, Annie falls ill for three and a half months and cannot leave her bed. Corresponding with her illness is an unusual period of heavy rains. Her illness distorts her perceptions, one time causing her to try to wash clean the imperfections in her framed photographs, ruining them. Annie's grandmother Ma Chess arrives and assures Annie's mother that the girl's sickness is not like her uncle Johnnie's, who died from a curse after laying two years in bed. Ma Chess, an obeah (or voodoo) woman, becomes Annie's primary caregiver. On the day the rains stop, Annie's illness disappears. During her illness, Annie has grown taller than her mother, and she now feels repulsed by the world in which she lives.

A Walk to the Jetty

Now seventeen and willing to go anywhere to escape Antigua, Annie is scheduled to leave for England to study nursing. She mentally sums up her life, concentrating on her relationship with her parents. She says a polite goodbye to Gwen, who will soon be married, something which Annie vows never to be. She then walks between her parents to the docks and surveys the world she is leaving, feeling both gladness and sharp pain. At her ship, she bids farewell to her parents, both crying with her mother and feeling suspicious of her. The novel ends with her in her cabin listening to the waves making "an unexpected sound, as if a vessel filled with liquid had been placed on its side and now was slowly emptying out."

Characters

Ma Chess

Grandmother embodies the traditions of the West Indies that Annie's mother abandoned when she left Dominica. Annie John's father's preference for Dr. Stephens indicates his desire to also leave these traditions behind. However, one day, Grandmother arrives and does not leave until Annie recovers.

Father
See Mr. Alexander John

Grandmother
See Ma Chess

Mr. Alexander John

Mr. Alexander John, Annie's father, is thirty-five years older than his wife and has many unacknowledged heirs. He is a carpenter builder who brings humorous tales about Mr. Oatie, his partner in the construction business, back to the lunch table. These daily reports have the effect of emphasizing the growing tension between mother and daughter. During the lunch routine, they behave properly to each other and Mother rarely fails to be amused by his stories. Mr. John represents the world of masculinity for which Annie's mother is preparing her. Until Annie is ushered into that world, however, it remains as distant as the haunting idea of boys playing marbles.

Mr. John built the family's house and made the furniture within. He protests against allowing the obeah woman to tend to Annie and he does not like Ma Chess. However, there is one moment of closeness between Annie and her father when he tells her of his own mother. Given the fears and obsession Annie has with her mother, this apparent empathy with Mr. John is actually a moment when Annie vicariously experiences the fantasy of being like her father—sleeping with mother until the age of eighteen when mother, then, conveniently dies.

Miss Annie Victoria John

The title character is a precocious young girl growing up in an Edenic garden governed by her loving mother. This changes with the onset of puberty and the declaration of independence her mother imposes on her. A civil war breaks out between them not unlike the Angelic war of *Paradise*

A nine-year-old girl carries water in St. John's, Antigua, after the 1995 storm Hurricane Luis cut off water and electricity to homes.

Lost. The more Annie struggles to be distant and different from her mother the more alike they become. In the end, Annie leaves the island with her own trunk, calling to mind the exodus her mother made from Dominca years before.

As the narrator of the story, Annie is at liberty to fabricate reality as she sees fit. Consequently, the line between myth or dream and reality is thin. She actively imitates her favorite literary personas, Satan and Jane Eyre, who moved into their own adult identities through rebellion and flight and recreated, in some way, the exact world from which they fled.

Annie also allows the traditional culture to exist with the present. She loves her grandmother and the magic her grandmother has. She is not afraid to give that as much importance as the magic of the schoolteacher and the doctor.

Finally, Annie dies to her childish self—the self that ruled the girls who gathered among the tombstones during recess and the child who hid marbles and stolen books beneath the house. This occurs during a three-month rain while she is ill. Recovery comes with the help of her grandmother

and the realization that she is too large for her home—she is now literally taller than both her parents. Not only does she want to leave, she must leave as a necessary step in her formation as a woman. She must take her trunk and go to a new place and build her world there.

Mrs. Annie Victoria John

Having fallen out with her father at age sixteen, Mrs. John packed her yellow-and-green trunk and left Dominica for Antigua. The boat she left in was hit by a hurricane and was lost at sea for five days. The boat was a ruin but Mrs. John and her trunk were fine. Annie's baby clothes and memories are kept in this same trunk beneath her bed. It is fitting that the mother's trunk comes to be used in this way because, as she says to Annie, "I loved you best."

Mrs. John is the benevolent goddess governing the garden from which little Annie observes the funeral, observes death. The paradise cannot remain such forever and gradually the mother introduces death and separation. She has formed Annie and she sends Annie away.

Mother's position is typical of Caribbean women. The women run the households and the men are sent out to work. Consequently, the children are indistinguishable from the mother while she goes about her tasks until it is appropriate to give the children their own identities. But in *Annie John* this situation becomes abnormally tense because there is only one identity. Furthermore, there is only one name. The mother fights to give it away while Annie struggles to take it.

Ma Jolie

A local obeah woman reccomended by Ma Chess. Mother calls her to come administer to Annie. Ma Jolie does not know as much as Ma Chess, however, and can do little. She prescribes traditional medicines, places appropriate candles in the room, and pins a foul-smelling sachet to Annie's nightie. The obeah concoctions are set behind Dr. Stephen's on the shelf above Annie's bed.

Gweneth Joseph

She is the first girl at the new school to notice Annie. It is not long before the two girls fall in love and become inseparable. But, eventually, Annie becomes bored with Gwen and in the end comes to see Gwen as a silly, giggling, schoolgirl come to bid farewell. She tells Annie of her engagement and receives a humored blessing. Annie stands inwardly amazed that she ever loved Gwen.

Little Miss

See Miss Annie Victoria John

Mineu

Mineu is a playmate of Annie's and the only boy close to her age in the narrative. When together, Annie and Mineu liked to reenact local events. This play leads Mineu to fake his own hanging in order to imitate an actual hanging. Annie watches as it goes wrong. She is unable to move. Luckily a neighbor comes and saves the boy. Years later she meets him in the street. They simply say "hello." Meanwhile, his friends snicker and poke each other while Annie's mother catches sight of the scene. Later, her mother calls her a slut for talking to him.

Mother

See Mrs. Annie Victoria John

Red Girl

The Red Girl embodies the very antithesis of what Annie has been taught to be proper. They meet when the Red Girl climbs a tree to collect a guava in a manner normally reserved to boys. She is dirty, smelly, and plays marbles with the boys. Annie embraces and kisses her, as the ultimate rebellion against her mother's notions. It is the temptation of the Red Girl that leads Annie into a "series of betrayals of people and things."

Ruth

The daughter of the Anglican minister doesn't fare well in Antigua. Ruth is one of the few English children in the community. She is an embarrassed blonde who is frequently the class dunce. Annie thinks that Ruth would rather be home in England "where no one would remind her constantly of the terrible things her ancestors had done."

Dr. Stephens

The family doctor is an Englishman named Dr. Stephens. He represents modern science and has served the family through Annie's other illnesses—like hookworm. Mother agrees with his theory that germs need to be rooted out and destroyed. He represents modern science and is approved of by Mr. John, but his medicinal prescriptions prove ineffectual against Annie's debilitating depression.

Media Adaptations

- An audio cassette was made of *Annie John* in 1994 by Airplay Inc.

Themes

Death

Death enters the frame of *Annie John* at the outset and never leaves. As a distant event observed by Annie, death serves as a counter reality to Annie's position as the beloved of her mother. Consequently, Annie's obsession with this other reality keeps the possibility of separation as the end of her blissful girlhood absolutely hidden. Death also serves to exaggerate the distance of the story and, thus, hide the narrator. In the first sentence, therefore, the adult narrator transforms into a girl fascinated by the apparently abstract concept of death.

There is a literal graveyard in the distance that Annie sees figures, not people per se, enter and leave. Death comes closer when Nalda, Sonia's mother, and then Miss Charlotte die. Annie is attentive to this facet of life and watches it. She observes funerals. She notes where death is. Yet she does not grieve. Annie wants to touch death by touching the hunched back of a dead girl whose funeral she attends for the purpose of observation. Disturbing Annie's peace, however, death nears her twice through the person of her mother who was holding Nalda and talking to Miss Charlotte when they died. These two events foreshadow the discovery of imperfection in Annie's universe.

Death does not come to Annie but she dies to three things: her girlhood, her mother, and her home. The first two take place through inevitable growth events. There is much that marks Annie as becoming a woman and, therefore, rivaling her mother for ownership of their shared name. The two primary events are her first menstruation and her illness. Her first menstruation is full of death images beyond the obvious significance of biological change—she faints because, she says, "I brought to my mind a clear picture of myself sit-

Topics for Further Study

- Working from the example of Annie and her mother, what is the psychological make up of the family? Is there one working model or do we all have individual relationships?

- Compare how families—especially mothers—are portrayed in today's media with the novel's portrayal. Use examples of television sit-coms, cartoons, and movies for your findings.

- Think about Annie's illness and the help she received from the obeah woman; does your family use any home remedies? Ask your parents what their parents did for them when they were not feeling well and compare that with how your family currently treats illness.

- Research the politics of travel or photographic hunting. What, if any ethics are involved with the pursuit of recreation or game? What impact does the multi-billion-dollar tourism industry have on native peoples and the environment?

- Respond to the following excerpt from Kincaid's essay, *A Small Place:* "Have you ever wondered why it is that all we seemed to have learned from you is how to corrupt our society and how to be tyrants … ? You came."

ting at my desk in my own blood." Her illness is a mock death. When she comes forth from her sick bed she is taller and no longer seems to be of the Antiguan world.

Identity

The central struggle, or agon, in Annie's story is her struggle to bring forth her own identity. That identity is fulfilled through the scripted story of the trunk—she will have her identity when she leaves bearing her trunk. This struggle involves mood swings, rebellious adventures, the awakening of sexuality, and a coming to terms with historical reality. However, the person on whom this struggle is focused, and who has some responsibility in its instigation, is her mother. The mother-daughter ten-

sion dominates the work. The tension is not eased though Annie's struggle meets with success. She gains an identity despite her adult telling of her story—in which she clearly becomes a woman in her mother's image—actual reconciliation is absent. Annie's trunk carrying identity, then, is a death to her self and loss of her mother.

Life as a child is set up as Edenic. Annie is indistinguishable from her mother and happiness reigns. That is, until the day her mother says they are now separate. The demand for Annie to suddenly be independent, to have her own subjectivity, is the high of the book. It arrives in Chapter 2; the central image is that of her parents having sex and particularly "The Circling Hand" of her mother on her father's back. At that point, Annie says, "To say that I felt the earth swept away from under me would not be going too far." Her model of the universe—a dual universe with two beings in one dress fabric—had suddenly become a universe of independent bodies all doing their own things to their own ends. The rest of the work details the way in which Annie puts herself back together and finds her own reflection. She had been seeing herself as a smaller version of her mother but gradually she sees her own reflection in a shop window. She reminds herself of "Satan just recently cast out of heaven." Eventually, identity formation leads her to a figurative death. Her recovery from her illness is also her arrival at her identity as a woman. Recovered, she is taller, conscious of her power as a woman who knows herself, and with her new wisdom she sees she has outgrown the very island of Antigua.

Annie uses several tools to form her identity. The first is her body. Her prowess and strength affords her respect from her classmates and captainship of the volleyball team. The other tool is her intellect. Being above average, she is not delinquent in opportunities to boost her confidence. But this does not prove as important as knowledge gained by observing people at home and hearing stories. One such story is of her mother's departure from Dominica. Annie knows the story well and, therefore, always has an example of strong womanhood before her. She also knows the story of her father, but she rejects his narrative although she empathizes with his tragedy. There are other narratives she rejects. Uncle John was a promising young man who died young. Annie notes that his belongings are kept in a trunk. Annie's things are in a trunk, too, but she decides to follow her mother's narrative and leave Antigua with a trunk—a new one—rather than follow the other narratives which both involve death. Re-enforcing her choice is Charlotte Brontë's story of *Jane Eyre,* whose heroine also strikes out on her own.

Post-Colonialism

Post-colonialism is a literary theory developed in response to the literature being written by people in countries previously governed by the British crown. In the years since the granting of independence, the people of these nations have had to reconcile their identity as educated British subjects with their awareness of their own subjugation by that government brought about by sudden self-determination. This resonates directly with Annie's identification with *Jane Eyre* as well as references to Milton and Shakespeare. Annie has been taught English literature—stories from the land of the former colonial administration. However, the postcolonial writer does not reject this literature; instead, she embraces it as her own. She also embraces the English tongue as her language, but now she will use them to tell her own story.

There are many references to the history of colonialism in *Annie John,* but two key moments involve a classmate named Ruth and Christopher Columbus. Both occur in Chapter 5, "Columbus in Chains," but resonate throughout the entire work. Being a good student with aspirations, Annie has trouble remembering the reality of her heritage or discerning whether she fits in "with the masters or the slaves—for it was all history, it was all in the past, and everybody behaved differently now." Still, there is some remembering and hard feelings over the past. Annie says of Ruth, "Perhaps she wanted to be in England, where no one would remind her [what] her ancestors had done."

Crucial to Annie's understanding of herself as a postcolonial subject is her crime against history. She is caught not paying attention to a history lesson, but she is punished for defacing her schoolbook in a way that was blasphemous. "I had gone too far this time," she says, "defaming one of the great men in history, Christopher Columbus, discoverer of the island that was my home." Annie is aware of how tenuous is the idea that this island is her home. She is here only as the curious result of Empire. Still, it is her home just as English culture is hers but with a little obeah thrown in.

Style

Point of View

The first person ("I") retrospective narrative is constructed with episodes. The prime person in *An-nie John* is, of course, Annie. Therefore, the Antigua shown the reader is that which is filtered through Annie. There are eight episodes highlighted in the chapter headings. During each episode more information is given about Annie. The timeline jumps but there is a steady progression from Annie as a young girl to her departure from home as a young woman.

This narrative, however, is ironic because an adult Annie establishes the reality of the story as if it was the perspective of little Annie. In other words, Annie knows her own story's outcome but tries not to reveal this. The novel opens by literally noticing figures in a distance and also by placing the story at a distance, "during the year I was ten." Thus the effort on the part of the young Annie to show her mother as an Old Testament deity is offset by the adult attempt to reconcile. The mother remains beautiful and loved though the literal story might say she is simply left behind.

Symbolism

The most important symbol of the work is the trunk. Each of the characters has a trunk—a place where their identity formation blocks are kept. In the case of Uncle John, it is all that is left. For Annie, the trunk with all of her baby things is a fun thing to clean out because she then hears stories about herself. When she leaves Antigua, Annie—like her mother when she left Dominica—takes a new trunk to build a new life. Father has a trunk but it is not solid. Father's trunk is everywhere. It is made up of all the women and illegitimate children that Annie and her mother run into. It is made up of the house and furniture he built. He adds to this trunk daily with stories about work because there is no one who wants to tell his story—Mother is busy with Annie's story.

Irony

Irony is akin to an "inside joke." It occurs when the intended meaning is the opposite of what is actually said. Kincaid offers many wonderful moments of irony. One example is in Chapter 5, when Annie says that colonialism is past and now "all of us celebrate Queen Victoria's birthday." It is a rather sudden cultural reference in the midst of a paragraph about the past. Many things happen in the phrase. Annie has been saying that the past is behind them, yet they still celebrate some queen's birthday. She is also noting that the personification of colonialism (the reign of Queen Victoria was the heyday of the Empire) remains as a national holiday.

More of these ironic moments involve works of literature. For example, on the desk of Miss Nelson, an Englishwoman, is an elaborate edition of Shakespeare's play *The Tempest.* She is reading this work while the girls are writing their autobiographical essays. The irony is that on the one hand, the teacher is simply reading one of the great plays of English literature. The deeper implication is very complex because that play has become a grand touchstone for all postcolonial writers, especially those of the Caribbean. The reason is this: many intellectuals of those islands read that play as the moment of conquest, as if Shakespeare was writing the reality of colonialism into effect with his play. Further, the figure of Caliban—a person brought to the island to labor—mixes his identity with the spirit of the island, Sycorax. Caliban is a slave who has learned English so that he can curse his master. The children writing their essays are a result of the same process—brought to the island and now expected to peacefully get along with their former masters. Particularly, Annie's narrative involves her being stranded on a little island—like the characters in the play—but unable to call to her mother. She, like Caliban, yells at her master but there can be no understanding.

Dream Vision

Unlike the culture whose literature she adores (in *Jane Eyre,* for example, mythology has been banished from England), Annie does not divide the mythical from reality. Kincaid uses this in the narrative itself, so that dreams and myth are written in and make up her characters. The result of this is the legitimating of oral tradition. The first instance of this appears early in the novel and concerns the dead. Annie reports that "sometimes they showed up in a dream, but that wasn't so bad, because they usually only brought a warning." Another example of this technique comes when Kincaid has Annie recite her autobiographical essay. This essay is atypical because in some sense it is a very mature psychological metaphor but it also mythologizes the mother-daughter relationship. A final example is the event of Annie's and Mother's "black things," subjective demons, wrestling on the lunch table only to return—never to grapple again—to their rightful owners. This blending of realities validates dreaming as a way of thinking; it carries on the traditions represented by the obeah woman and Ma Chess.

Historical Context

Contact, Colonialism, and Independence

Originally inhabited by the Siboney people, the Island of Antigua, the setting for Kincaid's *Annie John,* was populated by Arawak and Carib Indians when Christopher Columbus arrived there during his second voyage in 1493. He named the island after a church in Sevilla, Spain, named Santa Maria de la Antigua. Thirty years later it became an outpost of the Spanish Conquistadors. In 1629, the French made a base there as Spanish power descended and the British had not yet taken control. French control was brief, however, and the English arrived in 1632. The Treaty of Breda formalized this situation in 1667.

From 1674 to 1834, the island was one large sugar plantation. Slaves were imported from Africa because the indigenous peoples fled or had been killed. The end of slavery brought freedom but no opportunity to be free. For the next hundred years, Antigua and surrounding islands were under the jurisdiction of one and then another federation. Greater independence was achieved in 1967, with statehood within the British Commonwealth granted in 1981. Finally the seven islands of the East Caribbean formed a merger. The single nation of the Organization of Eastern Caribbean States (OECS) came into being in 1987 and included the former British colonies: Antigua, Barbados, Dominica, Grenada, Jamaica, Montserrat, St. Kitts-Nevis-Anguilla, St. Vincent, Tobago, and Trinidad.

Latin America and the Caribbean

The 1980s was a troubled decade for the nations of Latin America and the Caribbean. Warily, they attempted to cease being the playground and raw material supplier of Europe and America. In doing so, they strengthened old trading alliances and forged new ones. Meanwhile, the United States began to create NAFTA with Canada and Mexico, while Europe moved closer to unionization. In addition to economic competition, the United States practiced active interventionism.

Acting out of the Monroe Doctrine—that the United States will not tolerate interference by any European power (including Russia) in the affairs of the Western Hemisphere—and the precedent set by President Theodore Roosevelt, the United States intervened everywhere to both good and bad effect. In the late 1990s, the U.S. still enforced a trade embargo against Cuba that had been in effect since

1959. It may never be known just how involved the United States was in the turmoil that disrupted life in El Salvador and Nicaragua throughout the 1980s. Nor will the full story of Haiti's troubles be known. Less mysterious, however, were the invasions of Grenada in 1983 and Panama in 1989. In the first case, the Reagan administration acted in reaction to a coup, the potential endangerment of U.S. medical students, and the fear of even closer ties between Grenada and Cuba. The leader of Panama, on the other hand, was accused of laundering drug money. He was arrested in the invasion and began serving a sentence of forty years in the United States.

The 1980s in the United States

The decade of the eighties was original only in the way that culture in the United States sought to blend its past into the now. It was marked by pastiche, superficiality, recreations of old movie serials, nostalgia for a golden age that only ever existed on television, and "culture wars." The economy hummed at the surface with any sort of lifestyle and time available for consumption. Meanwhile, corporate mergers, downsizing, and an abrupt shift toward service economy left industrial America partially unemployed and the labor movement—beginning with the air-traffic controllers's strike of 1981—drastically weakened. To offset this industrial downsizing, the government embarked on an awesome weapons program. The result was an incomprehensible debt and a huge pile of nuclear warheads that nobody wants to ever, ever, use. It seemed to be a decade of deciding what to do—no clear answer has yet emerged.

Race Relations

The Civil Rights movement encountered a backlash in the 1980s for which it was unprepared. Leaders of the movement knew the highpoint and victories of the 1960s were past but they could hardly believe that the Miami riots of 1980 announced a decade of violence. Membership in neo-Nazi and Ku Klux Klan groups rose while racially motivated hate-crimes increased in frequency. Normally tolerant environments, like college campuses, reflected this trend. The climate of the nation had suddenly become conservative.

Elections in the 1980s reflected the drastic change. Reverend Jesse Jackson, considered by many to be the successor to Martin Luther King Jr., ran twice for president in 1984 and 1988 as a Democrat. But the 1980s instead saw Republican Pres-

Map of the island of Antigua, which in 1981 became part of the independent state of Antigua and Barbuda.

ident Ronald Reagan complete two terms of office that were succeeded by George Bush. Reagan won in a landslide because the populace felt that change might have occurred too fast. The brakes were applied and civil rights victories began to be overturned. In 1987, legendary civil rights activist and the first black to serve on the U.S. Supreme Court, Justice Thurgood Marshall, expressed his opinion that President Reagan was ranked at the bottom in terms of civil rights for all Americans, black or white. In a symbolic capping off of the decade, the elections of 1989 brought Republican David Duke, a former Ku Klux Klan grand wizard, to the Louisiana state legislature. Much to the relief of everyone, including the embarrassed Republican Party, Duke's bid for the U.S. Senate was unsuccessful.

Critical Overview

Response to *Annie John* has been unanimous in its praise. Reviewers focus on Kincaid's successful writing of a girl's coming of age as well as the wonder and excitement of a historic epicenter—the Caribbean. More serious views of the work simply explore this theme further by investigating the family as represented in the story and as existing in the West Indies. Critics have also noticed aspects of the novel which break new ground. For example, the harmony with which Kincaid treats the blending of obeah and modern medicine.

First reviews of the work in 1985 were excited, glowing, and attentive to Kincaid's prose ability. Paula Bonnell wrote in *The Boston Herald,* that the publication of Kincaid's first two books were "eagerly awaited events." Both, she continues, "are recreations of the self in that emotional country where dreams and what might have happened are part of the truest story of one's life." Jacqueline Austin agreed. She wrote a review in *VLS* months later saying, "Kincaid does write what she knows, what she knows is rare: pure passion, a past filled with curious events, a voice, and above all a craft." Austin also comments in passing about heritage. She names other writers from the West Indies to say that Kincaid is in a group trying to "encompass two traditions." She doesn't go much further nor does she say which two traditions. John Bemrose is more particular in his review for *Maclean's Magazine.* He says, "The instrument of Kincaid's success is a prose style whose subtly varied cadences suggest the slow, dignified pace of life in colonial Antigua. She also knows her way around the human heart." In the *Times Literary Supplement* in the fall of 1985, Ike Onwordi adds nothing new. He glosses over the fact that Kincaid's work is an "episodic" autobiography using "language that is poetic without affectation."

Heavier analysis of *Annie John* followed slowly. In 1990, H. Adlai Murdoch wrote an article for *Callaloo,* entitled, "Severing the (M)other Connection: The Representation of Cultural Identity in Jamaica Kincaid's *Annie John*" where he attempted to reconfigure the Oedipal tools of Freud for an utterly matriarchal order. Murdoch argues that as Caribbean writers began to create their own literature free of the burden of empire, they must confront the Oedipal tensions of identity formation. Such a reading assumes that the only route to the child's, or the newly independent nation's, subjectivity is by confrontation and overthrow of the father, or ruling power. Only then can the child own his culture, or mother. "The issue of subjectivity, beset with problems such as recognition of self and other and oedipal conflict under the most conventional circumstances, is complicated further here given the additional factors of colonialism and pluralism which continue to mark Caribbean society and culture." Fortunately, Murdoch does not belabor Freud's script but adds Lacan's notion of mirror as well as the more deconstructionist notion of phallic signifier. Together they enable a reading in which Annie's mother is the main power broker against whom Annie struggles, as would the son against the father in traditional Freudian readings, to attain her independent subjectivity. This analysis stays within the realm of psychological interpretation despite its promise to link postcolonial facets as well.

More recent criticism reflects postcolonial theory and views Kincaid as a postcolonial writer. Bill Ahscroft, Gareth Griffiths, and Helen Tiffin wrote the book on postcolonialism in 1989—*The Empire Writes Back: Theory and Practice in Post-Colonial Literatures.* The theory arises out of the historical fact that English literature as a discipline arose concurrently with the pressures of Empire. Consequently, previously colonized people found themselves independent but speaking English. They were not returned to pre-colonialism. They had to create a new cultural identity at peace with the unpleasantness of colonialism and new sovereignty. With the realization of this phenomenon, critics like James Nagel reread Kincaid's *Annie John* as more than a bildungsroman or coming of age story. Thus in his 1995 article, "Desperate Hopes, Desperate Lives: Depression and Self-Realization in Jamaica Kincaid's *Annie John* and Lucy," he builds upon Murdoch's insight. The mother becomes blended with the greater powers and the Oedipal constructs fracture beneath the pressure. The family's dynamics are now linked to the greater historical event that is Antigua.

Nagel notes the traditional bildungsroman aspects of the novel and then includes the background: "a legacy of slavery and deprivation and the rich texture of Annie's family life ... as well as the English cultural overlay on the social patterns of Antigua ... the eminence of the Anglican Church ... European Christianity ... folk rituals of potions and curses.... Everything in this society has a dual foundation, even the local dialect." The novel is seen here for its complexity and applauded for its ability to express the multiplicity of Antigua through the charm of a little girl. But that is art— to show how people live in their own circumstances. Allen Vorda quotes Henry Louis Gates saying this about Kincaid: "she never feels the necessity of claiming the existence of a black world or a female susceptibility. She assumes them both. I think its a distinct departure that she's making, and I think that more and more black American writers will assume their world the way that she does. So that we can get beyond the large theme of racism and get to the deeper themes of how black people love and cry and live and die. Which, after all, is what art is all about."

Beyond the areas where Kincaid subtly breaks new ground—as in her casual blending of traditional and modern medicine through the meeting of the obeah and pharmaceutical medicines—there is the serious craft that Gates describes. Kincaid's writing is wonderful and her story captivatingly emotional because, while she is expressing a political transformation, she focuses on the human effect—the effect on the little girl.

Criticism

Darren Felty

Darren Felty is a visiting instructor at the College of Charleston. In the following essay, he examines the struggles of Annie John, Jamaica Kincaid's protagonist, to define her own character in relation to her family and culture.

Critics often characterize Jamaica Kincaid's *Annie John* as a bildungsroman, or a coming-of-age narrative that traces the protagonist's quest for both self-knowledge and a distinct place in the world.

Such a description proves apt for Kincaid's largely autobiographical novel, since her work revolves around a series of conflicts related to her young protagonist's search for emotional stability and self-definition. Growing up worshiping her mother and living in a nurturing, almost blissful environment, Annie loses a secure sense of herself with the advent of puberty and her mother's insistence on emotional separation.

In addition to Annie's familial life, Kincaid also explores the cultural dynamics of Antigua through Annie's confrontations with the island's colonial legacy and her depictions of persistent African belief systems.

By focusing the work through Annie's eyes, Kincaid allows the reader intimate access to Annie's attempts to define herself in relation to others and to her culture. Yet despite this point of view and the lyrical, evocative style of Annie's narration, Kincaid does not romanticize Annie's conflicts or strain for reader sympathy. Instead, Kincaid insists on honestly portraying Annie's multiple reactions to her dilemmas, whether they evoke the reader's compassion or reproach. By doing so, she invites the reader to share her main character's negotiation of her turbulent adolescence and to witness the slow, painful development of inner resources that allow her to embark on a journey into the unknown.

Throughout the novel, Annie's relationship with her mother remains at the heart of her most pressing conflicts. The older Annie who narrates the book describes her early years as Edenic, with only fleeting doubts to interfere with her intense love for her mother. In fact, basking in her mother's attention, Annie recognizes the "paradise" of her existence and pities those people who lack such love.

Soon, however, Annie becomes one of these people herself when she enters puberty. Recognizing the end of her daughter's childhood, Annie's mother forces her to move beyond their close relationship, to begin the process of becoming independent. Yet Annie is not prepared for such a sudden transition and what it implies about her future. Confused over her bodily changes and in need of reassurance, she instead finds, in her eyes, betrayal.

Her most troubling and significant moment of transition comes when she unwittingly discovers her mother's sexuality. Returning early from Sunday school, Annie finds her parents making love and focuses her feelings of betrayal on her mother's hand. Horrified, Annie sees the hand as "white and bony, as if it had been left out in the elements. It seemed not to be her hand, and yet it could only be her hand, so well did I know it. It went around and around in the same circular motion [on Annie's father's back], and I looked at it as if I would never see anything else in my life again."

For Annie, the hand that had nurtured her and was always full of life and strength now appears dead as she recognizes her exclusion from her parents' lives. She no longer resides within the comforting "circle" of her mother's hand and is figuratively expelled from her Eden.

After this time, Annie's feelings for her mother remain intense, but they are twisted toward anger, hatred, and mistrust. Annie never stops loving her mother, despite her youthful assertions to the contrary, but she cannot recover the purity of the love she felt in her early youth, and she remains ever cognizant of this loss.

Annie soon finds a partial means of filling this emotional void: friendships with girls her own age. While Annie enjoys being a leader among her peers, she saves her most intense feelings for her private relationships.

With Gwen Joseph and, later, the Red Girl, she often keeps herself apart from the other girls. Such

What Do I Read Next?

- A story similar to that of Annie's is Kincaid's more recent *Lucy* (1990). This novel tells the story of a young woman (17-19) as she struggles to form herself in her new life in America. Many of the themes developed in *Annie John* are further explored here. Especially evident is the affinity of the young girl with the biblical and Miltonic Lucifer, whence Kincaid took the character's name.

- Written twenty–four years earlier than *Annie John, Miguel Street,* by V. S. Naipaul, is set in similar surroundings and with a similar plot. The author wrote in absentia, as did Kincaid, but his story was that of a boy growing up in the pseudo-Victorian society of Trinidad.

- Derek Walcott, poet of the Caribbean and Nobel prize winner in 1992, has two collections dealing directly with the themes in Kincaid's work—writing in absentia, in America, and being estranged from home. The two works are *The Fortunate Traveller* (1981) and *MidSummer* (1984).

- Annie refers to her favorite writers throughout her narration. One writer referred to is Charlotte Brontë and her novel *Jane Eyre.* The comparison is revealing as Jane must also struggle to form her identity but against dead parents and an overbearing, cruel step-family. Curiously, Jane becomes the governess for Mr. Rochester's little girl whose West Indian step-mother is kept in the attic—she is *insane.*

- Linking again with the same themes of the Caribbean and colonialism is Jean Rhys' *Wide Sargasso Sea* (1966). Born in Dominca, Rhys moved to Europe and took part in the writing circles of pre-WWI. She then disappeared in Cornwall to emerge with an answer to Charlotte Brontë's *Jane Eyre.* Rhys writes directly back to the center of empire by explaining the circumstances of the insane woman in Rochester's attic.

---

isolation emulates, however incompletely, her childhood feelings of being a privileged extension of her mother. Her ardent friendship with Gwen, for instance, clearly functions as a substitute for Annie's lost maternal relationship. Like Annie's mother, Gwen is neat and self-controlled, and she also makes Annie the center of her world, which Annie craves. Yet, like a Lucifer who was expelled from Heaven (to whom Annie refers later in the book), Annie ultimately embraces rebellion as the means to reconcile herself to her exile from her mother's affections.

Hence her attraction toward the Red Girl, who represents the opposite of what Annie's mother values. She bathes and changes clothes only once a week, does not attend Sunday school, and plays the forbidden game of marbles. Free from rigid parental dictates and constraints, which Annie wants to be, the Red Girl becomes the embodiment of Annie's resistance to parental authority. By playing marbles with the Red Girl and then lying about it to her mother, Annie asserts an independence won through deception, which she sees as the only means open to her.

Yet Annie's open rebellions against her mother, while they help define her independence, they also highlight Annie's continuing reliance on her mother for guidance. Ironically, to assert her own break with (and hurt) her mother, she models her behavior on what she has learned from her mother. In the contest of wills over the marbles, for instance, Annie adopts negative characteristics like subterfuge and manipulation that she believes her mother uses against her.

Kincaid further portrays this element of their relationship through her use of the trunk. For Annie as a child, her mother's trunk was a symbol of familial intimacy and her own significance, since her mother would recount Annie's youth by describing the history of its contents. It also betokened strength and independence, since her mother used it when escaping her childhood home. After a caustic argument, Annie requests her own trunk, a gesture that stresses her desire to overthrow her mother's influence. What Annie does not acknowledge, however, is her evident desire to emulate her mother. By requesting a trunk, she chooses her mother's method of rebellion against unwanted parental control and places herself on the path to independence that her mother has tread before her.

While familial conflicts are central to Annie's maturation and self-discovery, they alone do not shape her character. Kincaid also emphasizes the impact of cultural forms and attitudes on Annie, and Annie's reaction to them helps the reader understand the sense of self she is developing.

Running throughout the book are features of English influence, such as the Anglican church, English holidays, Annie's British textbooks, and even her middle name, Victoria. Annie recognizes her colonial status, but such knowledge does not lead her to feel inferior. In fact, she considers her slave heritage as a moral strength in comparison to the English colonizers, upon whose graves she and her friends daily walk.

Indeed, Annie is overtly contemptuous of the European colonizing mentality that enabled the Spanish and English to enslave others for their own aggrandizement. Contrary to her teachers, she does not revere Columbus and particularly relishes the picture of him as a captive in a ship. She underscores her enjoyment at his humbling by writing "'The Great Man Can No Longer Just Get Up and Go'" under the picture, drawing the words and sentiment from her mother's statement about her own father's debilitating illness.

Such a renunciation of colonial power parallels, in part, her attempts to reject parental authority. As with her familial relationships, she chafes at the implied cultural constraints that European institutions and attitudes have placed upon her. She cannot, however, completely escape them, as revealed by her love for the British novel *Jane Eyre,* her writing in Old English script under Columbus's picture, and her ultimate voyage to England itself. In fact, while her insolence toward colonial symbols reflects her desire for autonomy, it also reveals her need to combat the continuing hold of the colonizer's views on her own self-definitions.

A more substantial form of resistance to European influence seems to come from the African cultural traditions still thriving in Antigua. Kincaid shows that the colonial figures in the work justify to themselves the degradation of others by privileging rationality and science over emotion and mystery.

In direct opposition to this philosophy is obeah, the West Indian descendant of African voodoo practiced by female figures in the book. Obeah involves a belief in transformation, especially of spiritual forms, and embraces the flux of the natural world rather than trying to control it. These elements of obeah prove particularly relevant to *Annie John,* since the novel addresses the inescapability of both change and the impulses of nature.

Like the colonial elements of Antigua, obeah beliefs help shape Annie's life and her sense of herself. She makes no distinction, for instance, between the waking world and the dream world, and her mother works to protect their home from outside curses and bad spirits. Annie herself, while she never outwardly embraces obeah practices like her mother and grandmother, never mocks or rejects them. Indeed, they offer her a compelling alternative to colonial belief systems and, perhaps more importantly, form a link to her maternal heritage that helps her through the darkest period in her life.

Annie's extended illness marks her most important transition in the book. The world's treacheries and corruptions seem to force her to retreat into a womb-like existence in which her perception of reality becomes warped. Kincaid accentuates the potency and mysteriousness of this illness by coupling it with a period of continuous rain, as if nature itself were in sympathy with Annie, providing her with the water for her womb environment.

Conventional medicine fails to relieve her condition, and her grandmother, Ma Chess, soon arrives, fearing that Annie has been cursed. Not bound by the strictures of Western rationality and attuned to life's emotional chords, Ma Chess immediately recognizes the true nature of Annie's distress and encourages Annie's return to virtual infancy while tending to her like a mother.

Thus, if only for a short time, Annie finally restores the undivided, nurturing existence she formerly shared with her mother and escapes the pain that has been plaguing her. These experiences seem to prepare her for the next stages in her journey, in which she will strive not to restore previous bonds, but to rend them.

Though she re-creates a sense of her former intimacy with her mother, Annie's illness does not relieve her resentment and suspicion. In fact, when she emerges from this state, she feels an even stronger separation from her family and environment and is ready to leave her home.

Her final day on Antigua reflects both her desire to escape and her remorse over another loss in her life. She contemplates her past and her home, and she measures the changes in herself by the stasis she believes she witnesses in others' lives, like her parents and Gwen.

The final lines in the book, while Annie waits to embark for England, underscore her sense of the fundamental alterations in her life and character: "I could hear the small waves lap-lapping around the ship. They made an unexpected sound, as if a vessel filled with liquid had been placed on its side and now was slowly emptying out." Such imagery proves telling, for Annie, too, is "emptying out" in order to become a vessel for new experiences.

Like the vessel placed on its side, this transformation proves disorienting as well as liberating. She is trying to move beyond her past and beyond her mother's influence in order to redefine (or "refill") herself, but is unsure of what may result. She cannot see who she will become, but she can see who and what she does not want to be.

Like her language and imagery, Annie's character has grown richer and more complex throughout the book, and her journey vividly portrays Kincaid's vision of the necessary and excruciating search for selfhood that, like Annie's quest, is never complete.

Source: Darren Felty, in an essay for *Novels for Students*, Gale, 1998.

James Nagel

In this excerpt, Nagel asserts that Annie John *is a classic* bildungsroman *(coming-of-age novel) in which the heroine experiences familial bliss, then ambivalent turmoil about her mother, and finally a permanent departure from home at seventeen.*

On the surface, everything about *Annie John* suggests the traditional *Bildungsroman:* it traces the central episodes in the life of a young girl from prepubescent familial bliss to her ambivalent turmoil about her mother and a permanent departure from home at seventeen. Along the way she struggles through alternate moods of embracing and rejecting her parents, the satisfying and troubling subterfuge of social expectations, the awakening of an uneasy sexuality, and the gradual formulation of an internal life that seeks release from the strictures of home and the culture of Antigua....

It is an exciting but painful journey. Essentially, it proves a tragic "coming of age in Antigua," despite the overlay of humor and charm throughout the narrative. The central issue from start to finish is Annie's relationship with her mother. The central image is that of the trunk, one that contained mementos of the mother's youth in Dominica and then comes to hold the treasured reminiscences of every stage of Annie's childhood. It is appropriate that Annie brings a similar trunk with her when she leaves Antigua at seventeen. In the matter of the trunk, as in so much else, Annie's life recalls that of her mother and brings them as close together in their separation as they were on their island. This is an awareness the adult narrator would have that the child would not. It is buttressed by the special irony that although the child Annie sees the mother as a heartless despot, the Annie who narrates portrays "no tyrant but a beautiful, loving woman who adores her only child and is wise enough to wish her daughter independent" [as Charlotte H. Bruner states in *World Literature Today* 59, 1985]. The act of telling a story of rebellion with such a loving portrait of a mother is, in effect, an act of psychological reconciliation that never achieves material fulfillment. For there is no indication that Annie ever returns home. On one level, she need not, for what her story reveals is the process by which, in striving for independence, she recapitulates the life of her mother. It is no small point that both the child and the mother share the same name, "Annie John."

The book begins with ten-year-old Annie's childhood fascination with death, a subject with somber values set off against the sunny and carefree world of her everyday life. Her conflicts are with the world of the supernatural, with the imponderable causal forces that live in shadow and sign and that wrest a comforting meaning from random events. Her preoccupation with death is a normative fixation and an attempt to understand the most profound developments around her. Beyond the charm of innocent grotesquerie, her fixation offers the revelation of Annie's character and of a lively and creative mind. It reveals also a love for storytelling, an unsentimental confrontation with the most unpleasant realities, and a child's faulty logic that accepts folklore as transcendent reality.

In a sense Annie must reach outward for conflict. The world she lives in, at least on her level of engagement, is prelapsarian, an antediluvian feast of family love and lore. Her mother is not so much long suffering as long rejoicing. She is so in love with her daughter and life as to celebrate even its most minute details, from routine household tasks to the bark she uses to scent Annie's bath water. Indeed, the artifacts of the young girl's existence speak of adoration: Her father built the house she lives in with his own hands. He even lovingly crafts the furniture in her room, the spoon she eats with, the entire household. It is a brilliant context in which to begin the story: For this caring household is the world that Annie will come to resent and rebel against in her final departure.

Although as narrator she stresses these details, at the time of the action Annie is oblivious to them. She is obsessed instead with her immediate concern for a progression of expirations—from Nalda to Sonia's mother to Miss Charlotte and the humpback girl, whose passing inspires in Annie not compassion but a desire to rap on the hump to see if it is hollow. Even these episodes bring her back under the sway of her mother, however. For it is the latter who tells the stories of death in the family, and it is she who is holding Nalda in her arms when she dies. This tragedy is given cruel interpretation by Annie:

> I then began to look at my mother's hands differently. They had stroked the dead girl's forehead; they had bathed and dressed her and laid her in the coffin my father had made…. For a while, though not for very long, I could not bear to have my mother caress me or touch my food or help me with my bath. I especially couldn't bear the sight of her hands lying still in her lap.

It is the first negative transformation in Annie's attitude toward her mother. Annie begins to visit funeral parlors, an obsession that brings her home late one evening without the fish she was supposed to deliver. She lies about the incident: "That night, as a punishment, I ate my supper outside, alone, under the breadfruit tree, and my mother said that she would not be kissing me good night later, but when I climbed into bed she came and kissed me anyway."…

When Annie turns twelve everything changes. She enters the first stages of the love-hate relationship with her mother that informs the central plot of the narrative [according to Bruner]. Ironically, it is not the terrors of death that lead to the schism but the act that brought her life: she discovers her parents making love and is revolted. To provide a context for this event, the narrator sketches a background of familial closeness, how mother and daughter would bathe together in water scented with flowers and oils. Annie tells of her mother's departure from Dominica with the trunk

and of the many times the mother later removed Annie's things from it, caressing each item as an emblem of her daughter's previous growth: "As she held each thing in her hand she would tell me a story about myself." In contrast, the father's background is rich in love of a more perverse and complex variety. He has loved and abandoned a series of women, leaving several with children he does not now acknowledge. This is a fact that hangs over their lives, seeking expiation. Abandoned as a small child, he grew up with his grandmother, sleeping with her until he was eighteen, when she died. The father weeps when he relates this story, and Annie experiences a sudden growth of sensibility in her compassion for him.

The turning point for Annie comes when her mother informs her that it is time for her to have her own clothes, not simply imitations of her mother's dresses. Annie is shocked at this demand for her discrete identity: "To say that I felt the earth swept away from under me would not be going too far." Here Annie would seem to be confronting the classic confusion of a girl in her relationship with her mother: She desires the closest possible identification and shows distress when the mother suggests any degree of separation…. Her mother exhibits disgust at Annie's many lies, but the event from which their relationship never recovers is the parental sex scene, particularly the image of her mother's hand, making a circular motion, on her husband's back. It proves an imagistic referent that lends the title "The Circling Hand," indicating that it is the preeminent event. This image is invested with Annie's confrontation with adult sexuality, a development that will prove more difficult for her than the discovery of death. In the absence of siblings, Annie must share love with the "other" parent, a fact that inspires not rivalry toward her father but a bitter resentment of her mother: "I was sure I could never let those hands touch me again; I was sure I could never let her kiss me again. All that was finished." In her place Annie proclaims her love for a schoolmate, Gwen, and this and other surrogate loves sustain her through the break with her mother.

Annie's ambivalence toward her mother intensifies in the second chapter devoted to Annie at twelve; the implication is that the year was pivotal in her development. Annie is in a new school, and much of the chapter is a description of a typical school day. Yet the salient dimensions of the episode deal with Annie's growing maturity. There is here a nostalgic look back at the unconditional love she has received throughout her childhood from her mother, as well as her compelling need to move beyond the family to the larger social world around her. The key document is an autobiographical essay she writes in school. In it she describes swimming with her mother and the profound sense of isolation and abandonment she feels when her mother momentarily slips from view. Annie is not simply puzzled or startled; she experiences a momentary crisis of being: "A huge black space then opened up in front of me and I fell inside it.... I couldn't think of anything except that my mother was no longer near me." When her mother sees her crying, she hugs her closely and promises never to leave her again, but Annie is left with the sensation of abandonment.

The depth of Annie's dependence and antipathy here adumbrates the more exaggerated passage she will make through her dark night of the soul in the penultimate chapter. Yet even now there are pathological implications to the depth of her emotion. That these events are juxtaposed with an account of her first menstruation is also important in that Annie's struggle toward emotional maturity is linked to her biological coming of age. Similarly, the intensification of Annie's love for Gwen is set against the diminution of her love for her mother, a diminution that continues until Annie reflects that "I could not understand how she could be so beautiful even though I no longer loved her."

From this point on every episode contains another expression of Annie's continuing rebellion and of her substitution of other emotional alliances for the close bond she formerly shared with her mother. Soon these ideas take the form of Annie's stealing and lying and playing marbles, all forbidden activities. There is also her infatuation with the Red Girl, who is the personification of familial anarchy in that she refuses to bathe more than once a week. Gwen, the socially correct young lady who has Annie's mother's full approval, is replaced by the Red Girl, who is free from convention and discipline: "Oh, what an angel she was, and what a heaven she lived in!" That this expression of betrayal contains portions of both pain and pleasure is expressed in Annie's relationship with the Red Girl. The latter pinches Annie and then kisses the injured spots: "Oh, the sensation was delicious— the combination of pinches and kisses." That all of this activity takes place at a time commensurate with the previous chapter becomes clear when Annie starts to menstruate, the second rendering of that event in the book. Once again it is a transitional event in that it coincides with the departure of the Red Girl and the cessation of playing marbles. But through this episode Annie has expanded the terrain of her rebellion. Embracing forbidden friends, and violating the most sacred shibboleths of social behavior, she masks her true nature behind a conventional facade. This double life will come to exact its bounty....

In "Somewhere, Belgium," a title derived from an escape fantasy, Annie has turned fifteen and has entered into a deep depression, the etiology of which would seem to be an emotional schism. Many aspects of her life are warm and protective. These include the stories of her father's youth and the many objects around her crafted by his own hands, as well as the familiar story of Annie's mother leaving home at her age. But on another level Annie's already tenuous circumstances have grown worse. Promoted two grades, she is no longer in the same class with Gwen. Their relationship falters while at the same time the younger Annie suffers in the company of older girls well into adolescence. Her own hesitant steps toward courtship all end badly, even the games she plays with neighborhood boys; in each instance her mother expresses not so much outrage as disgust. When she stops on the way home to flirt with one of the boys from her youth, her mother observes the event and later accuses her of behaving like a slut. Her words move Annie to say "like mother like daughter" and the mother to respond that "until this moment, in my whole life I knew without a doubt that, without an exception, I loved you best."

Annie becomes deeply torn: she is filled with a sense of her mother's love for her, which moves her to tears; at the same time she wishes the older woman were dead. Their duplicitous relationship— outward harmony concealing a deep inner antipathy—is now an obstacle to any integration of self for Annie: "I could not be sure whether for the rest of my life I would be able to tell when it was really my mother and when it was really her shadow standing between me and the rest of the world." Annie needs desperately to be part of the rest of the world, hence the fantasy about escaping to Belgium.

These unresolved conflicts lead to Annie's dark night of the soul at fifteen, a sleep that continues throughout a long rain of more than three months. Caused by no discoverable physical illness, Annie's sleep is a mechanism to escape emotional irresolution. It is also an episode that allows for one last family summation, even the mysterious appearance of the maternal grandmother, who comes, still dressed in black since the death of her son decades before, with ritual cures and potions.

It is clear, however, that the causative factor does not lend itself to these cures nor to those of Western medicine: "I looked inside my head. A black thing was lying down there, and it shut out all my memory of the things that had happened to me." This illness resembles in many respects the archetypal pathology in the female *Bildungsroman:* "Sleep and quiescence in female narratives represent a progressive withdrawal into the symbolic landscapes of the innermost self.... Excluded from active participation in culture, the fictional heroine is thrown back on herself" [according to Marianne Hirsch in *The Voyage In: Fictions of Female Development,* 1983]. In this case, however, Annie's conflict results less from the problems of acculturation than from the more fundamental issue of growing up in her family.

Annie's illness takes her back through the progression of her life, with her parents' tender solicitations; they treat her like an infant, seeing to her every need. The complexity of her feelings toward her parents is omnipresent, as when Ma Jolie suggests that the cause of the illness may be the curses of the women Annie's father abandoned. Other familial objects also possess a negative resonance for her, as does the photograph of her in her communion dress, wearing shoes her mother had forbidden. It was another confrontation that had led Annie to wish her mother dead. Annie's need to break free of the constraints of this heritage is exemplified by her washing the images off the family photographs, except for her own portrait and that of the forbidden shoes. All of this is consistent with the theories of Nancy Chodorow, who postulates [in *Reproduction of Mothering: Psychoanalysis and the Sociology of Gender,* 1978] that

> mothers feel ambivalent toward their daughters, and react to their daughters' ambivalence toward them. They desire both to keep daughters close and push them into adulthood. This ambivalence in turn creates more anxiety in their daughters and provokes attempts by these daughters to break away.

The illness does not abate, however, until Annie begins to realize that she never wants to see her mother again, that her world has become an "unbearable burden." As soon as she is able to articulate this awareness, she quickly recovers. It has been a transforming respite, one that leads to the resolution of the book in the last chapter.

Source: James Nagel, "Desperate Hopes, Desperate Lives: Depression and Self-Realization in Jamaica Kincaid's *Annie John* and *Lucy,*" in *Traditions, Voices, and Dreams: The American Novel Since the 1960s,* edited by Melvin J. Friedman and Ben Siegel, University of Delaware Press, 1995, pp. 237–53.

Jacqueline Austin

In the following excerpt, reviewer Austin compares Jamaica Kincaid's first novel, Annie John, *with her collection of short stories. Austin states that Kincaid writes well-crafted, passionate accounts of a past filled with curious events.*

"Write what you know," says the experienced author to the younger one. Hence the critic's 10-mile bookshelf of breathless first novels about growing up normal: meager accounts, bitter, adoring, or pompous, of parents and school; death and love; television, baseball, dry or wet dreams. Jamaica Kincaid's first novel is not, thank the Muse, one of these: instead, it is one of those perfectly balanced wanderings through time which seem to spring direct from Nature. The parents and school, death and love are there, but oh, with what a difference, and 148 pages become 300 when you read a book twice. In her collection of stories, *At the Bottom of the River,* and here, in *Annie John,* Kincaid does write what she knows. What she knows is rare: pure passion, a past filled with curious events, a voice, humor, and above all a craft.

Ten-year-old Annie John lives in a paradise: a backyard in Antigua overseen by a benevolent goddess—her mother. "That summer, we had a pig that had just had piglets; some guinea fowl; and some ducks that laid enormous eggs that my mother said were big even for ducks. I hated to eat any food except for the enormous duck eggs, hard-boiled. I had nothing to do every day except to feed the birds and the pig in the morning and in the evening. I spoke to no one other than my parents ..." Into this Eden come twin serpents: death and separation from the mother. At first they seem innocent. From the yard, Annie observes, with curiosity, "various small, sticklike figures, some dressed in black, some dressed in white, bobbing up and down in the distance": mourners at a child's funeral. Gradually, death comes closer. One day, an acquaintance dies, a deformed girl. "On hearing that she was dead, I wished I had tapped the hump to see if it was hollow." Annie surreptitiously views the corpse and then lies about it to her mother. This is the first in a series of evasions for which she is punished.

Until now, Annie and her mother were almost one. They wore dresses cut from the same cloth; they went shopping together; they even bathed together. "Sometimes it was just a plain bath.... Other times, it was a special bath in which the barks and flowers of many different trees, together with all sorts of oils, were boiled in the same large caldron ... my mother would bathe different parts of my body; then she would do the same to herself." They took these baths after her mother and an obeah woman had interpreted the world's signals: "the way a dog she knew, and a friendly dog at that, suddenly turned and bit her; how a porcelain bowl she had carried from one eternity and hoped to carry into the next suddenly slipped out of her capable hands and broke into pieces the size of grains of sand … one of the many women my father had loved, had never married, but with whom he had had children was trying to harm my mother and me by setting bad spirits on us." Occasionally the pair would spend a gorgeous afternoon lingering over the objects in Annie's trunk—objects redolent of a shared past which seemed to promise to continue always.

But one day the mother cuts Annie a dress of fabric different from her own; this shock precipitates a slow decline in their relationship. They still keep the appearance of unity, but it's hypocritical: their smiles are false, and mask the most intimate kinds of treachery. The full break comes when Annie reaches puberty. She is now a stranger even to herself. Everything about her, from her nose to her habit of lying, is a mostly unpleasant surprise. This alienation worsens into disease, and ultimately into a total break with Antigua.

Derek Walcott has a poem, "Love After Love," in which he prophesies to himself, and we listen in: "The time will come / when, with elation, / you will greet yourself arriving / at your own door, in your own mirror, / and each will smile at the other's welcome …" The poem closes with a command. "Peel your own image from the mirror. / Sit. Feast on your life." Though Annie John replaces her mother with different objects of desire, first with the conventional schoolgirl Gwen and then with the wild Red Girl, she never does realize that both are reflections of herself, never experiences elation, except at her impending escape, and never feasts on her life—though Jamaica Kincaid does.

At the end of the book, Annie has just gone through a long illness. Having been treated by both doctors and obeah women, she rises from her sickbed several inches taller than her mother—that many inches farther from Eden. She decides to leave Antigua and become a nurse. As Annie embarks for England, the mother hugs her fiercely and declares, "in a voice that raked across my skin, 'It doesn't matter what you do or where you go, I'll always be your mother and this will always be your home.'" Annie hides her revulsion and goes to lie down in her berth, where "everything trembled as

if it had a spring at its very center. I could hear the small waves lap-lapping around the ship. They made an unexpected sound, as if a vessel filled with liquid had been placed on its side and now was slowly emptying out."

The past always threatens to contain the future; it's impossible for the future to break free while still embraced by the past. The daughter must tell her mother, "No, I am not you; I am not what you made me," and this, whether truth or a lie, precipitates sexuality, originality, an honest relationship to personal truth. Annie is clearly an autobiographical figure, not perhaps in specific detail, but certainly in her internal development, her emotions, the tempering of her mind, the changes in her image from within the skin. How has Kincaid broken free? How has she acknowledged her past?

First novelists usually try to cope with their heritage: Kincaid has had to encompass two traditions. This has been the plaint, and the strength, of writers from the West Indies—both black, like George Lamming, and white, like Jean Rhys. In her two books, Kincaid makes an impressive start, fusing folk tale with novel, poetry with fiction, West Indian locutions and rhythms with "European" ones. She has proven herself to be a big, exotic fish in a small, brightly colored pond—the personal interior narrative. It will be interesting to see what happens once she throws herself into the ocean.

Politics, colonial history, the theme of expatriation: these would be natural extensions for Kincaid. Like an old-time cartographer, she seems to avoid some territory. "There be dragons here." In one scene, Annie defaces a picture of Christopher Columbus by scrawling an inscription in Old English-style lettering. She is caught by her prunes-and-persimmons teacher. Her punishment? To copy out part of John Milton's *Paradise Lost.* The white teacher, who equates Columbus practically with God, the old English lettering, Annie's hatred of Columbus and his so-called "discovery"—all these are literary plums ripe for the plucking.

There are many ways in which Kincaid could arrange the plums in her particular literary dish. She could walk farther down her folkways or, like George Lamming in his 1953 *In the Castle of My Skin,* further relate her experience to "universal" mythic history:

"The scent of the air … filled the nostrils and the ears and the eyes so that everything smelt and looked and felt like iodine and raw fish and the liquid of the grape leaf … Bob arched his back and we heard the syllables stumbing past his lips. 'Sea Come No Further,

Sea Come No Further.' His voice went out like the squeak of an insect to meet the roar of the wave ..."

What the waves erase here, other than the boys' toeprints, are the imaginary footprints of King Canute.

Kincaid could also give up her Eden. *At the Bottom of the River* and *Annie John* are wonderful books, but they are, in subject, very much alike. These books epitomize elegy to a particular place and state of being, an impulse which can only sustain itself so long before it becomes redundant. For most writers, personal interior vision is not enough to precipitate a full break from the past. It is significant that the happiest moments in *Annie John* are moments of stasis:

> "Soon after, I started to menstruate, and I stopped playing marbles. I never saw the Red Girl again. For a reason not having to do with me, she had been sent to Anguilla to live with her grandparents and finish her schooling. The night of the day I heard about it, I dreamed of her ... I took her to an island, where we lived together forever, I suppose, and fed on wild pigs and sea grapes. At night, we would sit on the sand and watch ships filled with people on a cruise steam by. We sent confusing signals to the ships, causing them to crash on some nearby rocks. How we laughed as their cries of joy turned to cries of sorrow."...

With *Annie John,* Kincaid has completed the themes begun in *River.* The two are companion volumes: an object lesson in showing how far a writer's technique can stretch. *River* seemed to be dictated straight from heart to hand, almost bypassing the mind. The voice in *"Girl,"* for example, quoted first mother, then daughter, in a rhythm so strong it seemed to be hypnosis, aimed at magically chanting out bits of the subconscious. Now *Annie John* fills in between the bits; it gives the passions of *River* a rationale. The surreality, imagination, internal and external detail are still there, but they now flow in a single narrative wave.

Kincaid's subject matter ... is so interesting that her style, sumptuous as it is, becomes transparent. She is a consummate balancer of feeling and craft. She takes no short or long cuts, breathes no windy pomposities: she contents herself with being direct. The reader feels that even if this writer had had the bad luck to be born elsewhere, she would have made it as wonderful as "her" Antigua.

Cynthia Ozick, Mary Gordon, and Susan Sontag have sighed over Kincaid's virtuosity with language, and they were right. Her language recalls Henri Rousseau's painting: seemingly natural, but in reality sophisticated and precise. So lush, composed, direct, odd, sharp, and brilliantly lit are Kincaid's word paintings that the reader's presuppositions are cut in two by her seemingly soft edges. Her wisdom, measured craft, and reticence will carry her on to more complicated and wider canvases, to larger geographies of the mind.

Source: Jacqueline Austin, "Up from Eden," in *Voice Literary Supplement,* Vol. 34, April, 1985, pp. 6–7.

Sources

Bill Ashcroft, Gareth Griffiths, and Helen Tiffin, *The Empire Writes Back: Theory and Practice in Post-colonial Literatures.* London; Routledge, 1989.

Jacqueline Austin, "Up from Eden," in *VLS,* No. 34, April, 1985, pp. 6-7.

John Bemrose, "Growing Pains of Girlhood," in *Macleans Magazine,* Vol. 98, No. 20, May 20, 1985, p. 61.

Paula Bonnel, " 'Annie' Travels to Second Childhood," in *The Boston Herald,* March 31, 1985, p. 126.

H. Adlai Murdoch, "Severing The (M)other Connection: The Representation of Cultural Identity in Jamaica Kincaid's *Annie John,*" *Callaloo,* Vol. 13, No. 2, Spring, 1990, pp. 325-40.

James Nagel, "Desperate Hopes, Desperate Lives; Depression and Self-Realization in Jamaica Kincaid's *Annie John* and *Lucy,*" *Traditions, Voices, and Dreams: The American Novel since the 1960s,* eds. Melvin J. Friedman and Ben Siegal. Newark: University of Delaware Press, 1995.

Ike Onwordi, "Wising up," in *The Times Literary Supplement,* No. 4313, November 29, 1985, p. 1374.

Allan Vorda, "Interview with Jamaica Kincaid," *Mississippi Review Web Edition,* http://sushi.St.usm.edu/mrw/9604/kincaid.html, 1996.

For Further Study

John Bemrose, "Growing Pains of Girlhood," *Maclean's Magazine,* Vol. 98, No. 20, May 20, 1985, p. 61.
   In this complimentary review, Bemrose praises Kincaid's graceful style and her depiction of Annie John's resistance to the constraints of her environment.

Paula Bonnell, " 'Annie' Travels to Second Childhood," *The Boston Herald,* March 31, 1985, p. 126.
   Bonnell commends Kincaid's rich rendering of life in Antigua and her ability to communicate the emotional reality of Annie John's struggles.

Selwyn R. Cudjoe, "Jamaica Kincaid and the Modernist Project: An Interview," in *Caribbean Women Writers: Essays from the First International Conference,* edited by Selwyn R. Cudjoe, Calaloux Publications, 1990, pp. 215-32.
   In this interview, Kincaid discusses her career, her familial relationships, Caribbean culture, and critical

responses to her work. She specifically addresses the ending of *Annie John.*

Wendy Dutton, "Merge and Separate: Jamaica Kincaid's Fiction," *World Literature Today,* Vol. 63, No. 3, Summer, 1989, pp. 406-10.

Dutton explores the connections between *At the Bottom of the River* and *Annie John,* seeing them as complementary texts that together develop one cohesive story.

Moira Ferguson, *Colonialism and Gender Relations from Mary Wollstonecraft to Jamaica Kincaid: East Caribbean Connections,* Columbia University Press, 1994.

Taking a grand historical view, Ferguson links Kincaid's work to the struggle over gender in English literature.

Moira Ferguson, *Jamaica Kincaid: Where the Land Meets the Body,* University Press of Virginia, 1994.

Ferguson's book-length study investigates Kincaid's connections between motherhood and colonialism, the harsh tone these connections produce, and her protagonists' struggles for self-determination.

David Barry Gaspar, *Bondmen and Rebels: A Study of Master-Slave Relations in Antigua,* Duke University Press, 1993.

Gaspar details the legacy of the colonial power dynamic in which Annie grows up.

Patricia Ismond, "Jamaica Kincaid: 'First They Must Be Children,'" in *World Literature Written in English,* Vol. 28, No. 2, Autumn, 1988, pp. 336-41.

Comparing *Annie John* to various stories in *At the Bottom of the River,* Ismond explores relationships between mothers and daughters in Kincaid's work, as well as Kincaid's reliance on childhood perception and fantasy.

Jamaica Kincaid, *A Small Place,* Plume, 1989.

Kincaid reflects on the place where she grew up and asks Western tourists to join her. In doing so, she reveals the Antigua tourists never see—the one without hospital and library.

H. Adlai Murdoch, "Severing the (M)other Connection: The Representation of Cultural Identity in Jamaica Kincaid's *Annie John,*" *Callaloo,* Vol. 13, No. 2, Spring, 1990, pp. 325-40.

Murdoch employs psychoanalytic concepts and Antiguan cultural conflicts to illuminate Annie John's rebellion against authority and her search for identity.

Roni Natov, "Mothers and Daughters: Jamaica Kincaid's Pre-Oedipal Narrative," *Children's Literature: Annual of the Modern Language Association Division of Children's Literature and The Children's Literature Association,* Vol. 18, 1990, pp. 1-16.

Natov explores Kincaid's use of imagery, particularly associated with Annie John's mother and with water, to illustrate Annie's changing relationships and perceptions.

Donna Perry, "Initiation in Jamaica Kincaid's *Annie John,*" in *Caribbean Women Writers: Essays from the First International Conference,* edited by Selwyn R. Cudjoe, Calaloux Publications, 1990, pp. 245-53.

Connecting Kincaid's novel with other works by women of color and Third World women, Perry relates the traditions of female storytelling, obeah, and intergenerational blood ties to Annie John's development.

Diane Simmons, *Jamaica Kincaid,* Twayne Publishers, 1994.

Simmons' book-length study focuses on Kincaid's treatment of loss and betrayal in her works, as well as her use of obeah (the magical power of transformation) and the rhythm and repetition in her prose. Her chapter on *Annie John* includes a comparison to J. D. Salinger's *Catcher in the Rye.*

Marilyn Snell, "Jamaica Kincaid hates happy endings," an interview in *Mother Jones,* September/October, 1997, pp. 28-31.

Kincaid explains to Snell that she feels it is her duty to bring people down a bit from their oblivious happiness.

Helen Pyne Timothy, "Adolescent Rebellion and Gender Relations in *At the Bottom of the River* and *Annie John,*" in *Caribbean Women Writers: Essays from the First International Conference,* edited by Selwyn R. Cudjoe, Calaloux, 1990, pp. 233-42.

Timothy examines the links between Caribbean cultural practices and beliefs and Kincaid's treatment of mother-daughter conflicts.

Evelyn C. White, "Growing Up Black," *The Women's Review of Books,* Vol. III, No. 2, November, 1985, p. 11.

White praises Kincaid's ability to evoke both life in Antigua and the painful struggles of adolescence. She contends that while Kincaid addresses colonialism, she foregrounds her young protagonist's internal dilemmas.

The Awakening

Kate Chopin
1899

The Awakening tells the story of Edna Pontellier and the changes that occur in her thinking and lifestyle as the result of a summer romance. At the start of the story, Edna is a young mother of two and the life of a successful New Orleans businessman. While the family is vacationing at a seaside resort, Edna becomes acquainted with Robert Lebrun, a younger man who pays special attention to her. Moonlit walks and intimate conversations with Robert spark feelings that Edna has forgotten. When she returns to the city, Edna throws off the trappings of her old life—devotion to family, attention to societal expectations, and adherence to tradition—to explore independence in love, life, and sexual fulfillment.

While this plot is common by today's standards, it caused a huge commotion when Herbert S. Stone and Company published *The Awakening* in 1899. The book was removed from library shelves in Kate Chopin's hometown of St. Louis, and the St. Louis Fine Arts Club expelled Chopin from its membership. Although there was some praise for the novel's artistry and insight, critics generally denounced Chopin for her failure to condemn Edna's actions and for allowing Edna to make her final choice in life.

As evidenced by the many reprints of the book, modern critics appreciate Chopin's skill and artistry—particularly her use of psychological realism, symbolic imagery, and sensual themes. The feminist movement lauds Chopin's portrayal of Edna and the restraints tradition places on women.

Kate Chopin

Author Biography

Kate Chopin was born in 1850 to the well-to-do St. Louis couple Eliza and Thomas O'Flaherty. She attended a convent school, took piano and French lessons, and delighted in her two years as a St. Louis debutante. Kate had a nonconformist side, too. For example, she spent many hours with her family's slaves and became St. Louis' "Littlest Rebel" when she took down and hid a Union flag. In addition, she retreated to the attic of her family's home and remained secluded there for about two years after the death of several of her family members.

Kate O'Flaherty's actions reflected the influence of her great-grandmother, who lived with the family until Kate was eleven. Kate learned from her the love of storytelling, an interest in history, and an inquisitive attitude. Encouraged by her great-grandmother, Kate read widely and pondered unconventional ideas. When she met a woman in New Orleans who was successful at having a career, family, and social life, Kate was thrilled by the possibilities. Kate later behaved in ways that showed she believed in a woman's having control over her own life. After she was married, for example, she ignored society's disapproval as she often walked alone through the streets of New Orleans, smoking cigarettes.

Kate married Oscar Chopin in 1870. Oscar was from New Orleans. He worked as an agent, a banker, and a broker in the cotton industry. As members of the Southern aristocracy, the Chopins owned a summer residence on the shore, had servants, and were involved in many social activities. Kate was an active socialite during this time but also helped Oscar run the business. This equal sharing of work and play by husband and wife was unusual for the time. Their luxurious life came to an end, however, when the business failed in 1879. With six children, the Chopins moved to Cloutierville—a small town in north-central Louisiana—where they lived on her father-in-law's property and helped manage the Chopin family plantations. They had only been there four years when Oscar died of swamp fever. Kate managed the business for a year on her own but then moved back to St. Louis to live with her mother.

When Kate's mother died in 1885, Kate had little money. Her few friends encouraged her to write professionally, having been impressed with her letter writing. At the time, Kate was reading such authors as Guy de Maupassant, Alphonse Daudet, Moliere, Charles Darwin, Thomas Huxley, and Herbert Spenser. Relying on her life experiences, her great-grandmother's wisdom, and the influence of great writers, Kate began to write about life in north-central Louisiana. While readers enjoyed her first collection of stories, Chopin wrote stories that challenged and conflicted with society's moral standards. Her novel, *The Awakening,* was widely criticized for this when it was published in 1899. Even fellow author Willa Cather condemned the book for having a "sordid" theme.

Understandably despondent over this criticism, as well as the subsequent rejection of her next book, *An Avocation and a Voice,* Chopin nevertheless did not at first give up on her writing. She composed a number of short stories, including "The Storm," a tale of two lovers and their infidelity during a rainstorm.

By 1904, however, the author began to abandon writing as her health worsened. She died of a cerebral hemorrhage on August 22 of that year. Today, Kate Chopin is recognized not only for her skills as a local colorist but also as a realist.

Plot Summary

Grand Isle

The Awakening opens at the summer resort of Grand Isle, a small hotel located fifty miles off of the coast of New Orleans. Grand Isle is populated by well-to-do families escaping the blistering New Orleans heat. The action begins as Léonce Pontellier, the husband of the novel's protagonist, Edna Pontellier, sits on the porch of his cottage reading his day-old newspaper. Léonce is a self-important man who accepts as his due the deference of others to his perceived superiority. As Léonce sits on the porch, his wife returns from the beach with Robert Lebrun, the son of the resort owner. After some bantering between Robert and Edna about their trip to the beach, which Léonce does not find amusing, Léonce leaves for his club to play billiards. He invites Robert to join him, but the younger man declines the invitation, choosing instead to remain with Edna. Robert prefers the company of women, choosing to spend the long summer afternoons reading to the married ladies and playing with their children, rather than pursuing the more manly endeavors of working in the city or socializing at the local men's club. Each summer, Robert "constitutes himself the devoted attendant of some fair dame or damsel," but always chooses women who are safe—either girls who are too young to marry or matrons.

Edna does not fit in with the Grand Isle crowd. She is the only person at the hotel who is not a Creole, and she is embarrassed by the Creole society's openness on subjects such as sex and childbirth. Edna's discomfort with the Creole community is aggravated by a growing dissatisfaction with her socially-prescribed role as a "mother-woman," a role which assumes that she will be completely fulfilled by caring for her husband and children. Instead of experiencing this fulfillment, Edna is restless and subject to spells of depression that she does not understand. Edna's performance of her motherly duties does not satisfy her husband, either. On more than one occasion, he berates her for neglecting their children, and for being unconcerned about keeping up social appearances. For example, when Léonce returns from his club late one evening, he awakens Edna, telling her that one of their young sons has a fever. Edna believes that the child is perfectly well, since she had only put him to bed a few hours before. When Edna does not immediately spring from her bed to minister to her son, Léonce accuses her of neglect. Edna's response is to cry long after her husband has smoked a cigar and gone to bed. Léonce's scoldings, however, begin to lose their effectiveness as the story progresses. The more Léonce chastizes Edna for her shortcomings, the more resentful she becomes until she finally dismisses his complaints altogether.

Edna's feelings of boredom grow, and the more restless she becomes, the more she finds herself drawn to Robert. The two become nearly inseparable, sitting together and talking in the afternoons, going to the beach to swim, and taking boat trips to neighboring islands. As Edna's infatuation with Robert becomes obvious, one of Edna's friends, Adèle Ratignolle, warns Robert to stop flirting with Edna, because she is not like the Creole women with whom Robert has flirted in the past. Adèle tells Robert that Edna is different because she might make the mistake of taking him seriously. Robert becomes angry at the suggestion that he is not a man who a woman should take seriously, but retreats from his position when Adèle reminds him that should he allow himself to become involved with a married woman, he would not be worthy of the trust that the families at Grand Isle place in him. Adèle's warning may ultimately precipitate Robert's premature departure from Grand Isle.

Edna's restlessness leads to a series of emotional awakenings from which she begins to gain a sense of the parts of her life that she must cast off. These awakenings cause her to try to break away from the traditional role of wife and mother that turn-of-the-century society prescribed for women. Her first awakening occurs in chapter nine, when she listens to the artist Mademoiselle Reisz play the piano. Edna is "fond of music" because it allows her to enjoy pleasant mental images. She sits on the edge of the gallery during a gathering of all the vacationers. In this scene, she is poised on the edge of two worlds, the family-centered world of Creole society, and the enticing gulf, with its "mystic moon" which "speaks to the soul." The "voice of the sea" exerts a strong influence in Edna throughout the novel, offering a salve to her restless spirit and "inviting" her "to wander for a spell in abysses of solitude" in an attempt to fulfill her inner self. As Edna sits looking out over the gulf and listening to the strains of Mademoiselle Reisz's haunting music, Edna experiences the "first passion of her life." Her awakening becomes apparent later in the evening as she effortlessly swims for the first time. Edna has tried to learn to swim all summer but has no success until after her awakening.

Following her initial awakening, Edna begins to depart from the prescribed "mother-woman" role. She returns to her family's cottage after her swim, drained and tired after experiencing both the "unlimited" in which her "excited fancy" wished to "lose itself," and a momentary flash of terror that she would be unable to regain the shore. Robert accompanies her to her cottage, where Edna reclines in a hammock, and Robert remains with her until the other bathers return from the beach. As he leaves, Edna experiences the "first-felt throbbings of desire" for him. She remains in the hammock after Léonce returns from the beach, despite his insistent demands that she enter the house and go to bed. She tells him to leave her alone, tired of his rude commands, and finally tells him that he should "not speak to [her] that way again" as she "shall not answer." Only after her husband seats himself outside with her, smoking the cigars which are symbols of his overbearing masculinity, does Edna enter the house.

The next morning, Edna summons Robert, inviting him to accompany her to a nearby island, the Chênière Caminada. While attending mass at the Chênière, Edna becomes ill. Robert takes her to the home of Madame Antoine, who offers Edna a place to rest. Later in the evening, Mme. Antoine tells stories of lovers and pirates that are so real to Edna that she can hear the "whispering voices of dead men and the clink of muffled gold." As they return to Grand Isle late that night, Edna and Robert lay plans for other excursions together, and their conversation implies that they are each considering embarking on an affair. Shortly after their trip to the Chênière, however, Robert suddenly decides to leave Grand Isle and go to Vera Cruz to seek his fortune with a family friend. Shocked by his abrupt departure, Edna begins to realize the depth of her feelings for Robert. He bids her a cold and distant farewell, which, coupled with his "unkind" departure, sends Edna into a depression from which she never fully recovers.

New Orleans

At the end of the summer, the Pontelliers return to their fashionable home in New Orleans. Edna's malaise deepens, leading her to ignore her household responsibilities in favor of "lending herself to any passing caprice." Edna neglects the supervision of the servants, leading to unpalatable meals. She paints and refuses to keep her "at home" days, demonstrating a general disregard for society's conventions. When Léonce chastises Edna for "letting the housekeeping go to the dickens," she does not become upset like she used to. Instead she tells Léonce to leave her alone because he "bothers" her. She begins roaming through the streets of New Orleans, on some days feeling happy and content, and on others feeling "unhappy, she did not know why—when it did not seem worthwhile to be glad or sorry, to be alive or dead." The change in

Edna becomes obvious to everyone around her, including her father when he comes to New Orleans for an extended visit. Edna in "some way doesn't seem like the same woman."

In the midst of Edna's turmoil, Léonce departs on an extended business trip. During his absence, Edna sends her children to stay with their maternal grandmother and continues to live for herself. She begins attending the races and other social outings with Mrs. Highcamp, whom her husband has discouraged her from socializing with, and Alcée Arobin, with whom she ultimately has an affair. She decides to move from her husband's home into a house around the corner, which is dubbed the "pigeon house" because it is so tiny. Before she leaves Léonce's home, Edna hosts an elaborate dinner party for a selected few of her friends. She is the consummate hostess, making even the irascible Mlle. Reisz content, until Robert's brother, Victor, begins singing a song that poignantly reminds her of Robert. The lethargy that she has suffered from since the previous summer once again falls over her, and when the young man refuses to stop singing the song, she becomes agitated and cries out for him to quit. The party breaks up quickly after her outburst. Léonce is horrified at her flaunting of societal conventions, but rather than casting her out, he covers her social *faux pas* by making a grand spectacle of remodeling the family home.

Edna misses Robert sorely after his departure from Grand Isle, yet it is only in the presence of Mlle. Reisz—"that personality which was offensive to her," but whose "divine art" reached Edna's spirit and "set it free"—that she admits that she is in love with the younger man. Edna experiences a second epiphany as a result of Mlle. Reisz. As she continues to slide into despair during the New Orleans winter, Edna decides to find Mlle. Reisz. She begins spending time with the artist, listening to her play the piano. Upon learning that Robert has been writing to Mlle. Reisz, she begs for news of the young man. After Robert returns to New Orleans, Edna inadvertently meets him at Mlle. Reisz's apartment; again, Mlle. Reisz unwittingly acts as a catalyst for Edna's emerging sense of what she must do to ease her restlessness. Edna discovers that the young man has been avoiding her, and although they go to a cafe to have some coffee, they part on strained terms. They later meet, again by coincidence as Robert has continued to avoid Edna, in a garden coffeehouse, and this time he accompanies her to the pigeon house. Edna confesses her love and passion for Robert very openly, telling him that they will "love each other." Just as they are on the verge of becoming intimate, however, Edna is called away to attend Adèle who is giving birth to her fourth child. Robert begs Edna not to leave, but Edna feels compelled to sit with her friend. She leaves, promising to return shortly.

Edna finds Adèle's ordeal exhausting and emotionally draining, and as she leaves Adèle's bedside, the attending physician recognizes her turmoil. He speaks of the tricks that nature plays in order to get "mothers for the race," and invites Edna to come and speak with him about what is troubling her. Still distressed by Adèle's pain, Edna returns to the pigeon house, expecting to find Robert. Instead, she finds a note which says "Good bye—because I love you. Good bye."

Return to Grand Isle

Edna spends the remainder of the night lying on her sofa, thinking. In the morning, she goes to Grand Isle. She encounters Victor, and tells him that she is going to the beach for a swim. She requests that he find some lunch for her. She then goes down to the beach, strips her clothes from her body, and "stands as a newborn creature under the sky." She walks into the gulf, which again "speaks to the soul, inviting the soul to wander in abysses of solitude." She swims out quite far, not realizing until it is too late that she has no strength to return to the shore. She drowns in the gulf, remembering key events from her life, and through her death becomes one with the sea which has so affected her.

Characters

Alcée Arobin

Alcée Arobin provides for Edna the distraction she needs from her involvement with Robert. Arobin is a "womanizer." A single man who is known to go from one woman to another, Alcée recognizes in Edna a vulnerability from which they can both benefit. He does not have to commit to Edna, and she does not have to deny herself for him. While he has no intentions of marrying Edna—nor she him—they satisfy each other's needs for companionship and sexual gratification.

Colonel

The Colonel is Edna's father, a man who believes in tradition and constancy. He visits briefly with the Pontelliers while in the city to purchase a wedding gift for another daughter. A retired Con-

Media Adaptations

- *The Awakening* is the basis for the film, *The End of August,* released in 1982. Produced by Warren Jacobson and Sally Sharp under Quartet Production Company, the film features Sally Sharp as Edna and David Marshall Grant as Robert.

- The book is also available as a sound recording. Narrated by Alexandra O'Karma, the four tapes offer the unabridged version of the story. The taped volume is published by Charlotte Hall, MD: Recorded Books, 1987.

federate who enjoys his "toddies," the Colonel is tall, thin, and rugged-looking with white hair and a mustache accenting his bronzed face. Every bit the military man, as well as the Southern gentleman, he expects to be waited on and catered to. He also expects Edna to attend her sister's wedding as a womanly gesture and a matter of family respect. When Edna refuses to attend, the Colonel tersely advises Léonce to control Edna with a firmer hand.

Doctor

See Dr. Mandelet.

Robert Lebrun

Robert Lebrun, though clean-shaven, has nearly the same brown coloring as Léonce, but his youth makes his common look appear handsome. Robert is single and enjoys his holidays on the Grand Isle with his mother, who owns the resort. He always spends time with one of the female vacationers. This year he chooses Edna Pontellier. They take walks together, have long conversations, and go swimming and boating on a daily basis. Robert finds that he and Edna have a great deal in common. They spend so much time together and enjoy each other so much, he realizes they are falling in love.

Creole men were often friends with other men's wives, but they would not think of having affairs with them. A true Creole, Robert does not believe that he should be a party to Edna's betrayal

A street scene in the French Quarter of New Orleans, Louisiana, the setting of Kate Chopin's The Awakening.

of her husband. He becomes concerned that people will see their relationship for what it really is. While Robert does love Edna, he is not strong enough to rebel against Creole honor and duty to prove it to her. Robert leaves for Mexico at the end of the summer to avoid the problems that would arise if he and Edna were to continue their relationship.

Robert returns to New Orleans and visits with Edna but does not consummate the relationship. Still unable to ignore the influence of his Creole upbringing, Robert can not accept Edna for the person she is. He is not strong enough to turn his back on traditional expectations to love the Edna who can make her own decisions.

Dr. Mandelet

Gray-haired with reading glasses, the round Doctor Mandelet is the picture of wisdom. When he taps the arms of his chair with his fingertips and raises his bushy eyebrows, he is busy pondering symptoms and possible diagnoses. In Léonce's presence, the Doctor attributes Edna's unusual behavior to a passing whim, or a womanly idiosyncrasy. The Doctor observes Edna, however, and detects in her only a radiant happiness. While he would not overstep Creole boundaries to say any-

thing to Léonce, the Doctor tells himself that Edna's "problem" is a man other than Léonce.

Edna Pontellier

Edna Pontellier, twenty-eight years old, is the conventional Southern wife of a successful businessman. She is a handsome woman with light brown hair and eyes to match. With thick eyebrows like her father's, her face is interesting—handsome and honest.

She dutifully manages two children and her New Orleans household and maintains her role in high society. While on summer vacation, however, Edna begins to feel that her life is too confining and that there might be more to it than marriage, motherhood, and image. This awareness is brought about in part by the attentions of Robert Lebrun, a younger single man. Edna allows herself to enjoy his company and flirtations and to start to consider some of her own needs and desires. Becoming more assertive, the formerly shy Edna opens up to Adèle Ratignolle, a fellow vacationer. Edna talks to Adèle about her life as well as her feelings related to being a woman and mother. Edna also learns to swim, something she has never before been courageous enough to try.

When the family returns to New Orleans, Edna decides to take charge of her life. Edna feels inspired by her accomplishments on the Grand Isle and by the bold thoughts she has allowed herself. She refuses to sleep with her husband, stops the socially-required receiving of guests, ignores household responsibilities, and resumes her painting. In a final act of assertion, she moves out of the house. Edna experiences a feeling of freedom that affirms for her that she has done the right thing.

Edna wants to be liberated, but she also needs love and appreciation. She desires the freedom to make her own choices and to determine her own direction. Unfortunately, she finds that society—not just her marriage—is too restrictive to allow her to do these things. Her new-found freedom is short lived. While she had hoped to find happiness in a sexual relationship with acquaintance Alcée Arobin, she discovers only regret that he is not Robert. While she had hoped to be successful as an artist, she finds that she has little talent. Her final discouragement comes when she realizes that she cannot separate action from emotion—that while she will not live for others, she cannot live without others.

Edna understands that her desires and her new-found true self will not be accepted by society. Unwilling to go back to being the conforming wife and mother, and really unable to, Edna chooses to commit suicide—a final act of self-determination.

Léonce Pontellier

Léonce Pontellier is the successful New Orleans businessman to whom Edna is married. His whole appearance suggests precision. He is a small, 40-year-old man who keeps his beard neatly trimmed and his part even in his straight brown hair. His slightly stooped shoulders hint at long hours doing paper work. He has achieved a respectable status in the social and professional communities. His friends and associates admire him and consider Edna lucky to be his wife.

Very much the typical Creole gentleman, Léonce believes strongly in traditional Creole values. Léonce expects Edna to be devoted to him, their children, and their social obligations. He feels that a married woman should want nothing more than to serve her husband and care for their children. Léonce asserts that he works hard to support his family. He shows them love and consideration through the home and status that he provides. Thus, he finds it difficult to understand his wife's disinterest in their life together.

Léonce does not, however, allow himself to be too concerned. He views her new interests as a passing mood or a temporary insanity. Shrugging off Edna's disdain for him, Léonce does not even begin to think that he might be part of her "problem." He does not have much patience with what he considers her lack of responsibility, but he seriously doubts that the new Edna is a permanent one. Rather than try to communicate with Edna, or to find out what has happened to the relationship, he consults the family doctor. Léonce lets the matter drop when he is satisfied that his own evaluation of Edna's behavior is correct.

Madame Adèle Ratignolle

Adèle Ratignolle is the Southern woman that Edna Pontellier will never be. Devoted to her husband and children, Adèle lives for them and through them. She is the typical beautiful and charming woman of Creole culture—helpless, domestic, and self-involved. Her fair complexion and voluptuous white-clad figure perfectly convey her angelic nature.

While she allows Edna to confide in her, Adèle can neither understand nor approve of Edna's yearnings and is shocked at Edna's confessions. Adèle sees a woman's role in life as being the refined wife of a Southern gentleman. She denies that she is anything but fulfilled. She relies on her husband's direction and approval to give definition to her life. Adèle can not and will not do anything without her husband by her side. She feels abandoned if her husband and family aren't continually attentive. Adèle spends her time cultivating her image of the dutiful wife and mother. True to her beliefs, Adèle exemplifies the Southern woman.

Mademoiselle Reisz

Mademoiselle Reisz wears her black lace and artificial violets in defiance of conformity. Unmarried and unattractive, she finds passion only in her piano playing and feels that Edna Pontellier is a kindred spirit. Edna understands her music. Edna understands the role Mlle. Reisz has chosen to play in life.

Mlle. Reisz listens to Edna without passing judgement and provides for her a haven where Edna can be carried away by music and thoughts about Robert. Because she is a lonely woman who pursues her talent in exchange for relationships, Mlle. Reisz relishes Edna's presence and her appreciation for Mlle. Reisz's music. Seen as eccentric, the shriveled Mlle. Reisz simply chooses to be herself. To conform to the role that society defines for women would mean that Mlle. Reisz would have to give up her music. That would mean death for Mlle. Reisz.

Themes

Flesh vs. Spirit

Edna's rediscovery of feelings that she has long repressed underlie her search for freedom, self-expression, and love. Her relationship with Robert Lebrun awakens forgotten physical needs and prompts Edna to think about her life. For the first time, she begins to open up to others. She shares confidences with Robert Lebrun and Adèle Ratignolle and allows herself to be stirred by Mlle. Reisz's music. She learns to swim, further experiencing the power of the connection between mind and body. She finally acknowledges her feelings toward Robert and realizes that she can take action to control her own life. The new Edna results from a marriage of flesh and spirit.

Freedom

The awakening that Edna experiences at the Grand Isle is the beginning of her quest for personal freedom. She realizes that she wants to live her life beyond the definitions of wife and mother. When she returns to New Orleans, she refuses to sleep with her husband and gradually withdraws from meeting social obligations with people who are important only to her husband and his social status. She ultimately moves out of the house and rents a place of her own. No longer limited to doing what society expects of her, Edna earns her own income through her painting and socializes with whom she chooses. She enjoys the freedom of venturing out on her own—discovering parts of the city she never knew existed and noticing people she previously would have ignored. For Edna, choice defines freedom.

Sexism

In acknowledging her personal desires and dreams, Edna realizes that double standards exist for men and women. While no one thinks anything of Robert's attention to Edna, people would be appalled at knowing how Edna feels about him. Adèle, for example, is shocked and tries to warn Edna to be careful of her reputation. It was unthinkable that a woman should have her own desires or want to do anything but supervise her household and participate in social functions. Men,

on the other hand, engaged in extramarital affairs, pursued business and personal interests, and virtually had the freedom to do as they pleased. To illustrate, Léonce shows no concern over Robert's relationship with his wife, yet is so perturbed by Edna's actions that he believes she is having a nervous breakdown and consults the family doctor. The roles that Edna, Robert, and Léonce play in the story point out the unfairness of sexism and the repression of individual freedom that it causes.

Search for Self

Edna's spiritual and physical awakenings herald her search for self. While Léonce can see her actions only as some sort of temporary insanity, Edna knows that she is discovering the person within who wants to be free of society's boundaries. In attempting to determine that person, she first tries out her assertive self by refusing to have sexual relations with her husband. She next taps her creative self by reviving her interest in painting. She tries to define her relative self by considering her feelings about motherhood and her relationships with people. Finally, she experiences her sensual self by allowing herself to feel and act upon her own desires. Edna succeeds in determining who she is but discovers that the price for having her own identity is more than she can afford.

Choices and Consequences: Free Will

From the time that she first meets Robert, Edna realizes that all choices have their consequences. Her choice to remain in a relationship with Léonce would result in her continuing dissatisfaction with life. Yet she really doesn't understand, initially, that she can make choices that will result in different consequences. When she does see that she can make changes, she experiences a freedom that she has never before felt. This exhilaration, however, is short-lived. Edna finds that free will carries with it responsibilities that are almost as confining as her marriage was. Her loveless affair with Alcée, and Robert's inability to reciprocate her love, lead Edna to see the final, dismal consequence of her life. No matter what choices she makes, Edna can never be totally free within the confines of the society in which she lives.

Sex

The choices Edna makes in her life result, largely, from her rediscovery of sexual pleasure. Robert's attention prompts Edna to ponder her life. As an initial result, Edna withholds sex from her husband. Then, her unfulfilled love for Robert and her loveless affair with Alcée demonstrate to her that love and sex are entirely separate entities. Edna discovers that while sex draws men and women together and can be physically satisfying, it does not necessarily meet one's emotional needs. Free sex has its price, and ultimately, Edna is not willing to pay it.

Alienation and Loneliness

Although people surround Edna on the Grand Isle, she feels separated by her thoughts. She believes that if she makes changes in her life to reflect her true self, she will be able to do what she chooses and associate with people who think like she does. Unfortunately, while her new companions do live their lives in their own ways, they also live isolated by society's rules. Mlle. Reisz is a prime example. She is a talented musician who has chosen the unconventional road. Because Mlle. Reisz is unmarried and living alone, people think she is odd. Few people appreciate her music and fewer still associate with her. Mlle. Reisz finds comfort and passion only in her music. Edna eventually feels the same kind of loneliness. Tantalized by what could be, she refuses to give up her dream of freedom and to sacrifice her newfound individuality. As a result, she alienates herself from all of society in her choice to create her own destiny.

Public vs. Private Life

Edna recognizes that she is unhappy with the life she is leading and all that it represents. She must answer to a husband who wants her to be nothing more than a household manager and nursemaid. She must perform the social duties expected from the devoted wife of a highly-respected man. She must appear to be the loving mother of children who demand her full and constant attention. To maintain this public image, Edna must deny herself the intimate pleasures of mutual love, the liberating acts of self-expression and creativity, and the joy of having friends with whom she can share her most private thoughts.

Edna finally tires of the masquerade. She realizes that she can no longer ignore her own desires, thoughts, and aspirations. She knows that her new attitude will be difficult to reconcile with a public life, but she pursues it with determination. No longer stifled by public expectations, Edna acts on her thoughts.

Unfortunately, her liberation does not last. She finds that there can be no true union of her public

Topics for Further Study

- Trace the history of the women's rights movement beginning with the first political convention held in 1848 at Seneca Falls, New York and ending with the current decade. By way of a pictorial timeline, relate significant incidents to other historical events of the times.

- Research the Creole culture. Explain how Creoles have both Spanish and French ancestry and how that ancestry affects their lifestyle. Describe the culture through the customs and traditions honored by Creole descendants as well as through their routines of daily life.

- Critics consider *The Awakening* a study in psychological realism. In an essay, address the following questions: How does Chopin use psychological realism to make her characters believable? Do her characters react in ways that you would expect? Explain.

- Compare and contrast New Orleans' Carondelet Street and New York's Wall Street in 1899. Does Carondelet Street still exist?

- Consider Leonce Pontellier, Robert Lebrun, and Alcée Arobin—the most prominent male characters in *The Awakening*. How do you see each man as representative of his culture and the times? What are each man's specific traits? Explain how and why you might relate to each man.

- The Grand Isle was destroyed by a storm in 1893. Investigate the storm that destroyed it. Develop a series of news items that might have appeared at the time that (a) predict the storm, (b) cover the news as it's happening, and (c) report the results of the storm.

and private selves. The world in which she lives is bound too much by social convention to accept long-term nonconformity. The public is not ready to embrace the private Edna, and Edna is unwilling to yield to public sentiment.

Style

Point of View

An objective third person narrates the story of Edna Pontellier and her search for self in *The Awakening*. The narrator does not criticize or applaud characters for their traits or their actions. Most importantly, the narrator withholds judgement of Edna and the choices she makes.

Conflict

The basic premise of *The Awakening* is conflict. Edna Pontellier discovers that she cannot be the person society expects her to be and seeks to resolve the problem by changing her life. Even as she recognizes the conflict within herself and begins to deal with it, the people with whom she associates present her with new challenges. Edna believes that she can be an artist and a lover and still be independent. Alcée and Robert prove her wrong. They reimpose the original conflict by proving to Edna that they can see her in only one way. While each has his separate view, both men reflect society's beliefs that women have certain functions in life. Edna is right back where she started.

Setting

The setting contributes to the conflict. The story takes place in the late 1800s. Most of the action is set in the heart of Creole society, New Orleans. The city bustles with social gatherings, business meetings, and the impersonal pace of busy people. However, it is Grand Isle, a resort near New Orleans, that has the most influence on Edna. The Grand Isle in the Gulf of Mexico offers an intimate and relaxed atmosphere for walks along the beach, leisurely swimming, and moonlit conversations. Edna falls in love on the Grand Isle and changes her life upon return to, and under the cover of, hectic city life.

Imagery

Imagery used in the story emphasizes the conflict with which Edna struggles. Edna realizes that she can not tolerate being confined to marriage and motherhood, but nor is she free to love and create. Society sees the two choices as complete opposites. Other opposing images emphasize the contradiction. New Orleans city life, with its stiff social rules, contrasts with the openness and ease of life on the Grand Isle. Birds fly freely on the Grand Isle, while they live in cages in the city. Edna's friends, Adèle and Mlle. Reisz, are complete opposites as well. Adèle exemplifies the traditional Southern woman while Mlle. Reisz represents the typical societal outcast. The final, and most significant, image is the seductive acceptance of the sea. It mirrors both birth and death.

Foil

Foil is used to emphasize the primary conflict by exaggerating the distinct differences among Edna, Adèle, and Mlle. Reisz. Edna knows that she does not want to be, and will not be, like Adèle. Adèle lives only for her husband and her children. While she loves her family and they love her, she has given up her own will and bows to the whims of those around her. Unlike Adèle, Mlle. Reisz has forsaken love and relationships for her music. Her lonely life revolves around playing for audiences who don't appreciate her talent. Edna does not want to be like either woman. She would like to combine the best of both of them. Edna wants to be needed and loved, like Adèle, but would also like to pursue her own interests, like Mlle. Reisz. The idea of having to remain in her marriage, with all its responsibilities and restrictions, smothers her. On the other hand, if loneliness is the price she has to pay for freedom, Edna does not want that either. The constant interplay among the three characters keeps the conflict alive.

Symbolism

All of the images found in *The Awakening* gain more symbolic meaning as the story progresses, but the sea is the primary symbol. The sea represents the differences between choice and blind obedience, self-determination and predestination, and ultimately, between life and death. It is while at the seaside resort that Edna first realizes that she can still feel love and that she can change her life. She learns to swim at this time, too, and experiences the power of the connection between mind and body. Both of these experiences contribute to Edna's determination to find herself. To Edna, the sea represents acceptance, comfort, and self-renewal. Later, a disillusioned Edna returns to the sea to try to renew the feeling of freedom that she experienced on learning to swim and on changing her life. The sea again beckons her, and Edna willingly releases to it the conflict within her.

Realism

The author honestly portrays Edna's conflicts. Edna faces her first dilemma when she is attracted to Robert Lebrun. She is sexually aroused and wants to consummate the relationship with Robert. She then ponders her role in life, does not like what

Suffragettes marching with children in tow to promote the voting rights of women.

she sees, and makes changes to redefine it for herself. Kate Chopin puts Edna in real-life situations and gives her real-life emotions. At the time the novel was written, this was unheard of. Now, critics recognize that Chopin was ahead of her time in her frank exploration of the relationship between self and society.

Historical Context

Creole Society

Kate Chopin lived in, and generally wrote about, life in the South. In *The Awakening,* she wrote specifically about Creole society in northern Louisiana. Creoles saw themselves as different from Anglo-Americans and maintained cultural traditions passed down from their French and Spanish ancestors. They enjoyed gambling, entertainment, and social gatherings and spent a great deal of time in these activities. The Creoles seldom accepted outsiders to their social circles and felt that newcomers should live by their rules. Men dominated the households and expected their women to provide them with well-kept homes and many children to carry on the family name. Women responded by bearing children and refining their so-

cial talents. While the Creole men caroused, their women kept well-run houses and perfected their accomplishments in music, art, and conversation. Such refined women enhanced their husbands' social status.

The Beginnings of the Women's Movement

The 1800s saw a change in the status of women. Chopin's character, Edna Pontellier, illustrates the independent nature that women began recognizing in themselves. Edna felt that there was more to life than living in her husband's shadow and stifling her own desires and dreams. Women of the time felt the same way. As early as 1848, women gathered in New York State to begin addressing issues of equality. This first convention of women set the groundwork for the women's rights movement. Women's groups continued to organize to educate women about social and political issues and to allow a forum for women's discussions. While women did not gain the right to vote until 1920, these pioneering efforts gained a voice in society that would not be quieted. Edna's actions in *The Awakening* reflect the times and the emotions felt by the many women who sought personal freedom.

Compare
&
Contrast

- **1890s:** The women's movement begins to gain a foothold on American society. However, women still do not have the right to vote, and women's issues were not part of the political platform.

  Today: Women have had the right to vote since the passage of the Twenty-second Amendment to the Constitution in 1920.

- **1890s:** According to the law, a married woman's property belonged to her husband, even if she had inherited land before being wed. If she later divorced her husband, the land would still be legally his.

Today: Women have equal legal rights to property, and divorce cases usually conclude with at least half—if not more—of a couple's possessions going to the wife.

- **1890s:** Advice columns for women had their beginning. With the advent of Dorothy Dix's column in 1895, advice columns appeared in newspapers and provided a forum for discussion of women's issues.

  Today: Not only do publishing companies print women's columns in newspapers, but they also dedicate entire magazines to women's issues.

Literary Criticism

Chopin's editors tolerated her daring themes and characters' actions more than did the critics and general public. Chopin wrote about life as it really was and did not shy away from subjects that were considered taboo. The characters in Chopin's short stories and novels often demonstrated the "dual lives" that women of the 1800s lived. In a time when women's roles were changing, Chopin's characters found themselves questioning conformity and duty versus freedom and personal identity.

Kate Chopin, herself, exemplified the spirit of the women's movement during the 1800s. While she was married to a wealthy Southern businessman, she defied tradition by assisting her husband with his business, taking walks by herself through the streets of New Orleans, and smoking cigarettes. Her blatant disregard for society's expectations peaked in *The Awakening*. Her character, Edna Pontellier, thinks and acts in many ways like Kate Chopin did. Edna thinks about herself as separate from her family and society. She challenges the role society has forced upon her and courageously turns her back on it.

Critics denounced Chopin for allowing Edna Pontellier the freedom to refuse conformity. They also criticized Chopin's seeming sympathy for her character. The outcry demonstrated that the literary world was not ready for the realism Chopin's novel portrayed. Even though women's roles in the real world were changing, Chopin's frank treatment of female sexuality, social impropriety, and personal freedom shook the literary world. Critics condemned the novel. Libraries removed it from their shelves. In spite of the freer climate initiated by the women's movement, the St. Louis Fine Arts Club removed Kate Chopin from their rolls. Chopin continued to write, however, and to allow her characters to stretch beyond the confining boundaries set by society. Today's critics recognize her artistry and applaud her realistic approach that helps define society in the late nineteenth century.

Critical Overview

Critics condemned *The Awakening* when it was first published in 1899. They criticized Chopin's frank treatment of such moral issues as extramarital affairs and female sexuality. Good literature simply did not discuss women's emotions. It ignored the fact that women have the same impulses as men. For Edna to admit, even to herself, that she was sexually aroused, was shocking. For her to actually engage in an affair was scandalous.

Critics also denounced Chopin's seeming acceptance of Edna's search for personal freedom. They were appalled at the choices Edna made to acquire her freedom. Women were expected to accept their station in life and to repress any feelings they might have that could be considered nonconformist. Edna not only disliked her role in life, she also blatantly refused to continue it. Readers naturally sided with Léonce when Edna refused to have sex with him. When Edna moved out of the house, readers criticized her for abandoning her children.

Critics felt Chopin was overstepping her rights to discuss Edna's thoughts and improprieties so objectively. They felt that Chopin should have punished Edna in some way. The public, too, took offense at Edna's passion and adultery and virtually cheered her ultimate suicide. Women who wanted to keep their social standing lived within the rules of society. While men could have affairs and still be respected, society despised women who did. Edna could have had her thoughts if she had kept them to herself. For Edna to openly air them and to act upon them was a moral outrage. The public disapproved not only of the character, but of the author who could write so dispassionately about such improper behavior. As a result, Chopin's hometown library removed the book from its shelves, and the St. Louis Fine Arts Club banned Chopin from its membership.

The Awakening remained unnoticed for several years after the commotion it initially caused. In the 1930s, however, the book came back into the limelight when literary critics changed their minds about it. An intense look at the work revealed its positive elements. The researcher who first studied it appreciated Chopin's attention to literary form—particularly her mastery of form and theme. Chopin's composition has a poetic unity to it that comes from her application of symbolic imagery to plot. An example of this is Chopin's use of the sea—as a symbol of life and death as well as the site for the main action in the plot.

Since this first new look at the work, other critics have applauded Chopin's use of psychological realism, symbolic imagery, and sensual themes. For example, Per Seyersted stated that Chopin was the first female to write about sex in an intelligent, realistic and nonjudgmental way. Other critics agree that Chopin used sex in *The Awakening* not to moralize, but to reveal certain psychological characteristics of her characters. Characters become real people with real emotions as a result of the way Chopin dealt with their sexuality. This attribute raised the book above the "sex fiction" that one critic accused Chopin of writing, according to Margo Culley who edited the second edition of Chopin's *The Awakening*. The book's form, style, characterization, and symbolism contribute to both its early opposition as well as to its acclaimed acceptance today.

The Awakening has taken on a new significance since the advent of the women's movement. Literary debates have raged over the significance of Pontellier's awakening, her suicide, and the conflict between motherhood and career for women in the nineteenth century. Many critics feel that Edna's suicide was an independent victory over society's limitations. Others feel that she killed herself because she felt defeated by society and did not want to disgrace her children.

Women's issues were still too new in the late 1800s for the book to have any impact at the time it was published. Feminists since the 1940s and 1950s, however, have recognized the book as an important contribution to the understanding of women's changing roles in an evolving society. Chopin was in tune to women's issues and in a broader sense interested in universal human nature. Through her characters, she explored the relationship between self and society.

Particularly aware of the conflicts women face—due in part to her French background and her female perspective—Chopin shared with her readers a view of women in American society that differed from other writers of her day. Her characters often held unconventional attitudes toward themselves and society's rules. These characters tried to fit into society and, at the same time, remain true to themselves. Edna Pontellier is no exception. She represents women in society both past and present. She joins other of Chopin's female protagonists in forming a basis for dialogue about a society that once devalued female sensuality and independence.

Criticism

Suzanne D. Green

Green, who is the co-author of Kate Chopin: An Annotated Bibliography of Critical Works, *discusses how Chopin's work, which was very controversial when it was published, has become a classic in American literature and a particularly important piece of fiction among feminist critics.*

What Do I Read Next?

- *Bayou Folk* is Chopin's 1894 collection of stories that present the people of Natchitoches Parish as they live and love in daily life. Chopin's skill as a local colorist as well as an adept storyteller is evident in her perfect rendering of people, places, and events of the area and time. She uses universal themes, such as prejudice and interracial relationships, that are not common in regional fiction.

- Another of Chopin's collections is *A Night in Acadie,* written in 1897. Critics recognize this collection, too, for Chopin's skill as a local colorist. The difference in this collection and *Bayou Folk* is that in *A Night in Acadie,* Chopin's characters express their individuality more and recognize and heed impulses that are socially unacceptable. Chopin emphasizes more sensuous themes, and reviewers voiced their concerns.

- Chopin's third volume of works, *A Vocation and a Voice,* was not published in its entirety until 1991. Publishers prior to this time continued to question the appropriateness of Chopin's choice of themes. They failed to recognize the work for its outstanding treatment of such psychological elements as human consciousness and its relationship to circumstance, motivation, and action. The stories in this collection reflect less of Chopin's ability as a local colorist and more of her skill at understanding individual motives.

- *The White Dove* is a 1986 novel written by Rosie Thomas. Set in Great Britain in the 1930s, the story is about Amy Lovell, a young woman of the upper middle class who chooses a career over a life of luxury. Amy falls in love with Nick Penry, who is not only from a vastly different background but who also is a fiery socialist. Amy's search for a useful and fulfilling life forces her to make difficult choices.

- G. J. Scrimgeour wrote *A Woman of Her Times* to portray a woman who is torn between the respectable roles of wife and mother and the necessity of leading her own life. This is a story about a woman who starts out in pre-World War I Ceylon as a young British colonial wife, becomes a London socialite in the twenties, moves through a period in the thirties of being an impoverished working mother, and reaches the place in life where she feels she has survived as herself.

- *Coming of Age in Samoa* was considered shocking when it was published in 1928 as a psychological study. Dr. Margaret Mead, anthropologist, was only twenty-three when she started the study of Samoan children to determine if stress experienced by American children is a "natural" part of growing up. The results of the study confirmed that actions we have often attributed to "human nature" are actually reactions to civilization's restraints. Mead emphasized every child's right to know and to choose freely.

Published in 1899, Kate Chopin's novel *The Awakening* is considered to be one of the cornerstone texts of both American realism and the feminist movement. Modern critics praise *The Awakening* for its daring treatment of traditional gender roles as they were defined at the turn of the century, and for its exploration of a woman's search for self-fulfillment. However, when Chopin's novel first appeared, it met with harsh criticism. Reviewers objected to the unwholesome content of the novel, and although many considered the writing style outstanding, most critics dismissed the book as trash because they perceived its protagonist as an immoral woman. One reviewer, commenting on Edna Pontellier's lack of moral substance, remarked in *Public Opinion* that "we are well satisfied when she drowns herself."

The harsh reviews that *The Awakening* received have led to a common misconception concerning the effect of its critical reception. The first biography of Kate Chopin, by priest Daniel Rankin, reports that Chopin was shunned by society and that *The Awakening* was banned by many libraries, including those in her native St. Louis. These reports circulated widely for several decades, and until 1990, were accepted as factual accounts. Emily Toth's authoritative biography of Chopin, which appeared in 1990 and was subsequently nominated for a Pulitzer Prize, refutes Rankin's claims. Toth offers evidence that although *The Awakening* was reviled in some circles, the book was never officially banned, nor was it removed from library shelves during Chopin's lifetime. While Chopin lost a pre-existing contract for a collection of short fiction which would have appeared after *The Awakening,* Chopin was not a social outcast as a result of writing the controversial novel.

Despite the fallacies surrounding the initial publication of Chopin's novel, the mixed critical reception that the novel received led Chopin's publishers to allow it to pass out of print soon after its initial publication. From 1906, the date of the second printing of the novel, until 1969, when Norwegian scholar Per Seyersted began studying Chopin's fiction and produced a volume of the writer's *Complete Works,* only a few of Chopin's short stories remained in print. The appearance of Seyersted's biography precipitated scholarly study of Chopin's texts, and much of this study has focused on *The Awakening.* Feminist critics, in particular, have looked at *The Awakening* with renewed interest, and have successfully included Chopin's works in the core group of texts that constitute the basis of American literature. Since Chopin's rediscovery in 1969, her writings have remained in print continuously and have gained popularity at a rapid rate. When Chopin's works began to be reprinted, they represented a marginal example of the Southern local color school. Three decades later, *The Awakening* is a classic of American literature that is read more frequently than Herman Melville's *Moby-Dick.*

In *The Awakening,* Chopin adopts the point-of-view of a third-person, omniscient narrator. The narrator primarily reports the thoughts, actions, and feelings of both the main character, Edna Pontellier, and occasionally of some minor characters, such as Leonce Pontellier and Robert Lebrun. An important departure from this point-of-view occurs in chapter six, when the author pointedly intrudes into the novel. It is at this point that the reader is introduced to the internal turmoil that is the source of Edna's unrest and which causes her to act "capriciously." Chopin interjects her own voice into the narrative to tell the reader that Edna is discovering her "relations as an individual to the

world within and about her" and that she is experiencing the dawning of a light which "showing the way, forbids it." Chopin takes great pains to assure that the reader does not miss the importance of this "beginning of things" that is taking place inside Edna's head, as it represents Edna's first steps on the road toward self-discovery and away from the restrictions of the gender roles which were prescribed for turn-of-the-century women. Chopin makes use of repetition, often of entire sentences or paragraphs, to point out important events in the narrative. She also very often uses oddly-constructed sentences to highlight key points in the action of the story.

The Awakening is most often read in the context of feminist criticism. While a variety of sub-schools exist within the feminist movement, much of the feminist critiques of literary texts focus on the ways that women are treated. Feminist literary texts illustrate the types of oppression that women experience and the ways in which they struggle to break free from this oppression, realizing that they are worthwhile individuals with something meaningful to contribute to society. Accordingly, feminist readings often discuss the "jobs" that are traditionally assigned to women, such as tending a home, caring for a husband, and bearing children, and the ways in which these jobs are used to keep women in a powerless position. Female sexuality, and the way that a patriarchal system—a societal system in which men are the authorities and control the power structure—controls that sexuality are also common themes in feminist criticism. *The Awakening* deals with many of these traditionally feminist concerns. For example, much of the plot of *The Awakening* hinges on Edna's dissatisfaction with her role as a wife and mother. She feels oppressed by it and tries many avenues to escape from its restrictions.

One of the major outlets that Edna pursues as she attempts to escape from her prescribed role is the development of her sexuality. In fact, some critics have argued that Edna's awakenings are little more than a series of passionate encounters with men who are not her husband. While Edna experiences a variety of awakenings that transcend the physical or sexual, her experiences with passion play a major role in her decisions to disregard her husband's wishes, to conduct indiscrete affairs, to leave her husband's home, and ultimately to swim to her death in the sea.

Edna's destruction comes about as an indirect result of her attempts to escape from being her husband's property, both financially and physically.

Early in the novel, she is identified as Leonce's property. For example in the first chapter of the novel, as Edna returns from the beach with Robert, she meets with Leonce's disapproval because she has allowed her self to be "burnt beyond recognition," a conclusion which her husband draws as he looks her over as "one looks at a valuable piece of personal property which has suffered some damage." We later find out that Leonce spends a good deal of his time admiring his "household goods," and that he numbers Edna among his possessions. However, we should not judge Leonce too harshly for his evaluation of his wife's value, because his attitude was the norm in the U.S. at the turn of the century. In fact, Edna's friends at Grand Isle consider Leonce the model husband, forcing Edna to admit that she knows of no men who treat their families with such consideration. Despite the fact that Leonce is well-to-do and gives his wife every imaginable luxury, Edna is compelled by the seductive voice of the sea to pursue the fulfillment of her inner self, even at the cost of her material possessions, her friends, and ultimately, her life.

Adele Ratignolle, Edna's close friend at Grand Isle, is a foil (or opposite) to Edna. Adele is the consummate mother-woman, who dotes on her husband, adores her children, and produces a new baby at regular intervals. Adele often pressures Edna to conform to societal standards, arguing with Edna about what a mother's responsibilities are and urging her to "think of the children" when she fears that Edna may take a rash action that would adversely affect her two small boys. Despite prompting from all sides to follow the expected path, Edna is incapable of conforming. All of her life, she has instinctively understood the "dual life" that was necessary for a woman of the late 1800s, a life which consists of "that outward existence which conforms, the inward life which questions." However, as the summer at Grand Isle progresses, Edna becomes increasingly incapable of keeping the inward life from spilling into, and eventually completely consuming, her outward existence.

Edna's inability to reconcile her inner and outer lives precipitates her final swim in the sea. Throughout the novel, Edna is inexplicably drawn to the sea. At first, she only splashes around, as she can not master even the most basic swimming strokes. Following her first epiphany, however, she begins to swim effortlessly. The sea is connected with many of her awakenings: Chopin invokes the sea in chapter six, describing it as "whispering, clamoring, murmuring, inviting the soul to wander," as a seductive enchantress which is "seduc-tive, enfolding the body in its soft, close embrace." Edna's final awakening, as she stands at the edge of the sea, invokes these same lines. These lines mark the starting and ending points of Edna's search for a different type of life. She is initially drawn to the sea, and finally is drawn into it permanently because of the freedom that it represents.

Scholars argue over the particulars of Edna's suicide, attempting to determine whether her death is intentional or accidental, and, by extension, whether Edna is a successful character or not. The text of *The Awakening* is ambiguous on each of these points. The text seems to support the conclusion that Edna intends to commit suicide. She strips naked before her swim; she swims very far away from the shore without once looking back; and she is in a state of despair when she arrives at Grand Isle, incensed that her husband and children presumed that they could "drag her into the soul's slavery for the rest of her days." However there is an equal measure of evidence that supports the argument that Edna drowns accidentally. For example, she discusses her meal and sleeping arrangements with Victor at some length before she goes to the beach, and the narration tells us that in spite of the blow that she has suffered at Robert's departure she is "not thinking of these things as she walked to the beach."

Edna's death also begs the question of whether she is a success or a failure. Many critics have argued that because she dies, she is by definition a failure. After all, she is dead. However, given the options open to women at the turn of the century, it can also be argued that death was the only viable alternative that Edna had not experienced. She could no longer survive as merely a wife and mother, and she did not find fulfillment in art or in casual affairs. The man that she loved had deserted her, and she quickly came to the realization that his departure did not mean much, as the day would come when "the thought of him would melt out of her existence." Her only alternative was the peace and freedom that would come with a painless death. Death represented one aspect of her life that she could take complete control over. While these questions will undoubtedly be debated at length for some time to come, no clear-cut answers are to be found in the text. Chopin's ending is ambiguous, and it would appear to be intentionally so.

The Awakening offers a stirring glimpse into the psyche of a woman, giving contemporary readers insight into both the social structures and the effects that these structures have exerted over generations of women. This novel also offers a female protagonist with whom we can identify, and for whom we can have a great deal of sympathy. Edna Pontellier's escape strikes a cord in many readers, in large part because she had the strength to act, to take control of her destiny. It is this very act, this empowerment, which has made *The Awakening* a mainstay in the American literary canon.

Source: Suzanne D. Green, in an essay for *Novels for Students*, Gale, 1998.

Carole Stone

In the following excerpt, Stone examines the growth of Edna's artistry and autonomy.

Many recent critics of *The Awakening* fail to see Edna's growing sense of power and control as signs of progress toward a new self-definition. They view her as a woman deluded by romanticism who is unable to make a conscious choice, such as the decision to become an artist, because her instincts are regressive....

In this essay I will argue that Edna's memories of her childhood, her immersion in the sea, and her search for a mother figure are emblems of regression in the service of progression toward an artistic vocation. Rather than returning to the dependency of childhood, she goes forward to a new conception of self, a definition of herself as artist. Further, I will suggest that Edna's romanticism is positive because it catalyzes her imaginative power. As the final step forward functioning as an autonomous human being, moreover, she sees through the delusion of romantic love after confronting the horror of giving birth.

Edna's artistic birthing is shown through the contrasting characters of two women, Adèle Ratignolle, a "mother-woman," and Mme. Reisz, a pianist. As Per Seyersted has observed [in *Kate Chopin: A Critical Biography,* Louisiana State University Press, 1969], "the novel covers two generations and births ... a finely wrought system of tensions and interrelations set up between Edna's slow birth as authentic and sexual being and the counterpointed pregnancy and confinement of Adèle." Adèle embodies female biology, always talking of her condition, for she has a baby about every two years. Adèle's opposite, Mme. Reisz, a serious artist, is unmarried. She exemplifies the solitary life of the dedicated artist.

A third influence on Edna's artistic development is Robert LeBrun, a young Creole man who, because he has not yet assumed the masculine values of his society, can be a friend to Edna as her husband cannot. He teaches her to swim, furthering her autonomy, and with his easy way of talking about himself, encourages her self-expression. Because he has aroused sexual desire in her, she eventually has an affair with another man, Alcée Arobin, an affair which functions as a rite of passage to sexual autonomy.

Each of these three figures has positive and negative qualities that help and hinder Edna's struggle to be creative. Adèle Ratignolle, a sensuous woman, awakens Edna to the sensuality of her own body. Also Adèle's candor in talking about such subjects as her pregnancy helps Edna to overcome her reserve. Furthermore, Adèle encourages her to express thoughts and feelings she had kept hidden, even from herself. For example, at Adèle's urging to say what she is thinking as they sit together by the sea, Edna recalls "a summer day in Kentucky, of a meadow that seemed as big as the ocean to the very little girl...."

In these early scenes by the sea Chopin also establishes the sea as a central symbol for Edna's birthing of a new self. The connection in her mind between the grass and the sea foreshadows the autonomy she achieves by learning to swim, as well as her final walk into the sea at the book's end. Symbolically, the sea is both a generative and a destructive force in *The Awakening;* it represents danger inherent in artistic self-expression—losing oneself in unlimited space—as well as the source of all life, facilitating rebirth, so that Edna in her first moments of being able to swim feels like a child who has learned to walk. The ocean has also been seen as a symbol of woman or the mother in both her benevolent and terrible aspects. Madame Ratignolle, in association with the sea, represents the benevolent mother who nurtures Edna and even inspires her to paint. Adèle seems to her, as she is seated on the beach, like "some sensuous Madonna," and she paints her picture.

At this beginning point in her artistic development Edna thinks of herself as a "dabbler." However, though Edna has had no formal training, Chopin establishes the fact that she is talented for "she handled her brushes with a certain ease and freedom which came not from a long and close acquaintance with them but from a natural aptitude." We also see early on that Edna has the capacity for self-criticism as "after surveying the sketch critically, she drew a broad smudge of paint across its surface and crumpled the paper between her hands." Later when Edna's critical faculties are turned against conventional values of home, husband, and family in the direction of autonomy,

Adèle will show the negative side of her mothering qualities. By constantly reminding Edna of her duty to her children, she binds her to society's rules and impedes her creative growth.

In these early scenes at Grand Isle where Edna's struggle to be an artist is beginning, Robert is another source of imaginative power. As she paints Adèle's portrait, he encourages her with "expressions of appreciation in French." While this may simply be Creole flattery, it is more encouragement than she has ever received from her husband. Like Adèle, he is sensual, and as she paints he rests his head against her arm. He also speaks about himself freely, telling her of his plans to go to Mexico. Under his influence she speaks to him about her life, and it is he who awakens her to the passions of her body. A few weeks after the painting scene on the beach, Chopin again uses the sea as a symbol of growth, and again in connection with Robert. One evening he proposes a night swim and we see him lingering behind with the lovers, "and there was not one but was ready to follow when he led the way." Robert's appearance is associated frequently with lovers; he becomes Cupid who awakens Edna to the force of Eros. This evening she learns to swim and feels herself "reaching out for the unlimited in which to lose herself." Loss of boundaries suggests orgiastic union which foreshadows Edna's final merging with the sea. Significantly, that evening as she lies in a hammock, an image of lovemaking, she feels herself "pregnant with the first felt throbbing desire" for Robert.

When her husband returns later she refuses to go inside when he asks her to. By now she has achieved mastery over her body by learning to swim and mastery over her environment by challenging his authority. She now has to achieve mastery over her imagination, but at this point can only "blindly follow whatever impulse moved her." Next morning, without much thought, she asks a servant to tell Robert she wishes him to take the boat with her to Cheniere for mass. Walking to the wharf, there are, as always when Robert appears, lovers who already stroll "shoulder to shoulder." Edna's imagination is subsumed by the romance phase of her creative growth as she spends an idyllic day with Robert....

The woman who represents a structured form of art is Mme. Reisz, the true artist Edna wishes to become. While Madame Ratignolle plays the piano solely for the pleasure of her family, Mme. Reisz plays Frederic Chopin with great feeling and art. Before hearing Mme. Reisz play, music had evoked pictures in Edna's mind. After listening to her play,

Edna's passions are aroused. But like such nineteenth century female artists as Emily Dickinson, Mme. Reisz is unmarried, childless, eccentric in manner and in dress, and alienated from society. She cannot serve as a role model for Edna. Nevertheless, Edna's creative development continues. After the family's return to New Orleans, she takes up her painting once more in spite of her husband's admonishment that she "not let the family go to the devil" while she paints. She works with "great energy and interest" though she feels she is not accomplishing anything....

There are factors beyond Edna's control, however, which limit her development. [Sandra] Gilbert and [Susan] Gubar [in *The Madwoman in the Attic,* Yale University Press, 1979], in a discussion of the woman writer in patriarchal society, describe "the loneliness of the female artist, her feelings of alienation from male predecessors coupled with her need for sisterly precursors and successors, her urgent need for a female audience." Certainly this describes Edna's situation as she seeks out her two contrasting women friends for validation, Mme. Reisz and Adèle Ratignolle. She brings her paintings to Adèle even though she knows in advance, "her opinion in such a matter would be next to valueness ... but she sought the words of praise and encouragement that would help her to put heart into her venture." Adèle, true to her character as a "mother-woman," tells her that her talent is immense, and Edna is pleased even though she recognizes "its true worth." She receives a much harsher judgement of her artistic capacity from Mme. Reisz. In reply to the question of what she has been doing, Edna tells her "I am becoming an artist" and her friend says, "Ah! an artist. You have pretensions, Madame." Sensing the insecurity which keeps her from total commitment to art, Mme. Reisz warns, "To be an artist includes much; one must possess many gifts—absolute gifts—which have not been acquired by one's own effort. And moreover, to succeed the artist must possess the courageous soul."...

Two events occur almost simultaneously at the novel's climax, events which portray the forces that finally defeat Edna's search for artistic wholeness. One is her witnessing of Adèle's suffering in childbirth and the other is Robert's admitting that he loves her and wants to marry her. Edna has gone to Adèle, leaving Robert just after he tells her he has dreamed of marrying her if her husband will free her. She has replied that she is no longer one of Mr. Pontellier's possessions to be given away. When she returns from Adèle's he is gone, having explained in a note that he has left not because he doesn't love her but because he does. Robert has been deeply connected to her sexual growth, which in turn affected the growth of her imagination. Through him she has begun to transfer the authenticity of her romantic vision to her paintings. Now, romantic illusions shattered, she loses the catalyst for her art.

The other illusion that is shattered is that of childbirth being a moment of joy. Edna does not remember her own pain when she gave birth, since she was chloroformed. Now, seeing Adèle's pain, she recognizes that she cannot rebel against nature. Adèle's parting words "think of the children" remind her of her mother-role which conflicts with her new-found freedom. Chopin was far ahead of her time in exposing the myth of bearing children as a woman's ultimate fulfillment, calling Adèle's "acouchement" a scene of torture. Almost a century later Sylvia Plath was to use the same image in *The Bell Jar* by describing the delivery room as "some awful torture chamber."...

The next morning Edna returns to Grand Isle and walks to her death in the sea. Is her suicide triggered by Adèle's suffering in childbirth? By the knowledge that it is futile to rebel against biology? Does she kill herself because Robert has left her? Or because she has failed to become an artist? Edna drowns herself because she cannot live as a conventional wife or mother any longer, and society will not accept her newfound self. The solitude she enjoys makes for artistic growth, but she is bound to children, home, social duty. She will not sacrifice her new autonomy because, as Anne Jones points out [in *Tomorrow Is Another Day: The Woman Writer in the South, 1859–1936,* Louisiana State University Press, 1981], "she will not relinquish the core of her vision, which is not finally romance, but rather her own autonomous being ... so she freely goes to the sea, losing her life. But she does not lose her self."

By beginning and ending *The Awakening* with the sea Chopin gives the book a wholeness that Edna cannot find in her life. Furthermore, Chopin's themes of sea/mother, love/lover, self/birth, sexuality/creativity are joined as Edna's birth of a new self is juxtaposed against Adèle's giving birth to another. In a moment of liberty she stands naked on the beach feeling like "some new-born creature" before entering the sea which becomes the universal Great Mother. To be sure, Chopin uses one image of defeat, the "bird with the broken wing," which Edna sees "reeling, fluttering, circling, disabled down down to the water." This was the image used by Mlle. Reisz when, as if predicting Edna's fall she said, "it is a sad spectacle to see the weakling bruised, exhausted, fluttering back to earth." But how strong must a woman be at this time in order to maintain her artistic vocation without any support from community?....

Yet Edna's final moment is one of autonomous sexuality, as the world of her imagination resonates with fertility—"There was the hum of bees, and the musky odor of pinks filled the air." Chopin repeats the description of the sea which describes Edna's first swim, "The touch of the sea is sensuous, enfolding the body in its soft, close embrace," and with this symbolic closure portrays Edna becoming whole in the only way she can, by immersion in the universal sea of love. But how can Edna's death be positive? Many critics think it is not.... Nevertheless, Edna Pontellier succeeds in giving birth to a new self even though the fact that she can not live on earth as this new self is tragic. The triumph of *The Awakening* lies in Chopin's depicting, when others did not, the conflicts faced by women who wish to become artists. Courageously, she built in her novel a bridge from past to future so that women might find their way across. Like her heroine, she too was a *pontellier,* a bridge-maker.

Source: Carole Stone, "The Female Artist in Kate Chopin's *The Awakening:* Birth and Creativity," in *Women's Studies,* Vol. 13, Nos. 1 & 2, 1986, pp. 23–31.

Kenneth Eble

In this excerpt, Eble relates background information about the author and re-evaluates themes and controversies aroused by Chopin's novel upon its publication at the turn of the century.

The claim of [*The Awakening*] upon the reader's attention is simple. It is a first-rate novel. The justification for urging its importance is that we have few enough novels of its stature. One could add that it is advanced in theme and technique over the novels of its day, that it anticipates in many respects the modern novel. It could be claimed that it adds to American fiction an example of what Gide called the *roman pur,* a kind of novel not characteristic of American writing. One could offer the book as evidence that the regional writer can go beyond the limitations of regional material. But these matters aside, what recommends the novel is its general excellence....

In a way, the novel is an American *Bovary,* though such a designation is not precisely accurate.

Its central character is similar: the married woman who seeks love outside a stuffy, middle-class marriage. It is similar too in the definitive way it portrays the mind of a woman trapped in marriage and seeking fulfillment of what she vaguely recognizes as her essential nature. The husband, Léonce Pontellier, is a businessman whose nature and preoccupations are not far different from those of Charles Bovary. There is a Léon Dupuis in Robert Lebrun, a Rodolphe Boulanger in Alcée Arobin. And too, like *Madame Bovary,* the novel handles its material superbly well. Kate Chopin herself was probably more than any other American writer of her time under French influence. Her background was French-Irish; she married a Creole; she read and spoke French and knew contemporary French literature well; she associated both in St. Louis and Louisiana with families of French ancestry and disposition. But despite the similarities and the possible influences, the novel, chiefly because of the independent character of its heroine, Edna Pontellier, and because of the intensity of the focus upon her, is not simply a good but derivative work. It has a manner and matter of its own.

Quite frankly, the book is about sex. Not only is it about sex, but the very texture of the writing is sensuous, if not sensual, from the first to the last. Even as late as 1932, Chopin's biographer, Daniel Rankin, seemed somewhat shocked by it. He paid his respects to the artistic excellence of the book, but he was troubled by "that insistent query—*cui bono?*" He called the novel "exotic in setting, morbid in theme, erotic in motivation." One questions the accuracy of these terms, and even more the moral disapproval implied in their usage. One regrets that Mr. Rankin did not emphasize that the book was amazingly honest, perceptive and moving.

The Awakening is a study of Edna Pontellier, a story, as the *Nation* criticized it, "of a Southern lady who wanted to do what she wanted to. From wanting to, she did, with disastrous consequences." Such a succinct statement, blunt but accurate so far as it goes, may suggest that a detailed retelling of the story would convey little of the actual character of the novel. It is, of course, one of those novels a person simply must read to gain any real impression of its excellence. But the compactness of the work in narrative, characterization, setting, symbols and images gives meaning to such an imprecise and overworked expression. Some idea of the style may be conveyed by quoting the opening paragraphs:

A green and yellow parrot, which hung in a cage outside the door, kept repeating over and over " *Allez vous en! Allez vous en! Sapristi!* That's all right."

He could speak a little Spanish, and also a language which nobody understood, unless it was the mockingbird that hung on the other side of the door, whistling his fluty notes out upon the breeze with maddening persistence.

Mr. Pontellier, unable to read his newspaper with any degree of comfort, arose with an expression and an exclamation of disgust. He walked down the gallery and across the narrow "bridges" which connected the Lebrun cottages one with the other. He had been seated before the door of the main house. The parrot and the mockingbird were the property of Madame Lebrun and they had the right to make all the noise they wished. Mr. Pontellier had the privilege of quitting their society when they ceased to be entertaining.

This is Mr. Pontellier. He is a businessman, husband and father, not given to romance, not given to much of anything outside his business. When he comes to Grand Isle, the summer place of the Creoles in the story, he is anxious to get back to his cotton brokerage in Carondelet Street, New Orleans, and he passes his time on Grand Isle at the hotel smoking his cigars and playing cards. When he is on the beach at all, he is not a participant, but a watcher.

He fixed his gaze upon a white sunshade that was advancing at snail's page from the beach. He could see it plainly between the gaunt trunk of the water oaks and across the strip of yellow camomile. The gulf looked far away, melting hazily into the blue of the horizon. The sunshade continued to approach slowly. Beneath its pink-lined shelter were their faces, Mrs. Pontellier and young Robert Lebrun.

It is apparent that a triangle has been formed, and going into the details of the subsequent events in a summary fashion would likely destroy the art by which such a sequence becomes significant. Suffice to say that Robert Lebrun is the young man who first awakens, or rather, is present at the awakening of Edna Pontellier into passion, a passion which Mr. Pontellier neither understands nor appreciates. Slowly Edna and Robert fall in love, but once again, the expression is too trite. Edna grows into an awareness of a woman's physical nature, and Robert is actually but a party of the second part. The reader's attention is never allowed to stray from Edna. At the climax of their relationship, young Lebrun recognizes what must follow and goes away. During his absence, Mrs. Pontellier becomes idly amused by a roué [a man devoted to sexual pleasure], Arobin, and, becoming more than amused, more than tolerates his advances. When

Robert returns he finds that Edna is willing to declare her love and accept the consequences of her passion. But Robert, abiding by the traditional romantic code which separates true love from physical passion, refuses the offered consummation. When he leaves Mrs. Pontellier, she turns once again to the scene of her awakening, the sand and sea of Grand Isle:

> The water of the Gulf stretched out before her, gleaming with the million lights of the sun. The voice of the sea is seductive, never ceasing whispering, clamoring, murmuring, inviting the soul to wander in abysses of solitude. All along the white beach, up and down, there was no living thing in sight. A bird with a broken wing was beating the air above, reeling, fluttering, circling disabled down, down to the water.
>
> Edna had found her old bathing suit still hanging, faded, upon its accustomed peg.
>
> She put it on, left her clothing in the bath house. But when she was there beside the sea, absolutely alone, she cast the unpleasant, pricking garments from her, and for the first time in her life she stood naked in the open air at the mercy of the sun, the breeze that beat upon her, and the waves that invited her.
>
> How strange and awful it seemed to stand naked under the sky! How delicious! She felt like some newborn creature, opening its eye in a familiar world that it had never known.
>
> The foamy wavelets curled up to her white feet, and coiled like serpents about her ankles. She walked out. The water was chill, but she walked on. The water was deep, but she lifted her white body and reached out with a long, sweeping stroke. The touch of the sea is sensuous, enfolding the body in its soft close embrace....
>
> She looked into the distance, and the old terror flamed up for an instant, then sank again. Edna heard her father's voice and her sister Margaret's. She heard the barking of an old dog that was chained to the sycamore tree. The spurs of the cavalry officer clanged as he walked across the porch. There was the hum of bees, and the musty odor of pinks filled the air.

Here is the story, its beginning a mature woman's awakening to physical love, its end her walking into the sea. The extracts convey something of the author's style, but much less of the movement of the characters and of human desire against the sensuous background of sea and sand. Looking at the novel analytically, one can say that it excels chiefly in its characterizations and its structure, the use of images and symbols to unify that structure, and the character of Edna Pontellier.

Kate Chopin, almost from her first story, had the ability to capture character, to put the right word in the mouth, to impart the exact gesture, to select the characteristic action. An illustration of her deftness in handling even minor characters is her treatment of Edna's father. When he leaves the Pontellier's after a short visit, Edna is glad to be rid of him and "his padded shoulders, his Bible reading, his 'toddies,' and ponderous oaths." A moment later, it is a side of Edna's nature which is revealed. She felt a sense of relief at her father's absence; "she read Emerson until she grew sleepy."

Characterization was always Mrs. Chopin's talent. Structure was not. Those who knew her working habits say that she seldom revised, and she herself mentions that she did not like reworking her stories. Though her reputation rests upon her short narratives, her collected stories give abundant evidence of the sketch, the outlines of stories which remain unformed. And when she did attempt a tightly organized story, she often turned to Maupassant and was as likely as not to effect a contrived symmetry. Her early novel *At Fault* suffers most from her inability to control her material. In *The Awakening* she is in complete command of structure. She seems to have grasped instinctively the use of the unifying symbol—here the sea, sky and sand—and with it the power of individual images to bind the story together.

The sea, the sand, the sun and sky of the Gulf Coast become almost a presence themselves in the novel. Much of the sensuousness of the book comes from the way the reader is never allowed to stray far from the water's edge. A refrain beginning "The voice of the sea is seductive, never ceasing, clamoring, murmuring, ... " is used throughout the novel. It appears first at the beginning of Edna Pontellier's awakening, and it appears at the end as the introduction to the long final scene, previously quoted. Looking closely at the final form of this refrain, one can notice the care with which Mrs. Chopin composed this theme and variation. In the initial statement, the sentence does not end with "solitude," but goes on, as it should, "to lose itself in mazes of inward contemplation." Nor is the image of the bird with the broken wing in the earlier passage; rather there is prefiguring of the final tragedy: "The voice of the sea speaks to the soul. The touch of the sea is sensuous, enfolding the body in its soft close embrace." The way scene, mood, action and character are fused reminds one not so much of literature as of an impressionist painting, of a Renoir with much of the sweetness missing. Only Stephen Crane, among her American contemporaries, had an equal sensitivity to light and shadow, color and texture, had the painter's eye matched with the writer's perception of character and incident....

It is not surprising that the sensuous quality of the book, both from the incidents of the novel and the symbolic implications, would have offended contemporary reviewers. What convinced many critics of the indecency of the book, however, was not simply the sensuous scenes, but rather that the author obviously sympathized with Mrs. Pontellier. More than that, the readers probably found that she aroused their own sympathies....

Greek tragedy—to remove ourselves from Victorian morals—knew well *eros* was not the kind of *love* which can be easily prettified and sentimentalized. Phaedra's struggle with elemental passion in the *Hippolytus* is not generally regarded as being either morally offensive or insignificant. Mrs. Pontellier, too, has the power, the dignity, the self-possession of a tragic heroine. She is not an Emma Bovary, deluded by ideas of "romance," nor is she the sensuous but guilt-ridden woman of the sensational novel. We can find only partial reason for her affair in the kind of romantic desire to escape a middle-class existence which animates Emma Bovary. Edna Pontellier is neither deluded nor deludes. She is woman, the physical woman who, despite her Kentucky Presbyterian upbringing and a comfortable marriage, must struggle with the sensual appeal of physical ripeness itself, with passion of which she is only dimly aware. Her struggle is not melodramatic, nor is it artificial, nor vapid. It is objective, real and moving. And when she walks into the sea, it does not leave a reader with the sense of sin punished.... How wrong to call Edna, as Daniel Rankin does, "a selfish, capricious" woman. Rather, Edna's struggle, the struggle with *eros* itself, is farthest removed from capriciousness. It is her self-awareness, and her awakening into a greater degree of self-awareness than those around her can comprehend, which gives her story dignity and significance.

Our advocacy of the novel is not meant to obscure its faults. It is not perfect art, but in total effect it provokes few dissatisfactions. A sophisticated modern reader might find something of the derivative about it. Kate Chopin read widely, and a list of novelists she found interesting would include Flaubert, Tolstoy, Turgenev, D'Annunzio, Bourget, Goncourt and Zola. It is doubtful, however, that there was any direct borrowing, and *The Awakening* exists, as do most good novels, as a product of the author's literary, real, and imagined life.

How Mrs. Chopin managed to create in ten years the substantial body of work she achieved is no less a mystery than the excellence of *The Awakening* itself. But, having added to American literature a novel uncommon in its kind as in its excellence, she deserves not to be forgotten. *The Awakening* deserves to be restored and to be given its place among novels worthy of preservation.

Source: Kenneth Eble, "A Forgotten Novel: Kate Chopin's *The Awakening*," in *Western Humanities Review*, No. 3, Summer, 1956, pp. 261–69.

Sources

Kate Chopin, *The Awakening,* edited by Margo Culley, 2nd edition, Norton, 1994.

For Further Study

Review of *The Awakening,* in *Public Opinion,* Vol. 26, 1899, p. 794.

This unfavorable review of *The Awakening* criticizes the immorality of the book, calling into doubt "the possibility of a woman of solid old Presbyterian Kentucky stock ever being at all like the heroine" and concluding that "we are well satisfied when she drowns herself."

Harold Bloom, *Modern Critical Views: Kate Chopin,* Chelsea House Publishers, New York, 1987.

This compilation offers perspectives from such distinguished critics as Larzer Ziff, Cynthia Griffin Wolff, and Susan Rosowski. Their interpretations run from an analysis of the author's "Flaubertian detachment" to a feminist's evaluation.

Carley Rees Bogarad, "'The Awakening': A Refusal to Compromise," in *The University of Michigan Papers in Women's Studies,* Vol. II, No. 3, 1997, pp. 15-31.

Bogarad reviews the novel and classifies it as a "novel of development." The review offers the idea that Edna's awakening is a double one. Her first awakening occurs when Edna realizes that she wants autonomy as a human being and conceives of a life that would allow her to follow her dreams and still be connected to society. Her second awakening begins when she concedes that she can not reconcile her definition of self with society's definition. The reviewer provides detailed support for her view.

Thomas Bonner, Jr., *The Kate Chopin Companion,* Greenwood, 1988.

Bonner compiles an encyclopedic dictionary of all of Chopin's characters. This volume also includes several of Guy de Maussapant's short stories, which were translated from French into English by Chopin.

"Books of the Day," in *The Awakening,* by Kate Chopin, *Chicago Times-Herald,* Vol. 1, June, 1899, p. 9.

Although the reviewer praises *The Awakening* for being "strong," the overall review is negative. The reviewer says of *The Awakening* that "it was not necessary for a writer of so great refinement and poetic grace to enter the overworked field of sex fiction. This is not a pleasant story, but the contrast between the heroine and another character who is utterly devoted to her husband and family saves it from utter gloom."

Lynda S. Boren and Sara deSaussure Davis, *Kate Chopin Reconsidered: Beyond the Bayou,* Louisiana State University Press, 1992.

This volume of essays offers multiple feminist readings of *The Awakening* and some of Chopin's short fiction.

Violet Harrington Bryan, *The Myth of New Orleans in Literature,* University of Tennessee Press, 1993.

Bryan discusses the influence of New Orleans culture on Chopin's fiction, focusing heavily on issues of gender and race.

Joyce Dyer, *The Awakening: A Novel of Beginnings,* Twayne, 1993.

Dyer analyzes the nature of female awakenings in Chopin's short fiction and in *The Awakening,* but since she sees Chopin as sensitive to male perspectives, she argues that Chopin's true subject is not limited to an examination of the female nature, but to human nature.

Anna Shannon Elfenbein, *Women on the Color Line: Evolving Stereotypes and the Writings of George Washington Cable, Grace King, Kate Chopin,* University Press of Virginia, 1989.

Elfenbein discusses the double-bind that many of Chopin's characters of mixed race find themselves in, and the ways in which they attempt to overcome the prejudices against them. Although Elfenbein focuses on the short fiction, her book is useful for gaining a sense of Chopin's attitudes concerning racial equality.

Barbara C. Ewell, *Kate Chopin,* Ungar, 1986.

Ewell analyzes *The Awakening* as a feminist novel. She also discusses biographical information and the short fiction.

Linda Huf, *A Portrait of the Artist as a Young Woman,* Ungar, 1983.

Huf discusses *The Awakening* as "a tale of a young woman who struggles to realize herself—and her artistic ability."

Louisiana Literature, Vol. 2.1, 1994.

An entire section of this journal is devoted to essays presented at the Biannual Kate Chopin International Conference. The introductory essay by Emily Toth discusses new issues in Kate Chopin's work, and is especially useful for those unfamiliar with Chopin's work.

Carol S. Manning, editor, *The Female Tradition in Southern Literature,* University of Illinois Press, 1993.

This volume of essays discusses, in passing, Chopin's contribution to the Southern Renaissance in literature.

Wendy Martin, editor, *New Essays on The Awakening,* Cambridge University Press, 1988.

Contains essays on the roles of the artist, of modernist thought, of Edna's dilemma and her potential solutions in *The Awakening.*

Perspectives on Kate Chopin: Proceedings of the Kate Chopin International Conference, Northwestern State University Press, 1990.

Collected papers from the 1988 meeting of the Kate Chopin International Conference. This volume is very difficult to locate, but has some excellent essays on lesbianism, local color, and philosophical influences on Chopin. It also includes an essay on Chopin's relationship to her publishers.

Anne Rowe, "Kate Chopin," in *The History of Southern Literature,* Louisiana State University Press, 1985.

This essay offers a brief biographical sketch of Kate Chopin.

Per Seyersted, editor, *The Complete Works of Kate Chopin,* Louisiana State University Press, 1969.

This volume contains all of Chopin's known fiction, including *The Awakening, At Fault* and over 100 short stories. It also includes essays, poetry, and a song. Although a few pieces of Chopin's work have been discovered since the *Complete Works* appeared, it is still a reasonably complete volume.

Per Seyersted, *Kate Chopin: A Critical Biography,* Louisiana State University Press, 1969.

This biography gives information about Chopin's life, but also relies heavily on explication of her texts. Seyersted sets right some of the inaccuracies of Daniel Rankin's early, discredited biography.

Helen Taylor, *Gender, Race and Region in the Writings of Grace King, Ruth McEnery Stuart and Kate Chopin,* Louisiana State University Press, 1989.

Taylor argues that Chopin's fiction is inherently racist and illustrates with copious examples.

Emily Toth, *Kate Chopin: A Life of the Author of The Awakening,* Morrow, 1990.

This authoritative biography of Chopin's life was nominated for a Pulitzer Prize. Toth's style is very readable, and the book is chocked full of personal anecdotes from those who knew Chopin.

Crime and Punishment

Fyodor Dostoyevsky

1866

When the first installment of *Crime and Punishment* appeared in the journal *Russian Messenger* in January of 1866, its debt-ridden author, Fyodor Mikhailovich Dostoyevsky, had not yet finished writing the novel. However, even before the entire work had appeared in serial form, the novel was a public success. Early Russian readers and critics recognized that, artistically and socially, *Crime and Punishment* was one of the most important novels of its time, and it was widely discussed.

On the surface, *Crime and Punishment* is the story of a murder, set in the city of St. Petersburg, then the Russian capital. It is not, however, a murder mystery: we know the murderer's identity from the very beginning. Moreover, although Dostoyevsky depicts the crime and the environment in which it takes place with great realism, he is more interested in the psychology of the murderer than in the external specifics of the crime.

Like many of the great nineteenth-century novelists, Dostoyevsky often uses a series of incredible coincidences to move the plot forward. Nonetheless, the story takes on a compelling life of its own. Dostoyevsky's use of parable and of dream sequences is also original and remarkable. Furthermore, Dostoyevsky creates a gallery of memorable characters, including the proud and tormented ex-student Raskolnikov and his two murder victims; the drunken civil servant Marmeladov and his daughter, the meek prostitute Sonya, whose love helps to redeem Raskolnikov; Raskolnikov's devoted sister, mother, and best friend (Dunya,

Pulkheria Aleksandrovna, and Razhumikhin); Dunya's scheming suitor Luzhin and the sinister Svidrigailov; and the canny police investigator, Porfiry Petrovich. Finally, beyond its powerful plot and colorful characters, *Crime and Punishment* is marked by its insightful treatment of several major themes. Among other things, the book is an expose of social conditions in nineteenth-century Russia, a satirical analysis of liberal and radical politics, and a religious call for redemption through suffering. As an intensely dramatic study of the nature of good and evil, it is commonly considered the quintessential Russian novel.

Author Biography

When Fyodor Mikhailovich Dostoyevsky wrote *Crime and Punishment* in the mid-1860s, he was already a well-known author. Nonetheless, he lived in near-poverty and was plagued by gambling debts. Born in Moscow in 1821, he was the second child in a family that eventually consisted of seven children. The family's life was unhappy: Dostoyevsky's father, a doctor, ruled the family with an iron hand; his mother, a meek woman, died when the boy was sixteen. Young Dostoyevsky developed a love of books and enthusiastically read Russian, French, and German novels. However, his father insisted that Dostoyevsky study engineering, and from 1838 to 1843 Dostoyevsky trained in this subject at the military engineering academy in St. Petersburg. During this time the elder Dostoyevsky was murdered by one of his serfs, an incident that had a profound impact on Fyodor.

In the mid-1840s Dostoyevsky embarked on a literary career, writing several short stories and novellas, including "The Double" (1846). The concept of the "double" — the notion that a person may have a divided personality, symbolized by a good or evil "twin" — surfaced in several of his later works, including *Crime and Punishment*. His early published works brought Dostoyevsky some recognition. In 1848 Dostoyevsky joined a group of radical intellectuals (known as the "Petrashevsky Circle" after their leader, Mikhail Petrashevsky). The group discussed literary and political ideas and advocated reforming the autocratic tsarist government. Dostoyevsky and several of his friends were arrested for treason, tried, and sentenced to death. Just as they were lined up in front of the firing

Fyodor Dostoyevsky

squad, a messenger arrived with news that the tsar had commuted the death sentence to a term of hard labor in Siberia. Dostoyevsky later alluded to this event in *Crime and Punishment* and in other books. (It is believed that the authorities intended a mock execution all along.) During his five years in prison, Dostoyevsky came to know many of the prisoners, the great majority of whom were ordinary criminals rather than political prisoners. Through his dealings with them, the writer developed an understanding of the criminal mentality and the Russian soul. His political views also changed. He rejected his earlier pro-Western liberal-socialist ideas and instead embraced a specifically Russian brand of Christianity. His prison experiences provided the material for his later book *The House of the Dead* (1861).

After his release from prison camp in 1854, Dostoyevsky had to spend several more years in Siberia as an army private. He returned to St. Petersburg in 1859 and resumed his literary career. In the early 1860s he traveled extensively in Western Europe. However, he was troubled by personal misfortune, including the death of his wife and his brother, with whom he edited a literary journal. He also was afflicted by epilepsy, a condition little understood at the time. Moreover, he was unable to control his compulsive gambling habit, and he found himself on the brink of poverty. His writing during this period was stimulated not only by an intense desire to express important ideas but also by a need to earn money. In 1864 he wrote *Notes from Underground,* whose narrator is a self-confessed "sick ... spiteful ... unattractive man," an embittered character who resents society. Immediately after this book, Dostoyevsky started work on *Crime and Punishment* (1865-66), regarded as his first true masterpiece. Important Russian critics hailed the work, and Dostoyevsky was acclaimed as one of Russia's most significant writers and thinkers. However, he still faced financial ruin, and the next year he wrote, in just one month, a novella called *The Gambler* in order to pay his debts. He subsequently married the stenographer to whom he had dictated the work, Anna Snitkina. She helped reform his life, and they lived abroad for several years. Foremost among his later novels are *The Idiot* (1869), *The Possessed* (also translated as *The Devils,* 1871), and *The Brothers Karamazov* (1880). With *Crime and Punishment,* these books express the essence of Dostoyevsky's social and moral philosophy and his insight into human character. In the last decade of his life, Dostoyevsky finally gained critical acclaim, social prestige, and financial security. He died in St. Petersburg in 1881.

Dostoyevsky's reputation and his influence remain strong to the present day. Virtually all his books have been translated into English and are in print. His insights into the complexities of human psychology anticipated the theories of Sigmund Freud and other early psychologists. (Indeed, Freud acknowledged Dostoyevsky's importance in this field.) Later novelists as diverse as Robert Louis Stevenson, Franz Kafka, Albert Camus, and Iris Murdoch all drew inspiration from Dostoyevsky's themes and characters, while Aleksandr Solzhenitsyn carries on with Dostoyevsky's unique brand of Russian nationalism and Christianity. Filmmakers Ingmar Bergman and Woody Allen have also acknowledged a debt to Dostoyevsky in their views of human nature. Some scholars have gone so far as to claim that Dostoyevsky's view of the Russian character and politics prophesied the Russian Revolution and the terrible deprivations that Russia suffered under Soviet Communist rule in the twentieth century. With his contemporary Leo Tolstoy, Dostoyevsky is today regarded as one of the two greatest nineteenth-century Russian novelists and indeed as one of the most important novelists of any nation or period.

Plot Summary

Part I

As the novel *Crime and Punishment* begins, an impoverished student named Rodion Raskolnikov sets out to visit a pawnbroker in a poor section of St. Petersburg, the Russian capital. This visit serves as a trial run for a sinister mission: Raskolnikov plans to murder and rob the old woman. After the visit, Raskolnikov feels miserable, so he stops at a tavern for a drink. There he meets a drunk named Marmeladov who tells him how his daughter Sonya became a prostitute to support her family. Raskolnikov helps Marmeladov home, and he is touched by the pitiful scene of poverty he sees there. After leaving the family some money, he returns to his cramped room.

The next day, Raskolnikov receives a letter from his mother. She informs him that Raskolnikov's sister Dunya is set to marry a bachelor named Luzhin. Raskolnikov realizes that his mother and sister are counting on Luzhin to give Raskolnikov financial assistance after the wedding. As he sees it, Dunya is sacrificing herself for her brother, a sacrifice that reminds him of Sonya's prostitution. He berates himself for his passivity. Soon afterwards, he falls asleep, and he dreams of watching a peasant beat an overburdened horse to death. When he awakens, he articulates for the first time his plan to kill the pawnbroker with an axe. Hearing that the pawnbroker's sister would be away from their apartment the next evening, he realizes that the time to execute his plan has arrived. The murder itself does not unfold as intended. Lizaveta, the pawnbroker's sister, returns home unexpectedly, and Raskolnikov kills her too. Distraught, he finds only a few items of value, and he is nearly discovered by two of the pawnbroker's clients who knock at the door. When they leave momentarily, Raskolnikov slips out of the apartment undetected.

Part II

During the next few days, Raskolnikov alternates between lucidity and delirium. He feels torn between an impulse to confess his crime and an impulse to resist arrest. He begins a game of cat-and-mouse with the examining magistrate, Porfiry Petrovich. Porfiry has read an article written by Raskolnikov in which Raskolnikov expounds the theory that a few select individuals may have the right to commit crimes if they think it necessary to attain special goals. Raskolnikov now explains his theory to Porfiry, beginning with the idea that there are two categories of people in the world—the masses and the elite.

> The first group, that is the material, are, generally speaking, by nature staid and conservative, they live in obedience and like it. In my opinion they ought to obey because that is their destiny, and there is nothing at all degrading to them in it. The second group are all law-breakers and transgressors, or are inclined that way, in the measure of their capacities. The aims of these people are, of course, relative and very diverse; for the most part they require, in widely different contexts, the destruction of what exists in the name of better things. But if it is necessary for one of them, for the fulfillment of his ideas, to march over corpses, or wade through blood, then in my opinion he may in all conscience authorize himself to wade through blood—in proportion, however, to his idea and the degree of its importance—mark that. It is in that sense only that I speak in my article of their right to commit crime.

(From *Crime and Punishment,* translated by Jessie Coulson, Norton, 1989.)

Porfiry wonders whether Raskolnikov might consider himself to be an "extraordinary man," and if so, whether the murder of the pawnbroker could be connected with his cynical theory. Porfiry hints that he suspects Raskolnikov of the murder, but he avoids making definitive accusations at first, thus keeping Raskolnikov on edge.

While this covert duel between Raskolnikov and Porfiry Petrovich continues, Dostoyevsky develops several subplots. Marmeladov is run over by a carriage, and when Raskolnikov takes the dying man home, he sees Sonya. Struck by her image of humble self-sacrifice, he feels drawn to her. In the meantime, Raskolnikov's sister Dunya breaks off her engagement to Luzhin, who has become insufferably demanding. Yet she now must contend with a new pursuer, her former employer Svidrigailov. Svidrigailov is rumored to have abused young women and to have beaten his wife. He had made advances to Dunya when she worked for him, and his scandalous behavior had unjustly given her a bad reputation. Now he turns up again.

Wracked by continuing anxiety, Raskolnikov makes two important visits to Sonya's apartment. In the first visit, he alternates between antagonizing her and seeking her sympathy. He wonders how she could go on living despite her humiliating profession. It occurs to him that the answer may lie in religion. He asks Sonya to read aloud the Gospel account of the raising of Lazarus. This story of a dead man restored to life perhaps suggests to Raskolnikov that he too may someday be able to return to normal life. He tells Sonya that on his next visit he will disclose to her the murderer's identity.

During his second visit, Raskolnikov reveals to Sonya his awful crime. The moment of confession takes place without words. In a scene that uncannily recalls the original murder of the pawnbroker and Lizaveta, Raskolnikov looks into Sonya's eyes, and she reacts with the same terror he had seen on Lizaveta's face. In an instant, she perceives his guilt. Instead of turning away with horror, though, she embraces him and shows that she understands how much he suffers. Her selfless acceptance of his suffering gives Raskolnikov new strength. He tells her that he committed the murder to find out whether he was someone special, someone with the right to step over conventional codes of behavior. He now asks her what to do. She tells him to go to the crossroads, kiss the earth, and make a public confession. God will then send him new life. Yet Raskolnikov is not ready to surrender, and he leaves her apartment in a renewed state of indecision.

Unbeknownst to Raskolnikov and Sonya, Svidrigailov had been eavesdropping on their last conversation, and he attempts to use Raskolnikov's confession as a tool to win Dunya's affections. Luring her to his apartment, Svidrigailov tells Dunya that he knows of Raskolnikov's crime, and he indicates that he will save Raskolnikov if Dunya gives herself to him. She tries to leave the room, but he has locked the door. She takes a revolver out of her pocket, and while he taunts her to shoot him, she pulls the trigger twice. The first bullet misses, and then the gun misfires. Although Svidrigailov gives her the opportunity to shoot again, Dunya throws the gun down. Svidrigailov hopes that she will now surrender to him, but she tells him that she will never love him, and he lets her go. Disheartened by her rejection, Svidrigailov spends a fitful night in a cheap hotel. A series of dreams reveals to him the extent of his internal corruption. In the morning, he leaves the hotel and shoots himself in front of an astonished watchman.

On that same day, Raskolnikov resolves to turn himself in to the police. He makes a final visit to Sonya and departs for the police station. Crossing a public square, he recalls Sonya's words about confessing to the world. He falls to his knees and kisses the ground. The mockery of the bystanders, however, quells his impulse to make a public confession, so he moves on to the police station. There he learns that Svidrigailov has committed suicide. He begins to leave the station, perhaps feeling the lure of suicide himself. Outside the building, however, he sees Sonya looking at him in anguish. He reenters the station and declares in a loud voice: "It was I who killed the old woman and her sister Lizaveta...."

Epilogue

The novel's epilogue focuses on Raskolnikov's experiences as a convict in Siberia. Raskolnikov initially feels a deep sense of alienation from his fellow prisoners. During Lent and Easter, he falls ill, and he has a strange dream in which everyone in the world becomes infected with a disease that causes each person to believe that he or she is the sole bearer of truth. The deluded people kill each other, and the world heads toward total collapse. After recuperating from his illness, Raskolnikov walks to a riverbank and gazes at the landscape. Sonya appears at his side. Suddenly, Raskolnikov is seized with an entirely new sensation of love and compassion. Both he and Sonya realize that something profound has occurred within his soul. Love has raised him from the dead, and he will become a new man. Dostoyevsky concludes his novel by stating that the story of Raskolnikov's regeneration might be the subject of a new tale, but that the present one has ended.

Characters

Pulkheria Aleksandrovna

Raskolnikov's mother. A widow, she is forty-three years old, but her face "still retains traces of her former beauty." When she arrives in St. Petersburg with her daughter Dunya and meets Raskolnikov, whom she has not seen for three years, she is deeply concerned about him. She finds his behavior puzzling, and she worries about him. Raskolnikov is embarrassed (among other things) by his mother's attention and attempts to rebuff her. In his final encounter with his mother, Raskolnikov reveals his love for her but does not tell her about his crime. However, with a mother's intuition, she is more aware of what is happening to her son than he realizes.

Dunechka

See Dunya Avdotya Romanovna

Alyona Ivanovna

A pawnbroker whom Raskolnikov murders. The widow of a college registrar, in Raskolnikov's eyes she is a suspicious, miserly old woman who preys on unfortunate people who are forced to pawn their few possessions with her. Raskolnikov reasons that she is a "vile, harmful louse" who is no good to anyone and who only causes pain and suffering to others (including her simple-minded sister, Lizaveta Ivanovna). Therefore, for Raskolnikov, her murder is justified. However, Dostoyevsky suggests that the murder of even such an unsympathetic character is a crime against humanity.

Katerina Ivanovna

The wife of Marmeladov. Marmeladov tells Raskolnikov that she is "full of magnanimous emotions" but "hot-tempered and irritable." The daughter of a military officer, she was a poor widow when she met Marmeladov, and since her marriage to Marmeladov she has been reduced to total poverty. She has three children from her previous marriage. She is "a thin, rather tall woman, with a good figure and beautiful chestnut hair." Raskolnikov guesses that she is about thirty years old. She suffers from consumption (tuberculosis) and has been driven to despair by her husband's drunkenness and extreme poverty. In this piteous state she abuses her children, and on her deathbed she refuses to forgive Marmeladov for his irresponsibility. After her husband's death, she retreats into the fantasy that she has an aristocratic background. She dies shortly thereafter.

Lizaveta Ivanovna

The simple-minded younger half-sister of the pawnbroker Alyona Ivanovna. Raskolnikov kills Lizaveta when the woman unexpectedly enters the apartment where Raskolnikov has just murdered Alyona Ivanovna. Ironically, Raskolnikov had earlier expressed some sympathy for Lizaveta, a poor soul who was abused by her sister. Raskolnikov had learned that Alyona would be alone when he overheard Lizaveta talking to someone in the market. Curiously, his unpremeditated killing of the innocent Lizaveta plays little part in his subsequent feelings of guilt. He later learns that Lizaveta was a friend of Sonya Marmeladova.

Andrei Semyonovich Lebezyatnikov

A former student of Luzhin, with whom Luzhin lodges temporarily in St. Petersburg. Lebezyatnikov belongs to a radical utopian organization. Luzhin attempts to enlist him as a witness when he accuses Sonya of robbery. However, Lebezyatnikov realizes that Luzhin has framed Sonya, and he speaks up on her behalf and tells the truth. Dostoyevsky ridicules Lebezyatnikov's naive political ideas, but the character is commended for his basic honesty and decency.

Media Adaptations

- The earliest film adaptation of *Crime and Punishment* was produced in France, released in 1935, and remade in 1958. The original title of this French-language black-and-white film was *Crime et Chatiment*. Written by Marcel Ayme, Pierre Chenal, Christian Stengel, and Wladimir Strijewski (based on Dostoyevsky's book), it was directed by Chenal. It starred Pierre Blanchar, Madeleine Ozeray, Harry Baur, Lucienne Lemarchand, and Marcelle Geniat. Available from Facets Multimedia, Inc.

- An American film version of *Crime and Punishment* was released one week after the French film mentioned above. Adapted from Dostoyevsky's novel by Joseph Anthony and S. K. Lauren, it was directed by Josef von Sternberg. The cast included Peter Lorre, Marian Marsh, Edward Arnold, Tala Birell, Elisabeth Risdon, Robert Allen, Douglas Dumbrille, Gene Lockhart, and Mrs. Patrick Campbell. Available from Columbia Tristar Home Video.

- A Swedish film of *Crime and Punishment* was released in 1948. Adapted by Bertil Malmsberg and Sven Stolpe, it was directed by Hampe Faustman. It starred Faustman, Gann Wallgren, Hugo Bjorne, and Sigurd Wallen. Distributed by Film Rights.

- A Russian-language film of *Crime and Punishment* was produced in the Soviet Union in 1970. Written and directed by Lev Kulidzhanov, it featured Georgi Taratorkin, Victoria Fyodorova, and Innokenty Smoktunovsky. Distributed by Ingram International Films, Discount Video Tapes, Inc., and Horizon Entertainment.

Pyotr Petrovich Luzhin

The manipulative fiance of Raskolnikov's sister, Dunya. Luzhin is related to Svidrigailov and Svidrigailov's wife, Marfa Petrovna, for whom Dunya previously had worked as a governess. In his early forties, Luzhin is depicted as a self-important dandy with uncertain government connections. He clearly does not love Dunya, and his motives for marriage are suspect. After a brief acquaintance, he has arranged for Raskolnikov's sister and mother (Dunya and Pulkheria Aleksandrovna) to follow him to St. Petersburg. However, his arrangements are less than satisfactory. Raskolnikov takes an instant dislike to Luzhin and insults him. Raskolnikov vows to stop his sister's marriage to a man whom he regards as a hypocrite and an opportunist. Luzhin later falsely accuses Sonya of having robbed him, but the charges are disproven and Luzhin is humiliated. For Dostoyevsky, Luzhin embodies superficiality and corruption.

Semyon Zaharovitch Marmeladov

A drunken civil servant; the father of Sonya and the husband of Katerina Ivanovna. In the novel's second chapter, Raskolnikov encounters Marmeladov in a tavern, where Marmeladov tells the former student the story of his degeneration. Despite his drunkenness, Marmeladov is intelligent and perceptive, but he has abandoned his job and lost all self-respect. Consequently, his family has fallen into dire poverty, and his daughter Sonya has resorted to prostitution in order to help support them. Marmeladov is fully aware of his irresponsibility and its disastrous consequences for his family. Indeed, he seems to take pleasure in his depravity and suffering. However, he is unwilling or unable to change his ways and reform himself. Marmeladov is later run over by a carriage and is fatally injured. Raskolnikov happens to come along and has the older man carried to Marmeladov's apartment, where he dies. Both comic and pathetic, Marmeladov is regarded as one of Raskolnikov's "doubles." Dostoyevsky may also intend him to be symptomatic of a Russian national tendency toward slothfulness and irrationality and an inability to reform or modernize.

Sonia Marmeladova

See Sonya Marmeladova

Still from the 1935 movie Crime and Punishment, *starring Peter Lorre as Rodion Raskolnikov.*

Sonya Marmeladova

A meek young prostitute to whom Raskolnikov first confesses his guilt. The eighteen-year-old daughter of the drunken civil servant Semyon Marmeladov, and the stepdaughter of Katerina Ivanovna, Sonya has become a prostitute in order to help support Katerina's children. She is thin, fair-haired, and has "remarkable blue eyes." Raskolnikov first learns about her from Marmeladov. Although other characters scorn Sonya because of her profession, Raskolnikov is drawn to her because of her innocence. She reads Raskolnikov the biblical passage about Jesus's raising of Lazarus from the dead. She also tells Raskolnikov that she was a friend of the murdered woman Lizaveta. When Raskolnikov confesses that he is the murderer, Sonya is horrified because she realizes that he has murdered his own human spirit. She forgives him and urges him to go to a public place and bow down and confess his sin to God. Sonya follows him to Siberia. Sonya represents Dostoyevsky's religious faith. Her Christianity emphasizes redemption through suffering.

Natasya

Natasya is the cook and only servant of Raskolnikov's landlady. Dostoyevsky describes her as a "country peasant woman, and a very talk-

ative one." She tells Raskolnikov that the landlady has been talking about calling the police because he has been behind in his rent and will not leave. She is very kind to the poor student, bringing him tea and urging her cabbage soup on him, rather than taking his money to buy sausage.

Nikolay

Nikolay is one of the workmen. He is a house painter who confessed to the murders and who is described by Porfiry as a "child ... responsive to influences." His false evidence serves to distract people from suspecting Raskolnikov and provides Porfiry with a chance to urge Raskolnikov to make a full confession for his own good.

Pawnbroker

See Alyona Ivanovna

Porfiry Petrovich

A police inspector whose interviews with Raskolnikov provide much dramatic tension in the book. A relative of Raskolnikov's friend Razumikhin, he is about thirty-five years old and pudgy. At times he seems a somewhat befuddled, comical character, but in fact he is extremely perceptive and intelligent. His investigative methods are highly unorthodox. He is more interested in criminal psychology than in standard police procedure or material evidence. Raskolnikov is uncertain how much Porfiry really knows about the crime, and he attempts to outwit the detective. However, Porfiry's friendly but persistent and all-knowing manner upsets and confuses Raskolnikov. In the end, Raskolnikov breaks down and confesses. Porfiry's emphasis on criminal psychology reflects Dostoyevsky's own ideas and interests as a novelist.

Rodion Romanovich Raskolnikov

The central character of *Crime and Punishment*. He is a poverty-stricken twenty-three-year-old. Described as an "ex-student," Rodion Romanovich Raskolnikov has dropped out of the university presumably because of his inability to pay his fees. Beyond this, he has been suffering from a spiritual crisis. Proud, aloof, and scornful of humanity, at the beginning of the novel Raskolnikov has become obsessed with the idea that he is a "superman" and therefore not subject to the laws that govern ordinary humans. He has published an essay on his superman theory. To prove this theory, he intends to kill an old pawnbroker, whom he regards as worthless. However, the murder goes horribly wrong: he also kills the old woman's simple-minded innocent sister (Lizaveta), who stumbles upon the scene of the crime. Moreover, the crime fails to confirm Raskolnikov's cool superiority. Tormented by feelings of guilt, he acts erratically, and he fears that his guilt will be obvious to others. Much of the novel centers on Raskolnikov's irrational state of mind and the eccentric behavior that follows from this. On several occasions he comes close to boasting that he could have committed the crime, and dares others (notably the detective Porfiry Petrovich) to prove that he did it. He insults his friend Razumihkin and deliberately offends his mother and sister. However, he also acts in ways that show he still has a moral conscience. For example, he defends his sister against her scheming fiance Luzhin. He gives money to Marmeladov's widow Katerina Ivanovna. He recoils in horror from the depraved Svidrigailov. Most significantly of all, he is drawn to the young prostitute Sonya Marmeladova, who is morally pure and innocent despite her terrible life. He ultimately confesses his crime to her and begins his journey to redemption. The Russian word *Raskol* means "schism." The term was used to describe a split in the Russian Orthodox Church that occurred in the mid-1600s. Dostoyevsky's Russian readers would have been aware of the significance of Raskolnikov's name, which suggests contradictions in his own personality as well as his rebellion against God. In the complex Raskolnikov, Dostoyevsky created one of the most interesting and most human of all fictional characters.

Dmitry Prokovich Razumikhin

Raskolnikov's best friend. A former student himself, Razumikhin helps to nurse Raskolnikov back to health after the latter's breakdown (following Raskolnikov's murder of the pawnbroker and her sister). His attitude toward Raskolnikov is complex: he often berates Raskolnikov, but he is also protective toward his wayward friend. Razumikhin falls in love with Raskolnikov's sister, Dunya, and he subsequently acts as her protector. He is a cousin of the police inspector Porfiry Petrovich, to whom he introduces Raskolnikov. On the surface, Razumikhin is himself no paragon of virtue. He is unkempt and ungainly, and when he meets Raskolnikov's mother and sister after a party he is drunk. Razumikhin's name derives from the Russian word for "reason". Some critics have compared Razumikhin and his role in this novel to Shakespeare's character Horatio, the friend of Hamlet.

Rodya

See Rodion Romanovich Raskolnikov

Dunya Avdotya Romanovna

Raskolnikov's sister. She bears a physical resemblance to her brother, but in contrast to his morbid character she is self-confident, strong, and straightforward. She is devoted to Raskolnikov, and initially decides to marry Pyotr Luzhin primarily for her brother's financial benefit. With her mother (Pukheria Aleksandrovna), she unexpectedly arrives in St. Petersburg from the provinces and visits Raskolnikov. Raskolnikov is horrified at the thought of her loveless arranged marriage to Luzhin and attempts to stop it. Indirectly through Dunya, Raskolnikov also encounters Svidrigailov, whom Dunya earlier had served as a governess and whose intentions toward Dunya are not entirely honorable. Raskolnikov's friend Razumikhin falls in love with Dunya and serves as her protector; he eventually marries her.

Sofya Semyonovna

See Sonya Marmeladova

Arkady Ivanovich Svidrigailov

A mysterious wealthy landowner, Svidrigailov is a shadowy, highly ambiguous character. He does not appear directly until the last third of the novel, although he is mentioned earlier. He is about fifty years old but looks younger. His "strange face" resembles a mask. He has blue eyes, a blond beard and blond hair, and ruby-red lips. Svidrigailov's background is thoroughly distasteful. He and his wife had employed Raskolnikov's sister Dunya as a governess, and he became obsessed with her. (Marfa Petrovna helped to arrange Dunya's engagement to Luzhin in order to get the girl away from Svidrigailov.) He confesses to Raskolnikov that his marriage to an older woman, Marfa Petrovna, was one of convenience. He is a shameless sensualist whose favorite activity was seducing young girls. There are rumors that he is responsible for the deaths of a servant, a girl whom he had raped, and his wife; he is occasionally visited by their ghosts. Svidrigailov has recently arrived in St. Petersburg. While lodging in the apartment next to Sonya's, he overhears Raskolnikov tell Sonya that he (Raskolnikov) is a murderer. Svidrigailov subsequently lets Raskolnikov know that he is aware of the young man's secret, and he attempts to blackmail Raskolnikov emotionally. Yet, for all his lurid interests, Svidrigailov is apparently capable of compassion. He gives much-needed money to both Dunya and Sonya, and he arranges for Katerina Ivanovna's children to be put in a good orphanage after their mother dies. (However, he hints that his motives for this last act may be entirely selfish.) After his last meeting with Raskolnikov he again attempts to seduce Dunya. When this fails, he spends a night in a run-down hotel and is troubled by dreams about his former victims. In the morning he goes outside, puts a gun to his head, and commits suicide. Svidrigailov is often considered Raskolnikov's "double." His utterly selfish, callous, and destructive nature points to what Raskolnikov might become if Raskolnikov were to abandon all conscience and follow his theories through to their logical conclusion.

Zametov

The police clerk who tells Porfiry of his suspicions that Raskolnikov is the murderer early in the story. When Raskolnikov asks for him at the end of the novel in order to make his confession, he learns that Zametov is no longer there.

Dr. Zossimov

Dr. Zossimov is a young physician and friend of Razumikhim who comes to treat Raskolnikov. Described as "a tall fat man with a puffy, colourless, clean-shaven face and straight flaxen hair," he is fashionably dressed and nonchalant in manner,

but he is known to be excellent at his work. Dr. Zossimov continues to look after Raskolnikov, "his first patient," he says, and is one of two friends to attend the wedding of Razumikhim and Raskolnikov's sister.

Themes

On the surface, *Crime and Punishment* belongs to the popular genre known as the crime novel. A young man (Raskolnikov) commits a murder and then tries to conceal his guilt and evade arrest. In the end he confesses, is arrested, and is sent to prison, where he begins a process of spiritual regeneration. The novel's suspense arises not only from the question "what will happen next?", but from Dostoyevsky's close and relentless examination of the murderer's psyche. Dostoyevsky is more interested in important philosophical questions than in the technical police procedures of bringing a criminal to justice. He is also interested in the criminal's motives, which are ambiguous. The title indicates Dostoyevsky's interest in opposites and in the duality of human nature. The nature of guilt and innocence, the role of atonement and forgiveness, and the opposition of good and evil (and God and the Devil) all play an important thematic role in the book. While Dostoyevsky also examines social and political problems in the Russia of his day, his concerns are universal.

Guilt and Innocence

In large part, *Crime and Punishment* is an examination of the guilty conscience. For Dostoyevsky, punishment is not a physical action or condition. Rather (much as in Milton's epic poem *Paradise Lost*), punishment inherently results from an awareness of guilt. Guilt is the knowledge that one has done wrong and has become estranged from society and from God. From the very beginning of the novel, Raskolnikov (whose name derives from the Russian word for "schism") suffers from this estrangement. In murdering the pawnbroker, he seeks to prove that he is above the law. But his crime only reinforces his sense that he is not a part of society.

Although she is a prostitute, Sonya is the embodiment of innocence. Her motive in becoming a prostitute was not one of lust. Indeed, in all of the novel, there is no indication that Sonya has any lustful or sexual inclination. On the contrary, she is embarrassed by, and ashamed of, her profession. In Dostoyevsky's eyes, she is not guilty of any transgression. She does what she does out of sheer necessity, not out of any base instincts or any hope for personal gain.

In contrast with Sonya's sense of shame over the life she leads, Pyotr Luzhin is shameless in the way he manipulates Raskolnikov's sister and mother (Dunya and Pulkheria Aleksandrovna). He is guilty of emotional blackmail as well as of fraud. Arkady Svidrigailov is an even more "guilty" character. Luzhin's crimes are calculated, whereas Svidrigailov's crimes result from his complete surrender to his evil nature. Rather than facing up to his guilt and its consequences, as Raskolnikov does, Svidrigailov partially acknowledges his guilt but evades the consequences by committing suicide. Although Raskolnikov is the central figure of *Crime and Punishment,* Dostoyevsky suggests that Raskolnikov may not quite be the book's most guilty criminal. Svidrigailov and Luzhin are also guilty of criminal misdeeds, and they are less open than Raskolnikov to the possibility of redemption.

Atonement and Forgiveness

The theme of atonement and forgiveness is closely related to that of guilt and innocence. As Dostoyevsky's title suggests, punishment is the only logical and necessary outcome of crime. Punishment, however, does not mean merely a legal finding and a sentence of imprisonment. In Dostoyevsky's view, the criminal's true punishment is not a sentence of imprisonment. Nor is legal punishment the definitive answer to crime. The criminal's punishment results from his own conscience, his awareness of his guilt. However, he must not only acknowledge his guilt. The criminal must atone for it and must seek forgiveness.

Raskolnikov at first tries to rationalize his crime by offering various explanations to himself. Foremost among these is his "superman" theory. By definition, the superman theory denies any possibility of atonement. The superman does not need to atone, because he is permitted to commit any crime in order to further his own ends. Raskolnikov also rationalizes his crime by arguing that the old pawnbroker is of no use to anyone; in killing her, he is ridding the world of an unpleasant person. Driven by poverty, he also claims that he wants to use her money to better his position in life. In the course of the book, he comes to realize that none of these excuses justifies his crime.

Raskolnikov's reasons for fearing arrest are equally complex. It is clear, however, that without the example and the urging of Sonya, he would not be able to seek forgiveness. He finds it remarkable

Topics for Further Study

- Research the city of St. Petersburg, Russia. How did the city arise and develop? What are St. Petersburg's main features and landmarks?

- Research the main political movements in Russia in the mid-1800s. Is there any similarity between the kind of political groups that existed then and political parties as they are known in America?

- Research the condition of serfs (peasants who worked for landowners) in nineteenth-century Russia. Compare serfdom in Russia to slavery in America. What were the main similarities and differences between the two institutions?

- Research the plea of insanity as a legal defense in murder cases. What circumstances are usually necessary for a jury to find a defendant insane? Why does a defendant's claim of insanity often cause controversy?

that when he confesses his crime to her, Sonya immediately forgives him. She urges him to bow down before God and make a public confession. This act of contrition, she believes, will enable him to begin to cleanse his soul.

Svidrigailov is aware of his own guilt, but he does not seek forgiveness. Unlike Raskolnikov, he does not believe in the possibility of forgiveness. In giving money to Sonya and others, he attempts a partial atonement for his sins. However, even these gestures are motivated partly by base self-interest. Because he is spiritually dead, he feels that the only atonement he can make is to commit suicide.

Ubermensch ("Superman")

Part of the motive for Raskolnikov's crime comes from a theory that he has developed. In an essay that he publishes, Raskolnikov argues that humankind is divided into two categories: ordinary people, and geniuses or supermen. Ordinary people must obey the law, but "supermen" — of whom there are very few in any generation — are entitled to break existing laws and make their own laws.

Raskolnikov cites the French emperor Napoleon as the epitome of the superman type. He argues that Napoleon rose to power by overstepping the laws that govern ordinary people. Napoleon made his own laws and achieved his goals by killing tens of thousands of people in wars. Because Napoleon was a genius, Raskolnikov reasons, he was not regarded as a criminal. On the contrary, he was hailed as a hero. Early in *Crime and Punishment,* Raskolnikov has become obsessed with the notion that he himself is a "superman." Therefore, he thinks, he is not subject to the laws that govern ordinary people. (In the original Russian text, Dostoyevsky frequently uses a word that means "overstepping" or "stepping over"—that is, transgressing. This word is closely related to the Russian word for "crime" (*prestuplenie.*) Raskolnikov decides to murder the pawnbroker Alyona Ivanovna partly to prove that he is a superman. However, his indecision and confusion throughout the novel indicate that he is not a superman. Moreover, in the course of the novel, Dostoyevsky seeks to prove that there is no such thing as a superman. Dostoyevsky believes that every human life is precious, and no one is entitled to kill.

Dostoyevsky's formulation of the superman theory (through Raskolnikov) clearly anticipates the ideas developed by the German philosopher Friedrich Nietzsche in the 1880s. For Nietzsche, the superman and his "will to power" were supreme ideals. Christianity stood in the way of the superman, and Nietzsche scorned Christianity as a "slave morality." Dostoyevsky's view of the superman is absolutely opposed to Nietzsche's. For Dostoyevsky, following the "superman" theory to its natural conclusion inevitably leads to death, destruction, chaos, and misery. Rather than seeing Christianity as a "slave mentality," Dostoyevsky views it as the true vision of the human place in the world and of the human relationship with God. In Dostoyevsky's view, all people are valued in the eyes of God.

Style

Narrative

Crime and Punishment is written in the third person. However, Dostoyevsky's narrative focus shifts throughout the novel. *Crime and Punishment* is widely credited as the first psychological novel and in many passages, Dostoyevsky is concerned with the state of mind of the central character, Ro-

dion Romanovich Raskolnikov. In these passages—including those that relate Raskolnikov's brooding, the murder itself, and his encounters with the inspector Porfiry Petrovich—Dostoyevsky puts us inside Raskolnikov's head. We view the action from Raskolnikov's viewpoint and share his often-disordered and contradictory thoughts. These passages read more like a first-person confession than a detached third-person fictional narrative. At the same time, he describes exterior events with clear realism.

Critics have pointed out that Dostoyevsky is essentially a dramatic novelist. He does not so much *tell* a story as enact it. *Crime and Punishment* is full of dramatic scenes, of which Raskolnikov's murder of the pawnbroker is only one. There are also a number of dramatic confrontations between characters. Dostoyevsky's characters rarely have calm discussions; rather, they have fierce arguments and verbal duels. Generally (but not always) Raskolnikov is at one end of these confrontations. At the other, in various scenes, are his friend Razumikhin, his sister and mother, his sister's corrupt suitor Luzhin, the police investigator Porfiry Petrovich, the innocent prostitute Sonya, and the cynical landowner Svidrigailov. These duels and pairings help to illustrate the idea of the double, discussed further below.

Setting

The action of the book takes place in St. Petersburg, the capital city of Russia, in the summer of 1865. (The brief epilogue is set in Siberia.) *Crime and Punishment* is a distinctly urban novel. In choosing a definite urban setting, Dostoyevsky was paving new ground for Russian fiction. His Russian predecessors and contemporaries such as Gogol, Turgenev, and Tolstoy generally set their stories on country estates. In confining the action of his novel entirely to St. Petersburg, Dostoyevsky was emulating the English author Charles Dickens, who set his well-known stories in the British capital, London. Moreover, St. Petersburg is not just a backdrop, but it is an inherent part of the novel. Dostoyevsky recreates St. Petersburg's neighborhoods and its streets, bridges, and canals with great realism. In his narrative, Dostoyevsky does not give the full street names, but uses only abbreviations. (In the very first paragraph, for example, he refers to "S—Lane" and "K—n Bridge.") Readers who were familiar with St. Petersburg would probably have been able to identify most of these specific locations, as modern scholars have done.

Much of the action takes place indoors, generally in cramped tenement apartments. With these settings, Dostoyevsky creates a tense, claustrophobic atmosphere. For example, in the weeks before he commits the murders, Raskolnikov has been lying in his tiny room and brooding. He retreats to this room after the murders, occasionally leaving his lair to wander the city's streets.

Most of the book's main characters are not natives of St. Petersburg, but have come to the city from Russia's far-flung rural provinces. Thus, they are not at ease in this urban setting. Provincial Russians might normally regard the capital city, created by Peter the Great as Russia's "window on the West," as a place of opportunity. However, for Raskolnikov, Katerina Ivanovna, Svidrigailov, and other characters, the city turns out to be a destination of last resort, a place where their diminished expectations are finally played out. (Svidrigailov remarks that "there aren't many places where there are as many gloomy, harsh and strange influences on the soul of man as there are in St. Petersburg.") This sense of the city as a dead-end is emphasized by the settings. The apartments where Raskolnikov and the Marmeladovs live are so small that there is scarcely enough space for a small group of visitors. Moreover, at several points in the novel, characters are threatened with eviction and fear that they will wind up on the streets. Near the end of the book, Katerina Ivanovna and her children beg on the streets by singing and dancing.

Most readers tend to think of Russia as a "winter" country, with lots of snow and cold weather. Dostoyevsky contradicts these expectations by setting his story during an unusual summer heat wave. The heat and humidity add to the general sense of discomfort that pervades the narrative. They also reflect and reinforce the feverish state that afflicts Raskolnikov throughout the book.

Structure

Crime and Punishment is divided into six parts plus an epilogue. Each part is broken further into several chapters. For the most part, each chapter centers around a self-contained dramatic episode. Much of this episodic structure is attributable to the fact that *Crime and Punishment* was written for serialization in a magazine. Magazine readers wanted each installment to be complete in itself and to contain colorful incidents. Many chapters end with the sudden, unexpected arrival of a new character. By introducing such developments at the end of many of the chapters, Dostoyevsky maintained a high level of suspense. He knew that his readers would be curious to know what would happen in the next chapter and that they would look forward to the

next installment. Moreover, an unresolved complication at the end of a particular chapter would also stimulate Dostoyevsky to write the next chapter. This method of writing helps account for the numerous abrupt shifts in the plot focus.

Coincidence

Like many other important nineteenth-century novelists, Dostoyevsky does not hesitate to use coincidence to advance the plot. Indeed, many of the crucial developments in *Crime and Punishment* depend on sheer coincidences that seem highly unlikely to the modern reader. However, coincidence was an accepted literary convention of the period. Dostoyevsky does not attempt to explain away his coincidences, but on the contrary he simply states them as matters of fact. He uses this technique as a short cut to bring together certain characters and set up dramatic situations.

While he is walking down the street, Raskolnikov comes upon the scene of an accident. The accident victim turns out to be Marmeladov, a drunken civil servant whom he had met earlier in the novel. Marmeladov has been run over by a horse-drawn carriage. Raskolnikov takes charge of the situation and has Marmeladov carried home, where the injured man dies. This coincidence leads to Raskolnikov's first meeting with Marmeladov's daughter Sonya, who has turned to prostitution to support the poverty-stricken family. Drawn to Sonya by her meek nature and pure heart, Raskolnikov will later confess to her. In another coincidence, Sonya turns out to have been a friend of Lizaveta. This disclosure serves to increase Raskolnikov's sense of guilt and further points up Sonya's selflessness.

It is also purely coincidence that the scheming Luzhin happens to be living temporarily in the same building as Katerina Ivanovna. This makes plausible his appearance at Katerina's funeral party and his attempt to frame Sonya for robbery. Later, Svidrigailov just happens by coincidence to be renting the apartment next door to Sonya's apartment. Thus, he is able to overhear Raskolnikov's murder confession. Svidrigailov's awareness of Raskolnikov's guilty secret helps set into motion another chain of events. There are many more such coincidences in the course of the story. That such coincidences involving a relatively small number of characters would occur in a large city like St. Petersburg is almost unbelievable. However, Dostoyevsky's narrative has such dramatic force that the reader is able to overlook the implausibility of these coincidences.

Symbolism and Imagery

As already discussed, Dostoyevsky's literary technique mixes narrative realism, dramatic scenes, and psychological analysis. He also uses symbolism and imagery, not so much for aesthetic effect as to emphasize certain points about his characters' psychology. One of his main symbolic devices is the pairing of certain characters. Early in his writing career, Dostoyevsky formulated the idea of the "double." That is, he believed that there may be two sides to a human personality. In giving a character like Raskolnikov several "doubles," Dostoyevsky emphasizes certain aspects of Raskolnikov's personality by contrasting him with these "doubles."

Among Raskolnikov's symbolic "doubles" are Marmeladov, Razumikhin, Dunya, Sonya, and Svidrigailov. Where Raskolnikov is obsessed with a theory, Marmeladov lives entirely by impulse. Where Raskolnikov is extreme, Razumikhin is reasonable. (The Russian word *razum* means "reason.") Raskolnikov cuts himself off from his family, while his sister Dunya is completely dedicated to the family. Sonya too sacrifices herself for her family. Furthermore, her meekness and faith contrast with Raskolnikov's pride and his rejection of God. Raskolnikov is literally sickened by his crime and does not give any indication that he will commit more murders, whereas Svidrigailov takes pleasure in his criminal lust and persists in it.

Appropriately enough, blood and blood imagery pervades the book. Before he commits the murder, Raskolnikov has a horrific nightmare in which a group of drunken men flog "a little grey mare" to death. The notion of "shedding blood" becomes quite literal. Raskolnikov's murder of the pawnbroker and her sister with an axe is naturally a bloody act. As he attempts to escape notice, Raskolnikov becomes obsessed with the idea that he is covered in blood and that this will give him away. Toward the end of the novel, his sister Dunya tells him that "you have blood on your hands"; Raskolnikov defiantly replies that the world is covered in blood. It can be noted, as well, that the novel's blood imagery is paralleled by frequent references to tears.

Dostoyevsky uses dreams to give insight into his characters' psychology, as well as for symbolic purposes. Critics have debated the meaning of Raskolnikov's nightmare about the horse, mentioned above. As well as indicating his tormented state of mind, this nightmare may also symbolize the brutality of murder and the helplessness of the

innocent. In the book's epilogue, in Siberia, Raskolnikov dreams that the world is swept by a terrible plague that turns people mad. This dream is generally believed to symbolize what would happen if all people rejected traditional morality and acted out Raskolnikov's "superman" theory. Svidrigailov, too, has terrible dreams and claims that he has seen the ghosts of his deceased wife and of a servant. The night before he kills himself, he dreams about a little girl whom he has victimized. In this dream, he sees the moral consequences of his crimes.

Historical Context

Dostoyevsky's Russia: Social and Political Background

For most modern Americans, the Russia of Dostoyevsky's time is almost incomprehensible. Sir Winston Churchill's comment in 1939 that Russia "is a riddle wrapped in a mystery inside an enigma" can apply equally to the Russia of the 1860s when Dostoyevsky wrote *Crime and Punishment*. In the most simple terms, much of Russia's historical difference from the West has to do with the fact that for centuries it was cut off from Western Europe. The Reformation, the Renaissance, and the Enlightenment that helped transform the countries of Western Europe from feudalism to modern nations with well-educated citizens and important cultural institutions barely touched Russia. Moreover, large-scale foreign invasions (from the Mongols in the thirteenth and fourteenth centuries to the Nazi armies in the early 1940s) periodically devastated the country. As a result, Russia has historically been suspicious of other nations. Also, early in its national history, Russia developed a tradition of government that centralized immense power in the hands of an emperor—the tsar—and a handful of his advisors. (The Russian title "tsar" derives from the Latin word "Caesar.") In the mid-1500s, Tsar Ivan IV (known as Ivan the Terrible) established what for more than the next four hundred years became the model for Russian government, alternating short-lived periods of ineffectual reform with periods of severe repression.

Relatively "liberal" rulers such as Tsar Peter the Great (reigned 1682-1725) and Tsarina Catherine the Great (who was actually German; reigned 1762-96) pursued a policy of "westernization." They attempted to import modern technology and manners from Western Europe. At the same time,

The Peter and Paul Fortress on the Neva River in St. Petersburg, Russia, stands in contrast to the city's poverty-stricken neighborhoods in which Dostoyevsky's novel is set.

however, they held tightly onto absolute power and ruthlessly suppressed any challenge to the established political order.

During the period when Dostoyevsky was receiving his education and then establishing his literary career—the 1830s into the 1860s—Russia was stirred by intense intellectual debate. The small class of the educated people recognized that major changes were needed if the huge but backward country was to address its social problems and find its way successfully in the world. One general approach to change was proposed by certain intellectuals collectively known as Westernizers. The Westernizers were influenced by German philosophy and by social ideas that developed in Western Europe during the Industrial Revolution. They were also influenced by contemporary European revolutionary movements. The Westernizers were not united in their goals or methods. There were various factions. Some favored gradual democratic reforms, while others called for revolution to replace the tsarist government with a socialist regime. Among the leading Westernizers was Vissarion Belinsky (1811-48), the most famous Russian literary critic of his day. Belinsky praised Dostoyevsky's first book, *Poor Folk* (1846), and declared that Dostoyevsky was the literary successor of Gogol.

Another group of thinkers, known as the Slavophiles, proposed an entirely different approach to Russia's problems. Broadly speaking, the Slavophiles felt that Western ideals of rationalism and modernization were dangerous and alien to Russia. Rather than relying on a program of legislation and material improvement, the Slavophiles argued that Russia could only fulfill its destiny when Russians returned to their native spiritual values. Although they disagreed with the Westernizers, the Slavophiles were also opposed to the existing Russian government. By Western standards, the Slavophiles could be considered romantic and reactionary, but they made an important contribution to the debate over the future of Russia.

As a young man, Dostoyevsky was influenced by the Westernizers. In the mid-1840s he joined the so-called Petrashevsky Circle, a small group that met weekly to discuss socialist ideas. The group demanded political reforms and generally opposed the government of Tsar Nicholas I. In the spring of 1849 the members were arrested. Twenty-one of them, including Dostoyevsky, were sentenced to death but were pardoned at the last minute. During his subsequent imprisonment in Siberia, Dostoyevsky underwent a profound spiritual and political change. He renounced political radicalism and came to be-

Compare & Contrast

- **1860s:** Russia's government is a monarchy, with a head of state called the "tsar." But even at the time of *Crime and Punishment*'s publication, changes in government were beginning to be seen with Tsar Alexander II's introducuction of reforms in the Russian military, the law courts, and local government.

  Today: The Russian Revolution of 1917, which led to decades of oppressive rule under a communist government, has given way to a struggling democracy after the collapse of the Soviet Union in 1989. President Boris Yeltsin has since introduced economic reforms, though his country's economy is still unstable.

- **1860s:** The Russian novelists Dostoyevsky and Ivan Turgenev spend much of their time travelling abroad. Dostoyevsky eventually returns to

  Russia, but Turgenev decides to remain an expatriate.

  Today: Russian author Alexander Solzhenitsyn, exiled from Russia in the early 1970s because of his opposition to the communist government, has returned to his native country. However, his calls for spiritual rebirth and a return to traditional Russian values have been met with little support.

- **1860s:** Dostoyevsky notes widespread drunkeness is a major problem in Russian society.

  Today: Alcoholism remains a serious national problem, affecting at least half of all Russian households, according to one survey. Government attempts to curb drinking face strong resistance from the Russian people.

---

lieve that Russia's hope lay in Slavic idealism. His travels in Western Europe in the 1860s and 1870s reinforced his distaste for modern industrial society. In the great novels of his mature period, including *Crime and Punishment,* Dostoyevsky expresses his sympathy with the Slavophiles and attacks the Westernizers and radicals. Raskolnikov reflects the viewpoint of the radical Nihilists (from the Latin word for "nothing"), who rejected all the traditional conventions of society.

By the time Dostoyevsky wrote *Crime and Punishment* Tsar Alexander II (reigned 1855-81) was in the midst of a significant reform policy. In 1861 the Tsar signed a proclamation that freed millions of Russian serfs (peasants who lived and worked in conditions similar to slavery). This was followed by reforms of local government, the courts, and the military. (The police inspector Porfiry Petrovich refers to these reforms.) However, these reforms failed to resolve the major problems in Russia and helped to create new problems. Again, the immense social problems facing Russia at the time—widespread poverty, ignorance, and social agitation—form the background to *Crime and Punishment.*

Crime and Punishment in a Literary Context

In the words of historian Nicholas Riasanovsky, "Literature constituted the chief glory of Russian culture in the first half of the nineteenth century." Like most educated Russians of his time, Dostoyevsky knew and revered the work of the great Russian poets Alexander Pushkin (1799-1837) and Mikhail Lermontov (1814-1841). In his verse novel *Eugene Onegin* (written 1822-31), Pushkin cast a clear light on Russian society and its problems. Dostoyevsky was also familiar with the work of the novelist Nikolai Gogol (1809-1852), the most important Russian novelist before Dostoyevsky himself. Gogol was a master both of realism and of the fantastic. In his masterpiece *Dead Souls* (1842), Gogol examined the state of Russia with deep psychological understanding. Significantly, certain elements in *Crime and Punishment* can also be traced to two non-Russian writers whose work Dostoyevsky knew and admired, the French novelist Victor Hugo (author of *Les Miserables*) and the English novelist Charles Dickens (author of *David Copperfield,* which Dostoyevsky read while in prison). Indeed, Dostoyevsky frequently mentioned Dickens in his letters and note-books. In *Crime and Punishment,* Dostoyevsky shares Dickens's concern with contemporary urban life, poverty, crime, and the sufferings of children and the innocent.

Among Dostoyevsky's Russian contemporaries, two other major novelists stand out. Ivan Turgenev (1818-83) sided with the Westernizers and lived in Western Europe for much of his life; however, his subjects are thoroughly Russian. In his best known novel, *Fathers and Sons* (1862), he examines the relations between the older Russian democratic reformers and the younger, more radical generation. He also coined the term *nihilist.* Count Leo Tolstoy (1828-1910) is often placed as Dostoyevsky's equal, though he was very different. His epic novel, *War and Peace* (1863-69) began to appear in installments around the same time as *Crime and Punishment.* In his later years, Tolstoy developed a unique philosophy of nonviolence that has been compared to the philosophy of Mohandas K. Gandhi. Interestingly, both Dostoyevsky and Tolstoy knew and respected Turgenev although both disagreed with him, but Dostoyevsky and Tolstoy never met.

Critical Overview

Crime and Punishment excited much attention when it started to appear in serial form in a Russian literary journal in early 1866. Reviewing the first installment, an anonymous critic declared that "the novel promises to be one of the most important works of [Dostoyevsky]." The British scholar and translator David McDuff notes that "as the subsequent parts of the novel began to appear it acquired the status of a social and public event." A Russian critic of the time, N. N. Strakhov, later recalled that *Crime and Punishment* was "the only book the addicts of reading talked about." Strakhov noted that the novel was so powerful that people became agitated when they read it.

Some Russian critics—especially liberals and "Westernizers"—disapproved of the book because of its implicit, controversial political viewpoint. They viewed the novel as an attack on the younger generation in Russia. One reviewer, G. Z. Yeliseyev, accused Dostoyevsky of "fanaticism." An anonymous reviewer in the journal the *Week* criticized Dostoyevsky for implying "that liberal ideas and the natural sciences lead young men to murder and young women to prostitution." D. I. Pisarev, a leading nihilist critic of the time, wrote

an in-depth analysis of Raskolnikov's motives. Pisarev understood the conflicting emotions that drove Raskolnikov, but believed that Raskolnikov was basically a product of his environment. Emphasizing a social view of the novel, Pisarev rejected Dostoyevsky's insistence on redemption through suffering. Instead, he called for social change through a revolution.

N. N. Strakhov, mentioned above, praised the novel for its important treatment of universal themes and disagreed with the interpretations offered by the Westernizers. The book did not mock young Russian idealists, said Strakhov, but was a "lament" over the way that these young people were the victims of nihilistic ideas. When Strakhov's article appeared, Dostoyevsky wrote to him and told him that "you alone have understood me."

After Dostoyevsky's death, his philosopher friend Vladimir Soloviev gave several speeches about the meaning of Dostoyevsky's work. Soloviev distinguished between the outward (legal) and inward (moral) definitions of the terms "crime" and "punishment." Soloviev interpreted Raskolnikov's inward sins as "pride" and "self-idolatry, which can only be redeemed by an inner moral act of self-renunciation." Another important assessment of the novel was given by Russian critic Vasily Rozanov in 1893. Rozanov remarked on the power with which Dostoyevsky gave readers a glimpse into the criminal soul. According to Rozanov, the book "lets us feel criminality with all the inner fibers of our being." Rozanov found that "the general mood of the novel ... is far more remarkable than any of its individual episodes."

As Dostoyevsky's work became more widely known, it began to influence writers outside of Russia. Robert Louis Stevenson was an early British admirer of Dostoyevsky. In 1886 he declared that *Crime and Punishment* was "the greatest book I have read in ten years." (Coincidentally, that same year Stevenson published *The Strange Case of Doctor Jekyll and Mr. Hyde,* which embodies the Dostoyevskyan theme of the double.) Stevenson went on to note, however, that "many find [*Crime and Punishment*] dull; Henry James could not finish it." James's dislike was shared by such British authors as Joseph Conrad, John Galsworthy, and D. H. Lawrence. However, Dostoyevsky was championed in England by the translator Constance Garnett (1862-1946). Between 1912 and 1920, Garnett translated *Crime and Punishment* and Dostoyevsky's other major novels into English. Despite the criticism of James, Conrad, and others, mentioned above, Garnett's translation proved enormously influential. It introduced this novel to a new generation of British and American readers, and the book's reputation soared. For many years, Garnett's translation remained the standard English-language version of *Crime and Punishment*. (Garnett's translation is now considered to be somewhat flawed and has been largely superseded by others, including the 1991 translation by David McDuff published by Penguin.)

Debate over the interpretation of *Crime and Punishment* has continued throughout the twentieth century to the present. Writing in 1939, scholar Helen Muchnic observed that what critics say about Dostoyevsky really tells more about those critics than about Dostoyevsky. McDuff agrees that "in many of the critical analyses of his work the operative factors are of an ideological rather than a purely aesthetic nature." Thus, Russian critics during the Soviet period hailed Dostoyevsky as a great writer, but they tended to overlook the book's Christian, anti-revolutionary, and anti-materialist sentiments. Instead, they praised it as an attack on the decadent bourgeoise society of pre-Revolutionary tsarist Russia. Similarly, the American critic Philip Rahv believed that the book's epilogue did not offer a satisfactory resolution. On the other hand, critics like Konstantin Mochulsky and Nicholas Berdyaev have emphasized the book's Christian and existentialist ideals. The French novelist Andre Gide believed that the ideas Dostoyevsky worked out in *Crime and Punishment* led directly to the author's subsequent novels. The Scottish poet and critic Edwin Muir wrote that "Dostoyevsky wrote of the unconscious as if it were conscious; that is … why his characters seem 'pathological,' while they are only visualized more clearly than any other figures in imaginative literature." Translator McDuff believes that "Raskolnikov, far from being a madman or psychopathic outcast, is an image of Everyman." And Ernest J. Simmons lauds the novel for "the characteristic spiritual glow that radiates through all the action and illuminates the darkest recesses of the minds of these tormented and suffering men and women."

Criticism

Julian Connolly

In the following essay, Connolly, a professor of Slavic Languages and Literatures at the University of Virginia, reveals how Raskolnikov's

plight is symbolic of Dostoyevsky's belief that those who seek a rationalistic solution to society's ills are doomed to failure if they neglect to understand the spiritual and emotional needs of humanity.

In *Crime and Punishment,* Fyodor Dostoyevsky created an unforgettable novel of haunting intensity. With its sustained focus on the emotions and thoughts of its young protagonist, Rodion Raskolnikov, Dostoyevsky's novel provides a harrowing portrait of human error and misfortune. Dostoyevsky had originally intended to write an account of murder from the perspective of the murderer himself. As he worked on the project in November 1865, however, he concluded that such a perspective might be too limited, so he chose an omniscient, third-person narrative mode instead. Yet traces of the original design remain: much of the novel offers direct insight into Raskolnikov's impressions and experiences. One of the ways in which Dostoyevsky allows the reader intimate access into his protagonist's mind is by describing Raskolnikov's dreams. Early in the novel, for example, Raskolnikov has a vivid dream in which he sees himself as a young boy accompanying his father on a visit to the grave of a younger brother who died in infancy. On the way to the grave, Raskolnikov and his father witness an enraged peasant beating an old, overburdened mare. The young boy is horrified to see how the peasant whips the horse across the eyes. Finally, the peasant kills the horse with an iron crowbar, and the shocked child runs over to kiss the horse's bloody muzzle. It is after he awakens from this dream that Raskolnikov utters aloud for the first time his plan to take an axe and smash open the old pawnbroker's skull. Clearly, Raskolnikov's vivid dream has brought to the surface his unexpressed, murderous intentions.

Dostoyevsky's treatment of this dream has additional significance, however. Some dream analysts might argue that every character in one's dream represents some aspect of the dreamer's personality or impulses. Therefore, not only does the figure of the murderous peasant evoke Raskolnikov's own murderous urges, but also, the figure of the murdered horse might represent some part of the dreamer. Indeed, Raskolnikov's crime not only has the effect of killing the pawnbroker and Lizaveta in a *physical* sense, it also has the effect of killing Raskolnikov himself in a *spiritual* sense. Long after the murder he would tell Sonya: "I killed myself, not that old creature!" Having "died" at the moment when he killed the pawnbroker and Lizaveta, Raskolnikov is faced with the challenge of be-

What Do I Read Next?

- Dostoyevsky wrote *Notes from Underground* (1864) just before *Crime and Punishment*. Narrated by a tormented, alienated anti-hero, it introduces the moral, political, and social ideas developed in *Crime and Punishment*.

- Among Dostoyevsky's later novels, *The Possessed* (1871-72) is noteworthy for its critical portrayal of young Russian revolutionaries.

- Dostoyevsky's last novel, *The Brothers Karamazov* (1880), is generally considered his masterpiece. A family tragedy of epic proportions, it too involves a murder. However, it is best known for its philosophical treatment of the nature of good and evil and the existence of God.

- The hero of *Fathers and Sons* by Dostoyevsky's contemporary, Ivan Turgenev, is a young radical. Turgenev's political and social views were the opposite of Dostoyevsky's. This novel aroused much controversy when it was published in 1862.

- Leo Tolstoy's epic novel *War and Peace* (1863-69) came out in serial form at about the same time as *Crime and Punishment*. It portrays upper-class Russian society during the Napoleonic wars. Tolstoy's clear, lucid style is often contrasted with Dostoyevsky's more intense and abrupt writing style.

- The American scholar Joseph Frank has written a definitive multivolume biography of Dostoyevsky. Volume One, *Dostoyevsky: The Seeds of Revolt* (1976), covers the novelist's early life and his involvement in radical Russian politics. Volume Two, *The Years of Ordeal, 1850-1859* (1983), covers Dostoyevsky's spiritual and political conversion in Siberia. Volume Three, *The Stir of Liberation, 1860-1865* (1986), covers the years that led up to the writing of *Crime and Punishment*.

- Alexander Solzhenitsyn (born 1918) is the twentieth-century Russian writer most often compared to Dostoyevsky. His novella *One Day in the Life of Ivan Denisovich* (1962; English-language translation published 1963) is an account of life in a Soviet prison camp in Siberia.

---

ing restored to "life," and much of the novel records his struggle with this problem.

Raskolnikov's interactions with Sonya play a significant role in this process. During the meeting in which he confesses his crime to her, Raskolnikov's conduct and words have the effect of creating a kind of psychological or emotional reenactment of the original murder. Just as Raskolnikov feels that he killed himself when he murdered the pawnbroker, so too must he now have a second victim: the innocent Sonya takes the symbolic place of the innocent Lizaveta. The unconscious aim of Raskolnikov's behavior during this scene is to see how Sonya handles the dreadful experience. Will she be devastated by her recognition of Raskolnikov's crime, or, on the contrary, will she find a way to go on living and thus serve as a model for Raskolnikov himself? Her religious faith and her love for Raskolnikov serve as a potent force for the criminal's regeneration.

Dostoyevsky's treatment of the theme of death and regeneration makes distinctive use of religious imagery, from the Gospel account of the raising of Lazarus (first mentioned to Raskolnikov by Porfiry Petrovich and then read aloud by Sonya to Raskolnikov) to the final scene of the novel, which takes place soon after the Christian holiday of Easter. During that final scene, Raskolnikov feels a surge of overwhelming love for Sonya, as if his soul has undergone a sudden cleansing or purification. Dostoyevsky's description of this moment emphasizes its religious dimensions. He writes that Raskolnikov and Sonya experience "a perfect resurrection into a new life" and that "Love had raised them from the dead."

In addition to its religious imagery, *Crime and Punishment* also incorporates other symbolic systems. Landscapes and physical settings often suggest a character's emotional or psychological conditions. Raskolnikov lives in a tiny, cramped room, an evocative emblem of how constricted his lifestyle and thinking have become. He buries the items stolen from the pawnbroker under a huge rock. This rock serves as a reminder of the crushing burden of guilt that Raskolnikov carries with him. Recognizing the cramped nature of Raskolnikov's lifestyle and thinking, Porfiry Petrovich tells him that he needs "air" and that he should learn to be a "sun." The only time that Raskolnikov feels some sense of ease is when he leaves the stifling city streets behind and walks out into the countryside. His spiritual conversion at the end of the novel takes place on the bank of a river with a wide, pastoral scene displayed in front of him.

Yet it is not only the physical landscape that amplifies and reflects Raskolnikov's inner condition. Dostoyevsky's handling of other characters also plays a key role in the development and exposition of the central figure. As Raskolnikov moves through the city, he seems to move through a charged atmosphere in which every encounter triggers a resonant response in his soul. Thus, his chance meeting with Marmeladov introduces the concepts of suffering and self-sacrifice, concepts that will become so important to Raskolnikov later in the novel. More importantly, the characters who surround Raskolnikov often seem to serve as potential doubles or alter egos. That is, the traits that these characters embody represent potential directions for Raskolnikov himself. On one side stands the humble Sonya. She is willing to sacrifice herself for her family, and she puts the ideals of love and service to one's fellow humans above any notion of self-glorification. On the other side stands the corrupt Svidrigailov. He indulges in extreme forms of debauchery simply to relieve his boredom. Svidrigailov tells Raskolnikov that he considers the young man to be something of a kindred spirit. Although Raskolnikov does not wish to admit it, he senses that there may be some validity to Svidrigailov's assertions. When Svidrigailov informs Sonya that Raskolnikov only has two paths to choose from, either "a bullet in the brain" or "Siberia," he has effectively identified the choices that lie in front of the wretched young man. Only Sonya's appearance outside the police station at the end of the main section of the novel prevents Raskolnikov from emulating Svidrigailov's example and committing suicide. Instead, he follows her advice, confesses his crime, and with her love and support he ultimately finds redemption in Siberia.

In addition to the main characters who reflect and amplify Raskolnikov's conflicting impulses, several secondary characters appear in the novel to convey Dostoyevsky's scorn for certain ideological trends in contemporary Russian society. The pompous Luzhin, for example, has come to St. Petersburg to curry favor with the new "progressive" elements among the intelligentsia. Dostoyevsky uses Luzhin's simplistic praise for scientific thought and the virtues of self-interest to mock the popular ideas of the progressive writer N. G. Chernyshevsky. Even more satirical in this regard is the character of Lebezyatnikov, who has been so impressed with scenes from Chernyshevsky's novel, *What Is to Be Done,* that he tries to outdo the behavior of characters from that novel. He tells Luzhin that if he had a wife, he would encourage her to take a lover simply so he could show his magnanimity and understanding in refusing to condemn her.

Dostoyevsky's disdain for the radical movement was perhaps fueled by his own early exposure to progressive social movements. As a young man in the 1840s he had belonged to a small circle devoted to the discussion and dissemination of utopian socialist thought. His participation in this group had led to his arrest and imprisonment in 1849. He was subsequently sentenced to prison camp and exile in Siberia, and a decade would pass before he could return to St. Petersburg. Through his portrait of the young Raskolnikov, Dostoyevsky wished to show the dangers of errant thought in contemporary Russia. Those who believed that society's ills could be cured through rationalistic schemes, without regard for the inner spiritual and emotional complexity of the human subject, were not only doomed to fail, but from Dostoyevsky's perspective, they represented a serious threat to society itself. Raskolnikov's crime, then, serves to illustrate the pernicious nature of the radicals' self-centered and self-elevating intellectual schemes. Yet Dostoyevsky's novel offers much more than a partisan ideological tract. His haunting description of Raskolnikov's desperate struggles and aspirations has resulted in one of the most memorable and thought-provoking works in all of world literature.

Source: Julian Connolly, in an essay for *Novels for Students,* Gale, 1998.

William J. Leatherbarrow

For Leatherbarrow, the principle of uncertainty is prevalent in many of Dostoevsky's novels but particularly in Crime *and* Punishment. *In the following excerpt, Leatherbarrow asserts that not only is the motive for the crime unclear to the reader and the perpetrator, but time, space, and point of view as well deliberately lack clarity and objectivity.*

As the novel [*Crime and Punishment*] grew under Dostoevsky's pen, his notebooks and drafts show that he went from uncertainty to uncertainty in depicting Raskolnikov and his crime, even jotting down reminders to himself to elucidate the murderer's motives more clearly. It would be easy enough to conclude from this that Dostoevsky ... had simply not suspected the full richness and potential of his character and his theme, but this would be too simple a conclusion. Uncertainty is an important artistic principle in much of Dostoevsky's work, and it is at the very heart of *Crime and Punishment*....

In *Crime and Punishment* Dostoevsky sacrifices to the principle of uncertainty many of the conventional prerogatives of the novelist: his most far-reaching sacrifice was that of omniscience.... In *Crime and Punishment* the narrator enjoys no consistent perceptual advantage over the participants: he sees the world through the same haze of subjective uncertainty as Raskolnikov does. It is this above all else that gives the novel its permanently nightmarish quality.

The most obvious manifestation of this kind of uncertainty is in the presentation of motive. Raskolnikov becomes a "criminal in search of his own motive"; he does not in the end know why he committed his crime, and neither does the reader. The narrator offers us no definite explanation, only a share in Raskolnikov's confusion.... Dostoevsky originally conceived Raskolnikov's crime as a means of exposing the absurdity of the moral utilitarianism characteristic of many leading intellectuals in the 1860s....

The utilitarian principle undoubtedly remains a major aspect of Raskolnikov's crime in the finished novel. Indeed, he does not finally renounce it until his conversion in the Epilogue. In a conversation with Dunya late in the novel he vigorously defends the morality of his crime in utilitarian terms: " 'Crime? What crime!' he cried in a sort of sudden frenzy. 'That I killed a vile, harmful louse, an old hag of a moneylender of no use to anybody, for whose murder one should be forgiven forty sins, and who bled poor people dry. Can that be called a crime? I don't think about it, and I have no desire to wipe it out.' " But the utilitarian ethic alone can satisfy the demands of neither the reader nor Raskolnikov himself for a comprehensive explanation of his act. In a sense, this affirms Dostoevsky's point that the complex and often contra-

dictory impulses behind human action cannot in the end be reduced to simple causal chains or primary motives. But Raskolnikov, as a "man of the sixties," cannot countenance the possibility that he has committed an irrational or irreducible act. He craves a comprehensive motive to restore his belief in the lucidity of human values and behavior. Yet rational utilitarianism is not adequate to the task, and he loses himself in the maze of his own personality. He embarks upon his crime ostensibly with the aim of robbery to further the fortunes of himself and other socially worthy people at the expense of a worthless parasite—a simple and logical adjustment of society's faulty arithmetic. Yet he fails to ascertain in advance the extent and whereabouts of his victim's wealth; he leaves with only a few cheap trinkets which he soon abandons under a stone and never reclaims. At no stage does he consider the possibility of appropriating the old woman's wealth without resorting to murder. It quickly becomes obvious that Raskolnikov has not murdered in order to steal; he has fabricated a shabby robbery in order to murder. He has only murder on his mind, not the appropriation and redistribution of wealth.

After the murder the utilitarian motive slips farther and farther into the background as Raskolnikov's probing intellect discerns the shapes of other and more disturbing implications of his act. It is worth remembering that he is rarely troubled by the murder of Lizaveta, the innocent victim of an unanticipated turn of events. This second killing does not engage his concern, for it was an unpremeditated, simple, even "innocent" slaying with a clear motive: Raskolnikov killed Lizaveta in order to escape. It is the "rationally justified" murder of the old hag that gnaws at his soul and that in the end he cannot account for.

Porfiry Petrovich, the examining magistrate, is the first to associate the murder with the ideas expounded in an article of Raskolnikov's on crime, and thus to open the way to an explanation of the crime, not in terms of Raskolnikov's professed utilitarian altruism, but in the light of his insane pride, egoism, and craving for power. Raskolnikov's article, published without his knowledge, is a product of the narrow, cloistered intellectualism which characterizes the young ex-student and makes it so difficult for him to enter the mainstream of life. It is composed of the cramped and arid thoughts engendered by the coffinlike room in which he leads only the ghost of a life. The article divides humanity into two distinct categories: the *Supermen,* such as Newton and Napoleon, who by virtue of their originality, strength of will, or daring, write their names boldly in the history of human achievement; and the *Lice,* the ordinary men and women who are the bricks and not the architects of history and who contribute nothing new. The former, according to Raskolnikov, have an inherent right to moral and intellectual freedom; they create their own laws and may overstep the bounds of conventional law and morality. The latter are condemned by their ordinariness to a life of submission to common law and common morality; their sole function is to breed in the hope of one day giving birth to a Superman.

Clearly belief in any such division of humanity must tempt the man of pride into a harrowing dilemma of self-definition; and Raskolnikov is a man of immense pride. Does he therefore murder in the conviction that, as a superior man, he has the right to brush aside conventional morality in order to expedite the contribution he must make to history? This is unlikely, for, although Raskolnikov is seduced by his pride into longing for the status of Superman, his persistent doubts as he plans and rehearses the murder reveal all too clearly his uncertainty and fear of the Superman's freedom. Is the crime therefore conceived as a grotesque act of self-definition, whereby by assessing his reaction to moral transgression Raskolnikov seeks to choose his true self from the differing options offered by his pride and his uncertainty? This affords a tantalizingly plausible explanation of the murder; after all, we would expect the abstract Raskolnikov to respond most readily to abstract motives. Somehow it is impossible to imagine this unphysical intellectual murdering in response to such physical needs as hunger or want; but we can imagine him chasing the specter of self-knowledge. Moreover, Raskolnikov's need of self-definition is acute; in the novel's early chapters he oscillates wildly between satanic pride and abject humility, between unbounded admiration for the strong and limitless pity for the weak....

But the crime could be an authentic attempt at the resolution of this duality only if Raskolnikov were genuinely uncertain to which category of humanity he belonged, and this is not the case. In his pride he might long to be a Napoleon, but he knows that he is a louse, knows it *even before he commits the crime,* as he later acknowledges: "and the reason why I am finally a louse is because I am perhaps even nastier and viler than the louse I killed, and I felt *beforehand* that I would say that to myself *after* I had killed her." The implications of this admission are startling: Raskolnikov embarked

upon the murder of the old woman knowing in advance that he had no right to kill and no clear motive, and, moreover, clearly anticipating the destructive effect such an act would have upon the rest of his life. Perhaps it is this he has in mind when he later asserts: "Did I really kill the old hag? I killed myself, not the old hag! At that moment in one blow I did away with myself for good!" This feature of Raskolnikov's behavior illustrates the incompatibility of knowledge and pride. Raskolnikov's knowledge that he is ordinary and has no special right to overstep conventional moral limits cannot contain his proud and essentially irrational need to assert himself. In the end his crime is an act of terrifying inconsequence: a proud, petulant, and meaningless protest against the certain knowledge that he is not superior; a moment when the demands of frustrated pride are so insistent that he is prepared to sacrifice the whole of his future to them. "I simply killed; I killed for myself, for myself alone, and at that moment it was all the same to me whether I became some sort of benefactor of humanity or spent the rest of my life catching people in my web and sucking the life forces out of them like a spider."...

In *Crime and Punishment* the principle of uncertainty encompasses more than the question of motivation. Even the spatial and temporal coordinates of the novel are blurred and at times distorted by a narrator whose precise nature and point of view are neither clearly defined nor absolutely fixed. The notebooks reveal that the adoption of a narrative point of view presented Dostoevsky with his greatest difficulty in writing the novel. He originally planned to use the first-person confession form, which would have allowed direct and easy access to the thought processes of the hero, but which would have created real difficulties when it came to filling in the objective details of the world in which the murderer moves. Dostoevsky wrestled with this form until the third and final draft, when a new approach occurred to him: "Narration from point of view of author, a sort of invisible but omniscient being who doesn't leave his hero for a moment." The third-person narrator anticipated in this comment is retained for the novel itself, but his omniscience is open to doubt. Complete omniscience would have robbed the novel of its haunting uncertainty and provided the reader too clear an insight into Raskolnikov's behavior and motivation.... The first chapter illustrates this particularly well, as the alleys of St. Petersburg, with their stifling heat, dust, stuffiness, and smells, are conveyed to the reader in terms of the impression they make upon Raskolnikov. These details of the physical world, in passing through Raskolnikov's awareness, lose their tactile and sensual authenticity and are transformed into psychological stimuli....

In much the same way our sense of real space is distorted by this subjective third-person narrative. Many years after the appearance of *Crime and Punishment* Einstein argued that we cannot experience space in the abstract, independent of the matter that fills it; and it is Raskolnikov's consciousness that fills this novel. Like a gravitational field, it warps the space around it. For example, the description of Raskolnikov's room as seen through Raskolnikov's eyes at the start of the novel is uncomfortably inconsistent with objectively narrated events which occur in this same room later. The room appears to shift its size with the narrative point of view. The early description is clearly conditioned by Raskolnikov's own sensations of claustrophobia: he is oppressed and haunted by ideas, theories, pride, poverty, and illness, and the room he describes with hatred upon waking from a restless sleep resembles a tomb. A mere six feet long, not high enough for a man to stand, littered with dusty books, its yellow wallpaper peeling from the walls, it is dominated by a huge, clumsy sofa. The description accords so perfectly with what we know of Raskolnikov's state of mind that we hardly distinguish where his consciousness ends and the outside world begins. Yet a few chapters later, as Raskolnikov lies in bed semidelirious after the crime and the narrative adopts a more objective course in order to permit the introduction of several new characters, our sense of the room's size is quite different. As the sick Raskolnikov is visited by his maid Nastasya, his friend Razumikhin, the doctor Zosimov, and his sister's suitor Luzhin, the "tomb" seems to open out in order to accommodate each new arrival.

Distance is equally intangible. When, in Chapter 1, Raskolnikov visits his victim's flat, we have no real sensation of his physically moving from one environment to another. Dostoevsky tells us that "exactly seven hundred and thirty" paces separate the pawnbroker's flat from Raskolnikov's hovel, but the precision of this figure is entirely numerical. Locked inside Raskolnikov's consciousness as he rehearses a multitude of doubts and hesitations, we measure the physical distance only in terms of the number of thoughts which flash through his mind.

But the most uncertain quantity of all is time. Nearly all readers of *Crime and Punishment* experience the loss of a sense of duration in the course of the novel. It seems hardly possible, but the entire action requires only two weeks, and Part I a mere three days. Directed by the narrative mode into the inner world of Raskolnikov's turbulent imagination, we lose our temporal reference points. Absolute time ceases to be; we know time only as Raskolnikov experiences it. At moments it is severely retarded—indeed, in Part I, as Raskolnikov prepares for the kill, its flow is all but arrested; later the sense of time is violently accelerated as Raskolnikov undergoes the vertiginous fall from his crime to his confession. In this way time becomes a function of consciousness.... We might go further and suggest an analogy with Einsteinian time, which, like Dostoevsky's, depends fundamentally upon point of view. For Einstein there could be no absolute time: the time experienced by separate observers differed according to their relative motion. Dostoevsky seems to be suggesting something very similar in a cryptic remark in the drafts for *Crime and Punishment:* "What is time? Time does not exist; time is only numbers. Time is the relation of what exists to what does not exist." This remark might perhaps be interpreted as meaning that there is no abstract, absolute time. Time exists only when actualized in an event or series of events. The importance of this for *Crime and Punishment* is that events and their duration are experienced differently by different observers. Through Raskolnikov's consciousness the reader of the novel observes only the hero's experiences of intervals between events. There are no events narrated with consistent objectivity which form reference points against which to judge Raskolnikov's sense of time....

Despite all the uncertainties upon which *Crime and Punishment* rests, one overriding certainty is sustained throughout the novel: the conviction, shared by author, reader, and hero, that the crime is in the final analysis wrong.

Source: William J. Leatherbarrow, "The Principles of Uncertainty: *Crime and Punishment*," in his *Fedor Dostoevsky,* Twayne, 1981, pp. 69–95.

George Gibian

In the following excerpt, associate professor of English and Russian at Smith College, Gibian, offers an authoritative study of pagan and Christian symbolism in Crime and Punishment. *Chief among them are the imagery of water, vegetation, sun and air, the resurrection of Lazarus and Christ, and the earth.*

It may seem paradoxical to claim that critics have not sufficiently concerned themselves with

Dostoevsky's attack against rationalism in *Crime and Punishment;* yet this aspect of the novel has frequently failed to receive adequate attention, not because it has been overlooked, but because often it has been immediately noticed, perfunctorily mentioned, and then put out of mind as something obvious. Few writers have examined the consequence of the anti-rationalistic tenor of the novel: the extent to which it is paralleled by the structural devices incorporated in the work.

Dostoevsky held that dialectics, self-seeking, and exclusive reliance on reason ("reason and will" in Raskolnikov's theories and again in his dream of the plague) lead to death-in-life. In *Crime and Punishment* he set himself the task of exposing the evils of rationalism by presenting a laboratory case of an individual who followed its precepts and pushed them to their logical conclusion. By working out what would happen to that man, Dostoevsky intended to show how destructive the idea was for individuals, nations, and mankind; for to him the fates of the individual and the nation were inseparably interlocked....

The underlying antithesis of *Crime and Punishment,* the conflict between the side of reason, selfishness, and pride, and that of acceptance of suffering, closeness to life-sustaining Earth, and love, sounds insipid and platitudinous when stated in such general fashion as we have done here. Dostoevsky, however, does not present it in the form of abstract statement alone. He conveys it with superb dialectical skill, and when we do find direct statements in the novel, they are intentionally made so inadequate as to make us realize all the more clearly their disappointing irrelevancy and to lead us to seek a richer representation in other modes of discourse....

Symbolism is the method of expression with which we are primarily concerned here, but it is far from being the only indirect, non-intellectual manner of expression on which Dostoevsky depends. Oblique presentation is another means which he uses; one example is the introduction of the subject of need for suffering. The idea is first presented in a debased and grotesque form by Marmeladov. His confession of how he had mistreated his family, of his drinking, and of the theft of money—to Raskolnikov, a stranger whom he has met in the tavern—is almost a burlesque foreshadowing of Raskolnikov's later penance, the kissing of the earth and his confession at the police station. Marmeladov is drunk, irresponsible, and still submerged in his selfish course of action; he welcomes suffering but continues to spurn his responsibilities; he is making a fool of himself in the tavern. His discourse throughout calls for an ambiguous response. Raskolnikov's reaction may be pity, agreement, laughter, or disgust; the reader's is a mixture and succession of all those emotions.

Thus the important ideas summed up in Marmeladov's "it's not joy I thirst for, but sorrow and tears" are introduced in a derogatory context and in an ambivalent manner, on the lowest, least impressive level. Yet the concept is now present with us, the readers, as it is with Raskolnikov—even though it first appears in the guise of something questionable, disreputable, and laughable—and we are forced to ponder it and to measure against it Sonya's, Raskolnikov's, Porfiry's and others' approaches to the same subject of "taking one's suffering."

A simple, unequivocal statement, a respectable entrance of the theme on the stage of the book, would amount to a reduction of life to "a matter of arithmetic" and would release the reader from the salutary, in fact indispensable task of smelting down the ore for himself....

In *Crime and Punishment* the reader, as well as Raskolnikov, must struggle to draw his own conclusions from a work which mirrors the refractory and contradictory materials of life itself, with their admixture of the absurd, repulsive, and grotesque....

Traditional symbolism, that is, symbolism which draws on images established by the Christian tradition and on those common in Russian non-Christian, possibly pre-Christian and pagan, folk thought and expression, is an important element in the structure of *Crime and Punishment.* The outstanding strands of symbolic imagery in the novel are those of water, vegetation, sun and air, the resurrection of Lazarus and Christ, and the earth.

Water is to Dostoevsky a symbol of rebirth and regeneration. It is regarded as such by the positive characters, for whom it is an accompaniment and an indication of the life-giving forces in the world. By the same token, the significance of water may be the opposite to negative characters. Water holds the terror of death for the corrupt Svidrigaylov, who confirms his depravity by thinking: "Never in my life could I stand water, not even on a landscape painting." Water, instead of being an instrument of life, becomes for him a hateful, avenging menace during the last hours of his life....

Indeed it will be in the cold and in the rain that he will put a bullet in his head. Instead of being a positive force, water is for him the appropriate setting for the taking of his own life.

When Raskolnikov is under the sway of rationalism and corrupting ways of thinking, this also is indicated by Dostoevsky by attributing to him negative reactions to water similar to those of Svidrigaylov. In Raskolnikov, however, the battle is not definitely lost. A conflict still rages between his former self—which did have contact with other people and understood the beauty of the river, the cathedral (representing the traditional, religious, and emotional forces), and water—and the new, rationalistic self, which is responsible for the murder and for his inner desiccation.... There is still left in Raskolnikov an instinctive reaction to water (and to beauty) as an instrument of life, although this receptivity, which had been full-blown and characteristic of him in his childhood, is now in his student days overlaid by the utilitarian and rationalistic theories....

But Raskolnikov also realizes that his trends of thought have banished him, like Cain, from the brotherhood of men and clouded his right and ability to enjoy beauty and the beneficent influences of life symbolized by water; hence his perplexity and conflict....

Related to the many references to the river and rain, and often closely associated with them, are two other groups of symbolic imagery: that of vegetation (shrubbery, leaves, bushes, flowers, and greenness in general) and that of the sun (and the related images of light and air).

In contrast to the dusty, hot, stifling, and crowded city, a fitting setting for Raskolnikov's oppressive and murderous thoughts, we find, for example, "the greenness and the freshness" of the Petersburg islands.... The natural surroundings reawakened in him the feelings of his youth, through which he came close to avoiding his crime and to finding regeneration without having to pass through the cycle of crime and punishment....

By the same token, vegetation exercised the opposite effect on Svidrigaylov: it repelled him. In the inn on the night of his suicide, when he heard the leaves in the garden under his window, he thought, "How I hate the noise of trees at night in a storm and in darkness." Whereas Raskolnikov received a healthy warning during his short sleep "under a bush," Svidrigaylov uses the sordid setting of an amusement park which "had one spindly three-year-old Christmas tree and three small bushes" merely for vain distraction on the eve of his suicide, and contemplates killing himself under "a

large bush drenched with rain." In him all positive elements had been rubbed out or transformed into evil.

Similarly to water and vegetation, sunshine, light in general, and air are positive values, whereas darkness and lack of air are dangerous and deadening. The beauty of the cathedral flooded by sunlight ought to be felt and admired.... Before the murder, he looks up from the bridge at the "bright, red sunset" and is able to face the sun as well as the river with calm, but after the murder, "in the street it was again unbearably hot—not a drop of rain all during those days.... The sun flashed brightly in his eyes, so that it hurt him to look and his head was spinning round in good earnest—the usual sensation of a man in a fever who comes out into the street on a bright, sunny day." The sun is pleasant for a man in good spiritual health, but unbearable for a feverish creature of the dark, such as Raskolnikov had become....

Absence of air reinforces the lack of light suggestive of inner heaviness. Raskolnikov, whom Svidrigaylov tells that people need air, feels physically and mentally suffocated when he is summoned to the police-station: "There's so little fresh air here. Stifling. Makes my head reel more and more every minute, and my brain too." Later he tells his friend Razumikhin: "Things have become too airless, too stifling." Airiness, on the contrary, is an indication of an advantageous relation between outward circumstances and Raskolnikov's inner state. The warning dream of the mare comes to Raskolnikov in a setting not only of greenness but also of abundance of fresh air: "The green vegetation and the fresh air at first pleased his tired eyes, used to the dust of the city, to the lime and mortar and the huge houses that enclosed and confined him on all sides. The air was fresh and sweet here: no evil smells."

When we turn to specifically Christian symbolism in *Crime and Punishment,* we find the outstanding images to be those of New Jerusalem, Christ's passion, and Lazarus. New Jerusalem is an important concept throughout Dostoevsky's work.... Porfiry asks Raskolnikov, "Do you believe in New Jerusalem?" The significance of Raskolnikov's positive answer lies in the fact that the New Jerusalem which he means is the Utopian perversion of it, to be built upon foundations of crime and individual self-assertion and transgression (*prestuplenie*). It is the "Golden Age," as Raskolnikov called it in the draft version in Dostoevsky's notebook: "Oh why are not all people happy? The picture of the Age of Gold—it is already present in minds and hearts. Why should it not come about? … But what right have I, a mean murderer, to wish happiness to people and to dream of the Age of Gold?"

The confession of Raskolnikov is described in terms reminiscent of Christ's passion on the road to Golgotha: he goes on "his sorrowful way." When Raskolnikov reads in his mother's letter of Dunya's having walked up and down in her room and prayed before the Kazan Virgin, he associates her planned self-sacrifice in marrying Luzhin with the biblical prototype of self-assumed suffering for the sake of others: "Ascent to Golgotha is certainly pretty difficult," he says to himself. When Raskolnikov accepts Lizaveta's cypress cross from Sonya, he shows his recognition of the significance of his taking it—the implied resolve to seek a new life though accepting suffering and punishment—by saying to Sonya, "This is the symbol of my taking up the cross."

One of the central Christian myths alluded to in the novel is the story of Lazarus. It is the biblical passage dealing with Lazarus that Raskolnikov asks Sonya to read to him. The raising of Lazarus from the dead is to Dostoevsky the best *exemplum* of a human being resurrected to a new life, the road to Golgotha the best expression of the dark road of sorrow, and Christ himself the grand type of voluntary suffering.…

The traditional emphasis of the Eastern Church is on Resurrection—of the Western, on the Passion. In *Crime and Punishment* both sides are represented: the Eastern in its promise of Raskolnikov's rebirth, the Western in the stress on his suffering. Perhaps at least part of the universality of the appeal of the novel and of its success in the West may be due to the fact that it combines the two religious tendencies.…

The Christian symbolism is underlined by the pagan and universal symbolism of the earth. Sonya persuades Raskolnikov not only to confess and wear the cross, but also to kiss the earth at the crossroads—a distinctly Russian and pre-Christian acknowledgment of the earth as the common mother of all men.… In bowing to the earth and kissing it, Raskolnikov is performing a symbolic and nonrational act; the rationalist is marking the beginning of his change into a complete, organic, living human being, rejoining all other men in the community. By his crime and ideas, he had separated himself from his friends, family, and nation, in one word, he had cut himself off from Mother Earth.

By the gesture of kissing the earth, he is reestablishing all his ties.…

Now that we have examined selected examples of symbolism in the novel, let us take a look at the epilogue as a test of insights we may have gained into the structure and unity of the novel, for the epilogue is the culmination and juncture of the various strands of images which we have encountered earlier.…

If we approach the epilogue with the various preparatory strands of images clearly in our minds, what do we find?… [We] see the state of the soul of the unregenerate Raskolnikov, the Lazarus before the rebirth, expressed by Dostoevsky through the symbolic imagery to which the novel has made us accustomed—water and vegetation. The love for life (which Raskolnikov does not yet comprehend) is represented by a spring with green grass and bushes around it.

When the regeneration of Raskolnikov begins, it is expressed in a manner still more closely linked to previously introduced imagery. His dream of the plague condemns Raskolnikov's own rationalism. It shows people obsessed by reason and will losing contact with the soil.… This dream of the plague, coming immediately before the start of the hero's regeneration, may also be another reminiscence of the Book of Revelation with its last seven plagues coming just before the millennium and the establishment of the New Jerusalem.

The epilogue then goes on to emphasize that it is the second week after Easter—the feast of Christ's passion, death, and resurrection; and that it is warm, bright spring—the season of the revival of dead nature, again a coupling of Christian and non-Christian symbolism of rebirth such as we have encountered earlier in the novel.

The crucial final scene which follows takes place on "a bright and warm day," and "on the bank of the river." The river which Raskolnikov sees now is no longer a possible means for committing suicide nor a sight inducing melancholy; it is the river of life.…

Then appears Sonya, and with her arrival comes the moment when Raskolnikov is suffused with love for his guide and savior.… Vivid response to all that lives is a joining with the creator in creating and preserving the world; Sophia is a blissful meeting of god and nature, the creator and creature. In Orthodox thought Sophia has come close to being regarded as something similar to the fourth divine person. Love for Sophia is a generalized ecstatic love for all creation, so that the images of flowers, greenness, landscape, the river, air, the sun, and water throughout *Crime and Punishment* can be regarded as being subsumed in the concept of Sophia and figuratively in the person of Sonya, the embodiment of the concept. Sonya sees that all exists in God; she knows, and helps Raskolnikov to recognize, what it means to anticipate the millennium by living in rapt love for all creation here, in this world.

It was Sonya who had brought Raskolnikov the message of Lazarus and his resurrection; she had given him the cypress cross and urged him to kiss the earth at the crossroads. On the evening of the day when, by the bank of the river and in the presence of Sonya, Raskolnikov's regeneration had begun, the New Testament lies under his pillow as a reminder of the Christian prototype of resurrection which had been stressed earlier in the novel. Against the background of all the important symbols of the book, Easter, spring, Abraham's flocks, the earth of Siberia, the river, the dream, and Sonya, the drama within Raskolnikov's mind assumes its expressive outward form.

There follow several explicit statements of what happened. We read that "the dawn of a full resurrection to a new life" was already shining "in their faces, that love brought them back to life, that the heart of one held inexhaustible sources of life for the heart of the other," and that "the gradual rebirth" of Raskolnikov would follow. But the power of the general, overt statements depends on the indirect, oblique, dramatic, and symbolic statements which preceded them and prepared the ground for our acceptance of them. If we sense the full significance of the statement that now "Raskolnikov could solve nothing consciously. He only felt. Life had taken the place of dialectics," for example, it is because we have seen dialectics and apathy dramatized in Luzhin, Lebezyatnikov, Raskolnikov, and Svidrigaylov, and resurrection in Sonya and various symbols throughout the novel of which the epilogue is a climax and a recapitulation.

Source: George Gibian, "Traditional Symbolism in *Crime and Punishment*," in *PMLA*, Vol. LXX, No. 5, December, 1955, pp. 970–96.

Sources

David McDuff, introduction to *Crime and Punishment*, Penguin Classics, 1991, pp. 9-29.

Helen Muchnic, "Dostoyevsky's English Reputation (1881-1936)," in *Smith College Studies in Modern Languages*, Vol. 20, Nos. 2/3, 1939.

D. I. Pisarev, "A Contemporary View," in *Crime and Punishment and the Critics*, edited and translated by Edward Wasiolek, 1961.

Philip Rahv, "Dostoevsky in *Crime and Punishment*," in *Partisan Review*, Vol. XXVII, 1960.

Ernest J. Simmons, introduction to *Crime and Punishment*, translation by Constance Garnett, Dell Publishing, 1959, pp. 5-22.

For Further Study

Mikhail Bakhtin, *Problems of Dostoevsky's Poetics*, University of Minnesota Press, 1984.

Bakhtin's analysis of language and point of view gives particular attention to the way in which voices and perspectives intersect and intermingle in Dostoevsky's novel.

Fyodor Dostoevsky, *Crime and Punishment*, edited by George Gibian, Norton, 1989.

This edition of the novel contains numerous essays and documents that illuminate various aspects of the novel, from its critical reception to its symbolic and literary attributes.

"Dostoevsky, Fyodor Mikhailovich," in *The Oxford Companion to English Literature*, fifth edition, edited by Margaret Drabble, Oxford University Press, 1985, p. 286.

Summarizes Dostoyevsky's relationship to English literature, including his travels in England, his admiration of Shakespeare, Dickens, and others, and British reactions to his own works.

Donald Fanger, *Dostoevsky and Romantic Realism: A Study of Dostoevsky in Relation to Balzac, Dickens, and Gogol*, Harvard University Press, 1965.

Fanger explores the relation of Dostoevsky's novel to the literary tradition which preceded it, and he focuses on the treatment of the setting of the novel, the city of St. Petersburg.

Joseph Frank, *Dostoevsky: The Miraculous Years, 1865-71*, Princeton University Press, 1995.

Frank provides a detailed account of the novel's themes, its genesis, and its relation to the literary and historical events of its day.

Michael Holquist, *Dostoevsky and the Novel*, Northwestern University Press, 1977.

This book discusses the way in which Dostoevsky's novel reflects narrative patterns of the past, including detective tales and wisdom tales.

R. L. Jackson, editor, *Twentieth Century Interpretations of Crime and Punishment*, Prentice Hall, 1974.

This book contains over a dozen insightful essays that are devoted to major themes and patterns in the novel.

Malcom V. Jones, *Dostoevsky: The Novel of Discord*, Harper & Row, 1976.

Jones discusses the underlying theme of psychological and emotional disorder in *Crime and Punishment*.

Janko Lavrin, *Dostoevsky: A Study,* Macmillan, 1947.
Lavrin discusses Dostoyevsky's technique, including his ability to weave profound psychological and spiritual insights into his complex narratives.

Konstantin Mochulsky, *Dostoevsky: His Life and Work,* translated by Michael A. Minihan, Princeton University Press, 1967.
Mochulsky's biography of Dostoevsky highlights the writer's spiritual quest.

Richard Peace, *Dostoyevsky: An Examination of the Major Novels,* Cambridge University Press, 1971.
Peace focuses on the symbolic division within Raskolnikov's personality and the way in which this division is reflected in the characters surrounding him.

Gary Rosenshield, Crime and Punishment: *The Techniques of the Omniscient Author,* The Peter De Ridder Press, 1978.
This book offers a close analysis of Dostoevsky's manipulation of point of view and narrative perspective in the novel.

George Steiner, *Tolstoy or Dostoevsky: An Essay in the Old Criticism,* Dutton, 1971.
Steiner places *Crime and Punishment* in the context of Dostoyevsky's lifetime achievement, stressing the novel's moral, dramatic, and psychological dimensions.

Edward Wasiolek, *Dostoevsky: The Major Fiction,* MIT Press, 1964.
Wasiolek's discussion of the novel focuses on its exploration of the central characters and their personalities.

Cry, the Beloved Country

Alan Paton
1948

Alan Paton's novel exploded on the English reading public in 1948. Since then, the society of South Africa has evolved dramatically. Still, Paton's *Cry, the Beloved Country* remains a classic expression of South Africa and one of the best known stories of that country. The implications of the steadfast appeal of the novel are not only a credit to Paton's ability to capture the human tragedy of the Kumalo family, but also testimony to the unfortunate fact that racial tensions still exist both within and without South Africa.

The story itself is about the land of South Africa and its people as it is expressed in one man's quest to find his son. This mission brings the man, Reverend Stephen Kumalo, to Johannesburg—the great center of the country. Unfortunately, the son, Absalom Kumalo, is found guilty of an awful crime. In the end, the tragedy of Absalom's execution becomes a background for the renewal of the impoverished land. This renewal is made possible by a change in the attitude of a rich white landowner whose son was murdered by Absalom. Alan Paton tells this tale in a simple manner which captures pre-apartheid South Africa in a parable. However, though the tale is one of forgiveness, hope, and learning, there is a feeling of resignation to the misguided policies of what the world would soon know as Apartheid.

Author Biography

Alan Stewart Paton was born in Pietermaritzburg, Natal (now part of South Africa), on January 11, 1903. At the age of twelve, he entered Maritzburg College (a secondary school). After graduating, he enrolled in courses at the University of Natal. While in college he published his first poems in the university's literary magazine. In 1922 he graduated with a degree in physics.

Two years later he held his first political role by representing the students of his alma mater at the first Imperial Conference of Students in London. After this, he taught mathematics and chemistry at Ixopo High School for white children until 1928. That year he joined the staff at Maritzburg College and married Doris Olive Francis. Together they had a son, David Paton, two years later.

In 1935, Paton moved to Johannesburg to serve as principal of Diepkloof Reformatory for African boys. This position was the result of his friend Jan H. Hofmeyr's dual role in the coalition government. Hofmeyr was both head of Education and the Interior. By the power of this position, Hofmeyr transferred juvenile reform from the Department of Prisons to that of Education. Paton, in other words, as an early proponent of racial harmony, was in an ideal position to influence the direction of South Africa. Unfortunately, the hope of a harmonious South Africa lasted only as long as Hofmeyr's reign in government.

One year after becoming principal, Paton joined the South African Institute of Race Relations. He then had another son named Jonathan. When World War II was declared, Paton volunteered but was found ineligible. In 1942, he was appointed to an Anglican Diocesan Commission whose function was to report on church and race in South Africa. In the following year, he authored a series of articles on crime, punishment, and penal reform. In 1944 he addressed the National Social Welfare Conference, and this paper was later published in 1945 as "The Non-European Offender." Then in 1946 he began his tour of penal and correctional institutions in Europe, the United States, and Canada. While on this tour, he began *Cry, the Beloved Country,* published in 1948. At the same time as this novel's publication, Jan Hofmeyr died, and the National Party won the election. Apartheid policies were almost immediately enacted.

The international success of *Cry, The Beloved Country* enabled Paton to be financially indepen-

Alan Paton

dent as well as allowing him to write in opposition to the government and travel abroad. Being known internationally as an author and spokesperson of the conditions in South Africa kept Paton out of trouble with the government. However, the government did confiscate his passport in 1960, not returning it until the early 1970s. In the 1950s he was amongst those who tried to form an opposition Liberal Party to the Nationalist apartheid government. Legislation against non-whites in government forced Paton, who was president of the multi-ethnic party, to disband rather than conform to the new laws in 1968. From his most famous novel of 1948, until his death by throat cancer in 1988, Alan Paton wrote novels, poems, nonfiction articles and biographies, spoke around the world, and remained a proponent of racial equality.

Plot Summary

Book I

Cry, the Beloved Country consists of three sections, Books I, II, and III, each presenting a different point of view about the same events. Book I is presented through the eyes of the main character, Stephen Kumalo, a native priest in Ndotsheni, a small community in the Ixopo district of South Africa. The time is 1947. There is a terrible drought that is forcing the young people of the region to leave their agricultural communities and to emigrate to Johannesburg to seek employment in the mines. The loss of so many young people has undermined the tribal traditions, which cannot be maintained in a large urban setting like Johannesburg. The action begins with a letter that comes to Kumalo from Johannesburg, telling him that his sister, Gertrude Kumalo, is ill and needs his help. Kumalo consults with his wife and decides to use their meagre savings to go to the big city to help his sister. His son, Absalom, has also disappeared into the city, and Kumalo hopes to gain word of him as well.

After a long and intimidating journey by train and bus to Johannesburg, Kumalo visits a parish priest named Theophilus Msimangu who helps him to locate his sister. After a long search from one address to another, Gertrude is found living in a shabby room with a young child. She has been working as a prostitute. Kumalo arranges for her and the child to stay with him before they return to Ndotsheni. Kumalo then goes to visit his brother, John Kumalo, who has become a political leader for black rights in Johannesburg. Kumalo's discussions with his brother illustrate the tension between the tribal culture of the past and the new way of living in the city. In the new way of life everyone is on their own with no community, but also without the limitations of living within the rules of the tribe. John Kumalo praises the opportunities available for enterprising people in the city, but Kumalo suggests that his brother John might have protected their sister Gertrude if he had remembered the values of the tribe.

Kumalo then tries to discover the whereabouts of his son, Absalom. As he goes about Johannesburg with Msimangu as his guide, the terrible conditions of the "kaffirs" (native people) are revealed: the overcrowding, the segregation from the white communities where the natives have to work, the lack of transportation, the rising prices and stagnant wages. In fact, the black people have initiated a bus strike to protest a fare hike, and Kumalo and Msimangu must walk many miles in search of Absalom. Sympathetic white people drive up and down the thoroughfares giving the kaffirs rides in their cars in order to support the strike, and Kumalo is greatly impressed by this generosity. Kumalo's search for his son ends at a reformatory where Absalom had been sent after being convicted of theft. The white man who runs the reformatory

has released Absalom early for good behavior and found him a job and a place to live. Absalom has a girlfriend with whom he is expecting a child, and he is to marry her soon. Though Kumalo is distressed that his son has broken the law, he is delighted that Absalom seems to be reformed and on his way to living a regular life. The white man and Msimangu lead Kumalo to Absalom's new home so that father and son can be reunited.

When they arrive at Absalom's home they discover that he has abandoned his pregnant girlfriend and resumed his life of crime. The white man is very disillusioned and angry, but Kumalo is grieved at this new evidence of the destruction brought on by the breaking of the tribe. It is discovered that Absalom has been involved in a terrible crime: he and two companions have broken into the home of a white man, Arthur Jarvis, and killed him when the white man surprised them in the middle of the robbery. The irony is that Arthur Jarvis was an important advocate among white men of native rights and was writing a book about how white mistreatment of blacks was the underlying cause of black crime. The magnitude of the crime and its consequences for his family and the black community weigh heavily on Kumalo's mind.

> There is not much talking now. A silence falls upon them all. This is no time to talk of hedges and fields, or the beauties of any country. Sadness and fear and hate, how they well up in the heart and the mind, whenever one opens the pages of these messengers of doom. Cry for the broken tribe, for the law and custom that is gone. Aye, and cry aloud for the man who is dead, for the woman and children bereaved. Cry, the beloved country, these things are not yet at an end. The sun pours down on the earth, on the lovely land that man cannot enjoy. He only knows the fear of his heart.

Book I ends as Kumalo visits his son in prison. Absalom is remorseful, but has no explanation for his behavior other than the temptations of the city and bad companionship. Kumalo turns for help to Father Vincent, a white Anglican priest who finds an attorney for Absalom, and helps Kumalo through a crisis of faith.

Book II

Book II is presented from the point of view of James Jarvis, the father of the murdered man. Jarvis lives in Ixopo and has a large estate, High Place, near the village of Ndotsheni where Kumalo is the priest. Jarvis is only vaguely aware of the kaffirs and their community, seeing ignorant, dirty people who exhaust and damage their own land with traditional farming techniques. When the news comes that his only child, Arthur, has been murdered in Johannesburg, Jarvis has the sad task of informing his wife and going to the city to stay with his daughter-in-law's family while the body is identified and the estate settled.

While going through Arthur's papers, Jarvis discovers that his son had a great admiration for Abraham Lincoln and believed that Lincoln had much to teach South Africa about race relations. Since Jarvis knew little of his son's opinions about the conditions of the natives, he makes an effort to understand his son's thinking on the race issue. Jarvis reads the Gettysburg Address and Lincoln's second inaugural address, as well as Arthur's writings about the "native question." Jarvis begins to realize that the prejudices he has held against the kaffirs have contributed to the deprivations that natives have suffered in South Africa. He comes to understand that the white ruling class has broken the tribal life of native people by using them as cheap labor in the cities and depriving them of community life by making them live in compounds without their families. Jarvis sees that his son was trying very hard to change the lot of the native majority by giving them a greater share in the benefits and opportunities that the white minority have always enjoyed.

One of Absalom Kumalo's companions in crime is the son of John Kumalo. Though Absalom has determined to tell the truth to the court, John Kumalo advises his son and the other culprit to lie and say they were not there. In spite of the fact that Absalom has the free services of Mr. Carmichael, a white lawyer who defends black clients as a public service, the court condemns Absalom to death by hanging. The two other culprits are acquitted for lack of evidence. Kumalo prepares to return to Ndotsheni to tell his wife the tragic news. When he goes to take Gertrude with him, he finds that she has been lured back into her old life, leaving her son behind. Kumalo returns to his village with the boy and Absalom's pregnant wife. Absalom was permitted to marry her in prison to give their child a name.

Book III

Book III is told from the point of view of both Kumalo and Jarvis, who have returned to their respective homes in Ixopo. Jarvis's grandson, the young son of Arthur Jarvis, makes friends with Kumalo in order to learn to speak Zulu. Because of this relationship, Jarvis learns of the deprivations being suffered in the kaffir village because of the drought. He sends milk to save the dying children,

hires an agriculture expert to restore the stricken valley and to teach the people effective farming techniques, and builds a new church in his wife's memory. The two fathers, white and black, become reconciled to one another. Together they represent the hope for South Africa's future.

Characters

Mr. Carmichael

Mr. Carmichael is a tall, grave, white man brought to Rev. Kumalo by Father Vincent. He agrees to take up the defense of Absalom "pro deo"—for God, for free. Carmichael agrees to defend Absalom because he is a just man and senses that Absalom is telling the truth but his companions are not. Thus, he tells Kumalo, he could never defend the other two. At once then, Mr. Carmichael is a "godsend" who will do what he can to persuade the court not to execute Absalom. However, he is more than a lawyer, he is a white man who calls Kumalo "Mr. Kumalo" and is all business—no awkward racism. The lawyer is a man of the law, not of nonsense, but still he is unable to get past the paranoia that recent reports of "native" crime has spread amongst the people. The punishment for Absalom is inevitable.

John Harrison

John Harrison is a minor figure who is representative of the "average" white person in Johannesburg. John is the brother of Mary, Arthur Jarvis' wife. As a businessman, he is a part of the white establishment. By association with Arthur, it could be imagined that John is a tolerant person but instead, he says to James Jarvis, "He and I didn't talk much about these things … I try to treat a native decently … [but] we're scared stiff." Once, he was asked by a government official to speak to Arthur about toning down his liberal speech. Now, due to the reports of increasing crime and the murder of his brother-in-law, Harrison quite frankly hopes that the police catch Arthur's killers "and string 'em all up."

Arthur Jarvis

Arthur is a white activist who works to further the cause of racial equality in South Africa. His murder, at the hands of Absalom Kumalo, drives much of the action of the novel.

James Jarvis

A white landowner and father of Arthur, Absalom Kumalo's victim. Jarvis's estate is adjacent to the village where Stephen Kumalo lives. The death of his only son hits him hard but does not fill him with vengeance. Instead, he goes to his son's house and reads through his son's papers. There he reflects and accepts his son's thoughts about living as equals among the native peoples. It is not that previously he was a bad man, a miser, or a racist—only that he had been passive and did not do anything to help solve the problems of South Africa. That all changes as he reads the writing of his son and passes this writing to his wife.

When he returns to his estate he begins to distribute milk for the relief of the children. Then he finds an advisor who will help to restore the barren valley. He does this with the big picture his son presented in his mind. He does this both because it is the right thing to do but also because it will benefit his own family. This later consideration is clearly represented by his grandson who is allowed to ride his horse to the Rev. Kumalo's house for impromptu Zulu lessons.

The fathers meet in a very dramatic moment and both sense the genuine sorrow of the other. One could say they are almost friends, brought together by the tragedy. Yet they are not friends and cannot be. Jarvis is wanting to do right and Stephen is a conduit for that. Stephen in turn can only pray and be a willing conduit—he houses the agricultural advisor, humors the grandson, supports change, and opens his church to Jarvis in the rain. Jarvis, though never an evil man, is the most profoundly changed in the novel. He becomes a crazy liberal rumored to be spending his whole fortune on improvements for the valley. He is a great source of hope to Kumalo and to the reader.

Margaret Jarvis

The mother of Arthur and wife of James Jarvis, Margaret is a representation of motherhood. She shared her son's vision with him when he was alive. His death, and the ensuing change in her husband, serve as the catalyst for her pursuing Arthur's vision. Unfortunately, she is not able to do as much as her husband because her illness worsens. However, her dying wish is that her husband build a new church for St. Mark's Parish where Stephen Kumalo is a minister. The church is built and her memory kept alive by the people of the parish.

Absalom Kumalo

Absalom Kumalo is a product of the changing South Africa. He goes to Johannesburg to find his

Media Adaptations

- In 1951, Alan Paton and Zoltan Korda produced a film version of *Cry, the Beloved Country* with London Films. Starring Sidney Poitier, the film was recently released on video by Monterey Home Video.

- In 1994, *Cry, the Beloved Country* was recorded on cassette by Blackstone Audio Books.

- In 1995 Miramax filmed a new version of *Cry, the Beloved Country,* starring James Earl Jones and Richard Harris. The film was directed by Darrell James Roodt and produced by Anant Singh.

Aunt Gertrude but instead finds himself with no prospects but mining or crime. He chooses crime more by default and association with others in a similar position. At one point he is in the reform school from which he is let out on account of excellent behavior. The reform authorities hope that he will take the job they arrange for him so he may provide for his young girlfriend who is pregnant. Instead, he abandons the woman he is to marry and goes with two friends into a white neighborhood to steal. The house belongs to Arthur Jarvis, who surprises the three boys and is killed by Absalom.

For this murder Absalom is sentenced to death and finds himself abandoned by his friends. Then he faces his father whom he has shamed. Though by law he must be hanged for his crime, there is a tremendous sense of injustice over the events of which Absalom finds himself the victim. Absalom remains sympathetic to the reader since he acted from fear and did not intend to kill Arthur. Jarvis, unlike Mr. Harrison, does not want Absalom's death for his son's death.

Gertrude Kumalo

Stephen Kumalo's sister Gertrude left home for Johannesburg in search of her husband who had gone for a job in the mines. Not finding him, she stays in the city and becomes a prostitute. She sells liquor, has a child, and serves time in prison. When

Still from the 1995 movie Cry, the Beloved Country, *starring Richard Harris (left) and James Earl Jones.*

she becomes ill, a kindly minister writes to Stephen asking him to come to the city and care for Gertrude. Stephen arrives and removes her to the safety of Mrs. Lithebe's house. In the end, the call of the city is too strong and she slips away, leaving Stephen to care for her son. Gertrude represents the fate of the many "natives" going to the city in the mid-1940s seeking a better life. Unfortunately, most of them are destroyed, irreparably, by the city.

John Kumalo

John Kumalo reveals to his brother Stephen the new morals of the city. This moral code includes leaving his wife, selfishly getting ahead, and believing only in politics because it enables self-gain. John's whole attitude is incomprehensible to Stephen. However, through contact with his brother, representative of this self-seeking code, he learns about anger and betrayal.

Stephen's brother is a politically active man but only because he has the gift of public speech. In fact, John is a self-seeking and corrupt man interested in politics for the power he can gain. John's selfishness is to use the power of his voice to gain respect and power in the community without en-

dangering his carpentry business. He is the voice of the more politically astute men who are organizing the opposition to the government. His son was with Absalom at the murder scene. However, in John's more "worldly" way, he finds a lawyer for his son who enters a not-guilty plea based on denying his presence at the scene. Through this lie, his son is free while his nephew is executed.

Mrs. Kumalo

She is the wife of Stephen Kumalo and mother of Absalom. Her primary function is as a "reality check" on Stephen. As such, she allows the truth of her son's not returning to finish school to be spoken. Having allowed it, the money they were saving for him can now be spent to find Gertrude.

Reverend Stephen Kumalo

Stephen Kumalo is a Zulu clergyman and pastor of St. Mark's Church in a rural district of South Africa. He journeys to Johannesburg because of a letter from Theophilus Msimangu expressing concern over the welfare of Gertrude Kumalo, the clergyman's sister. Concern for her and a verbalization from his wife that his son is not going to return brings Stephen to use the money they had been saving for their son's schooling and go to Johannesburg to find Gertrude and hopefully Absalom. The novel follows his journey to the city, his retrieval of his sister and her son, and the horrifying discovery of his son's crime. Just as he begins to look for his son, he discovers his son has committed murder.

Through Stephen, whose name recalls the martyred saint, the reader can transverse the lines of tension existing in South Africa in the mid-1940s: race relations are deteriorating while nobody wants to admit the reasons why; the land becomes more and more impoverished with the associated problems of hunger and illness among native peoples; society is in upheaval as the culture of the Zulu tribe is dismantled by the economic siren song of the city. Stephen Kumalo, through all this, encounters doubt but then overcomes doubt with hope. He embodies hope, for Africa, for Mr. Jarvis, for the agricultural specialist who has come to help them. This hope, aided by the very generous gift of Msimangu's bank book, dampens the sense of tragedy Kumalo faces all around him.

Kumalo changes throughout the novel because he is subjected to many new experiences. He encounters the city with all its misery, and he gains insight into the effects of segregation on his people. He also sees the efforts being made to better his people. Kumalo is quite surprised by the bus boycott under the direction of Dubula. He is impressed by the organization of the Shanty Town. Then, he encounters within himself some very human passion that he, as a good pastor, did not know. He is angry and almost cruel with the girl that is his son's wife. He is also angry with his brother John. It seems to Kumalo that in the city one cannot be passive nor can one love pastorally or blindly. He brings this back home where he can no longer simply accept the destitution of the people. Fortunately, neither can Jarvis. Stephen Kumalo, then, is on a quest to understand the world, gain peace with it, and create resolution within his own family. None of these goals are met because they each depend on the other and though he might try, Stephen cannot heal South Africa.

Napoleon Letsitsi

Formerly an over-qualified village school teacher, Napoleon Letsitsi is employed by James Jarvis to teach agricultural methods to the people of Kumalo's village. Though employed by a white man, Letsitsi is fervent in his view of himself as working for Africa. He is one of the new generation of blacks (like Dubula and Mandela) who work for equality and whose anthem is *Nkosi Sikelel'*

iAfrika. He mirrors the hope Arthur Jarvis wrote about, that South Africa would one day be a harmonious and just society. His role, however, is to see that the land be rejuvenated and, with that process, the people.

Mrs. Lithebe

A widow with a large house, she is wealthy enough not to have to take in boarders. However, Mrs. Lithebe boards Stephen because she thinks it is good to have a priest in the house. She is very kind to him and very sympathetic to his sad tale. She takes in Gertrude, the boy, and the nameless girl on account of Stephen. She does all this because she is a "mother"—a type of person who creates home and hearth for those needing to be nurtured. Again and again she refuses to believe that she is doing anything extraordinary, saying simply, "Why else do we live?" She says this both as a "mother" but also as a symbol of human generosity. That is, she believes that people live to help people.

Reverend Theophilus Msimangu

He is a clergyman at the Mission House in Sophiatown, Johannesburg. A bit of a cynic, Msimangu is extraordinarily compassionate. He offers Stephen reasons for his search and assistance at every step along the way. He is a guide through the city not unlike Virgil who guided Dante through hell in the *Inferno.* And again, like Virgil, he offers explanations for the confusion that Kumalo finds in the city (which itself is set up in a circular pattern not unlike Dante's Hell). For example, Msimangu explains to him the politics of the bus boycott as well as the role of John Kumalo; he opens the eyes of Kumalo to the life that women, like Absalom's girlfriend and Gertrude, lead; he also has a wider understanding of the change occurring in South Africa—an understanding not unlike that of Arthur Jarvis. At the end, he has decided to give up all worldly goods and withdraw to an ascetic life. In doing so, he gives Stephen his life savings. This money not only happily replenishes all that Stephen had to use for the journey, but puts Stephen ahead.

Msimangu, as a guide, is humble, generous, and wise. He is not unbelievably good because, as he admits, God touched him and that's all. At each stage of Stephen's search he handles details, gains information, and leads him to the next stage. He brings him to trial and supports him throughout. Then, with the gift of the money, he is gone from the story though remembered in the prayers of Stephen.

Father Vincent

Father Vincent is a jolly Anglican priest from England who warmly befriends Stephen at the Sophiatown Mission House. Being a foreigner, Father Vincent portrays the European who is sympathetic to the plight of South Africa. He helps Stephen out with prayer and diverts his thoughts onto the beauty of the land. They discuss South Africa and Vincent tells Stephen about England. When Stephen finds his son in prison and sees that he needs a lawyer, he asks Father Vincent for help. Father Vincent goes to the best lawyer for the job—Mr. Carmichael.

Themes

Nature and Its Meaning

The tone of the novel, set from the first paragraph, is like a parable told of a distant place of beauty. Yet within that idyllic setting something is going horribly wrong. By the end of the second paragraph, the tone has changed to show that nature's lush greenness is actually fragile and interdependent with humans. "Destroy it and man is destroyed." *Cry, the Beloved County* is first and foremost the story of a land exploited and left to suffer by a people running after gold. Paton's story contains hope that a balance can be regained by raising awareness about the state of things so that the "natives" will have hope and men like Jarvis will make concessions so as to help them help themselves. It is a hope that the children will not care so much for ownership of the land or things, but for the beauty of the land and for each other.

From the start of Stephen Kumalo's journey to retrieve his family from Johannesburg, there is the unsettling presence of the land. Some critics have said that the land itself is a character in the novel whose pit of illness is the city. First, the land is described as lovely grass and hills, but then attention is drawn to the jarring effect of the road cutting through them. Next, as Kumalo journeys towards the city, the scars of industry are more pervasive as are the burdens on his people. Finally, the city is all noise and pollution and people. Africa is a sick person needing rescue from all those who depend upon it. Like Gertrude, the ill sister Stephen searches for, Africa is calling for

someone to rejuvenate it. However, though Jarvis begins by sending an expert, Mr. Letsitsi, the reader can only hope that the land will have more success than Gertrude.

Clearly, the land's health or illness is isomorphic, that is having similar appearance, to the healthy state of the tribe and the nation. The land is the only concern of the tribal leader since most of his people have left for the city. The land is a common conversational topic amongst black and white farmers who are concerned at the growing length of time between rains. There is something very wrong in Africa, and people feel it. The land is ill and society seems to be out of order with itself. Unfortunately, the people decide to worsen things by increasing the burden on the majority of its population—the non-whites—and by doing little to restore the vitality of the withering beauty of the land.

Fear

Fear, the emotion that never seems to diminish throughout the novel, is ever present to Stephen. He fears for the land, for his son, for Jarvis, for all he sees in the city. Everyday a new fear arises and the greatest is his faith is somehow pointless. This fear is a very important element at a crucial juncture in the novel. At the Mission House they have all just heard the news report of Arthur's death, but it is yet unknown who the culprit is. A sense of foreboding descends and Kumalo says privately to Msimangu, "Here in my heart there is nothing but fear...." Here Paton cleverly broadens the scope of this fear to include people generally.

Chapter twelve opens, "Have no doubt it is fear in the land," and the reader is allowed to know this because Paton provides bits of conversations of white people. The whites fear the blacks, and Kumalo fears that his son may be the one who killed Arthur Jarvis, thus setting off the most recent wave of hysterical paranoia in the city. Then there is the obvious fear of the white man's law and the impossibility of Absalom escaping death.

At the end of the novel, Paton lays all his cards on the table. Through Kumalo he suggests that the only reason Africa is not happy and healthy is fear. It is because people, white and black, are afraid of Kumalo and his wife, the young demonstrator, and Msimangu—afraid that such people would walk upright in the land, might be "free to use the fruits of the land," might sing *Nkosi Sikeleli' iAfrika*, God bless Africa.

Race and Racism

James Jarvis allows the reader the best insight into race relations in South Africa when he reads his son's work. In contrast to Arthur's sensitive theories is the more general outcry over the crime of Absalom. Arthur gives a reason for both the poor state of race relations and general hysteria. In the manuscript Arthur was working on at the time of the crime, Jarvis reads, "The truth is that our civilization is not Christian; it is a tragic compound of great ideal and fearful practice, of high assurance and desperate anxiety, of loving charity and fearful clutching of possessions." In other words, Arthur felt that it was the inaction of able people like himself that allowed South Africa to deteriorate to its present state. Arthur's suggested solution, one that Mr. Letsitsi would appreciate, was the creation of the South African. Indeed, Arthur felt that the biggest problem was that the English bore English, the Afrikaners more Afrikaners, and the natives were general labor. To get around this, a unified South Africa would have to be created. Mr. Letsitsi, on the other side, was working for Africa too—thus he sang the yet little known anthem *Nkosi Sikelel' iAfrika.*

The political rhetoric and the newspapers are not so logical or sober as the writings of Arthur Jarvis. Instead, as the pressure on the state increases due to the migration of blacks from the broken tribes to the city, the whites call for more separation and more exploitation. An effect of this pressure is visible in the hysterical pronouncements made in response to Absalom's crime in chapter twelve. People call for absolute separation by the division of Africa into white and black areas. Others call for the stricter enforcement of pass laws. Well-meaning whites seek to provide more money for education in hopes that this will give blacks more positive goals, thus preventing future crimes. However, none cry for integration, none call for the difficult investigations into the causes of South Africa's woes. Such causes, as Arthur hints, are too deep to be easy. Consequent to these calls, the political party favoring more separation was gaining adherents. In this way, the book prophesied the victory of the National Party. In fact, all throughout the book, the majority of whites are not like Arthur or his father but like Mr. Harrison, who sees the natives as "savage" and not as people with complex personalities and problems like the struggling Kumalo, the intelligent Msimangu, or the motherly Mrs. Lithebe.

Topics for Further Study

- Research the system of apartheid. Find out what the system meant legally as well as culturally and then try to find out the justifications, moral and ethical, for its existence. In what ways was it like Jim Crowism in the American South? In what ways did it differ?

- Watch *Cry Freedom* and compare it to *Cry, the Beloved Country.* Among other similarities, consider to what extent both works are examples of a white sympathizer exploiting black oppression or how they celebrate the role of the white outsider to raise awareness of the downtrodden other.

- Research the international politics of 1948, especially any tensions between the United Nations' Declaration of Human Rights and the installation of Apartheid in South Africa.

- In the last sections of the novel there is a great deal of concern about the environment. Research the problems caused by population displacement and refugee migration in Africa. What is the condition of the environment in South Africa today? Has the land been replenished or has the situation worsened?

- Find out what is going on in South Africa today and consider the place of Paton's novel now that Apartheid has been dismantled.

Style

Point of View

Paton tells his story as if from a dream. The opening, "There is," implies the story is happening right now, though it is not. The use of the present tense makes the story seem distant, yet possible. The story is a third person narrative. The narrator, however, is not omniscient (all-knowing)—only giving necessary information or as much as would be known in the situation. That is, readers do not ever know a great deal about any of the characters, only how they behave given the plot of the story. The words used to tell this story are reminiscent of Biblical language. The prose is simple and intermixed with religious intonations and references. This is due both to the main characters being Anglican clergymen but also because South Africa, as a Christian nation, might best understand itself represented in a parable fashion. Taking this into account adds even more significance to the comments of Arthur Jarvis as well as the overall complex self-reflection of the novel. The novel is aware of itself as novel— as a story being told far from Africa about the affairs of Africa. This distance is also important to the point of view; it may be third person but it is also written far away from the scenes that the author describes. *Cry, the Beloved Country* was popular, in fact, abroad before it was even known at home.

Dialect

The diction of the novel is influenced by the Zulu and Xosa tongues—not surprisingly as the novel takes place amongst members of those peoples colonized by speakers of the English language. Curious phrases from those languages are rendered into English to sound beautiful yet medieval. For example, women who are mature are greeted as "mother"; at parting they say, "go well, stay well" or just "stay well." Today, this choice of prose style sounds old-fashioned. Then again, some critics of the 1940s remarked that Paton was a bit too old-fashioned and sentimental for their taste. Another example of native-influenced syntax is the way simple words are used and repeated: "This thing, he said. This thing. Here in my heart there is nothing but fear. Fear, fear, fear." Such adoption of local dialect is also symptomatic of the author's effort to capture emotion. To capture emotion in words effectively demands simplicity, repetition, and terse exchanges between characters. Thus, rather than come off as patronizing, Paton accomplished emotional density by staying simple and adopting local phrases.

Apostrophe, Aphorism, and Parallelism

Paton's writing has much in common with the style typical of Hebrew poetry. For this reason, *Cry, the Beloved Country* was often said to be quasi-Biblical. Three rhetorical devices found both in the Bible and in Paton's novel are apostrophe, aphorism, and parallelism. For an example of the apostrophe, one need go only so far as the title, taken from a passage within the text. This technique involves the direct address of the inanimate for sympathy or aid. The passage which gives us the title begins, "Cry, the beloved country for the unborn child." That is, the country is being asked to have mercy on the future.

The second device is aphorism. An aphorism is the use of a wise saying. This technique is employed often in the speech of Msimangu. For example, "It suited the white man to break the tribe … but it has not suited him to build something in the place of what is broken." Or again, "It is fear that rules this land." Msimangu is authoritatively pronouncing a wisdom he has discovered through careful reflection.

The third technique occurs when Msimangu gives a sermon in chapter thirteen and the narrator attempts to describe his incredible voice. The narrator does this by a parallelism wherein an object (in this case, Msimangu's voice) is related to many things instead of being defined: "For the voice was of gold, and the voice had love for the words it was reading. The voice shook and beat and trembled, not as the voice of an old man shakes and beats and trembles, but as a deep hollow bell when struck…." Parallelism links descriptive phrases in a series so as to compound the complexity and amplify the impression of the object being described. With these serial phrases, the narrator embellishes the power of the voice by hypothesizing what else the voice does or what else the voice is like. The voice is related to things which the reader already knows to be valuable like "gold" and "love." Due to the associations, the reader imagines that he or she has arrived at the idea of the voice's magnificence independent of the help of the narrator but simultaneously with Kumalo.

Dramatic Irony

Dramatic irony is a moment of high drama that occurs when at least one character is lacking information known to the reader. Paton employs this technique expertly in chapter twenty-five when, by chance, Kumalo and Jarvis meet. Jarvis has no idea who the black clergyman is. The two fathers meet at Barbara Smith's on a day when the court is not in session. Kumalo is looking for Sibeko's daughter who was rumored to have worked there. It is on this errand for Sibeko that Stephen finds the father of his son's victim. Jarvis, however, sees only a poor, old, black clergyman. For the reader, as for Stephen, this is a highly charged encounter precisely because one of the participants is unaware of the identity of the other.

Historical Context

Post-World War II

Though World War II had been over for several years, the war was still in the minds of people

An example of the poor housing conditions for native Africans in Johannesburg, South Africa, where Gertrude and Stephen Kumalo live in Alan Paton's book Cry, the Beloved Country.

all over the globe in 1948. The economies of nations directly involved in the war were still recovering and the United States Congress voted for the implementation of the 1947 Marshall Plan to help rebuild Europe. Meanwhile, the Soviet Union and the United States were beginning what Bernard Baruch, advisor to President Truman, called the "Cold War." The first action of this war began where World War II ended. Soviet forces blockaded access to Berlin on June 24, 1948. In a nonviolent act to ignore the blockade, the United States and Britain countered with a great airlift of 4,500 tons of food and necessities per day until the Soviets allowed normal transit to return on September 30, 1949. At home, this "cold war" fueled political suspicion by the formation of the "Un-American Activities Committee." This committee was formed to investigate anyone who had Communist affiliations. The most famous 1948 case before this committee involved Alger Hiss. The case is still controversial today though Hiss is dead and Moscow has said he was never a spy.

As the two superpowers began their arms race, the colonies of the British empire began to struggle for independence. India struggled free with the help of Mahatma Gandhi, who was once a resident and prisoner of South Africa. In 1948, Gandhi was assassinated by those resentful of his allowance of partition with Pakistan. Other newly independent nations included Burma and Israel.

Apartheid in South Africa

South Africa was formed in 1910 when the former British colonies of Natal and the Cape joined with the republics of Transvaal and the Orange Free State. It was at this time that the descendants of early Dutch speaking settlers began to refer to themselves as Afrikaners, their dialect as Afrikaans, and their party as the Afrikaner Nationalists. Yet another force in South Africa in 1910 was the African population that outnumbered the whites, were still largely tribal in their political makeup, and lived in rural communities. However, a population shift was occurring that mirrored population shifts everywhere—away from the traditional rural community to the city. In South Africa, due to the dramatic expansions of mining and industry in general, that meant a shift to Johannesburg. This large city was built upon the mining fields where gold had been discovered in 1886.

The Afrikaner Nationalists ruled South Africa from 1924 until 1939. In that year, the liberal agenda of men like Jan H. Hofmeyr took over and people began to have hope that South Africa would

Compare
&
Contrast

- **1948:** Winning the national election, the National Party institutes a system of apartheid, officially segregating the black majority from the white minority.

  Today: Nelson Mandela, having served twenty-seven years in prison, is sworn in as the President of South Africa in 1994. In 1996 he signs the new Constitution which, among other things, guarantees equal treat ment before the law for all citizens—black or white.

- **1948:** Those in opposition to Apartheid policies take hope in a brighter future by singing *Nkosi Sikelel' iAfrika.*

  Today: The anthem of hope, *Nkosi Sikelel' iAfrika,* has become the national anthem of South Africa.

- **1948:** The British Empire is crumbling as former colonies declare independence.

  Today: The Soviet Union has collapsed and its republics have declared independence.

be a more equitable and just society. World War II began and South Africa fought on the side of the Allies against the Germans. After the war there was an even greater influx of Africans into the cities and into Johannesburg. It is at the post-World War II moment that Alan Paton sets his novel *Cry, The Beloved Country.* As that novel showed, there were two sides to South Africa in 1945. On one side were the Africans struggling to carve out a living in shanty towns or in rural areas whose soil was depleted. White men like Arthur Jarvis were awakening to the problems that inequality had created and joined with other whites to do what was possible to improve the situation of the natives. On the other side, the influx of people and the increase in crime in the city created a degree of paranoia amongst the enfranchised citizens. Thus in the election year of 1948, after the death of Hofmeyr, the Afrikaner Nationalists were voted back to power because they promised to restore order.

In 1948, the Afrikaner Nationalists began a system of government called apartheid. This system was similar in many ways to Jim Crow discrimination policies in America against African Americans. However, one very important difference was that it was a national policy legally discriminating on the basis of race. Under this system native Africans lived in designated areas and were required to carry "passes" and identity papers on them at all times. The inability to provide an enquiring official with one's papers meant jail or

fines. These passes said where the individual could go. Generally, the system of apartheid aimed to keep the nonwhite people living under South African rule a disciplined pool of workers. Thus they did not tolerate dissent or organization into labor unions or political parties. They did so by imprisoning men like Nelson Mandela and Steven Biko for crimes against the state. Recently, Nelson Mandela was released from prison, resumed his political place as head of the African National Congress, and was elected President of South Africa. In 1996, he signed a new constitution for the Republic of South Africa.

Critical Overview

The critical reputation of *Cry, the Beloved Country* in the international community has been overwhelmingly positive. Alan Paton's novel, both written and submitted to publishers while on a tour, received much praise the moment it was released. It sold out on its first day of appearance and entered its sixth print run by the end of the year. Back home in South Africa, however, the newly independent Paton was not so warmly embraced. The novel was critical of the new regime and Afrikaners because of their narrow vision and fear-ridden pride. Conversely, black South Africans could never forgive Paton for being a white and could never see the book as anything but a parable written by a white man—sympathetic though he was. The most positive reviewer from this camp was Dennis Brutus, a poet who was a prison inmate with Nelson Mandela. Brutus attributed a new sort of writing in South Africa to Paton and his novel. Paton, said Brutus, set in motion a writing that viewed apartheid critically in such a way as to move people and awaken them to our blight of inhumanity. Unfortunately, Brutus's valuation was retrospective as well as a minority opinion. Martin Tucker, in his book *Africa in Modern Literature,* said that few writers were indebted to Paton. Even so, *Cry, the Beloved Country* outsold all other books except the Bible in South Africa.

Though the first print run was small, the critics picked up the novel and sounded its triumph. The *New York Times Review,* the *New York Herald Tribune Weekly Book Review,* and the *Yale Review* were all enthusiastic in 1948 when the novel was released. They applauded the new sense of lyricism which Paton had brought English literature by the adoption of the Zulu and Xosa syntax. They praised the breadth of the subject matter yet simple style of the book. While still positive, there were those critics who seemed to miss the point of the novel. One example was Harold C. Gardiner's review in which he says, "the story is preeminently one of individuals. There are no sweeping and grandiose statements about 'the race problem.'" Apparently, he would have preferred a normal protest novel to the more poetic parable Paton wrote.

In 1957, Sheridan Baker wrote an interpretive article which found that the geography of Paton's story was not only symbolic but that it was the same type of Christian allegory to be found in Bunyan's *The Pilgrim's Progress* and Dante's *Divine Comedy.* This would not have been so bad, says Edward Callahan in his 1991 book, but Baker used his idea about Paton's work in an educational packet wherein children were instructed by Baker to make ludicrous associations in the novel. Fortunately, the article by Harry A. Gailey entitled "Sheridan Baker's 'Paton's Beloved Country,'" in which Gailey says that the interpretation of Baker is textually baseless, is also included in the anthology of Baker.

A more rational approach to the novel was close by. Edmund Fuller wrote glowingly of the novel in his *Man in Modern Fiction.* There he wrote that *Cry, the Beloved Country* "is a great and dramatic novel because Alan Paton, in addition to his skill of workmanship sees with clear eyes both good and evil, differentiates them, pitches them in conflict with each other, and takes sides." Thus, while moving only slightly beyond the obvious

praise for Paton's political stance, a critic was seeing the story as that of an individual quest for meaning and not just a political protest.

Most criticism of the book simply sides with Paton due to the political tension of the work. In fact, there is little variation amongst the reviewers when it comes to what it is in the novel which deserves praise. Mostly, it was felt that the quasi-Biblical language of the novel was an emotional catalyst that helped to place the reader on the side of the Kumalos and only secondarily with the Jarvis family. Typical of these reviews is that by Edwin Bruell in "Keen Scalpel on Racial Ills." In that article he compared Paton's novel with Harper Lee's *To Kill a Mockingbird* because both novels present children as the innocent victims of society's molding forces. Another review by Myron Matlaw in *Arcadia* simply sums up the critical view of Paton: "Understatement, deceptive simplicity, repetition, selectivity of narrative, episode, and setting, as well as the emotional charge of Paton's style—all these are manifested in Paton's characters as well."

In a recent book by Edward Callan, *Cry, the Beloved Country: A Novel of South Africa,* the view is taken that the book is a classic because of its endurance. After forty years and two movies, Paton's novel is still widely read. He also cites the work as having a universal appeal because of its poetic language and its theme of human responsibility. The setting for the novel, adds Callan, has changed incredibly in that span of time but he makes no prediction about how this will affect the reception of the work.

Criticism

Sharon Cumberland

In the following essay, Cumberland, an assistant professor at Seattle University, asserts that although Cry, the Beloved Country *was written by a white man, it successfully and artistically presents in human terms the plight of native African people suffering under apartheid.*

Cry, the Beloved Country made a tremendous impact on the international community when it was first published in 1947 by showing, in human terms, the effects of apartheid on its victims. "Apartheid" means "apartness" in Afrikaans, the language spoken by the white descendants of Dutch people who settled in the region now known as South Africa. Once known as Boers, these Afrikaners instituted

What Do I Read Next?

- First published in 1965, *117 Days: An Account of Confinement and Interrogation under South African Ninety-Day Detention Law,* is Ruth First's account of her imprisonment by the Government of South Africa. She was the wife of Joe Slovo, leader of the Communist Party in South Africa, and one of the first to be imprisoned during the crackdown of the 1960s. After her release, she continued to oppose the government until a letter bomb killed her in 1982. Her story of imprisonment is the story of a white South African who opposed apartheid.

- A recent account of South Africa's treatment of blacks is the 1987 novel by John Briley, *Cry Freedom.* Later made into a film by the same title, this work tells the true story of Donald Wood, a concerned white journalist, who is trying to interview Steven Biko. Unfortunately, Biko is imprisoned by the government and dies while in jail. Lately, amidst amnesty hearings in South Africa, it has been revealed that he was killed by the guards just as human rights defenders had always claimed.

- Although Nelson Mandela signed a new constitution into existence in South Africa, Albie Sachs's writings on the issues of such an undertaking are still worth reading. His *Protecting Human Rights In a New South Africa,* printed in 1991, is interesting because he explains the legal and social complexities inherent in the writing of a constitution which will safeguard all of South Africa's people.

- Information on Apartheid housing policies can be gained from *Homes Apart: South Africa's Segregated Cities,* published in 1991. Editor Anthony Lemon details the way in which, "South African cities were established by white settlers, who regarded the cities as their cultural domain." Therefore, the settlements were always thought of as a permanent situation of racial separation in order to guard the purity of white culture.

- For further information on the environmental problem in South Africa, see *Apartheid's Environmental Toll* by Alan B. Durning, released by the World Watch Institute. This work details the environmental policy of the National Party since its victory in 1948.

- A good feel for daily life in apartheid Africa, can be gained from the play *Woza Albert!,* published in 1983. This play by Percy Mtwa, Mbongeni Ngema, and Barney Simon depicts the average experiences in South Africa from riding the train to working for white bosses.

- Paton's 1953 novel *Too Late the Phalarope* focuses on the effects South Africa's Immorality Act of 1927 has on private lives. Afrikaner Pieter van Vlaanderen violates the Immorality Act by having an affair with a black woman, is sent to jail, and shunned by his family. *Too Late the Phalarope* demonstrates to readers how the South African system of apartheid degrades all citizens.

---

a system of rigid segregation between the black tribal people and the white settlers. White supremacy allowed the Afrikaaners and white people of other nationalities to become wealthy on the natural resources in South Africa, using tribal people for cheap labor.

The evil consequences of the apartheid system in South Africa were widely understood as political phenomena in 1947. Yet Alan Paton evoked the dilemma of tribal people so movingly that no one

who read his novel could fail to understand from an emotional point of view the terrible injustices built into the legal system—a system which held sway in South Africa until 1990. Though *Cry, the Beloved Country* stands alone as a compelling plot with memorable characters, it is a book which needs to be placed in historical context to achieve its full impact.

Alan Paton (1903-1983) was a white man of English descent, raised in Natal, a region of South

Africa which is the "beloved country" of the title. South Africa as a whole can also be understood to be the "beloved country" for which its natives, both white and black, must "cry," or weep for in sorrow and guilt. Paton understood that racial injustice, in which the blacks, who made up seventy percent of the country's population, worked to enrich the white Afrikaaners. It was a crime which led all South Africans, and especially the black natives, to disastrous consequences.

South Africa's history is the history of European colonialism in Africa. The Dutch East India Company came to the region in 1652 and began to displace the Bantu-speaking black Africans who lived there. Dutch farmers (Boers) who came from the Netherlands to settle the South African interior engaged in a long series of wars with the Xhosa people. But they were displaced in turn when the British took over the region in 1814. The Boers then settled even farther inland in Natal, the Orange Free State, and the Transvaal. When diamonds and gold were discovered in these regions in the 1860s and 1880s, making them more attractive for business than for farming, the British attempted to take over the regions. This prompted the Boer War (1899-1902). The British won the war and established the Union of South Africa in 1910. South Africa gained its independence from Britain in 1931. When the Boers, now called Afrikaaners, assumed power from England, they imposed the most strict apartheid laws, isolating the black natives in "homelands" which deprived them of their civil rights, as well as their ability to achieve economic and social stability.

When Paton wrote *Cry, the Beloved Country,* it was not clear how South Africa would solve the increasing injustices between its black and white inhabitants. Paton achieved two purposes in his novel. He depicted these injustices by showing how white commercialism dismantled the tribal customs which had given the black natives their stability, and he proposed an alternative to apartheid that was moral and religious rather than political. Through the reconciliation of his black protagonist, Stephen Kumalo, with the white land owner, James Jarvis, Paton proposes that natural charity and justice will emerge when members of both races see each other as fully human.

Paton did not merely write novels to propose solutions. He became actively involved in implementing his vision by helping to found the Liberal Party in South Africa in 1953. With the worldwide prestige, income, and authority he gained from the success of *Cry, the Beloved Country,* Paton was able to join with others to fight the increasingly harsh laws that limited Bantu education, access to jobs, freedom of movement, and property rights. At the same time, however, the African National Congress (ANC), originally formed in 1912, initiated the mass movements against the white regime that led eventually to armed conflict and guerrilla warfare. For forty years the ANC led the fight for black rights, resulting in the National Conference in 1991 at which Nelson Mandela was elected president. Mandela became the leader of the Government of National Unity in South Africa, which seeks to exercise justice for all races. Though Paton's hope for nonviolent change for his "beloved country" died with the failure of the Liberal Party, he is still credited with bringing powerful force to early efforts to organize reform.

Reading *Cry, the Beloved Country* is like reading a certain type of poetry, in that every word has significance and beauty. It is not a novel to be skimmed or read rapidly, even though it is fairly short. It is a book to be savored for its truthfulness, its carefulness, and its importance.

Cry, the Beloved Country is truly unique because it does not follow in a literary tradition, nor does it launch a tradition. Later South African authors who have gained the world stage, such as Nadine Gordimer, Athol Fugard, and Andre Brink, have been writing in an environment of open hostility between blacks and whites after the militarization of the African National Congress. Since *Cry, the Beloved Country* predates this period, it stands alone as an appeal for peaceful reconciliation between the races—a stance which the later authors could not realistically take. It also stands alone as a work about suffering and love that is timeless in its relevance to the human condition. Fifty years after its publication, when many of the worst offenses addressed in *Cry, the Beloved Country* are being solved by the Government of National Unity in South Africa, it is still a work to be read and cherished by new generations.

It is significant that in the novel the symbol of a hopeful future is situated in a white child. Though Paton appropriates the voice of a black minister, Stephen Kumalo, to tell most of his story, Paton himself is white. His lifetime of living among the Zulu gave him the authority to adopt Kumalo's voice accurately in terms of its particular sound and expression. In 1947, before the multicultural movement in literary theory, such an appropriation of voice would not be questioned, especially when it is done as well as Paton does it. Today, however, the critical reader must always be aware that the black voice is subject to the agenda of the white author.

For instance, one can speculate that the mind of the white man intrudes into his black characters at certain points when the black characters notice the generosity of white drivers during the bus strike, when they accept the decisions of white authority figures like Father Vincent without question, and when they seek for reconciliation with white characters such as James Jarvis. When compared to black African authors such as Chinua Achebe, the reader can see that Paton wishes to highlight those attributes upon which racial reconciliation can be built rather than simply to paint the terrible destructiveness of racial injustice. Thus, Paton's symbol for the next generation, the white child who reflects his father's respect for the Zulu, is a distinctly white perception of peace. One can speculate that a black writer on the same subject would see the hope of South Africa in a black child, one who might grow up in a country in which Africans had reclaimed their land from white intruders, and who might turn to tribal belief systems for their values rather than the transplanted Christian values which predominate in Paton's novel. There is no sense of irony in Paton's narration, for instance, that the broken tribes are broken, in part, by the imposition of a non-native religion.

The greatest theme of *Cry, the Beloved Country* is the Christian reconciliation of the races in the face of almost unforgivable sin. How can the black natives ever forgive white people for stealing their country and its resources while destroying their culture? On the other hand, how can white people ever come to face the enormity of their crimes, especially when the initial crimes were not committed by those who are living now? How can white South Africans not regard the land as their own when they and their ancestors have lived on it since 1652? Before a peaceful solution can be found, a race war might break out. As the character Msimangu says about the white people, "I have one great fear in my heart, that one day when they are turned to loving they will find that we are turned to hating."

This theme is expressed in three subthemes that can be described as "memory," "breaking the tribes," and "secrets." It is the memory of Ixopo that gives Kumalo strength while he is in the alien and evil city, because the hills and valleys of the "beloved country" represent the order and stability of the tribe. Likewise, it is the memory of his son Arthur that compels James Jarvis to overcome his prejudice and loathing in order to achieve under-

standing of his radical racial views and to carry on his son's work for racial justice.

The breaking of the tribes is a disaster brought on by several forces, including the relentless drought that forced agricultural people into the cities, as well as the exploitation of those people by the white mine owners. In Book I the reader can see the devastation in every character which is brought about by the breakdown of tribal customs. In Book II it is clear that the white "tribe" has thrived on the destruction of the black tribes, who have provided the white people with their maids, laborers, and mine workers. Paton suggests that a new tribe must rise out of this cycle of destruction and exploitation: a tribe based upon mutual respect between black and white. How this respect is to develop is a "secret"—one of the mysteries of life that will only be clear when it manifests itself in leaps of faith and acts of generosity.

As Kumalo tries to come to terms with the execution of his son for the murder of Jarvis' son— a crime which the reader understands to be the product of the breaking of the tribe—he turns away from what appear to be irreconcilable mysteries: the persistence of happiness under such conditions and the resilience of people who have suffered beyond endurance. When he fears he will lose his faith, Father Vincent tells him not to dwell on injustice: "And do not pray for yourself, and do not pray to understand the ways of God. For they are secret. Who knows what life is, for life is a secret." This theme is taken up at the end of the book, which ends on this note: "But when that dawn will come, of our emancipation, from the fear of bondage and the bondage of fear, why, that is a secret." Though it is a mystery why some people dominate and sin against others, it is also a mystery why there is forgiveness, reconciliation, and reform. Paton tries to show the progress of such sin and forgiveness in the Jarvis and Kumalo families as a model for the entire nation. Because the characters are so fully realized, their stories become models of suffering and reconciliation for all times and places.

Source: Sharon Cumberland, in an essay for *Novels for Students,* Gale, 1998.

Edward Callan

In the following excerpt, Callan examines the variety of literary styles Paton employs in Cry, the Beloved Country, *and provides a plot summary.*

It would be difficult to imagine a landscape or a point on the earth's surface so different in every way from South Africa as Trondheim, Norway. Yet it may have been fortunate for the artist in Alan Paton that Trondheim was the place where he undertook to compose *Cry, the Beloved Country*. This was not because of any direct influence other than that of loneliness and longing for home. True, he had read John Steinbeck's *The Grapes of Wrath* in Stockholm, and his sidetrip to Norway was prompted by a wish to visit the countryside depicted in Knut Hamsun's grimly realistic novel *Growth of the Soil;* but he says [in *Towards the Mountain* (1980)] he did not consciously adapt anything from either work except Steinbeck's "style of rendering conversations, indicating by a preliminary dash that a speech was about to begin, and omitting all inverted commas." What may have mattered more was that distance permitted a perspective that allowed him to see his own country and the struggles of its diverse peoples as a whole. It is essentially this overall point of view that makes *Cry, the Beloved Country* a unique artistic object: a dramatic manifestation of the agony of a country in which the spirit of South Africa hovers always on stage and dominates the human actors like the ever-present, threatening and life-giving force of the sea in J. M. Synge's play *Riders to the Sea.*

Many readers of *Cry, the Beloved Country* are struck by the simplicity of its language and the rhythmic quality of its prose style. Some of its rhythms—dependent on parallel phrases and repetitions—evoke translations of the Psalms. Because of this, the style of *Cry, the Beloved Country* has frequently been described as "biblical." This description is only partly accurate because it implies that Paton's is a naturally rhythmic style, and that the whole novel is written in one style.

But the novel has a wide variety of styles. The element that may strike readers first as having a flavor of originality is the evocation of the rhythms of Zulu speech that appears, chiefly, in Stephen Kumalo's speech and thought, and in dialogue among African characters. For an obvious contrast, however, one should look at the style of the elder Harrison in Book Two. Harrison is almost a caricature of the typical colonialist-minded United Party man from Johannesburg's English-speaking commercial community, hidebound by prejudice. He parrots hackneyed ideas about "the native problem." He speaks almost wholly in clichés, and is quite incapable of examining them from a fresh viewpoint. He is like the "stone age" neighbor in Robert Frost's "Mending Wall," who cannot go behind his father's saying: "Good fences make good neighbors."

For a stylistic counterpoint to Harrison's conventional commonplaces, one should turn to the documents left behind by the murdered man, Arthur Jarvis. Anyone familiar with the writings of Alfred Hoernlé—whose spirit frequently walks abroad in the novel—would probably recognize in their trenchant arguments, not only echoes of the ideas, but of the personal "synoptic" style that Hoernlé sought to develop. One could pursue these instances of characterization through style further: to the speech of James Jarvis, for instance, or of the village schoolmaster in Ndotsheni, and find that Paton's ear seems extraordinarily well tuned to the varied rhythms of speech, and also that he employs differences in speech patterns to give individuality to his characters, and to the cacophonous voices that clamor in his choruses.

Even though *Cry, the Beloved Country* is not written in one style and rhythm but in many styles and rhythms, there is, nonetheless, a dominant style associated with the book. This is the pattern of speech with a marked poetic quality accorded to Kumalo and the African characters generally, and also to some extent employed in the lyric passages voiced from outside the action. This quality, depending to a degree on the sound and syntax of spoken Zulu, can be viewed as a poetic invention designed to carry over into English the effects of the sound and idiom of African speech....

The plot of *Cry, the Beloved Country* combines three related quests corresponding largely to Book One, Book Two, and Book Three of the work itself. Book One, the Book of Kumalo, is concerned at first with the physical quest of the Reverend Stephen Kumalo, who travels from the African village of Ndotsheni to Johannesburg in search of his sister Gertrude, his son Absalom, and his brother John, who have all "disappeared" in the metropolis. His guide to these regions of lost people is another Anglican priest, a fellow Zulu of wholly different background, the Reverend Theophilus Msimangu. Msimangu, as has been pointed out, is a man with a deep philosophic bent and clear logical mind whose secular hero was the sharp-witted philosopher Alfred Hoernlé. He guides Kumalo down among the lost people as Virgil guided Dante through the infernal regions, opening his eyes and his understanding to the meaning of enigmatic things. They find Stephen's sister Gertrude, his brother John, and, finally, his son Absalom, only to discover that he is the confessed murderer of Arthur Jarvis.

Book Two is the Book of James Jarvis, father of the murdered man. He sets out from the closed mental world of his own habitual assumptions and prejudices and seeks to understand the liberal spirit revealed to him in his son's reputation and writings. Again, on the analogy of Virgil led by Dante, James Jarvis, "seeking his way out of the fog into which he has been born," is guided by the voice of his dead son who had "journeyed … into strange waters" and set down his philosophy in "A Private Essay on the Evolution of a South African."

Book Three is the Book of Restoration. In it, the physical and psychological quests of the earlier books turn toward the spiritual path of redemption. This is the region where, after guiding him through the horrors of hell and the mount of purgatory, Virgil left Dante to proceed alone with no guide but love.

In Book One, Stephen Kumalo journeys to Johannesburg and experiences manifestations of good and evil in this strange new industrial world. He is robbed, and he is treated with kindness; he visits places of despair like Claremont where he finds his sister Gertrude, and places of hope like Ezenzeleni where the blind are rehabilitated; he witnesses his brother John's self-seeking corruption and Msimangu's selfless dedication; he becomes aware, too, of conflicting good and evil impulses within himself. He is a good man seeking lost sheep, yet he lies to his fellow-passengers on the train to protect his self-esteem; and he is cruel to the nameless girl who is to bear Absalom's child, as he is later cruel to his brother John whose cunning has saved his own son at Absalom's expense.

In Book Two the reader observes James Jarvis's deep experience as he returns again and again to the writings on social justice left by his murdered son. These papers argue the case for racial conciliation in South Africa from the Christian and liberal standpoint that Paton shared with Jan Hofmeyr. They open James Jarvis's eyes for the first time to the real plight of both rural and urban Africans—the destruction of their tribal social organization without provision for its replacement by something better: "It was permissible to allow the destruction of a tribal system that impeded the growth of the country…. But it is not permissible to watch its destruction, and to replace it by nothing, or by so little, that a whole people degenerates, physically and morally." They also open his eyes to the need for restitution and restoration: "Our civilization has therefore an inescapable duty to set up another system of order and tradition and convention.…"

The writings of his son's hero, Abraham Lincoln, guide James Jarvis in deciding the form the memorial to his dead son should take, for he returns more than once to the Gettysburg Address, in which he encounters: "It is rather for us to be here dedicated to the great task remaining before us—that from these honored dead we take increased devotion to that cause for which they gave the last full measure of devotion; that we here highly resolve that these dead shall not have died in vain.…"

James Jarvis realizes that his son had journeyed into deep waters, but he also realizes that he must honor and carry forward his son's work as far as it is possible for him to do so. He is not equipped to do his son's work, but he does "the next best thing." He therefore gives practical financial help to the African Boys' Club and to the drought-stricken village of Ndotsheni. And he learns to respect the sufferings of the old man whose son had murdered his son.

The theme of restoration pervades Book Three on several levels. There is a beginning made on the restoration of the land through the work of a young agricultural demonstrator; there is the restoration of Kumalo's leaky village church through the generosity of James Jarvis; and this, in turn, is a halting step towards the restoration of brotherhood—one human being reaching out toward another across the barriers of fear and prejudice. The climax of the theme of spiritual restoration is reached when Kumalo, who in Book One neared despair, makes his lone pilgrimage to the mountaintop to share his son's agony on the morning set for his execution.

Book Three, seeking to evoke a Christian sensibility, may be open to the dual danger of uncritical applause from those who share Paton's faith, and to charges of sentimentality from those who do not. Yet Paton does not permit the reader either to applaud Jarvis's "conversion" or to smile tolerantly on it as a matter beyond the limits of practical sociological concern. At this very point in the novel he quite deliberately raises the question: "What courses of action are the concern of a practical man, and what courses of action are impractical?" His answer ironically contrasts two ways of undertaking the relief of present suffering.

One way is to hope for an ideal, utopian solution through the intervention of some agent of authority or impersonal force, such as the state, equipped with blueprints and long-range theories. Another way is, meanwhile, to do "the next best thing" and take those practical steps, however small, that lie within reach. The "good" characters in the novel do not accept evils passively. They act, not only for "humanitarian" reasons, but because as human beings they are involved in mankind, and are in a real sense their brothers' keepers. It is, indeed, a simple personal action—an assumption of the responsibility of priestly brotherhood that opens up the whole Pandora's box: namely, Msimangu's letter to Kumalo informing him of his sister Gertrude's "sickness." Kumalo learns in Johannesburg that he, too, bears a measure of personal responsibility for alleviating suffering; and must *act* like Msimangu, and the people at Ezenzeleni and the reformatory, and like Dubula who set up Shanty Town. He decides on the unprecedented, if unrewarding, step of seeking an interview with the chief to propose some practical steps to alleviate the suffering caused in Ndotsheni by the drought. And he does this because "the great city had opened his eyes to something that had been begun and must now be continued."

Next he seeks out the headmaster of the local school, where, as the chief reminded him, "we have been teaching these things for many years." There is a fine irony in Paton's portrait of the headmaster that satirizes the impracticality of theoretical schemes. Paton even employs a singsong rhythm—like those who parrot, by rote, things uncomprehended—that mocks the headmaster: "his office was filled with notices in blue and red and green." When Kumalo sought his advice about practical measures, he was answered in theoretical educational jargon pitifully far removed from reality: "The headmaster explained that the school was trying to relate the life of the child to the life of the community, and showed him circulars from the Department in Pietermaritzburg, all about these matters. He took Kumalo out into the blazing sun, and showed him the school gardens, but this was an academic lecture, for there was no water, and everything was dead." It is against this background of futile, high-sounding schemes and theories that Jarvis's simple, practical act of providing milk for the sick children is set with purposeful, yet profound, irony. For it was not only because of the drought that "there was no water, and everything was dead"; but, symbolically, because the schemes and theories themselves were arid. It is only when Jarvis and Kumalo meet humbly as two human beings, each aware of the weight of the other's suffering, and therefore of their common humanity, that the drought breaks and the rain comes at last to the valley of Ndotsheni.

Paton's *Cry, the Beloved Country* offers no blueprint for a utopian society. It offers instead recognition of personal responsibility. The crucial

development in the characters of both Jarvis and Kumalo is that each comes to recognize how individual fear or indifference infects society with moral paralysis; and that the antidote for this paralysis is individual courage willing to go forward in faith. They do not wait, therefore, for some miraculous healing of this paralysis to be brought about by the direct intervention of God, or through the implementation of some scheme for a final solution, or through the flowering of the promises of some manifesto. They act by taking whatever steps are possible to them as individuals in the immediate present. A road taken in faith has no certainty of arrival; if it did, faith would be unnecessary. *Cry, the Beloved Country,* therefore, rightly concludes with an acceptance of uncertainty: "But when the dawn will come of our emancipation, from the fear of bondage and the bondage of fear, why, that is a secret."

Source: Edward Callan, "Of Faith and Fear: *Cry, the Beloved Country*," in his *Alan Paton*, revised edition, G. K. Hall & Company, 1982, pp. 32–41.

Fred H. Marcus

In the following excerpt, Marcus explores the hopeful and optimistic aspects of Cry, the Beloved Country.

[*Cry, the Beloved Country*] emerges out of the racial problems in South Africa. We must assess it—not for its sociological content, nor outside its sociological content—as a work of art attempting to recreate experience in a world ordered by the writer. [In his introduction to *Cry, the Beloved Country,* Scribner's, 1948] Lewis Gannett credits the novel with being "... unashamedly innocent and subtly sophisticated. It is a story; it is a prophecy; it is a psalm." His observations merit comment. The words *prophecy* and *psalm* imply a Biblical quality. Even a relatively unsophisticated reader will sense the Biblical roll of the language, the Old Testament-sounding place names, and the technique of sonorous repetition, in which the plaintive cry of humanity merges with a paean of hope for a brighter tomorrow. The opening sentence of Book I—a sentence repeated in the opening of Book II— combines simplicity and directness with a rhythmic pulse. "There is a lovely road that runs from Ixopo into the hills." The breaks after *road* and *Ixopo* are natural and inevitable—establishing a simple chant through intonation. If this is the beginning of a love song, a drumming yet tender cadence of geographical loveliness, the tenderness applies even to the unpleasant. The grass which is not kept, or guarded, or cared for—in the valleys where the natives live—"... no longer keeps men, guards men, cares for men. The titihoya does not cry here any more." For Alan Paton the love song remains tender, but more and more forlorn. "The great red hills stand desolate, and the earth has turned away like flesh.... the dead streams come to life, full of the red blood of the earth." This is a poetry of compassion filled with wailing, notes of desolation and sadness. The short first chapter closes, "They are valleys of old men and old women, of mothers and children. The men are away, the young men and the girls are away. The soil cannot keep them any more." The psalm embedded in the novel yearns forth, "Cry for the broken tribe.... Cry, the beloved country.... The sun pours down on the earth, on the lovely land that man cannot enjoy. He knows only the fear of his heart."...

While the details of Alan Paton's novel encourage the flaring up of anger at man's inhumanity to man, the prevalent tone is hopeful. Africans are exploited, mistreated, harried unmercifully; the whites are responsible for unfair land distribution, slum growth, unjust laws, and the disintegration of native tribal structure. Against this background of provocation, Msimangu, a black priest, speaks the most significant words of the novel: "I have one great fear in my heart, that one day when they turn to loving they will find we are turned to hating." In the baleful light of reality these words are incredible. Yet, like Steinbeck before him—whose novel, *The Grapes of Wrath*, spurred the writing of *Cry, the Beloved Country*—Paton portrays people as a wonderful mixture of toughness and tenderness, men and women who love and lose their land but are revitalized by man's unquenchable humanity.

Nor can Alan Paton be dismissed as a sentimentalist. If the attitudes above sound "unashamedly innocent," that is because Christian doctrine about loving one's neighbor is rarely consistent with practice. *Cry, the Beloved Country* confronts the paradox of love and fear coexisting in South Africa. It confronts the inevitable complexity of human beings torn by conflicting principles. For example, Msimangu, who fears the turning of love to hate, preaches with a voice of gold.

> Yet he is despised by some.... They say he preaches of a world not made by hands, while in the streets about him men struggle and suffer and die. They ask what folly it is that can so seize upon a man, what folly it is that so seizes upon so many of their people, making the hungry patient, the suffering content, the dying at peace? And how fools listen to him,

silent, enrapt, sighing when he is done, feeding their empty bellies on his empty words.

And from Paton's point of view this picture of Msimangu has some validity. Contrasting with Msimangu in the novel is John Kumalo, a carpenter, owner of his own shop, a resident of the sinful city of Johannesburg. John stands for a more militant philosophy. He believes that "... what God has not done for South Africa, man must do." John understands the political and economic power structure; he recognizes the profit motive underlying the exploitation of native labor; he even recognizes the techniques of subjugation designed to keep the black man in his place. He says,

> I do not say we are free here ... at least I am free of the chief ... an old and ignorant man, who is nothing but a white man's dog.... the Church too is like the chief.... It is true that the Church speaks with a fine voice, and that the Bishops speak against the laws. But this they have been doing for fifty years, and things get worse, not better.

It would be impossible not to recognize the validity of much of John Kumalo's argument. Yet, Paton presents John Kumalo as "cunning," as a self-seeking, self-aggrandizing man who seeks power but lacks courage. His "great voice growls" in his "bull throat" and he symbolizes a potential native leader with the raw power to awaken his fellow Africans. But the policemen who have heard his speeches stand relaxed. They know he can paint "... pictures of Africa awakening from sleep, of Africa resurgent, of Africa dark and savage.... But the man is afraid, and the deep thundering growl dies down...." Even Msimangu concedes that many of John Kumalo's statements are true. But he perceives the essential corruption of the man's bid for power. "Perhaps we should thank God he is corrupt," he adds; "... if he were not corrupt, he could plunge this country into bloodshed. He is corrupted by his possessions, and he fears their loss, and the loss of the power he already has." Paton's characterization recognizes the complexity of people. Msimangu—whom he approves—symbolizes a theology comfortable to Paton; John Kumalo—whom he disapproves—symbolizes a political and economic awareness attractive to Paton. Kumalo might plunge South Africa into revolt if he had the courage. Paton finds this possibility abhorrent; he hopes for evolutionary progress. Msimangu preaches golden words; yet as a spokesman for love and religion, he represents little immediate pragmatic hope. At the end of the novel he retires to a monastic order, thus forfeiting a share in the continuing struggle. Yet even this detail contains a paradox. He will join a white communal group—thus symbolically helping to unravel another strand of the color line between men.

Early in the novel Msimangu says, "I am not a man for segregation, but it is a pity that we are not apart." The statement calls for segregation despite the speaker's demurrer. Msimangu is torn between a theoretical position disavowing segregated living and the emotional impact of real injustices with immediate impact. In one specific scene white men come to the aid of Africans. During a native boycott of buses a white man offers Msimangu and Stephen Kumalo free transportation. Later, when another white man renders the same help to black men, a policeman attempts to interfere. The white man challenges him, "Take me to court." In each of these incidents Msimangu marvels at the existence of brotherly love in action—almost as though his ritual preaching were words without application in actual instances. His incredulity belies his idealism. Stephen Kumalo's response to this latter incident conforms to Paton's affection for the innocent. "Kumalo's face wore the smile, the strange smile not known in other countries, of a black man who sees one of his people helped in public by a white man, for such a thing is not lightly done." The force of conformity to maintain an unjust *status quo* recurs in the novel. The upsetting of such conformity also recurs—thus giving support to Paton's optimism, an optimism sometimes hard-pressed by blatant injustice.

One dramatic symbol in the novel helps to crystallize the South African quandary and laissez-faire solution. The language reads like a parable:

> There is a man sleeping in the grass, said (Stephen) Kumalo. And over him is gathering the greatest storm of all his days…. People hurry home past him, to places safe from danger. And whether they do not see him there in the grass, or whether they fear to halt even a moment, but they do not wake him, they let him be.

Kumalo's statement foreshadows tomorrow's violence. The alternative to the unpleasant reality requires a love that casts out fear, a fear that flourishes among whites and blacks. The whites fear the overwhelming numbers of blacks in South Africa; the blacks fear the power of the entrenched minority. With great compassion, a compassion tinged with disillusion, Paton writes, "Who can enjoy the lovely land, who can enjoy the seventy years, and the sun that pours down on the earth, when there is fear in the heart? Who can walk quietly in the shadow of the jacarandas, when their beauty is grown to danger?" Sometimes, bitterness mutes Paton's optimism. For example, bitterness erupts in his description of foolish rationalizing.

> We shall live from day to day, and put more locks on the doors, and get a fine fierce dog when the fine fierce bitch next door has pups … and the beauty of the trees by night, and the raptures of lovers under the stars, these things we shall forego. We shall forego the coming home drunken through the midnight streets, and the evening walk over the star-lit veld. We shall be careful, and knock this off our lives, and knock that off our lives and hedge ourselves about with safety and precaution. And our lives will shrink, but they shall be the lives of superior beings.…

Paton's sarcasm draws perilously close to despair. He knows the rampant fear permeating South Africa and the foolishness it promotes; *Cry, the Beloved Country* confronts reality in detail after detail. Yet the transcending merit of the novel is its poetic rendering of experience. Paton welds incongruous elements effectively. He describes man's inhumanity to man in powerful, realistic descriptions tempered only by a vein of unsubdued tenderness. His realism is rooted in sociological and psychological insights communicated explicitly and through characterization. Secondly, he perceives love as a redeeming force; however, his faith is sometimes blunted by the realities of multiple injustices. Paton clings to a hope that good may come from evil. Out of the death of Arthur Jarvis, an indomitable force for social justice, murdered—ironically—by an African, good emerges. James Jarvis, hitherto uninterested in the problems of deterioration at Ndotsheni, catches a hint of his son's convictions. Thus, James plays a God-like role in the restoration of the small village, a role symbolizing man's capacity for change. More important, perhaps, his grandson, a "small boy with the brightness inside him," begins to learn the Zulu language and symbolizes a hope for better future relationships between black and white in South Africa.

The novel closes on an ambiguous note. Paton returns to geographical place names but invests them with obvious symbolic meaning.

> Yes, it is the dawn that has come. The titihoya wakes from sleep, and goes about its work of forlorn crying. The sun tips with light the mountains of Ingeli and East Griqualand. The great valley of the Umzimkulu is still in darkness, but the light will come there. Ndotsheni is still in darkness, but the light will come there also. For it is the dawn that has come, as it has come for a thousand centuries, never failing. But when that dawn will come, of our emancipation, from the fear of bondage and the bondage of fear, why that is a secret.

Paton's symbols affirm a dawn of hope. Only the "when" is clouded. Since African natives live in the valleys, not in the highlands, the rising sun must first dispel the mists of fear hanging over those valleys. But Paton's guiding symbol, the inevitable, never-failing oncoming of light, marks his faith in evolutionary progress—geographical and human.

Source: Fred H. Marcus, *"Cry, the Beloved Country* and *Strange Fruit:* Exploring Man's Inhumanity to Man," in *The English Journal,* Vol. 51, No. 9, December, 1962, pp. 609–16.

Sources

Sheridan Baker, "Paton's Beloved Country and the Morality of Geography," in *College English,* Vol. 19, November, 1957, pp. 56-61.

Edwin Bruell, "Keen Scalpel on Racial Ills," in *English Journal,* Vol. 53, December, 1964, pp. 658-61.

Edward Callan, *Cry, The Beloved Country: A Novel of South Africa,* Twayne, 1991.

Edmund Fuller, *Man in Modern Fiction: Some Minority Opinions on Contemporary American Writing,* Random House, 1958, p. 40.

Harry A. Gailey, "Sheridan Baker's 'Paton's Beloved Country,'" in *College English,* Vol. 20, December 1958, pp. 143-44.

Harold C. Gardiner, *In All Conscience: Reflections on Books and Culture,* Hanover House, 1959, pp. 108-12.

Myron Matlaw, review of *Cry, the Beloved Country* in *Arcadia,* Vol. 10, No. 3, 1975.

Martin Tucker, *Africa in Modern Literature: A Survey of Contemporary Writing in English,* Ungar, 1967.

For Further Study

Graham Hough, "Doomed," in *London Review of Books,* December 3-16, 1981, pp. 16-17.
    Rather than praise the novel for its political place, this critic restates the reason for this novel being viewed as a classic: it is the story of an individual grappling to understand the complexity of life in a society so obviously unjust as a racist one.

Tom McGurk, "Paton's Nightmare Came True," in *New Statesman,* Vol. 115, No. 2977, April 15, 1988, pp. 7-8.
    Written when things looked their worst in South Africa, McGurk feels that Paton's novel foreshadowed the increased racial oppression under Apartheid. He also tells the story of Paton's work being taught in school although he does not see this as the hopeful glimmer it will eventually prove to be.

William Minter, "Moderate to a Fault?" in *New York Times Book Review,* November 20, 1988, p. 36.
    In this article, Minter examines the concept of justice in Paton's novels and in his personal life.

Herbert Mitgang, "Alan Paton, Author and Apartheid Foe, Dies of Cancer at 85," in *New York Times,* April 12, 1988, pp. A1, D35.
    In this obituary, Mitgang chronicles the achievements of Paton's life as a writer, teacher, and political leader.

Democracy

Joan Didion
1984

Democracy, Joan Didion's fourth novel, published in 1984, takes a sardonic look at the relationship between politics and personal life. The tension between the public and private persona of the novel's main character, Inez Victor, is examined in the context of a life led in the glare of mass media. As the wife of an ambitious congressman, senator, and aspirant to the Presidency, Inez has been groomed in playing to the public. She is not at all comfortable in this role.

The novel is at its most biting when Inez and Billy Dillon, her husband's political adviser and public relations operator, are goading one another. Although she appreciates Dillon's ironic abrasiveness rather more than her husband's woolly political jargon, Inez resents, for example, interviewers deciding in advance the angle of their profile on the basis of library cuttings. It is as if she has lost all personal claim to her past. Her own memory, and hence her history, have been fictionalized. The main events of the novel occur in 1975, the year of the United States's withdrawal from Vietnam. It is therefore impossible to read the story of Inez's marriage, and her affair with the elusive Jack Lovett, as pure personal drama.

Democracy, as the title implies, is also the story of the way in which a nation has lost touch with its own past and with the principles that once guided it. Many of those who commented on the novel when it was first publication greeted it as Didion's best novel to date. It was seen as a book that combined the barbed observational precision

of her journalism with the broader scope of the novelist. Others were put off by the tentative nature of its composition, and in particular by the intrusive voice of the narrator, who regularly informs the reader of directions previous versions of the book might have taken.

Author Biography

Joan Didion was born in Sacramento, California, on December 5, 1934, into a family that had put down roots in the region during the mid-nineteenth century. Her great-great-great-grandmother, Nancy Hardin Cornwall, had travelled part of the way west with the members of the ill-fated Donner-Reed wagon train, most of whom died while trapped in the Rocky Mountains during the winter of 1846-47. Sensibly, as it proved, Didion's ancestor parted company with the main group and took the northern trail through Oregon. Critics often refer to this ancestral heritage, arguing that Didion has the frontier in her blood and the confidence to take her own course. Both thematically and stylistically, these are observations which are relevant to a study of the novel *Democracy.*

Didion's childhood became nomadic during World War II. Her father was moved from one Air Corps base to another, and the family had spells in Washington, North Carolina, and Colorado. By the time they were re-settled in Sacramento, Didion was already developing a serious interest in writing. As a young teenager she spent hours typing out entire chapters from the novels of Ernest Hemingway, Henry James, and Joseph Conrad. She enrolled at the University of California in February, 1953, and it was there, at Berkeley, that she had the first of her own works published—a short story entitled "Sunset," which appeared in the student magazine *Occident.*

In her senior year Didion won *Vogue* magazine's Prix de Paris Award, and, after her graduation in 1956, she went to work in the magazine's New York office. She was quickly made an associate editor. In addition to her work for *Vogue,* she contributed articles to *National Review* and *Mademoiselle.* In 1958 she met John Gregory Dunne, a graduate of Princeton and staff writer at *Time.* They married in January, 1964. Didion's first novel, *Run River,* had been published (and hardly noticed) the previous year. The newly-married couple both resigned from their magazine positions and moved to California.

Joan Didion

Working as freelancers, they earned only seven thousand dollars between them in their first year. However, Didion's reputation as a columnist with an individual voice grew steadily, and her essay collection, *Slouching Towards Bethlehem,* published in 1968, brought her fully into the public eye. Her second novel, *Play It As It Lays,* became a bestseller two years later. Didion spent much of the seventies collaborating with her husband on screenplays, including a version of her second novel and the much-more successful *A Star is Born.* This was a lucrative decade, but not a satisfying one for Didion, who preferred working on her own as a novelist.

The novel which Didion published in 1977, *A Book of Common Prayer,* concerned a detached narrator trying, and failing, to find some coherence in the life of the book's protagonist. Didion's second essay collection, *The White Album,* reflected a mood of personal and clinical depression. *Democracy,* Didion's fourth novel, did not appear until 1984. The difficulties and false starts encountered in its composition form an essential part of the book's texture.

Both Didion's fiction and nonfiction are characterized by self-consciously stylish prose and attention to circumstantial detail.

Plot Summary

Part I

Joan Didion's *Democracy* chronicles a woman's search for identity during America's turbulent 1960s and 1970s. It is a quest that is completed in 1975, soon after the final evacuation of American troops from Vietnam and Cambodia. Didion, who identifies herself as the narrator of the story, compiles fragments of Inez Christian's life in an effort to help order Inez's experiences, and thus provide meaning to her life.

The novel focuses on Inez's marriage to Harry Victor, a prominent politician, and her long love affair with Jack Lovett, a CIA freelancer. She first meets Jack in Hawaii on her seventeenth birthday and begins a brief affair. A few years later, she marries Harry Victor and adopts the role of a politician's wife. Though Inez finds little fulfillment in her private or public life, she dutifully supports her husband, who eventually wins a seat in the U.S. Senate. She and Jack see each other intermittently during the next twenty years, until the death of her sister, Janet. When her sister dies, Inez finally leaves her husband for Jack and a new life in the Malaysian city of Kuala Lumpur, where she helps resettle Vietnam war refugees.

The novel opens in the spring of 1975 in a bar outside Honolulu, where Jack and Inez watch the evacuation of South Vietnam on television. Jack describes the colors of the sunrise and the scent of the air during nuclear tests in the Pacific in 1952 and 1953. Then, commenting on her situation, he exclaims, "Oh shit Inez … Harry Victor's wife."

Didion introduces herself as the author of this account of Inez's life and jumps forward to the present, when she is struggling to arrange the bits and pieces of what she knows and what she has heard about Inez Christian. She explains that she abandoned the "novel" she had intended to write about Hawaii and Inez's family history there, deciding instead to focus on Inez's life from the time she met Jack Lovett in 1952 to her relocation to Kuala Lumpur in 1975.

After explaining Inez's reason for staying in Kuala Lumpur—"colors, moisture, heat, enough blue in the air"—Didion relates brief but significant details of Inez's childhood and her family gained from Inez's memory, from photographs, and from her own knowledge of the family. She introduces Inez as the daughter of a prosperous Hawaiian family: her mother, who abandoned Inez and her sister when they were teenagers; Inez's sister,

Janet, and her husband, Dick Ziegler, who "made a modest fortune in Hong Kong housing and lost it"; her uncle Dwight, who caused Dick's financial ruin; and her father, Paul, who was arrested in the spring of 1975 after fatally shooting Janet and her suspected lover, Hawaiian congressman Wendell Omura. She then introduces Jack Lovett, who has "waited for twenty years for Inez."

During the 1960s Harry Victor, Inez's husband, plotted his political career, participating in protest marches and sit-ins. He successfully campaigned for Congress in 1964, 1966, and 1968. In 1969 he won an appointment to the Senate, and in 1972 lost a bid for the presidency. During those years, Inez fulfilled the duties of a politician's wife. She expressed a desire to help refugees, but her husband and his aides considered this work "an often controversial and therefore inappropriate special interest." Inez tells Didion that she has a difficult time recalling all the details of her past, admitting that her memory has faded.

Didion next introduces Inez's two children: her son, Adlai, who has crashed two cars and seriously injured his passenger, and her daughter Jessie, a heroin addict who has attempted suicide.

Didion returns to 1975 and to a class she taught in Berkeley, California, on the theme of democracy in literature. She relates her students' views on Vietnam and her own scouring of the papers for news of the evacuation, when she comes across the details of the murder of Janet Christian and Wendell Omura.

Part II

Didion describes Jack meeting Inez at the Honolulu airport in March, 1975, as Janet clings to life in the hospital after being shot by her father. She then flashes back to Inez's seventeenth birthday in 1952, the first time Jack and Inez met. Although Jack was married, the two began a short affair soon after. Inez married Harry Victor in the spring of her sophomore year at Sarah Lawrence College; she was two months pregnant with his child. She lost the baby, but was quickly swept up in the responsibilities of being a politician's wife.

Inez meets Jack on several occasions over the years, including once in Jakarta, Indonesia, in 1969 on a trip with Victor, her children, Victor's campaign manager Billy Dillon, and Frances Landau, Victor's aide. During that trip a grenade exploded at the American embassy, and Jack moved the family to a safer location.

Returning to 1975, Didion reveals specific details of the shootings and of Paul Christian's confinement to a mental hospital in Honolulu soon after. Inez's family and Billy Dillon try to downplay both incidents to the press. Inez visits her father in jail and her comatose sister in the hospital, and afterwards she begins to remember bits and pieces of her childhood, especially memories of her mother.

Jessie refuses to come to Honolulu after hearing about the shootings. She walks out of a drug treatment clinic in Seattle and, with the help of a fake press card, boards a transport to Saigon, Vietnam, where she hopes to find a job. Didion then returns to the scene that opens the novel—Inez and Jack at a bar outside Honolulu trying to find information about Jessie. Later that night, the two take a flight to Hong Kong.

Part III

Inez waits in Hong Kong while Jack tries to find Jessie in Saigon. While she waits, she takes long walks in the rain, reads American newspaper reports about the evacuation, and spends time watching Chinese children playing outside a nursery. Jack finds Jessie waiting tables at the American Legion outside of Saigon.

Part IV

Eight months later, Didion interviews Inez in Kuala Lumpur. During that time, Paul Christian is found mentally unfit to stand trial and Jessie is sent back to the United States. Didion had previously spoken to Harry, Billy Dillon, Dick Ziegler, Jessie, and Adlai about Inez and the events that spring. Inez tells Didion that Jack died of a heart attack in her arms after swimming in a hotel pool in Jakarta. She buried him in Honolulu and then flew immediately by herself to Kuala Lumpur. Jack's presence in Vietnam had been questioned, but his death quieted the rumors. Didion repeats Inez's reason for staying in Kuala Lumpur—"colors, moisture, heat, enough blue in the air"—and her insistence that she will remain there "until the last refugee was dispatched."

Characters

Betty Bennett

Betty Bennett, introduced as a "Honolulu divorcee," was a close neighbor of Janet and Dick Ziegler. For eighteen months, between 1962 and 1964, Betty is Jack Lovett's second wife, an experience which "left little impression on either of them."

Carol Christian

Carol Christian, who is married to Paul Christian, is the mother of Inez and Janet. Although it is Inez and Janet who become the two main female characters, Didion admits early on in the novel that she "was interested more in Carol Christian than in her daughters." Having arrived in Honolulu as a bride in 1934, Carol Christian is always an outsider on the islands, and stubbornly lonely in her marriage. She leaves dark red lipstick marks on her cigarettes, which she stubs out after barely smoking them, and spends hours at her dressing table, which is strewn with paper parasols from cocktails. She dies in a Piper Apache plane crash near Reno, Nevada, soon after her daughter Janet's marriage to Dick Ziegler.

Dwight Christian

The brother of Paul Christian, and therefore uncle to Inez and Janet, Dwight has a moral saying ready for every occasion, a characteristic which Didion treats mockingly. The quotations come from extracts torn from a weekly column, "Thoughts on the Business Life," subsequently typed up on index cards by Paul's secretary to form a file. Paul is described as having more significance in the early life of Inez and Janet than their father, but the sympathetic qualities of his character are never properly explored.

Paul Christian

Paul Christian, husband of Carol Christian and father of Inez and Janet, kills Wendell Omura with a .357 magnum and fatally injures his own daughter Janet. The shooting is motivated by business, family, and racial jealousies, but it is described in terms of a cold assassination. Having developed an eccentric objection to his family's financial dealings in Honolulu, Paul Christian has taken to living off canned tuna. The description of his actions immediately before and following the murder (living in a single YMCA room, going for a swim in the YMCA pool) gives the impression of a man turned clinically insane, a fact that Billy Dillon is keen to make the most of in his efforts to contain the situation.

Ruthie Christian

Ruthie Christian, Dwight's wife and aunt to Inez and Janet, is rarely mentioned in the novel.

Evacuees struggle for spots on a plane leaving Nha Trang, Vietnam, on April 1, 1975.

Sybil Christian

Known in the family as "Cissy," Sybil is Inez and Janet's grandmother.

Billy Dillon

Billy Dillon is a major character, but one whose exact role is shadowy and only gradually discerned. On a first encounter with the novel, a reader will only gradually identify the full and politically sinister part that Dillon plays in the narrative. Initially, Billy appears as a mere business assistant and personal friend of Harry Victor. He is a witness at the wedding of Harry and Inez in 1955. The key events of the novel take place twenty years later, but Billy Dillon is still there, the archetypal, political backroom-boy, image-controller, and manipulator. His concern is for appearances and surface-gloss. His advice to Inez, after she has listened to her father confessing to two shootings and showing no remorse, is typical: " … trot out the smile and move easily through the cabin, babe, O.K.?"

Frances Landau

Frances makes only brief appearances in the novel—at a dinner at Jakarta airport with Harry Victor—but she is representative of a type of woman who will hang on to public figures, "deprecating their own claims to be heard."

Carla Lovett

Carla Lovett, a druggist's daughter from San Jose, California, was Jack Lovett's first wife. They were married from 1945 to 1952.

Jack Lovett

Jack Lovett is an undercover operator with a finger in many pies. An opportunist, he makes the best of a given situation. The exact nature of his operations is kept vague, but the reader is given the strong impression that he makes his living by arms-dealing and similar activities. In particular, towards the end of the novel he is implicated in profiting from events surrounding the American withdrawal from Vietnam. However, Didion is at pains to exempt him from accusations of treason: "It would be accurate only to say that he regarded the country on whose passport he traveled as an abstraction, a state actor, one of several to be factored into any given play."

For Jack, Inez is certainly not an abstraction. He falls for her on their first meeting, which is on her seventeenth birthday, during the intermission of a ballet. They have a brief affair. His marriage to Carla Lovett ends in the same year. But Jack is much older than Inez. She has her young life to lead, and the two of them meet only sporadically across a span of more than twenty years. At each encounter it is apparent that the old spark is still alive. However, Inez, despite the shallowness of her life with Harry, will not leave her husband for Jack. His entreaties are always charmingly understated. Finally, in the melodramatic closing of the book, Jack is able to seize the initiative, and Inez surrenders to his man-of-action prowess.

The renewal of intimacy between Jack and Inez is short-lived. Jack dies in a swimming pool in Jakarta. The timing and circumstance of his death are suspicious, but not belabored by Didion. However, the reader is clearly intended to note the fact that Jack's name had been increasingly mentioned in government investigations into wrongdoing during the American withdrawal from Vietnam. After Jack dies, a certain Mr. Soebadio takes over (from Inez) all matters pertaining to the death.

Narrator

It is tempting to identify the first-person-voice narrator as Joan Didion herself. She mentions her time at *Vogue* in the early 1960s, and ventures several opinions about the art and complexities of narrative construction that are known to be representative of Didion's own views as a novelist. However, if Janet, Inez, and the other characters are accepted as fictional, it is perfectly possible to accept the first-person voice as a fictional construct, too. The construct serves two purposes: It allows Didion to speak directly to the reader, and it suggests that she is passing on information that has been intimately communicated to her by certain characters in the novel.

Wendell Omura

Wendell Omura is a black political activist. He is shot by a deranged Paul Christian, who has become unhinged by Omura's apparent involvement with his daughter Janet.

Mr. Soebadio

Mr. Soebadio is a mysterious gentleman who appears at poolside following Jack Lovett's death and takes over (from Inez) all responsibility for dealing with the removal and transportation of the body.

Frank Tawagata

Frank Tawagata is a lawyer. He is married to a cousin of Wendell Omura, and represents the Omura family during the period following the arrest of Paul Christian. In Part Two, section 9, pressure is put on Frank to lobby for Mr. Christian to be committed to an asylum. Although Inez's father is certainly mentally incapacitated, she and Billy Dillon's apparent motive is to avoid the embarrassment of the case going to trial.

Adlai Victor

Adlai Victor is the twin brother of Jessie Victor. Both were born February 23, 1957. Adlai is involved in a serious accident in June, 1973, in which a "fifteen-year-old from Denver lost her left eye and the function of one kidney"—an example of carefully-placed, circumstantial detail not later developed by Didion. Adlai is less important to the novel than his sister, Jessie.

Harry Victor

Harry Victor, Inez's husband, is a creature consumed by political life and personal ambition. After successful campaigns for Congress in 1964, 1966, and 1968, he is made a senator in 1969, following the death of the incumbent. After his attempt to become the 1972 presidential nominee of his party fails, his life revolves around public dinners and public speaking. He lectures at Berkeley during the spring of 1973; and, estranged from his wife, he dines in London in the company of a glamorous woman. At the end of the book, his political ambition and personal life are in tatters. Harry Victor is seen as a pathetic figure who is powerless to prevent his wife from taking off with another man.

Inez Victor

Inez Victor, Harry Victor's wife, was born Inez Christian on January 1, 1935. She is the mother of twins: Adlai, a boy, and Jessie, a girl. She is the strongest character in the novel, and the one whose point of view the reader most frequently shares. Indeed, the author testifies that Inez was to have been the first-person narrator of an abandoned version of the book. As the wife of an ambitious politician, Inez has to develop mannerisms peculiar to people in the public eye. She is the primary focus for one of the book's most insistent themes: the insidiously destructive nature of public life. Inez, like others in her position, has "lost track." In playing a part for so long, in so diligently ensuring that her every gesture is tailored for general scrutiny, she has lost all memory of what being herself means.

Inez met and fell in love with Jack Lovett in 1952, before leaving Honolulu to start an art course at Sarah Lawrence College. But she marries Harry Victor in 1955. The private story told by the novel concerns Inez's repeated encounters with Jack, and her apparent resistance to his entreaties, up until the climax of the novel in which she finally walks out on her husband.

Jessie Victor

Jessie Victor, born Jessica Christian Victor on February 23, 1957, is the twin sister of Adlai and daughter of Inez and Harry Victor. Another victim of her father's immersion in public life, Jessie becomes a heroin addict. In June, 1973, she is found in a state of collapse, and the following year is placed in a clinic. Quite bizarrely, at just the point when American troops and civilians are pulling out of Vietnam, she decides to go and work in its capital city, Saigon. She flies out the night before her aunt Janet's funeral. Significantly, it is not her father who goes to fetch her back, but Jack Lovett (accompanied by Inez), using his clandestine connections. Jessie is found working as a bar girl at the Legion club.

Kiki Watt

A fading beauty who is interviewed by *Vogue* in the early part of the novel, Kiki is just a walk-on player. The single interlude in which she is featured is a significant one, however. Kiki rattles away in an amusingly well-captured banter, communicating nothing. The other characters present— Inez, Jack Lovett, and the novelist—say little but communicate a great deal. Kiki is a colorful, minor character used as an effective foil, or contrast, for the more important players.

Janet Ziegler

Janet Ziegler, born Janet Christian, is Inez's younger sister. Janet is a less significant character than Inez, although she figures in many of the flashbacks to the two sisters' childhood and early adolescence. This is especially so at the end of the novel, when Janet has been shot and is in hospital on a life support machine.

Themes

Truth and Falsehood

Didion's self-conscious intrusion of herself, the author, into the novel's narrative is fundamental to one of the book's major themes: the degree to which meaning can be ascribed to events by telling a story. Linked to this theme is consideration of its mirror image: the degree to which meaning can be eroded by telling a story falsely. Didion

is not simply experimenting with the narrative method, though she acknowledges that the reader has certain expectations, some of which may not be satisfied by her own peculiar narrative approach. Declaring that she understands traditional techniques, Didion writes in Book Two, Chapter 11, "I know the conventions and how to observe them, how to fill the canvas I have already stretched; know how to tell you what he said and she said and know above all, since the heart of narrative is a certain calculated ellipsis, a tacit contract between writer and reader to surprise, how not to tell you what you do not yet want to know."

The reader has already been told that an earlier version of the novel was modeled on nineteenth-century family sagas. There was to be a great deal of family background and provincial Honolulu detail. The early focus of the book was to have been on the older generation, or so the "author" would have the reader believe. In fact, the final structure of the novel is so perfectly wedded to its themes that it is difficult to believe this other version of the book ever existed. The author's presence in the narrative, referring as it does to known details from Didion's own biography—her time at *Vogue,* her teaching at Berkeley—is intended to prompt the reader to ask: "Does that mean the other characters are real too?" The issue of the border between reality and fiction is also raised by Didion's specific references to media coverage of the political events in the novel, and the increasing impossibility of separating truth from falsehood. Nearly every character in the book is adept at projecting a phony veneer. Billy Dillon makes an art of it. Harry Victor is an impassively deceiving political animal. Jack Lovett is direct but secretive. Young Adlai pompously puts on airs. Perhaps the only character "true" to an inner self is Jessie, who has utterly rejected the values of her environment to become a waitress and heroin addict. At the end of the novel, she is declared to be well, living in Mexico City, and writing a novel.

American Dream

At the end of the 1970s, Didion was in a depressed mood. Her sour look at the 1960s—the essay collection *The White Album*—was published in 1979. *Democracy,* published five years later, was created out of the same feelings of pessimism. Thomas R. Edwards said in his *New York Review of Books* review of the novel, "The devastating personal and public consequences of the loss of history are Didion's theme." The scramble to get out of Saigon is implicitly seen as the deeply humili-

Topics For Further Study

- Read some of the firsthand accounts of the American withdrawal from Saigon and identify details which Didion has used in her novel.

- Didion's novel was originally going to be "a study in provincial manners" centered on one particular family in Honolulu. Investigate the business and social history of Honolulu during the 1940s and 1950s.

- Didion's essay collection *The White Album* contains a piece about Honolulu—"In The Islands"—in which she writes at length about Schofield barracks and *From Here To Eternity* by James Jones. Reading extracts from Jones's novel and watching the 1953 Columbia movie version of the book, identify parallels and contrasts in Didion and Jones's portrayals of life in Honolulu.

- The opening sentence of the novel refers to the testing of nuclear devices in the Pacific. Re-

search the history of nuclear testing, and on a map of the Pacific area mark and date all places used for such tests.

- Inez Victor is a study of the effect that being in the public eye has on a character. Researching the lives of Jacqueline Kennedy, Diana Princess of Wales, and other women subjected to public scrutiny through association with their husbands, attempt to analyze what Didion means when she suggests that the "major cost" of public life is "loss of memory."

- Carry out a statistical analysis of Didion's one-line or very short paragraphs (do not include dialogue). You will need to set your own parameters for this study—will you look at paragraphs of ten words or less? Eight words or less? Carry out a sentence analysis on each paragraph in your sample and attempt to show the results graphically, using computer software.

---

ating consequence of a political system that has become riddled with humbug and secrecy. Inez, in her private life, has lost the thread of her existence and only barely clings to a sense of self by remembering simple moments from her childhood. The nation is in a similar state. Clinging to simplistic notions of manifest destiny and freedom of the individual, and led by politicians who mouth jargonized platitudes, the country has had to come to terms with defeat. The novel is not about the rights and wrongs of being in Vietnam. Its theme is the difficulty of holding on to the thread of history, the problem of constructing a continuous story in which the present is linked to the past. Its depiction of the unravelling of the American Dream makes it a resignedly philosophical book, rather than a fierce diatribe. Indeed, in its happy, epilogue-type ending, it is almost forgiving.

Search for Self

Having lost touch with her inner self for so much of the novel, Inez appears to have found ful-

fillment at the end by ministering to refugees in Kuala Lumpur. She has been through the mill, and only an act of selflessness such as she has undertaken can bring her satisfaction (for the rest of her days, it would appear, for "Kuala Lumpur is not likely to dispatch its last refugee in Inez's or my lifetime"). Inez's nunlike change of life is peculiar to her. The other survivors of the novel go on in ways that suggest that, for them, the search for self-fulfillment means simply carrying on. Billy Dillon has a new congressman to groom for the Presidency. Harry Victor has become a special envoy to the Common Market (what is now called the European Union). Adlai has a lowly clerical position, working for a federal judge. Jessie ("her weakness is for troubled capitals") is in Mexico City, living with a *Newsweek* reporter, and writing, of all things, a historical romance. In other words, the difficulties of modern life, of existence as an American citizen, have touched them all. The conclusion of the novel would therefore appear to be saying that only by consciously removing oneself from the structures of contemporary life can true self-discovery be made.

Betrayal

Most characters in the novel prefer to play the system—to stay within the structures and gain whatever personal advantage they can. If this means cheating, they cheat. If this means being secretive and underhanded, they are secretive and underhanded. If it means betraying those who are close to them, they betray them. Most of all they betray themselves, but only the thin-skinned, such as Inez, are aware of their self-betrayal. Political candidacy has so hardened Inez's husband that he can cheat on his wife and on his principles without the slightest sign of remorse. As far as politics are concerned, he has probably forgotten he ever had principles. Billy Dillon relishes the game so much—he is so slick a public relations man—that for him conventional morality is turned on its head. It would be a betrayal of the game to give the honest answer; it would be a betrayal to act naturally.

The wealth of the Christian family makes them paranoid about business betrayals. The important subplot concerning Wendell Omura and Inez's sister, Janet, adds further to the pervasiveness of the betrayal theme. In addition, the reader is never sure whether Jack Lovett is a secret agent, a loose cannon, or a mixture of the two. The appearance at the poolside, immediately following Lovett's fatal collapse, of the significantly-named Mr. Soebadio ("So-bad"), and the things that Mr. Soebadio just "happened to know" about getting a body out of Indonesia, suggest that Lovett belonged to a network of covert intelligence operators that made possible the breaching of protocol. The questions being asked about him at the end of his life, regarding possible profiteering from the American withdrawal from Vietnam, amount to a treasonous and undemocratic betrayal of his country.

Style

Narrative/Point of View

"This is a very hard story to tell," the narrator declares at the end of Chapter 1. Immediately after this, Chapter 2 begins, "Call me the author," an echo of the famous opening line "Call me Ishmael" from *Moby-Dick*. This is immediately undermined by a playful pastiche, or imitation, on the intrusive voice of nineteenth-century British novelist Anthony Trollope. On the same page, there is a quotation from a Wallace Stevens poem: "A gold-feathered bird/Sings in the palm, without human meaning,/Without human feeling, a foreign song." Didion is at pains to establish that the narrator of *Democracy* is not a fictional character, but the author herself. Although the rest of Chapter 2 is largely about problems she, as author, has supposedly encountered with the structure of her story, the reader is also asked to accept her as a character in her own book, playing an important role as witness and reporter (the passer-on of direct evidence).

This dual presence of Didion the novelist and Didion the character—the artist constructing her fiction vs. the reporter recording true-life events—has a disconcerting effect upon the reader. The strongest presence is of Didion the novelist, so that although the reader is made vividly aware of several of the characters, there is never any serious attempt to tell events from their point of view. The unbroken awareness of the novel as artifice—of something being self-consciously manufactured by the writer—is compounded by Didion's stylistic quirks, which again draw the reader's attention to the author. The reader is kept at a cool distance from the characters and events by the narrative voice, an effect which (if the quotation from Wallace Stevens is kept in mind) would appear to be intentional, rather than a failure of engagement.

Structure

The book is divided into four sections. Section 1 has twelve chapters; Section 2 has fourteen; Section 3 has three; and Section 4 has four. Chapters are usually short, focusing on one key scene, or on the musings of the author. The main narrative action takes place during 1975—before, during, and after the American withdrawal from Saigon, Vietnam. But Didion's narrative method, especially in the first two sections of the novel (which together comprise eighty per cent of the whole book), is not a consecutive one. She visits and revisits, in no particular chronological order, other important years in the lives of her characters: 1934, the year in which Carol Christian, Inez's mother, arrives in Honolulu as a bride; 1952, the first meeting between Inez and Jack Lovett; 1955, Inez's marriage to Harry Victor; 1960, the year in which Inez and the author worked together at *Vogue;* 1972, the year of Harry's failed attempt to win his party's presidential nomination; and 1973, when Adlai has a serious accident and Jessie's heroin addiction is revealed.

Didion's circling around this narrative material evoke in the reader thoughts of the investigative journalist. The book is not a mystery or a thriller. Told conventionally it would be a family saga with a political edge. Indeed, it is easy to imagine a popular novelist using the same material to work up a fat, five-hundred-page, episodic bestseller. The structure Didion chooses suits her own purpose, which is to explore connections and continuities between the past and the present. She wishes to make the reader aware that life experiences are often connected with events fairly distant in time, rather than those immediately preceding. To this end, the narrative structure works well, and it is something of a surprise when the two short, final sections of the novel deliver a conventional episodic conclusion.

Style

The use of repetition which occurs in the opening lines of *Democracy*—recurring from time to time throughout the novel—is one of the novelist's stylistic trademarks. She takes the words from the end of one sentence and uses them to begin the next. Cadenced repetition is not a new technique. One of Didion's early influences was Ernest Hemingway. As a teenager she copied out whole sections from his novels. The opening paragraph of *A Farewell to Arms* is a famously effective example of the use of repetition. But Didion's use of repetition has prompted criticism more than praise. Commentators find it over-formulaic. Her habit of separating repeated phrases so that each is on a separate line, in a paragraph of its own, has been called "padding."

Dialogue

Critics do not always consider Didion's use of poetic repetition effective. However, the consensus is that she is excellent at writing dialogue, although she chooses to transcribe it idiosyncratically; sometimes with quotation marks, sometimes without. In *Democracy* her use of dialogue is highly edited. She uses only those exchanges between characters that illuminate the themes she is developing. Snatched conversations are Didion's most effective means of characterisation. The reader understands Inez through her conversations with Billy Dillon and Jack Lovett, rather than through any direct comment from the novelist. Didion makes use of two types of dialogue. One (the kind presented without quotation marks) is overtly impressionistic and not intended to be literal. The other, and the kind in which Didion excels, is presented conventionally, and purports to be the direct transcription of words actually spoken.

Historical Context

The Legacy of the 1970s

Democracy was published in 1984, but the major part of the narrative focuses on the previous decade. An important political theme—the existence of individual wheeler-dealers brokering deals with the connivance of government, and sometimes at the government's bequest—touches upon one of the major political stories of the 1980s: the Iran-Contra crisis. The scandal was first revealed in 1986, when a secret CIA operative was shot down over Nicaragua. His cargo was a load of weapons intended for the Contras, a group of anti-Communist rebels. Further investigation into the matter revealed that this illegal shipment had been funded by secret sales of arms to Iran —a country under an arms embargo since hostages were seized at the U.S. embassy in Iran in 1979. High-ranking members of President Ronald Reagan's administration were later implicated in the scandal, but most received pardons or were granted immunity for their testimony.

When Didion chose to write explicitly about this story in her 1996 novel, *The Last Thing He Wanted,* she set the events in 1984. *Democracy*'s first readers were able to read the book with detail and background to the Iran-Contra events unfolding in realtime. Inevitably, early reviewers and commentators on the book drew attention to this. However, the primary political and social focus of the novel is still the 1970s and, to a lesser extent, the 1960s.

From many points of view the 1970s was a featureless or transitional decade. One commentator, Peter Carroll, named his 1984 survey of the decade *It Seemed Like Nothing Happened.* During the first half of the 1970s, the cultural and political trends of the 1960s remained dominant. In the second half, many of the trends that were to characterize the 1980s began to manifest themselves. However, deeper analysis reveals it to be possibly the most important decade in the postwar history of the United States. Two ideological positions were challenged at the time. The first of these—the belief in the expansion of American influence overseas— had before been taken for granted by both Democrats and Republicans. The second—support for liberal civil rights programs—had been more rigorously debated. But the legacy of the Lyndon Johnson administration, and the cultural climate of the closing years in the 1960s, seemed to protect such programs from attack. These basic principles

Democratic Former Vice President Walter Mondale (left) shakes Republican President Ronald Reagan's hand during the presidential debates of 1984, the same year Didion's novel was published.

of national self-belief were given a severe jolt by defeat in Vietnam. It was not so much the fact America lost the war as the ignominious and chaotic nature of civilian withdrawal that dented national pride most profoundly.

Vietnam

The concept of "Manifest Destiny"—that Americans had been divinely chosen to spread their influence and belief in freedom of the individual to all parts of the globe—had been axiomatic in American political affairs since the 1840s. In the nineteenth century, this belief had mainly fed the frontier spirit during the period of westward expansion. In the twentieth century, and particularly after World War II, America had extended its influence overseas, such as to the Philippines in Asia. In the 1960s a further frontier had been confronted, with manned flights to outer space and the Moon.

In conquering this latter frontier, America was in direct competition with the Soviet Union, its Cold War enemy. Initially, involvement in Vietnam had been explicitly explained as a stand against communism and a defense of the free world. It had become complicated by America's importation of corporate capitalism into South Vietnam (so that

business interests jockeyed for position with political and ethical factors) and, during the Richard Nixon administration, by increasing signs of detente (an easing of political conflict) between the two superpowers. At home presidential and national attention on the war was diverted by the Watergate affair, in which Nixon tried to cover up the illegal break-in at the Democratic National Committee office in Washington, D.C. The incident eventually led to Nixon's resignation.

Didion refers repeatedly in her novel to the exact circumstances of the American withdrawal from Vietnam in April 1975. The hectic and frantic helicopter flights out of Saigon are vividly described in a firsthand account by Stephen Klinkhammer, published in Al Santoli's *Everything We Had: An Oral History of the Vietnam War.* In this account Klinkhammer repeatedly describes the withdrawal as "total chaos" and "really a mess." Further details from this and other firsthand accounts are also used by Didion. In the novel, there are several references to money changing hands, and to certain people profiting out of the situation. Klinkhammer describes the Vice President of South Vietnam escaping with "an immense amount of gold bars." Didion implies that some American civilians also profited from the situation.

Watergate and Secrecy

As reported in the June 4, 1973, edition of *Time* magazine, President Nixon issued a four thousand word statement attempting to explain his actions with regard to Watergate. This statement explicitly attempted to defend political espionage because of a climate in which sensitive political matters were brought into the open for the sake of openness. "I think it is time in this country to quit making national heroes out of those who steal secrets and publish them in newspapers," Nixon is reported (in the same article) to have said to a rapturous audience of ex-P.O.W.s. And in the statement itself: "By mid-1969, my Administration had begun a number of highly sensitive foreign policy initiatives aimed at ending the war in Vietnam, achieving a settlement in the Middle East, limiting nuclear arms, and establishing new relationships among the great powers. These involved highly secret diplomacy. They were closely interrelated. Leaks of secret information about any one could endanger all. Exactly that happened. News accounts appeared in 1969 which were obviously based on leaks—some of them extensive and detailed—by people having access to the most highly classified security materials. There was no way to carry forward these diplomatic initiatives unless further leaks could be prevented."

In such a way did those at the helm in public life defend secret, undemocratic methods—in the name of the democracy that those methods and "diplomatic initiatives" so flagrantly flouted. There is not a polemical point running through Didion's novel relating to its title. Rather, she takes for granted her audience's experience of contemporary political life and allows readers to draw their own conclusions from the focus of the narrative. Didion was writing the novel from the perspective of a disenchanted Republican.

Critical Overview

A tendency for critics of Didion's fiction to draw upon knowledge of her public and private character was taken to the limit in 1980 by Barbara Grizutti Harrison. In a witheringly unsympathetic essay included in her 1980 book *Off Center*, Harrison accused the author of being self-consciously neurotic, a reactionary, and a stylistic trickster. Reviewers of *Democracy* were not disposed to receiving Didion's intrusions of herself into the narrative with much sympathy. Many of them were convinced that these intrusions weakened the novel. But a number of early reviewers were more positive about Didion's style than Harrison. Phoebe-Lou Adams, reviewing the novel in the *Atlantic,* described it as being "striking, provocative, and brilliantly written." Janet Wiehe, despite thinking that the book had the "immediacy of journalism" rather than the emotional depth of a great novel, nevertheless summarized it in *Library Journal* as "sophisticated political fiction, written with skill and wit."

One of the book's staunchest early supporters (and one of the few defenders of Didion's intrusive narrative device) was Thomas R. Edwards, who reviewed the novel at length in the *New York Review of Books*. Treating it as serious fiction, and drawing on its echoes with the book of the same name by Henry Adams, he wrote: "*Democracy* is absorbing, immensely intelligent, and witty, and it finally earns its complexity of form. It is indeed a 'hard story to tell,' and the presence in it of 'Joan Didion' trying to tell it is an essential part of its subject." A different point of view was expressed by Thomas Mallon in *The American Spectator*. In this review Mallon complained about a lack of range in Didion's female characterisation. "Inez Victor has in the past gone by the names of Lily Knight McClellan, Maria Wyeth, and Charlotte Douglas. They were the heroines of Didion's first three novels, and they're still the heroine of this one. All four women have the same frayed psychic wiring." About Didion's entry as a character in certain scenes of her story—for example, a conversation she has with Inez in the office of *Vogue*—Mallon writes, "There's a sort of desperation to the device." And about Didon's characteristic short sentences and repetitions, he observes, "One can sit down with the same syntax too many times, just as one can bump into the same heroine once too often."

The novel has been the subject of several critical essays. In "A Hard Story to Tell—The Vietnam War in Joan Didion's *Democracy,*" Stuart Ching analyses both the fragmentary nature of the novel and its factual correspondences: "Jessie's flight to Vietnam illustrates the confusion in Southeast Asia during the last few weeks before the final evacuation of Saigon. For example, between April 15 and April 28, 277 whites and blacks without identification or passports who spoke English and presented themselves as Americans at evacuation sites were evacuated without question." The cumulative conclusion of Ching's analysis is that "the fragmentation of the fictive world—Inez's flight to Hong Kong—concurs with the collapse of the external world—the fall of Saigon."

The novel's political themes were considered by Michael Tager in his 1990 essay "The Political Vision of Joan Didion's *Democracy*." The concluding paragraph of this essay states: "Didion's novel portrays a democracy vitiated by a secretive national security apparatus and image-conscious national politicians. Both use euphemisms and vague phrases to disguise or justify their questionable activities to the public.... The plot of *Democracy* illustrates [George] Orwell's claim from his essay 'Politics and the English Language' that the misuse of language contributes to sloppy thought and misconceived action, and that indefensible acts require misleading language for justification." In "Postwar America and the Story of Democracy," an essay concentrating on the novel's structure, another critic, Alan Nadel, explores how the language of justification affects the tone of the novel as a whole. "By foregrounding her roles as author and as character and by mixing the levels of fact, Didion denies the reader the same distance she has denied herself."

Criticism

Wendy Perkins

Perkins is an Assistant Professor of English at Prince George's Community College in Maryland. In the following essay she examines how the form of Democracy *illustrates the problematic search for identity.*

Some critics read Joan Didion's *Democracy* as a romance novel that centers on Inez Christian's love affair with Jack Lovett. Others consider it a political novel, finding a relationship between Inez's internal and external worlds. Didion's innovative construction, in fact, highlights both of these aspects as it reinforces and helps develop the novel's main theme: the problem of identity, especially in gaining a clear view of self and others in a society that encourages concealment and deception. The novel's fragmented form and shifting point of view illustrate on three levels the difficulties inherent in separating fact from fiction: Inez, the narrator, and the reader all struggle to understand Inez and her world.

Mary McCarthy, writing in her *New York Times Book Review* article, "Love and Death in the

What Do I Read Next?

- *The Last Thing He Wanted,* Joan Didion's 1996 novel, was her first work of fiction after *Democracy.* It develops several of the same political themes.

- Didion is admired as an essayist as well as a novelist, and the work in *The White Album,* her 1979 essay collection, evolved from state of mind similar to the one which created *Democracy.*

- *From Here to Eternity* (1951) by James Jones is a popular wartime novel set in Honolulu in the period leading up to the bombing of Pearl Harbor.

- A reading of *Democracy,* the 1880 novel by the nineteenth-century historian Henry Brooks Adams, helps to throw into sharper relief some of the cultural and political concerns which Didion's later novel of the same name explores.

Pacific," suggests that the "construction of *Democracy* feels like the working out of a jigsaw puzzle that is slowly being put together with a continual shuffling and re-examination of pieces still on the edges or heaped in the middle of the design." Didion creates this "jigsaw puzzle" by replacing traditional chronological order with flashbacks and flashforwards of fragmented scenes that allow us only glimpses of her characters. Our view is further complicated by Didion as narrator. She identifies herself as a journalist but insists she is writing a "novel" about Inez. As she begins the story, she admits she lacks "certainty ... conviction ... patience with the past and interest in memory" and feels she has "lost her authority as a novelist." Her confessions reveal the tension between fact and fiction, truth and imagination—a tension that the characters and the readers also feel.

Didion is not a traditionally omniscient narrator in the novel. She continually questions her ability to present an accurate portrait of Inez, acknowledging that she gains much of her information from unreliable sources: her own memory, interviews with Inez's friends (Jack, Billy Dillon) and family members (Harry, Adlai, Jessie), press clippings, and Inez's memory. Didion's and Inez's memories have faded, press clippings have provided only distorted images of her, and she doubts the truthfulness of other people.

The narrator begins Inez's story with a fragment of the scene where Jack and Inez stop at the bar outside Honolulu. They are trying to gather information about Jessie's flight to Vietnam. The narrator finds it difficult to continue, however, insisting that she has "no memory of any one moment in which either Inez Victor or Jack Lovett seemed to spring out, defined. They were equally evanescent, in some way emotionally invisible, unattached, wary to the point of opacity, and finally elusive." For several pages the narrator explains how hard it is to even begin to tell Inez's story. At one point she had intended to write a history of Inez's family in Hawaii, but decides instead to shift her focus to Inez's life in the United States. Ultimately, the narrator takes on the task of telling Inez's story, piecing together the collage of images and "fitful glimpses" in an attempt to provide shape and order to Inez's life and thus to help establish her identity.

As the narrator assembles the parts of Inez's story, she weaves in glimpses of other characters that impact Inez's life. However, the contradictory images we gain cloud our vision of these characters. We cannot fault the narrator entirely for this ambiguity, however, since the characters themselves invent fictions to cope with the realities of their lives.

Carol Christian, Inez's mother, explains her husband's frequent absences from their home in Hawaii by insisting "When a man stays away from a woman, it means he wants to keep their love alive." The narrator later suggests that infidelities kept her husband away. Inez's grandmother considers Carol's abandonment of her teenage daughters "a sudden but compelling opportunity to make the first postwar crossing on the reconditioned *Lurline.*" Elsewhere the narrator hints that Carol's "stubborn loneliness" while living as an "outsider" in the islands triggered her departure. Inez's married sister Janet, who maintains a "defensive veneer of provincial gentility" is suspected of having an affair with a Hawaiian. Paul Christian, who had "reinvented himself as a romantic outcast" after his wife left him, murders his daughter and her suspected lover. The shadowy Jack Lovett has been identified as an "army officer" by his first wife, an

"aircraft executive" by his second, a "businessman" on his visa application, and a "consultant in international development" on his business cards. The narrator leads us to suspect he is a CIA agent but never actually confirms this.

Harry Victor also invents fictions about himself, but the narrator provides us with a clearer vision of him and his contribution to his wife's loss of self. This self-seeking, ambitious politician creates an image of himself as a moral crusader, while in his private life he commits adultery and thwarts his wife's search for identity. On a family trip to Jakarta that includes his mistress, he appears more concerned about his press conference than the safety of his family. As a result, Jack Lovett tells him, "You don't actually see what's happening in front of you. You don't see it unless you read it. You have to read it in the *New York Times,* then you start talking about it."

The narrator complicates our view of Inez by revealing only fragmented scenes of her life. Inez and others also contribute to our confusion, as well as her own, as personal and public pressures help strip her of her identity. During her marriage, Inez is defined by the press as the ideal politician's wife. Yet this role confines her. For twenty years, she acts solely in her husband's political interests, not in her own. Her husband and advisors suppress her desire to work with refugees, since that special interest was "often controversial and therefore inappropriate" to the political image they had created for her.

The press helps reinforce this image as it reports her "very special feeling for the arts" and "very special interest in education"—interests manufactured for her by her husband's political machine. As a result of fabricating appropriate stories for the press and viewing her life as a series of "photo opportunities," Inez's memory fades to the point where she loses a true sense of herself. She admits that during this process "you drop fuel. You jettison cargo. Eject the crew. You lose track." While being interviewed, she tells a reporter "Things that might or might not be true get repeated in the clips until you can't tell the difference.... You might as well write from the clips ... because I've lost track."

Inez's memory also fades because she suppresses painful facts like her abandonment by her mother, her son's two car crashes (one of which left his passenger seriously injured), her daughter's heroin addiction, and her husband's frequent infidelities with the ever-present political groupies.

Inez's apparent indifference to these past events often makes her appear cold.

Inez's family and Billy Dillon also suppress the truth at times, but for a different reason. They conceal details of "uncomfortable" events to avoid hurting Harry's public image and thus his career. Michael Tager, in "The Political Vision of Joan Didion's *Democracy*," notes that "media scrutiny requires that one establish a pleasant past for public consumption while concealing or eliminating those elements that clash with the desired image." An example of this process occurs after the shootings, when the family rallies to downplay the incident to the press, to "manage" the situation for Harry and to "contain [it] to an accident."

The deception and lack of clarity in Inez's private and public life become comparable to and intertwine with larger political issues. The novel begins with a focus on this link as Jack describes to Inez the breathtaking sunrises and sweet-smelling air during nuclear testing in the Pacific in the mid-1950s, without commenting on the devastation that soon followed. The narrator offers contrasting views of the fall of Saigon in 1975, when the main action of the story takes place. While many in the United States considered the evacuation disastrous for the South Vietnamese, the narrator's students interpreted it as their "liberation from imperialism."

Tager argues that "democracy" is the "name we have given to a narrative of American global politics … [that] placed Americans in the roles of reader and viewer of a series of adventures, in which the heroes and villains were clear, the desirable outcomes known, and the undesirable outcomes contextualized as episodes in a larger narrative that promised a happy ending." The Vietnam War, however, had no such happy ending. Both the novel's political and personal narratives fall apart during the evacuation of Saigon. The idealistic vision of America as defender of world democracy, and of the Victors as a model American family, crumbles.

This process begins when Inez's father shoots Janet, an incident that jolts Inez's memories to the surface and prompts her to begin to sort out truth from fabrication. After she leaves with Jack to find Jessie, she breaks from her family, deciding "she was not particularly interested in any of them." While she waits in Hong Kong for Jack to ship Jessie home, she begins to separate herself not only from her family, but her country as well: "The world that night was full of people flying from place to place and fading in and out and there was

no reason why she or Harry or Jessie or Adlai or for that matter Jack Lovett … should be exempted from the general movement…. Just because they were Americans." When Inez decides to stay in Kuala Lumpur to work with the war refugees, ironically, she becomes a refugee herself, from her family, her country, and her past.

This separation allows Inez to begin to find freedom and a sense of identity. She permits her love for Jack to surface, and they find happiness for a short time, until his accidental death. At the end of the novel, Inez seems content with her new life, noting the "colors, moisture, heat, [and] enough blue in the air" to keep her in Kuala Lumpur "until the last refugee was dispatched." Yet, the narrator tells us she learned of Inez's intention of staying on from an article in the newspaper—not, as she has proven, a reliable source.

While Inez seems to gain a clearer vision of herself by the end of the novel, the narrator leaves the reader with only a partial view of her, attained through the fragmented narrative. We have only gained glimpses of Inez, and thus are not sure whether or not Inez has completed her search for identity and meaning in her life. The narrator voices her uncertainty as well, when she concludes: "Perhaps because nothing in this situation encourages the basic narrative assumption, which is that the past is prologue to the present, the options remain open here. Anything could happen."

Source: Wendy Perkins, in an essay for *Novels for Students*, Gale, 1998.

Janis P. Stout

In the following excerpt, Stout examines the narrative technique that the author employs in Democracy. *The critic contends that the narrator, named "Joan Didion," includes hesitations, blanks, gaps, and other "silences" in her narration as a means of both implying more than what is said and emphasizing the ways in which a male-dominated American society inhibits the expression of women.*

[In] *Democracy,* Didion writes in the terse, elliptical style [her] novels had taught us to expect of her, but with a somewhat different and more highly politicized import. As in *A Book of Common Prayer,* the narrative strategy involves a first-person narrator only slightly distanced from the author herself. Indeed, the distance is even less here. The narrator of the earlier book is particularized with a name, Grace Strasser-Mendana, and a personal background clearly distinct from Didion's own. The narrator of *Democracy* is a thinly fictionalized Joan Didion; we might call her "Joan Didion": a persona in only the most circumstantial of ways. This persona advances and retreats. At those points when she is at the narrative fore, she addresses the reader directly, calling our attention to the difficulties entailed by getting and presenting the story. Several chapters open abruptly with terse one-line "paragraphs" focusing on the act of telling—imperatives:

"Call me the author," "See it this way," "Let me establish Inez Victor"; personal declarations: "I also have Inez's account," "I am resisting narrative here." The directly accostive narrative voice that such openings establish creates the sense of urgency avowed in the narrator's "warning" to the reader,

like Jack Lovett and (as it turned out) Inez Victor, I no longer have time for the playing out.

Call that a travel advisory.

A narrative alert.

The issuance of a "narrative alert," an overt tactic for gaining reader involvement, is a part of the entire strategy by which "Joan Didion" is placed within the novel. The narrator's struggle to understand her characters' story becomes part of the fiction, which is a fiction of reporting rather than creating. "Joan Didion" is here, like Joan Didion in fact, an interpretive journalist, trying to get at the truth and communicate it before the failure of the social situation, represented in the fall of South Vietnam, makes investigation and interpretation impossible. When she says that she does not have time for a fully elaborated narrative, we feel not only the wildly accelerating events of the evacuation of Hanoi and the family tragedy being played out against it but also the impending breakup of the social order and the brevity of human life. The urgency "Didion" asserts is communicated to us, in part, by the rapid succession of terse, often fragmentary phrases....

In all Didion's work, the breaking into brief stand-alone sentences or phrases, or often strings of such sentences or phrases, is a device for emphasis, usually an ironic twist of emphasis. But in *Democracy,* the device gains a faster pace and a more hard-bitten, slangy tone. The rapidity is largely a matter of achievement of a sense of fast-breaking events, even of events being out of control. This is true both of family events and of events on the large scale. Social structures collapse more rapidly than politicians, generals, and weapons

dealers can shore them up. The fast verbal pace is achieved also through associative listing of items....

Rapid exchanges of smart dialogue, often in brief, slangy phrases tossed off sarcastically, also contribute to the fast pace of the dramatized scenes and to the harsh tone. The narrative voice, as well, often employs bitten-off slang to convey a mocking commentary or a sense of world-weariness....

The narrator's hard-bitten phrases, not quite hiding a fullness of emotions sensed behind them, often, though not consistently, emulate the glibness of sarcasm of this campaigning, image-building circle in which Inez moves as Harry Victor's wife. Mulling her story, she comments mockingly: "Cards on the table"; "Water under the bridge" "The Alliance *qua* Alliance"; "His famous single room at the Y." At other times, it is the laconic, tough yet nostalgic voice of Jack Lovett that we hear in the narrator's brief phrases. The beautifully taut opening of the novel, for instance, starts in Lovett's voice, then elides into Didion's own terse identification of the character, emphasizing (significantly) Inez's marital state, then returns to Lovett's distinctive blend of nostalgia and hard-boiled realism....

In part, Didion adopts Lovett's savvy understatement as a way of conveying, through its own cadences, some sense of an elusive personality, as if, though the mystery cannot be analyzed, it can be glimpsed....

In part, however, she adopts this tone, with its characteristic curtailments, as a protection from the pressure of emotion—just as, we suspect, Lovett himself adopts it. Indeed, all the people we respect in this book—Lovett, Inez, and the narrator—are "wary to the point of opacity." They adopt a tough exterior—such as Lovett's exclamation, conveying a lifelong caring and a lifelong frustration, "Oh shit, Inez, Harry Victor's wife" (repeated or echoed [several times])—to cover their vulnerability, knowing full well even as they do it that toughness "never stopped any plane from crashing." Disaster happens despite the surface toughness that they nevertheless maintain because, like the Hemingway hero's style, that is the way to do it, or at any rate their way to do it.

The narrator tells things in a compressed short-hand, sometimes imagistic but sometimes carefully abstract, both for impact and for control, for protection from the disorder. Inez's mother, Carol Christian, she tells us, clung to an assortment of romantic notions "in the face of considerable contrary evidence." It is not necessary to specify what that evidence was; we get the idea well enough, and she would rather not go into it. Just as the device of curtailed references is a means of refraining from specification, implying that that specification would be too unpleasant, so silences in the text, blanks or gaps, serve the same purpose, conveying ideas without spelling them out. In this novel, many blanks are structural, signaling shifts in the action. Many [blanks], however, ... tacitly invite the reader's particularized understanding even as they imply the narrator's brooding. After a long, wordy sentence conveying, in its cadences, the jumbled, densely populated quality of Harry Victor's politicizing, the narrator sums up,

> These people had taken their toll.
>
> [space]
>
> By which I mean to suggest that Inez Victor had come to view most occasions as photo opportunities.

After an account of Inez's conference with her daughter Jessie's first therapist, ending in "'What I don't do is shoot heroin,' Inez said," there appears a gap on the page, then, "The second therapist believed...." In the gap occurs the whole messy process of breaking off with one and finding the second, a process the narrator spares us all. Indeed, the gap says something that a full account could not say, that that messy process is not worth repeating and that it is so obviously unavoidable at this point that it goes without saying.

Inez Victor herself, in this way a typical Didion heroine, is equally reticent. In part her silences and the oddity of her speech when she does express herself are a result of being squelched. As the daughter of a son of a powerful family in a relatively closed society (Hawaii) and the wife of a powerful man with presidential ambitions, she has had to preserve appearances throughout her life. Her expression of self is subordinated to the building of her husband's political image. She has had to calculate every word, every facial expression, to ensure that that image is not damaged, playing a role in a planned script, repeating empty enthusiastic phrases—"'Marvelous day.' 'You look marvelous.' 'Marvelous to be here'"—and "fixing her gaze in the middle distance." When traveling she always has to go through a routine of phony accessibility, to "'trot out the smile'" and, as her husband's public relations aide puts it, "'move easily through the cabin.'" So well trained is she in playing the "tennis" game of public relations that Billy Dillon, the aide, has only to "mim[e] a backhand volley" to get her back on track if she slips into real communica-

tion. What she says gets smoothed over and reinterpreted, polished for press release beyond all recognition. Even the personal interests she is allowed to pursue are selected for their political appeal: a trumped up "special interest" in selecting the paintings to be hung in American embassies is safe; her real interest in "work with refugees" is off-limits because it is controversial and therefore "inappropriate." This is why it is so significant at the end that after Jack Lovett's death she devotes herself, in an almost saintly way, to the administration of refugee relief in Kuala Lumpur: it is the most emphatic possible way to express her independence from her husband's control.

Inez's public self has been an "impenetrable performance" protecting the mystery and the vulnerability of her private self. At times she uses silence, as she uses diversionary performances, to protect her self from manipulation and from the intrusion of a curious public, largely the intrusion of journalists. Within that protection, she has developed a "capacity for passive detachment," avoiding verbal acknowledgment of unacceptable things. But she also uses silence more aggressively. After a party at which her husband passes off empty, stale rhetoric she has heard him use "a number of times before" to cover lack of knowledge, she drives fast and says nothing until he finally notices and gets the point. Defensively, he taunts her for her "quite palpable unhappiness." They go to bed in silence. On another occasion, seeing her husband condoning what she regarded as specious activities by their son, she again spoke tersely and then "said nothing." Again Harry gets the point: "'Very eloquent. Your silence,' he says."

Inez Victor, like other women in Didion's novels, and like Didion as narrator, manages to say more than she says and to speak by not speaking. This, of course, is a time-honored way with women—women writers and women generally. Inez Victor speaks out of the frustration of feminine roles that inhibit her self-realization and interfere with her freedom of action. When she tries to assert her own judgment, as a free and intelligent adult, she is muffled and manipulated and her sexual relations with her husband deteriorate: they "had gone to bed in silence, and, the next morning, ... Harry left ... without speaking"; they had "slept in the same room but not in the same bed." The marital relation hinges on her being constrained in her self-assertion, on her foregoing a lifelong love relation with another man even though she had repressed her own reactions to her husband's succession of affairs because "girls like that come with the life." Her achievement of communication with "Joan Didion," the narrative persona, despite all the negative constraints of a lifetime of resisting honest personal communication and honest public statements, has to be regarded as a victory—like her victory in asserting her right to pursue the social service work to which she feels drawn. The end of the book, with Inez still in Kuala Lumpur, speaking to whomever she wants to when she wants to, stating her reasons in her own terms and with an edge of mockery (asked by Billy Dillon for "one fucking reason" why she is there, she writes back tersely, *Colors, moisture, heat, enough blue in the air. Four fucking reasons."*), is thus, in a limited way, a happy ending, despite its solemnity.

As in the other novels, the frustrating and repressed nature of the central character's life is not hers alone, but a condition she shares with other women....

The narrator, too, "Joan Didion," shares the frustrations of being a woman in what continues to be a man's world, and a disordered world as well. Because of the unusual narrative strategy, with the author's real self represented in a fictive world that includes events, people, and places we also recognize from the daily newspaper, the figure of "Joan Didion" ("call me the author," the narrator says, but particularizes herself by quoting textbook comments on Didion) becomes a bridge between fiction and fact. Naturally, by the creation of verisimilitude in her fictive world, the author invites (as do authors generally in realistic fiction) a sense of identification which generalizes the import of the story. To the extent that we recognize aspects of the characters' lives as resembling our own, we say that the story represents general experience. Accordingly, women readers will recognize the silences in the marriage bed, the conversational slightings, and other experiences of the fictional Inez and will validate the representational character of her story. But the bridging effect of "Joan Didion" accomplishes such generalizing in a much more direct way.

Clearly, the narrator objects to aspects of her world that are not gender-related. Her difficulty in telling her story does not stem simply from the fact that she is a woman, writing about a woman. The main burden of the story is a stringent objection to the ebbing of traditional values, family values, and a moral horror at the spectacle of America's role in Vietnam. It is an objection to dishonesty. Didion affirms the importance of what we must consider traditional values and traditional sources of satisfaction for women as well—stable relationships with men and with extended family, motherhood. Whether there has ever been a time when these roles alone did in fact provide adequate sources of fulfillment is a question she does not address. At the same time, Didion does not ignore the need for other satisfactions as well, means of achieving personal autonomy and self-definition. At any rate, the uncentered state of American society that undermines public and private honor also makes traditional role-fulfillment impossible. Gender problems are implicated in Didion's broad social criticism, even when they are not specified.

Within the novel, "Joan Didion" is drawn to the story of Inez Victor largely by her own need. Obviously it is, in a journalistic sense, a good story, with interesting social trappings and an odor of scandal. But it is not those aspects that keep the novelist working to find the right narrative approach to what is "a hard story to tell." Those externals are aspects of the story that she has "abandoned," "scuttled," "jettisoned" in favor of a focus on Inez's feelings and on her achievement of a personal value perspective on a world falling apart. That "Joan Didion" shares the need for such a perspective is clear from her account of the genesis of the novel: "I began thinking about Inez Victor and Jack Lovett at a point in my life when I lacked certainty, lacked even that minimum level of ego which all writers recognize as essential to the writing of novels, lacked conviction, lacked patience with the past and interest in memory; lacked faith even in my own technique." She focuses, in the early part of the novel, on the powerful emotional pull of a daughter's feelings toward a mother who has abandoned her and on the liminal position of looking with regret at a disappearing world, giving the "last look through more than one door." If she finds it a "hard story to tell" because of its complexity, occupying as it does the intersection of many issues, she also finds it hard to tell because its emotional impact evokes her own shared feelings.

The narrator's feelings are apparent in her hovering, circling style, with its tone of stiff-upper-lip compression. Her own experience of the breakup of American pretenses and the revelation of the hollowness at the core, epitomized in the fall of Vietnam, leads her to reinterpret the behavior of Inez Victor, also experiencing that breakup in a very direct way, so as to see it as a coping mechanism. "After the events which occurred in the spring and summer of 1975 I thought of it differently. I thought of it as the essential mechanism for living a life in which the major cost was memory. Drop fuel. Jettison cargo. Eject crew." In the same way as Inez jettisons the troubling cargo of memory, "Joan Didion" jettisons the cargo of superficial approaches to the story and Didion jettisons the cargo of excess verbiage. She retains only the words that epitomize emotional states and qualities of experience, not elaborated descriptions of those states and qualities, and the terse sarcasms that pronounce her judgment in the shortest possible fashion. The quickness of her verbal step shows her distaste for the moral muck. These few summary phrases she sets off as significant units ("drop fuel" and the parallel phrases quoted above) and repeats in meditative litanies. Her sense of the preciousness of Inez's long love for Jack Lovett, for instance, is conveyed in the sequence,

to keep the idea of it quick.

Quick, alive.

Something to think about late at night.

Something private.

She always looked for him.

The reader's sense of such a sequence encompasses not only its realization of Inez's emotion but its evidence of the narrator's involvement. The selection of the few emphasized phrases conveys a correspondence of feeling which goes far to explain the powerful emotional hold of the story of "Joan Didion," evidenced by her "examining this picture for some years now" to understand Inez's motivation, including Inez's motivation for first concealing and then revealing her memories to the writer "Joan Didion."

We may conjecture that the answer to that puzzle, the puzzle of why Inez finally shares her memories after long concealment, lies in her final achievement of an autonomous personal space. Released from the confusions and trivialization imposed on her by others, notably by both her natal family and her husband, she can at last achieve emotional balance and pursue work that she herself finds important. Only the sense of security gained by achieving that space allows her to communicate freely with "the author." "Didion," too, needs to find such a space, and does find it vicariously in her relationship to Inez—thus becoming enabled to write her novel. "Didion's" relation to Inez, then, becomes a kind of daughter-to-mother relation, a version of the relation that had first drawn her into the story. Inez, through her suffering and her eventual achievement, gives birth to and nurtures the eventual achievement of "the author."

Joan Didion represents a very different achievement in using strategies of reticence than the achievement we see in Austen, Porter, or Cather. Her strategy is more directly aggressive than theirs, employing sarcastic barbs to undermine the dishonesty and specious values that are her target. Conversational sarcasm, too, is often, of course, conveyed in brief phrases and monosyllables. Didion's interrupted style lends itself to our "hearing" a voice of sarcastic stringency, with anger and grief seething in the interstices. At the same time, sarcasm does not attack its object directly, but obliquely. It is another means of saying without saying, of speaking—virulently—by indirection or by not speaking. Didion's acerbic voice is a radical transformation of the traditional female reticence we see brought to fullness in Austen. It is also a continuation of that female strategy.

Source: Janis P. Stout, "Joan Didion and the Presence of Absence," in *The Critical Response to Joan Didion,* edited by Sharon Felton, Greenwood Press, 1994, pp. 147–87.

Thomas R. Edwards

In the following review, Edwards favorably assesses Democracy *and how Didion articulates its theme of "the devastating personal and public consequences of the loss of history."*

Joan Didion is one of those writers—Norman Mailer, Mary McCarthy, and Gore Vidal are others—who are so good at the higher journalism that their status as novelists may sometimes seem insecure. Do they, we may wonder, keep writing fiction out of professional pride, as if only the novel could truly certify their literary talent and seriousness? Are not their novels, however fine, shadowed by a suspicion, however baseless, that the form is not quite the best form for such powers?

Certainly *Democracy,* Didion's new novel, opens with an ominously awkward display of self-consciousness about the basic moves of fictional narrative:

The light at dawn during those Pacific tests was something to see.

Something to behold.

Something that could almost make you think you saw God, he said.

He said to her.

Jack Lovett said to Inez Victor.

Inez Victor who was born Inez Christian.

This self-revising fumbling with the identity cards that novels are supposed to slip quietly under the door seems a little like having a magician confess that the rabbit came not from the empty hat but from inside his vest. "This is a hard story to tell," complains the last sentence of this first chapter, and the manner of this opening makes one wonder if for Didion the old game is still good enough to play.

But what we have here is clearly a "chapter"— it began with a "1," and after some blank space and the turn of a page we find a new block of text headed "2." Despite the authorial shufflings, a story begins to get told, as if impelled by the stubborn conventions of narrative itself, the odd necessity of continuing once you have, for whatever reason, started. The devices of anti-fiction don't disappear. "Call me the author," the second chapter begins, followed by a glimpse of a writer named "Joan Didion" (done in the manner not of Melville but, of all people, Trollope) who is struggling to get her story started: "Consider any of these things long enough and you will see that they tend to deny the relevance not only of personality but of narrative, which makes them less than ideal images with which to begin a novel, but we go with what we have."

So indeed we do, but counter-illusion has begun to generate its own, second-order kind of credence—if this narrator is the Joan Didion who went to Berkeley, worked for *Vogue* in 1960, now lives in Los Angeles but travels to far-off places as a reporter, and so on, then Inez Christian Victor and Jack Lovett and the other people in this book may be real after all, since Joan Didion says she knew them. Maybe she does have nothing up her sleeve.

For a critic this is good material, but most readers of novels want the puppets to come to life, and in *Democracy* they blessedly do so before long, despite the continuing maneuverings of the author. Inez Christian, we learn, is a child of privilege. She was born in 1935, in Hawaii, to a mainland girl from Stockton who, while modeling at Magnin's in San Francisco, was swept off her feet and over the seas by Paul Christian, the footloose and increasingly odd son of one of those rich old families whose economic conquest of the Islands was an early, if relatively benign, instance of Yankee colonialism. As Didion pieces together Inez's story, we learn that she went to Sarah Lawrence, married (two months' pregnant) an ambitious young lawyer named Harry Victor, had twins, worked in New York with Joan Didion, and then settled, uncomfortably, into the quasi-public role of political wife.

Harry Victor, who has a keen eye for the main chance, became an activist lawyer in the 1960s, got elected to Congress and then the Senate, came close to winning a presidential nomination in 1972, and now devotes himself to something called the Alliance for Democratic Institutions. He is an odious man, full of a liberal self-importance that views the world and himself in it as "incorporeal extensions of policy," over-responsive to the young women who swarm around him and his causes (one of them, a pop singer, is winningly modest about her talents—"I just do two lines of coke and scream"), deeply attracted to his own untested slogans and the joys of radical chic. He is, in fact, almost a cartoon, but Didion allows him just enough semblance of humanity to suggest, in case we hadn't noticed, how really cartoon-like are the politics manufactured by television and the press.

Harry is less successful as paterfamilias than as public image. His son, the marvelously named Adlai, is a pompous lunkhead who barely gets into an obscure college near Boston but likes to talk grandly about what's what in "Cambridge." Adlai's twin, Jessie, equally dumb but somewhat sweeter, becomes a heroin addict in prep school, not out of rebellion against her parents or society but simply as a "consumer decision." Sent off to Seattle for methadone and work-therapy, she, perhaps too neatly, makes her way to Saigon just as the last Americans are being evacuated, because someone told her you could find interesting jobs there.

Inez herself deals with her marriage by becoming more and more numb to what happens to her. She comes to consider "most occasions as photo opportunities"; she works dutifully for good causes and is rumored to have a drinking problem; she reflects that she has been "most happy in borrowed houses, and at lunch." Asked by an AP reporter what the greatest cost of public life is, she answers "memory, mainly," and when urged to explain, she simply says, "you lose track." This seems an acute comment on the plight of politicians and others in public life—having to say and do so much just to hold your audience, you cease to care about, and then even to remember, what really happened. That may be why presidential advisers and others close to power seem so genuinely surprised that discrepancies in the record bother other people.

The devastating personal and public consequences of the loss of history are Didion's theme. The significant relations of events wash away in a flood of facts, those equally circumstantial details that news reporting democratically represents as being about equal in import:

I would skim the stories on policy and fix instead on details: the cost of a visa to leave Cambodia in the weeks before Phnom Penh closed was five hundred dollars American. The colors of the landing lights for the helicopters on the roof of the American embassy in Saigon were red, white, and blue. The code names for the American evacuations of Cambodia and Vietnam respectively were EAGLE PULL and FREQUENT WIND. The amount of cash burned in the courtyard of the DAO in Saigon before the last helicopter left was three-and-a-half million dollars American and eighty-five million piastres. The code name for this operation was MONEY BURN. The number of Vietnamese soldiers who managed to get aboard the last American 727 to leave Da Nang was three hundred and thirty. The number of Vietnamese soldiers to drop from the wheel wells of the 727 was one. The 727 was operated by World Airways. The name of the pilot was Ken Healy.

The voice heard here is Joan Didion's, not Inez Victor's, but the malady it reflects is also Inez's and of course our own. Vietnam is the most dramatic recent evidence of where an appetite for imperium can lead democracy; but the larger subject must be the evanescence of thought and moral judgment in a world of ceaselessly unsortable information.

It is the reading of this particular news story, on March 26, 1975, that leads Joan Didion to another story, a report of what becomes the crucial event of Inez's life. This is the murder in Honolulu, by Inez's now-insane father, of her sister Janet and Wendell Omura, a local anti-war congressman who may have been Janet's lover. This violent mixing of domestic self-destruction and racial chauvinism leads Inez toward something like moral freedom; and it gives the novel some justification of its intricate method in what seems to me its most daring and impressive stroke of political imagination.

The temporal circlings of Didion's narrative began, if just barely, with the conversation between Inez and Jack Lovett about the H-bomb tests in the Pacific in the early 1950s. That conversation, we later learn, took place in 1975, after the murders. Jack Lovett, a considerably older man, met Inez in Honolulu in 1952, before she left for college; they then had a brief affair which both remember fondly but do not continue when they occasionally meet in later years. Lovett is the antitype of Harry Victor, not a theorist and rhetorician but a sometime army officer and nominal diplomat who works in the demimonde where the CIA, private corporations, and plain criminals consort together for obscure purposes of profit and national policy. He has "access to airplanes"; when Joan Didion meets him in New York in 1960, he is "running a little coup

somewhere"; wherever he goes (and he goes everywhere) he strikes up conversations and asks questions, treating "information as an end in itself."

According to one version—a cartoon version, no doubt—of the world of power, Jack Lovett ought to be a bad man. He is certainly a tough man, whose arms deals and insurrections Joan Didion rather gently sees as expressing an interesting and almost admirable "emotional solitude, a detachment that extended to questions of national or political loyalty." Compared to the ungrounded ideological sparking of loose wires like Harry Victor, Lovett's illusionless concern for how to do things, what combinations of people and materials will have the needed result, is in a way refreshing. Though Lovett isn't made immune to the obvious objections, Didion breathtakingly elects him to be the one who cares and remembers, the one in whom information becomes knowledge, understanding, and even love.

Lovett remembers those bomb tests, not as horrifying displays of technique but as occasions of beauty:

He said: the sky was this pink no painter could approximate, one of the detonation theorists used to try, a pretty fair Sunday painter, he never got it. Just never captured it, never came close. The sky was this pink and the air was wet from the night rain, soft and wet and smelling like flowers, smelling like those flowers you used to pin in your hair when you drove out to Schofield, gardenias … never mind there were not too many flowers around those shot islands.

His memory of the tests gets entangled with his memories of loving Inez at about the same time, but he does remember her; and when her life goes fully to pieces after the murders in 1975, Lovett is there to help her escape the obligations to her corrupt husband and family that—or so we are to gather from Didion's cool observation—have been visibly destroying her.

I doubt that Didion means to suggest some comprehensive typology of character in making the otherwise rather sinister Jack Lovett a man of genuine sentiment in a political world where nominal good guys like Harry Victor have trouble feeling anything. She seems to have a weakness for male realists, however—Lovett has in effect a double in Billy Dillon, Victor's tough and amusingly cynical advisor, who understands Inez's feelings, takes care of her when her family flounders, and has secretly loved her all along. If there is a point to Lovett's combination of qualities, it may simply be that public performances don't reliably fit the contours of the private self inside. Lovett's self comes to an abrupt end before *Democracy* is over, but only after he has led Inez to about as much freedom as she can hope to manage. She remains in Asia, quietly looking after Vietnamese refugees, a choice people like Harry Victor would have difficulty understanding.

Democracy is absorbing, immensely intelligent, and witty, and it finally earns its complexity of form. It is indeed "a hard story to tell," and the presence in it of "Joan Didion" trying to tell it is an essential part of its subject. Throughout one senses the author struggling with the moral difficulty that makes the story hard to tell—how to stop claiming what Inez finally relinquishes, "the American exemption" from having to recognize that history records not the victory of personal wills over reality (as people like Harry Victor want to suppose), but the "undertow of having and not having, the convulsions of a world largely unaffected by the individual efforts of anyone in it."

This grim message supports the assumption that a novel by another American pessimist, Henry Adams's *Democracy,* is somewhere in Didion's mind. (She in fact quotes from the *Education,* and Adams's ambitious, venal, magnetic, and illusionless Senator Silas P. Ratcliffe may vaguely foreshadow both Harry Victor and Jack Lovett.) Both novels deal with the perilous maturing of a political culture which the national rhetoric ceaselessly represents as vigorous and young. Adams put a slightly different formulation of "the American exemption" into the mouth of a European diplomat unable to tolerate that rhetoric any longer:

> "You Americans believe yourselves to be excepted from the operation of general laws. You care not for experience. I have lived seventy-five years, and all that time in the midst of corruption. I am corrupt myself, only I do have the courage to proclaim it.... Well, I declare to you that in all my experience I have found no society which has had elements of corruption like the United States.... I do much regret that I have not yet one hundred years to live. If I then could come back to this city, I should find myself very much content … *ma parole d'honneur!*" broke out the old man with fire and gesture, "the United States will then be more corrupt than Rome under Caligula; more corrupt than the Church under Leo X; more corrupt than France under the Regent!"

Now, 104 years later, this seems a fairly chilling forecast, and the America of Joan Didion's *Democracy* seems amply to confirm it. Our decline has reached the Pacific—a name of consummate irony—and across it. Inez Victor's businessmen relatives are still making big money in construction around the Persian Gulf, but back home in the

Islands their real-estate developments are going bankrupt, and it is Wendell Omura's relatives who run things in Honolulu. And of course farther west, past the test-blast atolls, Southeast Asia produces its refugees. Like Henry Adams, we gave up on Washington long ago.

With due allowance for the distances between Quincy and Sacramento, Henry Adams and Joan Didion may have something in common. In both of them, irony and subtlety confront a chaotic new reality that shatters the orderings of simpler, older ways. Both face such a world with an essentially aristocratic weapon, the power to dispose language and thought, at least, against those empowered to dispose just about everything else. And both, I suppose, understand that such a weapon is only defensive, and that it may not suffice.

Source: Thomas R. Edwards, "An American Education," in *The New York Review of Books,* Vol. XXXI, No. 8, May 10, 1984, pp. 23–24.

Sources

Phoebe-Lou Adams, review of *Democracy* in *Atlantic Monthly,* May, 1984, p. 122.

Stuart Ching, "A Hard Story to Tell—The Vietnam War in Joan Didion's *Deomocracy,*" in *Fourteen Landing Zones—Approaches to Vietnam War Literature,* edited by Philip K. Jason, University of Iowa Press, 1991, pp. 180-87.

Thomas R. Edwards, "An American Education," in *New York Review of Books,* May 10, 1984, pp. 23-24.

Barbara Grizutti Harrison, compiler, "Joan Didion: Only Disconnect," in *Off Center: Essays,* Dial Press, 1980.

Stephen Klinkhammer, "The Fall of Saigon, April 1975," in *Everything We Had: An Oral History of the Vietnam War by Thirty-three American Soldiers Who Fought It,* edited by Al Santoli, Random House, 1981, pp. 252-56.

Thomas Mallon, review of *Democracy,* in *The American Spectator,* August, 1984, pp. 43-44.

Mary McCarthy, review of *Democracy,* in the *New York Times Book Review,* April 22, 1984, Sec. 7, p. 1.

Alan Nadel, "Postwar America and the Story of *Democracy,*" in *Boundary 2,* Vol. 19, No. 1, Spring, 1992, pp. 96-120.

"Nixon's Thin Defense: The Need for Secrecy," *Time,* June 4, 1973, pp. 17-23.

Michael Tager, "The Political Vision of Joan Didion's *Democracy,*" in *Critique,* Vol. XXI, No. 3, Spring, 1990, pp. 173-84.

Janet Wiehe, review of *Democracy,* in *Library Journal,* April, 1984, pp. 821-22.

For Further Study

Peter Carroll, in *It Seemed Like Nothing Happened: The Tragedy and Promise of America in the 1970s,* Holt, 1984.
 A full-length social and historical study of the 1970s.

Martha Duffy, review of *Democracy,* in *Time,* May 7, 1984, p. 114.
 This review criticizes Didion's placement of herself in the novel. Overall, Duffy considers the novel "flawed" yet "very fast and shrewd," especially in the depiction of the minor characters.

Sharon Felton, editor, *The Critical Response to Joan Didion,* (Critical Responses in Arts and Letters, No. 8), Greenwood, 1993.
 A very useful compilation of reviews and other critical responses to Didion's work.

Ellen G. Friedman, "The Didion Sensibility: An Analysis," in *Joan Didion: Essays and Conversations,* Ontario Review Press, 1984.
 Friedman argues that while Didion's characters are often unable to find meaning in their lives, they do have an "immense capacity for commitment and love," even when that love is doomed.

Katherine Usher Henderson, "Joan Didion: The Bond between Narrator and Heroine in 'Democracy,'" in *American Women Writing Fiction: Memory, Identity, Family, Space,* edited by Mickey Pearlman, University Press of Kentucky, 1989, pp. 69-86.

Henderson compares the character of the narrator and Inez Christian and argues that both search for meaning "in a world where society and politics are defined by artifice and self-seeking."

Al Santoli, editor, *Everything We Had: An Oral History of the Vietnam War by Thirty-three American Soldiers Who Fought It,* Random House, 1981.
 Santoli's book was almost certainly used by Didion as source material for her portrayal of the chaos surrounding American withdrawal from Saigon.

Susan Stamberg, "Cautionary Tales," in *Joan Didion: Essays and Conversations,* edited by Ellen G. Friedman, Ontario Review Press, 1984.
 In this interview, Didion discusses her belief that "experience is largely meaningless" and talks about how that view has affected her novels.

Janis P. Stout, *Strategies of Reticence: Silence and Meaning in the Works of Jane Austen, Willa Cather, Katherine Anne Porter and Joan Didion,* University Press of Virginia, 1990.
 An example of an academic title placing Didion in the continuum of American female novelists.

Anne Tyler, review of *Democracy,* in *New Republic,* April 9, 1984, Vol. 190, pp. 35-36.
 This review comments on the narrator as a character and on the fragmented structure of the novel.

Mark Royden Winchell, in *Joan Didion,* revised edition, Twayne, 1989.
 A biographical and critical survey of Didion's career.

Ellen Foster

Kaye Gibbons

1987

When Kaye Gibbons published *Ellen Foster* in 1987, the novel—her first—met with an enthusiastic audience. Critics admired Gibbons's skillful creation of Ellen's narrative voice, acknowledging its accuracy in representing a child's point of view. Gibbons won two literary awards for *Ellen Foster,* the Sue Kaufman Prize for First Fiction and a citation from the Ernest Hemingway Foundation. While some readers criticized the events of the novel as being melodramatic, others asserted that Ellen's wisdom, resilience, and tenacity save her narrative from becoming a sentimental tearjerker. Gibbons has said that some of the events of the novel—Ellen mother's suicide and Ellen's subsequent movement from one relative's home to another—reflect her own childhood experiences. Ellen is indeed a lonely child, quietly observing the happiness of other families, yearning to belong, and making mental notes about what her perfect family should be like. *Ellen Foster* is ultimately a coming-of-age story, as Ellen engineers for herself a place in the secure, nurturing family she has craved and simultaneously comes to understand herself better through her friendship with Starletta, her black friend. Against the Southern backdrop of racism, Ellen moves from feeling she is superior to Starletta into a new understanding that color has nothing to do with a person's character. *Ellen Foster* belongs not only to the Southern tradition in American literature, with its distinctive voice and its treatment of racism, but also to that of first-person coming-of-age narratives, in which the narrator's innocence is also his or her wisdom.

Kaye Gibbons

Author Biography

When Gibbons first published *Ellen Foster* in 1987, journalists writing about the book—her first novel—wanted to know whether narrator Ellen's troubled childhood reflected in any way the early experiences of her creator.

Born in 1960 in Nash County, North Carolina, Gibbons, not wanting to draw attention to her own life as a means of publicizing the book, was reluctant at first to discuss her childhood with the press. Eventually though, she revealed that her mother, like Ellen's, had committed suicide when Gibbons was ten, an event which led to her family's breakup and to Gibbons's having to live in a succession of relatives' homes.

Gibbons went on to graduate from Rocky Mount High School in North Carolina, and while a college student at the University of North Carolina at Chapel Hill, she began writing a poem in the voice of Starletta. Gibbons told Bob Summer in a *Publishers Weekly* interview that she wrote from Starletta's perspective because "I wanted to see if I could have a child use her voice to talk about life, death, art, eternity—big things from a little person." The poem about Starletta eventually evolved into *Ellen Foster.*

Gibbons gave up her plans for a teaching career once it was clear that *Ellen Foster* was a success. She won the Sue Kaufman Prize for First Fiction from the American Academy and Institute of Arts and Letters, as well as a citation from the Ernest Hemingway Foundation, for *Ellen Foster.* She cites both Flannery O'Connor and James Weldon Johnson as important literary influences on her work.

In *Hungry Mind Review,* Gibbons admits that an editor's one-time prediction that she "would always write about women's burdens," has mostly come true. She writes, she says, "in part, to discover what those burdens are and how a character's load can be lessened, her pain mitigated." In *Ellen Foster,* Gibbons discovers that Ellen, just on the verge of young womanhood, finds comfort and relief from her burdens within herself.

Plot Summary

The Beginning
Ellen Foster is told from young Ellen's point of view. The narrative shifts between memories of her abusive past and descriptions of her present life in a foster family.

The book opens with Ellen's confession that she used to think of ways to kill her daddy, but she did not kill him. He drank himself to death. She just wished him dead. She then shifts to talking about how much happier she is now that she lives with her foster family in a clean home with plenty of food.

Shifting into the past again, Ellen relates how her sickly mother came home from the hospital but could not rest because she had to tend to her drunken, abusive husband. Ellen tries to shield her mother from her father, effectively serving as parent to both of them, but she cannot save her mother, who overdoses on pills. Ellen tries to call for help, but her father threatens to kill both Ellen and her mother if Ellen leaves the house. He convinces Ellen that all her mama needs is sleep, so Ellen takes her mother back to bed and curls up beside her. Even after she feels her mother's heart stop beating, Ellen continues to lie there, wanting to hold on to her mother for a little longer.

Ellen's Daddy
After the death of his wife, Ellen's father stops doing anything but eating and sleeping. His brothers bring him some papers to sign, and after that

they bring him an envelope with money once a month. Ellen makes sure to get to the money before her father does so that she can pay the bills and buy food. Ellen's only friends are Starletta and her parents, a black family that lives nearby. Ellen struggles with her prejudices as she likes Starletta and her family, but secretly feels superior to them and fears that if she drinks from the same cup or eats their food she will catch something from them. Ellen spends Christmas day with them, but although she is hungry she will not eat dinner with them. She returns home, relieved not to find her drunken father there and spends Christmas night alone. This lonely scene is juxtaposed with a scene from Ellen's present life in the foster home, where all of the children are building a terrarium together.

On New Year's eve Ellen's father and other drunken men show up at Ellen's house. Ellen hides when the drunken men make lewd comments about her. When she comes out of hiding and tries to sneak out of the house her father grabs her, calling her by her mother's name. She runs to Starletta's home and asks to spend the night, offering to pay a dollar, which Starletta's mother refuses.

Ellen then decides to leave her father's house. Packing all of her things in a box, she calls her aunt Betsy and asks if she can stay with her. Betsy picks her up and they spend a pleasant weekend together but when Betsy discovers Ellen wants to stay permanently, she refuses to take Ellen in and drives her back home. The narration then abruptly shifts from this scene of rejection to Ellen's description of how her "new mama" shops for all of her foster children, always providing them with plenty of food and a safe place to stay.

Back at her father's house Ellen decides she will have to lock herself up to avoid her father's advances. Sometimes, however, he gets to her anyway and she has to struggle to escape. When Ellen's teachers notice a bruise on her arm they decide she cannot stay with her father anymore.

Julia and Roy

Ellen moves in with her art teacher, Julia, and Julia's husband, Roy. Roy and Julia are former hippies who moved to the rural south to find themselves. With them, Ellen is able to relax and enjoy herself. They garden, cook, paint, and draw together, and Ellen has her first birthday party, with Starletta as her guest. Ellen's life seems to be improving, until her father shows up one day at her school. Drunk as usual, he drops his pants and stands in the schoolyard shouting for her. Shortly after, the court takes Ellen from Julia and Roy and

awards custody to her grandmother, a bitter, angry woman who blames Ellen and her daddy for the death of Ellen's mama.

Again the novel shifts, from the loneliness of Ellen's past to the comfort and companionship of her present. Ellen describes the good food at her foster home and how enjoyable it is to be with her new mama and all the other children.

Mama's Mama

The period spent at her grandmother's house is a bad time for Ellen, who quickly learns that her grandmother hates her and blames her for the death of her mama. Ellen is put to work in the fields. The work is physically demanding, but through it Ellen meets Mavis, a black farmhand who grew up on the farm with Ellen's mama. Talking to Mavis, Ellen learns a lot about her own family, and watching Mavis and the other fieldhands, she learns a lot about what a family should be.

Ellen's father drinks himself to death and then her grandmother gets sick. Ellen must now leave working in the fields to take care of her. She believes Ellen helped her father to kill her mama, and so she tells Ellen "you best take better care of me than you did of your mama."

Ellen figures out that after her mother's death her grandmother took over the farm deeds belonging to Ellen's father and his brothers. It was she who provided the monthly envelope full of money, and then slowly killing off Ellen's daddy by giving him less money each month, knowing he would waste it all on alcohol.

Ellen cares for her grandmother to the best of her ability and when she dies Ellen even tries to revive her. But when she cannot resuscitate her she tells her " … the score is two to one now. I might have my mama's soul to worry over but you've got my daddy's and your own. The score is two to one but I win."

The Foster Home

After her grandmother's death, aunt Nadine and cousin Dora Ellen reluctantly taken Ellen in. Attending church with them one Sunday, Ellen sees her new mama for the first time. She asks Dora who the woman with all the girls is and Dora tells her they are the foster family. Ellen naively assumes that this means their last name is "Foster." Ellen knows from the woman's dignity and compassion that this is the mother for her, so when Nadine throws her out on Christmas day, Ellen walks to the foster home. She asks if she can stay there, offering all the money she has saved, one hundred and sixty six dollars, as payment. Ellen's new mama refuses the money, but gladly takes in the love-starved child.

In her new foster home Ellen is no longer forced to care for others, and is instead cared for. She is happy, but begins to miss Starletta, who is growing up and whom she fears will not always want to be friends with her. Growing up, Ellen leaves behind old prejudices. She begins to make plans to bring Starletta to spend the night at the foster home.

The book ends with Starletta's visit to Ellen's new home. Ellen confesses her old prejudices to Starletta, and in apologizing for them reveals how much she has learned and matured over the course of the novel.

Characters

art teacher
See Julia

Aunt Betsy

One of Ellen's mother's two sisters, Aunt Betsy is willing to have Ellen come stay with her for a weekend, but ultimately won't help her or take responsibility for her.

Aunt Nadine

Ellen's mother's sister, Aunt Nadine, is a self-important, selfish phony who treats Ellen as if she is beneath her. Aunt Nadine avoids the truth, refusing, for instance, to admit that her daughter Dora still wets her pants at the age of ten. Nadine takes charge at Ellen's mama's funeral, but Ellen is disgusted by her pretension and cheerfulness as she chats with the undertaker. According to Ellen, when Aunt Nadine "is not redecorating or shopping with Dora she demonstrates food slicers in your home."

When Ellen goes to live with Dora and Aunt Nadine after her grandmother dies, she sees that she is not welcome and decides to keep to herself as much as possible. For Christmas, after Ellen gives Nadine and Dora a painting she worked hard to make, they ridicule the painting behind her back. Ellen's Christmas gift from them is a pack of white art paper, a meager gift next to Dora's mountain of toys and clothes. Crushed and angered by their selfishness, Ellen tells Nadine she is crazy and that she and Dora are "the same as the people who would

Media Adaptations

- *Ellen Foster* was adapted as a Hallmark Hall of Fame television movie starring Glynnis O'Connor, Jena Malone, Julie Harris, and Debra Monk, 1997.

- Kaye Gibbons reads *Ellen Foster* on an audio cassette (three hours), published by Simon & Schuster (Audio), 1996.

not believe the world was round." Aunt Nadine thereupon tells Ellen to get out, that she never wanted Ellen to come, and that she and Dora just want to live in their house alone. This is Ellen's impetus to make her move to find herself a new family.

big lady
See Mavis

Dora

Ellen's first cousin, the daughter of Ellen's mother's sister, Aunt Nadine. Dora is ten years old and still wets her pants, according to Ellen. A spoiled only child, Dora is taught by her mother to look down on Ellen and not to see the truth.

Dora's mama
See Aunt Nadine

Ellen's daddy

Abusive toward his wife and daughter, Ellen's daddy is a self-destructive and selfish alcoholic. For Ellen, he is "a monster," "a mistake for a person." His cruelty to Ellen's mother is the reason for her suicide.

Following her death, he neglects Ellen, staying away from home for long periods and leaving Ellen alone in the house. When he is home, he often brings groups of friends home with him to drink. They take over the house and frighten Ellen, who hides when they are around. When her father begins to make sexual advances toward her, Ellen runs away. In the book's opening sentence, Ellen

A scene from the Hallmark Hall of Fame adaptation of Ellen Foster, *starring Jena Malone as Ellen and Julie Harris as her grandmother.*

confesses "When I was little I would think of ways to kill my daddy." She hates him for the way he treats her mama and her. Ellen's mama's family also hate Ellen's daddy because they feel their daughter and sister married far beneath her and they condemn his cruel treatment of her.

Ellen's mama

Ellen's mama dies in the second chapter of the novel, and it is her loss that sets in motion the disintegration of Ellen's world. A gentle woman who married beneath her in the eyes of her well-to-do family, Ellen's·mama endures the abuses of her husband; returning home from the hospital after heart surgery, she drags herself around the kitchen, waiting on him as he yells insults at her. Unable to stand her life with him any longer, Ellen's mama swallows nearly the whole bottle of her heart pills and dies, lying in her bed with Ellen beside her.

Ellen's mama's mama

Mean, angry, and vengeful, Ellen's mama's mama—her maternal grandmother—hates Ellen's daddy for his treatment of Ellen's mama—her daughter—and extends her hostile feelings to Ellen. A wealthy woman, she had not wanted her daugh-

ter to marry Ellen's daddy, whom she felt was beneath them socially, and now that he has caused her daughter's death, Ellen's grandmother is enraged.

When Ellen's daddy makes sexual advances toward Ellen, she runs away, and Ellen's case ultimately ends up in court, where a judge sends her to live with her grandmother because he believes families should stay together. Ellen thinks, "He had us all mixed up with a different group of folks," but she goes to live with her grandmother, who sends her every day to work in her cotton fields to get rid of her and to get revenge on Ellen's daddy. Her grandmother accuses Ellen of helping her daddy kill her mama and of being "in cahoots" with him. When her grandmother becomes desperately ill with the flu, Ellen nurses her and is by her side when she dies.

Ellen's new mama

Ellen notices the woman who is to become her "new mama" in church and it becomes clear to Ellen that this woman has dignity and character and "eyes that would flush all the ugly out of your system." After her own mama dies, Ellen thinks constantly about how to get a new, better family, and once she starts noticing the woman in church, she is determined to make this woman her new mama.

Once she does take Ellen into her home, which turns out to be a foster home for children, Ellen's new mama is all that Ellen could have hoped for in a mama: she is warm, nurturing, and supportive, and yet her home has structure and discipline. She is "always willing to help if it matters to you"; she not only allows Ellen to invite Starletta to sleep over, she also embroiders towels with Starletta's initials at Ellen's request, so that Starletta will feel especially welcome. In her new family—"the Foster family"—Ellen is made to feel she belongs.

Ellen Foster

Ellen, the eleven-year-old narrator of the novel, renames herself "Ellen Foster" when she decides she wants to be part of the "Foster family"— or foster family—she sees at church. Ellen is wise beyond her years because of the cruel treatment she has received from her "real" family, and she dreams and plans constantly about how to get herself a new family. She is a determined, resilient, resourceful girl who knows what she needs and how to fulfill those needs. She buys her own Christmas gifts and mix-and-match clothes, and she cooks frozen TV dinners for herself when her daddy isn't around.

But while Ellen is self-reliant, she also knows when she needs help, and she is driven to find the right place for herself in the world. She studies other families—Starletta's family, the "Foster family," Mavis's family—and makes mental notes of what she does and does not want in a family. As she watches Mavis and her family, Ellen declares she "would bust open if [she] did not get one of them for [her] own self soon."

She is troubled by her conflicting feelings about Starletta. At first she believes she is superior to Starletta because she is white and Starletta is black, but she comes to realize that the ones to watch out for are "the people you know and trusted they would be like you because you were all made in the same batch." Skin color does not determine what is inside that skin. White people can be low and evil.

After Ellen moves into her new mama's home, and finds her safe haven at last, she has the capacity to think about her relationship with Starletta in larger terms. She does the unthinkable in this racist Southern town and invites her black friend to sleep over at her new house. As they wait for supper in Ellen's room, Ellen recognizes that "I came a long way to get here but when you think about it real hard you will see that old Starletta came even farther…. And all this time I thought I had the hardest row to hoe."

Julia

Julia, the art teacher at Ellen's school, kindly takes Ellen home to live with her after she notices a bruise on Ellen's arm and Ellen admits her father has been hurting her. Julia is a goodhearted free spirit who loves to garden and be silly. Ellen says "she used to be a flower child [in the sixties] but now she is low key so she can hold a job." She treats Ellen like she is special.

Mavis

Mavis is a large, strong, African American woman who comes to Ellen's rescue. She helps her do the hard work in the cotton fields when Ellen's grandmother puts her to work after she comes to live with her. Ellen observes that Mavis's family is happy, and this prompts her to make "a list of all that a family should have."

psychologist

"The man [who] comes and asks me questions about the past," according to Ellen. He meets with her at school but she hates talking to him. She notices that he twists what she says to suit himself.

Roy

Julia's husband, Roy, amazes Ellen with his ability to cook, wash dishes, and clean. He is an enthusiastic organic gardener. Like Julia, Roy is kind to Ellen.

Starletta

She is Ellen's only friend. Younger than Ellen, she is an African American girl whose intact, happy family is a temporary refuge for Ellen when life with her father becomes unbearable. Starletta "hates to talk," according to Ellen, and she does not speak throughout the novel; rather, Ellen projects her emotions and longing for security onto her silent friend. Ellen loves Starletta and says of her "She is not as smart as I am but she is more fun." But Ellen is also confused about her feelings for Starletta because Starletta is "colored" and Ellen has been conditioned by her white Southern world to feel superior to her.

Starletta's daddy

Like Starletta's mama, her daddy is hospitable and warm toward Ellen. He is a family man, and Ellen notices that "he is the only colored man that does not buy liquor from my daddy."

Starletta's mama

Starletta's mama is kind to Ellen. Understanding that Ellen's life alone with her father is hard, she welcomes Ellen into her home. She and Starletta's father provide a warm and loving home for Starletta, a fact that does not escape Ellen's notice.

Stella

The unmarried "official mama" of baby Roger, Stella is also in the seventh grade. Stella and Roger live together at Ellen's new mama's house.

Themes

Alienation and Loneliness

Ellen Foster's story is one of movement, from alienation and loneliness to acceptance and belonging. Ellen herself effects this major change by force of her own will. Realizing her own family "is and always has been crumbly old brick," not meant to stick together, she targets a "foster" family that looks nice and decides to belong to them. She saves her money and on Christmas Day appears on the foster family's doorstep, ready to present $160 to her new mama and secure a place in the family.

Topics for Further Study

- Research the history of race relations in the American South during the second half of the 20th century. How did integration change the lives of blacks and whites in the South, and how have both races felt about these changes?

- Investigate the effects of foster care on American children who live in foster homes. Explore autobiographical narratives as well as research studies about life in foster care. How might living in foster homes impact—positively or negatively—a child's ability to build relationships with others?

- Has the incidence of child abuse increased in the last 25 years of the 20th century, or has increased reporting of child abuse made it seem as though child abuse is on the rise in American society? What social conditions might make child abuse a more likely occurrence?

- The definition of "family" and "family values" changed dramatically in the 20th century. Research views of the family from each twenty-five-year period of the 1900s: what was the "typical" American family like from 1900-1925? from 1926-1950? from 1951-1975? from 1976-the present? Who has been responsible for defining what is "typical" during each of these periods? How realistic is the "typical" family from each period?

Before Ellen targets the foster family as the one she wants, she is nearly alone in the world—her own mama is dead, her father neglects and abuses her, her aunts and grandmother don't want her, and her only friend, Starletta, is a little black girl who eats dirt and appears not to speak. While Starletta's parents are kind, Ellen is always aware they are "colored" and, in the context of the Southern town where they all live, she is not "supposed to" be friendly with them.

Her outsider status is emphasized by the fact that most of the happy families she knows are black and she "wanted one [that is] white." She feels she cannot be a part of either Starletta's or Mavis's families, both of whom are so closeknit. Ellen's sense of herself as "not just a face in the crowd," but as someone deserving of a place in a loving family, finally enables her to find such a place and gain a sense of belonging.

Coming of Age

Ellen Foster is a coming-of-age novel in the sense that it portrays the defining events of Ellen's young life: her mother's death when Ellen is ten, her subsequent discovery that her remaining family isn't really a family at all, her planning and achieving acceptance into a new, better family, and her learning, through it all, that her black friend Starletta is worthy of her love and admiration in spite of her skin color and background.

Ellen's coming of age begins when she is propelled into the world after her mother dies and her father attempts to sexually abuse her. She struggles to find a new family and her subsequent discoveries about life and people come from her distinct way of seeing the world. She is empowered by what she learns.

Living with the remaining members of her mother's family, she learns that cruelty comes in many forms and also what she does not want in a family. Similarly, she discovers what she does want by observing other, happier, families. She notes that the happier families she sees are usually "colored" and concludes that racism is meaningless and based on lies.

At age eleven Ellen begins to shape her own life with a vision of what she wants and then she goes after it.

Friendship

Ellen's friendship with Starletta, a black girl younger than herself, is a refuge for Ellen through much of the novel. In spite of Starletta's silence, she and her family represent a kind of safety net for Ellen. Starletta and her mother attend Ellen's mother's funeral, and Ellen wishes she could sit with them because they are the only mourners that Ellen can't condemn for being mean-spirited.

When Ellen is alone on Christmas or when her father becomes abusive, she goes to Starletta's house, knowing that Starletta's family will welcome her and make her feel safe.

Starletta's presence makes Ellen feel secure in another way too. Ellen feels superior to Starletta, criticizing her for eating dirt, picking at her bug bites, and breaking her crayons. She tells Starletta, "when I thought about you I always felt glad for myself."

Ellen knows she is not "supposed to" be friends with a black girl, but she says Starletta is "more fun" than she is and she knows Starletta will always be glad to see her. Through her friendship with Starletta, Ellen learns empathy and humility. She comes to see Starletta's life as more difficult than her own, and that she has no right to feel superior to anyone. Ellen also learns about happy families from her association with Starletta, and it is this understanding that enables her to find her own secure place in the world.

Race and Racism

Ellen is conditioned by her environment—the rural South—to look down on black people. She tries to figure out whether "colored" people are different from her. Are their germs different, is their food different? At Starletta's house, Ellen avoids drinking out of the same glass as Starletta or eating the "colored" biscuits Starletta's mother offers her. She likes Starletta even though she feels superior to her and sorry for her.

Ellen scrupulously observes Mavis and Starletta's families. She sees the love and kindness they have for each other, and knows her own extended family is not this way.

By the end of the novel, Ellen realizes color doesn't matter. Her own white family, given the chance, would stab her in the back. "Sometimes I even think I was cut out to be colored and I got bleached and sent to the wrong bunch of folks."

Her desire to have Starletta sleep over at her new house reflects how far she has come. She wants to entertain Starletta and make her feel special by having her new mama embroider towels with Starletta's initials. At first, Ellen is self-conscious about breaking "every rule in the book" by having a black girl sleep over, but then she remembers "that they changed that rule. So it does not make any sense for me to feel like I'm breaking the law." Ellen has learned that what she thinks is more important than what "the rules" are. She has seen how those in authority don't always know what is right or what is best for her.

Style

Point of View

The first-person narration in *Ellen Foster* makes the book distinctive. Ellen's unique perspective—that of a child lost amidst the swirling anger and cruelty in her family—is like the eye of a storm. Though only eleven, wise Ellen quietly perceives that her dysfunctional family "never was the kind that would fit into a handy category." Through her eyes we see that the adults around her are less capable of nurturing her than she is herself. She is sensible enough to know she needs a family and a "new mama" to take care of her.

Ellen's wisdom about the world contrasts with her often-incorrect vocabulary and grammar, emphasizing the concept that insight and authority can come from unlikely places. While a third-person rendering of Ellen's wretched circumstances might become maudlin, Ellen's good humor and resourcefulness are revealed in her dogged yet spirited first-person narration.

Setting

Ellen Foster takes place in the post-Civil Rights South, yet the racist values that Ellen struggles with throughout the novel reflect her upbringing in a South still divided by color. The racism of Ellen's world permeates the novel. Ellen's mother's funeral procession has "to drive through colored town to get to church," and Ellen's maternal grandmother calls her white father "a nigger and trash"—the worst insults she can think of—because she believes he is responsible for Ellen's mother's death.

Ellen is self-conscious about her friendship with Starletta, knowing that "every rule in the book says" she should not be friends with a "colored" girl, yet Ellen herself feels superior to Starletta because she is white and Starletta is black.

The setting is crucial to Ellen's story because the racist values of her larger world reflect the way her family treats her like a second-class citizen. As Ellen moves away from her harsh, chaotic family and toward the secure life she wants so badly, her own racism begins to fall away. She no longer needs to look down on someone in order to feel better about herself. Her change of circumstances allows her to see Starletta as a real person.

Structure

Throughout the novel, Ellen's narrative moves back and forth in time, from her present life to the events of the past year that lead up to it.

The present consists of Ellen's new life with her "new mama" in "the Foster family." This time period is marked by passages describing how orderly, nurturing, and secure life is in this new family.

Ellen's descriptions of her recent past begin with her mother's final illness and suicide, then moves through the downward spiral her life follows after this devastating event.

Gibbons's use of flashbacks to reveal the most painful times in Ellen's life allows Ellen as narrator to shape her past experiences around her happy ending. From her secure vantage point in the foster family, Ellen looks back at the turmoil and pain she lived through in her own family and feels "glad to rest" in her new home, as if she "would not ever move from there."

Images/Imagery

"Mamas" and food images permeate *Ellen Foster,* both reflecting Ellen's deep need for nurturing and love. Ellen's "real mama" commits suicide in chapter two, and the loss reverberates throughout the novel. Following her mother's death, Ellen notices "mamas" everywhere, refering to many of the women she knows not by name but in terms of their status as mothers. Her grandmother is "mama's mama," Aunt Nadine is "Dora's mama," Starletta's mother is known only as "Starletta's mama," young Stella is baby Roger's "official mama," and Ellen's foster mother is her "new mama."

"Mama," often a baby's first word, illustrates Ellen's very basic, almost infantile, need for a mother. After her mother swallows most of and too much of her heart medicine, Ellen snuggles close to her mother's side in bed and says, "I will crawl in and make room for myself. My heart can be the one that beats." This moment suggests Ellen's desire both to return to the safety of the womb and to reverse roles with her mother so that she provides life for her.

A similar hunger for nurturing and sustenance is reflected by Ellen's preoccupation with food throughout the novel. Following her mother's funeral, she goes home alone and eats "right out of the bowls" the food the ladies from church have sent. When her father neglects her and forgets to buy food for her, Ellen buys herself frozen dinners, "the plate froze with the food already on it. A meat, two vegetables, and a dab of dessert." Yet, in spite of her constant hunger, Ellen will not eat the food Starletta's mama makes because it is "colored" food. When she stays with her mama's mama, there is plenty to eat but no sense of togetherness at mealtime. "We both picked at our little individual chickens or turkeys and did not talk." Even when she is living at her new mama's house, where making and eating food are central activities, Ellen says "I stay

starved though" and predicts "I know that in ten years from now I will be a member of the food industry." Her hunger and preoccupation with food, as well as her fixation on mother figures, reflect her twin needs: to be taken care of and to belong.

Bildungsroman

Ellen Foster is a *bildungsroman,* or coming-of-age novel, tracing Ellen's movement from isolation into community, from abandonment into nurturance and her own role in making this transformation occur.

Ellen learns from her experiences. Her family teaches her what she does not want in a family, and she goes on to find one in which she can succeed. Her larger world, permeated by racism, tells her she should feel superior to black people simply because she is white, but eventually she sees the error and injustice of that view. Ellen grows into a self-empowered, empathetic girl by virtue of her ability to think for herself and her will to effect change in her world.

Historical Context

Conservatism in the 1980s

The existence of Julia—the former 1960s flower child turned respectable art teacher—helps to locate the action in *Ellen Foster* within the late 1970s or early 1980s. Gibbons began working on her ideas for the novel around 1980 while in college and published the novel in 1987.

A conservative political agenda centered on dismantling liberal programs and beliefs that held sway during the 1930s and the 1960s serve as the backdrop while Gibbons wrote her novel in the 1980s.

The civil rights and feminist movements, having accomplished much in the 1960s, now faced uphill battles against a conservative government of the 1980s. Efforts to help the homeless, fund AIDS research, and prevent drug abuse and urban violence met with resistance. The poor grew poorer while the rich grew richer. Helping those in need was viewed as encouraging the needy not to help themselves.

The contrast between Julia's flower child past and her present "low key so she can hold a job" demeanor speaks to the conservative political and social climate of the 1980s. Julia's free spirit and social-mindedness are portrayed as ultimately doing her no good in the present world of the novel. Recalling the 1960s, Julia describes herself as wanting to "change the world," but here in the 1980s her efforts to change Ellen's world fail, crushed by a court system which senselessly sends Ellen to live with a cruel, manipulative grand-mother.

Conservatives in the 1980s leaned heavily on "traditional family values," values culled from a nostalgic view of family life as it supposedly was in the past. The judge who places Ellen with her grandmother "talks about family [as] society's cornerstone," but Ellen protests in her mind that hers "was never a Roman pillar but is and always has been crumbly old brick."

Ellen and Julia both know that real families are not based on the myth of a particular set of values. The outcome of Ellen's quest for a "normal" family is ironically a group of people who are not blood-related but can still call themselves a family, thus contesting the conservative image of the "traditional" family.

Child Abuse

Reported incidents of child abuse in the United States rose dramatically during the 1980s. The number of cases reported in 1988 was four times the number reported in 1980, and in 1989 the number of reported cases stood at 2.4 million. Although these figures clearly show the prevalence of child abuse, this apparent increase may not be quite what it seems. The Child Abuse Prevention and Treatment Act, passed in 1974, requires more diligent reporting of child abuse than had previously been required. The increase in numbers may be indicative of the number of cases that professionals would not have reported previous to the passage of the 1974 act.

In the 1980s, Social Service agencies, already overburdened with the increase of child abuse cases, found they were up against a conservative social climate inhospitable to efforts to address child abuse as a social problem. Ellen Foster's abuse by her father occurs against the background of this social conservatism that includes a repulsion for families who didn't adhere to so-called "traditional family values."

Consequently, Ellen falls through the cracks of the system. Her father's neglect and abuse do not come to light until Ellen's teacher notices a bruise on her arm and for awhile she goes to live with Julia, her art teacher. When the judge sends her to live with her grandmother, Ellen is verbally and

Lorraine Lafata outlines the house rules at the Safe House for battered women and abused children in Ann Arbor, Michigan.

psychologically abused by other members of her extended family. The only sign of intervention comes from an ineffectual psychologist who she despises. He meets with her at school to discuss her "high degree of trauma."

Ellen finally achieves security not because anyone has helped her, but because she has helped herself. The irony of an abused child having to help herself find a home speaks of the harsh social climate of the 1980s, in which society's unfortunates received little help from those in power.

Racial Tensions

The gains made in race relations in the United States during the 1960s experienced a backlash in the 1980s. African Americans lost ground as the gap in income between blacks and whites grew. Racial tension accompanied the widening economic breach between the races, creating fear and anger on both sides.

When Ellen talks about "the law" that dictates separation between her and her black friend, Starletta, she could be referring to the Jim Crow laws of the South abolished during the 1960s civil rights movement. The reference could also be about the separation of the races that accompanied pre-Civil

War slavery. "I figure that if they could fight a war over how I'm supposed to think about her then I'm obligated to do it."

In spite of her affection for Starletta, Ellen is open about her feelings of superiority over Starletta and her fear of catching "colored germs." Her matter-of-fact attitude towards her own racism—repented as the novel nears its end—reflects a larger social trend in the 1980s toward open hostility of whites toward blacks.

Critical Overview

Critics responded favorably to *Ellen Foster* when it first appeared in 1987, praising Gibbons' skill crafting Ellen's narrative voice and the sensitivity she portrayed in Ellen's struggle with racism. Some critics deliberated the believability of Ellen's position as narrator, questioning whether she is too wise for her years. A critic for *Kirkus Reviews* suggested that Ellen's instinctual wisdom belies her eleven years yet in her "innocence" and "tough stoicism" the voice of this young narrator "rings true" A *Publishers Weekly* reviewer spoke in the same vein, calling Ellen's narrative voice a correct portrayal of the world from a child's view but one that was sometimes "too knowing."

Other critics focused on Gibbons's treatment of her subject matter, commenting that the terrible events of Ellen's young life could be read as melodramatic if not for Ellen's narrative voice. The *Publishers Weekly* reviewer, unsure about Ellen's capacity for saving the narrative from insipidness, claimed the book's plot is similar to a "Victorian tearjerker." But Brad Hooper, reviewing the work for *Booklist,* wrote that it was "never weepy or grim, despite the subject matter." Deanna D'Errico, in *Belles Lettres,* referred to "the artful, humorous style with which Ellen tells her tale," commenting specifically on Gibbons's use of "interweaving past and present in alternate chapters."

In agreement with both Hooper and D'Errico, Alice Hoffman wrote in *The New York Times Book Review* that "What might have been grim, melodramatic material in the hands of a less talented author is instead filled with lively humor ... compassion and intimacy." Hoffman went on to point out that the novel "focuses on Ellen's strengths rather than her victimization, presenting a memorable heroine who rescues herself."

Other critics, such as Pearl K. Bell, credited Gibbons for not falling into familiar traps by giving narrative authority to a child. Bell wrote in *The New Republic,* "Gibbons never allows us to feel the slightest doubt that [Ellen] is only 11. Nor does she ever lapse into the condescending cuteness that afflicts so many stories about precocious children." Linda Taylor asserted in *The Sunday Times* of London that Ellen is believable "because although she has a dark tale to tell, she will not engineer sympathy for her effects."

Some early critics found the theme of racism in *Ellen Foster* particularly compelling and skillfully handled by Gibbons. *Publishers Weekly* noted that the author artfully brings a reflective Ellen, given her own set of troubles, to know the injustice of discrimination by color. Again, in *The New Republic,* reviewer Pearl K. Bell claimed that "Gibbons, unlike so many writers of the New South, doesn't evade the racism of Southern life, which she subtly reveals through the tenacious child's mind." In addition to racism, Linda Taylor, critic for *The Sunday Times* saw Gibbons presenting a number of difficult social issues "through revelation rather than moral axe-grinding."

Ellen Foster suggests itself as part of the American literary tradition to some critics. The reviewer in *Kirkus Reviews* saw in Ellen's humor, intelligence, and resourcefulness, a likeness to Huck Finn and in the abusive, neglectful, alcoholic behavior of Ellen's father, a strong resemblance to "Huck's Pap." Veronica Makowsky, in *Southern Quarterly,* took the comparison further, contending that "although [Ellen's] gutsy, vernacular voice recalls Huck Finn, she does not light out for the territories in an attempt to maintain ... autonomy." Rather, Makowsky suggested, Ellen's self-reliance is demonstrated in her new mama's home by her "act of faith in others ... that allows [her] to contribute to, as well as receive from, the female tradition of community and nurturance." The novel, according to Makowsky, is "Gibbons's attempt to rewrite the saga of the American hero by changing 'him' to 'her' and to rewrite the southern female *bildungsroman* by changing its privileged, sheltered, upper-class heroine to a poor, abused outcast."

Criticism

Donna Woodford

Donna Woodford is a doctoral candidate at Washington University and has written for a wide variety of academic journals and educational publishers. In the following essay she discusses

What Do I Read Next?

- *The Adventures of Huckleberry Finn* (1883) novel by Mark Twain (Samuel Langhorne Clemens). The sensible and resourceful Huck narrates this story, in which he, a poor near-orphan, becomes the moral center when everyone around him seems to be hypocritical or corrupt. Against what he knows is the law, Huck befriends Jim, an escaped black slave, and Huck struggles with his conscience as he helps Jim make his way to freedom.
- William Faulkner's *As I Lay Dying* (1930) follows the difficult Anse Bundren and his children as they travel through Mississippi, bringing their dead wife and mother, Addie, to her birthplace for burial. The disjointed narrative is told through the interior monologues of fifteen different characters, among them the Bundren children.
- *Sights Unseen* by Kaye Gibbons (1995) is narrated by Hattie, who looks back from adulthood at how her mother's mental illness affected their family when Hattie was a girl. Like Ellen Foster, Hattie at 12 wants to be normal and to belong, and is wise beyond her years.

- Dorothy E. Allison's novel *Bastard Out of Carolina* (1992) is the first-person story of Bone, a young girl born out of wedlock into a poor South Carolina family who is sexually abused by her stepfather. Bone's voice captures the sensitive perceptions of a girl who is coming of age.

- *Lost in the System* (1996) by Charlotte Lopez with Susan Dworkin is the true story of Lopez's experiences as a foster child moved from one foster home to another, hoping to find love and security. Lopez emerged successfully from her difficult beginnings and went on to win the 1993 Miss Teen USA title.

---

the narrator's search for a mother figure in Ellen Foster.

Noting the many similarities between Kaye Gibbons's childhood and that of Ellen Foster, critics often focus on the autobiographical nature of Gibbons's first novel. In a 1993 interview with *Publishers Weekly,* Gibbons admits that *Ellen Foster* is "emotionally autobiographical," but she spent many years denying the parallels between the book and her own life, afraid that a focus on her own unhappy childhood would detract from the novel. But even when she was denying the autobiographical nature of *Ellen Foster,* Gibbons always credited her mother with having influenced her decision to become a writer. In "My mother, literature, and a life split neatly into two halves," she notes that the "writing urge" began with her mother, even though her mother never read to her or specifically encouraged her to write.

> Her name was Shine, which is exactly what she did through all the heat and poverty and the sad certainty that life would not be any other way. Her strength

was a fine thing to see, to remember. If I had not known that strength, that pure perseverance, I could not have become a writer. I would have chosen something that takes far less courage.

It therefore comes as no surprise that *Ellen Foster,* which is dedicated to Gibbons's mother, is largely about a young girl's quest to find a mother figure and to learn how to nurture herself and others. Ellen's story is, in fact, a coming of age story, but one in which the protagonist must achieve the childhood of which she has been deprived before she can begin to truly mature.

Ellen's recurring memory of working with her mother in the garden suggests the type of nurture for which she is searching. Describing her mother's tender care of the garden and of her, Ellen says.

> She nursed all the plants and put even the weeds she pulled up in little piles along the rows. My job was to pick the piles up and dispose of them. I was small my own self and did not have the sense to tell between weeds and plants.
>
> I just worked in the trail my mama left.

This remembered moment is one of the few times, prior to the foster home, that Ellen is allowed to behave as a child. Being small, she is not expected to take on the responsibilities of an adult. Rather she is given her own, age-appropriate job, and it is her mother who nurses the plants and leaves a trail in which her young daughter can work. But her mother's illness and her father's abuse soon rob Ellen of her nurturing mother figure. Her mother becomes unable to care either for Ellen or for herself, and Ellen is expected to serve as a parent for both her mother and father. Watching the way her father treats her invalid mother, Ellen describes him as "more like a big mean baby than a grown man," and when he is drunk she says, "you got to be firm when he is like this."

In this strange reversal of roles, the ten-year-old Ellen becomes the "firm" disciplinarian for her "mean baby" of a father. With her mother, Ellen is gentle and loving, but the roles of mother and daughter are still disturbingly reversed. Ellen helps her mother to undress and get into bed, just as a mother would do with a young child: "We peel her dress off over the head and slip on something loose to sleep in." Most disturbing of all, however, is Ellen's role as her mother's protector.

> I try not to leave her by herself with him. Not even when they are both asleep in the bed. My baby crib is still up in their bedroom so when I hear them at night I throw a fit and will not stop until I can sleep in the baby bed. He will think twice when I am around.

By climbing into her crib in order to protect her mother, Ellen simultaneously regresses to infancy and becomes a parent and protector. The fact that the screaming child in a crib is the only one who will make her father "think twice" is symbolic of the disturbingly reversed parent-child roles in their family.

The death of Ellen's mother only makes matters worse for Ellen since her father expects her to take her mother's place. Ellen takes control of paying the bills and preparing the food, but her father also expects her to take her mother's place sexually. He literally mistakes her for her mother, calling her by her mother's name: "he does not listen to me but touches his hands harder on me. That is not me. Oh no that was her name. Do not oh you do not say her name to me." Though this scene is shocking, it is only the most extreme example of the many ways in which the young Ellen is expected to take on the role of an adult woman long before she is ready to do so.

Neither does Ellen's extended family offer her the nurturing shelter which she needs. Her aunts are unwilling to care for her, and her grandmother not only fails to provide Ellen with the love and nurturing that she needs, but repeats the mistakes of Ellen's parents by expecting Ellen to take on the responsibilities of an adult.

Just as Ellen's father expected Ellen to take on her mother's role, Ellen's grandmother sees Ellen's father in her and transfers all her hate and resentment of him to his daughter. When she looks at Ellen she sees not her granddaughter, a young girl and the child of her daughter, but the accomplice of the man who took her daughter from her. Playing on the child's own guilt over her mother's death, she blames her for being "in cahoots" with her father and accuses her of having helped him to murder her mother. She refuses to see that Ellen was only a child and incapable of caring for her mother or standing up to her violent father.

Furthermore, Ellen's grandmother again places Ellen in the position of having to parent an adult: "And through all the churning and spinning I saw her face. A big clown smile looking down at me while she said to me you best take better care of me than you did of your mama." Once again, the adults in Ellen's life are reduced to absurd, childlike figures. Her grandmother is the "big clown" who saddles Ellen with the adult responsibility of caring for a dying woman.

Julia and Roy offer Ellen a brief respite from her adult responsibilities. While living with them she is allowed to enjoy childhood pleasures and does not have to care for anyone else. But though the three of them could "pass for a family on the street," Julia and Roy cannot provide Ellen with the stability and long term nurture that she needs. They are unable to protect her from the violence of her father or the anger of her grandmother, and when the judge takes Ellen from them they are as helpless as she is.

> All the arrangements are made they said so why bring me in here and do this in front of everybody like Julia who wants to scream she says. What do you do when the judge talks about the family society's cornerstone but you know yours was never a Roman pillar but is and always has been crumbly old brick? I was in my seat frustrated like when my teacher makes a mistake on the chalkboard and it will not do any good to tell her because so quick she can erase it all and on to the next problem.

Once again Ellen feels betrayed by adults who do not take adult responsibility. Teachers can erase their mistakes, and a judge can decide a child's fate even when he has her family "all mixed up with a different group of folks." In the face of such bureaucracy Julia can do nothing but "scream," and then relinquish Ellen and send her a letter "when you least expect it." Though well meaning and caring, Julia and Roy are not the stable, nurturing parents that Ellen seeks.

Throughout Ellen's troubled childhood, the two most positive examples of families in her life are Starletta's and Mavis's families. Starletta's parents are the first ones to offer Ellen shelter from her abusive father, and they are the ones who give her a Christmas present and offer to feed her on Christmas day. And just as Ellen's new mama will later refuse Ellen's money, Starletta's mother takes Ellen in when she needs protection and tells her to "put [her] money up that they do not take money from children." They are the first people to recognize that Ellen is only a child and still needs to be protected and nurtured. Mavis's family provides a similar example of a loving home. By watching Mavis's family Ellen begins to learn what a family should be.

> Of course there is the mama and the daddy but if one has to be missing then it is OK if the one left can count for two But not just anybody can count for more than his or her self.

> While I watched Mavis and her family I thought I would bust open if I did not get one of them for my own self soon.... I only wanted one white and with a little more money.

Ellen's inability to recognize that the nurturing qualities of these families are not diminished by the color of their skin merely demonstrates that although she has been forced to assume many adult responsibilities, she is not yet mature enough to make adult judgments. She will later realize that it was Starletta's family that offered her shelter when her own father threatened her.

> I wonder to myself am I the same girl who would not drink after Starletta two years ago or eat a colored biscuit when I was starved?

> It is the same girl but I am old now I know it is not the germs you cannot see that slide off her lips and on to a glass then to your white lips that will hurt you or turn you colored. What you need to worry about though is the people you know and trusted they would be like you because you were all made in the same batch. You need to look over your shoulder at the one who is in charge of holding you up and see if that is a knife he has in his hand. And it might not be a colored hand, but it is a knife.

But that realization will come only after she has found a parent who will nurture her as a child and allow her to mature at a natural pace.

She finds that parent in her "new mama." In the foster home Ellen finally has someone to care for her and love her. Describing life in the foster home Ellen says, "Nobody has died or blamed me for anything worse than overwatering the terrarium. But you can always stick some more ferns in the dirt. My new mama said it was not the end of the world." Ellen's only responsibilities here are age-appropriate, as they were in the garden with her mother. Once again she has a mother in whose path she can work.

Once Ellen reaches this safe, nurturing home, she is able to mature and begins to care for others. She puts aside her prejudices and reaches out to Starletta now that she realizes that her own difficult childhood has not been "the hardest row to hoe." In this coming of age story, Ellen must return to a safe and sheltered childhood in which she is nurtured by a mother before she can progress to the adult responsibilities of caring for others.

Source: Donna Woodford, in an essay for *Novels for Students*, Gale, 1998.

Diane Andrews Henningfeld

Henningfeld is a professor at Adrian College and has written widely for academic journals and educational publishers. In the following essay, she applies reader-response theory to Ellen Foster *in order to explore how Ellen's reading of her life parallels a reading of* Ellen Foster.

Ellen Foster is Kaye Gibbon's first novel. Published in 1987, the novel has been well received by critics and readers alike. Set in a rural Southern community, it is the story of an eleven-year-old child who endures grief and abuse before settling herself in a loving foster family.

The novel can be read as a coming-of-age story, a genre in which the main character passes from a child-like understanding of the world to an adult maturity. Books such as *Huckleberry Finn* and *Catcher in the Rye* represent this genre and are two novels to which *Ellen Foster* has been compared.

Some critics have viewed *Ellen Foster* as a story of Ellen's search for atonement. These reviewers argue that Ellen tries to redeem herself from the guilt she feels over her mother's death. In addition, these critics suggest that it is Ellen's quest for atonement that leads her to invite Starletta to her new home at the end of the novel. Ellen, they say, is attempting to atone for her earlier, racially biased attitudes that may have hurt Starletta and her family.

Finally, some critics read *Ellen Foster* as a study of free will and destiny. From the opening inscription from Ralph Waldo Emerson's "Self-Reliance" through Ellen's decision to find a home for herself, Gibbons addresses the question of personal responsibility. Although Ellen apparently believes that she is in charge of her own destiny, the question of control seems to remain ambiguous for the author.

That it is possible for *Ellen Foster* to be read in so many different ways illustrates the "openness" of the text. An open text is one which encourages readers to actively interpret rather than simply accept the text passively as something with a single meaning, complete and apart from the reader's action. Such an idea is at the heart of a literary practice known as "reader-response criticism."

Reader-response theorists argue that a text has meaning only when it is read. That is, a reader and a text work together to establish meaning. They believe that the most interesting texts are those with "gaps" that the reader must fill in. Further, literary critic Stanley Fish argues in his 1972 book, *Self-Consuming Artifacts: The Experience of Seventeenth-Century Literature,* that texts themselves are "self-consuming artifacts." Because reading is an event that takes place in time, each reading produces a unique meaning, informed by the reader's background and experience. Second readings of the same text by the same reader produce different meanings. Thus, as a reader works with a text to produce meaning, this meaning "consumes" itself nearly in the moment of its own creation. In some ways, this is parallel to the production of a play. The same group of actors performing the same script night after night will never produce two identical performances. Likewise, as we read, our understanding of earlier passages changes as we read later passages.

How might we apply these ideas to *Ellen Foster?* There are a number of strategies that illuminate the novel as not only a book in which reading takes place, but also a book about the act of reading itself. Kaye Gibbons' story is a text filled with gaps, one that requires active participation on the part of the reader. She creates gaps through the use of a limited point of view, shifts in the time sequence, and the lack of punctuation in the dialogue.

Ellen is the narrator of her own story. Consequently, everything we learn about the story is filtered through Ellen's eyes. This limited point of view hides the "big picture" from us. Rather, we are forced to piece the story together, bit by bit. Gibbons, however, offers us additional clues by allowing Ellen to report on the reactions of others, reactions that are interpreted one way by Ellen and another way by readers. Thus, we know more about the situation than Ellen does. For example, when Ellen's mama's mama dies, Ellen wants her to look nice when people arrive. She does this to atone for her own lack of response to her mother's death:

> Anybody with decency would honor the dead and fix them up in their own bed. Especially after my experience.
>
> You learn by your mistakes.
>
> But I had this one fixed pretty as a picture. I did not want a soul to say I had not done my part even down to the decorations.
>
> I found her Sunday hat she never wore and tilted it on her head the way a live woman might pop a hat on to ride to town in. Then the best part I will always be proud of was the nice frame I made all around her body. I put all the artificial flowers I could find from all those show jars around her end to end so she looked set off like a picture.

While we are within Ellen's limited point of view, this makes perfect sense. We are reading the scene in the same way she reads it. However, we shift out of this perspective when Ellen tells us, "The colored boys that loaded her up got a big kick out of my project but Nadine said I was sick to do such a thing." Suddenly, we realize how odd this little girl must appear to others. Likewise, when Ellen tells us that her new mama sits and holds Ellen's hands until her breathing slows and she stops shaking, we know that Ellen is far more traumatized than her narration leads us to believe. These moments allow us to read Ellen as other characters read her.

Gibbons also opens gaps in the text by using a chronologically-fragmented time structure. In the opening chapter, we are catapulted between Ellen's present in the home with her new mama and her past with her real mama who dies. In this first chapter, we discover that it will be our task to organize the details into a coherent story, a story that will allow us to understand Ellen's journey from past to present.

Gibbons' choice to omit punctuation around the dialogue also opens gaps. It is often unclear how much of the dialogue is spoken aloud, and how much occurs only in Ellen's head. Further, there are shifts in just who is being addressed, as in this scene just after the death of Ellen's mama's mama:

You two go ahead and fight over who did not take care of the other one's mama. You two pass the blame back and forth like butter at your tables and I'll stay out of this circle…. And even when she was so dead I could not help her anymore I made her like a present to Jesus so maybe he would take her. Take this one I got prettied up and mark it down by my name to balance against this one I held back from you before.

Here, at the beginning of the paragraph, Ellen seems to be talking to her two aunts. Suddenly, we realize that she is praying to God. Such devices force us to reread passages, and as we reread, our understanding of the text shifts and grows.

Another strategy used by reader-response critics is to examine instances of reading in the text. Certainly, *Ellen Foster* is filled with such instances. Ellen is a reader, although she "can hardly tolerate the stories we read for school." The happy families in her school books hold no interest for her; she would rather read "old books." One of her early favorites is the "laughing Middle Ages lady that wore red boots." This reference is clearly to Chaucer's Wife of Bath, a character who believes that experience, not authority, ought to be at the heart of learning. The Wife, a victim of spousal abuse, tells a story in which the main character must discover the answer to the question, "What do women most desire?" The answer is control over their own lives. The inclusion of this small allusion offers us insight into Ellen and into what she desires most herself.

There are many instances of reading in *Ellen Foster* that do not concern books, however. Her teacher "reads" a bruise on Ellen's arm, using her understanding of the bruise to fill in Ellen's story of her treatment at her father's hands. This reading demonstrates the power of text: by fixing meaning on the bruise, the teacher is able to effect real change in Ellen's life, leading to removal from her father's home.

Further, Ellen's "reading" of the ink blots put in front of her by the school social worker (the "man who comes and gets [her] out of social studies") clues us in to the depths of her distress, even as she denies it:

Then I saw big holes a body could fall right into. Big black deep holes through the table and the floor. And then he took off his glasses and screwed his face up to mine and tells me I'm scared.

I used to be but I am not now is what I told him. I might get a little nervous but I am never scared.

Ellen also reveals that she has a sophisticated understanding of the reading process and the importance of text. She understands that the made-up stories Nadine and Dora tell each other offer them some comfort, and that these stories "help them get along." Ellen also understands the ways texts change as the reader rereads. She revisits her own experiences with Starletta's family, changing the way she reads race and its importance in human relationships.

Ellen's rereading of Starletta and her family offers us a final focus on the reading process. Certainly, Ellen's reconstruction of her interactions with Starletta's family allows her to reach a better understanding of race; but we need to remember that Starletta has not participated. As Ellen lies in bed next to the silent Starletta, she reads Starletta in much the same way that the school social worker reads Ellen:

And then he will not let go of a word but he has to bend and pull and stretch what I said into something he can see on paper and see how it has changed like a miracle into exactly what he wanted me to say.

Ellen reads Starletta's life as a text, bending, pulling, and stretching that life in order to make meaning out of her own life. Further, Ellen uses Starletta's life as a yardstick against which to measure her own journey toward adulthood: "I came a way to get here but when you think about it real hard you will see that old Starletta came even farther."

Likewise, as readers, we want this to be a story with a happy ending about racial harmony and maturity. We, too, read like Ellen, (and like the school social worker), as we make meaning out of her relationship with Starletta. However, although this is the ending we want (and perhaps need), we ought to recall Starletta's difficulty with reading, and with speaking. When we do this, we see that the text is here at its most open. Starletta's life is an open text in the same way that *Ellen Foster* is an open text, offering the reader multiple avenues for interpretation, and raising the moral implications of reading another's life in order to make meaning of one's own.

Source: Diane Andrews Henningfeld, in an essay for *Novels for Students,* Gale, 1998.

Veronica Makowsky

In the following excerpt, critic Veronica Makowsky explores Kaye Gibbons's use of food as a major metaphor to describe the main character of Ellen Foster as she develops in Gibbons's novel of the same name.

Ellen Foster is Gibbons's attempt to rewrite the saga of the American hero by changing "him" to "her" and to rewrite the southern female *bil-*

dungsroman by changing its privileged, sheltered, upper-class heroine to a poor, abused outcast.... Ellen faces the psychological and spiritual problems of growing up, but she must also confront sexual abuse, homelessness and, above all, hunger....

The novel opens with ten-year-old Ellen trying to shield her sick mother from her father's abuse. Ellen's mother has just returned from the hospital for treatment of the chronic heart condition she acquired in her youth from rheumatic fever, which Ellen calls "romantic fever." Ellen's malapropism is actually quite accurate since her mother married beneath her class in what she must have believed to be a romantic escape from her own overbearing mother. Her mistake is glaringly obvious as Ellen's boorish father insists that her invalid mother make dinner, though she is plainly incapable of feeding anyone. Ellen comments that her mother "would prop herself up by the refrigerator" and "looks like she could crawl under the table." Because these props of domesticity—the refrigerator and kitchen table—are inadequate, Ellen herself must act as substitute homemaker. Her thoughts turn more to contamination, however, than to nurture: "What can I do but go and reach the tall things for her? I set that dinner table and like to take a notion to spit on his fork."

With Ellen's help, her mother gets dinner on the table and fulfills her physical role as nurturer, but she never learns to nurture herself. All she wants to ingest is an overdose of her medication in order to escape her unbearable marriage. Again, Ellen takes on the parental role as she implores: "Vomit them up, mama. I'll stick my finger down your throat and you can vomit them up. She looks at me and I see she will not vomit. She will not move." Ellen's mother is so debilitated physically and mentally that she poisons herself and can look at, but not nurture, her only child. Her father refuses to allow Ellen to call for help and later, as Ellen rests in bed beside her dying mother, she asserts, "And I will crawl in and make room for myself. My heart can be the one that beats." Ellen is expressing contradictory desires: to return to the womb's safety where she was fed and to take over the life-sustaining role of the mother's heartbeat and nourishing bloodstream.

Although Ellen's mother is totally unable to nurture her child at the beginning of the novel, in her earlier seasons of relatively good health she taught Ellen the lessons about life to which Ellen clings after her death. Ellen's favorite memory is of gardening with her mother.

She nursed all the plants and put even the weeds she pulled up in little piles along the rows. My job was to pick the piles up and dispose of them. I was small my own self and did not have the sense to tell between weeds and plants.

I just worked in the trail my mama left.

When the beans were grown ready to eat she would let me help pick. Weeds do not bear fruit. She would give me a example of a bean that is grown good to hold in one hand while I picked with the other. If I was not sure if a particular bean was at the right stage I could hold up my example of a bean to that bean in question and know.

Once again, through the production of food, Gibbons suggests that from her mother Ellen learned not only right from wrong, beans from weeds, but also what an exemplary adult is, a model who has grown "to the right stage." After her mother's death, Ellen desperately needs these lessons as she confronts a series of caretakers who cannot or will not feed her, physically or mentally.

Ellen's father has plainly not grown to the "right stage"—he still expects others to nurture him. When her mother was in the hospital, Ellen had to supply her place as nurturer: "If I did not feed us both we had to go into town and get take-out chicken." After her mother's death, he expects ten-year-old Ellen to replace her mother sexually as well. The perverse immaturity of his sexuality is evident in his focus on Ellen's body as baby food, milk and candy. "You got girl ninnies he might say.... Somebody else calling out sugar blossom britches might sound sweet but it was nasty from him." Although we might like to believe Ellen's father is a rare monster, Gibbons evidently intends him to represent a socially pervasive view of women as objects for consumption. His black drinking buddies advise him, again in eating imagery, on the night that he rapes her: "Yours is just about ripe. You gots to git em when they is still soff when you mashum."

While her father is attempting to consume her, Ellen is trying to feed herself.

The only hard part was the food. The whole time I stayed with him he either ate at the Dinette in town or did without. I would not go to the restaurant with him because I did not want to be seen with him. That is all.

I fed myself OK. I tried to make what we had at school but I found the best deal was the plate froze with food already on it. A meat, two vegetables, and a dab of dessert.

Ellen is not just putting food in her stomach; she is attempting to maintain her standards. She will not eat with her father, especially in public, but she still manages to fulfill the nutritional requirements she learned in school. Although she may be keeping her dignity before the outside world, eating the proper food groups, and physically starving, the "froze food" indicates spiritually cold comfort.

Not all the standards she retains from her past help nurture her. Ellen's refuge is the house of her black friend Starletta which "always smells like fried meat" and where Starletta's "mama is at the stove boiling and frying." Starletta's parents welcome Ellen, assure her of a haven against her father's abuse and even take her shopping for clothes, but Ellen cannot accept them as a substitute family because, as she says, "I would not even eat in a colored house." The tenacity with which Ellen clings to her standards betrays her in this instance because she cannot differentiate between the content of nourishing love and the packaging color: "No matter how good it looks to you it is still a colored biscuit."

By court order Ellen is sent to live with her maternal grandmother who, unfortunately, is not a sweet, white-haired old lady ready to feed the poor child milk and cookies, as Ellen quickly perceives: "My mama's mama picked me up in her long car that was like the undertaking car only hers was cream." Ellen's recognition of her grandmother's poisonous propensities is evident in her association of her grandmother's car with a hearse and food ("cream"), as well as her refusal to use the word "grandmother." Ellen's intuitions are accurate since her grandmother is taking Ellen not to nurture her, but to punish her for her mother's death, persisting in the belief that a ten-year-old child could and would connive with her father to poison her mother. Ellen's grandmother will not acknowledge that her mistreatment of her daughter helped precipitate her fatal marriage but projects the blame on Ellen and makes the small girl work in the fields in the intense heat of summer.

Ellen's grandmother provides her with sufficient food "just because she did not have it in her to starve a girl" but does not mind starving her for affection. "We ate right many miniature chickens or turkeys. I do not know the difference. But they were baked and not crunchy the way I most enjoy chicken. When we both ate at the same Sunday table we both picked at our little individual chickens and turkeys and did not talk. And still it was OK by me."

Her grandmother upholds class distinctions at the expense of pleasure and communion as they eat baked chicken, instead of the satisfyingly vulgar fried, and "individual chickens and turkeys" instead of food from a common serving dish. Ellen's insistence that she was glad they did not talk shows how much she has lost hope in her grandmother as nurturer. She had early decided that "she might be a witch but she has the dough"; later, "I called her the damn witch to myself and all the money she had did not matter anymore. That is something when you consider how greedy I am." Ellen has learned that there is more to a meal than food on the table and that society's substitution of money for "dough" produces an inedible mess.

Once again Ellen is placed in a situation in which she must nurture an adult, first mentally and then physically. Her grandmother feeds her hate on the sight of Ellen. "Her power was the sucking kind that takes your good sense and leaves you limp like a old zombie.... She would take all the feeling she needed from somebody and then stir it up with some money and turn the recipe back on you." Ellen is force-fed her grandmother's hate, but is unable to regurgitate it because she cannot separate the hatred from her identity. "It is like when you are sick and you know all the things you ever ate or just wanted to eat are churning in you now and you will be sick to relieve yourself but the relief is a dream you let yourself believe because you know the churning is all there is to you."

Although she recognizes her grandmother's hatred, Ellen takes care of her in her final illness and follows the doctor's advice to "feed her particular foods." Ellen does not feed her grandmother out of love but because her grandmother has perversely fed Ellen's feelings of irrational guilt over her mother's death, consuming Ellen's "good sense" in knowing that a ten-year-old child could not prevail against her father.

Despite Ellen's care, her grandmother dies, and she is reluctantly taken in by her mother's widowed sister Nadine, who has a daughter about Ellen's age. As Ellen expects, Nadine is solely concerned with nurturing Dora and regards Ellen as an intruder on their relationship, much as her late husband must have been. Ellen comments, "I stayed in the spare bedroom Nadine's old husband lived in. He did not die flat out but he had a stroke or something and wasted away in here." Ellen forsees a similar starvation for herself but tries to avert it. "I thought about taking my meals in my room but I did not like the picture of me eating off a tray slid to me like I was on death row. So I would eat at the table like normal." "Like normal" appears to be a false simulacrum because Nadine rids herself of the indigestible intruder by throwing Ellen out of the house on Christmas day.

Having learned that blood ties do not necessarily nurture, Ellen tries a nontraditional family. She throws herself on the mercy of a woman who takes foster children. Naively, she believes that "foster" is the family's name and renames herself accordingly, but once again her linguistic error points to truth since "to foster" means to further growth, or, in other words, to nurture. The reader knows Ellen's hunch about this woman is correct when Ellen smells fried chicken as she enters the house, picking up a three-day-old scent that she, in her desperation, apprehends.

Ellen repeatedly refers to her new home in terms of gratified hunger. "There is a plenty to eat here and if we run out of something we just go to the store and get some more." Cooking becomes associated with the rituals of community and love as the children and their foster mother cook their week's lunches on Sunday and receive individual cooking lessons during the week. The kitchen is no longer a place of conflict or empty routines, but is filled with affection. Ellen says of her foster mother that "she is there each day in the kitchen and that is something when you consider she does not have to be there but she is there so I can squeeze her and be glad."

Although Ellen is certainly much happier, her continuing obsession with food shows how deeply traumatized she is from years without nourishing affection.

> If I am very hungry my dress comes off of me in a heartbeat. Sometimes I hurry too fast and I forget to unzip my back. It is helpless to smell lunch through a dress that is hung on your face. I have busted a zipper and ripped two neck collars trying to strip and my new mama told me some things about patience.
>
> I stay starved though.

This comment comes approximately midway through the novel, which is narrated in a series of contrasting flashbacks to Ellen's life at her foster home. As the novel continues, Ellen's references to food decline dramatically, as if she begins to feel secure about food and affection.

By the end of the novel Ellen has learned the folly of social distinctions according to class and race, in addition to those she had learned about "blood" kin. She can assert that if Starletta "tells me to I will lick the glass she uses just to show that I love her and being colored is just the way she is." When her foster mother allows her to invite Star-

letta to spend the weekend and to request her favorite dishes, Ellen remarks that Starletta "could see how I enjoy staying laid up in my bed waiting for supper to cook. And you can guess what all is on the menu." Since Ellen is now nurtured by an adult, she can share that nurturing with someone younger and less privileged than herself, as evidenced in the last lines of the novel. "And all this time I thought I had the hardest row to hoe. That will always amaze me." The imagery recalls Ellen's favorite memory of growing beans with her mother and indicates that she sees woman's lot as hard, "work[ing] in the trail [her] mama left," but she can lend a hand to the next woman down the trail, so that all will be fed.

Ellen has certainly mastered Emerson's lesson of self-reliance, but that is not an end in itself, and although her gutsy, vernacular voice recalls Huck Finn, she does not light out for the territories in an attempt to maintain that autonomy.... Through Ellen, Gibbons redefines self-reliance, not as a willed and threatened isolation, but as the maturity that enables an act of faith in others and, in turn, that allows a girl to contribute to, as well as receive from, the female tradition of community and nurturance.

Source: Veronica Makowsky, "'The Only Hard Part Was the Food': Recipes for Self-Nurture in Kaye Gibbon's Novels," in *The Southern Quarterly,* Vol. 30, Nos. 2–3, Winter-Spring, 1992, pp. 103–12.

Sources

Pearl K. Bell, "Southern Discomfort," *The New Republic,* Vol. 198, No. 9, February 29, 1988, pp. 38-41.

Deanna D'Errico, Review in *Belles Lettres: A Review of Books by Women,* Vol. 3, No. 1, September-October, 1987, p. 9.

Review of *Ellen Foster,* in *Kirkus Reviews,* Vol. LV, No. 6, March 15, 1987, p. 404.

Review of *Ellen Foster,* in *Publishers Weekly,* Vol. 231, No. 11, March 20, 1987, p. 70.

Stanley Fish, *Self-Consuming Artifacts: The Experience of Seventeenth-Century Literature,* University of California Press, 1972.

Alice Hoffman, "Shopping for a New Family," in *The New York Times Book Review,* May 31, 1987, p. 13.

Brad Hooper, review in *Booklist,* Vol. 84, No. 1, September 1, 1987, p. 27.

Veronica Makowsky, "'The Only Hard Part Was the Food': Recipes for Self-Nurture in Kaye Gibbons's Novels," in

Southern Quarterly, Vol. 30, Nos. 2-3, Winter-Spring 1992, pp. 103-112.

"On Tour: Kaye Gibbons," in *Hungry Mind Review: An Independent Book Review,* November 22, 1997, http://www.bookwire.com/hmr/REVIEW/tgibbons.html.

Linda Taylor, "A Kind of Primitive Charm," in *The Sunday Times,* London, May 8, 1988, p. G6.

For Further Study

Leonore Fleischer, "Is It Art Yet?," in *Publishers Weekly,* Vol. 231, May 8, 1987, p. 34.
    An account of how *Ellen Foster* was written and published.

Kaye Gibbons, "My Mother, Literature, and a Life Split Neatly into Two Halves," in *The Writer on Her Work, Vol. II,* edited by Janet Sternburg, Norton, 1991, pp. 52-60.
    An autobiographical account of how Gibbons became a writer and the influence her mother has had on her.

Veronica Makowsky, "Walker Percy and Southern Literature," in *The Walker Percy Project,* December 3, 1997, http://sunsite.unc.edu/wpercy/makowsky.html.
    Focusing mainly on the works of Walker Percy, this article answers the question "What is Southern Literature?," giving rich historical and cultural background to this literary tradition. Gibbons is mentioned as an example of a writer in the Southern women's tradition.

Julian Mason, "Kaye Gibbons (1960-)," in *Contemporary Fiction Writers of the South: A Bio-bibliographical Sourcebook,* edited by Joseph M. Flora and Robert Bain, Greenwood Press, 1993, pp. 156-68.
    Mason provides a brief biographical account of Gibbons, along with an analysis of some of the major themes in her writing.

Don O'Briant, "Seeing Beyond Illness," in *y'all the arts: arts, entertainment, fun and silly things people do,* December 2, 1997, http://www.yall.com/thearts/quill/gibbons.html.
    An interview with Gibbons that touches on her beginnings as a writer, her family life, her novels, and her manic depression.

Bob Summer, "PW interviews," in *Publishers Weekly,* Vol. 240, February 8, 1993, pp. 60-61.
    An interview with Kaye Gibbons in which she discusses the autobiographical aspects of *Ellen Foster* and the difficulties she encountered when writing her fourth novel, *Charms for the Easy Life.*

The Giver

Lois Lowry
1993

When *The Giver* was first published in 1993, Lois Lowry was already a previous Newbery Medal winner (for her 1989 World War II novel, *Number the Stars*). She was also widely admired and greatly appreciated by an avid following of young readers for her comic series of Anastasia books. *The Giver* was immediately recognized as a very special novel. It too won the Newbery Medal. And a large number of commentators concluded that it was the best book Lowry had written.

Lowry's other work is mostly grounded in the cut and thrust of family life. The narrative of *The Giver,* because of the futuristic and allegorical themes in the novel, is a considerably more spartan affair. Readers are made immediately aware that they are in the realm of fabulous rather than realistic fiction, and that Jonas is the principle player in a moral fable with political and social overtones.

Lowry spent a good part of her childhood living near the Amish people of Pennsylvania. Later she moved to Tokyo and lived in an American compound within the city. Both experiences seem to have made her suspicious of attempts by communities to protect a rigid self-identity. She is careful in *The Giver* to make the community she is describing extremely plausible. From many points of view, it represents a well-managed social order. But as the reader discovers, along with Jonas, more and more about the principles on which that social order is based—infanticide, enforced euthanasia—it becomes impossible to read

the novel as anything other than a savage critique of such systems.

Author Biography

Lois Lowry was born March 20, 1937, in Honolulu, Hawaii. Her parents, Katharine (Landis) and Robert E. Hammersberg (an army dentist), were separated at the onset of World War II. Lowry spent the war years in Pennsylvania, where her mother's family lived. Early childhood influences included the presence of the Amish and an adoring grandfather. In 1948, when Lowry was eleven, the family was reunited in Japan, where her father was then stationed. In her 1994 Newbery Medal Acceptance Speech, she identified her experiences in Tokyo—living in the close confines of an American enclave named Washington Heights and making exciting forays on her bicycle into the Japanese streets—as amongst the significant memories which led to the writing of *The Giver*.

Lowry was educated at boarding school and Pembroke College. She attended Brown University but left after two years to marry an attorney, Donald Grey Lowry. She began writing seriously in the early 1970s, after all of her four children (born within a span of five years) were in high school. She was divorced in 1977, the year in which her first novel, *A Summer to Die,* was published. Prior to that, she had written two textbooks and a number of magazine articles and short stories.

This first novel described the relationship of two adolescent girls—thirteen-year-old Meg and her older sister, Molly, who is dying of leukemia. Meg gains sympathy and therapeutic friendship from an old neighbour, Will Banks, who encourages her interest in photography. (Lowry was, at the time of writing the novel, pursuing a parallel career as a semi-professional photographer. Her photographic work was used in a 1978 book called *Here in Kennebunkport* and on the dust jacket for *The Giver*.) The relationship between the two sisters in the novel also had a real-life correlation. Lowry's own elder sister, Helen, had died of cancer at a relatively young age.

Lowry's second novel, *Find a Stranger, Say Goodbye* (1978), confronted the issue of an adolescent, adopted child's search for her natural mother, but her third children's book was lighter in tone, and turned out to be the first in a series

Lois Lowry

of comic novels about Anastasia Krupnik. In the first, eponymous title, Anastasia Krupnik is a feisty and rebellious ten-year-old. By the time the series had reached its ninth title—with *Anastasia, Absolutely* (1996)—she was an equally rebellious, but increasingly self-doubting thirteen-year-old.

Lowry had won several awards for previous novels, but it was her 1989 war novel, *Number the Stars,* which brought her her first really prestigious prize, the Newbery Medal. Set in Nazi-occupied Denmark, the book tells about the adventures of ten-year-old Annemarie Johansen, as her family helps the resistance movement to convey Jews into the safety of neutral Sweden. The Newbery Medal was awarded to Lowry a second time for *The Giver,* a book completely unlike the Anastasia stories. Those, in the words of Michael Cart, writing in the *New York Times,* colorfully depict a "believably flourishing functioning family," whereas the Community in *The Giver* functions clinically, according to a strict set of principles. One by one the rules and routines of the Community are clearly delineated. Jonas's apprehension as his twelfth birthday (the end of childhood and the time when the Chief Elder will announce individual Assignments) approaches is matched by the reader's growing unease at the description of community life.

Plot Summary

The Allure of a Perfect World

Lois Lowry's *The Giver* tells the story of Jonas, who lives in a futuristic society and who, until the age of twelve, has led a peaceful and normal, albeit regulated, life. Jonas has two parents, a mother who is happily employed at the Department of Justice, and a father who is happily employed as a Nurturer. He occasionally quarrels with his younger sister Lily, and he enjoys riding his bicycle, visiting with his friends Asher and Fiona, and musing about his future. In Jonas's world, everything (from an individual's desire, to the weather, to a person's career) is regulated. The community's rulers see to it, for example, that every member of this nameless, timeless community occupies a productive role in the society. The plot of *The Giver* develops out of Jonas's changing perceptions towards his community after he is selected to be the Receiver of Memory and discovers that nothing about his idyllic community is what it seems to be.

In Jonas's community, a child receives a professional assignment at the Ceremony of Twelve, at which time s/he becomes an adult. Jonas, who has waited apprehensively to find out what his assignment will be, grows increasingly agitated during his long-awaited Ceremony. His friends have received desirable and appropriate assignments like "Fish Hatchery Attendant," and "Assistant Director of Recreation," but it appears that he, Jonas, has been bypassed. Finally, after all of the other Twelves have received their assignments, Jonas learns that he, because the elders recognize his intelligence and courage, and because he has the "Capacity to See Beyond" (the ability to see colors), has been selected to become the next Receiver of Memory.

The Horror of a Perfect World

When Jonas is selected to become the next Receiver of Memory, his life is instantaneously altered. He had prepared himself to be separated from his friends, but Jonas had no way of preparing for the loneliness and challenges of his unexpected new job. The Chief Elder warns him at the Ceremony of Twelve, in front of all his friends and family, that his training will involve pain. "Physical pain ... of a magnitude that none of us here can comprehend because it is beyond our experience." Jonas's friends all know what they are to become and what will become of them. Jonas's heart, however, is "filled with fear"; the last Twelve appointed to be Receiver of Memory failed.

Jonas's foreboding deepens when he receives his first training instructions. He learns that he is no longer allowed to share his dreams with anyone, and that he may lie. Both rules go against everything he has been taught up until this point. It feels like his world has been turned upside down. The only person who understands his fears is the current Receiver of Memory, a "bearded man with pale eyes," who tells Jonas to call him the Giver. The Giver's job is to consult his memories of "the whole world" in order to advise the Committee of Elders when they must come to a decision. The Committee of Elders needs the Giver's guidance because they, not having any memories of the past, or of Elsewhere, cannot imagine a world other than it is, and therefore have trouble addressing "new" problems.

The Giver begins to transmit his memories to Jonas. He begins with pleasant memories of snow, sledding, sun, and sailing. Gradually, he adds memories of injuries, of war, of hate, of horrors. Jonas begins to feel irrational anger at his group mates, who are "satisfied with their lives which had none of the vibrance his own was taking on." He is angry at himself, too, because "he could not change that [shallow living] for them." Suddenly Jonas's family, who tell each other their dreams and share their feelings every day, begin to seem shallow. None of them have any comprehension of what Jonas has been learning every day. "They have never known pain," Jonas thinks one night. The realization makes him feel "desperately lonely." When his mother says she feels sad, Jonas feels sadder because he "had experienced real grief," yet there is no "quick comfort" for how he feels, as there is for his mother's childish feelings. He begins to "lie easily" to his family about how pleasant his job is. In return, they smile and "lie easily," too. As Jonas begins to experience colors, and new sensations of both pain and pleasure, he grows more and more estranged from his community, and to feel increasingly disturbed. Who are his people, and how can they love if they lack depth of feelings and emotions and, even in a very fundamental way, choices?

Jonas's alienation from his community is complete when he witnesses, with the help of the Giver's closed-circuit television, his father "releasing" unwanted babies. Always before Jonas had assumed that babies who were released went "Elsewhere." It had never occurred to him that his father gave babies who were different (because they were twins, or because they, like his baby stepbrother, Gabriel, were difficult to care for) a lethal injection. As one of two "enlightened" members of the community, Jonas now feels a terrible responsibility to right his community's wrongs. He decides to escape. He believes that, when he leaves, his memories will be transmitted to the other citizens; his community will, therefore, finally regain its links to the past.

Jonas's Escape

Jonas's plans to escape during the Ceremony of Twelve are foiled when he learns that his temporarily adopted brother, Gabriel, is in danger of being released. Motivated by his knowledge that release is a euphemism for death, Jonas steals his father's bicycle and, with Gabriel in tow, rides towards Elsewhere. Their journey is cold, dark, painful, and hungry. Jonas twists an ankle, has little to eat, and must do the best he can to care for the weakening Gabriel. His only comforts are the knowledge that all of his memories will be returned to the community, and his own memories of sunlight and warmth, which he shares with Gabriel.

Jonas finally comes to a sled on top of a hill, which he recognizes as the sled in his memory. He and Gabriel get onto the sled and sail toward Elsewhere. Writes Lowry,

> The runners sliced through the snow and the wind whipped at his face as they sped in a straight line through an incision that seemed to lead to the final destination, the place that he had always felt was waiting, the Elsewhere that held their future and their past.

The novel's ending is ambiguous, but circular. Reunited with memories of light, snow, and sleds that the Giver gave him, reunited with memories of music, peace, joy, and freedom of choice that he found within himself, Jonas, along with Gabriel and the community that he left behind, has finally arrived in a better, more wholesome, place.

Characters

Andrei

As with all the characters, in the novel, Andrei is mentioned only by his first name. A contemporary of Jonas's father, he became an engineer and designed the bridge that crosses the river to the west of the community.

Asher

Asher is Jonas's best friend. He has a habit of mixing up his words; a habit which early chastisement with the Discipline Wand at the age of three did not eradicate. In one recollected scene, he asks for a "smack" instead of a "snack" and is repeat-

Media Adaptations

- *The Giver* was produced in an unabridged audiotape version in 1995, published on dual cassette by Bantam Books-Audio.

edly hit. This treatment caused him to stop talking altogether for a time, but essentially he remains an easygoing boy with a good sense of fun. At the ceremony of Assignment, he is made Assistant Director of Recreation, an occupation which everyone feels will be entirely appropriate for him. After Jonas has been assigned to The Giver, the two friends fall out, Asher not being able to understand Jonas's objections to a goodies-baddies game he has been playing with friends.

Benjamin

Benjamin is the same age as Asher and Jonas. For the past four years he has done his voluntary service after school in the Rehabilitation Center, where he has devised important new equipment.

Bruno

A very minor character. The brother of Fiona, a girl Jonas is especially fond of.

Caleb

Caleb is described as a replacement child. In Chapter 6 he is presented to a couple in place of their previous child, who had wandered off and fallen into the river. Fatal accidents, such as this, are rare in the Community. The choice of the same name for the replacement child is quite intentional. At the time of the original Caleb's loss, the entire community joined together in a slowly fading murmur of the drowned boy's name. Since then it has been used by no one. Then, at the naming ceremony of the new Caleb, the murmuring begins again, this time increasing in volume, "as if the first Caleb were returning."

Chief Elder

The Chief Elder, elected every eleven years, is the leader of the community, and responsible for

Cover of the first edition of Lowry's award-winning dystopia novel, The Giver.

addressing the annual ceremonies, at the culmination of which the Assignments are announced. The Chief Elder announcing Jonas's Assignment is female.

Edna

Edna is an old person who has been recently "released." She had been a Birthmother, and then worked for years in Food Production, without forming a family unit.

Father

For most of the time the reader is entirely sympathetic towards Jonas's father. He works as a Nurturer, looking after very young children before their naming and allocation to family units. His concern for one baby boy, Gabriel, who is not progressing well, is touching, especially when he decides to bring the child home for several weeks in order to build up his body weight. This gesture is thoroughly approved by Jonas. But total disillusion with his father sets in, when Jonas discovers the truth about "release," and witnesses his father's casual, businesslike approach towards deciding the fate of a pair of twins, only one of whom is allowed to grow up in the Community.

Fiona

Fiona is in the same year-group as Jonas and Asher. She and Jonas are special friends and often cycle to places together. She does all her voluntary work in the House of the Old and is officially made a Caretaker of the Old at her twelfth Ceremony. As a Caretaker she becomes party to the true meaning of "release" but, unlike Jonas, accepts it as the way of the community.

Fritz

Fritz is a clumsy boy who lives next door to Jonas. He receives a new bicycle at the ceremony of Nine, in Chapter 6, and immediately bumps into the podium with it. Jonas and his parents fear that the new bike will "probably too often be dropped on the front walk instead of wheeled neatly into its port." Fritz is a minor character but is used to emphasize the community's obsession with order and conformity. Minor infringements, such as shoes on the wrong feet, become major transgressions in such a world.

Gabe

See Gabriel

Gabriel

One of the children being "nurtured" by Jonas's father is not putting on weight. The boy is in danger of being declared "inadequate" and hence being set aside for "release." The father's concern is genuine. He secretly discovers the name that has been allotted to the child (Number Thirty-six in his year group), and uses it prior to the naming ceremony, hoping it will help the little fellow's development. In Chapter 3 Jonas's father actually brings the baby home at night, together with the child's comfort object (a hippo), and later he successfully lobbies for "Gabe" to be granted an additional year of nurturing.

Gabriel is pale-eyed. Although Jonas is also pale-eyed, this is a rarity in the Community. There is a suggestion that the two of them may have shared the same birth-mother. Certainly a fraternal bond develops between them, especially after Jonas offers to let Gabriel sleep in his room, so that he can be the one to comfort him in the night, if necessary, his Mother and Father having become worn out.

On being transferred for a trial night back to the Nurturing Center, Gabriel cries inconsolably, and it is decided he shall, after all, be "released." This announcement, at a family evening meal, cruel falsehoods——none more cruel than the ceremony of Release, which turns out to be the application of a lethal injection. He watches a video of his father dispatching one of two twins in this way, and he and the Giver plan an escape.

The planned escape has to be put in motion prematurely, so that Jonas can save the young child, Gabriel. They flee the community together and in the final pages of the book struggle through harsh terrain and elements, finally sledding down a snowy slope towards twinkling, colored lights. The book ends with readers having to make up their own minds whether Jonas and Gabriel survive, and if so in what kind of environment.

Larissa

Larissa is one of the old people. Jonas helps to bathe her in Chapter 4. Later, in Chapter 14, the reader learns that Larissa, who had memorable sparkling eyes and a soft voice, has been "Released." Jonas, at this stage, does not know the truth about "Release" and imagines her in the pleasant land of Elsewhere.

Lily

Lily is Jonas's little sister, four years younger than him. She still has a comfort object—a stuffed elephant.

Madeline

Significant for being Number One in Jonas's year group and therefore the first to receive an Assignment. She is made a Fish Hatchery Attendant.

Mother

Jonas's Mother holds a prominent position at the Department of Justice and is depicted as being more concerned about her job than about raising children. Early in the book she is distracted with thoughts about a court case in which she might be required to release a repeat offender. Later in the book she is only too glad to let Jonas look after Gabriel at night so that she can be refreshed for work.

Natasha

A very minor character, mentioned by Lily in Chapter 3. Natasha does her voluntary hours at the Birthing Center.

Philippa

Philippa is the female child in Asher's family unit; in the community's terms, his sister. She has no other part to play in the story.

Pierre

Pierre is numbered Twenty, to Jonas's Nineteen. Jonas has never liked Pierre. He is "serious, not much fun, and a worrier and tattletale, too." After Jonas's number has been skipped, he does not even hear what Assignment Pierre is given.

Receiver

See Giver

Roberto

An old person who has played a prominent part in the life of the community. He has worked as an Instructor of Elevens; has served on the Planning Committee; and was responsible for the landscaping of the Central Plaza. Despite these services, his "release" passes without notice, and when the name "Roberto" is re-assigned there is no Murmur-of-Replacement ritual.

Rosemary

Rosemary was the last person selected to be Receiver of Memories, some ten years ago. After five weeks, distressed by the painful memories passed on by The Giver, she had gone to the Chief of Elders and requested Release (forbidden in Jonas's rules, but not in hers). On her demise, the five weeks' worth of memories had come back to the people, causing them much anguish. The outcome is remembered as a terrible failure.

In Chapter 20 The Giver tells Jonas, in a dramatic declaration, that Rosemary was his daughter. Whether he means this figuratively or literally is another matter readers will decide for themselves.

Speaker

The Speaker is the person who makes all public announcements to the Community. Every room in every building has a loudspeaker which remains permanently switched on so that such messages can be assured transmission. It is a mark of The Giver's stature that he is able to turn his loudspeaker on or off, as he wishes.

Tanya

Another eleven/twelve year old, she is amongst those playing the game of goodies and baddies with Asher.

Thea

Another female in Jonas's year group, briefly mentioned in Chapter 6.

forces Jonas to bring forward his planned escape. He races away from the community on his Father's bike, with Gabriel in the child-seat on the back.

Giver

The Giver is fair-eyed, like Jonas, and like the previous Receiver, a girl called Rosemary. The Giver claims Rosemary as his daughter.

In her Newbery acceptance speech, Lowry talked about a painter she had met in 1979, while working on an article in a magazine. Something fascinated Lowry about the painter's face, especially his eyes. "Later I hear that he has become blind. I think about him—his name is Carl Nelson—from time to time. His photograph hangs over my desk. I wonder what it was like for him to lose the colors about which he was so impassioned. I wish, in a whimsical way, that he could have somehow magically given me the capacity to see the way he did." (Lowry's photograph of Carl Nelson was used on the front cover of the first American edition of the novel.)

The Giver, who describes himself as not as old as he looks, provides just such a magical transfer of powers. He has been made tired by the burden of knowledge and memories, the assimilation and storage of which have consumed his life. As soon as Jonas meets him (in Chapter 10), The Giver is at pains to point out that it is not the memory of nostalgia—not the recollections of childhood normally indulged in by the old—that he must transmit. "It's the memories of the whole world."

His apartment is book-lined, at first giving the impression that The Giver's knowledge is professorial, and that the relationship between him and Jonas will be one of sage and student. But this impression is quickly undermined when The Giver announces that he is going to transmit the memory of snow. This involves a ritualistic laying on of hands and an extra-sensory simulation of the sensation of cold.

After similar transmissions, both pleasurable and painful, The Giver concludes his education of Jonas in a very different fashion. He shows him a videotape recording of a "Release," and then, clearly having become opposed to the community himself, helps Jonas plan an escape.

Inger

Inger is described as "a nice girl, though somewhat lazy, with a strong body." Number Two in Jonas's year, she is made a Birthmother.

Instructor

A minor, anonymous char Asher's apology for lateness ir ter.

Isaac

Another minor character, the course of the Ceremony, i made an Instructor of Sixes (ch Assignment which "obviously p well-deserved."

Jonas

Jonas, the main character (his friend Asher, is careful a searches for the right words to ings. The opening of the book aged eleven, apprehensive abo December, when the annual Cere and Assignments will be given year group.

He gets on reasonably well has friends of both sexes (Ash he feels different. Physically whereas nearly everybody else Other eleven-year-olds are abl likely Assignments, which are c of observed inclinations and ap developed no special interest (h of the Old only to be with Fiona to her work there) and has no id will consider him cut out to beco prehensiveness.

Apart from this, Jonas co shares his family's distaste for and untidy boy who lives next Nineteen in his year group, Jon; at the Ceremony, while the lowe their Assignments. All are give aptly chosen tasks in life. His ne; The tension (both for Jonas and ; comes almost unbearable when skips Jonas's number. His is the to be announced. It is entirely hugely daunting. Jonas has bee next Receiver of Memory.

As such he has to spend man in the company of an old man v holder of Memories. The old man Giver. In the course of their sessi are opened to many things—in pleasurable things, then increasing Eventually he sees that the Comn

Yoshiko

A friend of Jonas's father, given as an example of someone who was surprised but thrilled by her Assignment (Doctor).

Themes

Coming of Age

A key characteristic of the particular community Lowry has created is the annual ritual in December when each year group, en masse, is declared one year older and given commensurate privileges and/or responsibilities. At the age of three, all children begin participating in the daily routine of "dreamtelling"—the requirement that, at the breakfast table, they describe the dreams they have had the previous night. It is also the age at which, educationally, the correct use of language is inculcated, regardless of individual development or speech skills. (Asher, who has specific problems with what educationists now call "word retrieval," has a good deal of trouble with this regime.) Up to the age of six, children wear jackets which fasten at the back. When they become seven they are given a front-fastening costume, as a mark of increasing independence. At the age of eight their "comfort object" is taken away. They are given another new jacket, this time with pockets: to indicate that they are now considered responsible enough to look after small belongings. And they must begin doing voluntary service outside of school hours. At the age of nine, girls remove their hair ribbons, and all children receive their own bicycle. At ten both boys and girls have their hair ceremoniously cut, and at eleven boys are given long trousers and girls "new undergarments."

But by far the most important rite of passage, and the one Jonas is in a permanent state of anxiety about in the early part of the book, is connected with becoming Twelve. This is the last time children are actively involved in the annual ceremony. After twelve, age is not considered important. Twelve is the age at which childhood is left behind, and an individual's adult calling is decided. Jonas is anxious because he has no idea what that calling is to be. It will be decided by the Elders and announced by the Chief Elder at the Ceremony.

There are two more Rites of Passage unrelated to age. They relate to Sex and Death.

Sex

Procreation is a purely mechanical affair in the community. If a girl is selected at the age of twelve to become a "Birthmother," she will eventually spend three years at the Birthing Center, giving birth to three babies. The babies are not brought up by their natural mothers but allocated to volunteer parents. No details are given as to the practical means of fathering children, but it is most likely to be by artificial insemination, since all sexual longing is eradicated at puberty, at the first sign of erotic dreaming. Indeed, the main purpose of "dreamtelling" is revealed to be the monitoring of "Stirrings"—the term given to sexual desire. When Jonas confesses one morning to an erotic dream, he is immediately prescribed a daily pill to purge such stirrings. Later in the book, when he stops taking this pill, it is a sign to the reader of open rebellion.

Death

The community refers to Death, euphemistically, as Release. The young are allowed to take this literally, believing that those "Released" are simply choosing to leave the community and go "Elsewhere." Release is the final Rite of Passage. A ceremony is held, which includes a "telling of the life," a toast, an anthem, a good-bye speech from the individual to be released (where appropriate), some farewell speeches from those who know him or her, then a walk through the door to the Releasing Room.

Not only the old enter the Releasing Room. Any infants that do not thrive are also sent there, as are persistent transgressors against the community's petty codes. Jonas eventually sees a video recording of what happens in the Releasing Room and discovers that the room is the scene of sordid executions. Individuals are given a lethal injection and their bodies disposed of down a garbage chute. His father's jaunty participation in the execution of an infant twin is particularly shocking.

The horrible truth of what goes on behind the door of the Releasing Room underpins any of the positive constructs defenders of the community might wish to put forward. Its social cohesion, its emphasis on law and order, its insistence that children develop at the same pace—all these are dependent upon infanticide, enforced euthanasia, and a justice system which administers the death penalty without qualm.

Difference

The community's weather is unvarying. Regulated by "Climate Control," it is in an unfluctuating state of "Sameness," so that amongst the first memories passed on to Jonas by the Giver, are the memories of snow and sunshine. The grey, climatic

Topics For Further Study

- A politician holding high office, after reading *The Giver,* decides that new laws should be passed outlawing cultish communities. These laws will also affect traditional communities, such as the Amish and the Bruderhof. As an attorney you are engaged by such communities to help defend their continuing existence. Prepare your defense.

- After collecting as many examples of attempts to build utopia as you can find (these should include both practical attempts, and fictional representations), plot them on a world map and on a timeline to determine whether they tend to occur in clusters.

- You are a television documentary producer. You have been asked to produce an outline for a 60-minute program on the subject of euthanasia, or voluntary suicide. Your professional brief requires you to present a balance of opinion, but as an individual you have very definite views. In your outline, you must construct the hour-long program so that you will be able to defend it in terms of balance, but in such a way that the balance of opinion supports your own beliefs.

- A dramatization of *The Giver* is to be shown on prime-time TV. Advertisers seem reluctant to sign up for the commercial breaks. As the advertising sales executive for the TV company, identify the manufacturers and service providers who might be interested in purchasing ads. Also identify creative links that could be made with the movie and their products and services.

- You are a medical practitioner in the community of The Giver. You discover that the pills taken to eradicate sexual longing ("Stirrings") have serious, indeed fatal, side-effects in later life. The Elders receive your report. Write an account of the debate which follows.

- You are directing a movie version of *The Giver.* Tomorrow you will be filming the Ceremony, closely following the description in Chapters 6 and 7. How will you plan the camera-shot sequence for each stage of the Ceremony?

"sameness" is an objective correlative of the community's strict regulation of difference and variety in all walks of life. The system of Assignments pays some regard to the temperamental and attitudinal differences between children. Observed through the early years of life, they are usually given an assignment that tallies with their chosen hobbies or interests. A child who likes to play with a construction set and does his volunteer hours on building sites, for example, is given the Assignment of Engineer. However, in effect, this makes children the victims of their early predilections. There is no recognition that individuals might develop different interests. Those first interests must become their life's work, to be pursued without change.

There are many other aspects of community life which enforce sameness—all family groups, for example, are allotted two children, one male and one female—but the fact that all individuals have crucial life-choices made for them (in particular, choice of career) is the most important.

Individual vs. Society

Superficially, the community is easy going about some of its rules and does allow individuals a degree of free choice. Most children do not wait till nine before they ride a bicycle. They borrow bikes from other children. Jonas's parents are allowed to bend the rules in order to take a third child into the house. But these are small matters compared with the fundamental loss of individual freedom represented by the announcement of Assignments. And in other small matters there are highly ritualized and formulaic expectations of behavior which support the will of the whole group as opposed to the individual. A child late for school makes an apology, and there is an immediate group response, "We accept your apology."

At any one moment individuals must be prepared to respond to announcements made through the ubiquitous loudspeakers. A day's holiday is proclaimed and everyone takes a rest from work. There is no opportunity for planning an individual vacation. There is nowhere to go; not much else to do. The community can only be successful in curtailing individual freedom by severely limiting the choices available to individuals. Hence, the community is paranoid in its insularity. Hence, the panic at the beginning of the novel, when an unidentified plane flies overhead.

The only character allowed any degree of personal freedom is The Giver. The power of his individuality is symbolized by the casual way in which he feels free to switch off the loudspeaker so that he cannot hear public announcements. This greatly impresses Jonas.

Style

Point of View

The book is written in the third person ("he/she"), but the narrative point of view is that of the main character, Jonas. From the first to final paragraph of the novel, the reader is always inside the head of Jonas, feeling with him the anxious moments leading up to the announcement of his Assignment, and feeling with him both the pleasurable and the painful memories passed on by The Giver.

Structure

The novel's structure is uncomplicated. The story is told in twenty-three, relatively short chapters, which describe a chronological narrative. The book is not divided into parts, but if it were there would be three.

Chapters 1 through 8 describe the events leading up to Jonas's selection as the next Receiver of Memories. These first eight chapters establish Jonas as a quiet boy who indulges in a fair amount of self-reflection. He is an easy character for the reader to identify with. The early chapters also establish the key attributes of the community and its social order. The piecemeal delivery of this information is important, because it allows the reader to begin reading the novel willing to give the community the benefit of the doubt, and therefore to share in Jonas's sense of disillusion when he later discovers some harsh truths. The time-scale of this section is quite condensed. The ceremony takes

place in December, and Chapter 1 begins with the words "It was almost December."

Chapters 9 through 20 describe Jonas's apprenticeship to The Giver. The passing-on of memories amounts to an education of the sensibilities. It is not an education which others in the community have enjoyed, and this means that Jonas's "childhood, his friendships, his carefree sense of security—all of these things seemed to be slipping away." Gradually he realizes just what the community has sacrificed in order to enjoy the placid, well-ordered way of life it has chosen for itself. This realization takes place over a number of visits to The Giver, culminating in an overnight stay in Chapter 20, following Jonas's discovery of what goes on in the Releasing Room. The time-scale of these chapters is looser than the earlier part of the book. In Chapter 16 we are told that almost a year has passed since Jonas became twelve.

Chapters 21 through 23 cover Jonas's flight from the community. Especially as exhaustion sets in, the narrative in these final chapters of the book becomes more impressionistic and less explicitly descriptive, so that the reader is unsure how far Jonas has travelled. The two fugitives' final sledride is described in such a way as to leave the ending of the book open, so that different readers can interpret it in their own way. It is almost as if Lowry wants to allow the reader freedom of choice at this crucial point in her story, in order to emphasize one of the key themes of the novel.

Allegory

There are not many highly-accomplished allegorical novels written for children. *The Giver* is one. Clearly the community in the novel is representative of all groups that try and close themselves off from the influences of the wider world. In particular it shares many of the social attributes found amongst Anabaptist or Amish communities: emphases on codes of dress, rites of passage, the subservience of the individual to the will of the group. But it would be wrong to read the novel simply as a critique of such communities. There is, for example, a more general allegorical message in the expectations of a pedagogy that expects all children to accomplish the same goals at the same age. And there is an even stronger allegorical message for any society contemplating euthanasia as a means of reducing the burden of caring for the old and infirm.

The novel is also an allegory about systems of arcane knowledge, and as such appears to be critical of Gnosticism (the idea that the deeper truths about our world are best reserved for a few, chosen minds—passed on to the few, but kept from the many). The relationship between The Giver and Jonas is redolent of that between sage and disciple.

Resolution

The exact fate of Jonas and Gabriel might be uncertain at the end of the book (although Lowry's choice of name for the baby boy would seem to load the argument in favor of an optimistic interpretation). Is the vision of lights at the bottom of the hill and the sound of voices singing a true apprehension, or a sign that Jonas is sinking into unconsciousness? In a sense, it does not matter how the reader decides to interpret the final paragraphs, the real resolution of the novel having occurred in Chapter 20, when the decision to escape was made, with all the consequences that this will have for the community. The memories of how life used to be, kept for safekeeping (quite why is never satisfactorily explained) by The Giver, will be released with Jonas's going amongst the community. Life there will never be the same again. That nasty world has been undone.

Historical Context

Bosnia

Lowry's novel was written against the backdrop of events in Bosnia, and in particular the ugly results of "ethnic cleansing." During the early 1990s, Serbian forces in Bosnia opened concentration camps and attempted to rid the country of Muslims. Muslim women were raped and Muslim men incarcerated and starved, all as a matter of social and political policy. These practices were made known to the world by investigative journalism. The community in Lowry's novel is similarly concerned to keep outsiders at bay. There is only a way out of the community, no way in.

Euthanasia

While writing her novel, Lowry will have been aware of a celebrated euthanasia case in 1990, involving Dr. Jack Kevorkian. Kevorkian had once proposed rendering death row prison inmates unconscious so that their living bodies could be used as the subjects of medical experiments. The suggestion had led to his dismissal, but he continued his preoccupation with euthanasia by writing on the subject for European medical journals. In an issue of *Medicine and Law,* he suggested setting up suicide clinics, arguing that the acceptance of planned death required the establishment of well-staffed and well-organized medical clinics where terminally ill patients can opt for death under controlled circumstances of compassion and decorum. In the late 1980s, he developed a suicide device that was basically a method of administering a lethal injection. In the novel, the Releasing Room, and the crude means of administering Release, bear all the hallmarks of Kevorkian's suicide device.

Kevorkian appeared on the Donahue talk show in April, 1990. A woman who had been diagnosed as suffering from Alzheimer's disease saw the show and got into contact with him. An English professor, she found the prospect of deteriorating mental faculties impossible to bear. Both she and her husband had been long-standing members of the Hemlock Society, which supports doctor-assisted suicide. On June 4, 1990, using Kevorkian's suicide machine, she terminated her own life.

Although attempts to punish Kevorkian with the law on this and subsequent occasions failed, the moral outcry was vociferous. Condoning suicide paves the way for society to abdicate its responsibility for improving conditions for the elderly and chronically ill, many argued. However, the woman's family and friends insisted that she was competent to make her decision and had every right to do so. They defended the doctor's part in her death. This particular case, and others Kevorkian has been associated with since then, have dramatized the issue of the right to die in a way that has demanded full media attention. Lowry's children's novel might well be advocated reading for any adult anxious to consider the full implications of doctor-assisted suicide.

Branch Davidian Raid

Early in 1993 the Branch Davidian compound in Waco, Texas, was raided by the Bureau of Alcohol, Tobacco and Firearms (ATF), after neighbors of the religious group complained of hearing machine-gun fire and a United Parcel Service employee reported delivering two cases of hand grenades and black gunpowder. The Branch Davidians were an offshoot of the Davidian Seventh-Day Adventists, a splinter group of the Seventh-Day Adventists.

David Koresh had joined the group in 1984 and immediately began a campaign to gain control. Under Koresh, the religious sect became a full-fledged cult. He incorporated a strict regime for the

The controversial Dr. Jack Kevorkian (called "Dr. Death" by some) at a press conference with attorney Geoffrey Feiger (left). Kevorkian has helped many terminally ill people die in his campaign to legalize physician-assisted suicides.

group, but excluded himself from his own discipline. After the first abortive raid by the ATF, the Federal Bureau of Investigations (FBI) swarmed the compound, hoping that cult members would surrender themselves voluntarily. Weeks of negotiations followed before the FBI asked Attorney General Janet Reno to authorize another raid on the compound.

The raid commenced at 12:05 p.m. Smoke was seen coming from the compound. Fire trucks were called, but they did not arrive for thirty minutes. By that time, most of the building had already collapsed. Eighty-six people perished in the fire, including seventeen children and Koresh himself. Only nine people survived.

Koresh was representative of individuals who cast a mesmerizing spell and gain supreme control of a sect. The community in Lowry's novel is a much more substantial body of people than this, and should not be referred to as a cult (Lowry herself does not use this word in the novel) any more than the Anabaptists or the Amish are cults. In this regard, although the events of the Branch Davidian Raid were closely contemporary with the book's publication, they are not particularly relevant to the themes of the novel.

Critical Overview

Despite its differences from Lowry's other work, *The Giver* was universally well-received on publication. Gary D. Schmidt, writing in *The Five Owls,* stated: "This is a fantasy novel that does what fantasy at its best can do: make us see the reality all the more clearly. The questions it asks about the costs of love, the structure of the family, the role of painful memories, the nature of the perfect society are all timely." In a much longer, but equally enthusiastic review of "this intricately constructed masterwork," Patty Campbell, writing for *Horn Book,* began by drawing attention to the departure from Lowry's usual style. "Up until now, much of Lowry's work has consisted of [what one reviewer called] 'contemporary novels with engaging characters that explore something very rare—a functional family.' But *The Giver* is a dystopia, 'driven by plot and philosophy—not by character and dialogue,' and the picture of the functional family turns disturbingly awry as the story proceeds." Campbell takes advantage of the space allowed for an extended review to delineate what she sees as the exceptional advance in narrative skill shown in the novel. The opening of the novel, she argues, shows a mastery of "innuendo, foreshadowing, and resonance." Quoting the opening sentence, Campbell goes on to explain: "The word December is loaded with resonance: the darkness of the solstice, endings, Christmas, cold.... The name Jonas, too, is evocative—of the biblical Jonah, he who is sent by God to cry against the wickedness of Nineveh, an unwilling lone messenger with a mission that will be received with hostility. In one seemingly simple sentence Lowry sets the mood and direction of her story, foreshadows its outcome, and plants an irresistible narrative pull."

Proceeding to compare the novel with Margaret Atwood's *The Handmaid's Tale,* Campbell then analyzed the skill with which Lowry slowly reveals the unpleasant edifice upon which the initially appealing community is based, before admiring the ingenuity of the novelist's handling of the denouement. Amongst a minority of reviews to question certain aspects of the novel, Jane Inglis, writing in *School Librarian,* wondered whether able readers might be frustrated "by the strict limits imposed by the author on her creative imagination." Inglis went on to recommend Lowry's book as "an admirable early venture into fictional dystopias, with lots of follow-up material available for the reader who craves for more." However, the review was out of kilter with the judgement of Campbell and others that Lowry's novel, though a children's book, deserved to be considered alongside the very best books written on a similar theme.

Lowry's Newbery acceptance speech identified the creative source of the book as memories bubbling up like springs and mountain streams, "each tributary bringing with it the collected bits and pieces from the past, from the distant, from the countless Elsewheres: all of it moving, mingled, in the current." She remembered living in an American enclave, situated in the centre of Tokyo, cocooned from the Japanese way of life. She remembered the way in which, at college, a fellow student had been ostracized simply for being different. There had been no teasing or unpleasantness. "We do something worse: we ignore her. We pretend that she doesn't exist. In a small house of fourteen young women, we make one invisible." She remembered meeting a painter, Carl Nelson, who later became blind. "I wonder what it was like for him to lose the colors about which he was so impassioned." In summarizing what these and other memories represented, Lowry has been her own most revealing critic. "I've never been a writer of fairy tales. And if I've learned anything through that river of memories, it is that we can't live in a walled world, in an 'only us, only now' world, where we are all the same and feel safe. We would have to sacrifice too much. The richness of color would disappear. Feelings for other human beings would no longer be necessary. Choice would be obsolete."

Criticism

Elyse Lord

Elyse Lord is a visiting instructor at the University of Utah and at the Salt Lake City Community College. In the following essay, she evaluates controversial themes in The Giver *and concludes that Lowry's novel, while terrifying in many ways, offers its readers hope and a constructive view of Jonas's world.*

Critics respond to Lois Lowry's novel, *The Giver,* with nearly universal praise. The book has received more than ten prestigious awards, including the highly coveted Newbery Medal, which the American Library Association awarded it in 1994. (The ALA awards the Newbery Medal to the best book published in the United States for children or young adults in the preceding year.)

One reason for the novel's nearly unprecedented acclaim is that its storyline captures the interest of a wide group of readers and critics. For example, many scholars consider the novel to be dystopian (about a miserable society), and compare it favorably to adult classics like *Brave New World* (1933), *Fahrenheit 451* (1953), and *1984* (1940) as well as to children's classics like *White Mountains* (1967) and *A Wrinkle in Time* (1962). Other scholars, like Patty Campbell, praise the novel for capturing the moral imaginations of its readers. Campbell lauds the novel for taking "hardened young-adult reviewers by surprise." The novel, she says, is so "rich in levels of meaning, so daring in complexity of symbol and metaphor, so challenging in the ambiguity of its conclusion, that we are left with all of our neat little everyday categories and judgments hanging useless."

While critics', librarians', educators', and students' responses to the novel seem like veritable fanfare, the novel has nevertheless become the center of a spirited censorship debate. To the surprise and indignation of many of the novels' enthusiasts, *The Giver,* according to a report by the People for the American Way, was the second most frequently challenged book in 1996. Parents in cities as geographically dispersed as Las Vegas, Nevada, Columbia Falls, Montana, Palm Springs, California, and Brecksville, Ohio, have protested use of the novel in public schools because it contains adult themes like infanticide (baby killing) and euthanasia (mercy deaths). In one particularly controversial scene, Jonas, the protagonist in the novel, watches as his father carefully directs a needle "into the top of newchild's forehead, puncturing the place where the fragile skin pulsed." His father says cheerfully, "I know, I know. It hurts, little guy. But I have to use a vein, and the veins in your arms are still too teeny-weeny." Jonas's father pushes in the plunger, then says, "All done," and sends the small corpse down a trash chute. Would-be censors object to the scene because it is so graphic, and because it transforms Jonas's once beloved father into a cold-blooded murderer.

The irony of censorship attacks on the novel is that *The Giver* dramatizes the plight of an individual living in a society that censors its peoples' language, emotions, and behaviors. This irony is compounded by the fact that most who would like to see *The Giver* censored confess that they have never read the novel in its entirety. However, would-be censors raise important questions, not just about Lowry's novel, but about all novels for youth. For example, parent Anna Cerbasi of Port Saint Lucie, Florida, who asked school board members to remove the novel from middle-school shelves, objected to the book because "Nobody is a family. They kill the baby who cries at night. I read it and thought—no way. Not for sixth grade. Maybe high school, maybe." Ms. Cerbasi's concerns about the novel raise legitimate questions about who should decide which books are appropriate for which children, and whether or not disturbing stories are appropriate for youth even if they teach a valuable lesson.

However, these large questions cannot be answered on the basis of one book. In fact, a surprising number of books written for youth contain graphic and disturbing materials. It seems likely that Lowry's novel has been more controversial than most, not because it is any more "dangerous" than other books, but because it has been so widely integrated into school curricula and has therefore caught more parents' attention than less accessible books. Given the size of the question—how can one evaluate whether or not terrifying materials are appropriate for a youthful reader—it is most realistic to respond to would-be censors' concerns by presenting a constructive reading of *The Giver*, a

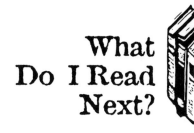

What Do I Read Next?

- *Anastasia Krupnik,* the first in Lowry's sequence of novels about a "crackle-brained, fizzle-headed, freckle-faced dynamo." The atmosphere in this novel could not be more different from *The Giver.* Can you identify *any* connections?

- One reviewer of *The Giver* compared it with Margaret Atwood's adult novel *The Handmaid's Tale* (1985), a dystopia in which women's roles are limited to either wife or bearer of children.

- There were several attempts to set up utopian communities in the nineteenth century. Nathaniel Hawthorne's *The Blithedale Romance* (1852) is based on personal experience of one such enterprise.

- Any futuristic tale must expect to be compared with George Orwell's 1949 classic, *Nineteen Eighty-Four.*

- *The Republic,* a description of Plato's celebrated political utopia, was written in the 4th century B.C.

reading which is consistent with educators' efforts to discuss controversial scenes in sensitive and responsible ways.

Critics and censors all agree that Jonas's situation in *The Giver* is horrifying. Through a series of shocking events, he discovers that "release" is actually murder, that his people literally have limited vision (they can only see in black and white, so do not notice racial differences, or colors of any kind), and that his people have no way to think for themselves, or to make decisions without the Giver's help. (They have no memories of pain and pleasure, and they are sedated so as not to feel the "stirrings" of their own desire.) Jonas is understandably concerned by these discoveries, especially when he learns that his step-brother Gabriel is going to be "released" (killed) because he cries during the night. Jonas knows that he must save

Gabriel, and he knows that he must do something to help his community to respond more creatively to the inevitable (and sometimes painful) variation of the human species.

Jonas's despair is, at this point, so profound that readers may fear he will be overcome by it. However, he does overcome his despair, and this is why the book is so important—and appropriate—for young people to read. Lowry has equipped Jonas with the qualities he will need to rise above his difficult circumstances. She has given him the ability to see color, the ability to grapple with imperceptible ideas (like memories and colors), and faith in his own ability to act morally. She has made Jonas's perceptual abilities a condition for him to act heroically in this story. Through Jonas, Lowry argues for the preservation of a kind of creative vision, a vision which every community needs if it is to benefit from its citizens' differences and input.

More specifically, Jonas is a hero worth emulating because, throughout the novel, he develops and refines his unusual ability to perceive and to understand ideas that are outside of his frame of reference. One day, for example, Jonas notices a "change" in an apple. When he tries to define this change, by observing the apple under a magnifying glass, he fails. The magnifying glass doesn't help him because what Jonas needs is "a new way of looking" at things in order to apprehend color; a magnifying glass does not allow him to apprehend what is new and different. Here Lowry is suggesting that the vision of an artistic boy, who is open to ideas that exist outside of current paradigms of thought, is of the utmost importance to a society that has lost the ability to perceive differences. Similarly, when Jonas admits to the community that he believes he has the capacity to "see beyond," the crowd begins to collectively murmur his name. Ironically, the community, which, as The Giver points out, has "never completely mastered Sameness," selects Jonas to help lead them *because* of his ability to perceive differences. Jonas's vision is all the more valuable because it is in such short supply. Lowry is arguing for the preservation of a particular way of looking at the world that is essential to the survival of the human(e) race.

Further evidence of the importance of Jonas's unique perceptual abilities comes when he discovers that his community's goodness is a sham. Had Jonas simply rejected his community (as a "lesser" character might have done), the novel would not have carried the same positive psychological impact. Jonas *does* initially feel contempt for his

community, but he quickly develops the insights he needs to channel his anger into constructive actions. For example, he sarcastically mimics his peoples' obedience.

> I will take care of that, sir. I will take care of that, sir.... I will do whatever you like, sir. I will kill people, sir. Old people? Small newborn people? I'd be happy to kill them, sir. Thank you for your instructions, sir.

But the Giver tells Jonas that "They can't help it. They know nothing." Jonas struggles to understand his community, and comes to recognize that it is made up of learned, civilized people, who have no awareness of their origins and very little knowledge of how rules are made. Jonas's people cannot perceive differences; they do not adapt well to change. And so they are simple, shallow, and murderous.

Yes, Lowry's novel is terrifying, but it is not irresponsible in its handling of sensitive materials. In fact, Lowry seems to be dramatizing a modern view of healing, as described by Louise Kaplan in her book *No Voice is Ever Wholly Lost.* After working with holocaust victims and their families, Kaplan concluded that, even though many holocaust survivors have never verbally shared their experiences with their children, their children feel compelled to physically reenact their parents' trauma (by developing anorexia, for example). The bodies and subconscious minds of holocaust survivors' children understand—without words—the nature of their parents' unwitnessable suffering. The only release for these children is to hear their parents' stories. This "truth telling" frees children from the compulsions they feel to "enact and concretize" their parents' unspeakable and painful pasts.

Kaplan's observations of how parents unknowingly transmit traumas to their children support a reading of Lowry's novel as powerful and positive. Jonas has been selected to receive memories because his community members prefer the comfort of virtually pain-free and comfortable living. However, Jonas discovers that if he leaves—or dies—his memories will be released and transmitted back to the community. Jonas chooses to give the community back its memories. If Kaplan's theory is right (and according to the logic of Lowry's story), the community needs its memories in order to heal itself; if members acknowledge both their pain and their joy, as well as the depths of their emotions, Jonas will be "released" (not killed) from the huge burden of serving as the Keeper of Memory.

Lowry's ending, though ambiguous, lends support to the idea that the novel embraces "wholeness" as a healing principle. In the end, Jonas, who has run away from home with Gabriel in tow, discovers a place that he remembers. He finds a sled that he remembers, mounts it, and its runners slice through the snow and take him towards "Elsewhere," the place that holds his and Gabriel's "future and … past." Jonas then hears music for the first time. He is able to hear the music, to recognize the music, because he has relinquished others' memories, and in so doing has opened the door to his own perceptions. It is now possible for his new thoughts and feelings to join with his old thoughts and feelings. Lowry foreshadows this perplexing but hopeful ending when she describes Jonas as Keeper of the "memories of the whole world." Her message, finally, is that one cannot ignore uncomfortable memories; one must embrace a "whole" vision, which contains joy as well as pain, if one (or one's children) is/are ever to feel "at home" in the world.

Though Lowry has consistently declined to interpret *The Giver's* ending, she has revealed that she is pleased by young readers who have perceived "the magic of the circular journey," and "the truth that we go out and come back, and that what we come back to is changed, and so are we."

Lowry's novel is compelling, terrifying, and above all, hopeful. Through reading about Jonas, a boy who has the courage and vision to help his people to acknowledge their pain and differences, Lowry's readers can experience the joy of pushing "open the gate" [Lowry's metaphor] that separates them from Elsewhere. It would be hard to find a more appropriate message for youth, who are immersed in making important decisions about what kinds of people they will one day become.

Source: Elyse Lord, in an essay for *Novels for Students,* Gale, 1998.

Lois Lowry

Lois Lowry explains the origins of The Giver *in this excerpt, taken from her 1993 Newbery Medal acceptance speech, given at the annual meeting of the American Library Association on June 26, 1994, in Miami, Florida.*

"How do you know where to start?" a child asked me once, in a schoolroom where I'd been speaking to her class about the writing of books. I shrugged and smiled and told her that I just start wherever it feels right.

This evening it feels right to start by quoting a passage from *The Giver* a scene set during the days in which the boy, Jonas, is beginning to look more deeply into the life that has been very superficial, beginning to see that his own past goes back further than he had ever known and has greater implications than he had ever suspected.

> Now he saw the familiar wide river beside the path differently. He saw all of the light and color and history it contained and carried in its slow-moving water; and he knew that there was an Elsewhere from which it came, and an Elsewhere to which it was going.

Every author is asked again and again the question we probably each have come to dread the most: How did you get this idea?

We give glib, quick answers because there are other hands raised, other kids in the audience waiting.

I'd like, tonight, to dispense with my usual flippancy and glibness and try to tell you the origins of this book. It is a little like Jonas looking into the river and realizing that it carries with it everything that has come from an Elsewhere. A spring, perhaps, at the beginning, bubbling up from the earth; then a trickle from a glacier; a mountain stream entering farther along; and each tributary bringing with it the collected bits and pieces from the past, from the distant, from the countless Elsewheres: all of it moving, mingled, in the current.

For me, the tributaries are memories, and I've selected only a few. I'll tell them to you chronologically. I have to go way back. I'm starting forty-six years ago.

In 1948 I am eleven years old. I have gone with my mother, sister, and brother to join my father, who has been in Tokyo for two years and will be there for several more.

We live there, in the center of that huge Japanese city, in a small American enclave with a very American name: Washington Heights. We live in an American-style house, with American neighbors, and our little community has its own movie theater, which shows American movies, and a small church, a tiny library, and an elementary school; and in many ways it is an odd replica of a United States village.

(In later, adult years I was to ask my mother why we had lived there instead of taking advantage of the opportunity to live within the Japanese community and to learn and experience a different way of life. But she seemed surprised by my question.

She said that we lived where we did because it was comfortable. It was familiar. It was safe.)

At eleven years old I am not a particularly adventurous child, nor am I a rebellious one. But I have always been *curious.*

I have a bicycle. Again and again—countless times—without my parents' knowledge, I ride my bicycle out the back gate of the fence that surrounds our comfortable, familiar, safe American community. I ride down a hill because I am curious, and I enter, riding down that hill, an unfamiliar, slightly uncomfortable, perhaps even unsafe—though I never feel it to be—area of Tokyo that throbs with life.

It is a district called Shibuya. It is crowded with shops and people and theaters and street vendors and the day-to-day bustle of Japanese life.

I remember, still, after all these years, the smells: fish and fertilizer and charcoal; the sounds: music and shouting and the clatter of wooden shoes and wooden sticks and wooden wheels; and the colors: I remember the babies and toddlers dressed in bright pink and orange and red, most of all; but I remember, too, the dark blue uniforms of the schoolchildren—the strangers who are my own age.

I wander through Shibuya day after day during those years when I am eleven, twelve, and thirteen. I love the feel of it, the vigor and the garish brightness and the noise: all such a contrast to my own life.

But I never talk to anyone. I am not frightened of the people, who are so different from me, but I am shy. I watch the children shouting and playing around a school, and they are children my age, and they watch me in return; but we never speak to one another.

One afternoon I am standing on a street corner when a woman near me reaches out, touches my hair, and says something. I back away, startled, because my knowledge of the language is poor and I misunderstand her words. I think she has said *"kirai-desu,"* meaning that she dislikes me; and I am embarrassed, and confused, wondering what I have done wrong: how I have disgraced myself.

Then, after a moment, I realize my mistake. She has said, actually, *"kirei-desu."* She has called me pretty. And I look for her, in the crowd, at least to smile, perhaps to say thank you if I can overcome my shyness enough to speak. But she is gone.

I remember this moment—this instant of communication gone awry—again and again over the years. Perhaps this is where the river starts.

In 1954 and 1955 I am a college freshman, living in a very small dormitory, actually a converted private home, with a group of perhaps fourteen other girls. We are very much alike. We wear the same sort of clothes: cashmere sweaters and plaid wool skirts, knee socks and loafers. We all smoke Marlboro cigarettes, and we knit—usually argyle socks for our boyfriends—and play bridge. Sometimes we study; and we get good grades because we are all the cream of the crop, the valedictorians and class presidents from our high schools all over the United States.

One of the girls in our dorm is not like the rest of us. She doesn't wear our uniform. She wears blue jeans instead of skirts, and she doesn't curl her hair or knit or play bridge. She doesn't date or go to fraternity parties and dances.

She's a smart girl, a good student, a pleasant enough person, but she is different, somehow alien, and that makes us uncomfortable. We react with a kind of mindless cruelty. We don't tease or torment her, but we do something worse: we ignore her. We pretend that she doesn't exist. In a small house of fourteen young women, we make one invisible.

Somehow, by shutting her out, we make ourselves feel comfortable. Familiar. Safe.

I think of her now and then as the years pass. Those thoughts—fleeting, but profoundly remorseful—enter the current of the river.

In the summer of 1979, I am sent by a magazine I am working for to an island off the coast of Maine to write an article about a painter who lives there alone. I spend a good deal of time with this man, and we talk a lot about color. It is clear to me that although I am a highly visual person—a person who sees and appreciates form and composition and color—this man's capacity for seeing color goes far beyond mine.

I photograph him while I am there, and I keep a copy of his photograph for myself because there is something about his face—his eyes—which haunts me.

Later I hear that he has become blind.

I think about him—his name is Carl Nelson—from time to time. His photograph hangs over my desk. I wonder what it was like for him to lose the colors about which he was so impassioned.

I wish, in a whimsical way, that he could have somehow magically given me the capacity to see the way he did.

A little bubble begins, a little spurt, which will trickle into the river.

In 1989 I go to a small village in Germany to attend the wedding of one of my sons. In an ancient church, he marries his Margret in a ceremony conducted in a language I do not speak and cannot understand.

But one section of the service is in English. A woman stands in the balcony of that old stone church and sings the words from the Bible: *Where you go, I will go. Your people will be my people.*

How small the world has become, I think, looking around the church at the many people who sit there wishing happiness to my son and his new wife, wishing it in their own language as I am wishing it in mine. *We are all each other's people now,* I find myself thinking.

Can you feel that this memory is a stream that is now entering the river?

Another fragment. My father, nearing ninety, is in a nursing home. My brother and I have hung family pictures on the walls of his room. During a visit, he and I are talking about the people in the pictures. One is my sister, my parents' first child, who died young of cancer. My father smiles, looking at her picture. "That's your sister," he says happily. "That's Helen."

Then he comments, a little puzzled, but not at all sad, "I can't remember exactly what happened to her."

We can forget pain, I thought. And it is comfortable to do so.

But I also wonder briefly: is it safe to do that, to forget?

That uncertainty pours itself into the river of thought which will become the book.

1991. I am in an auditorium somewhere. I have spoken at length about my book *Number the Stars,* which has been honored with the 1990 Newbery Medal. A woman raises her hand. When the time for her question comes, she sighs very loudly, and says, "Why do we have to tell this Holocaust thing over and over? Is it really *necessary?*"

I answer her as well as I can, quoting, in fact, my German daughter-in-law, who has said to me, "No one knows better than we Germans that we must tell this again and again."

But I think about her question—and my answer—a great deal.

Wouldn't it, I think, playing devil's advocate to myself, make for a more comfortable world to *forget* the Holocaust? And I remember once again how comfortable, familiar, and safe my parents had sought to make my childhood by shielding me from Elsewhere. But I remember, too, that my response had been to open the gate again and again. My instinct had been a child's attempt to see for myself what lay beyond the wall.

The thinking becomes another tributary into the river of thought that will create *The Giver.*

Here's another memory. I am sitting in a booth with my daughter in a little Beacon Hill pub where she and I often have lunch together. The television is on in the background, behind the bar, as it always is. She and I are talking. Suddenly I gesture to her. I say, "Shhh," because I have heard a fragment of the news and I am startled, anxious, and want to hear the rest.

Someone has walked into a fast-food place with an automatic weapon and randomly killed a number of people. My daughter stops talking and waits while I listen to the rest.

Then I relax. I say to her, in a relieved voice, "It's all right. It was in Oklahoma." (Or perhaps it was Alabama. Or Indiana.)

She stares at me in amazement that I have said such a hideous thing.

How comfortable I made myself feel for a moment, by reducing my own realm of caring to my own familiar neighborhood. How safe I deluded myself into feeling.

I think about that, and it becomes a torrent that enters the flow of a river turbulent by now, and clogged with memories and thoughts and ideas that begin to mesh and intertwine. The river begins to seek a place to spill over.

When Jonas meets The Giver for the first time, and tries to comprehend what lies before him, he says, in confusion, "I thought there was only us. I thought there was only now."

In beginning to write *The Giver* I created, as I always do, in every book, a world that existed only in my imagination—the world of "only us, only now." I tried to make Jonas's world seem familiar, comfortable, and safe, and I tried to seduce the reader. I seduced myself along the way. It did feel good, that world. I got rid of all the things I fear and dislike: all the violence, prejudice, poverty, and injustice; and I even threw in good manners as a way of life because I liked the idea of it.

One child has pointed out, in a letter, that the people in Jonas's world didn't even have to do dishes.

It was very, very tempting to leave it at that.

But I've never been a writer of fairy tales. And if I've learned anything through that river of memories, it is that we can't live in a walled world, in an "only us, only now" world, where we are all the same and feel safe. We would have to sacrifice too much. The richness of color would disappear. Feelings for other humans would no longer be necessary. Choice would be obsolete.

And besides, I had ridden my bike Elsewhere as a child, and liked it there, but had never been brave enough to tell anyone about it. So it was time.

A letter that I've kept for a very long time is from a child who has read my book *Anastasia Krupnik*. Her letter—she's a little girl named Paula from Louisville, Kentucky—says:

> "I really like the book you wrote about Anastasia and her family because it made me laugh every time I read it. I especially liked when it said she didn't want to have a baby brother in the house because she had to clean up after him every time and change his diaper when her mother and father aren't home and she doesn't like to give him a bath and watch him all the time and put him to sleep every night while her mother goes to work … "

Here's the fascinating thing: *Nothing that the child describes actually happens in the book.* The child—as we all do—has brought her own life to a book. She has found a place, a place in the pages of a book, that shares her own frustrations and feelings.

And the same thing is happening—as I hoped it would happen—with *The Giver.*

Those of you who hoped that I would stand here tonight and reveal the "true" ending, the "right" interpretation of the ending, will be disappointed. There isn't one. There's a right one for each of us, and it depends on our own beliefs, our own hopes.

Let me tell you a few endings which are the right endings for a few children out of the many who have written to me.

From a sixth grader: "I think that when they were traveling they were traveling in a circle. When they came to 'Elsewhere' it was their old community, but they had accepted the memories and all the feelings that go along with it."

From another: "Jonas was kind of like Jesus because he took the pain for everyone else in the community so they wouldn't have to suffer. And, at the very end of the book, when Jonas and Gabe reached the place that they knew as Elsewhere, you described Elsewhere as if it were Heaven."

And one more: "A lot of people I know would hate that ending, but not me. I loved it. Mainly because I got to make the book happy. I decided they made it. They made it to the past. I decided the past was our world, and the future was their world. It was parallel worlds."

Finally, from one seventh-grade boy: "I was really surprised that they just died at the end. That was a bummer. You could of made them stay alive, I thought."

Very few find it a bummer. Most of the young readers who have written to me have perceived the magic of the circular journey. The truth that we go out and come back, and that what we come back to is changed, and so are we. Perhaps I have been traveling in a circle, too. Things come together and become complete.

Here is what I've come back to:

The daughter who was with me and looked at me in horror the day I fell victim to thinking we were "only us, only now" (and that what happened in Oklahoma, or Alabama, or Indiana didn't matter) was the first person to read the manuscript of *The Giver.*

The college classmate who was "different" lives, last I heard, very happily in New Jersey with another woman who shares her life. I can only hope that she has forgiven those of us who were young in a more frightened and less enlightened time.

My son, and Margret, his German wife—the one who reminded me how important it is to tell our stories again and again, painful though they often are—now have a little girl who will be the receiver of all of their memories. Their daughter had crossed the Atlantic three times before she was six months old. Presumably my granddaughter will never be fearful of Elsewhere.

Carl Nelson, the man who lost colors but not the memory of them, is the face on the cover of the book. He died in 1989 but left a vibrant legacy of paintings. One hangs now in my home.

And I am especially happy to stand here tonight on this platform with Allen Say because it truly brings my journey full circle. Allen was twelve years old when I was. He lived in Shibuya, that alien Elsewhere that I went to as a child on a bicycle. He was one of the Other, the Different, the dark-eyed children in blue school uniforms, and I was too timid then to do more than stand at the edge of their schoolyard, smile shyly, and wonder what their lives were like.

Now I can say to Allen what I wish I could have said then: *Watashi-no tomodachi desu.* Greetings, my friend.

I have been asked whether the Newbery Medal is, actually, an odd sort of burden in terms of the greater responsibility one feels. Whether one is paralyzed by it, fearful of being able to live up to the standards it represents.

For me the opposite has been true. I think the 1990 Newbery freed me to risk failure.

Other people took that risk with me, of course. One was my editor, Walter Lorraine, who has never to my knowledge been afraid to take a chance. Walter cares more about what a book has to say than he does about whether he can turn it into a stuffed animal or a calendar or a movie.

The Newbery Committee was gutsy, too. There would have been safer books. More comfortable books. More familiar books. They took a trip beyond the realm of sameness, with this one, and I think they should be very proud of that.

And all of you, as well. Let me say something to those of you here who do such dangerous work.

The man that I named The Giver passed along to the boy knowledge, history, memories, color, pain, laughter, love, and truth. Every time you place a book in the hands of a child, you do the same thing.

It is very risky.

But each time a child opens a book, he pushes open the gate that separates him from Elsewhere. It gives him choices. It gives him freedom.

Those are magnificent, wonderfully *unsafe* things.

I have been greatly honored by you now, two times. It is impossible to express my gratitude for that. Perhaps the only way, really, is to return to Boston, to my office, to my desk, and to go back to work in hopes that whatever I do next will justify the faith in me that this medal represents.

There are other rivers flowing.

Source: Lois Lowry, "Newbery Medal Acceptance," in *The Horn Book Magazine,* Vol. LXX, No. 4, July-August, 1994, pp. 414-22.

Patty Campbell

In this excerpt, Patty Campbell, noted author, critic, and general editor of Twayne's Young Adult Author series, discusses the unexpected elements in Lowry's The Giver, *with its multilevels of meaning, complex symbolism, and ambiguous conclusion, so radical a change from previous works by the author.*

Once in a long while a book comes along that takes hardened young-adult reviewers by surprise, a book so unlike what has gone before, so rich in levels of meaning, so daring in complexity of symbol and metaphor, so challenging in the ambiguity of its conclusion, that we are left with all our neat little everyday categories and judgments hanging useless. Books like Robert Cormier's *I Am the Cheese* or Terry Davis's *Mysterious Ways* are examples of these rare treasures. But after the smoke of our personal enthusiasm has cleared, we are left with uneasy thoughts: Will young adults understand it? Will the intricate subtleties that so delight us as adult critics go right over their heads? Will the questions posed by the ending leave them puzzled and annoyed, rather than thoughtful and intrigued? It all depends—on the maturity of the particular young adult, on how well we introduce the book and follow up with discussion, and on certain qualities in the book itself. In the past year young-adult literature has been blessed with two such extraordinary works: *The Giver* by Lois Lowry and *You Must Kiss a Whale* by David Skinner.

The Giver is particularly surprising because it is a major departure from the style and type of book we have come to expect from Lois Lowry, as *Horn Book* Editor Anita Silvey pointed out in her July/August 1993 editorial. Up until now, much of Lowry's work has consisted of "contemporary novels with engaging characters that explore something very rare—a functional family." But *The Giver* is a dystopia, "driven by plot and philosophy—not by character and dialogue," and the picture of the functional family turns disturbingly awry as the story proceeds. Indeed, it is Lowry's skill at depicting cheerful, ordinary reality that makes the revelation of the sinister difference in this alternate reality so chilling.

Most surprising of all is the leap forward Lowry has made in mastering the creation of a subtext by innuendo, foreshadowing, and resonance.

Take, for example, the opening sentence. "It was almost December, and Jonas was beginning to be frightened." The word *December* is loaded with resonance: the darkness of the solstice, endings, Christmas, cold. *Almost* and *beginning* pull forward to the future source of his fear, "that deep, sickening feeling of something terrible about to happen." The name Jonas, too, is evocative—of the biblical Jonah, he who is sent by God to cry against the wickedness of Nineveh, an unwilling lone messenger with a mission that will be received with hostility. In one seemingly simple sentence Lowry sets the mood and direction of her story, foreshadows its outcome, and plants an irresistible narrative pull.

The fascinating gradual revelation of a world and its interlocking rationale as explained by a protagonist immersed in the culture is reminiscent of Margaret Atwood's *Handmaid's Tale.* Lowry plays with our perceptions and our emotions, creating tension by presenting details of this community that win our approval, and then hinting at something terribly wrong. The family, for instance, seems ideal: a gentle, caring father and mother and the one child of each gender that tells us that this community has solved the population problem; the scenes of their warm, bantering conversations around the dinner table; their formal sharing (as required by the Rules) of feelings from their day and dreams from their night; the comfort and support they offer one another. But then we hear of Birthmothers and applications for children and spouses; we begin to wonder why there are no grandparents and to suspect what lies behind the parents' talk of "release."

Lowry has structured the intriguing details of this planned community with meticulous care, focusing particularly, through Jonas's eyes, on the education system that produces a society which functions by internalized values. At first it seems to be an autocratic state—an impression that is given credence by Orwellian images such as the rasping voices that chastise from ubiquitous speakers. But soon it is revealed that the community is ruled by an elected Committee of Elders and that the citizens long ago chose this controlled life. Each peer group of fifty children is called by their ages— Fives, Elevenses—and is distinguished by certain clothes, haircuts, and required behaviors that are appropriate for their stage of development. At eight they begin to spend their afterschool hours volunteering in the various work of the community, and at twelve they are each given an Assignment, based on the careful observation of the Committee of Elders, which will be their job for life.

When the fateful December ceremony comes, Jonas is stunned to learn that he has been appointed the new Receiver of Memory, the highest position in the community. Each day he goes to the rooms of the old Receiver of Memory, a reclusive elderly man whom he comes to call the Giver. There his innocence is gradually transformed as the old man transmits to him, often with great pain for Jonas, the memories of experiences and emotions that the people have chosen to banish from their minds so that they might sustain the illusion of social order and success. Jonas's first memory-lesson is a sled ride that teaches him the concepts of cold and snow and of "downhill"—ideas that are new to him because the community has abolished weather and irregular terrain in the interests of efficiency. As the days wear on, Jonas experiences war and pain and love, and begins to understand how his society has given up choice and freedom for control and predictability.

And then one day he asks to view a videotape of a "release" that his father has that morning performed on an unwanted baby at the community nursery, and learns to his horror that the euphemism covers engineered death—for the old, for rule-breakers, and for surplus or difficult infants. Watching his father sweetly wave bye-bye to the small corpse as it slides down the disposal chute, Jonas realizes with cold shock that his nurturing family is a sham, held together by trained reactions, not love, and that there is only hollowness at the heart of the society's life. He and the Giver hatch a plot to force the community to change. Jonas will flee, so that the memories he has assimilated will return to the people, forcing them to suffer and grow. But that night Jonas's father announces that Gabriel, the difficult toddler who has been temporarily sharing their home and whom Jonas loves, will be "released" the next morning. There is no time to carry out the plot; in the night, Jonas and Gabriel bicycle away.

And now we come to the inherent difficulty of every dystopia story—how to end. Basically, there are three possibilities. The protagonist escapes as the society collapses; the protagonist escapes with the intention of returning with the seeds of change; or the protagonist escapes, but it turns out to be an illusion. Lowry opts for elements of all three. Jonas journeys for days and days and, finally, at the end of his strength, comes to a place where there is snow, and a hill, and a sled. Here the story, which up till now has been readable as an adventure tale, becomes symbolic and ambiguous as Jonas and the dying baby begin the sled ride toward the faint distant Christmas lights which are part of his memory of love. Is it a dream? Are they already dead? Or will they find a new life? Will the community they left behind reshape itself in a more human mold? Lowry refuses to provide a tidy ending. The challenge of the ambiguity is appropriate for the stature of this intricately constructed masterwork....

Source: Patty Campbell, "The Sand in the Oyster," in *The Horn Book Magazine,* Vol. LXIX, No. 6, November-December, 1993, pp. 717-21.

Sources

Patty Campbell, review in *The Horn Book Magazine,* Vol. LXIX, No. 6, November-December, 1993, pp. 717-21.

Jane Inglis, review in *The School Librarian,* Vol. 43, No. 1, February, 1995, pp.31-32.

Lois Lowry, Newbery Medal Acceptance speech, delivered at the American Library Association's annual meeting June, 1994, printed in *The Horn Magazine,* Vol. LXX, No. 4, July-August 1994, pp. 414-22.

Gary D. Schmidt, review in *The Five Owls,* Vol. VIII, No. 1, September-October, 1993, pp. 14-15

For Further Study

Michael Betzold, *Appointment with Doctor Death,* Momentum Books, 1993.

A journalist gathers together the evidence and background relating to cases involving Dr. Kevorkian.

Joel D. Chaston, "The Giver," in *Beacham's Guide to Literature for Young Adults, Volume 6,* edited by Kirk H. Beetz, Beacham Publishing, Inc., 1994, pp. 3255-63.

This excerpt from a reference book surveys Lowry's life and work, suggests ideas for reports, papers, and discussions related to *The Giver,* and summarizes the novel's plot, setting, themes, characters, and literary qualities.

Joel D. Chaston, *Lois Lowry,* Twayne's United States Author Series, edited by Ruth K. MacDonald, Prentice Hall, Intl., 1997.

Chaston tracks Lowry's development as a writer, beginning with her childhood and her sense of story and values, and progressing through her literary career and reputation.

Ilene Cooper, "Giving and Receiving," in *Booklist,* Vol. 89, April 15, 1993, p. 1506.

An early review that finds the conflict between sameness and freedom in the novel to be thought-provoking, but finds Lowry's message "forced," and her ending too ambiguous.

Mary Ellen Flannery, "Parents Want *The Giver* Off Shelves," in *The Palm Beach Post,* June 19, 1996.

Flannery reports on the ongoing controversy between Northport Middle School and concerned parent, Anna Cerbasi, who objects to use of *The Giver* in a public school setting.

Louise Kaplan, "Images of Absence, Voices of Silence," in *No Voice Is Ever Wholly Lost,* Simon & Schuster, 1995, pp. 216-37.

Psychologist Kaplan discusses the difficulties, yet importance, of bearing witness to traumatic events, and suggests that, since survivors of the Holocaust had to psychically absent themselves in order to survive trauma and abuse, their children must "testify as to what happened" to their parents.

Seymour R. Kester, *Utopian Episodes: Daily Life in Experimental Colonies Dedicated to Changing the World,* Syracuse University Press, 1996.

An extremely detailed and critical look at the way of life endured by participants in the three principal American utopias of the nineteenth century.

Walter Lorraine, "Lois Lowry," in *The Horn Book Magazine,* Vol. 70, July-August, 1994, pp. 423-26.

Lowry's editor reminisces about her fiction, which he praises for being immediately accessible to "very broad" audiences.

Lois Lowry, "Calling It Quits," in *The Writer,* Vol. 102, April, 1989, pp. 13-14, 47.

Lowry discusses the importance of ending a story in the right place, so that readers will want to continue writing the story in their own minds.

Lois Lowry, "Remembering How it Was," in *The Writer,* Vol. 100, July, 1987, pp. 16-19.

In this exploration of the importance of memory to storytellers, Lowry says that, while the details in a story need not be truthful, the emotions that are connected to the details must be true. She also says that using painful memories in writing is a way to get over them.

Lois Markham, *Lois Lowry (Learning Works Meet the Author Series),* Learning Works, 1995.

Published for Lowry's young readers, this book shows how the author incorporates significant autobiographical experiences into her fiction.

Donald E. Pitzer, editor, *America's Communal Utopias,* University of North Carolina Press, 1997.

A collection of essays on the full range of American communities, including the Shakers, George Rapp's Harmony Society and the Oneida Perfectionists.

Karen Ray, "The Giver," in *The New York Times Book Review,* October 31, 1993, p. 26.

An early review that finds the novel's themes "provocative," despite the novel's "occasional logical lapses."

Michael Sadowski, "Lois Lowry and Allen Say Take Newbery, Caldecott Medals," in *School Library Journal,* Vol. 40, No. 3, March 1994, p. 123.

An early announcement that Lowry had won her second Newbery medal.

Scott Shane, *Dismantling Utopia: How Information Ended the Soviet Union,* Ivan R. Dee, 1994.
A first-hand account of the disintegration of the communist state written by a correspondent of the *Baltimore Sun.*

Amanda Smith, "PW Interviews: Lois Lowry," in *Publishers Weekly,* Vol. 229, No. 8, February 21, 1986, pp. 152-53.
An exploration of Lowry's life and work that considers her philosophy of writing for children, and her

thoughts about laughter, adaptability, and human relations.

Lesley J. Smith *Forced Exit: The Slippery Slope from Assisted Suicide to Legalized Murder,* Times Books, 1997.
Openly opposed to euthanasia on principle, Smith has a response to every conceivable argument in defense.

Laura M. Zaidman, "Lois Lowry," in *American Writers for Children Since 1960: Fiction* (Dictionary of Literary Biography, Vol. 52), edited by Glenn Estes, Gale Research, 1986, pp. 249-261.
This essay summarizes Lowry's personal and professional life, summarizes criticism of Lowry's pre-1986 work, and includes an excerpt from one of her manuscripts that shows her revisions.

Grendel

John Gardner
1971

Completed in 1970 and published the following year, *Grendel* was the first of John Gardner's novels to bring him not just critical but popular success. The novel was praised as a literary *tour de force* and named a book of the year by *Time* and *Newsweek* magazines. As a professor of English specializing in medieval literature, Gardner had been teaching *Beowulf,* the source of inspiration for *Grendel,* for many years at various colleges. A relatively minor character in *Beowulf,* Grendel is a symbol for "darkness, chaos, and death," according to critic John M. Howell in *Understanding John Gardner.* In Gardner's version, however, Grendel becomes a three-dimensional character with, in Howell's words, "a sense of humor and a gift for language." Grendel even has a weakness for poetry. As a would-be artist, Grendel strives, however comically, to escape from his baseness. Such is the power of art, Gardner seems to be saying, that even a monster can be affected by it. Gardner also develops the theme of heroism as another moral force that enables society to advance by elevating Unferth, a minor character in the original poem, to a major character and foil for Grendel. Similarly, Gardner builds up the role of Grendel's mother to emphasize, through her inarticulateness, the importance of language in the development of civilization. Gardner also creates a relationship between Grendel and the dragon (another minor character in the original epic) in order to expand the concept of nihilism—the belief that there is no purpose to existence. Through these changes, Gardner

is able to develop themes that recur not only in *Grendel* but throughout his other works: the struggle between good and evil, the clash between order and disorder, the hero's sacrifice and achievement of immortality, and the importance of art and the artist as a means of affirming the moral meaning of life.

Author Biography

Grendel reflects two of Gardner's major interests: his belief in fiction as a moral force for good, and his passion for the medieval period in history. Gardner was born in 1933 and grew up in Batavia, New York. His mother was an English teacher and his father a farmer and lay preacher, so it is perhaps not surprising that Gardner was eventually drawn to the medieval period, when society was largely agricultural and the Church played a central role in life. As a boy he was attracted not only to language but also to music and chemistry. His father's passion for opera rubbed off on young John, who sang in various choirs as a boy and later wrote several opera libretti on medieval subjects. Having decided that English was his field because he did well at it, Gardner attended DePauw University from 1951 to 1953. The latter year he also married Joan Louise Patterson, with whom he had two children. Transferring to Washington University in St. Louis, Gardner received his A.B. in 1955. He also took an M.A. at the State University of Iowa in 1956 and a Ph.D. in 1958. As his doctoral dissertation, Gardner wrote an unpublished novel, *The Old Men.*

After receiving his Ph.D., Gardner pursued a teaching career while continuing his writing. He held positions at a number of colleges and universities before settling at Southern Illinois University from 1965 to 1974. His first published novel, *The Resurrection,* was published in 1966, though it attracted little notice, and his second, *The Wreckage of Agathon,* appeared in 1970. Gardner had been writing fiction fairly steadily from an early age, and he described *Grendel* (1971) as a "late work" in an interview in 1974. Though *The Sunlight Dialogues* (1972) and *October Light* (1976) were published after *Grendel,* both were actually written prior to it. *Grendel* was the first book to bring Gardner widespread recognition. The novel was named one of the ten best books of 1971 by *Time* and *Newsweek.*

During this period the author also published (with Lennis Dunlap) a textbook, *The Forms of Fic-*

John Gardner

tion (1961); a translation, *The Complete Works of the Gawain-Poet* (1965); *Jason and Medeia* (1972), a novel in verse; the collection *The King's Indian: Stories and Tales* (1974); and other scholarly works on medieval literary subjects.

Both *The Sunlight Dialogues* and *Nickel Mountain* (1973) were well received by the popular press. *October Light* won the National Book Critics Circle Award for fiction and was named one of the best books of 1976 by both *Time* and the *New York Times.* Gardner's reputation went down, however, after the publication of *On Moral Fiction* in 1978. While stating his own philosophy of moral affirmation eloquently, to many critics the book seemed arrogant and dismissive of many of Gardner's contemporaries.

From 1974 to 1978, Gardner held several short-term appointments in New York and New England colleges. During this period and the following four years, Gardner also published poetry, scholarly and children's books, a novel titled *Mickelsson's Ghosts* (1982), and a collection of stories. In 1978, he founded the writing program at the State University of New York at Binghamton. He served as its director until the time of his death, in a motorcycle accident, in 1982.

Plot Summary

Background: The Epic Beowulf

John Gardner's *Grendel* is a retelling of the first part of the Anglo-Saxon epic, *Beowulf*, with an important difference. In *Grendel*, the monster gets to tell the story. Because this is a retelling, however, Gardner assumes that his reader is familiar with the story of *Beowulf*. Indeed, without such familiarity the reader would be lost. Accordingly, the following is a very brief summary of the Anglo-Saxon story.

Beowulf is the oldest long poem in English, written as early as perhaps the seventh century A.D., with the only manuscript version dating to around 1000 A.D. The Danish King, Hrothgar, has built a fabulous meadhall, Heorot, for himself and his retainers. However, Heorot is not safe: each night the monster Grendel attacks the hall and kills Hrothgar's men. Beowulf, a Geat, hears of Hrothgar's distress and travels the land of the Danes to help rid Heorot of the monster and to garner fame for himself.

Beowulf fights with Grendel when the monster attacks the hall. He rips off Grendel's arm, and the monster flees, dying. Grendel's mother later attacks Hrothgar's men in retaliation for her son's death. Beowulf also fights Grendel's mother and kills her.

In the last section of *Beowulf*, set some fifty years later, old Beowulf, now king of the Geats, does battle with a gold-hoarding dragon who has been savaging the Geats. In this final battle, Beowulf and the dragon kill each other.

Chapters 1-4: Grendel and the World

Gardner's *Grendel* is a book of twelve chapters, the number recalling Grendel's twelve-year battle with Hrothgar, the months of the year, and the signs of the zodiac. The book, however, is not in straight chronological order. Rather, Gardner uses devices such as flashbacks, allusions, and foreshadowing to help relate the story. The present tense passages of the book move the reader chronologically through the twelve months of the twelfth year of Grendel's war with Hrothgar. Interspersed among the present tense passages are past tense passages telling of the years leading up to the present. Throughout, as the first person narrator of his own story, Grendel grows in his understanding of the nature of language and its power to create and destroy worlds.

The book opens in April, the month of the ram. It is in the present tense with Grendel observing the world around him, watching a ram on a mountain. Immediately his concern with language becomes evident: "Talking, talking. Spinning a web of words, pale walls of dreams, between myself and all I see."

Grendel lives in a cave under a burning lake with his mother, a mute, beast-like creature who cares for and protects him. There are other "shadowy shapes" in the cave, but Grendel alone can speak. In Chapter 2, Grendel recalls an important moment: trapped in a tree, crying for his mother, Grendel encounters men for the first time. The most important thing about the encounter is that the men speak words that Grendel understands, although the men do not understand Grendel's words.

After his rescue from the tree by his mother, Grendel begins watching the men and their actions. The third chapter is a summary of what he sees throughout the years as the Danes slowly develop human civilization. Hrothgar becomes the most powerful of the kings, because, Grendel tells the reader, he has a theory about the purpose of war that makes his battles effective.

About this time a blind poet arrives at Hrothgar's hall. The poet is called the Shaper. The Shaper does more than make poetry, according to Grendel. Through his retelling of Hrothgar's history, "The man had changed the world, had torn up the past by its thick, gnarled roots and had transmuted it, and they who knew the truth remembered it his way—and so did I." The Shaper's arrival is particularly significant for Grendel. In his songs, he names Grendel as one of the race of Cain, a representative of all that is dark and evil. For Hrothgar's men and for Grendel himself, this is what he becomes.

Chapters 5-7: The Dragon, Unferth, and Wealtheow

Grendel, unhinged by the Shaper's words, visits the dragon to find answers to his questions about order, language, and truth. (This is the same dragon who will kill and be killed by Beowulf in the Anglo-Saxon epic.) The dragon tells him that the Shaper's words are an "illusion of reality," and that they only serve to make the men think that there is meaning in the universe. According to the dragon, the men's religion, ritual, and songs are nothing more than nonsense whose only purpose it to make them believe that life is not random accident. The dragon denies the existence of God and meaning, advising Grendel to "seek out gold and sit on it."

Grendel discovers after leaving the dragon that the dragon has put a curse on him: he cannot be injured by the men's weapons. He begins raiding Hrothgar's meadhall, killing and eating men. On one occasion, he encounters Unferth, who stands up to him with bold words of heroism. Unferth's goal is to make his reputation by either killing or being killed by the monster. Grendel, instead of fighting, answers in words, and Unferth is shaken to realize that Grendel has language. Grendel engages in banter until Unferth, in frustration, says, "No more talk!" and rushes him with his sword. Uninjured, Grendel responds by throwing apples at him. By behaving in this unexpected way, Grendel completely humiliates Unferth. As a further insult, Grendel does not kill Unferth, but leaves him to his shame. Later, Unferth tracks Grendel to his lair and there confronts him on the meaning of heroism. Grendel demonstrates to Unferth that life is indeed meaningless by refusing to engage him in combat. Instead, he returns Unferth to the hall, kills two guards, and in future raids, spares Unferth's life. As Grendel reports, "So much for heroism."

In the next chapter, Grendel reveals in flashback the circumstances of the arrival of Wealtheow, the Queen at Hrothgar's court, during the second year of his raiding. At that time, Hrothgar was at war with the Helmings, Wealtheow's people. Her brother offered her to Hrothgar as a means of weaving a peace. Wealtheow's name means "holy servant of common good," and her role in *Beowulf* as well as *Grendel* is clearly that. Grendel attacks the hall and the Queen, but decides not to kill her.

Chapters 8-12: Grendel's End

In the eighth chapter, Grendel relates how Hrothgar's nephew, Hrothulf, arrived at the meadhall after the murder of his father. His resentful attitude and desire for power gives Grendel the opportunity to consider "the idea of violence" which grows in the young man. The following chapter features Grendel's encounter with a priest, which leads to several observations on the nature of religion. In the tenth chapter, Grendel feels tormented by boredom, and observes the death of the old poet Shaper. Meanwhile, his mother has become strangely protective of him and tries to prevent Grendel from leaving the lair.

In the next-to-last chapter, strangers arrive by sea. This is the unnamed hero that the reader knows to be Beowulf. Grendel is strangely excited by the presence of the strangers. He attacks the hall late at night and makes a fatal error: he allows Beowulf to grab him by the wrist. Beowulf tells him about the cycles of existence. Although everything in this world will be destroyed, something will remain and will grow again. Although Grendel cannot be harmed by steel weapons, he is killed by the strength of Beowulf's grip. Beowulf rips off Grendel's arm at the shoulder socket. Grendel screams again for his mother, then staggers to edge of his cliff. To the end, he attributes his death to random accident. As he falls into death and over the cliff, he says to the animals watching him, "Poor Grendel's had an accident." The last words of the novel are enigmatic: *So may you all.* Whether this is curse or a prediction is unclear. Grendel, however, dies.

Characters

Beowulf

Beowulf is the hero with the "strength of thirty thanes" (Chapter 10) who finally slays Grendel and brings peace to the land of the Scyldings. Significantly, Beowulf's coming is not only prophesied by the old woman who speaks of a "giant across the sea" but is also alluded to in the dying words of the Shaper: "I see a time when the Danes once again—." Beowulf's arrival is also foretold by the lengthening of the days, which is a traditional sign of hope and new life. When Beowulf, the son of Ecgtheow, lands among the Danes, he introduces himself and his party as Geats who are "hearth-companions of King Hygilac" (Chapter 11). Beowulf has come specifically to kill Grendel, but Hrothgar's court realizes, of course, that whoever slays the monster will no doubt soon have a fair claim to the land of the Scyldings and Helmings as well. When Beowulf finally confronts Grendel, he tricks the monster into thinking he is asleep with the other thanes (warriors) in the mead hall. Beowulf then grabs Grendel's arm and twists it behind the monster, which slips in a pool of blood he himself has created in slaughtering weaker thanes. After forcing Grendel to acknowledge his own mortality by commanding him to "sing of walls" (Chapter 12), Beowulf rips off Grendel's arm, and the monster dies from loss of blood. While carrying out this deed, Beowulf intones these lines: *"Though you murder the world ... strong searching roots will crack your cave and rain will cleanse it: The world will burn green, sperm build again. My promise. Time is the mind, the hand that makes (fingers on harpstrings, hero-swords, the acts, the eyes of queens). By that I kill you.*" Thus does Beowulf catalogue all the acts that he believes are stronger than the forces of evil, alluding to all the characters in the story who have acted in the common good—including the Shaper, Unferth, and Wealtheow.

Dragon

The Dragon, who first appears in Chapter 5, may be real or just another figment of Grendel's imagination. Nevertheless, it plays an important role in the story as an exemplar of a philosophy of nihilism (the idea that existence is meaningless), solipsism (the idea that only the self exists), and chaos. The dragon's advice to Grendel—"Seek out gold—but not my gold—and guard it!" (stated twice in the chapter)—only begins to suggest his cynical view of the world. For the dragon, there is no real meaning in life, only accidental incidents, each one a "foolish flicker-flash in the long dull fall of eternity." While the Dragon himself claims to be able to see all space and time (however weary he is of the sight), ordinary mortals must struggle along with their illusions of connection, meaning, and reality. Nevertheless, the Dragon's power is such that after meeting him, Grendel is impervious to the weapons of men (Chapter 6).

First priest

The high priest Ork's company includes four other priests who serve under him. The first priest focuses on the words of the gospel, not the philosophy behind them. He is especially fond of quoting scripture to support every thought and action. Thus, when Ork says that he has seen Grendel—"The Great Destroyer"—the first priest replies: "Blasphemy! It is written, 'Ye shall not see my face'" (Chapter 9).

Fourth priest

Only the fourth priest, who is younger than the others, seems genuinely moved by Ork's responses to Grendel's questions about the nature of the "king of the Gods" and the meaning of life. Somewhat comically, the younger man exclaims, "The rhythm is re-established! Merely rational thought ... leaves the mind incurably crippled.... But now at last, sweet fantasy has found root in your blessed soul!" (Chapter 9) and *The gods made this world for our joy!*" (Chapter 10).

Freawaru

She is Hrothgar's daughter by "a woman who'd died" (Chapter 8). Hrothulf blushes when-

Media Adaptations

- *Grendel* was adapted as an animated cartoon titled *Grendel, Grendel, Grendel* by Alexander Stitt in 1981. Sir Peter Ustinov was featured as the voice of Grendel.

ever she speaks to him, indicating a fondness for her. Hrothgar, however, plans to marry her off to the ruler of another rival fiefdom.

Grendel

While the monster Grendel was a less important character than Beowulf in the Old English epic on which Gardner's novel is based, as the title character here he has become the star attraction. Grendel is violent, cruel, cynical, and degenerate—in short, monstrous. Yet, like the humans who speak a similar language to his, Grendel has feelings, too. Like any mother's child, he cries when he is caught in the tree trunk (Chapter 2). Most important, he is moved by the words of the Shaper—the human poet whose words, though they no doubt embellish the truth, yet live through time to change the world and inspire the Scyldings to do great deeds (Chapter 3). Grendel is a monster, yet uses language as humans do, to try to define and explore his world.

As narrator, Grendel recounts the story of his life from birth to death. His search for meaning in his existence takes him to the home of the dragon and drives him to spy on the meadhall of Hrothgar. But when Grendel, inspired by the Shaper, tries to join the human race by leaving the "dark side" to which he believes he has been banished, he is misunderstood and turned on by fearful men. As a result, Grendel reverts to his former nihilism—believing there is no purpose to existence. He becomes vengeful, though remaining haunted by the Shaper's words.

Grendel is the author of numerous acts of violence and cruelty. By telling events from his point of view, however, the monster is still able to elicit sympathy from the reader. This sympathy has led some critics and readers to consider Grendel as the "hero" of the novel. Careful consideration of the entire text, however, allows for a different interpretation.

Grendel's mother

She has no name, and may be only a dim memory in Grendel's mind rather than an actual living character in the story. Yet Grendel's mother plays an important role as the monster's comforter and savior. She also serves to highlight the importance of language in the novel. Grendel's mother communicates only in inarticulate sounds that even Grendel cannot understand—although he often says, and then denies, that her sounds might mean something. The shadowy cave where Grendel's mother dwells represents her ignorance. Similarly, the bone pile she is constantly picking through suggests that those without the ability to communicate are left to scraps of others. Although Grendel's mother does not possess language, unlike her son she seems to have found some purpose in life: as Grendel says, "I was, in her eyes, some meaning I could never know and might not care to know" (Chapter 2).

Halga the Good

The younger brother of Hrothgar, Halga the Good is murdered, leaving his son Hrothulf to reside as an orphan in Hrothgar's court.

Herogar

The king of a neighboring fiefdom to that of Hrothgar (Chapter 1).

Holy servant of common good

See Wealtheow

Hrothgar

King of the Scyldings, he first appears in the story as a tall man in a long black beard who inspects the tree in which Grendel is trapped (Chapter 2). When Grendel shouts at Hrothgar and his men, Hrothgar throws an ax at the monster, who is finally saved by his mother. Hrothgar gradually learns that the secret to power is not killing your neighbors but collecting tribute from them and making them your allies. He also is smart enough to build roads to connect his fiefdoms and bring peace and order to formerly warring bands. Finally, when threatened by Hymgod of the Helmings, neighbors who are potentially more powerful than he, Hrothgar realizes that the solution to his problem is to accept Hymgod's offer of his sister, Wealtheow, as his bride. In the twilight of his rule,

Hrothgar is subjected to the trials of various forms of political philosophy—from the traditional heroism of the feudalistic age, seen in his Hrothgar's subject Unferth, to the Machiavellian beliefs and anarchism of his young nephew Hrothulf and his mentor Red Horse (a pun on the name of the radical French philosopher Georges Sorel).

Hrothulf

One of Halga the Good's two sons, Hrothulf comes at the age of fourteen to live at Hrothgar's mead hall after the death of his father. He is sullen and brooding: "already a God-damned pretender," Grendel observes (Chapter 8). Though exposed to the philosophy of anarchism by his mentor, Red Horse, Hrothulf is not totally taken in by the old man's violent beliefs. "Nobody in his right mind would praise violence for its own sake, regardless of its ends," says Hrothulf (Chapter 8). Perhaps more telling, Hrothulf remains kind to his young cousins, the children of Hrothgar and Wealtheow, though they stand ahead of him in line to the kingship.

Hygmod

Hrothgar's challenger from a neighboring fiefdom is a young king whose power is symbolized by the bear he leads on a chain (Chapter 7). Rather than wait for Hygmod to grow in strength and challenge him, Hrothgar takes his army to Hygmod. Hrothgar is wise enough to know that Hygmod's offer of gifts will not be sufficient to buy peace between the two rivals. But by the same token, Hygmod is smart enough to realize that his ultimate offer—the gift of his own sister, Wealtheow, as Hrothgar's bride—will not be refused. Hrothgar realizes that despite his current advantage, his kingdom is on the decline and that this new alliance may be the only way to save it.

King of the Scyldings

See Hrothgar

Lord of the Helmings

See Hygmod

Ork

The "eldest and wisest" of Hrothgar's priests by his own description, Ork is a blind prophet who encounters Grendel in Chapter 9. Ork takes his name from a recurring character in William Blake's poetry who seems to represent, at different times, Prometheus, Christ, or, in the words of critic Northrop Frye, the "dying and reviving god of

[Blake's] mythology" (Frye, *Fearful Symmetry,* as quoted in Howell, *Understanding John Gardner*). Ork's eloquent and heartfelt descriptions of the principles of his philosophy puzzle Grendel. His expectations defied, the monster hesitates to murder the priest as he had planned. Among Ork's memorable descriptions of his philosophy is his description of God's purpose ("the evocation of novel intensities. He is the *lure for our feeling*") and the ultimate Evil ("'Things fade' and 'Alternatives exclude'").

Red Horse

Red Horse is the old peasant who is young Hrothulf's counselor. Red Horse delivers almost verbatim the anarchistic philosophy of the French thinker Georges Sorel, as written in his *Reflections on Violence* (1908). "The total ruin of institutions and morals is an act of creation. A *religious* act. Murder and mayhem are the life and soul of revolution" (Chapter 8). While Hrothulf finds some of the old man's ideas attractive, he is not completely convinced.

Scyld Shefing

Scyld Shefing is the ancient Danish King who, according to a legend, was found as a castaway by the "first men." Scyld Shefing grew up to win the "glory of men," uniting a kingdom that had been "lordless" for many years. His great deeds are still sung by the Shaper (Chapter 3).

Second priest

The second priest's main concern seems to be physical, not spiritual. He believes that he and his fellow priests should follow a strict physical regimen so that they can each put their best efforts into their daily work. Thus he scolds Ork for being outdoors at night with snow falling on him. "A man should try to be more regular," he exclaims (Chapter 9).

Shaper

The Shaper is the name the author gives to the king's poet-musician-historian, for he can shape reality just with his words. The poet is a special person in the court, who through words and music alone makes the great deeds of humanity seem even greater, thus inspiring people to take risks for what they believe in. When the blind harper in Hrothgar's court sings of the deeds of the great Scyld Shefing, "men wept like children: children sat stunned" (Chapter 3). The Shaper may manipulate the truth as much as the politician, Gardner seems

to be saying. Yet the Shaper's ability to capture the emotions of his listeners and harness their energies, so that they may live their lives in service to the highest ideals, make him higher than others in the pantheon of human heroes. When the blind singer gets old and dies, his last thought, though unfinished, suggests hope: "I see a time when the Danes once again—" (Chapter 10).

Son of Ecglaf
See Unferth

Third priest

The main concern of the third priest is with appearances, not spirituality. He worries about how Ork's behavior will affect the perception of priests by people in general. The third priest says of Ork: "Lunatic priests are bad business. They give people the willies. One man like him can turn us all to paupers" (Chapter 9).

Unferth

The bravest of the thanes in Hrothgar's court, Unferth challenges Grendel on one of his invasions of the meadhall. The monster mocks the hero's brave words, and shocks Unferth when he reveals he can speak. Instead of dignifying Unferth with combat, he throws apples at the man before leaving the hall. To Grendel's surprise, Unferth follows him home and swims through the pool above Grendel's cave to challenge his power with the hope of dying a hero. Unferth, despite his brutish side, represents the author's philosophy that "except in the life of a hero, the whole world's meaningless. The hero sees values beyond what's possible" (Chapter 6). Grendel humiliates Unferth by carrying him back to Hrothgar's meadhall alive and intact. Later in the story (Chapter 7), it is revealed that Unferth apparently murdered his brothers, an event which moved him to "put on the Shaper's idea of a hero like a merry mask." His bitter demeanor is healed by the queen's forgiveness. Despite his unresolved conflict with Grendel, Unferth remains "top man in Hrothgar's hall" (Chapter 11) until Beowulf appears. Unferth challenges the newcomer by mocking his reputation, but Beowulf refutes the story convincingly and then puts Unferth in his place by referring to his bloody past.

Wealtheow

As her description, "holy servant of common good" (Chapter 7), suggests, Wealtheow has given up her personal life for the sake of keeping peace between the Helmings and Scyldings. Though she occasionally longs for her childhood home, she never lets these feelings show to the Scyldings. In offering to sacrifice herself for the good of all, Wealtheow is a true heroine in Gardner's terms. As such, she arouses mixed feelings of love and hatred in Grendel. He resolves to kill her, but at the last moment decides against it because it would be "as meaningless as letting her live."

Themes

Artists and Society

The artist in *Grendel* is the Shaper, the court harper. His singing of great men's deeds, no matter how embellished or even falsified, renders both men and deeds immortal. Individual artists may come and go as others with greater gifts appear: this happens when the old harper in Hrothgar's hall is displaced by the Shaper, a newer and more talented bard (Chapter 3). Nevertheless, the power of art remains. While it is kings who unite countries politically, Gardner seems to be saying that they could not do so without the courage and selflessness of individuals who are inspired by the Shaper to accomplish great deeds. Such is the power of the poet that he affects even Grendel. After hearing the blind harper "sing the glory of Hrothgar's line," Grendel flees the scene, a "ridiculous hairy creature torn apart by poetry." Even though Grendel ultimately rejects the Shaper's fable, Grendel himself is still driven back to poetry in his quest to be understood. Having destroyed Hrothgar's meadhall in Chapter 6, Grendel realizes now that "as never before, I was alone." In his new role as "Wrecker of Kings," he is nothing once he runs out of kings to wreck, because "physical destruction is finite," as Howell notes. Thus later, when Grendel wants to punish Hrothgar, instead of planning some physical act of destruction, he thinks of insinuating into the king's sleep a bad dream about a "heavy blade in flight" (Chapter 8). These words (which are actually a quote from Thomas Kinsella's poem "Wormwood") are meant to evoke in the old king a nightmarish recollection of the moment he threw an ax at Grendel and began their war.

Death

There is a marked contrast in attitudes toward death between the various monsters and Beowulf and the thanes (warriors), especially Unferth. With this contrast, Gardner makes the point that personal death is insignificant to the hero if it brings a chance

for immortality. For Grendel, the solipsist (one who believes nothing exists but the self), killing others means nothing. When Grendel himself faces even the slightest threat of physical harm, however, it is enough to send him wailing to his mother (Chapters 2, 12). Although Gardner embellishes the character of the dragon considerably, he does not include the scene from the original epic in which the dragon kills Beowulf. Instead, Beowulf lives to preach a gospel of death and rebirth: "The world will burn green, sperm build again. My promise. Time is the mind, the hand that makes (fingers on harpstrings, hero-swords, the acts, the eyes of queens). By that I kill you" (Chapter 12). In other words, it is through creation, imagination, and inspiration that one may kill evil and achieve immortality—even if heroic acts only live on through poetry and song.

Language and Meaning

According to Gardner, art—and especially poetry—is the only thing that gives meaning to an otherwise meaningless universe. Language is the only way that humans can break through the wall that isolates them from other humans and from the world of meaning. The wall is a recurring image in *Grendel* (see, for example, Chapters 2, 3, 8, and 12). The importance of language in *Grendel* in breaking through this wall is signaled not only by the significance of the Shaper's character but by the degree to which language plays a part in several other major characters. Most significant of these is Grendel himself, who begins the story as an inarticulate character like his mother but who rises at different points in the story to new levels of poetic intensity, however misunderstood by humans. (See, for example, Chapters 7, 8, 9, and 12.) Perhaps the most pathetic character in the story is Grendel's mother, who speaks no language at all, and who cannot even be understood by her own son. Though she does venture out of her cave at least once, to rescue her son, for the most part she is confined to a dark cave that symbolizes her total linguistic isolation.

Morals and Morality

The struggle in *Grendel* can be characterized as one between the forces of good and evil, morality and immorality. This struggle can be seen both within a single person, such as Grendel, and between individuals. Grendel, no matter how he may despise himself or seek to change, can be seen as representing the forces of evil. This would make Wealtheow and Beowulf, as well as Hrothgar and

Topics For Further Study

- Comment on Grendel's progress as a poet, under the influence of the Shaper, by evaluating the style and poetic effects of the doggerel he produces in Chapter 7; the verse play in Chapter 8; the free verse at the end of Chapter 9; and finally the poem in Chapter 12.

- Research the antiwar movement during the U.S. war in Vietnam, during which time *Grendel* was written. Relate the struggle between good and evil as depicted in *Grendel* to the struggle between different sectors of American society.

- Compare the philosophy of William Blake, as expressed in his poem *The Mental Traveller* and in the character of Ork, with the anarchistic philosophy of Georges Sorel, as expressed in his book *Reflections on Violence* and in the character of Red Horse, whom Gardner based on Sorel.

- Gardner added references to the twelve astrological signs to *Grendel,* focusing on one sign in each of the twelve chapters. Analyze how Gardner uses the meaning and symbolism of each astrological sign to lend unity to his overall story.

- In *Grendel,* Gardner has taken his point of departure from the classic Old English poem *Beowulf.* Compare and contrast the two stories. How are they the same? In what ways are they different?

- In *Grendel* we can see the contrast of two philosophies of government. Compare the feudal system represented by Unferth and Wealtheow in the kingdom of Hrothgar to the anarchism propounded by Red Horse, counselor to the young Hrothulf.

Unferth (despite their sometimes cynical or comical appearances), represent the forces of morality. Critics Helen B. Ellis and Warren U. Ober suggest in *John Gardner: Critical Perspectives* that Gardner is like the poet William Blake by implying that "the case for a particular set of values can best be made by positing an 'ironic set' of contrary values." As even Grendel recognizes, "balance is everything" (Chapter 7). Thus Hrothgar, despite his cold-blooded attempts to hold onto his throne, represents the forces of society against the threat of anarchy. We see another form of goodness in Wealtheow's comforting of the aged king, to whom she has sacrificed all personal comfort for the sake of keeping peace between potentially warring kingdoms. And of course Beowulf's slaying of Grendel at the end represents the ultimate triumph of good over evil. For Grendel, for all his artistic attempts, at the end still remains a person who believes there is no purpose in existence: a nihilist who insists that the result of his fatal fight was just an "accident" (Chapter 12) in a world with no real meaning.

Style

Point of View

Grendel is told in the first person ("I") from the point of view of the title character. Grendel is a monster with poetic aspirations whose every attempt to communicate with ordinary humans is met with misunderstanding and hostility. By focusing on the monster, the author elicits some sympathy for an otherwise thoroughly repulsive character who eats humans for pleasure. Because the point of view is that of Grendel, instead of the omniscient narrator of the original poem, the reader must deduce the story's theme from the monster's limited perspective. Fortunately Grendel is not just an aspiring poet but a good writer. In this respect he resembles Gardner's philosophical nemesis, John-Paul Sartre, whose philosophy of existentialism Gardner despised. Gardner told interviewer Marshall L. Harvey in *Chicago Review* that he wished "to present the *Beowulf* monster as Jean-Paul Sartre." According to Sartre, human beings are basically isolated individuals in an accidental world where God does not exist. Man must therefore create his own values, even though these values have no meaning outside the individual consciousness. Thus, when Grendel is attacked by the bull while trapped in a tree, he realizes that "the world was nothing: a mechanical chaos of casual, brute enmity.... I understood that, finally and absolutely, I alone exist" (Chapter 2). From that moment until the end of the story, in which Grendel describes his fatal wound as an "accident" (Chapter 12), the monster articulates Sartre's bleak philosophy.

Structure

The story begins in the "twelfth year of my idiotic war" against Hrothgar (Chapter 1) and uses the technique of flashback to tell the story of the monster's life. Grendel's long reminiscence covers from "when I was young" (Chapter 2) to the moment when he lies dying from Beowulf's fatal attack (Chapter 12). Within that frame, Gardner has ambitiously structured his tale around the twelve years of Grendel's war (one for each of the twelve chapters). He has also given each chapter an event associated with one of the twelve signs of the zodiac and their associated ruling planets and houses. (In an *American Literature* article, Barry Fawcett and Elizabeth Jones explicate each of these items.) For example, Chapter 1 opens with Aries the ram, representing Spring. Aries is associated with the planet Mars, the god of war—hence the references to Grendel's war with Hrothgar. Aries also corresponds to the first house in astrology, that of life— hence the funeral scene in which Hrothgar celebrates the life of the victims of that war. Beowulf's inspiring speech in Chapter 12, with its images of spring ("strong searching roots will crack your cave and rain will cleanse it: The world will burn green ... ") recalls the Spring imagery of Chapter 1. In this way the author is suggesting a cyclical pattern, which reinforces Beowulf's words of rebirth. As Kathryn VanSpanckeren has analyzed at length (in *John Gardner: Critical Perspectives*), Gardner used such "embedded structures" as the narrative frame in all of his novels except *Nickel Mountain*.

Other critics, such as Craig J. Stromme in *Critique*, have noted that each chapter is designed to highlight a different school of philosophy. After Gardner's introduction to the astrological idea of endless cyclical repetition in Chapter 1, Grendel begins as a solipsist in Chapter 2—"I exist, nothing else." In Chapter 3, Grendel is exposed to the sophistry of the Shaper, who can by the power of his words make his hearers believe anything. In Chapter 4, the Shaper articulates the theology of the Old Testament, in which the children of light are contrasted to the descendants of Cain, the children of darkness. In Chapter 5, the dragon expresses English philosopher Alfred Whitehead's philosophy of the fundamental connection of all things, but Grendel can't understand it. In Chapter 6, Grendel emerges as a skeptic who, in Stromme's words, "accepts that beings other than himself exist, but ... has postulated them all as enemies." Similarly, Grendel is exposed to Christianity by Wealtheow in Chapter 7, Machiavellian statecraft by Hrothulf in Chapter 8, the hypocrisy of the young priests in Chapter 9, the pessimism of Nietzsche in Chapter 10, and the nihilism of Sartre in Chapter 11. Thus *Grendel* is structured as a survey of philosophical ideas.

Parody

In Gardner's hands *Grendel* is a parody that is used both to imitate and to ridicule or admire specific pieces and forms of literature and specific authors. Most obviously, *Grendel* is a respectful tribute to its source of inspiration, the Old English classic *Beowulf*. Gardner borrows most of the plot and characters directly from the original poem. Where the author has expanded the role of a character, as in the case of Grendel or the dragon, it is generally to ridicule or act as a foil for specific philosophers and their works. For example, Grendel represents a "case history of a bad artist" whose words are constantly misunderstood by others, according to David Cowart in *Arches and Light: The Fiction of John Gardner*. He inspires only acts of violence, whereas the Shaper's words inspire hearers to do great deeds. Thus we see Grendel, inspired by the Shaper, try his own hand at poetry, which at first results in ridiculous doggerel (Chapter 7). This awkward attempt gives way to somewhat better rhymed verse (opening of Chapter 8); still more creative and metrically freer verse (end of Chapter 8); and lastly, truly inspired, alliterative verse (Chapter 12), albeit composed as Beowulf smashes Grendel against a wall. Similarly, by ridiculing the Shaper's lack of a "total vision, total system" (Chapter 5), the dragon seems to be advocating Whitehead's philosophy of connectedness, though as Howell notes, the dragon's "sneering tone seems to undercut the validity of Whitehead's vision as well as the Shaper's." Gardner, however, is using both Grendel and the dragon in a parodic manner to bring out the prominent points of contrasting philosophies.

A young protestor confronts the National Guard during a 1968 demonstration in Chicago.

Historical Context

American Society in the Late 1960s

The heady days of the early 1960s, with their promise of peace abroad, political change in Washington, and economic boom throughout the country, had given way by the end of the decade to a series of gloomy developments. The prospect of an unwinnable war in Vietnam was compounded by numerous protests that often ended in violence. Disillusion with the American political system was symbolized by several assassinations: first, that of President John F. Kennedy in 1963, then the 1965 murder of Black Muslim leader Malcolm X, then those of Robert Kennedy and Martin Luther King, Jr. in 1968. Early advances in civil rights stood in contrast to riots by urban blacks, whose expectations had been raised but not met by President Johnson's promises of a "Great Society." Economic uncertainty was reflected in a stagnant and inflationary economy that was unable to support both the war in Vietnam and the needs of President Johnson's domestic agenda.

Protests and Politics

The 1960s saw numerous protests, particularly over issues concerning civil rights and U.S. in-

volvement in the Vietnam War. By 1968, dissatisfaction with the Johnson administration's responses to these concerns led to a record number of protests, particularly on college campuses. Although President Lyndon Johnson declined to run for reelection in 1968, the Democratic National Convention was seen by many groups as the ideal protest forum, one which could gain them a wider audience. Several antiwar protest groups, as well as the Southern Christian Leadership Conference (SCLC), the civil-rights group once led by Dr. Martin Luther King, Jr., showed up in Chicago to protest. This led to several conflicts with Chicago police, who had been instructed by law-and-order mayor Richard Daley to stop any such protests. One legal rally led to violence when a group of police attacked not only protesters but innocent bystanders and members of the media who were covering the event. The whole conflict was captured by television cameras and broadcast nationally. In the aftermath, several leaders of activist groups—the "Chicago Seven"—were charged by the U.S. Attorney General with conspiracy to riot, even though most of them had never met before the convention.

Richard Nixon was elected president in 1968, in part aided by his "law and order" platform and his promises to bring an "honorable end" to the Vietnam War. In 1970, however, Nixon announced

Compare & Contrast

- **Sixth-century A.D. Scandinavia:** Using Scandinavian chronicles and sagas, it is possible to date the historical events in the original *Beowulf,* the basis for *Grendel,* to this time and place. The basic political conflict in *Beowulf* is between the Danes (represented by Hrothgar's house) and the Geats (represented by Beowulf and his visiting party). Similarly, the rivalry between Hrothgar and Hrothulf over what would happen to the throne when Hrothgar died are also recounted in the Scandinavian analogues.

  1960s-1970s United States: Political turmoil in the United States reaches a peak with students protesting the Vietnam War at the Democratic National Convention in Chicago in 1968. The Chicago police, under Democratic Mayor Richard Daley, repress the demonstrations with great force, leading to disillusionment not only in the Democratic Party (whose candidate, Hubert Humphrey, eventually lost the presidential election to Richard Nixon) but also in the whole democratic process.

  Today: Widespread disillusionment with the political process continues, with record numbers of eligible voters not voting and widespread cynicism among both politicians and voters about the effectiveness of the democratic process. Today, cynicism feeds on the controversy surrounding the ways in which political campaigns and candidates are financed. Cynicism also flourishes because of the decrease in bipartisan spirit on many issues between the two major political parties. Nevertheless, there is agreement that the U.S. system of government still seems to work as well or better than any system others have been able to devise.

- **Sixth-century A.D. Scandinavia:** The political tribes of the area have little interaction with cultures outside of Europe; the fall of the Roman Empire in 476 A.D., while creating new political realities throughout Europe, is scarcely felt in Scandinavia (which had never been a part of the Roman Empire) either politically or economically.

  1960s-1970s United States: This period sees the beginning of an increasingly inflationary economy (where prices rise quickly). The high inflation of this stagnant economy, combined with the oil embargo by Arab nations, produces a serious economic recession in 1973 and 1974.

  Today: Fueled by low inflation and interest rates, the steady growth of the U.S. economy leads to a period of economic prosperity and optimism unequaled since the early 1960s. In 1997 the influence of a worldwide economy can be seen in a sudden drop in the U.S. stock market, caused by economic downturns in Asian countries.

- **Sixth-century A.D. Scandinavia:** Power rests on wealth from raids and trading, although trading eastward is cut off during this period by the Huns and Avars. Society consists of a landed aristocracy and farmer tenants and a local court system.

  1960s-1970s United States: Young people, particularly students, challenge the authority of those who govern at all levels. There is a general questioning of the right of a power elite, composed largely of white males, to make policy for an increasingly younger and more diverse citizenry. Civil rights groups continue to fight for the rights of minorities, while others focus on equal rights for women and homosexuals.

  Today: There is a greater representation of women and minorities in various areas of life, including government and the workforce. Nevertheless, some inequalities remain, particularly economic ones, and racial issues are prominent in politics. A country containing individuals of diverse social, sexual, and ethnic identities, the United States remains more a "salad bowl" of many separate ingredients rather than a "melting pot" containing one definition of "American."

that U.S. military forces had invaded Cambodia, another Southeast Asian country, in order to find and destroy enemy Vietcong bases. This triggered massive demonstrations on college campuses and often rioting. The Ohio National Guard was called to quell unrest on the campus of Kent State University, and on May 4, shots were fired into a crowd, killing four students and injuring nine others, including some students who had not even participated in the protest. Investigations later showed that, contrary to official claims, none of the victims had been physically threatening the Guards, or even been closer than sixty feet. A similar situation occurred at Jackson State University in Mississippi eleven days later, leaving two women dead. The result of these two incidents was a student strike that shut down over two hundred colleges and universities nationwide, and a country embroiled in conflict over political protest.

Literature of the 1960s

As befitted an era of conflict and protest, much of the literature of the 1960s was concerned with political issues. Socially conscious artists saw their work as a means to communicate their ideas, criticisms, and protests. Black humor, such as that found in the antiwar novels *Slaughterhouse-Five* by Kurt Vonnegut or *Catch-22* by Joseph Heller, was often employed to satirize issues of the day. Writers also experimented with form, trying new and different techniques to push the boundaries of traditional fiction. These more literary works often ended up on best-seller lists, adopted by a reading public open to new literary possibilities and new ideas. By the end of the 1960s, however, many artists became frustrated with what they felt was a lack of effectiveness in using art to achieve social reform. They adopted a nihilistic viewpoint—that existence is pointless. Literary works reflected this view either by focusing only on a work's form, not its content, or by using absurdity to deal with the hopelessness of life.

Gardner's *Grendel,* written at the tail end of this era, attempted to refute this nihilistic viewpoint. While the twelve-chapter structure is an important part of the novel, this form serves to highlight and support the content, not replace it. Gardner also makes an argument for the importance of the artist in society. Through the character of the Shaper, the author points out the positive influence an artist may have on those around him. In this way, Gardner's work reflects the spirit of many other literary novels of the day, and achieved similar success.

Critical Overview

Gardner's first two published novels, *The Resurrection* (1966) and *The Wreckage of Agathon* (1970) generated little response, although Geoffrey Wolff did praise the latter in *Newsweek.* With *Grendel* (1971), however, as David Cowart noted in *Arches and Light,* "the critical tide of caution began to turn. Reviewers were charmed, and *Time* and *Newsweek* cited it among the year's best novels. After a first printing of 7500 copies, it went through nine hardback and thirteen paperback printings in this country and England by the end of 1977. It had also, by then, been translated into French, Spanish, and Swedish." No doubt some of this attention was due to readers' familiarity with Grendel's literary source, the classic epic poem *Beowulf,* known especially to high school and college English students and their professors. Academics in particular respected the author, who was already an established scholar in medieval studies, having edited four books and translated two other works in this field.

But critics generally also felt, as David Cowart wrote in the *Dictionary of Literary Biography,* that in *Grendel* Gardner "burnishes the classic at the same time that he creates a new masterpiece." Academic critics in particular responded to Gardner's scholarship in drawing not only on medieval sources but also poets from William Blake to Thomas Kinsella and philosophers from Plato to Whitehead and Sartre. Critics also relished unravelling the novel's structure, with its allusions to the signs of the zodiac and various school of philosophical thought. The character of Grendel received special attention, with a lively debate ensuing over whether that monster, who is certainly the central character in the story, is not also its real hero. Like the Shaper, Grendel is engaged in a struggle to create poetry. (As these critics noted, Beowulf, the ostensible hero of the novel, makes only a relatively brief appearance toward the end.) Some critics went as far as to consider Grendel an absurd hero whose violent nihilism is the only sane reaction to the chaos of modern society.

Gardner himself lent insight into this debate in his treatise *On Moral Fiction.* In this 1978 work (which according to *New York Times Magazine* contributor Stephen Singular was actually written in 1965), Gardner criticized contemporary novelists like Saul Bellow, John Barth, John Updike, and Thomas Pynchon for not practicing "moral art." By this term he meant art which "in its highest form holds up models of virtue, whether they be heroic models like Homer's Achilles or models of quiet endurance like the coal miners ... in the photographs of W. Eugene Smith." In a similar vein, a year earlier Gardner had told *Atlantic Monthly* interviewers Don Edwards and Carol Polsgrove that "if we celebrate bad values in our arts, we're going to have a bad society. If we celebrate values which make you healthier, which make life better, we're going to have a better world." These statements would seem to indicate the author's intent lay in rebuking Grendel's nihilist viewpoints. That the work has been interpreted in exactly the opposite fashion is, according to various critics, either a testament to Gardner's ability to invent a powerful and sympathetic protagonist or an indication of his problems in clearly presenting his ideas.

Despite the fervency and highmindedness of such views, *On Modern Fiction* elicited mostly negative reactions from both reviewers and fellow writers, as summarized by Cowart in *Arches and Light.* Not surprisingly, the novelists who were attacked in the essay fought back in print in widely read forums like the *New York Times.* And since Gardner had boldly and unapologetically set a high standard for artists, his own novels, especially his later ones, were soon being judged by this same standard and found wanting. Critic John Romano, for example, claimed in the *New York Times Book Review* that *Freddy's Book* (1980) wasn't moral since its exuberance threatened to "slip over into immorality at any turn" and that Gardner's moral aesthetic contradicted his medievalist love for "the fabulous, the enchanted."

Thus far, however, Gardner's *Grendel* has, for the most part, escaped such criticism. As Fawcett and Jones stated in *American Literature,* "Somewhere in our cavernous hearts the old heroic ideals continue to haunt and illumine us. Grendel's conflict, as he holds fast to skepticism yet sways toward vision, turning and twisting between mockery and anguish, poetry and black humor, continually ironizing his ironies, is our own as inhabitants of the twentieth century."

Criticism

Diane Andrews Henningfeld

Henningfeld is an English professor at Adrian College and has written for a wide variety of academic journals and educational publishers. In the following essay, she reads Grendel *from a feminist perspective, demonstrating the importance of language and gender to the text.*

Grendel, John Gardner's retelling of the first part of *Beowulf,* offers the reader a host of interpretive possibilities. As an Anglo-Saxonist scholar and as a post-modernist writer, Gardner's work is both allusive and complex. Nonetheless, Gardner, known for his experimental fiction as well as his poetry and philosophical writings, left behind a raft of interviews and articles regarding his fiction when he died unexpectedly in 1982 as the result of a motorcycle accident. Consequently, critics can find ample support for a variety of readings.

Critical approaches to *Grendel* are thus varied and wide-ranging. Some critics choose to concentrate on Gardner's sources for his novel. Gardner weaves in allusions to such writers as Chaucer, Browning, and even Kurt Vonnegut. The strongest connection between his novel and another work is William Blake's *The Marriage of Heaven and Hell.* A number of critics focus on Blake's phrase, "the contraries of existence" to demonstrate that Grendel's vision is not coincidental with Gardner's. Blake, writing at the close of the eighteenth century, stated "Without contraries is no progression. Attraction and Repulsion, Reason and Energy, Love and Hate, are necessary to Human Existence." In addition, these critics posit Grendel's ultimate failure on his rejection of life's contradictory meanings. For Grendel, life has meaning, or not. For Grendel, the absolutist, contradictory elements cannot exist simultaneously.

Other critics choose to examine Gardner's structuring of the novel. Most obviously, the novel is structured around the signs of the zodiac. Each of the twelve chapters contains a controlling image connecting the chapter to its sign. For example, when the book opens, Grendel is observing a ram, and "the first grim stirrings of springtime come." From this the reader can determine that it is April, the month of Aries the ram. (Additionally, such an opening ironically recalls Chaucer's first lines of the *Canterbury Tales.*) When the unnamed hero (whom the reader knows to be Beowulf) finally arrives by boat, it is in the eleventh chapter, the month of February, under the sign of Aquarius, the Water Bearer. Such symbolism offers the reader a rich range of possibilities.

Finally, still other critics concentrate on the philosophic ideas underpinning Gardner's work. Certainly, *Grendel* is nothing if not a novel of ideas. Gardner seems particularly concerned with exam-

What Do I Read Next?

- *Beowulf* is the oldest epic narrative in any modern European language. As the major inspiration for Gardner's *Grendel*, it will be of great interest to any reader who enjoyed Gardner's version. One of several good translations is that by Charles W. Kennedy (Oxford University Press, 1940). It also contains a helpful introduction with sections on historical background, the history of the manuscript itself, and the influence of the classical epic and various folk sources.

- Gardner's best-known nonfiction work, *On Moral Fiction* (1978), is concerned with the purpose and craft of fiction and is basically a statement of Gardner's philosophy. Passionate, blunt in tone, and sometimes contradictory, it found favor with those who agreed with the author about the essential humanity of great literature. Nevertheless, Gardner riled some critics who felt that his judgments on some of his fellow contemporary novelists were too harsh.

- Gardner's *The Sunlight Dialogues* (1972) explores on a massive scale the theme of order versus chaos, with eighty characters and an intricate plot set in Gardner's hometown of Batavia, New York. In this novel, described by David Cowart in the *Dictionary of Literary Biography* as "possibly his finest," Gardner sets in opposition the Sunlight Man, a mercurial and mysterious criminal who represents absolute freedom, and Fred Clumly, a local police officer who espouses law and order.

- *The Legacy of Heorot* (1987) is a science-fiction version of the first part of *Beowulf* that is set on Earth's first stellar colony. The spot seems like paradise, until dogs and cattle begin to disappear, devoured by a monster. Authors Larry Niven, Jerry Pournelle, and Steven Barnes have combined forces to create a frighteningly realistic horror story à la Stephen King.

---

ining existentialism, a twentieth-century philosophy which suggests that there is nothing more to human life than existence itself. No larger meanings or order control human destiny, and it is human duty to choose how life will be lived. For the existentialist, even not choosing represents a choice. That Gardner explicitly connects Grendel with existentialist thought and specifically with John Paul Sartre, the French existentialist, is clear from a 1978 interview with Marshall Harvey:

> I use Sartre a lot. What happened in *Grendel* was that I got the idea of presenting the *Beowulf* monster as John Paul Sartre, and everything that Grendel says Sartre in one mood or another has said, so that my love of Sartre kind of comes through as my love of the monster, though monsters are still monsters—I hope.

There is, however, yet another way to read *Grendel.* In recent years, feminist critics have begun to reread the canon of Anglo-Saxon poetry, including *Beowulf.* In spite of the dearth of female characters, there is much to be learned by reexam-

ining the Anglo-Saxon epic through this lens. Likewise, *Grendel* can be read from a feminist perspective, concentrating on Grendel's mother, Wealtheow, and the role language plays in ordering a culture.

French feminists in particular have used the theories of psychoanalytic philosopher Jacques Lacan to explain the ways language creates and maintains the patriarchal power structures of a society. What we call "language" is public discourse, a male construction that maintains the hierarchies of a culture. That is, the very language a culture uses serves invisibly to preserve and protect the power systems of the culture. For example, in English, the masculine pronoun has always been considered the correct form in sentences such as this: "Does everyone have his book?" Further, the word "man" stands in for the human race as the normative term. Likewise, while we may speak of "women writers," we rarely speak of "male writers."

Further, Lacan maintains that children "fall" into language at about the same time that they rec-

---

ognize themselves as separate beings from their mothers. Certainly, the second chapter of *Grendel* illustrates graphically both Grendel's separation anxiety and his growing awareness of the function of language. When he speaks of his understanding of himself and his mother early in the chapter, he reports, "We were one thing, like the wall and the rock growing out from it." Later, however, Grendel finds himself trapped in a tree, unable to remove himself. Immediately he screams for his mother, who does not appear. It is in this moment that he states, "I understood that, finally and absolutely, I alone exist." A bit later he describes himself as "an alien, the rock broken free from the wall." These are clear signs of his separation from his mother. Significantly, it is at this moment of separation that Grendel hears men speaking for the first time. "The sounds were foreign at first, but when I calmed myself, concentrating, I found I understood them: it was my own language, but spoken in a strange way."

Lacan further suggests that the male child will begin to identify himself with his father as spokesman of cultural values at about the same time that the child learns language and separates from the mother. For Grendel, however, there is no father. Into this absence, then, steps Hrothgar. Grendel attempts to identify with the king and with his men. On the night that he first hears the Shaper, Grendel tries to join Hrothgar's band with disastrous consequences: "Drunken men rushed me with battle axes. I sank to my knees, crying, 'Friend! Friend!' They hacked at me, yipping like dogs." Although Grendel understands his language to be the same as the men's, they do not understand his speech. Thus, he is an outsider to their community and a threat. For Grendel, the identification with a father, and thus with a culture, remains incomplete.

Further, it is also possible to explain Grendel's fascination with Wealtheow by considering his separation from his mother. French feminists argue that male language is the language of desire. Further, they suggest that male language idealizes and fantasizes about the feminine. This idealization and fantasy is caused by the absence of the mother. The separation from the mother causes an emotional lack in the male child. That Grendel feels an emotional lack is clear as he contemplates his mother, and the separation between them; he says explicitly, "I am a lack." Further, Grendel idealizes and fantasizes about the Queen, Wealtheow. In his eyes, she is all beauty, and offers some hope for meaning in the world. His understanding of Wealtheow, however, is conditioned by the Shaper's songs,

more male language. It is not the woman Wealtheow that Grendel wants, but rather the ideal created by the language of the Shaper. Grendel observes that the ultimate act of nihilism would be to kill the Queen. Yet he is unable to contemplate this until he raids the hall and pulls her legs apart. He decides to kill her because of "the ugly hole between her legs." His confrontation with her body destroys his notion of the ideal, but not entirely. Ultimately, he chooses not to kill her, in spite of her body and the sexuality that both fascinates him and repels him. And yet he still finds one of his two minds insisting, "she was beautiful."

In *Grendel,* language is repeatedly shown to be the province of men. All speakers are masculine. The Dragon, the Shaper, Hrothgar, Unferth, and finally Beowulf each offer Grendel a system for understanding the universe and his place in it. The dragon is a nihilist. That is, he believes there is no meaning to life and that all events are nothing more than random accident. The Shaper is a poet. He creates meaning in the world through his songs; the world becomes what he sings. His is the voice of art. Hrothgar is a politician. His world is constructed by the words of treaties and oaths of fealty. His words reveal to Grendel a world of plots and counterplots, devoid of morality. Unferth is a hero. He argues that only in heroism does the world have meaning. The words that constitute a hero's reputation and fame construct his vision of the world. Finally, at the very end of the tale, Beowulf explains to Grendel the cycles of existence: life has meaning because it continues, in spite of death and destruction. (Tellingly, Beowulf speaks of sperm, not ova.) What these voices all have in common is their masculinity. In each case, their words construct and maintain the power system. What none of these voices includes is room for feminine language or for feminine understanding of the world.

Grendel chooses to look for answers in these systems, ultimately rejecting all but the dragon's view. He clearly sees himself as a superior creature to his mother, primarily because he is a maker of words, someone who possesses language. He walks on two legs; she walks on all four. Yet care should be taken to distinguish Grendel's position on this from Gardner's. Gardner seems to suggests that the language of Grendel's is somehow primeval and pre-existent, outside the system of male language. Grendel states, "She'd forgotten all language long ago, or maybe had never known any. (How I myself learned to speak I can't remember; it was a long, long time ago.)" Grendel, trying to find meaning through masculine language, fails to recognize that his mother finds meaning in her own creation, even as he states, "I was, in her eyes, some meaning I could never know and might not care to know." Further, Grendel's mother's language is bound up in her body. Her response to Grendel's despair is to clasp him to her breast, offering nurture and sustenance.

Wealtheow, for her part, has little to say in either *Beowulf* or *Grendel*. She finds meaning not through the masculine language of politics, treaties and war, but rather through her feminine role as peace-weaver and mother. She creates a truce between her people and her husband's people. Further, as the mother of Hrothgar's children, she engenders new life, opening the possibility of meaning in the world. Because Grendel is repelled by the "ugly hole between her legs," he overlooks the pun that the phrase implies: the "whole" is indeed between her legs. Through her body, Wealtheow weaves together the whole world, at least while she lives. It can thus be argued that the feminine creates and sustains life while the masculine creates words.

It can be argued that Grendel's ultimate failure to find his place in the world springs first, from his separation and longing for his mother; and second, from his incomplete identification with a father figure. He never fully learns to use the language of men in such a way that he can be understood. Instead, he remains suspended between the dark, pre-verbal cave of his mother and the world-as-text of the masculine characters, ultimately falling from the cliff, a fall that mirrors his earlier "fall" into language.

Source: Diane Andrews Henningfeld, in an essay for *Novels for Students*, Gale, 1998.

Robert Merrill

In the following excerpt, Merrill argues that many of the critics who see Grendel *as an absurdist novel with the monster as hero are supporting an interpretation that is contrary to the author's intentions. Instead, the critic suggests, Gardner meant to present the character of Grendel as a negative example: the creature's "nihilistic rationalism is what Gardner wants to caution us* against."

Nothing has become more unfashionable in the last ten years than *explication du texte*. No doubt in reaction against the New Critics, we have tended to stress "broader" considerations, whether historical, psychological, or philosophical. Sometimes, however, questions of textual interpretation must

be faced if we are to avoid the most basic misunderstandings about the works we read and teach. A case in point is John Gardner's *Grendel* (1971). Gardner is one of our more respected contemporary writers, and *Grendel* is his most popular work, yet I think this book is usually read in such a way as literally to reverse Gardner's intended meaning. Insofar as *Grendel* deserves its emerging status, the interpretive problem is unfavorable....

> "If the traditional hero is insane, then, who becomes the modern hero? As John Gardner realizes, it *must* be Grendel—the monster who rejects all traditional values of his world needs only a few slight alterations to become a perfect absurd hero. Gardner's novel fits neatly into the category of contemporary absurdist literature."
>
> Jay Ruud ["Gardner's *Grendel* and *Beowulf*: Humanizing the Monster," *Thoth,* Spring-Fall, 1974]
>
> "What *Grendel* does is take, one by one, the great heroic ideals of mankind since the beginning and make a case for these values by setting up alternatives in an ironic set of monster values. I hate existentialism."
>
> John Gardner ["Backstage with *Esquire*," *Esquire,* Oct., 1971]

As these two quotations suggest, there is disagreement as to Gardner's meaning in *Grendel*. Indeed, the quarrel between Gardner and his critics is nearly absolute. Robert Detweiler has written [in *Contemporary Literature,* Winter, 1976] that "*Grendel* is a retelling of the Beowulf legend from the monster's point of view that depicts him as a relatively sympathetic character and Beowulf as a psychopath." W. P. Fitzpatrick [in *Notes on Contemporary Literature,* January, 1977] has seen Grendel as an "absurdist hero," comparable to Camus' Caligula, with the following results: "Not only does *Grendel* challenge our perspective of medieval heroism, but it destroys whatever wisp of the 19th century visionary gleams might remain." And [in *Critique,* Vol. 23, 1981] Michael Ackland has summarized the experience of most readers: "... by the end of the narrative, the reader shares the deterministic insight that marked Grendel's opening reference to life as being 'Locked in the deadly progression of moon and stars'." These and other critics have agreed with Bruce Allen's assertion [in *Sewanee Review,* Summer, 1977] that "the meaning is existential," whereas Gardner has said that he hates existentialism. How are we to account for such a drastic difference of opinion?

At this point it is customary to do one of two things. Either one quotes Lawrence's famous dictum that we should trust the tale and not the teller, or one dismisses the many quoted critics as wrongheaded or somehow lacking that crucial insight which will clarify everything. I would prefer to do neither. I happen to think that Gardner's version of *Grendel* is more reliable than that of his critics.…

The standard reading of *Grendel* assumes that Gardner chose to retell the story of *Beowulf* because he wanted to champion Grendel's "modern" point of view. In the first chapter, as if to emphasize the point, Gardner has Grendel repeatedly express his haunting sense of life's meaninglessness. Grendel believes that life is a mechanistic process in which "The sun spins mindlessly overhead, the shadows lengthen and shorten as if by plan," although there is no plan, no order, no organizer: "The sky says nothing, predictably.… The sky ignores me, forever unimpressed." It is one of Grendel's central arguments that mankind imposes its hopes and fears on mindless reality, thus establishing an artificial order by means of what Grendel calls "some lunatic theory." Grendel himself is a theorizer, but the difference between him and others is that he *knows* there is no connection between theory and reality—the heroic ideals that we associate with *Beowulf* are no more than whistlings in the dark designed to conceal the fact that "The world is all pointless accident."

In this reading Gardner establishes Grendel as a dark but poetic witness in order to comment on man's pretensions to civilization. Grendel has observed Hrothgar's rise to power, for instance, so he offers a sardonic account of how roving bands evolved into savage tribes. Here Grendel's point of view is in dramatic contrast to that of Hrothgar's *scop*, the Shaper. Where Grendel sees "crafty-witted killers that worked in teams," the Shaper commemorates "the glorious deeds of dead kings … his harp mimicking the rush of swords, clanging boldly with the noble speeches, sighing behind the heroes' dying words." Grendel is contemptuous of the Shaper's influence on Hrothgar's men ("Did they murder each other more gently because in the woods sweet songbirds sang?"), yet he concedes that even he is "swept up" by the Shaper's music. Grendel's observations on the Shaper are thus thought to point up the dangerous allure of art (the Danes are said to have "gone mad on art"), or, in broader terms, to expose the irrepressible human tendency to substitute consolatory myths for unpleasant realities.

As Grendel reports other attempts to explain or justify the Scyldings' travails, we come to see that what the Shaper does so artfully is indeed a universal practice. The episodes involving Unferth, Wealtheow, Hrothulf, and Ork illustrate this widespread desire to rationalize life's apparent evils by means of saving fictions: that the life of the hero "makes the whole struggle of humanity worthwhile" (Unferth); that "Meaning as quality" is a viable philosophy despite life's quantifiable futility (Wealtheow); that revolution is a religious activity, amply justified as a visionary alternative to corrupt social norms (Hrothulf); that religion is a "sweet fantasy" which offers relief from the crippling structures of "merely rational thought" (Ork). Grendel's role is to qualify or undermine these efforts to establish objective values in a meaningless world. Therefore Grendel humiliates Unferth, nearly kills Wealtheow, remarks Hrothulf's swinish conspiracy with an anarchist, and dismisses Ork and the other priests as lacking any real conviction. In this way Gardner "inverts the perspective of the heroic *Beowulf*" [according to Fitzpatrick]—an inversion climaxed by his ironic treatment of Beowulf's victory over Grendel. For most readers, Gardner's Beowulf is a moral cipher: a "cold-blooded fanatic," "strangely mechanical, even mad," a "hired mercenary" who is in reality "a *moral* monster." Beowulf triumphs over Grendel only because the monster slips—a mere accident, as Grendel argues. The point is that the legendary Beowulf is for us an unbelievable, certainly an unsympathetic character. The true hero, as we suspected all along, is Grendel himself.

Two crucial assumptions inform this reading of *Grendel*. The second, that Grendel is a sympathetic and reliable narrator, follows naturally from the first: that Gardner is a "modern" who shares the vision of such writers as Beckett and Sartre. In fact, however, Gardner has said that Beckett is "wrong" and that Sartre is "a handy symbol of what has gone wrong in modern thinking." The most relevant of Gardner's pronouncements appear in his recent book on contemporary writing, *On Moral Fiction* (1978). Throughout this treatise Gardner keeps up a running attack on the very writers with whom he has been associated in most readings of *Grendel*. He berates "the cult of cynicism and despair," arguing that an "art which tends toward destruction, the art of nihilists, cynics, and merdistes, is not properly art at all." Nor does he refer to minor, unrepresentative figures—Mailer, Vonnegut, Heller, and Pynchon are among the many recent writers who are condemned. Such judgments follow from Gardner's belief that "Great art celebrates life's potential, offering a vision unmistakably and unsentimentally rooted in love." As this would suggest, Gardner's literary credo is unabashedly traditional; for him art is good "when it has a clear positive moral effect, presenting valid models for imitation, eternal verities worth keeping in mind, and a benevolent vision of the possible which can inspire and incite human beings toward virtue." For this reason, among others, Gardner insists that "again and again the ancient poets seem right, and 'modern sensibility' seems a fool's illusion."

Everything Gardner has written makes it clear that the "nihilistic" reading of *Grendel* is improbable, but we do not have to rely on general remarks to determine Gardner's intentions. In a review [in *American Scholar,* Winter, 1974–75] of Gardner's critical study of the Wakefield Cycle, Martin Stevens objected to "Gardner's apparent low esteem for the medieval consciousness," a view he also found in *Grendel,* "justly praised ... as a 'revisionist' fiction for its bold, inventive, and keenly humorous perspective of the Anglo-Saxon heroic ideals." Gardner was sufficiently unhappy to respond in the next issue [Spring, 1975] of *American Scholar:* "Those who have read *Grendel* will recognize, I hope, that [Stevens] is quite wrong about the book. My monstrous central character, Grendel, will believe in nothing he cannot logically justify. Scorning the Anglo-Saxon *scop* who reshapes reality into noble ideals, scorning the great Anglo-Saxon values, he grows more and more vicious, more and more helpless, more and more existential until he commits a kind of suicide ... I have been as faithful as possible to the Christian spirit of the epic." We should now see what kind of sense the book makes if it is read as Gardner intended.

At the time of the first chapter Grendel has been at war with Hrothgar for twelve years, so the ensuing narrative is an extended flashback designed to explain how Grendel came to believe that the world is all pointless accident. The crucial episode is Grendel's visit to the dragon in chapter five. Gardner's dragon is a remarkable character, given to quoting Sartre, Heidegger, and Whitehead (without acknowledgment), and certain of one basic truth: that ultimately nothing matters. The dragon "knows" this because he is able to see all time at once, rather like Vonnegut's Tralfamadorians. And what he sees is no cause for celebration. His credo is "Ashes to ashes and slime to slime, amen"; life,

he argues, is "a brief pulsation in the black hole of eternity." So much for human aspirations! The youthful Grendel is drawn to the Shaper's ideals, so he protests: "Why shouldn't one change one's ways, improve one's character?" But the dragon will not take the question seriously: "'Why? Why?' Ridiculous question! Why anything?" The dragon's influence on Grendel is decisive, for after visiting his cave Grendel finds that "Futility, doom, became a smell in the air, pervasive and acrid as the dead smell after a forest fire." Grendel's war with Hrothgar follows, inspired by the monster's now firm conviction that human values are insubstantial myths designed to get us through the night. The Grendel we meet in chapter one is the product of this encounter, where "the old dragon, calm as winter, unveiled the truth."

For Gardner, however, the dragon's "truth" is despicable. "The Dragon looks like an oracle," Gardner has said, "but he doesn't lay down truth.... He tells the truth as it appears to a dragon—that nothing in the world is connected with anything. It's all meaningless and stupid, and since nothing is connected with anything the highest value in life is to seek out gold and sit on it.... My view is that this is a dragonish way to behave, and it ain't the truth. The Shaper tells the truth, although he lies." Grendel makes the wrong choice, then, when confronted with "the alternative visions of blind old poets and dragons." The dragon despises mankind for living according to consoling myths, but Gardner believes that "Real art creates myths a society can live instead of die by, and clearly our society is in need of such myths." Indeed, Gardner has insisted that we should deny "the myth of blind mechanics" in favor of "the myth of connectedness." If the choice is ours why choose chilly visions of an abandoned world and skies which are forever unimpressed? Why not choose such "myths" as love and courage?

Having made his fatal choice, Grendel proceeds to mock Unferth's belief in heroism, Wealtheow's personal integrity, and Ork's religious theory that good comes from evil. These actions do not so much expose man's predilection for comforting illusions as they reveal the disastrous consequences of accepting the dragon's point of view. When he dies, for example, the Shaper is mourned by a female admirer who presents what is obviously a superb image of human dignity. Grendel's response is to regret never having physically abused the poet: "I should have cracked his skull midsong and sent his blood spraying out wet through the meadhall like a shocking change of key." Grendel should have done this to "prove" that the dragon was right—everything is arbitrary, all values are fictional, nothing matters. In fact, of course, he would only have proven how pernicious the dragon's influence had been. From his encounter with the dragon to his death at the hands of Beowulf, Grendel acts very much like one of those contemporary writers Gardner has condemned for celebrating ugliness and futility.

Gardner has characterized the Grendel of *Beowulf* as a "cosmic outlaw," "a creature of *sinnihte,* perpetual night." Of the poem itself he has said, "It is just as clearly, on one level, a celebration of the best possible human being living by the best possible human—perhaps divinely inspired—code." If we recall that Gardner wanted to be as faithful as possible to the Christian spirit of the epic, we can only conclude that Beowulf is the novel's true hero. Once again Gardner has been admirably clear about his aims [in *Papers on Language and Literature,* Summer, 1970]: "So I write a book in which there is a dragon who says everything a nihilist would say, everything the Marquis de Sade would say; and then at the end of the book there is a dragon who says all the opposite things. He says everything that William Blake would say. Blake says a wonderful thing: 'I look upon the dark satanic mills; I shake my head; they vanish.' That's it. That's right. You *redeem* the world by acts of imagination every time you pick up a baby." The dragon who says all the opposite things is of course Beowulf, whose superiority is not an accident or a matter of physical strength, as Grendel supposes, but rather his commitment to that healthy life of faith which Gardner has so explicitly praised.

The connection between Beowulf and the dragon is made by Beowulf himself as he takes physical control of Grendel. His first words are an exact repetition of the dragon's despairing description of life as a random movement of atoms: "*A meaningless swirl in the stream of time, a temporary gathering of bits, a few random specks ... Additional refinements: sensitive dust, copulating dust....*" This startling parallel suggests that Beowulf's long speech to Grendel is a conscious refutation of the dragon's beliefs:

> As you see it (the world) is, while the seeing lasts, dark nightmare-history, time-as-coffin; but where the water was rigid there will be fish, and men will survive on their flesh until spring. It's coming, my brother. Believe it or not. Though you murder the world, turn plains to stone, transmogrify life into I

and it, strong searching roots will crack your cave and rain will cleanse it: The world will burn green, sperm build again. My promise. Time is the mind, the hand that makes (fingers on harpstrings, hero-swords, the acts, the eyes of queens). By that I kill you.

In this eloquent speech Beowulf accuses Grendel of "murdering" the world by denying his own deep but non-rational connections with it. Beowulf's "promise" is that spring will indeed come again, so long as the human mind (imagination) keeps faith with itself, as it has in the exemplary acts of the Shaper ("fingers on harpstrings"), Unferth ("hero-swords"), and Wealtheow ("the acts, the eyes of queens"). Grendel's denial of life's "strong searching roots" has produced that very rigidity he mistakenly perceived as inevitable.

Beowulf's message is indeed Blakean, which should surprise no one familiar with Gardner's other writings. Gardner's Blake is a poet who stands for the redemptive power of the imagination—Gardner's own theme, as he once told John Howell. Blake's message, as Gardner and many others have understood it, demands that we reject the dictates of pure reason (Urizen) and heed instead the creative impulses of the imagination (Los or Orc). Grendel, however, "will believe in nothing he cannot logically justify." This is to say that Grendel accepts the Urizen-like authority of the dragon. It should now be apparent that this nihilistic rationalism is what Gardner wants to caution us *against* by means of Grendel's negative example. Indeed, Gardner's point is that the logical and despairing Grendel is all too representative. Though we may protest (like Grendel himself), we moderns have become monstrous precisely to the extent that our assumptions parallel those of the *Beowulf*-poet's—and John Gardner's—Grendel.

Source: Robert Merrill, "John Gardner's Grendel and the Interpretation of Modern Fables," in *American Literature,* Vol. 56, No. 2, May, 1984, pp. 162–80.

Craig J. Stromme

In the following excerpt, Stromme examines how Gardner uses each chapter of Grendel *to illustrate a different philosophical principle. The critic suggests that the circular nature of the novel's astrological motif is mirrored in Grendel's philosophical experience, as he travels from believing that only he exists to accepting that all external things he experiences also exist.*

In an interview [in *The New Fiction* by Joe David Bellamy, 1974] John Gardner says of *Grendel* that he "wanted to go through the main ideas of Western Civilization ... and go through them in the voice of the monster, with the story already taken care of, with the various philosophical attitudes (though with Sartre in particular), and see what I could do." Gardner goes even further to explain the organization of the novel: "It's got twelve chapters. They're all hooked up to astrological signs, for instance, and that gives you nice easy clues." These statements seem to be an instant explication of the novel, but they really only add up to a clue. The problem with the "nice easy clues" is that no two astrologers agree on anything. For example, one tells us that Arians are "outgoing," another that they "like to live in the mind," and a third that they are "originators" and "sympathetic." It is difficult to see how one could blend these traits into a coherent whole, but even more difficult to see how the whole would point inexorably to some main idea of Western Civilization.

In examining each of the twelve chapters, we shall attempt to discern the philosophical center of each. By studying the philosophical discussions that occur between characters and in the musings of Grendel, we should be able to arrive at conclusions at least as reliable as those suggested by astrological charts. The first thing we need to do is to forget everything about *Beowulf* except its basic plot. True, *Grendel* is based on *Beowulf* and the dramatic action is very similar, but the motivation for actions in *Grendel* is completely different. In *Beowulf* the focus is always on heroic action and beastly malfeasance; in *Grendel* the focus is on philosophical ways of living in the world. Grendel dies in each work, but the meaning of his death is radically different....

In *Grendel* philosophical ideas are always linked to ways of living in the world: a character does not simply describe an idea, he lives it.

Grendel is the arbiter of twenty-five centuries of philosophy because he is not human. Grendel has no vested interest in any one philosophy; he is searching for the best way to live in the world. The ideas that Grendel judges are not presented in a uniform format. Some of the ideas Grendel himself lives for a time; some of the ideas other characters live; and some of the ideas are so subtle that they need to be explained to us. If Grendel completely changed philosophies every chapter, the novel would be as much a story of character as philosophy, but if he never changed character at all, the novel would not show philosophy as having any real effects on action. The mixture of Grendel's action and observation, his mastery over others and others' mastery over him, then, allows us to see a history of philosophy in action.

Aries begins the astrological block and also begins the first chapter of *Grendel*: "The old ram stands looking down over rockslides." The symbolic importance of Aries is that it marks the beginning of a new cycle just like the cycle that has ended. Grendel tells us he is in "the twelfth year of my idiotic war," and this year appears that it will be substantially the same as the last. The ram acts the same way he did "last year at this time, and the year before, and the year before that." Grendel realizes that he is caught in the same endless pattern: "So it goes with me day by day and age by age.... Locked in the deadly progression of moon and stars." He will go down the hill and attack Hrothgar's village again, and after he has broken down their door they will build a new one to replace it "for (it must be) the fiftieth or sixtieth time." All has happened before; all will happen again. Grendel and his world are trapped in the "progression of moon and stars," the cycle of astrology. Grendel presents us in this chapter with the theory of the world as repetition and endless cycles, a philosophy, one of the oldest in the West, first presented by the Orphic sages.

Chapter Two, a flashback to Grendel's youth, begins Grendel's journey into the world of men. He leaves the cave of ignorance and enters the world of sunlight for the first time (an obvious reference to Plato's parable of the cave). Because the sunlight blinds him, Grendel always returns to the cave at daybreak. One night, he catches his foot in the crotch of a tree and is unable to free himself. When he accepts that his mother will not come from the cave to rescue him and that he is alone against the world (represented by a bull—this is the chapter of Taurus—charging him), Grendel concludes "that the world was nothing: a mechanical chaos of casual, brute enmity on which we stupidly impose our hopes and fears. I understood that I alone exist.... I create the universe blink by blink." When men arrive at the tree and begin to torture him, in order to determine what manner of beast he is, his shrieks of pain bring his mother to save him from the men. Safe in the cave, he repeats, "The world is all pointless accident.... I exist, nothing else." From these statements, Grendel clearly begins his life in the world as a solipsist. His claim of unique existence is the fundamental basis for that philosophy....

Grendel's solipsism is challenged when the Shaper, a poet-minstrel, arrives in Hrothgar's village. Shaper brings history to the village and forces Grendel to acknowledge exterior reality. Shaper creates a better world with his songs, an order untainted by the unpleasantness of certain facts of existence. He creates an order out of the pointless accident, and Grendel confesses that "even to me, incredibly, he had made it all seem true and very fine." Shaper's visions transform the grubby little village into a growing city-state, merely by changing the villagers' perceptions about themselves, their past, and Grendel. Shaper "had torn up the past by its thick, gnarled roots and transmuted it, and they, who knew the truth, remembered it his way—and so did I." Geminis, symbolized by the "wobbly twins" Grendel sees, are supposed to be versatile, superficial, and inventive—all part of their dual-nature. Shaper is all these things, as were the Sophists, who were so skilled at argument that they could argue any side of any question and win. They remade the world with their arguments just as Shaper does with his songs. All who hear Shaper's visionary history believe in it, even though they remember what actually happened. Grendel wants to believe in it but cries out, *"Lost!"* because he cannot let the dream replace the reality of his experience.

Chapter Four, Cancer the nourisher, shows us the growth of the religion that will nourish the new world Shaper has made Hrothgar's villagers see.

> [Shaper] told of how the earth was first built, long ago: said that the greatest of gods made the world, every wonder-bright plain and the turning seas, and set out as signs of his victory the sun and moon … and gave life to the every creature that moves on land.

> The harp turned solemn. He told of an ancient feud between two brothers which split all the world between darkness and light. And I, Grendel, was the dark side…. The terrible race God cursed.

God created all things in the world and all was good, but an evil force arose that divided the world into good and evil. The man who follows the good shall go to heaven and "find peace in his father's embrace," but the evil man shall burn forever—basic Old Testament theology. Grendel, the recognized evil of creation, is symbolized as brute nature—not really intelligent at all, merely a force that attempts to draw the villagers into evil. The vision is so compelling that Grendel desires it even if he "must be the outcast, cursed by the rules of this hideous fable." Grendel even rushes into the midst of the villagers and asks for their forgiveness for his role in the fable, but they simply hack at

him with swords. Grendel wants the vision to be true because it gives some order and purpose to the world, even if the order demands the vilification of his image.

In Chapter Five, the chapter of Leo the dramatizer, Grendel learns what his role will be in the new order Shaper has provided. Grendel goes to a dragon to ask about his part in this world and meets a metaphysician who explains everything's place in the world. Gardner says that the dragon is "nasty" and "says all the things that a nihilist would say." Much of the dragon's advice is nihilistic and much is materialistic, but the most important part comes from [Alfred North] Whitehead. The dragon begins his explanation of Grendel's place in the world by describing the fundamental connectedness of things and deploring the common-sense notions of reality. He then tells Grendel that:

> Importance is primarily monistic in its reference to the universe. Limited to a finite individual occasion, importance ceases to be important…. Expression, however, … is founded on the finite occasion.

The dragon is explaining the way in which eternal objects are expressed in actual entities, taking his explanation directly from Whitehead [in *Modes of Thought,* 1938]:

> Importance is primarily monistic in its reference to the universe. Importance, limited to a finite individual occasion, ceases to be important….

> But expression is founded on the finite occasion.

The dragon uses Whitehead's metaphysics to explain an ordering of the world even more comprehensible and sensible than the one Shaper provides. The problem is that Grendel can understand Shaper, but not the dragon. The dragon needs to stoop to particulars:

> You improve them, my boy! Can't you see that yourself? You stimulate them! You make them think and scheme. You drive them to poetry, science, religion, all that makes them what they are for as long as they last…. You *are* mankind, or man's condition.

The dragon prevents Grendel from accepting the simplified theological world-view offered by Shaper—"What god? Where? Life force, you mean? The principle of process?"—and helps Grendel recognize a more complex order in the world.

In Chapter Six Grendel finds his role in this order:

> I was transformed. I was a new focus for the clutter of space I stood in…. I had become, myself, the mama I'd searched the cliffs for once in vain…. I had *become* something, as if born again. I had hung be-

tween possibilities before, between the cold truths I knew and the heart-sucking conjuring tricks of the Shaper, now that was passed: I was Grendel, Ruiner of Meadhalls, Wrecker of Kings!

The most familiar formulation in existentialist thought is "existence precedes essence." This phrase means that people exist as things long before they create themselves as entities capable of acting coherently in the world. Before his realization, Grendel had possessed no real sense of himself: he accepted the images others had of him (his mother's image of him as "son," the villagers' image of him as "monster," and Shaper's image of him as "devil") for his self-image. Thus, Grendel is reborn but reborn into scepticism. He accepts that beings other than himself exist, but he has postulated them all as enemies. Grendel is a sceptic, one who doubts everything with moral fervor, and has decided that his new role is to be the destroyer of all the hypocritical orders men have created. Grendel feels that all orders blind men to the truth: "So much for heroism. So much for the harvest-virgin. So much, also, for the alternative visions of blind old poets and dragons."

Chapter Seven is the story of Wealthow, "holy servant of the common good." She is given to Hrothgar by her brother as a tribute to Hrothgar's power. She brings such a great sense of peace and has a faith so deep that she protects the village from Grendel's ravages. Libra is the sign of conciliators, and Wealthow brings harmony not only between the two peoples, but within the village as well. Chapters Six and Seven are the heart of the novel just as Virgo and Libra are the center of the astrological year. What we have is the scepticism of Grendel balanced by the faith of Wealthow. He is willing to sacrifice nothing; she "would give, had given her life for those she loved" and has "lain aside her happiness for theirs." He is a sceptic; she is the closest thing we see to a Christian in *Grendel*. Shaper brought the Old Testament to the village, but Wealthow brings the New Testament ideals with her. At the center of the novel, then, we have the two contrasting ways of viewing the world: Grendel's belief in chaos and futility balanced by Wealthow's belief in order and purpose.

The first seven chapters have transformed Grendel from a frightened solipsistic child into an angry sceptical monster. The village has evolved from a small collection of huts into a city-state. Everything necessary for Beowulf's arrival has been given to us, but Beowulf does not arrive for four more chapters. The plot has been developed;

the next four chapters develop philosophical ideas Gardner is interested in. Gardner says that "at about Chapter 8 there is a section in which you are no longer advancing in terms of the momentum toward the end.... it's just the wheels spinning. That is *not* novelistic form; it's lyrical form." Gardner stretches *Grendel* to elucidate certain ideas about philosophy and the growth of society, not to add convolutions to the traditional plot. These chapters should reveal just how different *Grendel* is from a more traditional novel, for its underlying purpose is to explore philosophies, not character.

The purpose is made clear in Chapter Eight when Machievelli's ideas enter the village. Hrothulf, the "sweet scorpion," learns statecraft from Red Horse:

> "Public force is the life and soul of every state.... The state is an organization of violence, a monopoly in what it is pleased to call *legitimate* violence.... All systems are evil. All governments are evil. Not just a trifle evil. *Monstrously* evil.... If you want me to help you destroy a government, I'm here to serve. But as for Universal Justice—" He laughed.

Hrothgar's village has arrived at the age of nation-states and all that matters during such an age is the maintenance of power, or, for the disenfranchised, the achievement of power. Hrothulf is an orphaned nephew adopted by Hrothgar and Wealthow, but sentiments and obligations play no part in Machievellian statecraft. With the replacement of Wealthow's love and charity by Hrothulf's scheming, we enter the modern age.

Chapter Nine shows us another indication that the village has entered the modern age. We saw the village's religion begin in Shaper's passioned delineation between the powers of good and evil, but we see now that the church has evolved into a pallid study of Whitehead's idea of process. Grendel hides among their idols one night and convinces an old priest to tell him the nature of the village's god. The priest tells Grendel,

> The King of Gods is not concrete, but He is the ground for concrete actuality. No reason can be given for the nature of God, because that nature is the reason for rationality.... The King of the Gods is the actual entity in virtue of which the entire multiplicity of eternal objects obtains its graded relevance to each stage of concrescence. Apart from Him, there can be no relevant novelty.

When the old priest tries to tell the other priests of his interview with "The Great Destroyer," as he had assumed Grendel to be, they laugh at him and his theories of god. The last great metaphysician speaks and no one will listen to him. Their religion has fallen from Shaper's dualism to Whitehead's process to hypocrisy—the young priests worry that "Lunatic priests are bad business.... One man like him can turn us all to paupers." Grendel is so disturbed by the sight of the younger priests ridiculing the old priest who still has faith that he leaves them all alone. He cannot understand that the young priests are able to preach what they do not believe.

In Chapter Ten we see Grendel once more puzzled by man's insensitivity. Just as Grendel was the only listener moved by the old priest's explanations, so he is the only one truly moved by the Shaper's death. Capricorns are supposed to be pessimistic—and in this chapter Grendel develops a Nietzschean philosophy. Because Shaper is dead, Grendel feels that "we're on our own again. Abandoned." They are alone because only Shaper's art made their world real. Shaper molded their reality and infused it with actuality. When Grendel says, *"Nihil ex nihilo,* I always say," he is recognizing the emptiness of their world without its creator. All of Grendel's despair and the conclusions he draws from his despair are parallel to Nietzsche's writings when he faced the death of god.

Grendel's journey thus far, then, has been from solipsist to sceptic to nihilist. He has listened to the great metaphysicians explain their systems, but he could never believe that an order corresponded to what they described. As Nietzsche is traditionally seen as a predecessor of Sartre, Chapter Eleven gives us the most succinct version of Sartre's thought in the novel. After Grendel sees Beowulf for the first time, he retires to his cave and meditates on his being:

> All order, I've come to understand, is theoretical, unreal—a harmless, sensible, smiling mask men slide between the two great, dark realities, the self and the world.... "Am I not free?" ... I have seen—I embody—the vision of the dragon: absolute, final waste. I saw long ago the whole universe as not-my-mother, and I glimpsed my place in it, a hole. *Yet I exist,* I knew. *Then I alone exist,* I said. *It's me or it.* What glee, that glorious recognition!... For even my mama loves me not for myself, my holy specialness ... but for my son-ness, my possessedness.

"All order ... is theoretical, unreal" is Grendel's explicit rejection of the dragon, the priests, and Shaper. Because "I alone exist," he feels that he must create his own order centered around himself and his perceptions of the world. He posits himself as the center of the world and arranges it accordingly: "For the world is divided, experience

teaches, into two parts: things to be murdered, and things that would hinder the murder of things." The ideas Grendel expresses of freedom, existence, and possessedness are all Sartre's ideas, all central to existentialism. In this chapter we can truly say that Grendel has become an existentialist. God (Shaper) is dead, and after his initial despair, Grendel has built a new world and new order without Him. Grendel's chosen essence, "absolute, final waste," does not seem very different from what it was before—the important thing is that now he moves beyond a received definition of himself and defines the world in his own terms.

Chapter Twelve, the chapter of Pisces, the end of the astrological cycle, shows us the battle between Grendel and Beowulf. Beowulf has come to Hrothgar's village to kill the monster and bring a new age to its people. Grendel wants to kill Beowulf in order to maintain the village as his fiefdom. Grendel creeps into the sleeping hall, hoping to kill Beowulf by surprise, but Beowulf, instead, tricks Grendel and seizes him. Beowulf twists Grendel's arm behind his back and forces him to listen:

> Though you murder the world, turn plains into stone, transmogrify life into I and it, strong searching roots crack your cave and rain will cleanse it: The world will burn green, sperm build again. My promise. Time is the mind, the hand that makes.... By that I kill you.... Grendel, Grendel! You make the world by whispers, second by second. Are you blind to that? Whether you make it a grave or a garden of roses is not the point. Feel the wall: is it not hard? *He smashes me against it, breaks open my forehead.* Hard, yes! Observe the hardness, write it down in careful runes. Now sing of walls! Sing!

Beowulf beats Grendel until he produces his first poem; satisfied with the poem, he lets Grendel wander off to bleed to death. As Grendel dies, he says, "Poor Grendel's had an accident.... *So may you all."*

About the last chapter Gardner says, "Grendel begins to apprehend the universe. Poetry is an accident, the novel says, but it's a great one." Grendel can no longer say "Only I exist" after he has sung of the beauty of walls. Beowulf forces Grendel to discard his existentialism and view the world without a screen. Beowulf beats Grendel against reality and turns him into an empiricist. Out of such contact comes poetry. Grendel can only understand that all knowledge, all truth, all art grows out of the contact with reality after he has been forced to give up his old philosophy. Grendel does not merely imagine the wall and posit that it is not-

Grendel; he has his head smashed against it until he rejects everything but experience.

Grendel's philosophical journey is almost circular, just as the cycle of astrology is circular. He begins with solipsism, "Only I exist," and ends with empiricism, for which only objects of experience are real. The major difference between the two is that empiricism accepts the existence of other objects while solipsism denies other objects concrete existence. These two schools are closely related historically and often difficult to tell apart in certain philosophers, Hume, for example. Once the empiricist questions the existence of external objects, he becomes a solipsist. The cycle of astrology, then, is important as a symbol for Grendel's philosophical development as well as for some clues in the chapters. Grendel's first teacher, the dragon, reveals the beauties of metaphysics and his final teacher, Beowulf, reveals the hard truths of empiricism. Grendel's awareness of the flaws of the former and the limits of the latter allow him to create poetry, a new way of ordering the world.

Grendel's journey is not the only important one in the novel. The village of Hrothgar's people is almost a main character itself, and its journey is also circular: from an unimportant village to the prosperous years of Shaper and Hrothgar, and finally into a decline with neither a great poet nor a great leader. Shaper "sang of a glorious mead-hall whose light would shine to the end of the ragged world." He sang of something that will happen in the future and then helped to bring it about. Grendel sings that "these towns shall be called the shining towns." Shaper's prophecy came true, but its time of truth is already over. The Shaper heralds the village's growth; Grendel's poem signals its decline. Moreover, Grendel's death destroys the last, great symbol of the village's struggle over adversity. Statecraft and religion had already been cheapened, and when Grendel dies even brute nature is gone. *Grendel* shows in all ways the passing of one age and the birth of the next, and so the novel becomes a complete history of man's progress.

Source: Craig J. Stromme, "The Twelve Chapters of Grendel," in *Critique: Studies in Modern Fiction,* Vol. XX, No. 1, 1978, pp. 83–92.

Sources

David Cowart, "John Champlin Gardner, Jr.," in *Dictionary of Literary Biography,* Vol. 2: *American Novelists since World War II,* edited by Jeffrey Helterman and Richard Layman, Gale, 1978, p. 177.

David Cowart, *Arches & Light: The Fiction of John Gardner,* Southern Illinois University Press, 1983.

Don Edwards and Carol Polsgrove, "A Conversation with John Gardner," in *Atlantic Monthly,* May, 1977, p. 43.

Helen B. Ellis and Warren U. Ober, "'Grendel' and Blake: The Contraries of Existence," in *John Gardner: Critical Perspectives,* edited by Robert A. Morace and Kathryn VanSpanckeren, Southern Illinois University Press, 1982, p. 47.

Barry Fawcett and Elizabeth Jones, "The Twelve Traps in John Gardner's *Grendel,*" in *American Literature,* Vol. 62, December, 1990, pp. 634-647.

John Gardner, *On Moral Fiction,* Basic Books, 1978, p. 82.

Marshall L. Harvey, "Where Philosophy and Fiction Meet: An Interview with John Gardner," in *Chicago Review,* Vol. 29, Spring, 1978, p. 75.

John M. Howell, *Understanding John Gardner,* University of South Carolina Press, 1993, pp. 61, 71-73.

John Romano, review of *Freddy's Book,* in *New York Times Book Review,,* March 23, 1980, p. 26.

Stephen Singular, "The Sound and Fury over Fiction," in *New York Times Magazine,* July 8, 1979, p. 36.

Craig J. Stromme, "The Twelve Chapters of *Grendel,*" in *Critique,* Vol. 20, No. 1, 1978, p. 87.

Kathryn VanSpanckeren, "Magical Prisons: Embedded Structures in the Work of John Gardner," in *John Gardner: Critical Perspectives,* edited by Robert A. Morace and Kathryn VanSpanckeren, Southern Illinois University Press, 1982, pp. 114-129.

For Further Study

Leonard Butts, "The Monster as Artist: *Grendel* and *Freddy's Book,*" in his *The Novels of John Gardner: Making Life Art as a Moral Process,* Louisiana State University Press, 1983, pp. 86-110.

Butts discusses Grendel as a failed artist who lives in his own first-person narrative, unable to make connections with humans or redeem himself through imagination and art.

Norma L. Hutman, "Even Monsters Have Mothers: A Study of 'Beowulf' and John Gardner's 'Grendel,'" in *MOSAIC: A Journal for the Comparative Study of Literature and Ideas,* Vol. 9, No. 1, 1975, pp. 19-31.

The author compares the two works and finds that Gardner's novel stands up well beside the older classic.

Jerome Klinkowitz, "John Gardner's 'Grendel,'" in *John Gardner: Critical Perspectives,* edited by Robert A. Morace and Kathryn VanSpanckeren, Southern Illinois University Press, 1982, pp. 62-67.

Characterizes the work as a product of its times and faults it for being Gardner's personal experiment instead of addressing its real audience.

Dean McWilliams, "*Grendel,*" in his *John Gardner,* Twayne, 1990, pp. 29-41.

McWilliams reads *Grendel* as an exploration of the role of dialogue in the creation of the self and the world.

Joseph Milosh, "John Gardner's *Grendel :* Sources and Analogues," in *Contemporary Literature,* Vol. 19, No. 1, Winter, 1978, pp. 48-57.

An essay connecting *Grendel* with Chaucer's *The Nun's Priest's Tale.*

Jay Rudd, "Gardner's Grendel and *Beowulf:* Humanizing the Monster," in *THOTH,* Spring/Fall, 1974, pp. 3-17.

A close analysis of the original poem and why it is so appealing to modern writers like Barth, Heller, and Beckett, as well as Gardner.

Obasan

Joy Kogawa
1981

Winning both the Books in Canada First Novel Award and the Canadian Authors' Association Book of the Year Award, *Obasan* was the first novel to deal with the Canadian internment of its Japanese citizens during and after World War II. Written by the poet Joy Kogawa, the novel appeared in 1981 while the efforts of Japanese Canadians to win redress from the Canadian government for internment were in high gear. The novel has been the focus of much criticism exploring its treatment of landscape, identity, and mother-culture.

The autobiographical work tells the story of a schoolteacher, Naomi, remembering the struggle to grow up as a third generation Japanese Canadian amid the hysteria of World War II. Being so young when internment began, she did not understand what was happening and nobody tried to explain it to her. She loses her mother as a result, she thinks, of her sexual abuse by a neighbor. Then she loses her father when all Japanese must go to the interior or to work camps. Given the circumstances and historical whims of her story, it is surprising that the novel is not a tragedy. It does not become so because of the silent strength of the title character, Obasan. She holds the keys to the past, to which Naomi must reconcile herself. She is finally successful in an epiphanic ending—a sudden revelation—as she embraces and is embraced by the Canadian landscape.

Author Biography

Born in Vancouver, Canada, in 1935 as the daughter of Lois (Yao) and Rev. Gordon Goichi Nakayama, Joy Kogawa is a poet, essayist, novelist, and a Nisei—a second-generation Japanese Canadian. When World War II broke out, she, like the rest of her family, was forced from the coast. Canada and its allies were at war with Germany, Italy, and Japan and regarded Canadians of Japanese heritage with suspicion. Due to these circumstances, Kogawa had to attend grade school in the internment camp at Slocan, British Columbia. Her 1981 autobiographical novel, *Obasan,* relates her life as a Canadian during World War II. The novel is the first, in Canadian letters, to deal with this painful time and has won several awards. In that novel, Kogawa makes peace with the injustice of the internment of herself and others whose ancestors originated in Japan. Her novel also reflects the anti-nuclear movement as well as the growing effort to seek redress for the treatment of Japanese-Canadians in World War II.

Because internment did not end with the war, Kogawa went on to school in Coaldale, Alberta. She then entered the university system and attended the University of Alberta, Toronto Conservatory of Music, the Anglican Women's Training College, and the University of Saskatchewan. In 1957, she married David Kogawa and had two children. Kogawa and her husband were divorced in 1968. From 1974 to 1976, Kogawa worked as a staff writer for the Office of the Prime Minister. In 1978, she was writer in residence at the University of Ottawa.

Before her autobiographical novel, Kogawa was, and remains, a well-regarded poet. Her first collection, published in 1967, *The Splintered Moon,* reflected upon her marriage. Her next three collections reflected upon the same themes found in *Obasan.* She wrote of living a hybrid life as a Japanese-Canadian Nisei; divorce; an abortion in 1971; deaths in her family, specifically her uncle and mother; the silence of Obasan, her aunt; and the militancy of women seeking justice and redress. Her recent collection of poetry, *Woman in the Woods* (1985), is her most balanced and refined collection to date.

Joy Kogawa

Plot Summary

Chapters 1–10

Joy Kogawa's *Obasan* centers on the memories and experiences of Naomi Nakane, a schoolteacher living in the rural Canadian town of Cecil, Alberta, when the novel begins. The death of Naomi's uncle, with whom she had lived as a child, leads Naomi to visit and care for her widowed aunt Obasan. Her brief stay with Obasan in turn becomes an occasion for Naomi to revisit and reconstruct in memory her painful experiences as a child during and after World War II. Naomi's narration thus interweaves two stories, one of the past and another of the present, mixing experience and recollection, history and memory throughout. Naomi's struggle to come to terms with both past and present confusion and suffering form the core of the novel's plot.

Obasan opens in August, 1972, with a visit by Naomi and her uncle Isamu to the coulee, a shallow grassland ravine to which they return "once every year around this time." Though Naomi seems unaware of it (until the end of the novel), her uncle returns to the "virgin land" of the prairie each year to mark the anniversary of the dropping of an atomic bomb on Nagasaki on August 9, 1945.

Naomi simply recalls that "the first time Uncle and I came here was in 1954, in August, two months after Aunt Emily's initial visit to Granton." Only at the end of the book does Naomi (and the reader) learn the news that Emily brought on that occasion, in the letters of Grandma Kato, about the suffering of Naomi's mother and grandmother in the aftermath of the Nagasaki bombing.

One month after her visit to the coulee, Naomi learns of her uncle's death. In the days following her return to Granton to attend to her aunt, Naomi tries to communicate with Obasan, to understand the silent "language of her grief," to penetrate a silence that "has grown large and powerful" over the years. At the same time, Naomi sifts through the documents, newspaper clippings, letters, and diaries kept by her aunt Emily, an outspoken political activist determined to air the truth about the Japanese-Canadian experience of persecution. That experience, recounted in *Obasan* largely through Naomi's memories of childhood, is rooted in the actual history of 20,000 Japanese Canadians (and 120,000 Japanese Americans). Viewed as a dangerous enemy during World War II, many of these individuals were stripped of their homes and possessions, compelled to relocate to ghost towns or concentration camps, forced to live and work under terrible conditions, and generally denied the rights of citizenship. Throughout *Obasan,* Naomi's quest to understand the painful personal story of her childhood intersects this larger communal history of suffering.

Between the influences of her two aunts, one suffering in silence, the other a "word warrior," Naomi feels driven to review her life as a child in all of its mystery, confusion, and pain. Naomi's recollections come to her in isolated phrases, scenes, stories, dreams, and fairy tales. A photograph of herself as a child with her mother, given to her by Obasan, prompts Naomi to remember her childhood home in Vancouver and the idyllic life it contained before her family was broken up and evacuated from the West coast. Naomi recalls steaming-hot baths with Grandma Kato, evenings spent in the family's music room, and bedtime stories told "night after night."

Chapters 11–23

But as the stories of Naomi's childhood unfold, the sources of her confusion and pain emerge. Repeated incidents of sexual abuse by a neighbor, Old Man Gower, produce feelings of shame and confusion in young Naomi that seem to separate her from

her mother for the first time. When her mother leaves on a trip to Japan, Naomi feels "an ominous sense of cold and absence," uncertain if her own wrongdoing caused her mother to "disappear." Finally, Naomi is troubled as a child by the growing racial tension that threatens the rest of her family with evacuation and internment, the "riddle" that made them "both the enemy and not the enemy."

When the evacuation commences and Naomi's father and uncle are ordered to report to work camps, Naomi, her brother Stephen, and Obasan board a train from Vancouver to the mountainous interior of British Columbia. In the ghost town of Slocan, Naomi and her surrogate family, along with many other relocated Japanese Canadians, attempt to reconstruct family and community life. In the face of tremendous obstacles, they succeed at least partially. Slocan comes alive, after a time, with new small businesses, new social ties, worship services and schools, and Naomi enjoys "Sunday-school outings, Christmas concerts, sports days, [and] hikes" with new-found friends. But life in Slocan is not free of suffering and confusion for Naomi. In the hospital, after being saved from drowning by Rough Lock Bill, Naomi dreams of all the brutishness and death that she has witnessed since leaving Vancouver. Her hallucinatory dream leads her to understand that "Death comes to the world in many unexpected places," even in the restored community of Slocan.

Chapters 24–39

After several years in Slocan, Naomi and Stephen are overjoyed by the end of the war and the unexpected arrival of their father. But their hopes for a reunited family and a return to their former life are short-lived. Their father is once again dispatched to a work camp, where he later dies before seeing his children again. Meanwhile, Uncle, Obasan, Stephen and Naomi are "relocated" to a sugar-beet farm in the harsh climate of the Canadian plains. On the Barker farm outside of Granton, Alberta, they struggle to survive under conditions far worse than those in Slocan, without the consolations of community that Slocan had allowed. Eventually, Uncle and Obasan manage to leave the Barker farm and move to a house in Granton, where they remain after Stephen pursues a career in music and Naomi becomes a teacher.

It is this home in Granton to which Naomi returns after her uncle's death to care for Obasan. And it is also in Obasan's home, more than twenty-seven years after the bombing of Nagasaki, that

Naomi finally learns the truth about her mother's suffering and the reasons for her silence. Naomi and Stephen had been spared of this knowledge by the wishes of their mother, who asked that the truth be kept secret "for the sake of the children" ("Kodomo no tame"). Even as an adult, Naomi is shielded from the truth, by Uncle (at the coulee), by Obasan (who gives her pictures in place of answers), and by Aunt Emily:

> "What do you think happened to Mother and Grandma in Japan?" I asked. "Did they starve, do you think?"
>
> Aunt Emily's startle was so swift and subtle it barely registered. But I could feel that somewhere, beneath her eyes, a shutter had clicked open and shut at my mentioning Mother and Grandma. It was as if my unexpected question was a sudden beam of pain that had to be extinguished immediately.
>
> She stared into the blackness. Sometimes when I stand in a prairie night the emptiness draws me irresistibly, like a dust speck into a vacuum cleaner, and I can imagine myself disappearing off into space like a rocket with my questions trailing behind me.

When, finally, the remnants of her family are reunited to mourn the death of her uncle, Naomi receives answers to the questions that have trailed behind her throughout her life. At Naomi's pleading, Nakayama-sensei reads the letters sent many years before by Grandma Kato, letters that Naomi had seen and touched but could not translate herself. The letters tell tales of horror, of unbearable experiences and unthinkable memories, and they explain the enduring silence, the "voicelessness," that has tormented Naomi since her mother left her as a child. Although the horror of her mother's fate allows no easy reconciliation with the past or with the powers that brought on that fate, Naomi finally understands that her mother's silence was inspired by her attempt to protect and love her children, not abandon or punish them. At the end of *Obasan*, Naomi returns to the coulee that she had visited each year with her uncle, now aware of the significance of his ritual and able to embrace the past in peace, to put aside "this body of grief," to recognize that "the song of mourning is not a lifelong song."

Characters

Aya-obasan
See Ayako Nakane

Mr. Barker
When the family is allowed to leave the camp at Slocan but still refused access to Vancouver, they move to Granton and work in the sugar beet fields for Mr. Barker. He represents the typical Canadian of the interior. The whole family—Isamu, Obasan, Stephen, and Naomi—work the field of sugar beets. Their work, joined with similar Japanese work across the Canadian heartland, wins the respect of the farmers because the harvest is a record crop. Mr. Barker appears toward the end of the novel to pay his respects to Obasan, but the scene is very awkward and his wife is extremely condescending.

Rough Lock Bill
Though his appearance is brief, the character of Rough Lock Bill is very important. He stands in direct contrast to the other male symbol of Canada, Mr. Gower. Rough Lock sees people as people and not as races. He also knows some of the stories of the land and it is not the first time that there is a link between the plight of the Japanese-Canadians and the Native Americans. Underlining the idea that there is good left in a hysterical Canada, it is Rough Lock who saves Naomi from drowning while Kenji runs away in fright.

Old Man Gower
The next-door neighbor of the house in Vancouver is Mr. Gower. Under the varying pretenses of scraped knees and treats, he lures Naomi close enough to be sexually caressed and undressed. He is also the one who is asked to watch the house when the family must leave. The irony is that all the adults know there will probably never be a return to the house. The experience with Mr. Gower haunts Naomi in Slocan. The forest for her hides his searching eyes and groping hands. Thus, through the horror of Mr. Gower, the wilderness of the Canadian interior is masculinized. This is a novelty on the part of Kogawa because in the history of literature the male protagonist masters a female universe. Here, Naomi will finally master the wilds of Canada when she embraces the earth at the coulee.

Dr. Kato
When Grandma would travel back to Japan, Grandpa would look after Emily. This explains why Emily is less traditional. Grandma's first trip was taken while he was still in medical school. As a doctor, he has certain privileges that his family can take advantage of when internment begins. Thus Emily is able to go to Toronto rather than the camp at Slocan. Emily is unable to take the Nakanes.

During World War II, thousands of Japanese Canadians were sent to internment camps far from their homes, where they were stripped of their rights as citizens and forced to work and live under harsh conditions.

Aunt Emily Kato

Governed by the old testament dictum, "Write the vision and make it plain," Aunt Emily Kato is the political firebrand. She bestows all her papers and zeal on Naomi in the hopes that she will pursue justice with her. At one point, Naomi describes Aunt Emily as "one of the world's white blood cells, rushing from trouble spot to trouble spot." Ironically, it is not Aunt Emily who makes the story known, it is the *daughter* of silent Obasan who tells the story. Nevertheless, Aunt Emily is the source of documentation. She offers the headlines, the executive orders, and the piles of letters. Aunt Emily is the character trying to make sense of the government's actions during World War II by gathering the facts. These facts, however, are little comfort to Naomi. Aunt Emily is the opposite female figure to Obasan. She will not be silent, she will demand that justice be done. Still, she kept silent about the death of Naomi's mother though Grandmother Kato couldn't.

Grandma Kato

The most traditional of the family, Grandma Kato never left Japan entirely. She returned quite often, and when Mother was old enough she went too. Consequently, Mother was like both Grandmas—yasashi. While on one of these trips, World War II broke out and they were stranded in Japan. Despite being traditional, she cannot bear the suffering of her daughter. Therefore, she writes to the family in Canada describing her horrific fate.

Grandpa Kato

See Dr. Kato

Kenji

Kenji is a playmate of Naomi's who tells her about the King bird who cuts off the tongues of those who lie. Kenji takes Naomi to the lake one summer day and entices her, with promises of caution, onto a raft. He swims her out accidentally beyond the drop-off. Out of fear at what he has done, he runs away, leaving Naomi adrift in the middle of the lake.

Mark

See Mr. Tadashi Nakane

Mother

See Mrs. Kato Nakane

Ayako Nakane

The title character of the book is based on Kogawa's aunt. She is the silent heart of the narrative—more an attitude than a person—and embodies the strength of silence. In the novel, Obasan is the daughter of a schoolteacher and was a well-educated music teacher. She immigrated to Canada where she met Grandma Nakane. They became fast friends and she married her son, Uncle Isamu. She believes in the tradition of keeping quiet and accepting whatever life offers without protest. She holds to this when her babies die, her in-laws suffer at Nagasaki, the government confiscates the fishing boats, they are removed to the camps, and when her husband dies. According to Obasan, who says little beyond "O," one must accept the injustice. In her character is also a tribute to women and mothers the world over:

> "Squatting here with the putty knife in her hand, she is every old woman in every hamlet in the world … Everywhere the old woman stands as the true and rightful owner of the earth. She is the bearer of keys to unknown doorways and to a network of astonishing tunnels. She is the possessor of life's infinite personal details."

For Naomi she becomes a mother figure when her actual mother is gone. Even so there always remains "an ominous sense of cold and absence." Obasan does her best and Naomi takes comfort from her softness and constancy.

Grandma Nakane

Grandma Nakane was yasashi, soft and silent. This means she was very traditional and, consequently, extremely powerful in nonverbal communication. She was the first to die in the camps, more out of a lack of understanding why she was there than the horrid conditions.

Grandpa Nakane

The first of Naomi's ancestors to come to Canada was a master boatbuilder. He quickly became famous and many fishermen came to his shop on Saltspring Island. He married a cousin's widowed wife. She brought him a son and bore him Naomi's father. The two sons built a beautiful boat which was soon taken by the Royal Canadian Military Police in 1941. Grandpa Nakane did not survive the internment camp.

Uncle Isamu Nakane

Born in Japan in 1889, Isamu was a boatbuilder, like his father, on Lulu Island. After the government confiscated the fishing fleet, the Nakanes sought refuge near the Katos. Because of his brother's learning, the government sent him to work camp leaving Isamu to be stepfather to his children—Stephen and Naomi.

For eighteen years, Naomi and Uncle Isamu made a pilgrimage to a certain coulee near their home in Granton. Not until the end of the story does she realize that Uncle was trying to reveal the fate of her mother. This site then becomes Naomi's touchstone or memorial to her family and to the lost community of Vancouver.

Mrs. Kato Nakane

Mother is yasashi—soft and traditional—like her mother, Grandma Kato. She is the absent presence in the novel. The horrific details of her struggle to protect children in her care at Nagasaki are heart-wrenching but she doesn't want her children to know. This wish leads to almost thirty years of mystery for Naomi.

Megumi Naomi Nakane

The narrator of the novel is thirty-six-year-old school teacher Naomi Nakane. She is called from her teaching by the Principal to receive the news of her uncle's death. She returns to her aunt's house to be with her and to remember. Her story jumps about in time but follows her through her story of being sexually abused, losing her mother, being interned, and working the beet fields. When the whole family is assembled for the funeral, Naomi and her brother Stephen finally hear the story of their mother's death.

In the telling of the story, however, the adult narrator still allows for the collusion of her abuse by Old Man Gower and the departure of her mother. Being so young, she is easily able to accept Obasan as a substitute mother. In addition to her secret, Naomi is haunted by the shadow of the King Bird which bites off the lying tongue and brings more caution to Naomi's speech. Naomi felt that her secret with Mr. Gower prompted her mother to leave and stay away. She wants the past to stay in the past and is quite bothered by Aunt Emily's insistence that all be told, that facts be known.

Naomi the child was very quiet. So much so that her relatives often thought she was mute. However, she did ask questions especially about her mother. She never received answers and ceased asking. Similarly, in the chaos of being interned to the camp in Slocan, she lost her doll but only asked about it once because she knew it was lost. This linguistic anxiety clearly marks Naomi throughout the story and even marks the adult Naomi whom we first see troubled by her students' questions about her. In her narration, on the other hand, her voice is steady. She has not raised her voice to tell about the injustice done her people as would her Aunt Emily, nor has she kept silent—which in a Euro-centric culture amounts to passive acceptance. Instead, her writing about a silence and through references to her own juvenile state and the many references to juvenile tales are an even-voiced, steady documentation of a history of a wrong. The result is a declaration of cultural enrichment. She is Canadian, oh Canada, ready or not.

Nomi Nakane

See Megumi Naomi Nakane

Stephen Nakane

The elder brother of Naomi is the musical prodigy Stephen. He has many advantages over Naomi, not least of which is his recourse to music as a voice. Thus he has two voices when Naomi has trouble enough with her own. Being older, Stephen also had more time to know his mother and he is better able to understand what is happening. Therefore, he is better able to handle her departure and he is also able to reject Obasan as a substitute. Through music he has a ready bond with his father, and when they play, Naomi sits and listens.

Stephen is angry with his family and with Japanese-Canadians generally. While growing up, this is exhibited in a sour behavior and is symbolized by his broken leg. This is yet another reason for rejecting Obasan—by doing so he rejects the mother-culture. His attitude is first displayed when he is beat up before the internment. He is frustrated because he is Canadian, he plays European music, and he has nothing to do with World War II. Still, he has to be shipped off to the camp in Slocan where he hobbles about in his cast, playing records again and again on the gramophone. Finally, though he does come to the funeral, Stephen stays away as much as possible and only brings his fiancee by for a few minutes. They do not stay to eat.

Mr. Tadashi Nakane

Father was brought up as a boatbuilder but he is also a musician. For some reason he is singled out for the camps, whereas his brother Isamu eventually arrives at Slocan. His marriage to Mother is the first non-arranged marriage in the community. Father dies of tuberculosis in the internment hospital after living in a work camp.

Nakayama sensei

Anglican minister based on the author's father, who had been a Buddhist before he became a Christian preacher. Nakayama is the spiritual leader of the Japanese Canadian community and is always willing to help anyone in need. He leads the service at Grandma Nakane's funeral, even though Buddhist rites are performed in accordance to Grandpa Nakane's wishes. At the end of the book, it is Nakayama Sensei who translates the letter Grandma Kato wrote to her husband after the war, revealing the tragic fate of Naomi's mother and the reason the children were never told.

Nesan

See Mrs. Kato Nakane

Nomura-obasan

She stays with the family at Slocan for a time. She is an old friend of the family's from Vancouver and as such is referred to as obasan, aunt. She is frail and has contracted TB. This causes a scene at the baths and is the reason why Naomi is not allowed to play with Reiko.

Obasan

See Ayako Nakane

Reiko

Reiko is another playmate in Slocan. But when her mother finds out that someone at Naomi's house is ill, they can be friends no more. Reiko shows how intolerance is spread because she has learned that sickness is a shame. Whereas, Naomi is taught that it is a misfortune.

Themes

Prejudice and Tolerance

The root of the internment lies in prejudice. Early in the novel when Naomi is first browsing through Aunt Emily's parcel, there is a nice encapsulation of the problem. Naomi has noted that every time the words "Japanese race" appeared in the new articles or in pamphlets, Aunt Emily has crossed them out and written "Canadian citizens." Therein lies the problem. Naomi's family were viewed as visitors and then, with the outbreak of war, as the enemy. There is no good reason for this. Asian immigrants to North America were as recent as the Irish and many of the European immigrants

Topics for Further Study

- Research the internment experience of people with Japanese ancestry in both Canada and the United States during World War II and compare them.

- Who was Sitting Bull? In what ways is the experience of Sitting Bull's people similar to Naomi's family? In what ways was it different?

- Do some research into the religion of Buddhism and then interpret some of the Buddhist references in Naomi's story. Is the narrator successful in blending Christianity and Buddhism?

- If you were going to make *Obasan* into a film, how would you handle Grandma Kato's letter from Japan?

---

who came after World War I. Yet neither the Italians nor the Germans were interned. The scapegoating of the Japanese appears directly in the confiscation of the fishing boats and then when Stephen gets beat up at school. It is also visible after the war. The Japanese Canadians are still not allowed to return to the coast and many signs along the highway say, "Japs Keep Out." Still, little sense can be made out of all that happened and Naomi thinks of Grandma Nakane in her stall in prison "too old then to understand political expediency, race riots, the yellow peril. She was told that a war was on."

These forms of intolerance are not the only ones seen by Naomi. There is her brother's developing dislike of his family and his heritage. But the example of Stephen is long in developing. There is one episode, however, that is clear. Near the end of their time in Slocan, Naomi's friend is not allowed to speak with her. Their meeting, therefore, is a very awkward moment in the baths. Once outside, Naomi hears from her friends, "we can't play with you … you're sick. You've all got TB. You and the Nomuras and your dad." This is news to Naomi but Uncle Isamu later explains to her, "For some people it is a shameful matter to be ill. But

it is a matter of misfortune, not shame." The attitude of some within the exiled community toward the less fortunate, being expressed by Reiko, lends a great deal of realism to the novel because it shows that the interned group is not faultless. Finally, it hints at how intolerance is transmitted. Reiko admits she knows only what "my mom told me." Just as Reiko is learning how to judge, Naomi learns to accept those who are ill like old Nomura-obasan, who lived with them for awhile on a cot in the kitchen.

Identity

The second chapter opens with Naomi receiving the third degree from her students about her love life. It is an uncomfortable but usual discussion to her as a teacher. Still, she feels the interrogation acutely because her identity is unresolved. Her tumultuous life has left her "tense" with "a crone-prone syndrome" and many mysteries, silences, and repressed traumas. Just as the young Naomi took a while to realize her father was dead, the mature Naomi has not understood how incredible was the trauma of her sexual abuse, the loss of her mother, and the disruption of community caused by war. She finally resolves these issues when she knows the whole truth and, consequently, faces her history. In the end, she is resolved when she runs out into the night wearing Aunt Emily's jacket to go to the coulee. There, inspired by the silence of Obasan and what Uncle tried to tell her, she finally feels at ease with the land and at ease with herself. The nightmares will now cease and she will bury her family in Canada, her home.

Justice vs. Injustice

Injustice in the novel is always mirrored by an accompanying act of violation. The official policy of scapegoating the Japanese violates the family in apparent and secret ways. The fishing boats are taken, their civil rights are taken, and Mother is trapped in Japan as war breaks out. But this is merely the background to the violation of innocence represented by the awful scene of the mother hen killing the chicks and Old Man Gower. The sexual abuse of Naomi initiates her into the sexual world at the same time as the world is going through tremendous upheaval.

Sexual violence is the symbolic gesture of injustice as well as being a very personal injustice—rape is the metaphoric and real violation of people in this book and all are silent as a result (all communications with the camps were censored or silenced). It is not only Mr. Gower. Later in Slocan, a boy named Percy is indiscrete with her. It is Mr. Gower, however, who haunts her and remains the one thing she cannot tell her mother. His assault on her, she fathoms, can be the only explanation for Mother leaving and not returning. Because of Mr. Gower, she feels eyes watching her in the woods and has nightmares of a saw separating her legs from each other and from her mother. Gayle Fujita wrote in *Melus,* "The resulting cleavage represents not only a natural separation of growing up, but unnatural guilt and fear due to the nature of initiation and its being complicated because it is 'around this time that mother disappears.'" Sexuality, Mother, and her identity are inextricably linked.

Memory and Reminiscence

"The past is the future," says Aunt Emily, and indeed it is the whole purpose of the book. One symbol of Naomi's revelation of the past is the sweep of her flashlight across the multitude of spider webs in Obasan's attic. Naomi has followed her aunt up to the attic in the middle of the silent night to find Aunt Emily's parcel that Naomi has been putting off reading for years. Instead, they find only dust and spiders in the attic. Thus the attic has served as the repository of memory and what it holds has been forgotten—left for the spiders. There is an additional reference to spiders in the "weaving" of stories. This theme recalls Penelope, the wife of Ulysses who wove and unwove a tapestry in an attempt to put off her suitors. Naomi's story itself is constructed like a web. Her mother and father are her needles but they leave and it is a long time before Naomi has the pieces from her aunts to finish herself. Also, her story jumps forward and backward, from center to edge, but, finally, as a web it catches the identity created by the story—Naomi.

There is another symbol of this telling in the King bird. He represents the narrator's fear at exaggerating or lying about the tale. This is the reason why the narrator gives way to explanation through fairy tales—Goldilocks, Heidi, and Momotaro. The latter is an oral story from Japan told to her at bedtime. It is the story of a young hero, similar to Hercules, who devotes his life to helping people in their battles against greater powers. In many ways, Kogawa's Naomi has a certain affinity with this hero. By her confessed remembrance, she gives strength to the anti-nuclear movement and, specifically, to the redress movement in Canada. As with Naomi, once all the pieces are present and the full story can be told, only then,

Obasan would say, "the time of forgetting is now come."

Style

Autobiography

The novel is a first person account of a woman who is breaking silence about several aspects of her life and the history she lived through. As the narrator, the adult Naomi is facing the death of her uncle Isamu, and Obasan feels it is time that Naomi read Emily's parcel full of factual anger. In other words, it is time to deal with the past. But Naomi's response is peculiar. She describes personal memories and childhood experiences that seem to have no place in the story's political commitment. As a result, reading time jumps from the present death of her uncle to points in the past, beginning with herself as a quiet little girl losing her mother. Due to the point of view being Naomi's, who rarely received answers to her questions when she asked them, the recollection is hazy and the characters often remain presences and never become personalities. The result is an almost pure recollection of girlhood whose testimony is more powerful than any of the facts collected by Emily.

Imagery

The images in the novel are a blend of Christian and Buddhist traditions, coming in the forms of allegorical moments and strict dream visions. However, the central symbol of the work is Naomi's mother. She is not a character in the story so much as a remembered tale. Naomi has few stories of her mother and she constantly asks others for their recollections of her mother. The effect is to make her more a governing spirit than a real person. Words that bring mother to the story are almost prayerful. For example, "Mother, I am listening. Assist me to hear you…. You are tide rushing moonward."

All such surrounding language matches the superhuman account of Nagasaki where Mother guarded the children in her care despite the radiation burns. This apocalyptic event, both linguistically and structurally, is the high point of the novel. Amazingly, it is very soft-spoken and written in simple sentences, "it was my mother." As the symbol of motherhood, mother-culture, and the pre-war bliss, she survived the ultimate weapon with horrible disfigurement. Her survival motivates Naomi to piece herself together and finally offer her story as therapy for the whole community.

Diction

The words forming the novel are carefully chosen and become active players in the plot structure in unusual ways. The reason for this is that the novel is breaking the silence that the victims were intended to keep. Naomi recalls, "We are the despised rendered voiceless, stripped of car, radio, camera and every means of communication." In keeping silent, however, the victims are not whole. "If you cut any of [your history] off, you're an amputee…. Don't deny the past." Those are words from Aunt Emily, whose succinct and inflammatory writing style stands in stark contrast to the poetics of the narrative as a whole. Aunt Emily means well, means to tell the truth. But like the two ideograms of love, there are different ways of telling the tale.

Due to the delicacy of the situation—so many want the story to stay silent and be forgotten while others want to scream it out—the words are carefully chosen and the writing makes liberal use of allegory. The stone bread made by Uncle is like the manna that nourished the Israelites. Uncle is also compared to Sitting Bull and thus the removal of the Japanese is compared to the earlier act of putting the indigenous people on reservations. Similarly, Emily's parcel is like the stone bread as it provides nourishment for the mind. Oftentimes, biblical writing is used. "When I am hungry, and before I can ask, there is food," recalls the Christian gospel. Allegorical language also serves to blend Buddhist imagery into the tale by introducing the "white stone" and the idea of nature's dancing. The effect of Kogawa's language is to make the barrier between dream or story and reality, present and past, and nature and individual almost nonexistent.

Dream Vision

There are many dreams in the work but all stem from the two forces driving the novel—sexual abuse and the loss of mother because of the war. The dreams grow out of Naomi's anxiety over sex due to early abuse and whether that initiation into sexuality caused her mother to leave. But her dreams also offer answers by showing the ways in which the family members are linked. Her uncle appears to be attempting to help her and thus the dream vision is not easily separated from the reality of the story. In one dream, Uncle is making a ceremonial bow as his part of the flower dance. It is Naomi's struggle, then, to realize what the ceremony is that she must complete in order to put the ghosts of the past to rest. She finally does this in the novel's closing epiphany.

Historical Context

Canada

Canada is a large and sparsely populated country and a member of the British Commonwealth and NAFTA. It is generally seen throughout the world as a relatively neutral, and therefore non-threatening, nation. However, the tales of Amerindian and Inuit removals and the internment of Canadians with Japanese ancestry in World War II remain whispered tales. Also, Canada's recent skirmishes with European countries, especially Spain, over fishing area hints at larger environmental faults.

Canada's constitution is surprisingly new and unsettled. After steadily gaining nominal independence, discussion of rescinding the British North America Act began in 1927 as the first step toward making Canada independent. Limbo existed until 1981, when the Constitution Act was passed under the Liberal Prime Minister Pierre Trudeau. The Act was in turn accepted by Queen Elizabeth II in the following spring. This effectively replaced the British North American Act as the working document of the Canadian government. Unfortunately, not all of the provinces were ready to accept the Act. Quebec wanted independence and would not sign. To keep Quebec in the union it was offered the special status of "distinct society" by the Meech Lake Accord of 1987. The Inuit and Amerindians of Canada were also granted "distinct society" status. Quebec's privilege angered the provinces of New Brunswick and Manitoba, who refused to ratify the Act. Another compromise came in the Charlottetown Accord of 1992, but that was rejected by referendum.

World War II

Canada under the premiership of William Lyon Mackenzie King entered World War II earlier than the United States. It contributed more than one million men to the Allies' war effort and lost 32,000 men. The anti-Asian sentiment in Canada had been prevalent in the late thirties and was officially expressed when the Canadian government confiscated the fishing fleet of its Canadians of Japanese ancestry. This racist policy increased to the point of hysteria with the news of Pearl Harbor's demise on December 7, 1941. In the United

Protests by Japanese Canadians eventually led to compensation by the government for the injustices done to them during the war.

States, President Roosevelt signed Executive Order 9066, calling for the immediate evacuation and internment of 110,000 West Coast Japanese despite the fact that fully two-thirds of them were American citizens. In Canada, where evacuation had been underway, the process was speeded up. Thus, 21,000 Canadians of Japanese ancestry were forced into work camps and interment camps far from the West Coast. Of those removed, 17,000 were Canadian born and, therefore, the removal was a gross violation of human rights and civil liberties. Unlike internment in America, Canada still restricted Japanese-Canadian movements for many years after the war. Furthermore, the United States returned confiscated property—Canada never did—and, therefore, the Japanese community in the United States recovered much faster.

The illegality of the removal was not unnoticed even by members of King's own government. Asian immigrants, however, had long been seen by both the United States and Canada as "sojourners," or as immigrants who would eventually return home. In addition, before the early part of this century, Asians were subject to various mandates that effectively barred them from citizenship and limited their property owning capacity. Therefore, the allowing of Asian-immigrants the same status as immigrants from anywhere else in the world was a recent development. This does not excuse the internment but it offers some explanation to the perception of Asians as foreigners and, consequently, as a potential threat to security during World War II. In other words, the resentment against "foreigners" taking away the jobs of citizens contributed to the enthusiasm for scapegoating certain people. The idea of ruining the prosperous Japanese-Canadian community by taking their land, ships, and fishing areas so soon after the depression years helped to drive the removal hysteria.

National Association of Japanese Canadians (NAJC)

The NAJC achieved the Redress Agreement in 1988 with the Government of Canada on behalf of all Canadians of Japanese ancestry. This agreement was a settlement of the conditions of restitution to those Japanese Canadians illegally interned and dispossessed of their property during World War II. As a result of the Agreement, the Government of Canada formally apologized for the violation of human rights committed by the act of internment and dispossession. In addition, the government paid out symbolic amounts to those Japanese Canadians affected; it established a $12 million community fund to be administered by the Japanese Canadian Redress Foundation. Lastly, the government established the Canadian Race Relations Foundation for the purpose of researching and fighting racism.

Canada's Liabilities

In addition to the demand for redress from those Canadians affected by the government's actions during World War II, Canada has had to deal with other cultural stresses. Throughout the 1960s, 1970s, and 1980s, the indigenous peoples of Canada won many court battles and were given money and land from the government. Their success was helped by the concurrent move in America by tribes to have treaties honored. But for a few exceptions, this remained a legal struggle with a happy outcome. Another problem that persists is oil revenue. Alberta and Newfoundland have various disagreements with the government over regulation, pricing, and revenue sharing. In Newfoundland, this prevented the exploitation of the vast Hibernia oil reserves offshore until the 1980s.

A more violent stress in Canada has been Quebec and French-speaking Canadians generally. The problem here is a larger one because it involves a problem in the working document of government and the status of Quebec. During the 1970s, the Quebec Liberation Front performed various terrorist acts which led to the invocation of the War Measures Act in peace time and the banning of the group. The declaration of French as the official language of Quebec helped calm some anxiety. In 1976, the separatist Parti Quebecois, under the leadership of Premier Rene Levesque, was elected to power in Quebec and immediately proposed independence. The ballot measure was defeated in a referendum with an 82% turnout.

Critical Overview

Critics and reviewers have found a lot to say about Kogawa's first novel because of its wondrous poetic prose and its successful attempt to express the Canadian hybrid as art. The most popular theme to pick up on in the critical literature is family and how Kogawa writes the family drama as non-Oedipal but a struggle of the mother-culture to survive in patriarchy. It is this struggle which either leaves the daughter devastated or barely intact. The other obvious focus for critics has been the cultural blending of the Japanese and the Canadian that Kogawa subtly accomplishes. Other interpretations

have focused on the landscape as a force in the novel which eventually overcomes the government's action.

Following the publication of the novel and the awards, the first reviews were bland. They were almost bothered by the silences of the novel. An early review in the *Canadian Forum* by Suanne Kelman positively assessed the novel for its ability to transcribe a very political history into a well-crafted piece of literature. Edward White repeated that praise in the *Los Angeles Times Book Review,* adding, "[the] novel must be heard ... [for] exposing the viciousness of the racist horror, embodying the beauty that somehow survives." Critics dealing with the work in the mid-eighties, however, had begun to delve into the complexities for which the novel was deservedly rewarded. The first of this wave was Erika Gottlieb's article in *Canadian Literature.* Since then there have developed five areas of critical focus: puzzle and cross-reference; the place of literature in politics and history; the role of landscape in identity; the difficulties of cultural clash in terms of language both body and tongue; and the psychological drama of mother-daughter relations.

With Gottlieb the novel becomes more than a historical novel making poetry of human injustice. Gottlieb writes, "The novel sets up these multi-dimensional questions as puzzles arranged in a concentric pattern—container hidden within container within container—creating a sense of mystery and tension." These containers, for Gottlieb, are the three riddles of hidden manna, hidden voice, and hidden reason. They reflect the three dimensions of Naomi, the cosmos, and Canada. It is Gottlieb who suggests that the spider webs in the attic mimic the time-jump in the narrative. More significantly, Gottlieb has taken the time to translate the intricacies of Japanese culture endemic in the novel. She suggests that the space of the novel is akin to the space in Buddhism for mourning. Thus the story is begun by news of Uncle's death and ends on the eve of his funeral. There is also the echo of the tea ceremony and the many icons that invoke the blend of Christianity and Buddhism in the work. Following her leads, many critics have attempted to further Gottlieb's solution to the Obasan puzzle or correct her translation. Teruyo Ueki, for example, in her article for *Melus,* reads the novel in terms of Aunt Emily's parcel. She first agrees with Gottlieb's interpretation, but then shows how "the riddles are arranged as 'the folder structure.'" She does this down to the very ribbons tying the parcel together. The grandest container is, of course, the landscape. Karin Quimby focuses on this aspect of the novel and draws the connection between Naomi's growth and the three locales of the story (Vancouver, Slocan, and Granton). These readings reveal that the dreams of flower and roots reconcile themselves in the last scene. There, Naomi is physically rooting in the Canadian prairie with her hands in the grass.

Readings of the novel focusing on culture clash, begin with Gary Willis's article in *Studies in Canadian Literature*. His thesis depends on Kogawa's comparison of Western versus Japanese forms of carpentry. The latter pulls "with control rather than push with force." King-Kok Cheung, in the collection of essays *Listening to Silences*, explains the power of silence and the way it functions in the novel. The key is to realize that silence does not mean passivity. Instead, the novel's silences articulate in literary form "the use of nonverbal expression." To read the novel's silences otherwise, says Cheung, is to fall prey to Orientalism or the stereotype of the submissive Asian. "The thematics and poetics of silence are tightly interwoven.... The narrator negotiates between voicelessness and vociferousness, embodied respectively by her two aunts." Calling the novel a *polyglossia* (because of the several layers of meaning, for example, contained in the ideogram for love), Cheung notices that Kogawa "deploys fables and dreams to spin a web of associations, of verbal and emotional echoes." Cheung ends by referring to the example of carpentry suggesting that Kogawa has carved a style with "the pull of silences." Gayle Fujita picks up on Cheung's insights and reads Kogawa in terms of the story of Momotaro.

Returning to the idea that the novel is historical, Marilyn Rose wrote for *Mosaic* that in a postmodern world literature is still able to convey human experience. She compares the novel to the documentary writing being produced in the late seventies about the internment. Rose argues that by creating Naomi as a "humble and tentative narrator" Kogawa's "argument against this historically specific injustice makes compelling art." Mason Harris has a similar view of the novel in his essay for *Canadian Literature*. His purpose is to pay closer attention not just to how the novel functions on a cultural level as novel or documentary but the way in which the novel itself struggles with that function. For him the novel not only reconstructs "a suppressed chapter of Canadian history" but the transformation of the immigrant family through several generations to adjust to the new culture and the pains that arise between the generations. Both

Robin Potter and Eleanor Ty offer a more exacting psychological reading of the novel with the assistance of Feminist theorists Luce Irigaray and Julia Kristeva. Ty also picks up on a neglected aspect of Kogawa's Naomi when she compares *Obasan* to Jamaica Kincaid's *Lucy* in the *International Fiction Review*. She writes that the mother "evokes an otherness fraught with sexual and racial overtones for Naomi." This condition, she continues, must be demythologized if Naomi is to create new forms of language and expression as a Canadian.

Criticism

Anthony Dykema-VanderArk

Anthony Dykema-VanderArk is a doctoral candidate in English at Michigan State University. In the following essay, he analyzes the importance of ambiguity, irony, and paradox in Obasan.

Since its publication in 1981, Joy Kogawa's *Obasan* has assumed an important place in Canadian literature and in the broadly-defined, Asian-American literary canon. Reviewers immediately heralded the novel for its poetic force and its moving portrayal of an often-ignored aspect of Canadian and American history. Since then, critics have expanded upon this initial commentary to examine more closely the themes and images in Kogawa's work. Critical attention has focused on the difficulties and ambiguities of what is, in more ways than one, a challenging novel. The complexity of *Obasan*'s plot, the intensity of its imagery, and the quiet bitterness of its protest challenge readers to wrestle with language and meaning in much the same way that Naomi must struggle to understand her past and that of the larger Japanese-Canadian community. In this sense, the attention that *Obasan* has received from readers and critics parallels the challenges of the text: Kogawa's novel, one might say, demands to be reckoned with, intellectually as well as emotionally.

Much about Kogawa's novel makes it difficult not only to read but also to classify or categorize. First, *Obasan* blurs the line between nonfiction and fiction. Kogawa draws from actual letters and newspaper accounts, autobiographical details, and historical facts throughout the novel, but she artistically incorporates this material into a clearly fictional work. In addition, Kogawa's narrative operates on multiple levels, from the individual and

What Do I Read Next?

- Kogawa's *Itsuka* (1992) continues the story of Naomi's family as they try to win redress from the Canadian government for the unjust internment.

- Leslie Marmon Silko's *Ceremony* (1977) is the story of a Native American man trying to recover from his experience fighting in World War II for the U.S. Army in the Pacific against the Japanese. His nightmares involve the frightening idea that as a sometime enemy of Americans he was killing an enemy that looked like him. Eventually he is able to regain his mental health by returning to his tribe's traditions.

- Jamaica Kincaid's *Lucy* (1990) is a tale of another girl coming of age while dealing with sexual nightmares. Lucy's sexual secrets, like Naomi's, make the already difficult task of coming to womanhood as a racial minority all the more difficult.

- An American who wrote of a character trying to restore the Japanese community to its pre-internment state was John Okada. His 1957 novel, *No-No Boy,* takes place in the United States.

---

familial to the communal, national, political, and spiritual. Stylistically, the novel moves easily between the language of documentary reportage and a richly metaphorical language, and between straightforward narrative and stream-of-consciousness exposition. This astonishing variety in Kogawa's novel can, at times, become bewildering and unsettling to the reader. But as many readers and critics have noted, Kogawa's style and method in *Obasan* also constitute the novel's unique strength. Kogawa writes in such a way that ambiguity, uncertainty, irony, and paradox do not weaken her story but instead—paradoxically—become the keys to understanding it.

The reader's experience of ambiguity in *Obasan* begins with the poetically-charged proem, preceding chapter one, which opens with these words:

There is a silence that cannot speak.

There is a silence that will not speak.

Does Kogawa intend these lines to introduce "silence" as a character of sorts? Does the second line clarify the first, or does it instead differentiate one silence from another, an involuntary muteness from a willed refusal to speak? These and other questions remain unanswered in the proem. Only after beginning the novel-proper does the reader recognize Naomi as the author of these words; and only after completing the novel can the reader begin to grasp the significance of the questions introduced in the proem, particularly the charged question of silence. *Obasan* dwells on many silences: the silence of history concerning the suffering of Japanese-Canadians during and after World War II; the silence of those who have died and "cannot speak" any longer; the "large and powerful" silence of Obasan; Aunt Emily's outspoken opposition to silence as a "word warrior" for the Japanese Canadian cause; the silence of Obasan, Uncle, and Emily who, in spite of Naomi's questions, "will not speak" of the fate of her mother; and, finally, Naomi's "Silent Mother" herself, who initially chooses not to speak of her horrific injuries at Nagasaki in an effort to protect her children from the truth, then is lost in the permanent silence of death. Naomi's persistent attempts to penetrate these various silences form the story at the heart of *Obasan*.

However, Kogawa also recognizes the paradoxical power of silence. Naomi wonders, for example, if Obasan's grief might represent a "language" with "idioms" and "nuances" all its own. While Obasan's silent suffering often brings her to isolation and a trance-like paralysis, Naomi also sees in her a representative figure of strength and endurance, "the bearer of keys to unknown doorways and to a network of astonishing tunnels." As King-Kok Cheung argues in her reading of *Obasan,* "one must avoid gliding over the tonalities of silence in the novel" in order to recognize the "quiet strength" of first-generation Japanese-Canadians like Uncle and Obasan.

Conversely, Kogawa illustrates that language is only a *potential* antidote to a dangerous silence: like silence, language can imprison just as it can liberate. Emily's bundle of written documents clearly exerts a powerful, positive influence on Naomi by urging her to "remember everything" and to come to terms with the pain of her childhood and adolescence. Yet Naomi also wonders if "all of Aunt Emily's words, all her papers" finally amount to little more than "scratchings in the barnyard." Emily may be a "word warrior," but her "paper battles" cannot bring Naomi's parents back to life or return the family to their idyllic Vancouver home, cannot address the deepest truth of Naomi's loss.

Similarly, when Emily writes "Canadian citizen" over "Japanese race" in a pamphlet, the gesture appears utterly futile next to the Canadian government's powerful naming. Those in power can, for example, call Japan the rightful "homeland" of Japanese-Canadians or mask official acts of racist persecution with deceptively-bland terms such as "evacuation," "relocation," and "assistance." Kogawa understands that the efficacy of language depends in part on the power to enforce words, to enforce a version of reality. At the same time, she powerfully depicts Naomi's struggle to find words of her own to describe her childhood experience. Naomi needs to find language to mark out a middle ground between Emily's solution, "spreading words like buckshot," and Obasan's retreat into silence.

Kogawa also uses the motif of language and silence to illustrate the paradoxical or ironic nature of Naomi's experience as a child. For instance, Naomi's abuse at the hands of Old Man Gower produces a particularly painful double-bind of silence. On the one hand, with Mr. Gower, Naomi feels that remaining silent is the only way to be "whole and safe": "If I am still, I will be safe…. If I speak, I will split open and spill out." On the other hand, her secret knowledge and shame threaten the wholeness and safety that Naomi feels with her mother: "If I tell my mother about Mr. Gower, the alarm will send a tremor through our bodies and I will be torn from her. But the secret has already separated us." But paradox and irony also characterize the experience of the Japanese-Canadian community as a whole during and after World War II. Stephen summarizes the situation of every Japanese-Canadian citizen when he tells Naomi, "It is a riddle…. We are both the enemy and not the enemy." In a similar fashion, Aunt Emily points to fundamental irony in the situation of the Japanese immigrant generation: "In one breath we are damned for being 'inassimilable' and the next there's fear that we'll assimilate." Finally, as Sauling Cynthia Wong notes, movement and mobility also take on ironic resonance in *Obasan*, since a people determined to settle down are forced to move repeatedly, leaving homes and possessions

behind, while those who resist relocation are imprisoned. In all of these painful, paradoxical situations, neither silence nor speech offer any effective means of resolution to Naomi or her community.

But Kogawa incorporates paradox in *Obasan* in more positive, life-affirming ways as well. When Aunt Emily says to Naomi, "it must have been hell in the ghost towns," she is only half correct: Naomi's memories of life in Slocan include not only disturbing images of cruelty and death but also compelling scenes of friendship and community. Just as memories of Mr. Gower disrupt Naomi's recollections of an idyllic childhood before the evacuation, so too the restoration of a sense of community in Slocan undermines Emily's single-minded view of its absolute destruction. Of course, Naomi's positive memories of Slocan do not lessen the crime of relocation and internment, do not excuse what the Canadian and American governments did to Japanese residents and citizens. But Kogawa's portrayal of Naomi's experience presents a more complicated vision of human suffering than any allowed by Emily's outspoken political protest.

In a review entitled "Impossible to Forgive," Suanne Kelman contends that *Obasan* illuminates "the most horrible of all human paradoxes," that "injustice provokes more guilt in its victims than in its perpetrators." However, a desire to believe that forgiveness is *not* impossible also runs throughout Kogawa's novel, spoken most clearly by Nakayama-sensei: "It is a high calling my friends—the calling to forgive." Naomi resists Nakayama-sensei's message, leaving the room when he speaks of Love, drowning out his voice when he speaks of forgiveness. But the resonance of his message is not lost, and his voice—though he speaks of paradoxical truths—is not, as some critics have argued, finally ironic. Instead, Kogawa instills in her novel faint echoes of hope, small but powerful signs of forgiveness, that persist even in the midst of a despair that will not ever be wholly overcome.

By the end of *Obasan*, Naomi does not miraculously resolve her painful struggle with the past or achieve any easy catharsis, but she does find a more positive, less paralyzing way of seeing. The double-bind of silence that Naomi suffered as a child because of Old Man Gower's abusive touch, a silence that threatened to separate her forever from her mother, now opens her eyes to her mother's own suffering and impenetrable silence. Though Naomi rejects her mother's decision to protect her children by "lies" and "camouflage," she recognizes the love that motivated it and the bond that joins mother and daughter: "Gentle Mother, we were lost together in our silences. Our wordlessness was our mutual destruction." Having learned the truth of her mother's suffering and death, Naomi can perceive her mother's immutable presence in her life even as she acknowledges her literal absence. She can envision a certain gentleness in Grief's eyes, a "brooding light" amidst the darkness of death, and an "underground stream" flowing around the "world of stone" that holds her lost loved ones.

At the end of *Obasan,* Naomi returns to the coulee to mourn her own deep loss, to grieve for her Uncle, and to carry on his ritual of remembering those lost forever to that "world of stone." But she goes with new insight into his grief and her own, having come to terms with the painful experiences and the troubling silences that have haunted her life. Fittingly, Kogawa captures Naomi's newfound peace in a paradoxical yet hopeful image of stone and water in harmony, in the reflection of the moon on the river: Though her own shoes are "mud-clogged" and heavy, Naomi can envision "water and stone dancing" in a "quiet ballet, soundless as breath."

Source: Anthony Dykema-VanderArk, in an essay for *Novels for Students,* Gale, 1998.

King-Kok Cheung

King-Kok Cheung is an author, educator, and associate director of the Asian American Studies Center at the University of California at Los Angeles. She not only points out the difference between a Eurocentric and Oriental understanding of "silence," but makes three further distinctions—protective, stoic, and attentive silences—and Kogawa's attitude toward them in Obasan.

Since the Civil Rights movement in the late 1960s, women and members of racial minorities have increasingly sworn off the silence imposed upon them by the dominant culture. Yet silence should also be given its due. Many Asian Americans, in their attempts to dispel the stereotype of the quiet and submissive Oriental, have either repressed or denied an important component of their heritage—the use of nonverbal expression. With many young Asian Americans turning against this aspect of their culture and non-Asians even less able to understand the allegedly "inscrutable" minority, it is not surprising that Joy Kogawa's *Obasan,* an autobiographical novel, has been subject to tendentious reviews. To Edith Milton [writing in the *New York Times Book Review,* Septem-

ber 5, 1982] the book is "a study in painful silence, in unquestioning but troubled obedience to the inevitable"; to David Low [writing in *Bridge,* 8:3, 1983] it is "clearly a novel about the importance of communication and the danger of keeping silent"; to Joyce Wayne [in *RIKKA,* 8:2, 1981] it is "a tale of the submissive silence of the oppressed." The resounding condemnation of silence reflects the bias of "translation" or of language itself which, as Paula Gunn Allen tells us [in *The Sacred Hoop: Recovering the Feminine in American Indian Traditions,* 1986], "embodies the unspoken assumptions and orientations of the culture it belongs to." In English, *silence* is often the opposite of *speech, language,* or *expression.* The Chinese and Japanese character for *silence,* on the other hand, is antonymous to *noise, motion,* and *commotion.* In the United States silence is generally looked upon as passive; in China and Japan it traditionally signals pensiveness, alertness, and sensitivity.

These differences are too often eclipsed by a Eurocentric perspective to which even revisionist critics may succumb. As Chandra Mohanty has argued [in *Boundary,* 1984], much of Western feminist representation of oppressed "third world" women is pitted against the implicit self-representation of Western women as educated, liberated and, I might add, verbally assertive: "These distinctions are made on the basis of the privileging of a particular group as the norm or referent." A similar norm frequently governs the assessment of racial minorities in North America. Marilyn Russell Rose, a sophisticated critic keenly aware of the danger of Orientalist discourse, nevertheless places inordinate blame on the victims in *Obasan:* "'Orientalism' has been so internalized by this Oriental minority, that their silence is an inadvertent bow to the occidental hegemony which legitimizes their abuse" [*Dalhousie Review,* 1987]. Undeniably, nikkei have been subject to political exploitation, but to view their reticence as no more than the internalization of Occidental stereotypes is to tune out the "other" perceptions of silence in the novel. Countering Orientalism means challenging Western reduction or homogenization of Asian traits, but not necessarily denying or denouncing the traits themselves.

Situated on the crossroads of cultures, Kogawa in *Obasan* shows a mixed attitude toward both language and silence and reevaluates both in ways that undermine logocentrism. Certainly, language can liberate and heal, but it can also distort and hurt; and while silence may smother and obliterate, it can also minister, soothe, and communicate. The verbal restraint that informs Kogawa's theme and style manifests not only the particular anguish of voicelessness but also what Gayle Fujita describes [in *MELUS,* 12:3, 1985] as the narrator's specific nikkei legacy—"a nonverbal mode of apprehension summarized by the 'term attendance.'" Where Fujita subsumes several forms of reticence under the rubric "attendance," however, I find it necessary to distinguish among protective, stoic, and attentive silences, which Kogawa regards with varying attitudes. Kogawa also deplores negative manifestations of silence, such as political oppression through censorship and enforced invisibility, and the victims' repression.

The thematics and poetics of silence are tightly interwoven. On the thematic level, the narrator negotiates between voicelessness and vociferousness, embodied respectively by her two aunts. The style of the novel likewise evinces a double heritage. The biblical injunction to "write the vision and make it plain"—advocated by one of the aunts—is softpedaled by the narrator's preference for indirection, a preference which sociologist Stanford Lyman associates with the nisei generally. Even as the narrator confronts the outrages committed during World War II, she resorts to elliptical devices, such as juvenile perspective, fragmented memories and reveries, devices which at once accentuate fictionality and proffer a "truth" that runs deeper than the official written records of the war years spliced into the novel. The gaps in the narrative demand from the reader a vigilance and receptivity that correspond to the narrator's attentiveness....

The novel is presented from the point of view of Naomi Nakane, a 36-year-old schoolteacher. It begins in 1972 when Naomi's Uncle Isamu is still alive in Granton, Alberta. A month later, Isamu dies and Naomi goes to comfort his widow Aunt Aya—the title character. *Obasan* is *Aunt* in Japanese, but it can also mean *woman* in general. The title thus implicitly "acknowledges the connectedness of all women's lives—Naomi, her mother, her two aunts" [according to Fujita, *MELUS,* 1985]. At Obasan's house Naomi finds a parcel from her Aunt Emily that contains wartime documents, letters, and Emily's own journal written between December 1941 and May 1942. (Many of Emily's letters of protest to the Canadian government are based on the real letters of Muriel Kitagawa, a Japanese-Canadian activist.) As Naomi sifts through the contents of this package, she reluctantly sinks into her own past. She recalls the uprooting and dissolution of her family during and after the war: her father died of tuberculosis; two of her grandparents died

of physical and mental stress. Naomi and her older brother Stephen were brought up by Uncle Isamu and Obasan. Hovering over the tale is the riddle of what has happened to Naomi's mother, who accompanied Grandma Kato (Naomi's maternal grandmother) to Japan on a visit shortly before the war, when Naomi was five. Only at the end of the book do Naomi and Stephen (and the reader) discover that their mother had been totally disfigured during the nuclear blast in Nagasaki and died a few years later. Before her death she requested Obasan and Uncle to spare her children the truth. The adults succeed all too well in keeping the secret; Naomi does not find out about her mother's fate for over thirty years.

The novel depicts Naomi's plight of not knowing and not being able to tell. Naomi has been speechless and withdrawn throughout childhood and adolescence—her quiet disposition tied to her mother's unexplained absence. As a girl she questions but receives no answer; as an adult she prefers to leave the question unspoken because she dreads knowing. As Magnusson has observed [in *Canadian Literature/Litterature Canadienne* 116, Spring, 1988], "Naomi's individual drama is closely caught up in her linguistic anxiety, which comes to serve as a synecdoche for her estrangement—from others, from her cultural origins, from the absent mother who preoccupies her thoughts, from her past."

In her quest for identity and for peace, Naomi is influenced by her two aunts' contrary responses to their harrowing experiences during the war. Obasan, the reticent aunt who raises Naomi, counsels her to forget and to forgive. Aunt Emily, the political activist, presses her to divulge the indignities endured by Japanese Canadians—to "write the vision and make it plain." Emily brings to mind the Old Testament prophets who cry for justice; Obasan, the New Testament preaching of humility, forgiveness, and charity. But both sets of behavior also have roots in Japanese culture. As Michiko Lambertson points out, "There are two poles in the Japanese way of thinking. One is a fatalistic attitude of acceptance, endurance, and stoicism and the other is a sense of justice, honour, and fair play" [*Canadian Woman Studies* 4:2, 1982]. Obasan's attitude is as much Buddhist as Christian; she moves with equal ease in Christian and Buddhist burial ceremonies, always ready with her serving hands. Emily's activism, though ascribed to her Canadian schooling, is also promoted in the Japanese tale, recounted in the novel, of Momotaro—the boy who defends his people valiantly against cruel bandits (see Fujita). Naomi remarks:

> How different my two aunts are. One lives in sound, the other in stone. Obasan's language remains deeply underground but Aunt Emily, BA, MA, is a word warrior. She's a crusader, a little old grey-haired Mighty Mouse, a Bachelor of Advanced Activists and General Practitioner of Just Causes.

Naomi feels invaded by Emily's words and frustrated by Obasan's wordlessness. She undercuts Emily's polemics with irony and strains to hear Obasan's inner speech....

If skepticism about language and interrogation of majority consensus aligns Kogawa with many a woman writer and postmodernist thinker, her ability to project a spectrum of silence is, as Fujita suggests, traceable to her bicultural heritage. To monitor this peculiar sensibility, one must avoid gliding over the tonalities of silence in the novel, or seeing them all negatively as destructive. The protagonist, to be sure, struggles against oppressive and inhibitive silence. She also feels divided about the protective and the stoic silence of the issei which has sheltered her as a child but paralyzes her as an adult. She continues nevertheless to cherish the communicative and attentive silence she has learned from several female forerunners.

Oppressive silence in the novel takes both individual and collective forms, inflicted on women and men alike. As a child Naomi was sexually abused by a neighbor—Old Man Gower—who forbade her to tell of the violation: "Don't tell your mother." Later, it is the Canadian government that harasses the Japanese Canadians and suppresses the victims. Emily notes: "All cards and letters are censored.... Not a word from the camps makes the papers. Everything is hushed up." Naomi tells: "We are the despised rendered voiceless, stripped of car, radio, camera and every means of communication."

Not an uncommon reaction to suppression is repression on the part of the victims. Instead of voicing anger at the subjugators, they seal their lips in shame. Child Naomi, whose relationship with her mother has been one of mutual trust, begins to nurse a secret that separates them after her molestation. Racial abuse similarly gags the victim. When Stephen is beaten up by white boys, he refuses to tell Naomi what has caused his injury. Naomi intuits, "Is he ashamed, as I was in Old Man Gower's bathroom?" Rape, Erika Gottlieb points out, is used here as "metaphor for any kind of violation" [*Canadian Literature* 109, Summer,

1986]. Like Stephen, many Japanese Canadians also refuse to speak about what Rose calls their "political and spiritual rape" by the Canadian government [*Mosaic* 21, Spring, 1988]. Naomi, for one, wishes to leave the past behind: "Crimes of history ... can stay in history." Her attitude of acceptance is, however, ultimately complicit with social oppression: her self-imposed silence feeds the one imposed from without. Naomi nonetheless learns that she cannot bracket the past, not only because it is impossible to do so, but also because it is self-destructive. "If you cut any of [your history] off you're an amputee," Emily warns. "Don't deny the past. Remember everything. If you're bitter, be bitter. Cry it out! Scream!"

What makes it especially difficult for Naomi to "scream" is her schooling in the protective and stoic silence of the issei, which she is gradually coming to regard with ambivalence. She appreciates the efforts of Mother and Obasan to create a soothing environment for the children. She recollects Mother's reassuring manner during a childhood crisis, after she tells her that a big white hen is pecking a batch of infant yellow chicks to death (an event that clearly foreshadows the pending interracial dynamics). Mother comes immediately to the rescue: "With swift deft fingers, Mother removes the live chicks first, placing them in her apron. All the while that she acts, there is calm efficiency in her face and she does not speak." Obasan also exhibits serenity in the face of commotion. Even on the eve of the evacuation, "Aya is being very calm and she doesn't want any discussion in front of the kids. All she's told them is that they're going for a train ride." An involuntary exodus is recast as a pleasant excursion—for the children's sake.

A point comes when such protective silence—a form of enforced innocence—infantilizes. Naomi, now an adult, is constantly frustrated by tight-lipped Obasan: "The greater my urgency to know, the thicker her silences have always been." When Naomi asks her about the letters written in Japanese—letters describing the bombing in Nagasaki—Obasan produces instead an old photograph of Naomi and her mother, once more substituting a sweet image for harsh facts. Her silence can be as misleading as words.

The stoic silence of the issei is presented with a similar mixture of appreciation and criticism. The issei believe in quiet forbearance, in dignified silence. During the war they mustered enormous strength to swallow white prejudices, weather the ravages of the internment, and, above all, shelter the young as much as possible from physical and psychological harm. To the dominant culture their silence suggested passivity and weakness, and encouraged open season on them. Kogawa capsulates these divergent perceptions of silence in two successive images from nature: "We are the silences that speak from stone.... We disappear into the future undemanding as dew." Stone connotes sturdiness, endurance, and impregnability; dew, by contrast, suggests fragility, evanescence, and vulnerability. Placed side by side, the two figures for silence reveal the complex attitude of the Japanese-Canadian narrator. She acknowledges the physical and inner strength of the issei: their sturdiness is a requisite to survival in taxing environments such as the ghost town of Slocan and the beet farm of Alberta. The silence exemplified by Uncle and Obasan attests at once to their strength of endurance and their power to forgive. At the same time, the narrator knows all too well that their magnanimity—redoubled by their Christian belief in turning the other cheek—lends itself to exploitation by the dominant culture. Like dew, they can become "wiped out."

Kogawa does not allow the negative implications of silence to engulf its positive manifestations, of which the most disarming is attentive silence. Fujita notes that attendance is instilled in Naomi since infancy, through the very decor of her prewar home: "Above my bed with the powdery blue patchwork quilt is a picture of a little girl with a book in her lap, looking up into a tree where a bird sits. One of the child's hands is half raised as she watches and listens, attending the bird." The girl's heedfulness is significantly inseparable from her thoughtfulness and poised hand. Far from suggesting passivity, this form of silence entails both mental vigilance and physical readiness. Complementing the visual aids are the actual examples set by Grandma, Mother, and Obasan. They supply positive reinforcement for Naomi. Their "alert and accurate knowing" has left a lasting impression on her:

> When I am hungry, and before I can ask, there is food. If I am weary, every place is a bed.... A sweater covers me before there is any chill and if there is pain there is care simultaneously. If Grandma shifts uncomfortably, I bring her a cushion.

> "Yoku ki ga tsuku ne," Grandma responds. It is a statement in appreciation of sensitivity and appropriate gestures.

There is neither explicit request nor open inquiry. At the point when her grandparents have been taken to the hospital and Obasan offers unspoken yet palpable solace, Naomi registers: "We must always honour the wishes of others before our own.... To try to meet one's own needs in spite of the wishes of others is to be 'wagamama'—selfish and inconsiderate. Obasan teaches me not to be wagamama by always heeding everyone's needs. That is why she is waiting patiently beside me at the bridge."

These instances trace attentive silence to a maternal tradition in Japanese culture. Naomi has learned it from Grandma, Mother, and her surrogate mother Obasan, all of whom have been raised in Japan. Yet it is also to be directed beyond one's kin, as is evident from what occurs on the train that takes Obasan and the children from British Columbia to Slocan. A young woman has given birth just before boarding, but she does not have a single baby item with her. Obasan quietly places in front of her a bundle that contains a towel and some fruit. Her kindness inspires another old woman to follow suit. Little Naomi, taking stock of these generous acts, is herself moved to charity: she notices her brother's unhappiness and slips a present (her favorite ball) into his pocket.

Grandma and Mother disappear from Naomi's life early on. The extant person, in whom the woe and wonder of silence converge, influencing Naomi into adulthood, is Obasan. Kogawa has set her name as the title of the book because Obasan "is totally silent." "If we never really see Obasan," the author has stated, "she will always be oppressed" [Wayne, *RIKKA*, 1981]. Kogawa realizes that Obasan's quiet fortitude makes her an easy target of subjugation, and she appeals openly to the reader to see Obasan and to hear "the silence that cannot speak" (epigraph). But she does not enjoin Obasan to emulate Emily. As readers, we must be wary of adopting the attitude of Stephen, who scorns Obasan's Japanese ways; or that of the chilling Mrs. Barker, whose "glance at Obasan is one of condescension." Or we may be guilty of the very blindness that the author attempts to cure. Dismissing Obasan as a victim would legitimize her victimization....

The narrator herself, unlike Stephen and Mrs. Barker, never regards Obasan arrogantly. She does not view her through Eurocentric or even revisionist eyes: "Obasan ... does not come from this clamourous climate. She does not dance to the multi-cultural piper's tune or respond to the racist's slur. She remains in a silent territory, defined by her serving hands." In portraying her aunt she pointedly departs from the view of silence as absence or as impotence. She divines unspoken meanings beneath Obasan's reticence and wishes to enter "the vault of her thoughts." She textualizes the inaudible: "The language of her grief is silence. She has learned it well, its idioms, its nuances. Over the years, silence within her small body has grown large and powerful." The quietest character in the novel, Obasan is also the most attentive. (She performs what Wordsworth in "Tintern Abbey" eulogizes as those "little, nameless, unremembered acts of kindness and of love.") One marked achievement of this novel is the finesse by which the author renders a wordless figure into an unforgettable character.

The destructive and enabling aspects of silence are recapitulated together in the climax of the novel. Naomi finally learns (from her grandma's letters) about her mother's disfigurement. Bewildered, she at first can only deplore her mother's protective silence: "Gentle Mother, we were lost together in our silences. Our wordlessness was our mutual destruction." Yet almost in the same breath that remonstrates against protective silence the narrator is invoking attendance which, as Fujita observes, "supports Naomi in her moment of greatest need." The act ushers in the process of healing: "Gradually the room grows still and it is as if I am back with Uncle again, listening and listening to the silent earth and the silent sky as I have done all my life…. Mother. I am listening. Assist me to hear you."

In this receptive state she hears "the sigh of … remembered breath, a wordless word." She is able to conjure up her mother's presence, and empathy restores the original bond: "Young Mother at Nagasaki, am I not also there?" The communion continues:

> I am thinking that for a child there is no presence without flesh. But perhaps it is because I am no longer a child I can know your presence though you are not here. The letters tonight are skeletons. Bones only. But the earth still stirs with dormant blooms. Love flows through the roots of the trees by our graves.

Naomi breathes life into the verbal knowledge transmitted by the letters ("bones only") by means of a nonverbal mode of apprehension. Her ability to grasp an absent presence through imaginative empathy is fostered by her sedulous heedfulness. She finally discovers the key to the cryptic epigraph: "To attend its voice, I can hear it say, is to embrace its absence."

Source: King-Kok Cheung, "Attentive Silence: *Obasan*," in her *Articulate Silences: Hisaye Yamamoto, Maxine Hong Kingston, Joy Kogawa,* Cornell University Press, 1994, pp. 126–167.

Edward M. White

White is an American educator and critic. In the following positive review, he praises Kogawa's depictions of suffering, injustice, and survival within the context of specific historical events in Obasan.

"Nisei," we learn from this extraordinary first novel, [*Obasan*], means "second generation," embracing the children of the Canadian and American first-generation immigrants from Japan. Everyone by now knows that the internment and theft of property suffered by Americans of Japanese descent during World War II represents a national disgrace second only to the massacres of Native Americans. It is a small comfort to realize that Canadian Nisei were treated at least as badly as the Americans, but the distance created by the Canadian setting perhaps will help make the pain this novel evokes more bearable for U.S. readers.

Joy Kogawa, a Canadian teacher and poet, has drawn upon her own experience as a displaced Canadian Nisei to write a unified story of a battered and broken family that endures under the worst conditions. The systematic outrages inflicted by the Canadian government on its own citizens echo the Nazi treatment of the Jews; the novel, in turn, shares some of the tone of *The Diary of Anne Frank* in its purity of vision under the stress of social outrage. This novel too has a magical ability to convey suffering and privation, inhumanity and racial prejudice, without losing in any way joy in life and in the poetic imagination.

The narrator is Naomi Nakane, now a 36-year-old teacher: "Marital status: Old maid. Health: Fine, I suppose…. Personality: Tense. Is that past or present tense? It's perpetual tense." Like her author, Naomi was torn at the age of 5 from a warm and loving family inside a secure Japanese–Canadian culture in Vancouver, British Columbia. Her mother is stranded in Japan, finally to encounter an atomic bomb, and her physician father's fragile health fails before the hardships of dispersal and brutal labor.

Naomi and her resentful brother Stephen (a musical prodigy) depend on their aunt, "Obasan," whose silence and strength form the solid center of the novel. The death of their uncle draws the family together, and draws Naomi's past into perspective as she reviews documents that expand her imperfect understanding of what has happened to her and her family. These documents include not only the diaries and notes collected by her irrepressible

Aunt Emily, but a series of chilling nonfictional official papers and newspaper accounts.

Part of the strength of this novel is in its historical particularity, but another part is in its larger resonance: This is also an account of human barbarity wherever it occurs. This motif is made explicit early on in a description of Obasan:

> Squatting here with the putty knife in her hand, she is every old woman in every hamlet in the world. You see her on a street corner in southern France, in a black dress and black stockings. Or bent over stone steps in a Mexican mountain village. Everywhere the old woman stands as the true and rightful owner of the earth. She is the bearer of keys to unknown doorways and to a network of astonishing tunnels. She is the possessor of life's infinite personal details.

"Now old," Obasan repeats; "everything old." The rhythms of the prose, when under extreme pressure, expand into Biblical patterns:

> We are leaving the B.C. coast—rain, cloud, mist—an air overladen with weeping. Behind us lies a salty sea within which swim our drowning specks of memory—our small waterlogged eulogies. We are going down to the middle of the earth with pick-axe eyes, tunneling by train to the Interior, carried along by the momentum of the expulsion into the waiting wilderness.... We are the silences that speak from stone. We are the despised rendered voiceless, stripped of car, radio, camera and every means of communication, a trainload of eyes covered with mud and spittle. We are the man in the Gospel of John, born into the world for the sake of the light.

The poetry remains quiet behind the prose, even as the universal theme radiates from the strong and driving plot. The story keeps unfolding, until its full sadness is complete. The next-to-last word is Nakane's:

> This body of grief is not fit for human habitation. Let there be flesh. The song of mourning is not a life-long song.... The wild roses and the tiny wild flowers grow along the trickling stream. The perfume in the air is sweet and faint. If I hold my head a certain way, I can smell them from where I am.

The last word in the book is from the memorandum sent by the Co-operative Committee on Japanese Canadians to the House and the Senate of Canada in April, 1946. It points out that the orders-in-council for the deportation of Canadians of Japanese racial origin are "wrong and indefensible" and "are an adoption of the methods of Nazism." This protest was ignored by the government and by the world at large.

Kogawa's novel must be heard and admired; the art itself can claim the real last word, exposing the viciousness of the racist horror, embodying the beauty that somehow, wonderfully, survives.

Source: Edward M. White, "The Silences That Speak from Stone," in *Los Angeles Times Book Review,* July 11, 1982, p. 3.

Sources

King-Kok Cheung, "Attentive Silence in Joy Kogawa's *Obasan,*" in *Listening to Silences: New Essays in Feminist Criticism,* edited by Elaine Hedges and Shelley F. Fishkin, Oxford University Press, 1994, pp. 113-29.

Gayle K. Fujita, "'To Attend the Sound of Stone': The Sensibility of Silence in *Obasan,*" in *Melus,* Vol. 12, No. 3, pp. 33-42.

Erika Gottlieb, "Silence into Sound: The Riddle of Concentric Worlds in *Obasan,*" in *Canadian Literature,* No. 109, Summer 1986, pp. 34-53.

Mason Harris, "Broken Generations in *Obasan,*" in *Canadian Literature,* No. 127, Winter, 1990, pp. 41-57.

Suanne Kelman, "Impossible to Forgive," in *The Canadian Forum,* Vol. LXI, No. 715, February, 1982, pp. 39-40.

Robin Potter, "Moral—in Whose Sense?: Joy Kogawa's *Obasan* and Julia Kristeva's *Powers of Horror,*" in *Studies in Canadian Literature,* 1990.

Karin Quimby, "'This is my own, my native land': Constructions of Identity and Landscape in Joy Kogawa's *Obasan,*" in *Cross-Addressing: Resistance Literature and Cultural Borders,* edited by John C. Hawley, State University of New York Press, 1996, pp. 257-73.

Marilyn Russell Rose, "Politics into Art: Kogawa's 'Obasan' and the Rhetoric of Fiction," in *Mosaic: A Journal for the Interdisciplinary Study of Literature,* Vol. XXI, Nos. 2-3, Spring 1988, pp. 215-26.

Eleanor Ty, "Struggling with the Powerful (M)Other: Identity and Sexuality in Kogawa's *Obasan* and Kincaid's *Lucy,*" in *The International Fiction Review,* Vol. 20, No. 2, 1993, pp. 120-26.

Teruyo Ueki, "*Obasan:* Revelations in a Paradoxical Scheme," in *Melus,* Vol. 18, No. 4, Winter, 1993, pp. 5-20.

Edward M. White, "The Silences that Speak from Stone," in *Los Angeles Times Book Review,* July 11, 1982, p. 3.

Gary Willis, "Speaking the Silence: Joy Kogawa's *Obasan,*" in *Studies in Canadian Literature,* Vol. 12, No. 2, 1987, pp. 239-49.

For Further Study

Cheng Lok Chua, "Witnessing the Japanese Canadian Experience in World War II: Processual Structure, Symbolism, and Irony in Joy Kogawa's *Obasan,*" in *Reading the Literatures of Asian America,* edited by Shirley Geok-lin Lim and Amy Ling, Temple University Press, 1992, pp. 97-108.
   This essay highlights the ritual structure and the "ironic narrative mode" of Kogawa's novel. Chua

also contends that *Obasan* "puts an ironic question to the Christian ethics professed by Canada's majority culture."

Andrew Garrod, interview with Joy Kogawa, in *Speaking for Myself: Canadian Writers in Interview,* Breakwater (St. Johns, Newfoundland), 1986, pp. 139-53.
> A lengthy interview in which Kogawa speaks revealingly about her childhood, her theological and political convictions, and her writing, especially her writing of *Obasan.*

Gurleen Grewal, "Memory and the Matrix of History: The Poetics of Loss and Recovery in Joy Kogawa's *Obasan* and Toni Morrison's *Beloved,*" in *Memory and Cultural Politics: New Approaches to American Ethnic Literatures,* edited by Amritjit Singh, Joseph T. Skerrett, Jr., and Robert E. Hogan, Northeastern University Press, 1996, pp. 140-74.
> This essay draws useful comparisons between *Obasan* and Toni Morrison's *Beloved* as novels that "enact the process of loss and recovery" through "ceremonial performances of memory."

Rachelle Kanefsky, "Debunking a Postmodern Conception of History: A Defence of Humanist Values in the Novels of Joy Kogawa," in *Canadian Literature,* Vol. 148, Spring, 1996, pp. 11-36.
> In her "defence" of a humanist vision in Kogawa's novels, Kanefsky poses a direct challenge to critics who interpret those novels in terms of postmodern views of history and language. Kanefsky contends that both Kogawa and her protagonist finally support a humanist conviction that "What's right is right. What's wrong is wrong."

Joy Kogawa, "Is There a Just Cause?," in *Canadian Forum,* March, 1984, pp. 20-24.
> In this compelling editorial, Kogawa writes of her own involvement in and understanding of social activism, affirming "the paradoxical power in mutual vulnerability" and arguing that "our wholeness comes from joining and from sharing our brokenness."

Joy Kogawa, "What Do I Remember of the Evacuation," in *Chicago Review,* Vol. 42, No. 3-4, 1996, pp. 152-53.
> This poem, originally published in 1973, offers an intriguing glimpse at Kogawa's reflections about the evacuation several years before she wrote *Obasan.* Like the later novel, this poem draws its expressive force from an ironic juxtaposition of "adult" realities and childhood perceptions.

Maryka Omatsu, *Bittersweet Passage: Redress and the Japanese Canadian Experience,* Between the Lines, n.d.
> Records the struggle of Japanese Canadians to obtain redress from the Canadian government.

Edward Said, *Orientalism,* Random House, 1979.
> Said details the history of the way in which the Western powers view eastern or oriental people. In other words, it is a history of stereotypes and the attitudes enabling policies like internment.

Ann Gomer Sunahara, *The Politics of Racism: The Uprooting of Japanese-Canadians During the Second World War,* Lorimer, 1981.
> A detailed work on the event of Canadian internment. It is a work that Aunt Emily would appreciate for its careful documentation.

Sau-ling Cynthia Wong, *Reading Asian American Literature: From Necessity to Extravagance,* Princeton University Press, 1993.
> Wong offers compelling "intratextual" and "intertextual" readings of *Obasan* in this study of Asian American literature, focusing in particular on Kogawa's use of the "stone bread" image and her "obsession with mobility" in the novel.

Mitsuye Yamada, "Experiential Approaches to Teaching Joy Kogawa's *Obasan,*" in *Teaching American Ethnic Literatures: Nineteen Essays,* edited by John R. Maitino and David R. Peck, University of New Mexico Press, 1996, pp. 293-311.
> Though primarily intended for teachers, this essay presents a useful model for reading Kogawa's novel through three different frames: "the aesthetic, the historical, and the experiential."

A Passage to India

E. M. Forster
1924

A Passage to India, published in 1924, was E. M. Forster's first novel in fourteen years, and the last novel he wrote. Subtle and rich in symbolism, the novel works on several levels. On the surface, it is about India—which at the time was a colonial possession of Britain—and about the relations between British and Indian people in that country. It is also about the necessity of friendship, and about the difficulty of establishing friendship across cultural boundaries. On a more symbolic level, the novel also addresses questions of faith (both religious faith and faith in social conventions). Forster's narrative centers on Dr. Aziz, a young Indian physician whose attempt to establish friendships with several British characters has disastrous consequences. In the course of the novel, Dr. Aziz is accused of attempting to rape a young Englishwoman. Aziz's friend Mr. Fielding, a British teacher, helps to defend Aziz. Although the charges against Aziz are dropped during his trial, the gulf between the British and native Indians grows wider than ever, and the novel ends on an ambiguous note. When *A Passage to India* appeared in 1924, it was praised by reviewers in a number of important British and American literary journals. Despite some criticism that Forster had depicted the British unfairly, the book was popular with readers in both Britain and the United States. The year after its publication, the novel received two prestigious literary awards—the James Tait Black Memorial Prize and the Prix Femina Vie Heureuse. More than seventy years later, it remains highly regarded. Not only do many schol-

ars, critics, and other writers consider it a classic of early twentieth-century fiction, but in a survey of readers conducted by Waterstone's Bookstore and Channel 4 television in Britain at the end of 1996, it was voted as one of the "100 Greatest Books of the Century."

Author Biography

When Edward Morgan Forster completed *A Passage to India,* he was in his mid-forties and was already a respected and relatively successful novelist. Between 1905 and 1910 he had published four well-crafted Edwardian novels of upper-middle class life and manners: *Where Angels Fear to Tread* (1905), *The Longest Journey* (1907), *A Room With a View* (1908), and *Howards End* (1910). However, although he had continued to write short stories as well as another novel, *Maurice* (published in 1971, after Forster's death), he published little in the decade after *Howards End.*

Born in London on January 1, 1879, E. M. Forster was an only child. His father, an architect, died when Forster was only a year old. The boy was raised by his mother, grandmother, and his father's aunt, who left Forster the sum of 8,000 pounds in her will. This large amount of money eventually paid for Forster's education and his early travels. Early in the new twentieth century it also enabled him to live independently while he established his career as a writer.

Forster grew up in the English countryside north of London, where he had a happy early childhood. He attended an Eastbourne preparatory school and then the family moved to Kent so that he could attend Tonbridge School (a traditional English public school), where he was miserable. However, he found happiness and intellectual stimulation when he went to Cambridge University. There, at King's College, he studied the classics and joined a student intellectual society known as the Apostles. Among his teachers was the philosopher G. E. Moore, who had an important influence on Forster's views. He made many friends and acquaintances, some of whom went on to become important writers and eventually became active in the Bloomsbury Group.

After graduating from Cambridge, Forster traveled in Italy and Greece. These experiences further broadened his outlook, and he decided to become a writer. He became an instructor at London's

E. M. Forster

Working Men's College in 1902 and remained with them for two decades.

In 1906, while living with his mother in the town of Weybridge, near London, Forster tutored an Indian student named Syed Ross Masood. The two developed a close friendship, and Forster became curious about India. In 1912 Forster visited India for the first time, with some friends from Cambridge University, and spent some time with Masood there. He stayed in India for six months and saw the town of Bankipore, located on the Ganges River in northeast India. Bankipore became the model for Chandrapore. Forster also saw the nearby Barabar Caves, which gave him the idea for the Marabar Caves. While in India he wrote first drafts of seven chapters of a new novel that would become *A Passage to India.* However, after returning to England he put the work aside and instead wrote *Maurice,* a novel about a homosexual love affair. Because its theme was considered very controversial at the time, Forster decided not to publish this book during his lifetime.

During World War I, Forster worked as a Red Cross volunteer in Alexandria, Egypt. In 1921 he made a second visit to India, where he spent six months as private secretary to the Maharajah of Dewas Senior, an independent Moslem state. He gathered more material about India, and after returning to England he finished writing *A Passage to India,* which he dedicated to Masood. Forster found the writing process difficult and feared that the book would be a failure. He was relieved by the book's favorable reception, and in the remaining forty-five years of his life he received many awards and honors. Although he continued to write short stories, essays, and radio programs, he turned away from the novel form.

Forster died of a stroke on June 7, 1970, in Coventry, England. Today, his literary reputation remains high, and all of his novels, except *The Longest Journey,* have been adapted into films.

Plot Summary

Part I—Mosque

Set in India several decades before the end of British Rule, *A Passage to India* by E. M. Forster explores the relationships that ensue when Dr. Aziz, an Indian doctor, is befriended by Mrs. Moore and Miss Adela Quested, two recently arrived Englishwomen. In the opening scene, Dr. Aziz is involved in a discussion about whether or not it is possible for an Indian to be friends with an Englishman. The conversation is interrupted by a message from the Civil Surgeon, Major Callendar, who requests Dr. Aziz's immediate assistance. Aziz makes his way to Callendar's compound but arrives only to be told that the Civil Surgeon is out. On his way back home, Aziz stops in a mosque to rest and meets Mrs. Moore. He is delighted by her kind behavior and accompanies her back to the Chandrapore Club. Mrs. Moore's son, City Magistrate Ronny Heaslop, quickly learns of his mother's meeting with the Indian doctor. He instructs her not to mention the incident to his fiancee, Miss Quested, because he does not want her wondering whether the "natives" are treated properly "and all that sort of nonsense."

Meanwhile, Adela, who travelled all the way from England to decide whether or not she will marry Ronny, expresses her desire "to see the real India." The Collector, Mr. Turton, makes plans to throw a Bridge Party—a party to bridge the gulf between East and West. But the event is not a great success and Adela thinks her countrymen mad for inviting guests and then not receiving them amiably. One of the few officials who does make a genuine effort to make the party work is Mr. Fielding, the Principal of the Government College. He hosts a gathering of his own a couple of days later, and it is then that Dr. Aziz first meets Adela and

invites her and Mrs. Moore to visit the nearby Marabar Caves. It is also on this afternoon that a friendship begins to develop between Aziz and Fielding.

Part II—Caves

The day of the visit to the Marabar Caves arrives and, except for the absence of Fielding and his assistant, Professor Godbole, who miss the early morning train, the expedition begins successfully. An elephant transports the party into the hills and a picnic breakfast awaits Aziz's guests when they reach their goal near the caves. However, things begin to change when they visit the first cave. Mrs. Moore nearly faints when she feels herself crammed in the dark and loses sight of Adela and Dr. Aziz. She feels something strike her face and hears a terrifying echo:

> The echo in a Marabar cave is … entirely devoid of distinction. Whatever is said, the same monotonous noise replies, and quivers up and down the walls until it is absorbed into the roof. 'Boum' is the sound as far as the human alphabet can express it, or 'bou-oum', or 'ou-boum,'—utterly dull. Hope, politeness, the blowing of a nose, the squeak of a boot, all produce 'boum'…. Coming at a moment when [Mrs. Moore] chanced to be fatigued, it had managed to murmur: 'Pathos, piety, courage—they exist, but are identical, and so is filth. Everything exists, nothing has value.' If one had spoken vileness in that place, or quoted lofty poetry, the comment would have been the same—'ou-boum.'

The echo lingers in Mrs. Moore's mind and begins "in some indescribable way to undermine her hold on life." She suddenly realizes that she no longer wants to communicate with her children, Aziz, God, or anyone else and sinks into a state of apathy and cynicism.

Meanwhile, Aziz and Adela are en route to visit more of the caves. Preoccupied by thoughts of her marriage and by the disturbing realization that she and Ronny do not love each other, Adela inadvertently offends her host by asking an ill-thought question. Aziz is momentarily annoyed and slips into one of the caves "to recover his balance." Adela loses sight of him and also enters one of the caves. When Aziz reappears, he catches a glimpse of Adela running down the hill towards an approaching car. Thinking that she has merely gone off to meet Ronny, Aziz returns to the camp and learns that Adela has unexpectedly driven away. The remaining members of the expedition take the train back to Chandrapore. Upon their return, Dr. Aziz is arrested and charged with making insulting advances to Miss Quested in the Marabar Caves.

That evening, there is a meeting at the Club and Fielding stands alone against his countrymen by stating his belief that Aziz is innocent. Adela remains ill for several days, hovering "between common sense and hysteria" and, like Mrs. Moore, is plagued by the sound of the echo. She begins to have doubts about what happened in the cave and eventually tells Ronny that she may have made a mistake. Mrs. Moore supports Adela's belief that Aziz is innocent but Ronny insists that the trial must proceed and sends his mother back to England. When Adela takes the stand, she feels herself returned to the Marabar Hills and finds the exact reply to all the questions put to her. However, she is unable to say for sure whether Aziz followed her into the cave; she could see herself in one of the caves, but could not locate Aziz. Finally she tells the court that she has made a mistake and that Dr. Aziz never followed her into the cave. The Superintendent withdraws the charges and Aziz is released "without one stain on his character."

After the trial, Adela receives the news of Mrs. Moore's death at sea and can no longer bear Ronny's company. He eventually breaks off their engagement because marrying her would now ruin his career. Before her voyage back to England, Adela is subjected to one final adventure when her servant, Antony, attempts to blackmail her by claiming she was Fielding's mistress. By this time, Fielding, who believes that Adela should not suffer for her mistake, has managed to convince Aziz to renounce his right to monetary compensation. Aziz begins to regret that decision when he hears the "naughty rumour" concerning his two friends. The misunderstanding is complicated when Aziz learns that Fielding is also returning to England. Aziz suspects that his friend intends to marry Adela for her money and leaves Chandrapore before Fielding can explain or say good-bye.

Part III—Temple

Two years later, Dr. Aziz and Professor Godbole are both living in Mau, a town several hundred miles west of the Marabar Hills and which is currently in the midst of Hindu religious celebrations. Dr. Aziz has learned that Fielding, along with his wife and brother-in-law, will soon be stopping in Mau on business. Fielding had sent his old friend a letter explaining all the details about his wedding to Stella Moore, Mrs. Moore's daughter, but Aziz never read it. As a result, he still thinks that Fielding has married Adela. All misunderstandings are finally cleared up when they meet, but Aziz does not care who Fielding has married; his heart is now

with his own people and he wishes no Englishman or Englishwoman to be his friend.

Later that day, Fielding and his wife borrow a boat in order to watch the religious procession. Aziz runs into Ralph Moore and brings him out on the water too, thereby repeating the gesture of hospitality he had intended to make through the visit to the Marabar Caves two years earlier. At the height of the ceremony, the two boats collide and all are thrown into the water. The accident erases all bitterness between Fielding and Aziz and the two go back "laughingly to their old relationship." A few days later, they go for a ride in the Mau jungles and Aziz gives Fielding a letter for Miss Quested in which he thanks her for her fine behavior two years back. They talk about politics and Aziz foresees the day when India shall finally get rid of the English. Then, Aziz tells Fielding, "you and I shall be friends."

Characters

Mahmoud Ali

A close friend of Dr. Aziz. A Moslem and a lawyer, he is often in the company of Aziz and Hamidullah. In Chapter II, Mahmoud Ali declares that it is not possible for Indians to be friends with the English; Hamidullah argues that such friendship is possible. Mahmoud Ali is generally cynical, and he often makes sharp comments about other characters. He helps to defend Aziz at Aziz's trial.

Mr. Amritrao

A famous Hindu barrister (trial lawyer) from Calcutta who is hired to defend Dr. Aziz at his trial. Mr. Amritrao, reputed to be one of the finest Indian lawyers in the country, has made his name as a radical who is "notoriously anti-British." His hiring causes some controversy, and the move is regarded as a political challenge to the British. During the trial, Amritrao objects to the fact that Adela's British supporters have been allowed to sit on a platform at the front of the courtroom, and they are forced to move.

Dr. Aziz

A young doctor who is the central Indian character in the novel. Dr. Aziz is a Moslem and a widower. His three children live with his wife's mother. He is described as "an athletic little man, daintily put together but really very strong." He works at the government hospital in Chandrapore, under the supervision of Major Callendar. In addition to his practical skill as a doctor, he also has a romantic side and writes poetry. His favorite poetic themes are "the decay of Islam and the brevity of Love." Although he is thoroughly Indian, he idealizes the cultures of Persia and Arabia, where the Islamic faith originated. He regards the historical Mogul emperors of India as his models. In the early part of the novel he is disdainful of Hindus; although they are Indians, he considers them foreign. Because of his good education and respected professional situation, Aziz believes that he can be accepted by the British as almost their equal. Despite a melancholy streak, Aziz possesses a sense of humor, and hospitality is important to him. He is eager to please and impress people whom he considers kind and thoughtful, and early in the novel he especially wants to make friends with Mrs. Moore and Mr. Fielding. However, his very goodwill and his somewhat impulsive nature get him into situations that cause him trouble. ("Aziz overrated hospitality, mistaking it for intimacy, and not seeing that it is tainted with the sense of possession.") He at first wants to invite Mrs. Moore and Fielding to his house, but then realizes that this is not a suitable place for entertaining Western guests. On the spur of the moment, he asks Mrs. Moore, Fielding, and Adela Quested to join him for a picnic at the Marabar Caves, a famous natural landmark outside the town. The picnic results in disaster, however, when Adela believes that Aziz has attacked her in one of the caves. He is brought to trial in Chandrapore. Although Adela drops the charges during the trial and Aziz is freed, his reputation is ruined. He becomes completely disillusioned with his position in life and develops a hatred of the British. In Part III of the novel, he has moved to the Hindu state of Mau and given up his medical ambitions; instead, he is content to be a simple "medicine man" to the state's ailing ruler. At the end of the book he is reconciled with his British friend Fielding but tells him that they can only be true friends after the British have left India.

Nawab Bahadur

A distinguished Moslem who is a leading figure in the Indian community in the Chandrapore district. ("Nawab" is an honorary title.) The Nawab Bahadur is an older man, "a big proprietor and a philanthropist, a man of benevolence and decision." A supporter of British rule in India, he is also known for his hospitality and loyalty to his friends. Ronny Heaslop and Adela Quested are riding in the Nawab's car when it runs off the road. Following

Media Adaptations

- *A Passage to India* was adapted as a film by David Lean, starring Judy Davis, Victor Banerjee, Peggy Ashcroft, James Fox, and Alec Guinness, Columbia, 1984. It was nominated for eleven Academy Awards, including Best Picture; Ashcroft was named Best Supporting Actress for her portrayal of Mrs. Moore. Available from Columbia Tristar Home Video.

- *A Passage to India* was adapted for the stage by Santha Rama Ran, produced in London, 1960, produced on Broadway, 1962; adapted for television by John Maynard, BBC-TV, 1968.

the incident at the Marabar Caves, the Nawab proclaims Dr. Aziz's innocence and attends his trial. After the trial he renounces his title and is known simply by his original name, Mr. Zulfiqar. A victory banquet is held at his mansion, where Aziz, Fielding, and Hamidullah lie on the roof and discuss the trial and its consequences.

Major Callendar

The head of the government hospital in Chandrapore and a figure of some authority in the Anglo-Indian (British) community. Major Callendar holds the post of civil surgeon and is Dr. Aziz's immediate superior at the hospital. The most arrogant of the British officials in Chandrapore, he is "dour," gruff, and plain-spoken to the point of offensiveness. In Chapter II he summons Dr. Aziz to his bungalow, interrupting Aziz's pleasant evening with his friends. When Aziz arrives after a short delay, a servant informs him that Callendar is not at home and has not left a message. After Aziz's aborted trial, Callendar makes some intemperate remarks about Indians at the club, where the members of the Anglo-Indian community have gathered. We later learn that Callendar has been replaced as civil surgeon by a Major Roberts.

Collector

See Mr. Turton

Still from the 1984 movie A Passage to India, *starring Judy Davis and Nigel Havers.*

Mr. Das

The assistant magistrate (judge) in Chandrapore and thus the assistant to Ronny Heaslop, the magistrate. Das, a Hindu, presides over the trial of Dr. Aziz. (Ronny has excused himself from sitting on the case because of his relationship with Adela Quested, who has brought the charges against Aziz.) Ronny expresses confidence in Das's ability to conduct an orderly trial, but Major Callendar declares that Das is not trustworthy because he is an Indian. Das follows correct procedures in the trial and does not show favoritism toward either the prosecution or the defense. After the trial Das visits Dr. Aziz for medical treatment and also requests a poem from Aziz for his brother-in-law's magazine. Das's friendly visit represents a new spirit of cooperation between the Moslem and Hindu communities.

Miss Nancy Derek

An unconventional Englishwoman. Young and single, Miss Derek is regarded with some distrust by the British community at Chandrapore because of her unorthodox behavior. She is not part of the civil station at Chandrapore, but serves as a personal assistant to the Maharani of Mudkul, an independent Indian state. When Adela Quested and Ronny Heaslop are in a minor car accident, Miss

Derek comes along and drives them back to Chandrapore. She again shows up in her car near the Marabar Caves as Adela is running from the caves and drives Adela back to Chandrapore. After Dr. Aziz's trial, Aziz and Fielding discuss a rumor that Miss Derek is having an affair with Mr. McBryde, the Superintendent of Police.

Mr. Cyril Fielding

The principal of the Government College (that is, a British-run school) in Chandrapore. Fielding develops a close friendship with Dr. Aziz during the course of the novel and is the only Englishman to publicly express his belief in Aziz's innocence. In contrast to such Anglo-Indian (British) career administrators as Mr. Turton and Major Callendar, Fielding arrived in India relatively late in his life—after the age of forty. By the time he arrives in India, he has already had a "varied career." He is described as "a hard-bitten, good-tempered, intelligent fellow on the verge of middle age, with a belief in education." Because of his more easy-going and broadminded attitudes, he is regarded with some suspicion by his fellow expatriates, especially the women. Indeed, he has no particular enthusiasm for the conventional social life of Chandrapore's Anglo-Indian community, and thus "the gulf between himself and his countrymen ...

widened distressingly." Moreover, he has "no racial feeling"—he regards Indians simply as people from another country, not as inferiors. He believes that people from different parts of the world can understand one another "by the help of good will plus culture and intelligence." He is "happiest in the give-and-take of private conversation." This emphasis on the importance of friendship and the personal over the professional life makes Fielding a representative of Forster's own views. In Chapter VII, Fielding gives a tea party attended by Aziz, Mrs. Moore, Adela Quested, and Professor Godbole (who teaches at the college). The party is a success, bringing together Christian, Moslem, and Hindu as equals. However, the party sets in motion the disastrous events of the excursion to the Marabar Caves. Fielding is supposed to travel to the caves with Aziz and the English women, but he misses the train. When Adela returns to Chandrapore with Miss Derek and claims that Aziz has attempted to rape her, Fielding goes to see Inspector McBryde. Fielding tells McBryde that there has been some misunderstanding and that Aziz is innocent, but McBryde becomes angry at Fielding's interference. Because he supports Aziz and insults Ronny Heaslop, Fielding is forced to resign from the English club in Chandrapore. Adela stays with Fielding after the trial. Fielding has a long conversation with Aziz at the post-trial victory party at the Nawab Bahadur's house, but their friendship cools. Fielding soon returns to England, and Aziz believes that he has married Adela. The friendship is revived somewhat when Fielding eventually returns to India with his new wife, Stella, the daughter of Mrs. Moore. However, Aziz tells Fielding that they cannot be true friends until the British have left India, and the novel concludes on this ambiguous note.

Narayan Godbole

See Professor Godbole

Professor Godbole

An Indian who teaches at the college in Chandrapore, where Mr. Fielding is the principal. He is a friend of Dr. Aziz. Godbole is a Hindu (of the Brahmin caste, the highest caste in the Hindu religion) and remains somewhat aloof. Godbole is supposed to take part in the trip to the Marabar Caves organized by Aziz. However, he and Fielding miss the train on which Aziz, Mrs. Moore, and Adela Quested are traveling because Godbole takes too much time saying his prayers before leaving for the station. In the third part of the novel, "Temple,"

Professor Godbole has moved to the Hindu state of Mau, where he is Minister of Education in the local government. Godbole is the central symbolic figure in this part of the book, representing the Hindu philosophy of acceptance. Ironically, he may also be more representative of the "real" India than is Aziz. He takes part in the ceremony held to celebrate the rebirth of the Hindu god Krishna.

Hamidullah

A Moslem Indian who is a good friend of Dr. Aziz. He was educated at Cambridge University in England and is "the leading barrister [trial lawyer] of Chandrapore." In chapter two, Hamidullah, Aziz, and Mahmoud Ali discuss whether it is possible for an Indian to be friends with the British. Hamidullah recounts his own experience in England some years earlier. He had been welcomed into the home of an English couple, whom he recalls with great affection. Hamidullah helps to organize Dr. Aziz's defense after Aziz is charged with having assaulted Adela Quested in the Marabar Caves.

Ronny Heaslop

A young Anglo-Indian (British) civil servant who is the city magistrate of Chandrapore. He is the son of Mrs. Moore by her first husband. At the outset of the novel, Ronny is expected to marry Adela Quested, whom he had originally met in England. Educated in an English public (the equivalent of an American private) school, Ronny embodies a narrow, rigid concept of duty and represses the personal side of his life. He expresses the view that the Indians are not capable of governing themselves, and that Britain rules India for India's own good. When his mother and Adela arrive in India, they are disappointed to find that Ronny has changed. Adela perceives that "India had developed sides of his character that she had never admired," such as "self-complacency," "censoriousness," and "lack of subtlety." She also finds that "when proved wrong, he was particularly exasperating." Ronny disapproves of his mother's and Adela's attempts to see "the real India" and to mix with Indians socially. He becomes impatient with what he considers their naive attitude toward India. According to Ronny, "No one can even begin to know [India] until he has been in it twenty years." The alleged attempted rape of Adela at the Marabar Caves and her subsequent withdrawal of the charges against Aziz during the trial cause Ronny much embarrassment, and he breaks off their engagement.

Dr. Panna Lal

A colleague of Dr. Aziz at the government hospital in Chandrapore. A Hindu, he is described as "timid and elderly" and "of low extraction." Dr. Aziz regards Dr. Lal as "Major Callendar's spy," and he and his friends make Lal the butt of some humor. Dr. Lal urges Aziz to go with him to the Turton's Bridge Party, but at the last minute Aziz decides not to go. In Chapter VI, Dr. Lal meets Aziz and asks why he was not at the party; Aziz makes up the excuse that he had to go to the post office. In Chapter IX, Dr. Lal goes to Aziz's bungalow to treat him for a mild illness.

Mohammed Latif

A poor distant relation of Hamidullah. He is described as "a gentle, happy, and dishonest old man" who "had never done a stroke of work." Mohammed Latif serves Dr. Aziz as a general servant and dogsbody. He is often present in the book but never speaks unless he is spoken to. He accompanies Aziz, Mrs. Moore, and Adela Quested on their picnic to the Marabar Caves. In the last section, "Temple," he has left Chandrapore with Aziz and settled in Mau.

Mr. McBryde

The district superintendent of police in Chandrapore. McBryde formally arrests Dr. Aziz after Adela Quested reports the incident in the Marabar Caves. Forster describes McBryde as "the most reflective and best educated of the Chandrapore officials." He was born in India (in the town of Karachi, in present-day Pakistan), not in Britain, and he has "read and thought a good deal." His experiences, including an unhappy marriage, have made him cynical; but unlike Major Callendar, he is not a bully. He is personally sympathetic toward Aziz and acts against him out of his professional duty, not out of malice. McBryde gets angry at Fielding when Fielding tries to tell him that Aziz is innocent. He acts as the prosecutor at Aziz's trial. Aziz and Fielding later hear that McBryde has been having an affair with Miss Derek and is divorcing his wife.

Mrs. Moore

An Englishwoman who is a central figure in the book. She is the most sensitive and reflective of the English characters. An elderly widow, she is the mother of Ronny Heaslop, the Chandrapore city magistrate, by her first marriage. She also has another son, Ralph, and a daughter, Stella, by her second marriage. Mrs. Moore has recently arrived in India with Adela Quested, who is expected to marry Ronny. Mrs. Moore is introduced in Chapter II when she encounters Dr. Aziz in the mosque in Chandrapore. Dr. Aziz has gone into the mosque after his unsuccessful attempt to find Major Callendar and is startled when he discovers that a stranger—an Englishwoman—is also there. The two talk, and a friendship develops: Aziz is happy to have met an English person who is sympathetic toward him and India, while Mrs. Moore finds Aziz charming, intelligent, and interesting. (Adela Quested later tells Aziz that Mrs. Moore "learnt more about India in those few minutes' talk with you than in the three weeks since we landed.") Uncomfortable in what she considers the superficial company of the English expatriate community, Mrs. Moore decides that she wants to see "the real India." Her plans to visit two Indian women are unsuccessful, but she enjoys Mr. Fielding's tea party. At the tea party, Aziz invites Mrs. Moore, Adela, Fielding, and Professor Godbole to join him on an excursion to the Marabar Caves. (At the tea party Mrs. Moore also discusses "mysteries and muddles"; these words take on a special significance in the book.) In the meantime, Mrs. Moore quarrels with Ronny, who she finds has become narrow-minded during his time in India. When it becomes clear that Ronny and Adela will not marry, Mrs. Moore realizes that "My duties here are evidently finished. I don't want to see India now; now for my passage back." By the time of their visit to the caves, Mrs. Moore has lost interest in the trip. Tired by the heat, she finds the caves "a horrid, stuffy place," hits her head, and nearly faints. Moreover, she is alarmed by "a terrifying echo." When she emerges from the cave "the echo began in some indescribable way to undermine her hold on life." For her, the echo's message is "Everything exists, nothing has value." Shortly thereafter—just before Aziz's trial—she leaves India; we later learn that she has died on the voyage back to England. However, her presence continues to be felt after her death. Although Dr. Aziz's career is ruined by Adela's false charge of rape and he develops a hatred of the English, Aziz continues to think fondly of Mrs. Moore. Indeed, on his acquittal, the Indian crowd acclaims her as "Esmiss Esmoor," transforming her into a Hindu goddess. (The Indians apparently believe that she had somehow intervened to testify on Aziz's behalf, and regard her as a deity of justice.) At the end of the novel, the spirit of Mrs. Moore returns to India symbolically in the form of her daughter Stella, who has married Cyril Fielding.

Ralph Moore

The son of Mrs. Moore by her second husband. He is thus the brother of Stella and half-brother of Ronny Heaslop. Ralph is mentioned several times in the book but does not appear until near the end of the novel, when he arrives in Mau with his sister Stella and her new husband, Cyril Fielding. Dr. Aziz meets Ralph and treats his bee stings.

Stella Moore

Mrs. Moore's daughter. Stella's father was Mrs. Moore's second husband; she is thus the full sister of Ralph and the half-sister of Ronny Heaslop. Stella is mentioned by Mrs. Moore and referred to at several points in the novel. She lives in England and does not actually appear until the end of the novel, when she arrives in the Hindu native state of Mau with Ralph and with her new husband, Cyril Fielding. Dr. Aziz had mistakenly assumed that Fielding had married Adela Quested. Aziz is surprised and pleased when he learns that Stella, not Adela, is Fielding's wife. However, Aziz's attitude toward Stella is ambiguous because she is related both to Mrs. Moore, whom Aziz had admired, and to Ronny, whom he dislikes. Fielding confides that Stella "has ideas I don't share…. My wife's after something." This suggests that she has a deeper understanding of life than either Aziz or Fielding.

Miss Adela Quested

A young Englishwoman who comes to India with Mrs. Moore. She is expected to marry Mrs. Moore's son Ronny Heaslop, the Chandrapore city magistrate. Adela is a catalyst for the central dramatic events of the novel, and her behavior in these events radically affects the lives of the characters around her. Her accusation against Dr. Aziz, followed by her recantation during the trial, exposes the deep divisions between the British and Indians. On a more symbolic level, Adela may also be seen to represent most people's inability to communicate or to understand the deeper patterns and meaning of life.

Adela is described as "plain." (Because of her very plainness, Aziz is not at all attracted to her, and he is later insulted by the idea that anyone could think he would have wanted to rape her.) Although initially she is well-intentioned toward India, she does not possess Mrs. Moore's sensitivity and imagination. As a newcomer, she is somewhat naive about the nature of relations between the Anglo-Indians (British) and the Indians. Ronny expresses his disapproval of Adela's desire to see "the real India." While she is at Fielding's tea party, she offhandedly remarks that she is not planning to stay long in India. Immediately she—and the reader—realizes that unconsciously she has decided not to marry Ronny. However, she changes her mind temporarily when she and Ronny are in a minor accident in the Nawab Bahadur's car.

Adela accompanies Dr. Aziz and Mrs. Moore to the Marabar Caves. Here, while she is in one of the caves, something unexplained happens and she hurriedly runs out of the caves. Miss Derek, who happens along in her car, drives Adela back to Chandrapore, where Adela tells the authorities that Dr. Aziz had attempted to rape her. Ill and confused after her experience, Adela stays with the McBrydes before the trial. Although earlier Adela had not endeared herself to the British officials and their wives, they rally around her and denounce Aziz because she is "an English girl, fresh from England." However, when she withdraws her charge against Aziz during the trial, she in effect renounces her own people. She breaks off her engagement with Ronny and stays with Fielding for a while before leaving India and returning to England. She does not reappear after this. However, in Part III, Dr. Aziz continues to harbor bad feelings toward her. He mistakenly believes that Fielding, who has also gone back to England, has married her—a misunderstanding that is not cleared up until just before the conclusion of the novel.

Mr. Turton

An Anglo-Indian (British) government administrator in Chandrapore. He holds the post of Collector, and is a generic representative of British authority in the district. Aziz uses the phrase "your Turtons and Burtons" to refer offhandedly to all British civil servants. Turton has been in India for twenty-five years, but his comments and actions show that he really does not understand the Indians. For example, he remarks that "India does wonders for the judgment, especially in hot weather." He organizes a "Bridge Party" so that Adela Quested and Mrs. Moore can meet some Indians. Although Turton is not particularly sensitive or imaginative, he is basically a decent man.

Mrs. Turton

The wife of the Collector at Chandrapore, Mr. Turton. She is a generic *memsahib*—the wife of an Anglo-Indian (British) official. She is something of a snob. Mrs. Turton prefers to socialize with other British wives and their husbands in the tight-knit Anglo-Indian community and does not socialize with Indians except at formal events. She disapproves of Adela Quested.

Mr. Zulfiqar

See Nawab Bahadur

Themes

Culture Clash

At the heart of *A Passage to India* —and in the background—is a clash between two fundamentally different cultures, those of East and West. The British poet Rudyard Kipling, who was born in India and lived there for several years as an adult, wrote: "East is East and West is West, and never the twain shall meet." Without quoting or acknowledging Kipling, Forster adopts this premise as a central theme of *A Passage to India.*

The West is represented by the Anglo-Indians (the British administrators and their families in India) in Chandrapore. They form a relatively small but close-knit community. They live at the civil station, apart from the Indians. Their social life centers around the Chandrapore Club, where they attempt to recreate the entertainments that would be found in England. Although these Westerners wish to maintain good relations with the Easterners whom they govern, they have no desire to "understand" India or the Indians. Early in the book Ronny Heaslop remarks that "No one can even begin to think of knowing this country until he has been in it twenty years." When Adela Quested rebukes him for his attitudes, he replies that "India isn't home"—that is, it is not England.

Mrs. Moore, Adela, and Mr. Fielding are three English characters who challenge this received wisdom. Significantly, Mrs. Moore and Adela are newcomers who have no experience of India and thus are not fully aware of the gulf that separates the two cultures: "They had no race-consciousness—Mrs. Moore was too old, Miss Quested too new—and they behaved to Aziz as to any young man who had been kind to them in the country." However, Adela shows her ignorance of Indian customs when she asks Dr. Aziz how many wives he has. The Turtons throw a "Bridge Party" to "bridge the gulf between East and West," but this event only emphasizes the awkwardness that exists between the two cultures. Mrs. Moore senses that India is full of "mystery and muddle" that Westerners cannot comprehend. Following Aziz's arrest, Turton tells Fielding that in his twenty-five years in India "I have never known anything but disaster result when English people and Indians attempt to be intimate socially."

The culture clash, however, is not only between Indians and Anglo-Indians, but also between two distinct groups of Indians—Moslems and Hindus. The narrative makes it clear that these two groups have very different traditions. Dr. Aziz is proud of his Moslem heritage and considers the Hindus to be almost alien. Hindus "have no idea of society," he tells Mrs. Moore, Adela, and Fielding. At the same time, although he is quite conscious of being an Indian, Aziz has a sentimental affection for Persia, the land from which Moslem culture originally spread to India. The Moslem-Hindu divide closes somewhat when a Hindu attorney, Mr. Amritrao, is called in to defend Aziz. After the trial, Hindus and Moslems alike celebrate Aziz's acquittal. In the book's final section, Aziz is living in a Hindu state, where he regards himself as an outsider.

Friendship

E. M. Forster considered friendship to be one of the most important things in life. He once remarked, controversially, that if he were faced with the choice of betraying his country or betraying his friends, he would betray his country. *A Passage to India* explores the nature of friendship in its various forms, and the word "friend" occurs frequently throughout the book. When we first meet Dr. Aziz and his friends Hamidullah and Mahmoud Ali, they are discussing whether it is possible for Indians to be friends with the British. Hamidullah, who is pleasant and easygoing, fondly recalls his friendship with a British family long ago. When Dr. Aziz meets Mrs. Moore at the mosque, he feels she is someone with whom he can develop a friendship. He also wants to make friends with Cyril Fielding, whom he regards as a sympathetic and enlightened Englishman. However, despite his general impulsiveness, Aziz realizes that "a single meeting is too short to make a friend."

Aziz has a curious friendship with Professor Godbole. He likes Godbole but is unable to understand him. Godbole himself has a friendly attitude, but he is vague and distracted. When Fielding tells him that Aziz has been arrested, Godbole seems unconcerned. Instead, he asks Fielding for advice about what name to give to a school that he is thinking of starting. Still, Fielding acknowledges that "all [Godbole's] friends trusted him, without knowing why."

Of all the British characters in the book, Fielding has the greatest gift for friendship. Mrs. Moore feels friendliness for Aziz when she first meets him, but she loses interest in friendship—and in life itself—when she loses her faith at the Marabar Caves. Among the other British characters, a sense of duty generally takes precedence over friendship. Although he had known her in England, Ronny is unable to sustain a relationship with Adela in India. In their words and actions, Anglo-Indian officials such as Ronny, Mr. Turton, and Mr. McBryde demonstrate that while they may get along with Indians on one level, it is impossible and indeed undesirable to be friends with them.

The book concludes with a conversation between Aziz and Fielding about the possibility of friendship—the theme that had been the subject of the first conversation. Aziz tells Fielding that they cannot be friends until the English have been driven out of India. Fielding replies that he wants to be friends, and that it is also what Aziz wants. The last paragraph, however, suggests that the impersonal forces at work in India will not yet allow such a friendship.

Public vs. Private Life

The various attempts at friendship throughout *A Passage to India* are frustrated not only by cultural differences but also by the demands of public life, or duty. These demands are strongest among the Anglo-Indian officials of Chandrapore. In general, characters such as Turton, Callendar, McBryde, and Ronny put their jobs above whatever personal desires they may have. The Turtons' "Bridge Party" is more a diplomatic exercise than a truly personal gesture. McBryde, the superintendent of police, prosecutes Aziz because it is his duty to do so; personal feelings do not enter into his decision. Ronny breaks off his engagement with Adela partly because her actions in the court are seen by the Anglo-Indians as a public disgrace. His marriage to her would offend the members of his community, who disapprove of Adela because of her behavior at the trial.

Cyril Fielding, the principal of the government college, seems to be the only British character willing to act out of personal conviction rather than public duty. The Anglo-Indian authorities believe it is important to keep up a public image of unity on the question of Aziz's guilt. In speaking up for Aziz, Fielding goes against the public behavior that is expected of him and is seen as "letting down the side." Because of this transgression, he is expelled from the English club at Chandrapore.

McBryde's affair with Miss Derek, revealed later in the book, is perhaps a minor instance in

Topics for Further Study

- Research a specific aspect of life in British India in the early twentieth century. Possible aspects for study include: the British colonial administration; the legal system; the Hindu caste system; the Native States and their relation to British India; Hindu-Moslem relations; the everyday lives of Anglo-Indian (British) families.

- Identify some of the various ethnic groups within India. In what regions do these people live? What languages do they speak, what religions do they practice, and what are some of their customs?

- Research Mohandas K. Gandhi and his philosophy of nonviolence and passive resistance. What were Gandhi's main beliefs and how did he practice them? What effect did his teachings and actions have?

which another British official chooses to fulfill a personal desire at the risk of his public image. However, we do not see the consequences of this choice.

Dr. Aziz himself is torn between his public life as a doctor at a government hospital and his private dreams. When he attempts to transcend the distinction between private wishes and the public constraints, "Trouble after trouble encountered him, because he had challenged the spirit of the Indian earth, which tries to keep men in compartments." Only in Professor Godbole does the division between public and private life seem to disappear. For Godbole, the two are simply different forms of one existence. Godbole's prayers, for example, have both a private and public function, and it is difficult to tell where one ends and the other begins.

Ambiguity

A Passage to India is full of ambiguity, and its most important characters—Dr. Aziz, Mrs. Moore, Cyril Fielding, Adela Quested—are beset by doubt at key points in the narrative. The terms "mystery" and "muddle" are introduced during Fielding's tea party and are repeated several times throughout the book. When Adela remarks that she "hates mysteries," Mrs. Moore replies that "I like mysteries but I rather dislike muddles." Mr. Fielding then observes that "a mystery is a muddle."

Doubt and ambiguity surround two key incidents in the book that occur at the Marabar Caves. On a literal level, Adela does not know if she has really been attacked in the cave or if she has only imagined this incident. If she has been attacked, was Dr. Aziz the attacker? While the reader might not doubt Aziz's innocence, there is a larger ambiguity about what really did take place. For Anglo-Indian authority figures such as Ronny Heaslop, Major Callendar, and Mr. McBryde, there is no doubt whatever; it is only characters such as Cyril Fielding who are capable of entertaining doubt and, thus, of thinking critically about events.

An even larger, more metaphorical ambiguity surrounds Mrs. Moore's experience at the caves. While she is inside one of the caves, she hears an echo and suddenly feels that everything—including her religious faith—is meaningless. So powerful is the doubt that fills Mrs. Moore, that she loses her grip on life.

God and Religion

E. M. Forster was not a religious man nor a religious writer. However, religion is a major preoccupation in the book. India is seen as a meeting point of three of the world's historic religions—Islam, Christianity, and Hinduism. Indeed, the three parts of the book—"Mosque," "Cave," and "Temple"—generally correspond to these religions. Aziz loves the cultural and social aspects of his Moslem (Islamic) heritage, but he seems less concerned with its theology and religious practice. He is aware that Moslems are in the minority in India, and he thus feels a special kinship with other Moslems such as Hamidullah. The Anglo-Indians are nominal representatives of Christianity, although there is little overt sign of such Christian virtues as charity, love, and forgiveness. Ronny Heaslop admits that for him Christianity is fine in its place, but he does not let it interfere with his civil duty. Mrs. Moore is basically Christian in her outlook. However, she experiences a crisis of faith during her visit to the Marabar Caves, and her belief in God or in any meaning to life is destroyed. Hinduism is the main religion of India, and Professor Godbole is the central Hindu figure in the book. He is also,

by far, the most religious character. For Godbole, Hinduism is "completeness, not reconstruction." The central principle of this religion is the total acceptance of things as they are. Forster suggests that this is the most positive spiritual approach to life. It is also most representative of the true spirit of India.

Style

Point of View

A Passage to India is written in the third person, with an impersonal narrative voice. This technique makes the narrative seem traditional and straightforward, especially when compared to the more obviously experimental narrative techniques that were being used at the time by such novelists as James Joyce and Virginia Woolf. The narrator here is apparently omniscient, telling the reader much about India at the same time as describing the situations in which the various characters find themselves. At the same time, however, the narrative withholds a full explanation of certain events, most notably the misadventures that befall Mrs. Moore and Adela Quested at the Marabar Caves. Indeed, in recounting these details, the narrator is ambiguous rather than omniscient. A degree of ambiguity also surrounds the depiction of certain characters. Often, relatively minor characters (such as Mr. Turton, Mrs. Callendar, Mahmoud Ali, and the Nawab Bahadur) will appear in a scene without much introduction. Forster seems to take their presence for granted. This technique mimics the way that people might come and go in real life. Forster also assumes that the reader will have some knowledge of the social nuances of British India.

At times, the narrative focus shifts from a depiction of external events and enters the consciousness of one character or another, almost without the reader noticing that such a shift has occurred. This stream-of-consciousness effect is evident when Forster writes about Mrs. Moore's experiences at the caves and when he reports Adela's perceptions during the trial. It is also used several times when the narrative records Aziz's thoughts about his Islamic heritage and about his place in India.

Setting

The action of the first two sections of the book takes place in the town of Chandrapore and at the

Marabar Caves, located outside the town. Within the town itself, which is fairly nondescript, Forster identifies several localized settings. When we see the Anglo-Indian officials such as Major Callendar and Mr. Turton and their wives, it is almost invariably at the Civil Station, the area where the Anglo-Indians live and work. Often they are at the Chandrapore Club, which is exclusively for the Anglo-Indians and their British guests such as Mrs. Moore, and which Indians cannot enter. Although this setting emphasizes the Anglo-Indian's superior social status, it also shows their isolation from the mass of Indians who live around them. By contrast, the Indians are often shown at their own homes or in public places. The third section is set in Mau, a Hindu state several hundred miles from Chandrapore. (The book's three section headings—"Mosque," "Caves," and "Temple"—indicate the symbolic settings; see "Structure" and "Symbolism," below.)

Apart from these specific settings, India itself is the larger setting of the book. Indeed, some critics have remarked that India is not only the setting: it is also the subject and might even be considered a "character."

Critics have argued about the extent to which *A Passage to India* reflects actual historical and political conditions of the time in which it is set. Indeed, there is some critical dispute over exactly when the novel takes place; Forster gives no dates in the narrative. One Indian who admired the book believed that it was more representative of India at the time of Forster's first visit, 1912. Several Western critics have agreed with this analysis, and one has claimed that the action of the novel occurs "out of time." It may be safe to assume that the time setting is an amalgamation of the early 1910s and the early 1920s.

Structure

A Passage to India is divided into three parts or sections. Each part has its own particular symbols, correspondences, and associations. Each is set in a different season and opens with a chapter that describes a particular aspect of India. Part I, titled "Mosque," takes place during the cool, dry season. The Mosque where Dr. Aziz meets Mrs. Moore corresponds to Islam and the Islamic or Moslem aspect of India, as represented by Dr. Aziz and his family and friends. Despite some hints of possible trouble, the prevailing mood is one of harmony. The main events of this part of the book are Aziz's meeting with Mrs. Moore and Mr. Fielding's tea party.

Part II, "Caves," takes place during the hot season. The focus shifts to the British domination of India and to a contemporary British Christian perspective. Adela Quested becomes the center of attention. This part of the novel is marked by misunderstanding and conflict (or mystery and muddle, to use Mrs. Moore's earlier terms). Mrs. Moore gives in to despair after she hears the echo while she is in the cave, and Adela becomes completely confused. The incident at the Marabar Caves and the trial of Dr. Aziz make up the main dramatic action.

Part III, "Temple," takes place during the rainy season several years after the action of Parts I and II. Dr. Aziz has settled in a Hindu state, Mau. Professor Godbole becomes a more prominent character. This part of the novel concentrates on the themes of rebirth and reconciliation. The primary events are the Hindu festival celebrating the rebirth of Krishna and Fielding's return to India. Part III is the shortest of the three sections of the novel and might be considered as an epilogue.

Motif

Just as the three-part structure gives the novel dramatic shape, the use of certain motifs helps to give the book dramatic unity. A *motif* is a recurring image or incident that has a suggestive and even a symbolic quality. One prominent motif in *A Passage to India* is the interrupted or delayed journey. This first occurs in chapter two, when Dr. Aziz is riding his bicycle to Major Callendar's bungalow at the English civil station and gets a flat tire. He has to find a tonga, or carriage, to take him the rest of the way. By the time he finally arrives, the major has left. Aziz's failure to arrive on time suggests the wide gulf that separates the Indians and the British. (To make matters worse, two English ladies appear and take Aziz's carriage, leaving him without transportation.)

Another interrupted journey is the ride that Adela and Ronny take in the Nawab Bahadur's car. There is a minor accident—in the darkness the car runs off the road, stranding the passengers until Miss Derek comes along and offers to take them back to Chandrapore in her car. (But she leaves the Nawab's chauffeur behind.) During this episode, Adela and Ronny decide that they will marry after all; but their engagement will prove to be temporary. This interrupted journey suggests their failure to marry.

In Part II of the novel, Cyril Fielding and Professor Godbole miss the train that they are intending to take on the trip to the Marabar Caves. This failure separates them from Aziz, Mrs. Moore, and Adela, who go on without them. The reader is left to imagine that if Fielding and Godbole had been able to accompany Aziz and the women as they had planned, the terrible and confusing incidents that befall the members of the party at the Marabar Caves might never have occurred. Later, Mrs. Moore dies on her voyage back to England.

In the final section, as they travel to the native state of Mau where Aziz and Godbole are living, Fielding, Stella, and Ralph are delayed by floods caused by the monsoons. Just before the end of the book, Aziz takes Ralph out on the river in a boat ("a rudderless dingy"); the oars had been "hidden to deter the visitors from going out." Fielding and his wife have already gone out in another boat, using long poles to push themselves. Aziz fears that the couple "might get into difficulties, for the wind was rising." The two boats collide and the passengers spill into the river. Despite the accident, this time the journey ends safely. The four characters have witnessed the Hindu celebrations, and their immersion in the water suggests not drowning but rebirth and renewal.

Irony

E. M. Forster has been called an ironic writer, and *A Passage to India* is perhaps the most ironic of all his works. Several layers of irony are evident. For example, it is ironic that Aziz has organized the trip to the Marabar Caves in order to entertain his English guests. Rather than being the pleasant outing that Aziz intended, the excursion ends in disaster for everyone concerned. Something happens to Adela while she is in one of the caves: she believes that she has been attacked by Aziz. Aziz, who had prided himself on his hospitality, instead finds himself punished for a crime he did not commit. (There is also a minor irony in that Aziz finds Adela physically unattractive and is offended that anyone could think that he would want to rape her.) Mrs. Moore too suffers a fate more terrible than Adela's. While she is in the cave she hears an echo that is simply a meaningless noise—"ouboum." She takes this to mean that everything is meaningless, and thus she loses her faith. It is also ironic that, although the caves are reputed to be famous, there is really nothing remarkable about them except their effect on the visitors.

A further irony occurs later in the book when Dr. Aziz assumes that his friend Cyril Fielding has married Adela Quested. In fact, Fielding has married Stella Moore, the daughter of the late Mrs.

Moore, whom Aziz greatly liked and admired. Also ironic is the suggestion that Stella, who has just arrived from England, may have a greater understanding of the mystery of India than does Aziz himself.

Symbolism

Although *A Passage to India* is a realistic novel, it also contains many symbolic elements. The most obvious symbols are those that give the titles of the book's three sections—mosque, cave, and temple. Both for Aziz and Mrs. Moore, the mosque is a symbol of refuge and peace, a place of sanctuary. The first meeting of Aziz and Mrs. Moore takes place in the mosque at night, under the moonlight. Mrs. Moore has gone to the mosque because she is bored with the play she has been attending at the Chandrapore club. The English play, *Cousin Kate,* seems artificial and out of place in India. The mosque, by contrast, is one symbol of the "real" India.

The cave bears some resemblance to the mosque, in that both are enclosed spaces. Here, however, the resemblance ends. The cave is dark, featureless, and menacing. Although there are many caves at Marabar, it is impossible to tell one from another; they are all alike. Critics have argued about the symbolic meaning of the cave. It is at least certain that whatever else they might suggest, they stand for misunderstanding and meaninglessness, or what Mrs. Moore calls "muddle."

Prominent among other symbols is the wasp. When Mrs. Moore goes to hang up her cloak at the end of chapter three, she sees a wasp. The symbolic significance of the wasp is not spelled out. However, it suggests the natural life of India, and also carries a hint of uncertainty. Much later, in Part III, Professor Godbole recalls "an old woman he had met in Chandrapore days." He then remembers "a wasp seen he forgot where.... He loved the wasp equally...."

Historical Context

Forster's England

Although the action of *A Passage to India* takes place entirely in India, it should be remembered that Forster was a British writer, and that most of his readers were British. Thus, the work reflects not only the contemporary India, which is its overt subject, but also England and the milieu in which Forster lived and wrote. Moreover, although Forster published the book in 1924 during the reign of King George V (r. 1910-36), he is commonly regarded as an Edwardian novelist. Forster's first four novels were written in the first decade of the twentieth century, during the reign of King Edward VII (r. 1901-10), and his values and outlook were developed during this period, before World War I. Thus, like Forster's earlier books, *A Passage to India* is commonly regarded as an Edwardian book (an Edwardian novel of manners, at that), even though it was not written during the Edwardian period.

Between the time Forster first visited India and began writing this novel (1912-13) and the time he finished it (1924), Britain had undergone the traumatic experience of World War I. Britain and her allies won the war, but more than 750,000 British soldiers were killed, along with another quarter of a million soldiers from other parts of the British Empire; another two million British and Empire soldiers were wounded, many of them severely. These losses affected people's attitudes toward tradition and authority. The self-confidence that earlier had marked Britain's attitude about its empire and its place in the world was replaced with doubt and uncertainty. Nonetheless, although there was some sympathy for the Indian cause, most British people at the time would have supported the British presence in India.

Between 1912 and 1924, the British political landscape had also changed. At the beginning of this period, the Liberal Party had been one of the two major parties in Britain. (The other major party was, and remains, the Conservative Party.) The Liberals had won the majority of votes in the election of 1908, and were in power from that time until 1915. However, during this decade the Liberals lost much of their support to the newer and more radical Labour Party, which favored a socialist program. The Labour Party had its first election victory in 1924; by this time, the Liberal Party had dwindled to a third-party status, and it never won another general election. (Forster and most of his circle, including the members of the Bloomsbury Group, were Labour supporters.) Although Labour remained in power for only ten months in 1924, the party had become the main alternative to the Conservatives.

During this period the British Empire was beginning to change. This change was most evident in Ireland, the only region of the British Empire that was right on Britain's doorstep. On Easter Sunday, 1916, a group of Irish rebels declared Irish in-

During the period when E. M. Forster was writing A Passage to India, *Mohandas Karamchand Gandhi, pictured on the left with Shrimah Sorojini Naidu, was leading India towards independence from British rule.*

dependence from Britain and attempted to seize control of Dublin. Although the British army quickly crushed the rebellion, a more widespread Irish independence movement soon arose, and in 1921 the British government signed a treaty recognizing self-rule for the twenty-six southern counties of Ireland.

The Indian Context

Although the Irish rebellion had no direct effect on British rule of India, the fact that Ireland had gained limited independence helped to strengthen the idea of possible Indian independence in the minds of many Indians. Forster's novel is set during a time of increased tension between the British and their Indian subjects. The British presence in India had begun in the 1600s, when a British trading company, the East India Company, gained a strong foothold in Madras, Bombay, and Calcutta. At this time, much of India was nominally governed by a royal Moslem dynasty, the Moguls. (It was the Mogul emperors and their court that Dr. Aziz in the novel idealized.) However, the Mogul government was weakened by infighting and was

Compare & Contrast

- **1910s–1920s:** The British Empire stretches around the world. British-ruled territory in Asia includes present-day India, Pakistan, Bangladesh, Burma, Malaysia, and Singapore. Such present-day African countries as Egypt, Nigeria, Kenya, Zimbabwe, and South Africa are also part of the Empire, as are many Caribbean islands.

  Today: Virtually all the former British colonies are independent nations. Many retain loose trade and cultural ties with Britain in an association called the Commonwealth of Nations. Hong Kong, one of the last remaining British crown colonies, returned to Chinese rule at midnight on June 30, 1997.

- **1910s-1920s:** Britain is a major world power with a large industrial base and dominates international trade. Much of the raw material for Britain's manufacturers comes from India and other British colonies.

  Today: Britain is a small nation with a largely service-based economy. It is a member of the European Union (formerly the European Economic Community), a close economic association of European nations. Britain trades widely with other European nations in the EU. After a period of economic change that saw the decline of traditional industries such as mining, manufacturing, and shipbuilding, Britain is now one of the most prosperous nations in Europe. Foreign-owned businesses operate successfully in Britain.

- **1910s-1920s:** The population of Britain is comprised almost entirely of English, Scottish, and Welsh people. A small number of elite students from India and other parts of the Empire are educated at British universities.

  Today: Immigrants from former colonies, and their descendants, make up approximately five percent of the British population. Some large British cities, including London, have substantial Indian, Pakistani, and Bangladeshi communities.

- **1910s-1920s:** Mohandas K. Gandhi, an Indian lawyer educated in Britain, develops his philosophy of passive resistance to British rule. By 1920 he has become a leading figure in the Indian National Congress, a political and cultural organization that works for fair treatment and increased civil rights for Indians. Support for independence grows.

  Today: India (predominantly Hindu) and Pakistan (Moslem), formed out of former British India, have been independent since 1947. The two nations have fought several wars against each other, and relations are peaceful but uneasy. There is also ethnic and political violence within both countries. In India, the Congress Party (the successor to the Indian National Congress) was the dominant political party until the 1990s. Among Hindus, Gandhi remains a revered historical figure.

---

unable to control all of India. The Indian population consisted of a number of different ethnic and religious groups, with little sense of an overall Indian identity. The British were thus able to increase their power in India.

In 1773, the English Parliament created the post of Governor General for India. Under Governor-General Cornwallis (1786-93), the British established a sophisticated colonial administration in India. (Cornwallis was also the British general who

had surrendered to George Washington at the end of the American Revolutionary War.) Cornwallis instituted a system of British rule that was still mostly intact at the time of *A Passage to India*. Indians were forbidden to hold high government office and were subject to other laws that kept them in a subservient position, both legally and economically. A number of areas of the country—known as Native States or Independent States—were not under direct British rule, but were governed by local Indian princes or maharajahs. However, the British authorities kept close watch on these states, which had friendly policies toward the British.

The British suppressed an Indian rebellion (known as the Indian Mutiny or Sepoy Rebellion) in 1857. By the time of *A Passage to India,* there was a significant organized movement for Indian equality and eventual independence, in the form of the Indian National Congress. In 1919, nearly 400 Indians were shot to death and another 1,200 wounded when soldiers under British command opened fire on a crowd that had gathered illegally in the northeast Indian town of Amritsar. The Amritsar Massacre, as it became known, caused a public outcry both in India and Britain. India stood poised on the edge of widespread violence. In this tense atmosphere, a British-educated Indian lawyer named Mohandas K. Gandhi began a long nonviolent campaign of civil disobedience against British rule. Gandhi advocated Indian equality as well as peaceful cooperation between the country's Hindu and Moslem populations. Forster does not mention Gandhi or the Amritsar Massacre, but the division between India's Hindus and Moslems is a major concern in the novel.

There is some critical dispute over the time period during which Forster's novel is set. One Indian who admired the book believed that it was representative of India at the time of Forster's first visit, 1912. One American critic has claimed that the action occurs "out of time." Most critics and readers feel that the action takes place in the early 1920s, contemporary with the time that the book was finished and published.

In any case, Forster's novel is not only concerned with its own time but also looks forward to the future. The novel hints that the two groups may be able to put aside their traditional differences and live in harmony as Indians. However, this did not turn out to be the case. As independence grew nearer, Moslems demanded the creation of a separate Moslem nation, Pakistan. Indian independence in 1947 was accompanied by violent clashes between Hindus and Moslems, with tens of thousands of deaths on both sides. The next year, Gandhi was assassinated by a Hindu fanatic who believed that Gandhi was making too many compromises with the Moslems. Ironically, today both India and Pakistan have relatively good relations with Britain and the British. So it is likely that Dr. Aziz and Mr. Fielding would today be able to have the sort of uninhibited friendship that is mentioned at the end of the book.

Critical Overview

When *A Passage to India* was published in 1924, E. M. Forster was already a well-known and highly respected novelist. However, he had not published a novel for fourteen years (*Howards End,* 1910, was his previous book). Upon its publication, *A Passage to India* was reviewed widely in British newspapers and literary journals, as well as in American magazines. Most of these early reviews were very favorable and helped to ensure the book's success.

Among the first reviewers of *A Passage to India* in Britain and America were the English novelists Rose Macaulay (*Daily News,* June 4, 1924) and L. P. Hartley (*The Spectator,* June 28, 1924); the British writer and publisher Leonard Woolf (*The Nation and Atheneum,* June 14, 1924); and the Scottish poet Edwin Muir (*The Nation,* October 8, 1924). All of these reviews were positive; in fact, these writers believed that *A Passage to India* was the best novel that Forster had written. A review in the London *Times Literary Supplement* concluded that Forster "portrays the super-sensitiveness, the impulsiveness, the charm and the weakness, of Mohammedan and Hindu India, in order to emphasize the honesty, the arrogance ... and the moral tremors of the governing caste." In the United States, Robert Morss Lovett wrote a favorable review in *The New Republic* (August 16, 1924). However, E. A. Horne in *The New Statesman* in London criticized Forster for his unsympathetic portrayal of the book's Anglo-Indian (British) characters and pointed out some inaccuracies in Forster's depiction of India.

Two of Forster's distinguished contemporaries expressed differing views of *A Passage to India* in personal remarks. The celebrated military hero T. E. Lawrence—Lawrence of Arabia—told Forster that *A Passage to India* was "universal: the bitter hopeless picture a cloud might have painted, of man in India." However, the novelist D. H. Lawrence (no relation to T. E. Lawrence) commented that the book was filled with "people, people, and nothing but people."

In the decades since its publication, *A Passage to India* has continued to receive close and respectful attention from many distinguished scholars and critics, often as part of a consideration of Forster's writing in general. With her husband Leonard, Virginia Woolf was an early—though not entirely uncritical—supporter of Forster's work. She discussed the book in a 1927 essay, "The Nov-

els of E. M. Forster," in the *Atlantic Monthly*. Rose
Macaulay, who like Forster was a graduate of Cambridge University, wrote one of the first full-length
books about Forster, *The Writings of E. M. Forster,*
published in 1938. That same year the influential
English critic F. R. Leavis wrote about Forster in
his Cambridge journal, *Scrutiny*. The famous
American critic Lionel Trilling discussed *A Passage to India* in 1943 in *E. M. Forster: A Study,*
thereby helping to revive American interest in the
work nearly twenty years after its publication.

More recent academic studies in both Britain
and America have focused attention on particular
aspects of Forster's book, such as its narrative technique, symbolism, and politics. Malcolm Bradbury
and Jeffrey Meyers are among those who have
made important contributions to scholarship on *A
Passage to India.*

Criticism

Jeffrey M. Lilburn

*Lilburn, a teaching assistant at the University
of Western Ohio, explores possible interpretations
of Forster's novel, including its political, racial,
and homo-erotic implications.*

A Passage to India is E. M. Forster's final and
perhaps finest novel. Forster visited India twice and
wrote another novel, the posthumously published
Maurice, before finally completing *A Passage to
India* in 1924—more than ten years after it was begun. Although Forster has stated that the novel is
not really about politics and that it is less concerned
with the incompatibility of East and West than it
is with the difficulty of living in the universe, the
novel does address issues such as colonialism,
racism, nationalism, and rape. As a result, much of
the critical analysis has focussed on political and
social themes. One of the major issues the novel
attempts to address is introduced in the second
chapter through a conversation in which Dr. Aziz,
Mahmoud Ali, and Hamidullah discuss "whether
or not it is possible to be friends with an Englishman." Shortly after this discussion, Dr. Aziz is befriended by two Englishwomen and the Anglo-Indian Principal at the College, Mr. Fielding. But
most critics tend to look beyond the relationships
between individuals and discuss the novel in terms
of its depiction of Anglo-Indian colonial society.
Debate over whether or not *A Passage to India* is

critical of colonialism is ongoing. Many critics
agree that the novel does attack the traditional justifications for British domination, but convincing
arguments can also be made that Forster's attempt
to represent India implicates him in the "muddle"
of imperial power.

At the centre of the novel is the visit to the
Marabar Caves. All the connections and friendships
established in the first section of the novel lead to
this expedition. Much has been written about what
actually happens in the caves but the mystery remains unsolved. One might read Mrs. Moore's and
Miss Quested's experiences in the caves as a breakdown of established values resulting from the exposure to "other" conceptions of culture and being.
Adela's experience in particular is often read as a
hallucination or hysterical reaction brought about
by sexual repression. But the mystery remains a
mystery because the pivotal scene involving Adela
and Aziz is never told. Mrs. Moore has a "horrifying" experience inside one of the caves and sinks
into a state of apathy and cynicism. All that is
known of Adela's misadventure is that she suffers
a maybe-real, maybe-imagined sexual assault and
that Aziz is charged with the crime. Whether or not
there even was a crime committed, either by Aziz
or by someone else, is never revealed.

After witnessing the unsuccessful Bridge
Party, Adela vows that she will never succumb to
Anglo-Indian ideology. Yet, as Jenny Sharpe has
noted in her article *The Unspeakable Limits of
Rape: Colonial Violence and Counter-Insurgency
in Genders,* the accusations Adela makes against
Dr. Aziz seemingly confirm the fears and racist assumptions used to justify imperialism—that the
"native" world is chaotic, uncontrollable and evil
and thus in need of English domination. Following
Aziz's arrest, many of these hateful and unfounded
fears are openly manifested. The District Superintendent of Police, Mr. McBryde, is not surprised
by Aziz's downfall because he believes that "all
unfortunate natives are criminals at heart, for the
simple reason that they live south of latitude 30."
At the Club, people begin to voice their concern
for the safety of the "women and children" and one
young woman even refuses to "return to her bungalow in case the 'niggers attacked.'" The prevailing attitude is best represented by McBryde's
words at Aziz's trial. He delivers his opening statement almost indifferently because he believes that
Aziz's guilt is already accepted as fact. The possibility that Aziz may in fact be innocent is never
even considered because, as McBryde tells the
court, it is a "general truth" that the "darker races

What Do I Read Next?

- E. M. Forster's first novel, *Where Angels Fear to Tread,* was published in 1905. Set it Italy, it concerns the tragic relations between an English family and a young Italian man.

- Forster's third novel, *A Room With a View* (1908), is also set in Italy. It too focuses on a clash of cultures, contrasting the conventional behavior of English characters with the more spontaneous life of the Italian characters.

- Considered second only to *A Passage to India* among Forster's novels, *Howards End* (1910) is a subtle study of English class distinctions and the uneasy relationship between aesthetic and materialistic outlooks on life. An Edwardian novel of manners, it is the most "English" of Forster's novels. In it, Forster coined the motto that best expresses his view of how to live a full life: "Only connect." ("Only connect the prose and passion, and both will be exalted, and human love will be seen at its height.")

- Forster expressed his ideas about the novel as a literary genre in a series of lectures that he gave at Cambridge University in 1927. These lectures were collected and published in the same year under the title *Aspects of the Novel.* Forster mentions particular novels by important writers and discusses the qualities that make a good novel.

- Forster gave a factual account of his travels in India in a nonfiction work, *The Hill of Devi,* published in 1953.

- Ruth Prawer Jhabvala's 1975 novel *Heat and Dust* traces the parallel experiences in India of an Englishwoman and her great-niece some sixty years apart. Jhabvala also wrote the screenplays for Ishmail Merchant and James Ivory's film adaptations of Forster's *Room With a View, Maurice,* and *Where Angels Fear to Tread.*

- The English writer Paul Scott wrote a series of four novels known collectively as *The Raj Quartet.* Set in India from 1942 to 1947, the books follow relations between the English and Indians in the years leading up to India's independence. The four books are *The Jewel in the Crown* (1966), *The Day of the Scorpion* (1968), *The Towers of Silence* (1972), and *A Division of Spoils* (1972).

---

are physically attracted by the fairer, but not vice versa."

But passages such as these do not lend authority to Adela's allegations against Dr. Aziz. On the contrary, the rhetoric used to justify imperialism is severely parodied. The scenes paint an ugly picture of the English officers sent to India to "do justice and keep the peace"; they become almost ridiculous when it is remembered that the colonizers' prejudices and fears are aroused by an event that may not have taken place. McBryde's "general truth" is based not on evidence or, as he claims, scientific fact, but on the assumptions and premises which are necessary to support notions of Western superiority.

Similarly, the mystery surrounding the caves and the events that transpired inside them undermine any sense of certainty in the novel. Adela herself becomes unsure about what actually happened in the caves and is plagued by the echoing doubt that her accusations may have been fabricated. Sharpe has argued that this element of uncertainty, introduced into a crime which supposedly confirms the "native's" depravity, reveals the fictionality of what she terms "colonial truth-claims." In other words, Sharpe illustrates how the declaration of Aziz's innocence "undermines the racist assumptions underpinning an official discourse that represents anticolonial insurgency as the savage attack of barbarians on innocent women and children." The novel's exposure of such politically constructed "truths" thus subverts the conventional justifications for British domination.

However, the novel 's condemnation of imperial ideology is not unproblematic. Benita Parry has noted, in *The Politics of Representation* in *A Pas-*

sage to India, from *E. M. Forster: Contemporary Critical Essays,* that while the text does lampoon colonial rhetoric, its overt criticism of colonialism is phrased in the feeblest of terms. One scene which several critics have singled out even suggests that colonialism might have been more acceptable had the British only been a little kinder: "One touch of regret ... would have made [Ronny] a different man, and the British Empire a different institution." The novel's ending is also troublesome. Fielding, the one man who stood against his countrymen to defend Aziz, finally throws in "his lot with Anglo-India by marrying a countrywoman" and "acquiring some of its limitations." He even begins to doubt whether he would repeat his defiance of his own people "for the sake of a stray Indian."

Moreover, there are instances in the novel where the narrator appears to be guilty of making broad generalizations about Indians. Compared to the loud and offensive remarks spoken by McBryde, the narrator's occasional reinforcement of racial stereotypes is easily overlooked. But seemingly harmless comments—"like most Orientals, Aziz overrated hospitality"—do contribute to the West's textual construction of the East. And, as alluded to above, it is this kind of fabricated report which can eventually become accepted as a "general truth." While narrative comments such as these do not necessarily invalidate the novel's criticism of colonialism, they do suggest that the Western novelist's prose about India, like the "pose of seeing India" criticized in the novel, can be a "form of ruling India."

Of course, it is possible to discuss the novel without emphasizing the political and colonial themes. A completely different reading is offered by Parminder Bakshi in *A Passage to India: Theory and Practice Series.* Bakshi argues that *A Passage to India,* like all of Forster's fiction, contains homo-erotic themes and was inspired not by colonial issues but by the barriers to male friendship. She contends that Forster strives to dissociate friendship from politics and illustrates how the novel moves towards creating intimacy between Fielding and Aziz. Central to her argument is the theme of friendship which, Bakshi believes, decenters the hollow and artificial convention of marriage because it poses a threat to male friendship.

Perhaps most convincing is Bakshi's reading of the novel's final scene. Although politics appear to be the reason for Fielding and Aziz's separation, Bakshi argues that politics are actually superfluous. More traditional readings of the scene interpret Aziz's final words as an acknowledgment that the colonial situation makes friendship between the English and Indians impossible. But Bakshi points out that it is only at the suggestion of male intimacy made by Fielding ("Why can't we be friends now? It's what I want. It's what you want.") that the entire universe rises in protest by hurling countless barriers between them: "the horses didn't want it—they swerved apart; the earth didn't want it, sending up rocks through which riders must pass single-file; the temples, the tank ... they didn't want it, they said in their hundred voices, 'No, not yet,' and the sky said, 'No, not there.'" Through Bakshi's reading, the novel transcends contemporary politics and becomes an indictment against the oppression of male love.

Still, it is impossible to read the end of the novel without also considering the political and colonial themes. Forster's text is not optimistic about the future of East-West relations, but it is prophetic. Early in the novel, when Aziz is making his way to Callendar's compound, he becomes depressed by the roads which, "named after victorious generals and intersecting at right angles, were symbolic of the net Great Britain had thrown over India." In his final meeting with Fielding, Aziz recognizes the immediate need to throw off this net and foresees that the time for Indian independence will come with the next European war. Will the act of driving "every blasted Englishman into the sea" make it possible for an Indian to be friends with an Englishman? The novel provides no simple answer. Forster was certainly aware that the repercussions of British authority would echo for years after the end of British domination, and while his novel's final words, spoken by a chorus of a hundred voices, do suggest the possibility of a better future, it is a future that, in 1924, remains uncertain.

Source: Jeffrey M. Lilburn, in an essay for *Novels for Students,* Gale, 1998.

Hunt Hawkins

In the following excerpt, Hawkins considers Forster's primary anti-imperial argument as the impossibility of personal relationships. Besides the bigotry of the English in India, he dwells on the self-interest and fear of betrayal on the Indian side. He also questions not only politics but nature itself as a power against human connection.

The chief argument against imperialism in E. M. Forster's *A Passage to India* is that it prevents personal relationships. The central question of the novel is posed at the very beginning when Mahmoud Ali and Hamidullah ask each other "whether or no it is possible to be friends with an Englishman." The answer, given by Forster himself on the last page, is "No, not yet.... No, not there." Such friendship is made impossible, on a political level, by the existence of the British Raj. While having several important drawbacks, Forster's anti-imperial argument has the advantage of being concrete, clear, moving, and presumably persuasive. It is also particularly well-suited to pursuit in the novel form, which traditionally has focused on interactions among individuals.

Forster's most obvious target is the unfriendly bigotry of the English in India, or the Anglo-Indians as they were called. At times he scores them for their pure malice, as when Mrs. Callendar says, "The kindest thing one can do to a native is to let him die." More tellingly, Forster shows up their bigotry as prejudice in the literal sense of pre-judgment. The Anglo-Indians, as Forster presents them, act on emotional preconceptions rather than rational and open-minded examination of facts. They therefore fall into logical inconsistencies which the author exposes with his favorite weapon: irony. For example, at the hysterical Club meeting following Dr. Aziz's arrest for allegedly molesting Adela Quested, the subaltern defends an anonymous native with whom he had played polo the previous month: "Any native who plays polo is all right. What you've got to stamp on is these educated classes." The reader knows, as the subaltern doesn't, that the native was Aziz himself. Against the bigotry of the Anglo-Indians, Forster urged tolerance and understanding in the widest sense....

Forster does much more in his book ... than simply deride the intolerance of a few accidental individuals. He carefully shows how this intolerance results from the unequal power relationship between English and Indians, from the imperialistic relationship itself.... The process is best shown in the book in the case of Ronny, who has only recently come out from England to be City Magistrate of Chandrapore.

Ronny was at first friendly towards the Indians, but he soon found that his position prevented such friendship. Shortly after his arrival he invited the lawyer Mahmoud Ali to have a smoke with him, only to learn later that clients began flocking to Ali in the belief that he had an in with the Magistrate. Ronny subsequently "dropped on him in Court as hard as I could. It's taught me a lesson, and I hope him." In this instance, it is clearly Ronny's official position rather than any prior defect of the heart which disrupts the potential friendship. And it is his position in the imperial structure which causes

his later defect, his lack of true regret when he tells his mother that now "I prefer my smoke at the club amongst my own sort, I'm afraid."

Forster tells us that "every human act in the East is tainted with officialism" and that "where there is officialism every human relationship suffers." People cannot establish a friendship of equals when the Raj is based on an inequality of power....

The one possible exception to this process of corruption among Englishmen is Fielding. He is partially immune to the influence of the imperialistic power relationship because he works in education rather than government, and because, as he puts it, he "travels light"—he has no hostages to fortune. Fielding establishes a friendship with Aziz and maintains it in defiance of all the other Anglo-Indians. There is some doubt, however, whether he can maintain this course and still remain in imperial India. He is obliged to quit the Club and says he will leave India altogether should Aziz be convicted. After Fielding marries Stella, thereby ceasing to travel light, and after he becomes associated with the government as a school inspector, he undergoes a marked change of attitude toward the Raj. It would surely be a mistake to continue, as several critics do, to identify Forster with Fielding past this point. The omniscient narrator pulls back and summarizes Fielding's situation: "He had thrown in his lot with Anglo-India by marrying a countrywoman, and he was acquiring some of its limitations." Like Ronny and the other English officials, Fielding begins to be corrupted by his position. Thinking of how Godbole's school has degenerated into a granary, the new school inspector asserts that "Indians go to seed at once" away from the British. Fielding almost exactly echoes Ronny's defense of the Raj to his mother when he excuses unpleasantness in the supposedly necessary imperial presence: he had "'no further use for politeness,' he said, meaning that the British Empire really can't be abolished because it's rude." Fielding certainly did not start with a defect of the heart, but, as a result of his new position in the imperial structure, he is acquiring one.

The English, of course, aren't the only ones corrupted by imperialism. Although most of the Indians in the book have a nearly unbelievable desire to befriend Englishmen, they are ultimately turned from it by the political reality. Some succumb to self-interest. Mahmoud Ali, for example, seems to have been the first to subvert his budding friendship with Ronny by advertising their smoke to potential litigants. More often the Indians succumb to the fear, largely justified but occasionally erroneous, that they will be scorned and betrayed. The prime example is Aziz. He makes the horrible mistake of assuming that Fielding back in England has married his enemy Adela and further that Fielding had urged him not to press damages against his false accuser so Fielding himself could enjoy Adela's money. Aziz, of course, has been conditioned to expect betrayal from his experience with other Anglo-Indians, and this expectation provides an undercurrent to the friendship from the very beginning. After Fielding returns to India, and Aziz learns he really married Stella Moore, their relationship is partially retrieved, but the damage has been done. The new school inspector has shifted toward the Raj, and Aziz, now leery of all Englishmen, has become a nationalist, saying of India, "Not until she is a nation will her sons be treated with respect."...

In 1924, when *Passage* appeared, the Indian movement led by Mahatma Gandhi was still not yet agitating for independence. They said they wished to achieve dominion status and remain within the empire. Forster took what was at the time a more radical position by declaring that India inevitably had to become free. In an article in *The Nation and the Athenaeum* in 1922, Forster stated that "ten years ago" Indians had looked to Englishmen for social support, but now it was "too late," and he anticipated "the dissolution of an Empire." These phrases are repeated at the end of the novel when Aziz cries, "Clear out, all you Turtons and Burtons. We wanted to know you ten years back—now it's too late."

Forster's novel does not explicitly spell out what has happened in the previous ten years, apart from Aziz's own trial and his blow-up with Fielding. However, the book is full of muted references to recent events. The most important among these was the 1919 uprising in the Punjab which the British brutally suppressed. At the town of Amritsar, General Dwyer ordered his troops to fire on an unarmed crowd, killing nearly four hundred. Later he issued an order requiring Indians to crawl through a street where an English girl, Miss Marcella Sherwood, had been attacked. In *Passage* Mrs. Turton, after the supposed attack on Adela, says of the Indians, "They ought to crawl from here to the caves on their hands and knees whenever an Englishwoman's in sight." After Amritsar, General Campbell issued an order obliging Indians to approach the houses of Europeans on foot. Thus Aziz, when he goes to visit Major Callendar, has to get out of his tonga before he reaches the verandah....

There are two important drawbacks in Forster's argument for independence on the grounds that it is necessary for friendship. The first is that his argument takes little account of the less personal, more abstract issues of imperialism, particularly the economic issues. Apart from a passing reference to "the wealth of India" allowed "to escape overseas," there is no mention of England's economic exploitation of India. We see no plantations or mines in British India. Collector Turton presumably takes in tax, but we never see him doing so. And, with the exception of the punkah wallah, we never see an Indian performing physical labor. Thus we have little sense of why the English are in India in the first place....

Forster may have omitted the economics of the Raj because he was ignorant of them or didn't see their significance. Or possibly he did so because he was following the Bloomsbury aesthetic of starting with characters and bringing in the material world only secondarily. In any case, he left out an important aspect of the Raj, and this omission has led the Marxist critic Derek S. Savage to attack him fiercely: "The ugly realities underlying the presence of the British in India are not even glanced at, and the issues raised are handled as though they could be solved on the surface level of personal intercourse and individual behavior." This criticism may be justified, but in defence of Forster it should be noted that his particular argument against the Raj, its disruption of friendship, was shared by the Indian leaders of his day. In a 1921 letter explaining the purpose of the Non-cooperation Movement, Gandhi wrote: "We desire to live on terms of friendship with Englishmen, but that friendship must be friendship of equals both in theory and practice, and we must continue to non-cooperate till ... the goal is achieved."

The second drawback to Forster's anti-imperial argument is perhaps more damaging. It is that even if the political barriers are overcome, Forster is still sceptical that friendship can be achieved. This scepticism has the effect of undermining the entire political argument and making us say, "Why bother?" *A Passage to India* suggests a number of non-political barriers to friendship: the selfishness inherent in human nature, cultural differences which cannot be bridged, and the human potential for insanity. The most important barrier, though, is the echo. There have been many interpretations of the echo in the Marabar caves, and it is difficult to explain in words since the echo intrinsically resists language, but it seems first of all to indicate the meaninglessness of the universe. For Mrs. Moore, the echo reduces all human expressions to the same dull "boum," and it says, "Everything exists, nothing has value."... In the political aspect of the novel, Forster attacked the prejudice of the Anglo-Indians by appealing to a reason which would find the true facts; but in the metaphysical aspect, he tells us that reason is useless.

The effect of the echo on Mrs. Moore is to make her abandon all attempts at human connection. After hearing it, she realizes she "didn't want to communicate with anyone.... She lost all interest, even in Aziz." Mrs. Moore withdraws into herself, leaves India without any further significant interaction with anyone, and finally dies. For her, the echo makes friendship impossible. Later, of course, the figure of Mrs. Moore undergoes a sort of apotheosis in which she is imagined as a benefactress of India. She becomes the Hindu demi-deity Esmiss Esmoor; Professor Godbole makes her part of his ecstatic devotion; and Aziz tells Ralph, "Your mother was my best friend in all the world." There is no objective basis, however, for this exaltation of her by the Indians, and Reuben Brower seems right in saying, "We can hardly accept this about-face in Mrs. Moore's role and its symbolic value. We cannot at the end of the novel regard Mrs. Moore as in tune with the infinite and conveniently forget the mocking denial of her echo." Whatever her effect on others, she seems irretrievably isolated by the echo. Although she senses that Aziz is innocent, she is indifferent to his plight and does nothing at all to help him. When asked to testify, she says irritably, "When shall I be free from your fuss? Was he in the cave and were you in the cave and on and on ... and ending everything the echo." She decides of all people, including Aziz, "They do not exist, they were a dream." Mrs. Moore's friendship for Aziz thus comes to an end. The disruption in this case has nothing to do with the Raj or any other political barrier; rather it is caused by something much more powerful and over-riding: the echo.

A Passage to India does suggest a solution to the echo, of course. There is some doubt, however, whether Forster himself subscribed to this solution. And the solution contributes nothing to the argument against the Raj since it transcends politics and all other worldly concerns. The solution is Hinduism, which is shown countering the echo by abandoning reason and embracing the muddle of the universe with irrational joy. The negative echo "boum" is thus transposed into the affirmative chant "OM," representing the Hindu trinity of Brahma, Vishnu, and Siva.

While Hinduism may provide a metaphysical solution, it does not, at least according to Forster's novel, provide a political one. Hinduism is shown embracing everything, including the British empire, with equal mindless affirmation. Professor Godbole points out that good and evil "are both of them aspects of my Lord." There are no villains: everyone attacked Adela. When Shri Krishna is born in the festival of Gokul Ashtami, he saves foreigners as well as Indians....

At the very end of the novel when Aziz tells Fielding, "We shall drive every blasted Englishman into the sea, and then ... and then ... you and I shall be friends," the Englishman asks him, "Why can't we be friends now? It's what I want. It's what you want." The question is never answered by either man because their horses swerve apart.... One interpretation of this closing paragraph is that Fielding and Aziz cannot be friends until India becomes a nation, but another interpretation, a far more chilling one, is that they can never be friends. Not only politics keep them apart. The very earth and sky do. All of existence and the echo prevent human connection.

Source: Hunt Hawkins, "Forster's Critique of Imperialism in *A Passage to India*," in *South Atlantic Review*, January, 1983, pp. 54–65.

Roger L. Clubb

In the following excerpt, Clubb proposes that the meaning of the Marabar Caves is the mystery of the origin of life and a conscious spirit beyond human powers of comprehension.

That E. M. Forster's *A Passage to India* should, almost forty years after its first publication, continue to have an enthusiastic reading public is not surprising, though as a political and sociological document it is often spoken of, even by Forster himself, as dated. The fact is, as many recent articles have made clear, that the theme of the novel— the resolution of chaos (or the possibility of such a resolution) through human or divine love—is one which has pervaded the literature of the West from the time of Aeschylus to the present. Furthermore, analyzed on almost any level—as social comedy, as penetrating study of character, as metaphysical discourse, or as patterning of detail and episode— the novel is a masterpiece. Even as political and sociological comment the novel is, I feel, not so dated as Forster was prepared to admit. Certainly the situation in India has altered since the book was begun in 1912; however if we take the conflict between England and India as a pattern of that between France and Algeria, Belgium and the Congo, Portugal and Angola, or African white and African Negro, we see that the political aspects of the novel are by no means dated, nor will be so long as political or economic domination leads to conflicts between peoples. This is not to say that all such conflicts are identical, but it is to say that wherever we find the exploitation of one people by another, we are likely to find political and social consequences which, if not worse, will be much like those portrayed in *A Passage to India*....

The importance of the Marabar Caves is indicated by the emphasis given them in the opening chapter, which begins, "Except for the Marabar Caves—" and continues with a description of the novel's main setting, Chandrapore on the Ganges River with the English civil station above. Towards the end of the chapter is mentioned the "immense vault" of the sky. The description of the sky naturally leads to the horizon and then to the only interruption of the straight line of the horizon, the "fists and fingers" in the south. The final sentence of the chapter returns us to the caves: "These fists and fingers are the Marabar Hills, containing the extraordinary caves."...

Throughout Part One of the novel Forster keeps the reader's attention on the caves by casual references and more particularly by Aziz's invitation to Adela and Mrs. Moore to visit them. However, the caves remain mysterious. Indeed they remain mysterious throughout the novel, but in Part One few details are given about them and no inkling whatever of their impact on the viewer. In Chapter Seven during Fielding's tea party, at which Mrs. Moore and Adela are present, the caves are discussed by Aziz and Professor Godbole, but only to leave them in a greater mystery than before. Aziz has never seen the caves himself and knows them only by hearsay. Godbole has visited the caves but for some unknown reason is not willing to reveal anything about them except for the most trivial and obvious facts....

The first extended treatment of the caves occurs at the beginning of Part Two, where Forster not only describes their appearance but also gives a brief geological history of the Indian sub-continent....

The caves are associated with the vast and unknowable expanse of geological time. They derive from the most remote ages of the Pre-Cambrian era, a period covering the first two or three billion years of the earth's history and a period of which geologists have merely the slightest knowledge, since only the lowest and most easily obliterated forms of life existed. The caves antedate even the most primitive fossils. Forster divests them of any relation to life—human, animal, or plant. "To call them uncanny suggests ghosts, and they are older than all spirit." The Hindus have made some scratches on them; some saddhus once tried to settle in them but failed. This is all....

[The] caves represent not only a primitive level of intellectual and emotional activity but also, I believe, those mysteries of our universe which human beings—because they are, after all, finite, at least in the physical world—will never understand. Particularly, they symbolize the riddle of life itself, the mystery which lies behind the creation or appearance of that nonmaterial essence that we call spirit or consciousness....

The description of the caves, then, offers one more example of this pushing back to the unknown. I have suggested above that the mystery here may be that which lies behind the existence of spirit itself. How can stone, in which spirit is apparently inherent (for the stones themselves seem alive during the journey of the Aziz party to the caves), give rise to those forms of matter which we call *life* and which exhibit so clearly the quality that we call *consciousness?* The question, of course, cannot be answered. The biologist can explain how the one-celled protozoan can evolve into man, but he cannot explain how the complex molecule becomes the protozoan. This is a crucial step. Professor Godbole, whose sympathies can comprehend the wasp, cannot make the imaginative leap to stone. One passage particularly in the chapter on the caves suggests the mystery inherent in the development of life from non-life. Forster writes of the visitor striking a match upon entering the cave....

Here we have the direct opposition of organic and inorganic matter. The response of the flame in the stone suggests that spirit is infused through *all* matter but that only the spirit or consciousness of living beings can know this; hence the flame in the stone is a *reflection* of the flame in the air. Ultimately the gap between stone and flame can never be completely closed because, in this life, the spirit of man can never be completely one with the spirit of inorganic matter, however broad his sympathies may be....

[The] caves should be understood as symbolic of the womb. Such a meaning reinforces the concept that the caves represent the mystery of the origin of life. We may say, then, that the caves symbolize this mystery on two levels: the metaphysical and the sexual.

This interpretation of the meaning of the caves helps to explain the reactions of Mrs. Moore and Adela to their experiences at the Marabar. For Mrs. Moore the metaphysical problem is dominant. In England her faith had apparently been that of the orthodox Christian, possibly of rather narrow persuasion. In India her sympathies instinctively broaden. She feels the presence of God in the Mosque, and she offers a kind of benediction over the wasp; thus she is becoming a mystic who sees the cosmos as an emanation of, or as infused with, the spirit of God, a universal God, not a specifically Christian God. In essence she is approaching the Hindu position, and it is significant that during the trial of Aziz she becomes deified among the Hindus as Esmiss Esmoor and that she and Professor Godbole are linked through the thoughts of Godbole at the end of the novel. Intellectually, however, Mrs. Moore finds herself dissatisfied....

Mrs. Moore finds God less efficacious because in her heart she no longer accepts her former religious beliefs as the final and absolute truth. In the caves and afterwards comes her spiritual crisis, for the caves represent an unsolvable mystery, a mystery which Mrs. Moore's Christianity cannot cope with. Because of her religious uncertainty she cannot accept the caves with equanimity like Aziz and Professor Godbole. She reacts almost violently, and for her the echo of the cave robs everything of truth and value: "Pathos, piety, courage—they exist, but are identical, and so is filth. Everything exists, nothing has value."...

And so Mrs. Moore, unable to come to grips with the riddle posed by the caves, falls into pessimism and selfishness. She becomes peevish and petty, unwilling to comfort Adela or to testify at the trial in behalf of Aziz, though she believes him innocent.

Forster has been criticized for resurrecting Mrs. Moore as a spiritual force later in the novel, through her children, Ralph and Stella. It is certainly difficult to overlook the dwarfing of her spirit after the episode of the caves, but Forster does not leave her in this barren state of mind and prepares, though perhaps not sufficiently, for her spiritual influence over later events. Just before her death as she is leaving India, the mystery of the Marabar is put in its proper perspective, for one must come to terms with the unknowable. During the overnight journey from Chandrapore to the port of exit, Bombay, she sees the mosque at Asirgarh. The train

makes a semicircle around the town, and the mosque appears to her once again....

The mosque, which in part represents the positive value of the love of man for man and which presided over the meeting and establishment of understanding between Mrs. Moore and Aziz, suggests the renewal of spiritual life. As she sails from Bombay the voices of India impress upon her that the Marabar Caves are a very small part of the whole of India and that the mystery of the Marabar is a relatively minor problem in the whole of life.... Her journey across India, on one level, is a journey from life to death, for she dies soon after leaving Bombay; but on the spiritual level it is a journey from death to life, from the Caves to the Mosque.

The effect of the caves on Adela is different. In Mrs. Moore the full impact of the experience builds up slowly, and her thoughts about it are more terrifying than the experience itself. Adela, however, is suddenly thrown into a state of mental shock from which she recovers only by reliving the experience at the trial through the Prosecutor's questioning, which has the effect on her of a kind of psychoanalysis. (Fielding refers to the process as an "exorcizing.") Adela, who on the whole is a rather literal-minded, no-nonsense young woman quite unaware of the power of suggestion or of the workings of the sub-conscious mind, enters her second cave having just come to the startling conclusion that she is planning to marry a man she does not love. But also she has been thinking in a rather disinterested way about Aziz—what a handsome man he is and what a beautiful wife and children he no doubt has. Then recalling that Mohammedans often have four wives, she asks a question that shocks Aziz deeply: "Have you one wife or more than one?" Aziz breaks away from her in anger and the two enter separate caves. Precisely what happens to Adela is not fully revealed. Did she have a hallucination? Did the guide attack her? Was she simply thrown into a panic by the echo? Certainly the echo, with its suggestion of mystery, continues to haunt her until the trial scene. But whatever may have happened to her literally, it is clear, I believe, what happened to her psychologically. Consciously she rejects Ronny, and subconsciously she desires Aziz. I do not wish to be misunderstood here. Forster states that Adela has nothing of the vagrant in her, and indeed she does not. Surely, however, the subconscious desire for Aziz is there. Why otherwise does she dwell on his physical beauty and why the question about his wives? Conflict is set up between the conscious and subconscious minds, and Adela resolves the subconscious desire into a supposed sexual attack on the part of Aziz. In rushing from the cave she is repudiating a part of herself, the cave symbolizing at this point the womb or sexual consummation....

In the cave, then, Adela faces a mystery of another kind, the mystery of the primitive workings of the subconscious mind. Like Mrs. Moore she comes to terms with the meaning latent for her in the caves, but unlike Mrs. Moore she is incapable of the breadth of love and sympathy necessary for universal brotherhood and she retires from India defeated, dissatisfied, and "at the end of her spiritual tether." Mrs. Moore had some concept of a realm of the spirit beyond the physical universe, but not Adela....

But even Mrs. Moore did not know all. The ultimate mystery of the Marabar Caves, the mystery behind the existence of conscious spirit in the universe, is beyond the powers of the human intellect to solve.

Source: Roger L. Clubb, *"A Passage to India:* The Meaning of the Marabar Caves," in *CLA Journal,* March, 1963, pp. 184–93.

Sources

Parminder Bakshi, "The Politics of Desire: E. M. Forster's Encounters with India," in *A Passage to India: Theory and Practice Series,* edited by Tony Davies and Nigel Wood, Open University Press, 1994, pp. 23-64.

Benita Parry, "The Politics of Representation in 'A Passage to India,'" in *E. M. Forster: Contemporary Critical Essays,* edited by Jeremy Tambling, MacMillan (London), 1994, pp. 133-50.

Review of *A Passage to India,* in *Times Literary Supplement,* June 12, 1924, p. 37.

Jenny Sharpe, "The Unspeakable Limits of Rape: Colonial Violence and Counter-Insurgency," in *Genders,* No. 10, Spring, 1991, pp. 25-46.

For Further Study

Malcolm Bradbury, "Two Passages to India: Forster as Victorian and Modern," in *Aspects of E. M. Forster,* edited by Oliver Stallybrass, London, 1969, pp. 124-25.

Bradbury sees Forster as "a central figure of the transition into modernism."

Tony Davies, "Introduction," in *A Passage to India: Theory and Practice Series,* edited by Tony Davies and Nigel Wood, Open University Press, 1994, pp. 1-22.

Davies discusses critical commentary on *A Passage to India,* from early reviews to contemporary analysis.

Philip Gardner, "E. M. Forster" in *British Writers, Vol. VI: Thomas Hardy to Wilfred Owen,* General Editor Ina Scott-Kilvert, The British Council and Charles Scribner's Sons, 1983, pp. 397-413.

Gardner identifies and analyzes several levels on which the action of the novel moves, with special attention to the symbolic element.

Philip Gardner, *E. M. Forster: The Critical Heritage,* Routlege & Kegan Paul, 1973.

A good survey of critical interpretations of and reactions to the works of Forster up to the early 1970s.

Francis King, *E. M. Forster,* Thames & Hudson, 1988.

This copiously illustrated biography in Thames and Hudson's popular "Literary Lives" series provides an engaging introduction to Forster's life and work. King discusses Forster's writing of *A Passage to India* in the context of the author's travels and concerns. For general readers.

Stephen K. Land, "A Passage to India," in *Challenge and Conventionality in the Fiction of E. M. Forster,* AMS Press, 1990, pp. 189-217.

Land's chapter on *A Passage to India* touches on many of the major issues in the novel and makes frequent comparisons to Forster's other works.

F. R. Leavis, "E. M. Forster," in *Scrutiny,* No. 7, September, 1938, pp. 188-202.

An essay by the influential British critic that helped to canonize Forster as a major twentieth-century novelist.

Rose Macaulay, *The Writings of E. M. Forster,* London, 1938.

James McConkey, *The Novels of E. M. Forster,* Cornell University Press, 1957.

McConkey's book remains valuable both for its close study of Forster's novels in general and for its perceptive and useful discussion of *A Passage to India*

Frederick P. W. McDowell, "E. M. Forster," in *Dictionary of Literary Biography, Vol. 34: British Novelists, 1890-1929: Traditionalists,* edited by Thomas F. Staley, Gale Research Company, 1985, pp. 121-51.

A survey of Forster's life and works, with a thorough synopsis of *A Passage to India* and a discussion of the book's symbolism.

Jeffrey Meyers, "The Politics of *A Passage to India,*" in *Journal of Modern Literature,* Vol. 1, No. 3, March, 1971, pp. 329-38.

Meyers calls attention to the political and historical references of *A Passage to India,* which he believes have been ignored or underestimated by previous critics.

Leland Monk, "Apropos of Nothing: Chance and Narrative in Forster's 'A Passage to India,'" in *Studies in the Novel,* Vol. 26, No. 4, 1994, pp. 392-403.

Monk examines the narrative techniques of each of the novel's three sections and contends that the third is concerned with the importance of chance.

Judith Ruderman, "E. M. Forster" in *Encyclopedia of World Literature in the 20th Century,* revised edition, Vol. 2, General Editor Leonard S. Klein, Continuum Publishing Company/Frederick Ungar Publishing, 1982, pp. 121-25.

Ruderman notes that Forster's novels move from speech into silence, and that in *A Passage to India* Forster "recognizes the limits of the humanistic creed" and suggests that "human intercourse may be impossible and language in vain."

Chaman L. Sahni, *E. M. Forster's Passages to India: The Religious Dimension,* Heinemann, 1981.

A study of Moslem-Hindu relations in the novel and the book's representation of religion and religious symbolism.

Wilfred Stone, *The Cave and the Mountain: A Study of E. M. Forster,* Stanford University Press, 1966.

A book-length analysis of all Forster's novels. Stone regards Forster as not only a liberal humanist but also a visionary prophet akin to D. H. Lawrence. In Stone's interpretation, the cave in *A Passage to India* is a symbol of the "underworld of human experience."

Virginia Woolf, "The Novels of E. M. Forster," *Atlantic Monthly,* Vol. 115, No. 5, November, 1927; reprinted in Woolf's *The Death of the Moth and Other Essays,* London, 1942, and in *E. M. Forster: The Critical Heritage,* edited by Philip Gardner, Boston and London, 1973, pp. 321-24.

An early assessment of Forster's output by one of his leading contemporaries. Novelist Woolf notes Forster's similarity to Jane Austen in the way he captures "the shades and shadows of the social comedy," but she finds that in *A Passage to India* the realistic and symbolic aspects of Forster's narrative technique do not mesh successfully.

Slaughterhouse-Five

Kurt Vonnegut Jr.
1969

In 1969, Kurt Vonnegut Jr. was not especially well known or commercially successful, despite having already published five novels and two short story collections. The publication of *Slaughterhouse-Five* in that year marked Vonnegut's artistic and commercial breakthrough. Based on Vonnegut's own experiences as a World War II prisoner who witnessed the Allied firebombing of Dresden, Germany, *Slaughterhouse-Five* is the story of Billy Pilgrim, a man who has come "unstuck in time." Without any forewarning, he finds himself suddenly transported to other points in time in his own past or future. In chronicling the extraordinary events that happen to Billy, from witnessing the Dresden firebombing to being kidnapped by aliens, *Slaughterhouse-Five* summarizes many of the themes of Vonnegut's work. These include the dangers of unchecked technology, the limitations of human action in a seemingly random and meaningless universe, and the need for people, adrift in an indifferent world, to treat one another with kindness and decency. Almost thirty years after its initial publication, *Slaughterhouse-Five* remains Vonnegut's most discussed and widely admired novel.

Author Biography

Kurt Vonnegut Jr. was born November 11, 1922, in Indianapolis, Indiana, to Kurt and Edith (Lieber) Vonnegut. Vonnegut's father was a successful architect, and his mother's family ran an equally successful brewery. However, the onset of Prohibition, followed by the Great Depression, as well as anti-German sentiment in the wake of World War I, put the Vonnegut family under severe economic and social distress. As an undergraduate at Cornell, Vonnegut wrote articles for the school newspaper opposing American entry into World War II. After Pearl Harbor, however, Vonnegut put aside his reservations about the war and joined the U.S. Army in January, 1943. World War II saw his family's fortunes sink even lower, leading to his mother's suicide in May, 1944. Vonnegut was taken prisoner during the Battle of the Bulge. In February, 1945, while in a German prison camp, he witnessed the Allied firebombing of Dresden, an experience which later became an important part of his novel *Slaughterhouse-Five.*

After being liberated by Soviet troops in April, 1945, Vonnegut returned to the United States and was awarded the Purple Heart. He married Jane Cox in September of that year and enrolled in the graduate program in anthropology at the University of Chicago. His master's thesis was rejected, however, and in 1947 Vonnegut moved to Schenectady, New York, where he went to work as a public relations writer for the General Electric Research Laboratory. His experiences at General Electric also found their way into his fiction, most notably his first novel, *Player Piano* (1952). While working for GE, Vonnegut was also writing fiction. After publishing several short stories and his first novel, he resigned from the company in 1951 and moved to Provincetown, Massachusetts, to become a full-time writer.

Through the 1950s and 1960s, Vonnegut published several novels and numerous short stories. Novels such as *The Sirens of Titan* (1959), *Cat's Cradle* (1963), and *God Bless You, Mr. Rosewater* (1965) increased his reputation from that of a little-known author of science fiction to an "underground" favorite with a small but loyal audience. After *God Bless You, Mr. Rosewater* appeared, Vonnegut taught at the prestigious Iowa Writers' Workshop, an experience which encouraged him to be more innovative and autobiographical in his writing. The result was *Slaughterhouse-Five,* the publication of which marked the beginning of Vonnegut's widespread fame.

Although Vonnegut's works of the 1970s received uneven critical response, his popularity continued to grow. In 1971, having separated from his wife, he moved to New York City. In that same year, the University of Chicago accepted *Cat's Cradle* in lieu of a thesis paper and finally awarded

Kurt Vonnegut, Jr.

Vonnegut his master's degree in anthropology. In 1979, he married photographer Jill Krementz. During the 1970s and 1980s Vonnegut continued to produce novels, such as *Breakfast of Champions* (1973), *Slapstick* (1976), *Jailbird* (1979), and *Galapagos* (1985), as well as various essays and articles collected in *Wampeters, Foma, and Granfalloons* (1974) and *Palm Sunday* (1981), and a play, *Happy Birthday, Wanda June* (1970). Through the 1980s and into the 1990s, Vonnegut has achieved a level of fame unusual for an American writer. As a commentator on social issues and an outspoken opponent of censorship and militarism, he continues to be not merely a well-known novelist, but a significant figure in American culture.

Plot Summary

Part I—Introduction

Slaughterhouse-Five tells the story of Billy Pilgrim, a man who has come "unstuck in time." At any point in his life, he may find himself suddenly at another point in his past or future. Billy's experiences as an American prisoner of war in Germany during World War II are told in more or less chronological order, but these events are continually interrupted by Billy's travels to various other times in his life.

At several points in the novel, including the whole of Chapter One, Vonnegut addresses the reader directly. In the opening chapter, the author mentions his own real-life experiences as a prisoner of war—in particular, his witnessing of the Allied firebombing of the German city of Dresden—and discusses the difficulties he had over the years in writing about his war experiences. He also tells of his visit with Bernard O'Hare, who was a prisoner along with Vonnegut, and of their trip back to Germany. When O'Hare's wife learns that Vonnegut is planning to write a book about he war, she becomes angry, thinking that Vonnegut will glamorize the war. The author promises her that he will not and that he will call his book "The Children's Crusade."

Part II—Billy Pilgrim in the War

Chapter Two begins Billy Pilgrim's story. Born in Ilium, New York, in 1922, Billy is drafted into the Army during World War II. Assigned to the post of chaplin's assistant, Billy is sent overseas to Europe, where, in 1944, his regiment is all but destroyed during the Battle of the Bulge. The only survivors are Billy, two experienced scouts, and Roland Weary, a sadistic bully whose hobbies include collecting instruments of torture. The other three soldiers are reasonably well-clad and armed, but Billy has "no helmet, no overcoat, no weapon, and no boots." While wandering with the other three soldiers, Billy has his first experience of being "unstuck in time," travelling in quick succession to several points in his past and future before returning to 1944.

Eventually, the two scouts desert Billy and Roland, for which Roland blames Billy. The two are quickly captured by a band of German soldiers who have ambushed and killed the two scouts. They are then transported to a prison camp aboard a horribly overcrowded train. Several prisoners die along the way, including Roland Weary, who has contracted gangrene. Before he dies, Weary blames Billy for his death and asks the other soldiers to avenge him.

After ten days on the train, Billy and the other prisoners arrive at a prison camp originally used to exterminate Russian prisoners. After being processed into the camp, the Americans are enthusiastically greeted by the British prisoners, who have been in the camp for over four years. While the Americans are in terrible shape physi-

cally and emotionally, the British have kept themselves in excellent condition. Appalled at the sorry state of the Americans, the British offer them food and clothing, and even entertain them with a play of *Cinderella.* The Americans are made sick by the rich food. Billy, who is in even worse shape than many of the others, falls into an hysterical fit during the play and has to be restrained and tranquilized. He is taken to the prison hospital, where he meets Paul Lazzaro, who had befriended Roland Weary on the prison train and promised Weary that he would one day kill Billy as an act of revenge.

The American prisoners are transferred to the German city of Dresden, an "open city" with no strategic value that is supposed to be safe from attack. They are housed in an abandoned slaughterhouse—Slaughterhouse-Five. At one point they are visited by Howard W. Campbell, Jr., an American who has gone over to the Nazis. When Campbell tries to talk the prisoners into switching sides, he is roundly condemned by Edgar Derby, a forty-four-year-old schoolteacher who has nursed Billy in the prison hospital and who is by now the unofficial leader of the American prisoners.

One night, while the Americans are underground in the slaughterhouse meat locker, Dresden is firebombed by the Allies, who have chosen to attack the city despite its lack of military significance. When the soldiers return to the surface the next morning, they find the entire city has been destroyed and almost all its inhabitants have been killed:

> The guards told the Americans to form in ranks of four, which they did. Then they had them march back to the hog barn which had been their home. Its walls still stood, but its windows and roof were gone, and there was nothing inside but ashes and dollops of melted glass. It was realized then that there was no food or water, and that the survivors, if they were going to continue to survive, were going to have to climb over curve after curve on the face of the moon.
>
> Which they did.
>
> The curves were smooth only when seen from a distance. The people climbing them had learned that they were treacherous, jagged things—hot to the touch, often unstable—eager, should certain important rocks be disturbed, to tumble some more, to form lower, more solid curves.
>
> Nobody talked much as the expedition crossed the moon. There was nothing appropriate to say. One thing was clear: Absolutely everybody in the city was supposed to be dead, regardless of what they were, and that anybody that moved in it represented a flaw in the design. There were to be no moon men at all.

135,000 civilians are killed in the raid, almost twice the number who would later die at Hiroshima.

The German guards who had been in the meat locker with the Americans march the prisoners to a suburb, where they are taken in by a blind innkeeper and housed in a stable. The Americans are then taken back into Dresden and forced to dig through the ruins for bodies. Edgar Derby, after being caught taking a teapot from the ruins, is executed by a firing squad. Eventually, however, the war in Europe ends, and Billy and the surviving prisoners return home.

Part III—Billy Back Home

Back in Ilium, Billy resumes classes at the Ilium School of Optometry, where he had been a student before the war. During his senior year, he becomes engaged to Valencia Merble, the wealthy daughter of the owner of the optometry school. Shortly after his engagement, Billy suffers "a mild nervous collapse," checks himself into a veteran's hospital near Lake Placid, and undergoes electroshock therapy. Six months after leaving the hospital and graduating from optometry school, he marries Valencia.

Billy's life from this point on is one of unexpected material prosperity, as his father-in-law sets him up in a lucrative optometry practice. He and Valencia have two children, Barbara and Robert. However, Billy continues to come "unstuck in time," periodically and without warning, a condition he does not discuss with anyone.

Part IV—Billy on Tralfamadore

In 1967, on his daughter's wedding night, Billy is kidnapped by aliens from the planet Tralfamadore. The aliens take him back to their home planet and display him naked in a cage. After being on display for some time, Billy is joined by Montana Wildhack, a movie actress. They become lovers and have a child together. Finally, Billy is returned to Earth, while Montana stays behind to take care of their child. When Billy returns, it is only a moment after he left. He has not even been missed.

While on Tralfamadore, Billy learns of the aliens' philosophy of time and death. For Tralfamadorians, time is not a linear progression of events, but a constant condition: "All moments, past, present, and future, always have existed, always will exist." Like Billy, the aliens can travel back and forth to different moments in time. They do not consider death a significant event, since

when a person dies he or she "is still very much alive in the past." The Tralfamadorians advise Billy "to concentrate on the happy moments of life, and to ignore the unhappy ones."

Part V—Billy Back on Earth

At first, Billy does not tell anyone of his kidnapping. A year later, however, while on a chartered flight to an optometrists' convention, his plane crashes, and everyone on board is killed except for Billy and the copilot. Valencia, desperately trying to get to the hospital to see Billy, is killed in an auto accident.

After his release from the hospital, Billy returns home, but soon travels to New York, where he shows up at a radio talk show and, mistaken for someone else, is allowed to go on the air. He tells the story of his captivity on Tralfamadore and is "gently expelled" from the studio. Billy's daughter Barbara and her husband come to New York and take Billy home, after which he begins to write letters to newspapers telling of his experiences with aliens.

Billy dies on February 13, 1976—the anniversary of the Dresden bombing. He is gunned down by an assassin hired by Paul Lazzaro, who is still alive and has never forgotten his promise to kill Billy. However, Billy the time traveller "has seen his own death many times" and is unconcerned. After the shooting, Billy "experiences death for a while" and then "swings back into life again" at a point in 1945, "an hour after his life was threatened by Lazzaro." Billy, like the Tralfamadorians, regards death with a shrug and a "So it goes." There will always be another moment.

Characters

Billy Pilgrim's father

Billy Pilgrim's father, whose full name is not given, is a barber in Ilium, New York. He dies in a hunting accident while Billy is in military training in South Carolina. Billy attends his funeral shortly before being shipped overseas.

Billy Pilgrim's mother

Billy's mother, whose name is not given, survives into old age. Billy visits her in a rest home in 1965.

Wild Bob

Wild Bob is an American prisoner of war who dies en route to Dresden. Shortly before he dies, he

Media Adaptations

- *Slaughterhouse-Five* was adapted for the screen by writer Stephen Geller and director George Roy Hill in 1972. The film stars Michael Sacks as Billy Pilgrim, Ron Leibman as Paul Lazzaro, and Valerie Perrine as Montana Wildhack. Available on MCA/Universal Home Video.

- The novel is also available in abridged form as a sound recording, read by the author, on Harper Audio, 1994.

gives a speech to imaginary troops encouraging them to continue fighting the Germans and inviting them to visit him in the United States after the war. His delusions as to his troops and the glories of combat represent the overall absurdity of both war and the attempt to control the uncontrollable.

Howard W. Campbell Jr.

An American who has gone over to the Nazis and works in the German Ministry of Propaganda, Campbell visits the American prisoners in Dresden and tries to convince them to leave the Allies. Campbell is also the main character in Vonnegut's earlier novel *Mother Night.*

Colonel

See Wild Bob

Edgar Derby

Derby is a high school teacher from Indianapolis who becomes the unofficial leader of the American prisoners in Dresden. He is a fundamentally decent man and a natural leader. He is also very kind to Billy Pilgrim. After the firebombing of Dresden, he is caught stealing a teapot and is shot by the Germans for plundering—a pointless death that underscores the absurdity and tragedy of war.

English colonel

See Head Englishman

Head Englishman

The head of the English prisoners of war is a colonel. He is friendly but slightly condescending to the Americans, who do not share the English prisoners' determination to remain disciplined, organized, and cheerful during their captivity.

Paul Lazzaro

Lazzaro is an American prisoner of war in Dresden who befriends Roland Weary and promises to avenge Weary's death, which Weary blames on Billy. Lazzaro survives the war and hires the assassin who kills Billy in 1976.

Lionel Merble

Lionel Merble is Billy Pilgrim's father-in-law. He sets Billy up in a successful optometry practice. He is killed in a plane crash when he and Billy are travelling to an optometrist's convention; Billy and the copilot are the only survivors. Although not a bad man, Lionel Merble may be seen as representing the callousness and shallow materialism of postwar America.

Bernard V. O'Hare

Bernard is Vonnegut's "old war buddy" with whom Vonnegut witnessed the Dresden firebombing. A real-life person with whom Vonnegut travelled back to Dresden in the 1960s, Bernard makes an appearance at the novel's beginning.

Mary O'Hare

Mary O'Hare is Bernard's wife and another real-life person to appear in the novel. Mary objects to Vonnegut's writing about Dresden, worrying that he might make war seem romantic and glamorous. Vonnegut promises that he will subtitle his book "The Children's Crusade."

Barbara Pilgrim

Barbara is Billy Pilgrim's daughter. It is on the night of her wedding that Billy is kidnapped by the Tralfamadorians. After her mother's death, Barbara assumes a parental role with the increasingly detached Billy and is both impatient with and embarrassed by Billy's stories about the Tralfamadorians.

Billy Pilgrim

At one point in *Slaughterhouse-Five,* Vonnegut writes, "There are almost no characters in this story … because most of the people in it are so sick and so much the listless playthings of enormous forces." This description certainly applies to Billy. From his earliest childhood memories of be-

Still from the 1972 movie Slaughterhouse-Five, *based on Kurt Vonnegut's book of the same name.*

ing tossed in the deep end of a pool to learn how to swim, or being dragged against his will on a family vacation to the Grand Canyon, Billy has been at the mercy of "enormous forces." As a soldier captured after the Battle of the Bulge by German soldiers, Billy is pathetically unprepared for the pressures of combat and reacts to the horrific events he witnesses, including the firebombing of Dresden, Germany, with varying degrees of disassociation and withdrawal. It is while he is a prisoner that he first becomes "unstuck in time," finding himself travelling into the past and future with no warning. This time travel is both a literal science-fiction event and a metaphor for the alienation and dislocation Billy, and contemporary humanity, feel in the face of overwhelming and inexplicable cruelty and violence.

Billy is later kidnapped by aliens from the planet Tralfamadore. The aliens' philosophy explicitly rejects the concept of free will. They believe that events cannot be changed by a person's actions. This idea reinforces the theme that Billy, and everyone else, is at the mercy of forces largely beyond our control. In fact, the only active response Billy has during the entire novel is his attempt to publicize his abduction by aliens. It is appropriate that the closest relationship Billy has is not with

his wife or family but with Kilgore Trout, a science fiction writer whose novels see through the illusion of logic and control.

After the war, Billy becomes an optometrist, marries, and has two children. His life is mundane, but he continues his time-traveling experiences, which are, like everything else, beyond his power to control. His time spent with the Tralfamadorians helps him to gain a peaceful perspective on life. In the end, Billy comes to accept the fact that he cannot change events, and he devotes life to teaching the philosophy of the Tralfamadorians to the people of Earth.

Robert Pilgrim

Robert is Billy Pilgrim's son. After having "a lot of trouble" in high school, Robert joined the military, became a Green Beret, fought in Vietnam, and "became a fine young man."

Valencia Merble Pilgrim

Valencia is Billy Pilgrim's wife. A wealthy but unattractive woman, she is hopelessly in love with Billy, but Billy never really loves her and sees her as "one of the symptoms of his disease." While Billy is hospitalized after surviving his plane crash, Valencia is killed in a traffic accident while rushing to be with Billy in the hospital—another inno-cent victim of an absurd and indifferent universe.

Eliot Rosewater

Eliot Rosewater is a friendly eccentric with whom Billy Pilgrim shares a hospital room after Billy's breakdown. Rosewater and Billy "both found life meaningless, partly because of what they had seen in the war." It is Rosewater who intro-duces Billy to science fiction, especially the nov-els of Kilgore Trout. Rosewater is also the title character of Vonnegut's earlier novel *God Bless You, Mr. Rosewater.*

Bertrand Copeland Rumfoord

A Harvard professor and official Historian of the U.S. Air Force, Rumfoord shares a hospital room with Billy Pilgrim after Pilgrim's plane crash. Rumfoord is a fervent patriot and an outspoken sup-porter of the Allied firebombing of Dresden. He is, like Roland Weary, yet another example of the delusional belief in the romance of war and hu-manity's ability to control the uncontrollable.

Tralfamadorians

The alien race that kidnaps Billy Pilgrim are from the planet Tralfamadore. Although never rep-resented as individuals, the Tralfamadorians pro-vide the philosophy of time and free will that un-derlies the novel.

Kilgore Trout

Kilgore Trout is a science fiction novelist and Billy Pilgrim's favorite writer. He lives in Illium and supports himself by delivering newspapers. Billy meets Trout for the first time in 1964 and be-friends him. Trout represents yet another way of try-ing to cope with the absurd tragedy of human exis-tence. Some critics have also seen him as a projection of Vonnegut's own anxieties about be-ing typecast as a science fiction writer. Both Trout and his novels are mentioned in other Vonnegut novels.

Kurt Vonnegut Jr.

One of the unusual aspects of *Slaughterhouse-Five* is that its author appears as a character in his on novel. Vonnegut appears throughout the first and last chapters, where he discusses his difficulty in writing the novel and his visit back to Dresden some twenty years after his imprisonment there.

Roland Weary

Weary is one of the three other soldiers cap-tured with Billy Pilgrim after the Battle of the Bulge. He is a sadistic bully who despises Billy and whose hobbies include collecting instruments of torture. He imagines that there is great camaraderie between him and the two scouts with whom he and Billy are lost, but the scouts eventually abandon both Weary and Billy. Weary dies of gangrene on the train to Dresden, blames Billy for his death, and asks other soldiers to avenge him. Weary's ag-gressively violent nature and delusional belief in the romance of war represent the militarism and ha-tred that Vonnegut is condemning in the novel.

Montana Wildhack

Montana is a twenty-year-old American movie star who is kidnapped by the Tralfamadorians to be a mate for Billy Pilgrim during his captivity. She and Billy have a child while they are being kept by the Tralfamadorians.

Themes

Kurt Vonnegut Jr.'s *Slaughterhouse-Five* tells the story of Billy Pilgrim, a man who is "unstuck" in time. The two central events Billy keeps return-ing to are his abduction by aliens from the planet Tralfamadore and his time as a prisoner of war dur-ing World War II, during which he witnesses the Allied firebombing of the German city of Dresden.

Alienation and Loneliness

Alienation may be defined as, among other things, an inability to make connections with other individuals and with society as a whole. In this sense, Billy Pilgrim is a profoundly alienated indi-vidual. He is unable to connect in a literal sense, as his being "unstuck in time" prevents him from building the continuous set of experiences which form a person's relationships with others. While Billy's situation is literal in the sense of being a science fiction device—he is "literally" travelling through time—it also serves as a metaphor for the sense of alienation and dislocation which follows the experience of catastrophic violence (World War II). This violence is, for Vonnegut and many other modern writers, a fact of life for humanity in the twentieth century. It is appropriate that what is ar-guably the closest relationship Billy has in the novel is with the science fiction writer Kilgore Trout, another deeply alienated individual: "he and Billy were dealing with similar crises in similar ways. They had both found life meaningless, partly because of what they had seen in the war."

Free Will

One of the most important themes of *Slaughterhouse-Five* is that of free will, or, more precisely, its absence. This concept is articulated through the philosophy of the Tralfamadorians, for whom time is not a linear progression of events, but a constant condition: "All moments, past, present, and future, always have existed, always will exist." All beings exist in each moment of time like "bugs in amber," a fact that nothing can alter. "Only on Earth is there any talk of free will." What happens, happens. "Among the things Billy Pilgrim could not change were the past, the present, and the future." Accordingly, the Tralfamadorians advise Billy "to concentrate on the happy moments of life, and to ignore the unhappy ones."

Apathy and Passivity

Apathy and passivity are natural responses to the idea that events are beyond our control. Throughout *Slaughterhouse-Five* Billy Pilgrim does not act so much as he is acted upon. If he is not captured by the Germans, he is kidnapped by the Tralfamadorians. Only later in life, when Billy tries to tell the world about his abduction by the Tralfamadorians, does he initiate action, and even that may be seen as a kind of response to his predetermined fate. Other characters may try to varying degrees to initiate actions, but seldom to any avail. As Vonnegut notes in Chapter Eight, "There are almost no characters in this story, and almost no dramatic confrontations, because most of the people in it are so sick and so much the listless playthings of enormous forces."

Death

Given the absence of free will and the inevitability of events, there is little reason to be overly concerned about death. The Tralfamadorian response to death is, "So it goes," and Vonnegut repeats this phrase at every point in the novel where someone, or something, dies. Billy Pilgrim, in his travels through time, "has seen his own death many times" and is unconcerned because he knows he will always exist in the past.

Patriotism

The world as depicted in *Slaughterhouse-Five* is a world in which patriotism twists into nationalism and militarism and becomes an excuse for acts of violence and mass destruction. Those who claim to be patriots, such as "Wild Bob," the American prisoner of war who gives speeches to imaginary troops, or Bertrand Copeland Rumford, an Air

Topics for Further Study

- Research the Dresden, Germany, firebombing of World War II and compare Vonnegut's account of the event with the historical record.

- Research the history of UFO sightings in the United States and compare Billy Pilgrim's experience with the Tralfamadorians to actual reported sightings and "abductions."

- Compare and contrast *Slaughterhouse-Five* with another well-known novel of war, such as *The Red Badge of Courage* or *All Quiet on the Western Front*.

Force historian who defends the Dresden raid, are deluded at best and malevolent at worst. More realistic is the reaction of the German soldiers in Dresden to the American prisoners: "There was nothing to be afraid of. Here were more crippled human beings, more fools like themselves."

War and Peace

Slaughterhouse-Five deals with many different themes, but it is most of all a novel about the horrors of war. For Vonnegut, war is not an enterprise of glory and heroism, but an uncontrolled catastrophe for all involved, and anyone who seeks glory and heroism in war is deluded. Although World War II is regarded by most as a justified conflict which defeated the genocidal regime of Nazi Germany, Vonnegut sees only victims on all sides, from the American soldier executed by the Germans for looting to the 135,000 German civilians killed in the Allied firebombing of Dresden. The horrors of the war are so overwhelming that Vonnegut doubts his ability to write about them. Speaking directly in the first chapter, he says of the novel, "It is so short and jumbled and jangled … because there is nothing intelligent to say about a massacre." The only response to the nightmare of war is a profound alienation and distancing, made literal by Billy Pilgrim's being "unstuck in time." Appropriately, Billy's condition offers the most striking image of peace in the novel, as he becomes unstuck in time while watching a war movie on television and sees it backwards:

> The bombers opened their bomb bay doors, exerted a miraculous magnetism which shrunk the fires, gathered them into cylindrical steel containers, and lifted the containers into the bellies of the planes…. The steel cylinders were taken from the racks and shipped back to the United States of America, where factories were operating night and day, dismantling the cylinders, separating the dangerous contents into minerals … [which] were then shipped to specialists in remote areas. It was their business to put them into the ground, to hide them cleverly, so they would never hurt anybody ever again.

Science and Technology

Although *Slaughterhouse-Five* does not deal as directly with issues of science and technology as do other Vonnegut novels such as *Player Piano* and *Cat's Cradle,* the limitations of technology remain an important theme. The destruction of World War II would not have been possible without "advances" in technology (the long-range bombers that destroyed Dresden; the poison gas used on concentration camp inmates). And the extraordinarily advanced technology of the Tralfamadorians not only cannot prevent the end of the Universe, but actually causes it: "We [Tralfamadorians] blow it up, experimenting with new fuels for our flying saucers."

Style

Structure

Perhaps the most notable aspect of *Slaughterhouse-Five*'s technique is its unusual structure. The novel's protagonist, Billy Pilgrim, has come "unstuck in time"; at any point in his life, he may find himself suddenly at another point in his past or future. Billy's time travel begins early on during the major experience of his life—his capture by German soldiers during World War II and subsequent witnessing of the Allied firebombing of Dresden, Germany. Both the centrality of this event and its radically alienating effect on the rest of Billy's life are represented by the novel's structure. Billy's experiences as a prisoner of war are told in more or less chronological order, but these events are continually interrupted by Billy's travels to various other times in his life, both past and future. In this way, the novel's structure highlights both the centrality of Billy's war experiences to his life, as well as the profound dislocation and alienation he feels after the war.

Point of View

Another unusual aspect of *Slaughterhouse-Five* is its use of point of view. Rather than employing a conventional third-person "narrative voice," the novel is narrated by the author himself. The first chapter consists of Vonnegut discussing the difficulties he had in writing the novel, and Vonnegut himself appears onstage as a character several times later in the novel. Instead of obscuring the autobiographical elements of the novel, Vonnegut makes them explicit; instead of presenting his novel as a self-contained creative work, he makes it clear that it is an imperfect and incomplete attempt to come to terms with an overwhelming event. In a sentence directed to his publisher, Vonnegut says of the novel, "It is so short and jumbled and jangled, Sam, because there is nothing intelligent to say about a massacre."

Symbolism

Slaughterhouse-Five is, among other things, a work of science fiction. As such, both Billy Pilgrim's travels through time and his abduction by aliens are presented as literal events. However, as in the best science fiction, these literal events also have symbolic significance. Billy's being "unstuck in time" is both a literal event and a metaphor for the sense of profound dislocation and alienation felt by the survivors of war, while the aliens from the planet Tralfamadore provide a vehicle for Vonnegut's speculations on fate and free will.

Style

Style—the way an author arranges his or her words, sentences, and paragraphs into prose—is one of the most difficult aspects of literature to analyze. However, it should be noted that *Slaughterhouse-Five* is written in a very distinctive style. In describing overwhelming, horrible, and often inexplicable events, Vonnegut deliberately uses a very simple, straightforward prose style. He often describes complex events in the language one might use to explain something to a child, as in this description of Billy Pilgrim being marched to a German prison camp:

> A motion-picture camera was set up at the border—to record the fabulous victory. Two civilians in bearskin coats were leaning on the camera when Billy and Weary came by. They had run out of film hours ago.
>
> One of them singled out Billy's face for a moment, then focused at infinity again. There was a tiny plume of smoke at infinity. There was a battle there. People were dying there. So it goes.

In writing this way, Vonnegut forces the reader to confront the fundamental horror and absurdity of war head-on, with no embellishments, as if his readers were seeing it clearly for the first time.

Black Humor

Black humor refers to an author's deliberate use of humor in describing what would ordinarily be considered a situation too violent, grim, or tragic to laugh at. In so doing, the author is able to convey not merely the tragedy, but also the absurdity, of an event. Vonnegut uses black humor throughout *Slaughterhouse-Five,* both in small details (the description of the half-crazed Billy Pilgrim, after the Battle of the Bulge, as a "filthy flamingo") and in larger plot elements (Billy's attempts to publicize his encounters with the Tralfamadorians), to reinforce the idea that the horrors of war are not only tragic, but inexplicable and absurd.

Dresden, Germany, after the Allied bombing attack during World War II. As a prisoner of war, Kurt Vonnegut witnessed the firebombing of the city.

Historical Context

The Firebombing of Dresden

The most important historical event which informs *Slaughterhouse-Five* took place almost a quarter of a century before the novel was published. On February 13 and 14, 1945, allied aircraft dropped incendiary bombs on the German city of Dresden—a so-called "open city" with no significant military targets. The bombing raid created a firestorm that destroyed the city and killed an estimated 135,000 people, almost all of them civilians. This was nearly twice the number of people killed by the first atomic bomb dropped on Hiroshima. The Dresden bombing remains the single heaviest air strike in military history. The raid remains controversial to this day, as many historians have suggested that the raid served no real military purpose and did nothing to hasten Germany's defeat. Approximately one hundred American prisoners of war, captured at the Battle of the Bulge, were in Dresden during the bombing. Vonnegut was one of them.

The Vietnam War

The war between communist North Vietnam and non-communist South Vietnam began in 1954 and ended in 1975 with a North Vietnamese victory and the reunification of Vietnam under communist rule. This same time period also covered most of the Cold War between the United States and the Soviet Union, a political conflict which led to the United States entering the Vietnam War on the side of South Vietnam. The year before Vonnegut's novel was published, 1968, saw the American presence in Vietnam peak at 543,000 troops. As American involvement increased, so did opposition to the war among Americans. By 1969, a sitting President, Lyndon Johnson, had chosen not to run for reelection because of his role in prosecuting the war. Also, antiwar sentiment had taken the form of mass demonstrations and the migration of thousands of young American men to Canada, Sweden, and other countries in order to avoid the draft.

Although Vonnegut's novel is centered on events which took place in the 1940s during World War II, it is very much a product of the Vietnam era. Vonnegut even makes direct references to Vietnam in Chapter Three, when Billy Pilgrim, in 1967, listens to a speech by a Marine urging increased bombing of North Vietnam. And in Chapter Ten Vonnegut refers to the 1968 assassinations of Martin Luther King, Jr., and Robert Kennedy while observing that "every day my Government gives me a count of corpses created by military science in Vietnam." It is perhaps no surprise that a novel which faced head-on the horrors of war, as well as

Compare & Contrast

• **1940s:** World War II was a decisive victory for the United States and its allies and was widely supported by Americans. Americans' knowledge of the war came from delayed accounts in newspapers, on radio, and in newsreels shown in movie theaters. By the end of the war, the United States was the top military and economic power in the world.

1960s: American involvement in the Vietnam War eventually lost the support of most citizens, perhaps in part because of extensive television news coverage, which brought the realities of war into American living rooms. The war concluded in 1975 with the United States withdrawing from Vietnam—the only war America ever lost. While still the "leader of the free world," the Vietnam War deals a strong blow to American prestige around the world.

Today: The United States's most recent military conflict, the Persian Gulf War against Iraq, was an overwhelming victory, in part because of American determination to avoid "another Vietnam." The war enjoyed widespread support among Americans. However, media coverage was carefully controlled by the military. Although the end of the Cold War after the collapse of the Soviet Union left America as the only true "superpower," its economic su-

premacy is being challenged by countries like Japan, China, and Germany. There is a reluctance within the U.S. government and the populace to commit U.S. troops to military conflicts overseas.

• **1940s:** Before the first wave of UFO sightings begins in 1947, popular awareness of "aliens from outer space" was mostly confined to the readers of pulp science fiction magazines.

1960s: The U.S. Air Force reports almost three thousand UFO sightings between 1965 and 1967; congressional hearings on the issue are held in 1966. The science fiction movies of the 1950s and 1960s, television shows such as "Star Trek" and "The Invaders," and the American space program all dramatically increase public awareness of the possibility of life on other planets.

Today: Claims of "alien abductions" become almost commonplace. Popular television shows and movies, such as "The X-Files" and "Independence Day," and extraordinary public events, such as the Heaven's Gate mass suicide, in 1997, bring public awareness of the UFO phenomenon to all all-time high. The first planets outside the solar system have been discovered, and scientists, led by such astronomers as the late Carl Sagan, now seriously speculate about the possibilities of life on other planets.

American responsibility for some of those horrors, struck a chord with the reading public at a time when many Americans were beginning to think their country had made a terrible mistake.

The UFO Phenomenon

An important element of *Slaughterhouse-Five* is Billy Pilgrim's abduction by aliens from the planet Tralfamadore. In the 1990s, "alien abduction" has become a well-recognized cultural myth, as countless individuals claim to have been abducted by aliens from outer space. Public speculation about UFOs (Unidentified Flying Objects) and

the possibility of life on other planets is at an all-time high, fueled by both popular entertainment (television shows such as *Star Trek* and *The X-Files,* movies such as *E.T.* and *Independence Day*), scientific discoveries (the identification of planets outside our solar system), and news events (the Heaven's Gate mass suicides of 1997).

Although Vonnegut's novel predates the current wave of popular awareness of UFOs, the phenomenon was already well-documented when *Slaughterhouse-Five* appeared in 1969. Beginning in 1947, reports of UFOs came in waves from all over the world. Between 1965 and 1967, the U.S.

Air Force received almost three thousand reports of UFO sightings. In 1966, there was even a congressional hearing on the subject, and the Air Force appointed scientist Edward U. Condon to investigate the matter. Condon's conclusion—that there was "no direct evidence whatever" that UFOs were in fact extraterrestrial spacecraft—was the subject of great controversy.

Science Fiction

Slaughterhouse-Five is, among other things, a science fiction novel, and it is also a novel with a strong awareness of the history of science fiction. Vonnegut began his writing career labeled as a science fiction writer, a classification he never fully escaped until the 1960s. In its use of the alien Tralfamadorians, his novel shows a keen awareness of the staples of both written "pulp" science fiction of the 1930s and 1940s and the popular movies of the 1950s. The character of Kilgore Trout is especially interesting in this regard. Some critics have seen Trout—a visionary writer doomed to poverty and obscurity because of his work in a literary genre considered to be inferior to "real" literature—as a projection of Vonnegut's own fears of how he might have wound up if he had not escaped the "science fiction" label. Others have suggested that Trout is modeled on actual science fiction writers of the 1950s, especially Philip K. Dick and Theodore Sturgeon.

Critical Overview

There is a substantial body of criticism on Kurt Vonnegut, Jr.'s work in general, and on *Slaughterhouse-Five* in particular. While critics have often found Vonnegut's fiction as a whole to be uneven in quality, they have frequently praised him for *Slaughterhouse-Five*, which is widely regarded as the author's finest work.

The tone for much of the criticism that followed the book's release was set by Robert Scholes in his review of *Slaughterhouse-Five*, which appeared in the *New York Times Book Review* shortly after the novel's publication in 1969. Scholes praised Vonnegut's humor, noting that it "does not disguise the awful things perceived; it merely strengthens and comforts us to the point where such perception is bearable." He asserted that the absurd elements of the novel are appropriate and necessary to deal with the absurdity of the world. He considered the novel to be "an extraordinary suc-

cess ... a book we need to read, and to reread ... funny, compassionate, and wise." The noted critic Granville Hicks, reviewing the novel in *Saturday Review,* compared Vonnegut to Mark Twain as both a humorist and moralist.

Much of the later criticism of *Slaughterhouse-Five* has emphasized the book's unusual and innovative structure. In *Vonnegut: A Preface to His Novels* (1977), Richard Giannone observed that "Vonnegut the witness draws moral force by undermining conventional narrative authority" and "comments on the reality of Dresden by treating the problems of fiction." In his 1990 study *"Slaughterhouse-Five": Reforming the Novel and the World,* Jerome Klinkowitz observed that the Tralfamadorian concept of time is also "the overthrow of nearly every Aristotelian convention that has contributed to the novel's form in English over the past three centuries." And in an earlier study of Vonnegut, Klinkowitz links the author's experiments with narrative form to those of other experimental writers of the 1960s, such as John Barth, Donald Barthelme, and Thomas Pynchon.

Several critics have also focused on *Slaughterhouse-Five* as a work of science fiction. Reviewing the novel in the *New Republic,* J. Michael Crichton compared it to works by such well-known science fiction authors as Robert A. Heinlein, J. G. Ballard, and Roger Zelazny, all of whom were, like Vonnegut, popular among the youth "counterculture" of the 1960s. James Lundquist spent a chapter of his 1977 study of Vonnegut examining Vonnegut's connections to science fiction, noting especially the character of science fiction novelist Kilgore Trout. Interestingly, critics from within the science fiction field are frequently uncomfortable with Vonnegut's use of science fiction devices. Thomas D. Clareson, writing in *Understanding Contemporary American Science Fiction,* agreed with noted British science fiction novelist and critic Brian W. Aldiss that Vonnegut's use of time travel and other science fiction devices is "intrusive."

While the critical reception of *Slaughterhouse-Five* has been overwhelmingly positive, some critics have expressed reservations concerning the novel's apparent endorsement of passive acceptance as an appropriate response to evil. Crichton suggested that Vonnegut "refuses to say who is wrong ... ascribes no blame, sets no penalties." And Tony Tanner, in his 1971 book *City of Words,* worried that Vonnegut's vision is one of "moral indifference." The overwhelming popular success of *Slaughterhouse-Five* has also been somewhat tempered by the fact that it is one of the novels most frequently banned from high school classrooms. This is presumably because of its unsparing violence and occasionally explicit language. Nonetheless, Vonnegut's novel has maintained a level of popular and critical success seldom achieved by any book. Most readers and critics have agreed with Tanner, who, despite his concerns about "moral indifference," concluded that Vonnegut's most famous work is "a masterly novel" of "clarity and economy—and compassion."

Criticism

F. Brett Cox

F. Brett Cox is an assistant professor of English at Gordon College in Barnesville, Georgia. In the following essay, Cox explains how Slaughterhouse-Five *represents Vonnegut's efforts to come to terms with his personal war experiences. Other aspects of the novel are of secondary concern when compared to Vonnegut's anti-war theme.*

In 1969, Kurt Vonnegut, Jr., had already published five novels and two short story collections, but he was not especially well known or commercially successful. The publication of *Slaughterhouse-Five* in that year was an artistic and commercial breakthrough for Vonnegut. According to the critic Jerome Klinkowitz, one of the leading authorities on Vonnegut, *Slaughterhouse-Five* was Vonnegut's "first bestseller. [It] catapulted him to sudden national fame, and brought his writing into serious intellectual esteem." Other critics have noted the novel as a summation of many of the themes of Vonnegut's work: the dangers of unchecked technology, the limitations of human action in a seemingly random and meaningless universe, and the need for people, adrift in an indifferent world, to treat one another with kindness and decency. Almost thirty years later, *Slaughterhouse-Five* remains Vonnegut's most discussed and widely admired novel.

Many critics and scholars have suggested that Vonnegut's breakthrough in *Slaughterhouse-Five* occurred because here, for the first time, he addressed directly the pivotal event of his own life. While serving in the U.S. Army during World War II, Vonnegut was captured by the Germans and, while a prisoner of war, witnessed the firebombing of the German city of Dresden—an "open city" with no significant military targets. On the night of

February 13, 1945, Allied bombers dropped incendiary bombs on Dresden, creating a firestorm that destroyed the city and killed an estimated 135,000 people, almost all of them civilians. This was nearly twice the number of people killed by the first atomic bomb dropped on Hiroshima. The Dresden bombing remains the single heaviest air strike in military history.

Vonnegut's effort to come to terms with such an overwhelming—and, in the view of many historians, unnecessary—catastrophe took the form of a novel with a highly unusual structure. Rather than employing a conventional third-person "narrative voice," *Slaughterhouse-Five* is narrated by the author himself. The first chapter consists of Vonnegut discussing the difficulties he had in writing the novel, and Vonnegut himself appears onstage as a character several times later in the book. In a sentence directed to his publisher, Vonnegut said of the novel, "It is so short and jumbled and jangled, Sam, because there is nothing intelligent to say about a massacre."

The novel's "short and jumbled and jangled" structure reflects the condition of its protagonist, Billy Pilgrim. Like Vonnegut, Billy is taken prisoner by the Germans and witnesses the Dresden firebombing. Billy's response, however, is not to write a novel but to become "unstuck in time." Beginning during this captivity behind German lines, Pilgrim finds himself liable at any time, suddenly and without warning, to travel to any given moment in his own past or future. Although the novel follows Billy's war experiences in more or less chronological order, a scene of Billy in a German prison camp may be followed immediately by a scene of his wedding night, or a time when his father taught him to swim as a child.

Billy's condition is, on one level, a symbol of the shock, confusion, dislocation, and desire for escape that result from the horrible experiences of war. His time travels could, perhaps, be interpreted as the delusions of an emotionally unstable man. It is important to remember, however, that several of Vonnegut's earlier novels, such as *Player Piano, The Sirens of Titan,* and *Cat's Cradle,* were science fiction novels. Billy's time travel may be symbolic, but it may also be interpreted as an actual event, an example of science fiction's ability to make metaphors concrete.

The most overtly science-fictional element in *Slaughterhouse-Five* is, of course, Billy's abduction by aliens from the planet Tralfamadore on his daughter's wedding night many years after the war.

What Do I Read Next?

- *Player Piano,* Kurt Vonnegut, Jr.'s 1952 novel, also deals with the limitations of science and technology.

- *The Red Badge of Courage* (1895) is Stephen Crane's classic story of the Civil War that, like Vonnegut's novel, portrays the horrors of war in an unromanticized fashion.

- Erich Maria Remarque's *All Quiet on the Western Front* (1928) is a classic novel of World War I that, like Vonnegut's novel, portrays German soldiers as ordinary people caught up in the horrors of war.

- Norman Mailer's *The Naked and the Dead* (1948) was one of the first major American novels based on its author's experiences in World War II.

- Tim O'Brien's *Going After Cacciato* (1978) was one of the first major American novels based on its author's experiences in Vietnam.

- Ray Bradbury's *Fahrenheit 451* (1953) is another example of science fiction as social criticism.

- Vonnegut's 1962 novel, *The Sirens of Titan,* also features the Tralfamadorians.

- Daniel Keyes' *Flowers for Algernon* (1966) uses both science fiction devices and an unusual narrative structure to tell a story of alienation and displacement.

- *More Than Human* (1953) is the most famous novel by science fiction writer Theodore Sturgeon, whom some have cited as a model for Kilgore Trout, Jr.

- *Venus on the Half-Shell* was published in 1975 with Vonnegut's permission as a science fiction novel by "Kilgore Trout, Jr." It was actually written by Philip Jose Farmer, a well-known science fiction writer who for much of his career, like Trout, wrote visionary works for little financial gain or popular recognition.

In using an alien civilization as a vehicle for commenting on humanity, Vonnegut is again using the traditions of science fiction. The Tralfamadorians also appear in Vonnegut's *The Sirens of Titan.* During his captivity on Tralfamadore—where he is displayed naked in a cage and, eventually, mated with a movie actress from Earth named Montana Wildhack—Billy learns of the aliens' philosophy of time and death. It is a philosophy that explains his own condition.

For Tralfamadorians, time is not a linear progression of events, but a constant condition: "All moments, past, present, and future, always have existed, always will exist." Like Billy, the aliens can travel back and forth to different moments in time. They do not consider death a significant event, since when a person dies he or she "is still very much alive in the past." Billy does, in fact, know when he is going to die, and is unconcerned. At the moment of his death, he finds himself returning to an earlier point in his life. The Tralfamadorian response to death is "So it goes"—a phrase Vonnegut writes at every point in the novel where death is mentioned. All beings exist in each moment of time like "bugs in amber," and there is nothing that can alter that fact: "Only on Earth is there any talk of free will." Accordingly, the Tralfamadorians advise Billy "to concentrate on the happy moments of life, and to ignore the unhappy ones."

Such a philosophy can, of course, lead to being passive and resigned rather than trying to oppose evil and make the world better. Some critics have noted this tension in the novel and worried that it could be read not as moral outrage but as, in the words of the critic Tony Tanner, "culpable moral indifference." A possible answer to this charge may be found in one of Vonnegut's direct comments to his readers: "There are almost no characters in this story, and almost no dramatic confrontations, because most of the people in it are so sick and so much the listless playthings of enormous forces." There are certainly characters and dramatic situations in *Slaughterhouse-Five,* but the characters are fragile, wounded people at the mercy of forces completely beyond their control.

Those characters who claim to have some degree of control are, almost without exception, clueless, or cruel, or both. Roland Weary, the soldier who torments Billy while they wander behind enemy lines, believes he is a great warrior. Along with the two scouts with whom he and Billy find themselves, he considers himself one of "The Three Musketeers," a closely-bound fighting unit. In fact, Weary is a sadistic, incompetent bully whom the experienced scouts abandon. "Wild Bob," a colonel on the prison train with Billy, delivers a speech in which he assures his nonexistent troops that they have the Germans on the run and invites the troops to a reunion in his hometown after the war: "If you're ever in Cody, Wyoming, just ask for Wild Bob!" Shortly thereafter, "Wild Bob" dies of pneumonia. The British prisoners of war, who make a great show of thriving in adverse conditions, owe their prosperity to a clerical error which causes the Red Cross to send them extra supplies. Years after the war, Billy shares a hospital room with Bertrand Copeland Rumfoord, an Air Force historian who has no patience with "bleeding hearts" and tries to convince Billy that the Dresden raid was justified. Billy responds by quoting another person with delusions of control: "'If you're ever in Cody, Wyoming,' said Billy Pilgrim behind his white linen screens, 'just ask for Wild Bob.'" Confronted by the inexplicable horrors of war, and by a world in which people like Weary and Wild Bob and Rumfoord find glory in wholesale death and destruction, Billy's passivity is, perhaps, understandable.

Slaughterhouse-Five is, then, not an answer to the tragedy of war, but a response. The novel's innovative structure, distinctive prose style, and skilled use of humor and satire have all been much commented upon by critics. But it is the horror of war, as represented by the Dresden firebombing, and the attempts of decent people to come to terms with those horrors, that lie at the heart of the book and provide its most memorable scenes. One such scene is when the American POW's emerge from the meat locker under Slaughterhouse-Five to see the charred wreckage left after the bombing:

> ... the survivors, if they were going to continue to survive, were going to have to climb over curve after curve on the face of the moon.... The curves were

smooth only when seen from a distance. The people climbing them learned that they were treacherous, jagged things.... Absolutely everybody in the city was supposed to be dead.... There were to be no moon men at all.

Slaughterhouse-Five was published during the height of the Vietnam War, a point in history when many Americans were beginning to think their country had made a terrible mistake. It is perhaps no surprise that a novel which faced head-on the horrors of war (and American responsibility for some of those horrors), while at the same time suggesting that the only proper response to these horrors was to maintain a degree of ironic distance while being kind to victims, struck such a chord with the reading public and made its author a cultural icon. That Vonnegut's novel has remained a classroom staple is a tribute to both its artistic achievement and the power of its message. *Slaughterhouse-Five* is, in the words of Tony Tanner, "a masterly novel" of "clarity and economy—and compassion."

Source: F. Brett Cox, in an essay for *Novels for Students,* Gale, 1998.

Charles B. Harris

In the following excerpt, Harris examines the author-as-character, and the distancing and buffers set up by Vonnegut as self-protection.

Carefully read, Chapter One [of *Slaughterhouse-Five*] emerges as a functional and illuminating part of the novel as a whole. For the chapter contains passages that suggest three important facts crucial to a proper understanding of Vonnegut's novel: (1) the novel is less about Dresden than about the psychological impact of time, death, and uncertainty on its main character; (2) the novel's main character is not Billy Pilgrim, but Vonnegut; and (3) the novel is not a conventional anti-war novel at all, but an experimental novel of considerable complexity.

Billy Pilgrim, the putative protagonist of *Slaughterhouse-Five,* does not even appear in this chapter. Instead, the focus is on Vonnegut, the author-as-character. Emerging is a portrait of the artist as an aging man, "an old fart with his memories and his Pall Malls, with his sons full grown." He is a man of nostalgia who makes late-night drunken phone calls to almost-forgotten acquaintances, calls that seldom make connection. He reminisces about his days as a university student and police reporter in Chicago, as a public relations man in Schenectady, and as a soldier in Germany. The wartime memories, particularly as they concern the mass deaths at Dresden, especially haunt his reveries and of course form the basis of plot for the subsequent nine chapters.

Yet for one so apparently obsessed with the fleeting nature of time—he even quotes Horace to that effect—Vonnegut seems at times curiously vague and indefinite about time. He cannot remember the exact year he visited O'Hare and, upon returning to bed after a night of drinking and telephoning, cannot tell his wife, who "always has to know the time," what time it is. "Search me," he answers. His forgetfulness seems a shield, a defense against a medium that oppresses him.

The Vonnegut of Chapter One appears simultaneously obsessed with and oppressed by time, the past, and death—particularly death. His preoccupation with death is reflected in the various figures he employs in Chapter One and throughout the novel. Among the most prominent of these is the flowing-frozen water metaphor. Vonnegut has used this motif before, especially in *Cat's Cradle,* when ice-nine, dropped accidentally into the ocean, ossifies everything liquid. But it recurs in a subtler though perhaps more pervasive way in *Slaughterhouse-Five.* Early in the novel, Vonnegut, on his way to visit Bernard V. O'Hare in Philadelphia, crosses the Delaware, then appropriates the river as a metaphor in his reflections upon the nature of time. "And I asked myself about the present: how wide it was, how deep it was, how much of it was mine to keep." Even before this association of time and the river, however, Vonnegut associates death with ice, frozen water. "Even if wars didn't keep coming like glaciers," he writes, "there would still be plain old death." Extending this metaphor throughout the novel, Vonnegut repeatedly portrays living humanity as water flowing, dead humanity as water frozen. "They were moving like water," he describes a procession of Allied POW's, "... and they flowed at last to a main highway on a valley's floor. Through the valley flowed a Mississippi of humiliated Americans." One of the POW's, a hobo, is dead, therefore "could not flow, could not plop. He wasn't liquid anymore." Later, Billy Pilgrim sees the dead hobo "frozen stiff in the weeds beside the track," his bare feet "blue and ivory," the color of ice. The phrase "blue and ivory" occurs seven times in *Slaughterhouse-Five,* twice to describe the frozen feet of corpses, five times to describe the feet of Billy Pilgrim, who, though still in the land of the flowing, is marked as mortal.

A similar figure applies to Vonnegut himself. Twice in Chapter One he refers to his breath as

smelling of "mustard gas and roses." The phrase appears again in Chapter Four when Billy Pilgrim receives a misdialed phone call from a drunk whose breath, like the drunken "telephoner" of Chapter One, smells of mustard gas and roses. The full implication of the image becomes clear only on the next-to-the-last page of the novel. In the "corpse mines" of Dresden, as the dead bodies begin to rot and liquify, "the stink (is) like roses and mustard gas." Like Billy Pilgrim's "blue and ivory" feet, Vonnegut's breath marks him as mortal. This, the image suggests, is what time does to us all, not only when we lie dead like the Dresden corpses, but while we breathe. Life is a state of gradual but perpetual decay.

Time, then, is the enemy harrowing the brow of the first character we meet in the novel. It is important to recognize that the Vonnegut of Chapter One is, indeed, a *character* in *Slaughterhouse-Five.* Of course he is very much like Vonnegut the author, has the same experiences, but he remains nonetheless the author-as-character. Moreover, he becomes the first-person narrator for the remainder of the novel, a fact obscured by the Billy Pilgrim plot, which is often read as the novel proper rather than the novel-within-the-novel-proper. Vonnegut-as-character introduces himself in Chapter One, informs us of his procedures in gathering materials for his novel, and confesses the difficulties he has had over the past twenty-three years in writing his story. Then, starting with Chapter Two, he begins narrating his novel, that is, the novel by the author-as-character *within* the novel by Vonnegut the author.

It is not until the Tenth and final chapter that Vonnegut-as-character again "appears." He has not changed much since Chapter One. He again remembers conversations with O'Hare, he is still confused about time, placing the assassinations of Robert Kennedy and Martin Luther King only a month apart; and he still harbors thoughts of death. The most significant aspect of this chapter, however, is that in describing the Dresden "corpse mines" the narrator shifts for the first time in the novel to first person *plural:*

> Now Billy and the rest were being marched into the ruins by their guards. I was there. O'Hare was there. *We* had spent the past two nights in the blind innkeeper's stable. Authorities had found *us* there. They told *us* what to do. *We* were to borrow picks and shovels and crowbars and wheelbarrows from our neighbors. *We* were to march with these implements to such and such a place in the ruins, ready to go to work. (italics added)

The shift in number insists, however subtly, that the story just related is not merely Billy Pilgrim's story, but the *narrator's* as well. He, too, had suffered capture and malnutrition and the devastating firebombing. He, too, worked in the corpse mines and saw a friend shot for "plundering" a teapot from the ruins.

And so, we realize, did Vonnegut the author. Indeed, many autobiographical similarities linking Billy Pilgrim to his "creator," Vonnegut-as-character, extend even more to Vonnegut himself. Both Pilgrim and Vonnegut were born in 1922, had fathers who hunted, are tall; both were captured in Luxembourg during the Battle of the Bulge, were sent to Dresden, where they stayed in *Schlachthof-funf,* worked in a plant that manufactured malt-syrup for pregnant women; both survived the Dresden holocaust and helped dig up the corpses afterwards; both were discharged in 1945, returned to college, and were married soon afterwards. Billy thus becomes a dual persona, a mask not only for Vonnegut-as-character (who is already a mask of sorts for Vonnegut), but for Vonnegut the author as well. Vonnegut has thus removed himself at least twice from the painful Dresden experience. By including himself as a character in his own novel, he achieves the distance that must exist between author and first person narrator, no matter how autobiographically based that narrator is. The further inclusion of Billy Pilgrim as protagonist of the novel-within-the-novel removes Vonnegut yet another step from the scenes he is recreating.

Nowhere is this need for distance more evident than when Vonnegut relates the actual firebombing itself. Since this scene constitutes the novel's *raison d'etre,* one might expect an extended and graphic presentation. The scene, however, is not only brief, but is couched in indirection, layered with multiple perspectives. At least one reviewer has criticized the scene's failure to describe more fully the Dresden catastrophe. But Vonnegut did not *see* the firebombing, he heard it, from within *Slaughterhouse-Five.* So does Billy Pilgrim.

> He was down in the meat locker on the night that Dresden was destroyed. There were sounds like giant footsteps above. Those were sticks of high explosive bombs. The giants walked and walked.... A guard would go to the head of the stairs every so often to see what it was like outside, then he would come down and whisper to the other guards. There was fire-storm out there. Dresden was one big flame. The one flame ate everything organic, everything that would burn.

Most significant about this scene is not its indirection, however, but the fact that it is a *remembered* scene. For the first time in the novel, Billy Pilgrim *remembers* a past event rather than time-travelling to it. Time-travel, it seems, would have made the event too immediate, too painful. Memory, on the other hand, supplies a twenty-year buffer. But if the firebombing, only indirectly witnessed, was distressing, the totally devastated city confronted the following day by the one hundred prisoners and their four guards must have been almost overwhelming. To relate that scene Vonnegut-as-narrator requires even more distance than memory can provide. So the scene is revealed through a story Billy remembers having told Montana Wildhack on Tralfamadore.... Vonnegut-as-character removes himself as much as possible from the scene he narrates, cushioning it with multiple perspectives, constructing what is finally a story within a memory within a novel. (Vonnegut the author removes himself yet one step further, achieving a story within a memory within a novel within a novel.) Moreover, before relating this important scene, Vonnegut-as-narrator withdraws to the protective fantasy of Tralfamadore. Only from the perspective of that timeless planet can he at last come to artistic terms with a scene that has haunted him for twenty-three years.

Source: Charles B. Harris, "Time, Uncertainity, and Kurt Vonnegut, Jr.: A Reading of *Slaughterhouse-Five,*" in Centennial Review, Summer, 1976, pp. 228–43.

David L. Vanderwerken

In the following excerpt, Vanderwerken discusses Billy Pilgrim, focusing on the causes of his breakdown and how he is influenced by Tralfamadorianism.

The reader's central problem in comprehending Vonnegut's *Slaughterhouse-Five* lies in correctly understanding the source of Billy Pilgrim's madness. Vonnegut continually undercuts our willing suspension of disbelief in Billy's time travel by offering multiple choices for the origin of Billy's imbalance: childhood traumas, brain damage from his plane crash, dreams, his shattering war experiences, and plain old fantasy. Yet if, as F. Scott Fitzgerald once observed, only a "first-rate intelligence" has the "ability to hold two opposed ideas in the mind at the same time, and still retain the ability to function," an inquiry into the two opposed philosophical systems that Pilgrim holds in his mind—Tralfamadorianism and Christianity—may lead us to the fundamental cause of Billy's breakdown. Clearly, Billy is no "first-rate intelligence," and he hardly can be said to "function"; he simply cracks under the strain of his dilemma. For some critics, however, Vonnegut's method of juxtaposing two explanatory systems, seemingly without affirming one or the other, becomes a major flaw in the novel.... I would argue that, on the contrary, Vonnegut's position is clear; he rejects both Tralfamadorianism and divinely oriented Christianity, while unambiguously affirming a humanly centered Christianity in which Jesus is a "nobody," a "bum," a man.

In the autobiographical first chapter, Vonnegut introduces the opposed ideas, which the narrative proper will develop, evolving from his twenty-three-year attempt to come to terms with the horror of Dresden. The Christmas card sent to Vonnegut's war buddy by a German cab driver, expressing his hope for a "world of peace and freedom ... if the accident will," dramatizes, in miniature form, a central tension in the novel. Human history is either divinely planned—Christmas signifies God's entrance into human history—and historical events are meaningful, or human history is a series of random events, non-causal, pure "accident," having no ultimate meaning as the Tralfamadorians claim. Both viewpoints deny free will; man is powerless to shape events.... Either position allows one serenely to wash his hands of Dresden. Billy Pilgrim washes his hands, so to speak, and becomes reconciled to his Dresden experience under the tutelage of the Tralfamadorians: "'[Dresden] was all right,' said Billy. '*Everything is all right, and everybody has to do exactly what he does. I learned that on Tralfamadore.*'"

The Tralfamadorians provide Billy with the concept of nonlinear time, which becomes the foundation for a mode of living: "'I am a Tralfamadorian, seeing all time as you might see a stretch of the Rocky Mountains. All time is all time. It does not change. It does not lend itself to warnings or explanations. It simply *is*. Take it moment by moment, and you will find that we are all, as I've said before, bugs in amber.'" Although men on earth are always "'explaining why this event is structured as it is, telling how other events may be achieved or avoided,'" Billy learns that "'there is no *why*.'"

In short, Tralfamadorianism is an argument for determinism. Yet, this is a determinism without design, where chance rules. The universe will be destroyed accidentally by the Tralfamadorians, and wars on earth are inevitable.... The upshot of the Tralfamadorian philosophy finds expression in a cliché: "Everything was beautiful, and nothing hurt."

When Billy, full of revelations, returns to Earth "to comfort so many people with the truth about time," the implications of Tralfamadorianism become apparent. Although Billy's first attempt to "comfort" someone, a Vietnam war widow's son, fails, Billy blossoms into a charismatic national hero at the time of his assassination in 1976. The public appeal of Tralfamadorianism is obvious. Simply, it frees man from responsibility and from moral action. If all is determined, if there is no why, then no one can be held accountable for anything, neither Dresden nor My Lai. In his personal life, Billy's indifference and apathy toward others are clearly illustrated. Chapter Three offers three consecutive examples of Billy's behavior: he drives away from a black man who seeks to talk with him; he diffidently listens to a vicious tirade by a Vietnam Hawk at his Lions Club meeting; he ignores some cripples selling magazine subscriptions. Yet the Tralfamadorian idea that we can do nothing about anything fully justifies Billy's apathy. When Billy preaches this dogma as part of his "calling," he does a great service for the already apathetic by confirming their attitude; he provides them with a philosophical base for their apathy. If one ignores the ghetto or the Vietnam War, neither exists. By exercising one's selective memory, by becoming an ostrich, one may indeed live in a world where everything is beautiful and nothing hurts. Perfect. No wonder Billy is a successful Comforter; he has fulfilled Eliot Rosewater's request that "new lies" be invented or "people just aren't going to want to go on living."

If Tralfamadorianism is a "new lie," it recalls an "old lie"—God. There is little difference between God's will and accident's will in the novel. For Vonnegut, man's belief in an all-powerful Creator, involved in human history, has resulted in two great evils: the acceptance of war as God's will; the assumption that we carry out God's will and that God is certainly on our side, which justifies all atrocities. Sodom, Gomorrah, Hiroshima, Dresden, My Lai IV—all victims of God's will. Vonnegut directs his rage in *Slaughterhouse-Five* at a murderous, supernatural Christianity that creates Children's Crusades, that allows men to rationalize butchery in the name of God, that absolves men from guilt. Since, for Vonnegut, all wars are, finally, "holy" wars, he urges us to rid ourselves of a supernatural God.

While Vonnegut indicts Tralfamadorianism and supernatural Christianity as savage illusions, he argues in *Slaughterhouse-Five* for a humanistic Christianity, which may also be an illusion, but yet a saving one.

Throughout the novel, Vonnegut associates Billy Pilgrim with Bunyan's Pilgrim and with Christ. A chaplain's assistant in the war with a "meek faith in a loving Jesus," Billy finds the war a vast Slough of Despond; he reaches Dresden, which "looked like a Sunday school picture of Heaven to Billy Pilgrim," only to witness the Heavenly City's destruction. Often, Vonnegut's Christian shades into Christ Himself. During the war, Billy hears "Golgotha sounds," foresees his death and resurrection, " 'it is time for me to be dead for a little while—and then live again,' " identifies himself fully with Christ: "Now his snoozing became shallower as he heard a man and a woman speaking German in pitying tones. The speakers were commiserating with somebody lyrically. Before Billy opened his eyes, it seemed to him that the tones might have been those used by the friends of Jesus when they took His ruined body down from His cross." After his kidnapping in 1967 by the Tralfamadorians, Billy assumes the role of Messiah: "He was doing nothing less now, he thought, than prescribing corrective lenses for Earthling souls. So many of those souls were lost and wretched, Billy believed, because they could not see as well as his little green friends on Tralfamadore." Vonnegut has created a parody Christ whose gospel is Tralfamadorian, who redeems no one, who "cried very little although he often saw things worth crying about, and in *that* respect, at least, he resembled the Christ of the carol." Indeed, Pilgrim's dilemma is that he is a double Savior with two gospels—a weeping and loving Jesus and a Tralfamadorian determinist. His opposed gospels drive him mad, render him impotent, result in his crackpot letters to newspapers and in his silent weeping for human suffering. Possibly Billy could have resolved his dilemma if he had paid closer attention to the human Christ in the novels of Billy's favorite writer—Kilgore Trout.

While Vonnegut often mentions Trout's books and stories for satiric purposes, Trout, "this cracked messiah" who has been " 'making love to the world' " for years, also serves as Vonnegut's spokesman for a humanistic and naturalistic Christianity. In Trout's *The Gospel from Outer Space,* a planetary visitor concludes that Christians are cruel because of "slipshod storytelling in the New Testament," which does not teach mercy, compassion, and love, but instead: *"Before you kill somebody, make absolutely sure he isn't well connected."* Trout's visitor offers Earth a new Gospel in which Jesus is not divine, but fully human—"a nobody." When the nobody is crucified: "The voice of God came crashing down. He told the people that he was adopting the bum as his son, giving him the full powers and privileges of The Son of the Creator of the Universe throughout all eternity." What Vonnegut suggests here is that Christ's divinity stands in the way of charity. If the "bum" is Everyman, then we are all adopted children of God; we are all Christs and should treat each other accordingly.

As mentioned earlier, both Tralfamadorian determinism and the concept of a Supreme Being calling every shot on Earth nullify human intention, commitment and responsibility. But Vonnegut's humanistic Christianity in the face of a naturalistic universe demands moral choice—demands that we revere each other as Christs, since all are sons and daughters of God. Not surprisingly, Vonnegut's position echoes that of Stephen Crane.... The correspondent's insight that we are all in the same boat adrift in an indifferent sea, and that once we realize that we have only each other, moral choice is "absurdly clear," is Kurt Vonnegut's insight as well. (Vonnegut mentions *The Red Badge of Courage.*) The courage, sacrifice, and selflessness in *The Red Badge* appear in *Slaughterhouse-Five* also.

While Vonnegut offers several versions of ideal brotherhood in his works—the Karass, the Volunteer Fire Department, and, despite Howard W. Campbell, Jr.'s assessment of American prisoners, moments of brotherhood in *Slaughterhouse-Five*—he also suggests an alternative for the individual, a slogan that becomes a way of living. On the same page where Vonnegut says, "Billy was not moved to protest the bombing of North Vietnam, did not shudder about the hideous things he himself had seen bombing do," appears the following prayer and Vonnegut's comment:

GOD GRANT ME

THE SERENITY TO ACCEPT

THE THINGS I CANNOT CHANGE,

COURAGE TO CHANGE THE THINGS I CAN,

AND WISDOM ALWAYS

TO TELL THE

DIFFERENCE

Among the things Billy Pilgrim could not change were the past, the present, and the future.

The Serenity Prayer, sandwiched between episodes concerning Vietnam, is Vonnegut's savage indictment of Billy Pilgrim. In short, Billy lacks the "wisdom" to see that Dresden is of the past and cannot be changed, but that the bombing of North Vietnam lies in the present and can be changed. However, to protest the bombing requires moral "courage," a quality obviated by his Tralfamadorian education.

The seemingly innocuous Serenity Prayer, the motto of Alcoholics Anonymous, appears once more in a most significant location—on the last page of Chapter Nine. The truth of Raymond M. Olderman's observation in his *Beyond the Waste Land* that "Vonnegut is a master at getting inside a cliché" is verified when we consider that Vonnegut has transformed the AA motto into a viable moral philosophy. Vonnegut knows that we have to accept serenely those things that people cannot change—the past, linear time, aging, death, natural forces. Yet the Prayer posits that, through moral courage, there are things that can be changed. War, for example, is not a natural force like a glacier, as Harrison Starr would have it. While Billy believes that he cannot change the past, present, or future, Vonnegut suggests that in the arena of the enormous present, we can, with courage, create change: "And I asked myself about the present: how wide it was, how deep it was, how much was mine to keep."

If there is a broad moral implication in *Slaughterhouse-Five*, it is aimed at America. Vonnegut, like his science fictionist Kilgore Trout, "writes about Earthlings all the time and they're all Americans." Vonnegut's message for America is this: America has adopted the Tralfamadorian philosophy, which justifies apathy. We have lost our sense of individuality; we feel powerless, helpless, and impotent; we consider ourselves the "listless playthings of enormous forces." What Vonnegut would have us do is develop the wisdom to discriminate between what we can or cannot change, while developing the courage to change what we can. We have met Billy Pilgrim and he is us.

Source: David L. Vanderwerken, "Pilgrim's Dilemma: *Slaughterhouse-Five*," in *Research Studies,* Vol. 42, No. 3, September, 1974, pp. 147–52.

Sources

Brian Aldiss with David Wingrove, *Trillion Year Spree: The History of Science Fiction,* Victor Gollancz, 1986.

Thomas D. Clareson, *Understanding Contemporary American Science Fiction: The Formative Period (1926–1970),* University of South Carolina Press, 1990.

J. Michael Crichton, review of *Slaughterhouse-Five,* in *New Republic,* April 26, 1969.

Richard Giannone, *Vonnegut: A Preface to His Novels,* Kennikat Press, 1977, pp. 82-97.

Granville Hicks, "Literary Horizons," in *Saturday Review,* March 29, 1969, p. 25.

Jerome Klinkowitz, *Kurt Vonnegut.* Methuen, 1982, pp. 63-69.

Jerome Klinkowitz, *"Slaughterhouse Five": Reforming the Novel and the World,* Twayne, 1990.

Jerome Klinkowitz and Donald L. Lawler, editors, *Vonnegut in America: An Introduction to the Life and Work of Kurt Vonnegut,* Delacorte Press/Seymour Lawrence, 1977.

James Lundquist, *Kurt Vonnegut,* Frederick Ungar, 1977, pp. 69-84.

Robert Scholes, review of *Slaughterhouse-Five, New York Times Book Review,* April 6, 1969, pp. 1, 23.

Tony Tanner, *City of Words,* Harper & Row, 1971, pp. 194-201.

For Further Study

Clark Mayo, *Kurt Vonnegut: The Gospel from Outer Space; or, Yes We Have No Nirvanas,* Borgo Press, 1977, pp. 45-52.

> Discusses *Slaughterhouse-Five* as a response to "the horror and absurdity of war" with emphasis on the novel's unconventional structure.

Leonard Mustazza, *Forever Pursuing Genesis: The Myth of Eden in the Novels of Kurt Vonnegut,* Bucknell University Press, 1990, pp. 102-15.

> Discusses *Slaughterhouse-Five* in terms of Billy Pilgrim's attempts "to construct for himself an Edenic experience" and the "linkage … between Eden and Tralfamadore."

Peter J. Reed, *Kurt Vonnegut, Jr.,* Crowell, 1972, pp. 172-203.

> Discusses *Slaughterhouse-Five* as "an effort to bring together all that Vonnegut has been saying about the human condition and contemporary American society." Reed calls the novel "remarkably successful" and "one of Vonnegut's best."

Stanley Schatt, *Kurt Vonnegut, Jr.,* G.K. Hall, 1976, pp. 81-96.

> A detailed summary and critique of the novel. The book also contains an extensive bibliography of critical works on Vonnegut.

Tess of the d'Urbervilles

Thomas Hardy

1891

When *Tess of the d'Urbervilles* appeared in 1891, Thomas Hardy was one of England's leading men of letters. He had already authored several well-known novels, including *The Return of the Native,* and numerous short stories. *Tess* brought him notoriety—it was considered quite scandalous—and fortune. Despite this success, the novel was one of Hardy's last. He was deeply wounded by some of the particularly personal attacks he received from reviewers of the book. In 1892, he wrote in one of his notebooks, quoted in *The Later Years of Thomas Hardy, 1892-1928,* compiled by Florence Emily Hardy, "Well, if this sort of thing continues no more novel-writing for me. A man must be a fool to deliberately stand up to be shot at."

In spite of his reputation, Hardy had difficulty finding a periodical willing to publish the book when he offered it for serialization to London's leading reviews. The subject matter—a milkmaid who is seduced by one man, married and rejected by another, and who eventually murders the first one—was considered unfit for publications which young people might read. To appease potential publishers, Hardy took the novel apart, re-wrote some scenes and added others. In due course; a publisher was secured. When it came time to publish the novel in book form, Hardy reassembled it as it was originally conceived.

Early critics attacked Hardy for the novel's subtitle, "A Pure Woman," arguing that Tess could not possibly be considered pure. They also denounced his frank—for the time—depiction of sex,

criticism of organized religion, and dark pessimism. Today, the novel is praised as a courageous call for righting many of the ills Hardy found in Victorian society and as a link between the late-Victorian literature of the end of the nineteenth century and that of the modern era.

Author Biography

Thomas Hardy was born in 1840 in a small village in Dorset, an area of southern England steeped in history. One of the local landmarks, Corfe Castle, was once home for the kings of the ancient Saxon kingdom of Wessex. Hardy chose the name Wessex for the setting of his most important novels, including *Tess of the d'Urbervilles*. Like the Durbeyfields in *Tess,* the Hardys fancied themselves descendants of a noble and ancient family line. The Dorset Hardys were presumably a branch of the Le Hardys who claimed descent from Clement Le Hardy, a fifteen-century lieutenant-governor of the British Channel island of Jersey. Remote ties to Vice-Admiral Sir Thomas Masterman Hardy, who served with the British naval hero Nelson during the decisive battle of Trafalgar in 1805, were also possible.

Besides his family name, Hardy's parents gave their son the love of literature, music (like his father, Thomas played the fiddle), and religion, which are evident in his works. A self-styled "born book-worm," Hardy could read at age three. He might have had a successful career as a scholar, but at age sixteen, his formal schooling ended when he was apprenticed to a local church restorer. He loved knowledge, however, and continued his education by rising early every morning to study Latin and Greek before setting off to work. He read voraciously, especially the Bible and, in 1859, Charles Darwin's *The Origin of Species*. In 1862, Hardy became an assistant to a London architect Sir Arthur Blomfield. He had thought about entering the ministry or becoming a poet, but by his early twenties his reading had converted him to agnosticism and his poetry had met with little success. For economic reasons, he decided to try his hand at prose. His first fictional piece was published in 1865; the manuscript of his first novel "The Poor Man and the Lady" was completed two years later. Although the book was never published, encouraging advice from George Meredith, a poet whom Hardy admired, convinced the aspiring novelist to try again. Hardy's first popular suc-

Thomas Hardy

cess occurred in 1874 when the first of his Wessex novels, *Far from the Madding Crowd,* was published. As with *Tess,* this work was noted for its spirited female protagonist and Hardy's use of his fictional landscape.

In 1885, Hardy moved, with his wife, Emma, into Max Gate, a home he had built in Dorset. There, only a mile or two from his birthplace, the novelist would live the rest of his life. Coming back to his native land seemed to stir Hardy's creativity, and the next ten years saw the publication of three volumes of short stories as well as five major novels, including *Tess*. His wife died in 1912, and he married again in 1914. As the years passed, he noticed how the encroachment of civilization, especially the coming of the railroad to Dorset some seven years after his birth, had changed forever his beloved rural world. In his novels he poetically recaptures the beauty of the region.

Plot Summary

Part One—An Insignificant Incident and Its Consequences

Thomas Hardy's *Tess of the d'Urbervilles* begins with a seemingly insignificant incident: John

Durbeyfield, a middle-aged peddler, is informed during a chance encounter on his way home one May evening that he is the descendent of an "ancient and knightly family," the d'Urbervilles. On learning this "useless piece of information," "Sir John" has a horse and carriage fetched for him so that he can arrive home in a manner more befitting his new station. He then goes out drinking, getting so drunk that he is unable to get up in the middle of the night to make a delivery to a nearby town for the following morning. Tess, his oldest daughter, accompanied by her young brother Abraham, attempts to make the delivery instead; but she falls asleep on the way, and the family's horse, unguided, gets into a grotesque freak accident and dies on the road.

Now deprived of their transportation, the family faces hard times. Tess's parents hit on the idea of having her solicit the wealthy Mrs. d'Urberville, whom they incorrectly assume to be a relative, for help. Feeling responsible for their current situation, Tess agrees to go. When she arrives at the d'Urberville estate, she is met by Mrs. d'Urberville's son, Alec. He is attracted to her good looks and soon arranges for her to care for his mother's chickens. He comes to fetch her, and on the ride back makes it clear that his actions were not motivated by charity. Alec's unwanted attention continues throughout the next three months, culminating one night when he coaxes her to accept a ride home from a dance. He intentionally takes an alternate route, gets them lost, and eventually rapes her in her sleep. Hardy was forced to cut this episode from the novel for serial publication, and even in its final form in the novel it is handled with extreme circumspection, as is evident from the following excerpt:

> "Tess!" said d'Urberville.
>
> There was no answer. The obscurity was now so great that he could see absolutely nothing but a pale nebulousness at his feet, which represented the white muslin figure he had left upon the dead leaves. Everything else was blackness alike. D'Urberville stooped; and heard a gentle regular breathing. He knelt and bent lower, till her breath warmed his face, and in a moment his cheek was in contact with hers. She was sleeping soundly, and upon her eyelashes there lingered tears.
>
> Darkness and silence ruled everywhere around. Above them rose the primeval yews and oaks of The Chase, in which were poised gentle roosting birds in their last nap; and about them stole the hopping rabbits and hares. But, might some say, where was Tess's guardian angel? where was the providence of her simple faith? Perhaps, like that other god of

whom the ironical Tishbite spoke, he was talking, or he was pursuing, or he was in a journey, or he was sleeping and not to be awaked.

A few weeks after this incident, Tess returns home. Falling into a depression, and pregnant, she remains in seclusion for the better part of the next year. She emerges in the following August to work in the fields, and soon thereafter her baby dies.

Part Two—Angel

After two more "silent reconstructive years" at home, Tess ventures forth again, this time to work as a dairymaid. At the dairy she attracts the attentions of Angel Clare, the youngest son of a vicar who has turned away from his father's faith and has settled on farming as a career. Angel is learning the ins and outs of the dairy business at Talbothays. Over the course of the summer the two are drawn to each other, until Angel finally makes his feelings known to Tess. Soon after he goes home to broach the topic of marriage with his parents, who are resistant to the idea at first but finally give him a qualified "go-ahead."

On his return to Talbothays, Angel wastes no time in proposing to Tess, but she, to his surprise, rejects him, and refuses to tell him why. Several such encounters follow, until her feelings for him overwhelm her shame, and she agrees to marry him. She continues to feel guilty about her past, however, and, unable to bring herself to confide in Angel, she declines for weeks to commit to a wedding date. With the time for his departure from Talbothays fast approaching, Angel finally persuades her and a date of December 31 is set. Shortly before the day arrives, Tess makes a final failed effort to confess her "stain" to him.

The wedding over, they drive on to an old mansion, which Angel informs Tess once belonged to her family. That night several things happen. First, the couple receives a parcel from Angel's parents containing several pieces of diamond jewelry willed to him by his godmother and to be presented to his wife. Soon thereafter their luggage arrives, along with bad news from Talbothays about three of Tess's fellow dairymaids, all of whom (unbeknownst to Angel) were also in love with him. Finally, Angel, recalling Tess's earlier wish to make a confession, himself confesses to a relatively minor past indiscretion, an "eight-and-forty hours' dissipation with a stranger." Thus fortified by her husband's apparent show of good faith and moved by the sudden fall of her three compatriots, Tess "enter[s] on her story of her acquaintance with Alec d'Urberville."

The consequences of her confession are cataclysmic. Angel is unable to accept her, claiming that, far beyond its being a matter of forgiveness, he feels as if she had become a different person. Divorce not being a viable option, they soon settle on a separation. Angel promises to keep her apprised of his whereabouts (his plans being to look for an estate to farm, either in the north of the country or abroad), provides her with what he assumes will be an adequate sum of money to maintain her, and drops her off at her home.

Angel ends up in Brazil. Tess, meanwhile, unable to bear staying at home, takes a series of temporary agricultural jobs, and by the fall of that year finds herself running out of money. Unable to land any more such jobs, she decides to join Marian, one of her friends from the dairy, at a farm at Flintcomb-Ash. The work there is grueling, and her employer, Farmer Groby, is a brutish man. She perseveres for a while but soon decides to apply to Angel's parents for aid (as he had said she could if she needed to). She walks the several miles to Emminster, where the Clares' vicarage is located, but as a result of two chance encounters there, loses her confidence, and she heads back to Flintcomb-Ash, leaving her mission unaccomplished.

Part Three—Renewing Old Acquaintances

Midway into her return journey, she chances on a "ranter," or Primitive Methodist preacher, addressing the inhabitants of a small village, and recognizes the man to be none other than Alec d'Urberville. Before she withdraws, he recognizes her and later catches up with her on her way home. He tells her about his recent conversion, begs her forgiveness for his past behavior, but continues to show some of his old interest in her as a lover. Though she makes him promise never to see her again, he appears at the farm several days later, and proposes to make up for his past wrongs by marrying her. She declines, and eventually informs him that she is already married (though she refuses to disclose her husband's name). On learning this, Alec proceeds to press her in this and several subsequent meetings, insisting that she is an abandoned wife, and that she is a fool for not allowing him to help her. Soon he has given up his preaching and resumed his role of young dandy. Tess vehemently refuses his advances and writes a letter to Angel pleading with him to return to her. Again, though, circumstances conspire against her. First, on hearing that her mother is seriously ill, she leaves her job and returns home; and while her mother soon

recovers, her father dies suddenly, as a result of which her family loses their house. Declining Alec's offer to put them up at his estate, Tess goes along with arrangements made by her mother to move to Kingsbere, the seat of the old d'Urberville family, but on arriving there they learn that their house has already been let. Thus, they are literally stranded, homeless and penniless.

Soon thereafter Angel returns home from Brazil. He has recently received Tess's letter, and because of it and his experiences abroad has forgiven her and wishes to rejoin her. He looks for her first at Flintcomb-Ash, then at her home village of Marlott, and finally at Kingsbere. There Tess's mother reluctantly directs him to the fashionable seaside resort of Sandbourne, which he heads to that evening. The next morning he looks Tess up at the lodging-house where he is informed she is staying, only to discover that she has married Alec. She begs Angel to leave her, which he very reluctantly does. The bitter irony of her situation soon overcomes her, though, and at a slight provocation from Alec she stabs him to death and leaves the lodging-house. She manages to catch up with Angel on his way out of town, confesses her deed to him, and reaffirms her love for him. This time, he promises to be her protector. The two proceed north along footpaths for the rest of the day and eventually settle in an unoccupied mansion, where they remain for several days. They then continue going north, Angel's plan being to reach a northern port, from which they will be able to safely leave the country. They walk well into the night, reaching Stonehenge, at which point Tess, pleading exhaustion, convinces Angel to let her stop for a while. Dawn soon breaks, and Angel perceives several figures approaching them from all directions—the local authorities. Tess is arrested, and shortly thereafter executed.

Characters

Mercy Chant

The only daughter of a friend and neighbor of the Clares, Mercy Chant, is the girl Angel Clare's parents hope he will marry. She is religious and holds Bible classes, but appears cold and unyielding. She ends up married to Angel's brother, Cuthbert.

Angel Clare

Angel is the youngest son of Rev. James Clare and his wife. He appears in the opening chapters

Media Adaptations

- *Tess of the d'Urbervilles* was adapted as a film directed by Roman Polanski, starring Nastassja Kinski, Leigh Lawson, and Peter Firth, 1980. The film received many Academy Award nominations, including one for best picture; it won Oscars for best cinematography, best art direction and best costume design. It is available from Columbia Tristar Home Video.

- It was also recorded on audio cassette, narrated by Davina Porter, published by Recorded Books, 1994.

of the book as a young man with upper-class bearings that dances with Tess's friends as they celebrate their May festival. He demonstrates immediately the differences between him and his brothers; while they hurry home to their studies, he pauses to dance and admire Tess's beauty. The two meet again at Talbothays Dairy where Angel is in apprenticeship for being a gentleman farmer. Although his father and his two older brothers are members of the clergy, Angel wants no part of their orthodox Christianity. To Tess, he is "educated, reserved, subtle, sad, [and] differing." He idealizes Tess as a "fresh, virginal daughter of nature," and asks her to marry him. When she hesitates, he asks again and again, and when she puts off a wedding date, he insists. At Talbothays he and Tess are portrayed as Adam and Eve where in the early mornings they notice "a feeling of isolation, as if they were Adam and Eve," and Angel plays his secondhand harp in a garden complete with an apple tree. Three of the other milkmaids at the farm worship Angel from afar and despair at the thought that Angel will never be theirs. Although he defends his choice of her for a wife before his parents, he seems not really to accept her as she is, and is secretly elated when she tells him she is of the d'Urberville family. His true feelings are revealed when, after their marriage, he confesses to "eight-and-forty hours' dissipation with a stranger" which Tess promptly forgives. He, however, is unable to for-

give Tess when she confesses what had happened with Alec. He gives her some money but leaves her to seek his fortune in Brazil. His total lack of concern for Tess is seen when he happens upon one of the milkmaids from the farm, Izz Huett, and asks her to go with him to Brazil. He changes his mind, however, when she tells him no one could love him as much as Tess. When he returns to England from Brazil, he is finally able to accept her as his wife. The two enjoy a few days of happiness together before Tess is captured. After her death, he follows her wishes and marries her sister.

Cuthbert Clare

A classical scholar, and a fellow and dean of his college at Cambridge, Cuthbert Clare is Angel's eldest brother. He seems to think of nothing but his academic work, and has little patience for those not sharing his interests. He marries Mercy Chant.

Felix Clare

Felix is the middle boy in the Clare family, being Angel's older brother, and Cuthbert's younger brother. As curate at a nearby town, he is as much a churchman as his older brother is an academician. When Tess hears Felix and his brother talking in a derogatory fashion about her and Angel's marriage, she decides not to try to contact Angel's parents for help. This, the narrator says, is "the greatest misfortune of her life."

Reverend James Clare

Angel's father, Reverend James Clare, is a respected minister who is known for "his austere and Calvinist tenets." He and his wife live a frugal existence in Emminster. Although he seems cold, "the kindness of his heart was such that he never resented anything for long." His compassion is demonstrated when, although he is disappointed that Angel doesn't want to go into the ministry like the rest of the family, he pledges to help his son financially in whatever he does by giving him the money he had saved to pay his university expenses. He and his wife hope that Angel will marry Mercy Chant, the daughter of their neighbor, but are resigned to Angel's choosing a wife for himself. He asks only that she be from "a truly Christian family."

Mrs. Clare

Angel's mother, identified only as Mrs. Clare, helps her husband with his duties as a parson. She believes in living a simple, faith-filled life, but unlike her husband, appearances are important to her. When Angel speaks of wanting to marry, Mrs.

Still from the 1981 movie Tess of the d'Urbervilles, *starring Nastassia Kinski as Tess Durbeyfield and Peter Firth as Angel Clare.*

Clare wants to know if the woman in question is a "lady."

Dairyman Crick

See Richard Crick

Mrs. Crick

Mrs. Crick looks after the help at Talbothays Dairy. She is somewhat snobbish—she considers herself "too respectable" to milk the cows herself. She shows her kind heart when she sends some black pudding and a bottle of mead home with Angel when he visits his parents.

Richard Crick

A master-dairyman, Dairyman Crick runs Talbothays Dairy and is portrayed as a warm, jovial man who is friendly with his help.

Car Darch

Described as "a dark virago," and called "Queen of Spades," Car Darch was the receiver of Alec d'Urberville's attentions until Tess appeared. Tess decides to go with Alec the night he seduces her, partially because she is afraid of what the jealous Car Darch might do to her.

Alec d'Urberville

See Alexander Stoke-d'Urberville

Tess d'Urberville

See Tess Durbeyfield

Abraham Durbeyfield

Tess's nine year old brother, Abraham, accompanies her on her early morning ride delivering the bee hives after her father becomes too drunk to take them. In an important scene, the two look up at the stars and Tess explains that most are "splendid," but some are "blighted." Then, Abraham asks, "Which do we live on—a splendid one or a blighted one?" Tess answers, "A blighted one." Soon after this, Prince, the family horse dies in an accident.

Eliza-Louisa Durbeyfield

Tess's sister, Eliza-Louisa, is twelve-and-a-half when the novel opens. Tess describes 'Liza-Lu as "gentle and sweet, and she is growing so beautiful," when she asks Angel to marry 'Liza-Lu after she dies.

Jack Durbeyfield

See John Durbeyfield

Joan Durbeyfield

Tess's mother, Joan Durbeyfield, is a simple woman, proud of the beauty that her daughter has inherited from her and anxious to have her "claim kin" at the d'Urberville estate. She has the common peasant attitude of accepting whatever fate comes her way, but is superstitious and consults the *Compleat Fortune-Teller* for advice. When Tess is distraught over her seduction and pregnancy, Joan tells her daughter. "Well, we must make the best of it, I suppose. 'Tis nater, after all, and what do please God!"

John Durbeyfield

Tess's father, John Durbeyfield, works as a peddler and a wagon driver. He is greatly impressed with the news that he is the last descendant of the once noble d'Urbervilles. He immediately orders a carriage to take him home and proceeds to celebrate for the rest of the evening, bringing about the scene of Prince's death. Durbeyfield seems to do as little work as possible, and the news that he is connected with nobility seems like a good reason to do even less. When Tess returns to Marlott to look after her sick mother, she finds her father ready to send all antiquarians in England a letter asking for a donation to keep the family going as a national treasure. He suffers a heart attack, and dies soon afterwards.

Tess Durbeyfield

Hardy's heroine is the daughter of John and Joan Durbeyfield of Marlott in Wessex; the eldest of seven children. The subtitle to the novel, "A Pure Woman" emphasizes her purity, but critics debate whether a woman who is seduced by one man, marries another one who abandons her, and then kills the first, could be considered "pure." But, purity aside, she is, with rare exception, praised by critics who admire her steadfast hope under adversity. To some, like Donald Davidson in the *Southern Review,* she is like a figure from a folk ballad "the deserted maiden who murders her seducer with a knife," while to others, including Irving Howe in *Thomas Hardy,* she is "a girl who is at once a simple milkmaid and an archetype of feminine strength." To Angel she is "a regular churchgoer of simple faith; honest-hearted, receptive, intelligent, graceful to a degree, chaste as a vestal, and, in personal appearance, exceptionally beautiful." She has "passed the Sixth Standard in the National School," and thinks about becoming a teacher. While she is unimpressed with the news that she has noble ancestors, she feels so much guilt when

she unwittingly causes the death of the family horse, that she follows her parents' wish that she "claim kin" at the nearby d'Urberville estate. She is shown as a hard worker, working in the fields after her baby is born, working at the dairy, and, later, working in the rutabaga fields at Flintcomb-Ash. But for all her strength, she is like a trapped bird. In her simplicity, she tries to do what is right, but her well-meaning actions often are futile. Her effort to help her family by going to the d'Urberville estate, ends with her seduction; when she tries to tell Angel about what happened between her and Alec, she is unable to until after the wedding. When Alec keeps pursuing her she tells him, "Whip me, crush me…. I shall not cry out. Once victim, always victim—that's the law." Later, she murders Alec in desperation, knowing that if he had only gone away when she told him to, she could have been happy with Angel. Before she is taken away by the police, she asks Angel to marry her sister, 'Liza Lu. As the book ends, she is hung for Alec's murder.

Farmer Groby

Farmer Groby is the owner of Flintcomb-Ash farm, where Tess finds work after Angel leaves her. A cruel man, he is particularly harsh with Tess because of an incident in which Angel punched him because he thought the farmer had insulted her. Groby's temperament seems to match the harshness of the land he keeps and serves as a contrast to the joviality of Talbothays Dairy.

Izz Huett

"The pale, dark-eyed" Izz Huett is one of the three other milkmaids besides Tess who fall in love with Angel Clare at Talbothays Dairy. After Angel leaves Tess, he asks Izz to go with him to Brazil, but her honesty betrays her when she tells Angel that Tess loved him more than anyone else. Hearing this, Angel tells her he can no longer take her with him.

Liza-Lu

See Eliza-Louisa Durbeyfield

Marian

The "jolly-faced" Marian is the eldest of the three milkmaids besides Tess who fall in love with Angel at Talbothays Dairy. She is despondent when Angel and Tess marry, and soon afterward loses her job at the dairy because she starts drinking heavily. Her friendship with Tess is strong, however, and when she finds out that Tess is separated from her husband, she asks her to come and work with her at Flintcomb-Ash.

Retty Priddle

The "auburn-haired" Retty Priddle is the youngest of the three milkmaids besides Tess who fall in love with Angel at Talbothays Dairy. When Tess and Angel get married, she tries to drown herself but is rescued.

Queen of Spades

See Car Darch

Mrs. Stoke-d'Urberville

A blind invalid, Mrs. Stoke-d'Urberville is Alec's mother and lives with him at the estate at Tantridge. A note written by Alec in her name, asking for someone to help her with her birds, brings Tess to work at the family's estate.

Alexander Stoke-d'Urberville

In his early twenties when he first appears in the novel, Alec is the son of the late Mr. Simon Stoke, who added "d'Urberville" to his name to conceal his real identity when the family moved from southern England. He seems immediately taken with his pretty "Coz," when she comes to the estate to "claim kin," and after she leaves, he sends a letter purported to be from his invalid mother to Tess's mother asking that Tess come to work for her. Tess tries to avoid him, but one night he follows her when she goes to a fair and market at a neighboring town. He cajoles her into accepting his offer of a ride in his buggy, because she fears to be out so late by herself. Taking advantage of the lateness of the hour and her fatigued condition, Alec seduces her. The next time he appears in the novel, he is a preacher, converted by Angel's father. When he and Tess accidentally meet, Alec's softer side is revealed as he seems to be particularly touched when Tess tells him for the first time of their child. Alec becomes once again obsessed by her and pursues Tess to Flintcomb-Ash where she reveals to him that she is married. She refuses to have anything to do with him, but when she sees him again he no longer wears his parson's frock. Instead he is described as a villain from a melodrama, twirling a "gay walking cane." He belittles Tess for being faithful to her absent husband. Infuriated, she hits him in the face with a leather glove. Although they part, when she returns to Marlott to care for her ailing mother Alec pursues her again. As she works in the family garden, in the light of fires of burning weeds, he appears as a devil with a pitchfork in hand and says to her, "You are Eve, and I am the old Other One come up to tempt you in the disguise of an inferior animal." His constant reproaching her for believing in Angel, his bestowal of gifts upon her family, and the family's desperate situation when Tess's father dies and the family is forced to leave their home, all contribute to Tess's final agreement to live with him as his wife. The pair go to Sandbourne, a fashionable resort area, where Tess finally kills him by stabbing him with a knife.

Themes

Fate and Chance

The characters in Hardy's novel of seduction, abandonment, and murder appear to be under the control of a force greater than they. Marlott is Tess's home and, as the name of the town implies, her lot in life appears be marred or damaged. As the novel opens, Tess's father, John Durbeyfield, learns that he is the last remaining member of the once illustrious d'Urberville family. The parson who tells him admits he had previously "resolved not to disturb [Durbeyfield] with such a useless piece of information," but he is unable to control his "impulses." This event, which starts Tess's tragedy, seems unavoidable, as do many others in the novel. In scene after scene something goes wrong. The most obvious scene in which fate intervenes occurs when Tess writes Angel a letter telling him of her past, but upon pushing it under his door, she unwittingly pushes it under the rug on the floor in the room. If only he could have found it and read it before they were married. If only Angel could have danced with Tess that spring day when they first met. But for Hardy, like Tess, the Earth is a "blighted star" without hope. At the end of the novel, after Tess dies, Hardy writes, "'Justice' was done, and the President of the Immortals, in Aeschylean phrase, had ended his sport with Tess." Tess was powerless to change her fate, because she had been the plaything of a malevolent universe.

Culture Clash

During Tess's time, the industrialization of the cities was diminishing the quality of life of the inhabitants of rural areas. Hardy explores this theme in many ways. The contrast between what is rural (and therefore good) and what is urban (and therefore bad) is apparent in Tess's last names. When

Topics for Further Study

- Imagine Tess's story taking place in today's U. S. society and analyze how her story would have ended up differently or the same, refer to specific scenes from the novel in your analysis.

- Research late-19th century British laws then, playing the role of either the prosecuting or defense attorney, plan your defense or prosecution of Tess for the murder of Alec d'Urberville using details from the novel.

- Compare American novelist William Faulkner's fictional Yoknapatawpha County with Hardy's Wessex, examining the personality and physical description of each literary environment.

Tess is unquestioningly innocent she is "of the field," as the name Durbeyfield implies. D'Urberville invokes both "urban" and "village," and because it belongs to a diminished ancient family, the name is further associated with decrepitude and decay. It is significant that Angel's "fall" happens when he was "nearly entrapped by a woman much older than himself" in London. When Angel and Tess leave Talbothays to take the milk to the train, Hardy writes, "Modern life stretched out its steam feeler to this point three or four times a day, touched the native existences, and quickly withdrew its feeler again, as if what it touched had been uncongenial." He uses the word "feeler" as if the train were a type of insect, indicating his disgust with the intrusion. Later, he calls the thresher at Flintcomb-Ash "the red tyrant" and says "that the women had come to serve" it. As the old ways fade away, people serve machines and not each other.

Knowledge and Ignorance

Knowledge—whether from formal education or innate sensibility—causes conflict between those who see the truth of a situation, and those who are ignorant. Tess and Angel feel isolated from their parents, who appear set in their ways, unable to grasp new ideas. The intellectual gap between Tess, who has gone to school, and her mother is

enormous, but Tess's strong sense of right and wrong widens the gap even more. With Angel, in particular, Hardy recognizes that true knowledge is not just a product of schooling. He contrasts Angel, who alone in his family is not a college graduate, with his brother Cuthbert Clare, a classical scholar who marries the "priggish" Mercy Chant. Although Angel has less formal education, he alone recognizes Tess's worth and wisely chooses her over Mercy's religiosity. When he rejects Tess after their marriage, he does so because her confession "surprised [him] back into his early teachings," the strict moralistic beliefs of his father. True knowledge, therefore, is understanding one another and one's self, and is an essential ingredient for happiness. The village parson refuses to preside at a Christian burial for Tess's infant because he "was a newcomer, and did not know her." When Angel leaves Tess, "he … hardly knew that he loved her still."

Natural Law

Hardy's contrast between false knowledge and knowledge that allows insight into the needs and desires of others, is also seen in his insistence on a natural law that exists independent of humanity. He repeats several times in the novel that what has happened to Tess has not offended nature, but merely society. When she returns pregnant to her home in Marlott from her visit with Alec, she likes to walk in the countryside in the evening away from the disapproving eyes of the townsfolk, but feels that because of what has happened she should not enjoy the beauty around her. "She had been made to break an accepted social law," Hardy observes, "but no law known to the environment in which she fancied herself such an anomaly." Later, Hardy notes that Tess's shame was "a sense of condemnation under an arbitrary law of society which had no foundation in Nature." Victorian society, with its strict code of appropriate and inappropriate social behavior, was anything but natural.

God and Religion

The "arbitrary law of society" that Hardy criticizes is a product of organized religion. His religious characters are pious hypocrites, except for Angel's father, who appears to have a good heart. The local parson's hypocritical attitude forces Tess to bury her child in the section of the cemetery reserved for drunkards and suicides. Alec's appearance as a preacher is a thinly disguised criticism of religious convictions that are held for appearances only. After seeing Tess again, Alec's true nature is again revealed. The stifled atmosphere of the Emminster parsonage where Rev. Clare and his wife live is contrasted with the lively warmth of the Talbothays dairy. In one of the novel's few humorous incidents, Angel sits down to eat with his parents and brothers, expecting to feast on the black puddings (a sausage made of blood and suet) and mead Dairyman Crick's wife had given to him when he left the dairy. On the contrary, he is told that the food has been given to the poor and the drink would be saved for its medicinal properties and used as needed. His disappointment is obvious.

Sex

Victorian society preferred to avoid talking about sex, but Hardy believed the elimination of sex from popular writing produced "a literature of quackery." In *Tess* sex is often associated with nature; it is presented as a natural part of life. The scene of Tess's seduction by Alec takes place in The Chase, an ancient stand of woods that dates from before the time of established societal morality. The valley of the Froom, where Talbothays is located, is described as so lush and fertile that "it was impossible that the most fanciful love should not grow passionate." Tess and Angel fall in love there. Tess's three milkmaid friends toss and turn in their beds, tortured by sexual desire. "Each was but a portion of the organism called sex," Hardy asserts. Later, when Tess forgives Angel his "four and twenty hours dissipation with a stranger;" Angel cannot forgive her similar fault. Hardy condemns such unequal treatment.

Style

Narrator

Tess of the d'Urbervilles tells the story of a girl who is seduced and has a child who dies. When she meets another man whom she wants to marry, she is unable to tell him about her past until after their wedding. Her husband abandons her, and Tess is driven by despair into the arms of her former seducer. When her husband returns, Tess kills the man she is living with. Hardy uses a third-person ("he"/"she") narrator with an omniscient (all-knowing) point of view to tell Tess's story. Thus the narrator not only describes the characters but can reveal their thoughts. Hardy also uses his power as narrator to offer his philosophical insights on the action. The novel's closing paragraph, which begins " 'Justice' was done, and the President of the

Immortals, in Aeschylean phrase, had ended his sport with Tess" is a good example of how Hardy comments on the action. Some critics believe the novel would have been better if Hardy could have remained silent and let the actions of the characters tell the story. At several spots in the novel, Hardy's narrator loses his omniscient ability and comments on the story through the eyes of a storyteller of local history. For example, when he tells the story of Tess and Angel's first meeting, when Angel chooses another girl to dance with him, the narrator says he does not know the lucky girl's name. "The name of the eclipsing girl, whatever it was, has not been handed down," he notes.

Setting

The story takes place in Wessex, an invented territory based on the Dorset countryside where Hardy was born and which fascinated him his entire life. Hardy gives Wessex its own vitality by depicting the region's folk customs (such as the "club-walking" in the scene in which we meet Tess), the "folklore dialect" with its colorful expressions like "get green malt in floor" (meaning to get pregnant), and its superstitions (such as the story of the d'Urberville coach). Hardy's settings seem to mirror the emotions of his characters. Talbothays Dairy, where Angel and Tess's love grows, is described as "oozing fatness and warm ferments" and there "the rush of juices could almost be heard below the hiss of fertilization." Everything about Talbothays drips with the moisture of fertility and sensuality. In stark contrast to the dairy are scenes at Flintcomb-Ash where Tess goes after she is abandoned by Angel. It is "a starve-acre place" where the fields are "a desolate drab" color and the work is exhausting and demeaning. The scene of Tess's capture is Stonehenge, the famous prehistoric ruins on the Salisbury Plain, consisting of large upright stones surrounding an altar stone. Significantly, it is on this altar stone, thought to have been the site of bloody sacrificial offerings, that Tess lies when the police come to arrest her for Alec's murder. Through his choice of settings Hardy is able to make additional comment on the action of the story without further narrative intrusions. By placing Tess on the sacrificial altar Hardy makes clear that he believes she is an innocent victim. Time of year is also important in the novel as Hardy uses the changing of the seasons over the period of about five years as representative of the changing fortunes of his heroine. It is "a particularly fine spring" when she goes to Talbothays; summer as Angel courts her; and finally winter at Flintcomb-Ash

Hardy set Tess of the d'Urbervilles *in a fictional county based on his native Dorset, England.*

where she tries to once more avoid Alec's advances. Time of day is equally as important: unhappy events usually happen in the evening or night.

Symbolism

The settings in *Tess of the d'Urbervilles* function as symbols in that their names have meanings more important than just geographical points. Marlott, Tess's birthplace, for example, alludes to her "marred" or disfigured lot or destiny. Flintcomb-Ash, as its name implies, is a hard, barren place. Several characters have symbolic names as well, including the girl that Angel's parents want him to marry, Mercy Chant, who is depicted as religious to a fault, and Angel Clare, who seems to be an "angel" to Tess and her three milkmaid friends, and even plays a harp. The harp, however, we are told is secondhand, and it symbolizes Angel's imperfect character. Throughout the novel, Angel and Tess are symbolically associated with Adam and Eve of the Bible. In one of the most commented on scenes in *Tess of the d'Urbervilles,* Tess approaches Angel, who is playing his harp, through the wildflowers and weeds in an unkempt garden with an apple tree. As she approaches, she is unaware of the "thistle-milk and slug-slime" and other disagreeable natural secretions that coat her skirts

and arms. Even though Talbothays may seem like Paradise, the reader understands that this Garden of Eden is one that has been spoiled. Later in the novel, more references appear that, again, equate Tess with Eve and Angel with Adam. Alec, on the other hand, appears to Tess as she plants potatoes in a Marlott field. Amid the fires of burning weeds, he appears holding a pitchfork and he says, "You are Eve, and I am the old Other One come to tempt you." Tess is also repeatedly identified with a captured bird. Other important symbolic images in the novel include a bloodstained piece of butcher paper caught in the gate of the Clare residence as Tess attempts to contact Angel's parents in Emminster, the bloody heart-shaped stain on the ceiling at "The Herons" after Tess kills Alec in the room above, and the capture of Tess on the stone of sacrifice at Stonehenge.

Historical Context

Darwin and Social Darwinism

The last fifty years of the nineteenth century saw innovations in science and technology that changed society to a greater degree than ever before. The theory of evolution popularized by nat-

Compare
&
Contrast

- **1890s:** The rural population was forced to move toward urban areas as low prices and industrialization of farm equipment made smaller farms less profitable.

  Today: Family-run farms are disappearing across the United States at the rate of several hundred a year, primarily due to large corporations controlling food production and pricing.

- **1890s:** The advent of rail transportation from rural to the teeming cities of the late nineteenth century made dairy farming more attractive than crop farming, since production was less weather dependent, costs were lower, and an ever-expanding customer-base was within easy reach.

  Today: While small dairies still exist, increasing production costs and lower prices have forced many dairy farmers to sell out to larger concerns, with an average dairy in the western United States milking one to two thousand cows.

- **1890s:** Women could not divorce their husbands, even for having an affair, unless they could prove their husbands had treated them cruelly or abandoned them.

  Today: All fifty states permit couples to divorce by mutual consent, although in twenty, pro-family groups have proposed, and in several cases passed, legislation for making divorce harder to obtain when children are involved.

- **1890s:** State supported education was provided for all children, with education being compulsory to age eleven.

  Today: Increasing dissatisfaction with public schooling has led to exploration of alternative educational methods, including independent public charter schools and 1.2 million students in home-schools.

- **1890s:** Teacher, rural worker, domestic helper, and nurse were some of the positions open to women seeking financial independence; those who chose nontraditional career paths, such as medicine, were ridiculed.

  Today: Although on the average women still earn less per hour than male workers, unlimited career opportunities are now available to them; in 1997, Madeleine Albright became the first woman to ever serve as U. S. Secretary of State, eliminating yet another barrier to advancement for women.

- **1890s:** Women who bore children out of wedlock were considered "ruined"; they and their children could hope for little more than social marginalization.

  Today: Single parenting has become commonplace, with more than 30% of U.S. children being born to fathers and mothers who are not married.

---

uralist Charles Darwin in his *On the Origin of Species by Means of Natural Selection*, published in 1859, had enormous cultural implications. The idea that humans were descended from apes changed accepted views of religion and society. It shook belief in the Biblical creation story and, therefore, all religious beliefs. It shocked the Victorians (those who lived during the reign of the British Queen Victoria from 1837 to 1901) to think that their ancestors were animals. They glorified order and high-mindedness, and thought themselves, as British subjects, the pinnacle of culture.

To make Darwin's theory more palatable, a complementary theory called Social Darwinism was formulated. Proponents of this social philosophy argued that Darwin's ideas of "survival of the fittest" also applied to society. The existence of lower classes could be explained by their inferior intelligence and initiative in comparison to that of the upper classes. Angel refers to this theory when he expresses his surprise that there is no "Hodge" amongst the workers at Talbothays. "The conventional farm-folk of his imagination—personified in the newspaper-press by the pitiable dummy known as Hodge—were obliterated after a few days' residences." He is surprised to discover in Tess "the ache of modernism." For Tess, Angel, and others of their era, the God of their childhood was no longer able to answer their questions. Darwin's book ended forever the security of a society that could offer unalterable answers to every question; like Angel, many began to put their faith in "intellectual liberty" rather than religion.

Industrialization and Rural England

When the railroad came to the area of southwest England where Tess was born, the area still led an isolated, almost medieval existence. The railroad made it easier for country folk looking for work to leave the towns where their families had lived for centuries. The railroad also fostered new types of agricultural use of the land. Large dairies such as Talbothays, where Tess worked as a milkmaid, could flourish only because the rapid trains allowed transport of fresh milk to heavily populated areas. When Tess and Angel take milk cans from the dairy to the nearest train station, Tess reflects that the next morning in London "strange people we have never seen" will drink the milk. The trains converted a closely-knit society into one where consumers never met the producers and where strangers lived together in larger and larger groups.

England entered an agricultural depression in the 1870s, brought on in part by the completion of the first transcontinental railroad across the United States in 1869. (This made it easier and cheaper for American goods to complete with British goods.) Rural workers unable to get jobs, flocked to British cities, causing urban population to double between 1851 and 1881. Less profitable farming, meant farms had to become larger in order to turn a profit, so smaller farms were bought out by larger farm owners. Machines, like the steam threshing machine at Flintcomb-Ash, made agricultural workers less in demand. The large landowners felt no connection with the families living on their land, so to not renew their leases—as was done to Tess's family on Old Ladies Day—was a question of economic good sense, nothing more. Hardy criticized this practice in "The Dorsetshire Labourer," an essay published in *Longman's* magazine in July 1883 quoted in Martin Seymour-Smith's biography of Hardy. "But the question of the Dorset cottager," Hardy notes, "here merges in that of all the house-less and landless poor and the vast topic of the Rights of Man."

Women in Victorian Society

In *Tess* Hardy considers both the "Rights of Man" and, with equal sympathy, the rights of women. Women of the Victorian era were idealized as the helpmate of man, the keeper of the home, and the "weaker sex." Heroines in popular fiction were expected to be frail and virtuous. The thought that Hardy subtitled his novel "A Pure Woman" infuriated some Victorian critics, because it flew in the face of all they held sacred. For while the Victorian era was a time of national pride and belief in British superiority, it was also an age best-remembered for its emphasis on a strict code of morality, unequally applied to men and women. The term Victorian has come to refer to any person or group with a narrow, uncompromising sense of right and wrong. Women were not only discriminated against by the moral code, but they were also discriminated against by the legal code of the day. Until the 1880s married women were unable to hold property in their own name; and the wages of rural workers would go directly to the husband, even if he failed to provide anything for his family. The —Matrimonial Causes Act of 1857 granted the right to a divorce to both men and women on the basis of adultery but, in order to divorce her husband, a women would have to further prove gross cruelty or desertion. Women who sought divorce for whatever reason were ostracized from polite society. Women, like children, were best "seen, but not heard," or as Seymour-Smith observes, "The Victorian middle-class wife ... was admired upon her pedestal of moral superiority only so long as she remained there silently."

Critical Overview

Tess of the d'Urbervilles was a great success, marred only by controversy over its frank treatment of sex and its pessimistic view of life. After a little over a year, more than twenty thousand copies of the book had been sold. Undoubtedly, sales were inflated by the curious who wanted to know what the controversy was about. Several foreign language editions were printed as well. While a popular success, critical opinion was mixed, with commentary ranging from highest praise to deepest contempt. Both the *Anthenaeum* and the London *Times* highly recommended the novel, but for different reasons. A critic in *Anthenaeum* not only found the novel "well in front of Mr. Hardy's previous work," but also praised the novelist's creation of Tess, "a credible, sympathetic creature." The same critic, however, did regret Hardy's excessive "use of scientific and ecclesiastical terminology." A reviewer in *Times* was moved by the story and praised Hardy's effective criticism of Victorian moral standards. On the negative side, a critic in *Saturday Review,* while identifying Tess as the most true to life character in the novel, found the other characters "stagy" or "farcical." He objected to what he saw as Hardy's excessive concern with descriptions of Tess's appealing physical attributes and deemed the story improbable. The critic admitted that even with a poor story, good technique could have saved the novel, but "Hardy, it must be conceded, tells an unpleasant story in a very unpleasant way." Public sentiment was such, however, that the those who disliked the novel felt outnumbered. In *Longman's* magazine, Andrew Lang found the characters in *Tess* to be "far from plausible," the story "beyond ... belief," and Hardy's use of "psychological terminology," unskillful, but resigned himself to the fact that "on all sides—not only from the essays of reviewers, but from the spoken opinions of the most various kinds of readers—one learns that *Tess* is a masterpiece."

According to novelist and critic Albert Guerard, Hardy critics before 1940 seemed to chide Hardy for many of the same points of style that later reviewers found admirable. That year the *Southern Review* celebrated the centennial of Hardy's birth with the publication of an issue devoted entirely to the author. Earlier critics such as Lang and Lionel Johnson, who wrote the first book length critique of Hardy, praise his ability to describe the country folk of Wessex, while condemning his fatalistic view of life. Guerard states in his introduction to *Hardy: A Collection of Critical Essays,* that, beginning with the essays in the *Southern Review,* modern reviewers enjoy Hardy because of his pessimism; they find Hardy's "mismatched destinies, the darkness of the physical and moral landscapes, the awareness of dwindling energies, and the sense of man's appalling limitations ... peculiarly modern." One *Southern Review* contributor, Donald Davidson, discovers in the fatalism of the novel, as well as in Hardy's controversial closing paragraph about "The President of the Immortals," reflections of Hardy's interest in the folk ballads of his native Dorset. Davidson contends that fateful coincidences are comparable to the supernatural occurrences that frequently occur in the ballads and that Hardy's closing paragraph functions merely as a closing state-

ment to the novel much like a traditional ballad ending. In *Jane Austen to Joseph Conrad,* John Holloway disregards Hardy's use of coincidence, saying that the scenes that might seem unrealistic are out of necessity so "in order that their other dimension take meaning, their relevance to the larger rhythms of the work, shall transpire." In *Tess* the "larger rhythm," as Holloway sees it, is in repeated identification of Tess with a hunted animal and a Darwinian vision that takes Tess, much like a developing species, from formation, through adaptation, to ultimate extinction. Dorothy Van Ghent notes in *The English Novel: Form and Function,* that "in the accidentalism of Hardy's universe we can recognize the profound truth of the darkness in which life is cast, darkness both within the soul and without."

For Guerard, "Hardy the novelist is a major transitional figure between the popular moralists and popular entertainer of Victorian fiction and the serious, visionary, often symbolizing novelists of today." Other critics also place Hardy in the doorway to modernism. Harold Bloom maintains that this is especially evident in *Tess of the d'Urbervilles.* "It can be asserted that Hardy's novel," he writes in his introduction to *Thomas Hardy: Modern Critical Views,* "has proved to be prophetic of a sensibility by no means fully emergent in 1891. Nearly a century later, the book sometimes seems to have moments of vision that are contemporary with us." In particular, critics have reevaluated the novel in the light of new emphasis on women rights and feminist issues. As Hardy biographer Martin Seymour-Smith concludes, Hardy's novel remains one of riveting validity even one hundred years after publication. "Tess was a *woman* who stabbed her *husband.* Then, as now, in the eyes of most judges, there is one law for men who kill their wives, and quite another for women who kill their husbands." For Seymour-Smith, Tess and her pitiful treatment by the men in her life are at the core of discovering the true importance of the work. "The question raised by the novel is this: what would a woman be if she were released from male oppression and allowed to be herself?"

Criticism

Stan Walker

In the following essay, Walker, a doctoral candidate at the University of Texas, notes that while some criticisms of Hardy's novel are justified, the

What Do I Read Next?

- Spanish playwright Federico Garcia Lorca's widely-performed lyrical folk tragedies, *Blood Wedding* (1933), *Yerma* (1934), and *The House of Bernarda Alba* (1936), dealing with sexual repression and tradition in rural Spain.

- *Madame Bovary*, Gustave Flaubert's 1857 best-selling satirical novel of Emma Bovary's search for romantic love in provincial France.

- Norwegian poet and playwright Henrik Ibsen's 1890 drama *Hedda Gabler*, about a woman who tries to live her life through a man, but finds it impossible to submerge her own desires and play the role of a housewife.

- Thomas Hardy's *The Return of the Native* (1878) in which Hardy explores the conflict between the forces of nature, represented by the Egdon Heath, and the area's inhabitants.

- Edith Wharton's Pulitzer-Prize winning novel of manners *The Age of Innocence* (1920), set in the New York City of the 1870s, examines the negative effects of social convention on three members of society's elite.

---

view of Tess *as a pessimistic work is not really valid.*

Tess of the d'Urbervilles was Thomas Hardy's penultimate novel, published in 1891 when he was fifty-one years old (*Jude the Obscure*, his final novel, appeared four years later). After *Jude*, Hardy returned to his original love, poetry, producing eight volumes of verse during the last thirty years of his life. In his two-volume autobiography (credited to his second wife, Florence Emily Hardy, but written predominantly by Hardy himself), he claimed to have taken up the writing of novels "under the stress of necessity," and to have "long intended to abandon [it] at some indefinite time." It was the troubles he experienced with the publication of *Tess*, however, that "well-nigh compelled

him, in his own judgement at any rate," to abandon novels. These troubles arose chiefly around his attempts to have the novel published serially (that is, in regular installments in a newspaper or magazine).

The cultural climate in England at the time was one of widespread prudery and intolerance, and "family values" were being promoted as the medicine to combat a perceived spread of sexual decadence, according to Elaine Showalter in *Sexual Anarchy: Gender and Culture at the Fin de Siecle.* As periodicals were by and large seen as family organs, some of the "adult" scenes in *Tess* were deemed inappropriate. Thus the novel was turned down by two periodicals. It was accepted by a third only after Hardy, with what he described in his autobiography as "cynical amusement," agreed to some significant changes. The novel was restored to its original form when it was published as a book later that year. Ironically, it proved to be perhaps the most popular of his novels with readers, while it was widely, though not universally, admired by critics.

Hardy viewed the writing of novels as being closely akin to the writing of poetry. He aimed, he said in his autobiography, "at keeping his narratives ... as near to poetry in their subject as the conditions would allow." By "near to poetry" he meant, more or less, "close to natural life," a condition to which he contrasted the production of "stories of modern artificial life and manners showing a certain smartness of treatment." Certainly Hardy is concerned in *Tess* with portraying the natural world: among the most memorable scenes in the novel are those in which he evokes the fields and woods of his beloved Wessex. Yet some critics have argued that on the whole *Tess* is hardly "close to natural life." Hardy's contemporary Andrew Lang wrote in a review in *Longman's* that by his own "personal standard," "*Tess* is not real or credible," and he characterized it as a "morally squalid fairy tale." Robert Louis Stevenson complained in a letter to fellow writer Henry James that Hardy's novel was "not alive, not true, ... not even honest!" In *Nineteenth-Century Fiction*, modern critic Hugh Kenner dismissed Hardy's "situations" as "melodrama" and his characters as "phases in the sociology of fiction."

A quick look at many of the incidents in *Tess,* particularly in the second half of the novel, lends at least some weight to these criticisms. The response of Tess' fellow dairymaids to her wedding Angel Clare; the scene in which Angel sleepwalks with Tess in his arms; the fact that Farmer Groby, Tess' employer at Flintcomb-Ash, was a man with whom Angel and she had had a previous run-in; and the fact that Alec d'Urberville's brief conversion to Primitive Methodism (unlikely in itself) is precipitated by a confrontation with Angel's father, as well as other events, all stretch the boundaries of credibility.

Critics have more generally agreed in their assessment of Hardy as a pessimistic writer. There is ample evidence in *Tess* to support such an assessment. It is clear, for example, that while Hardy honors the practice of truly pious people like Angel Clare's parents, he recognizes little if anything in their creed to support its claims to possessing an exclusive hold on truth. In this Hardy was very much in step with his time: the nineteenth century had witnessed the waning of the Christian faith in the face of mid-century discoveries in geology (Charles Lyell) and biology (Charles Darwin), and the rise of comparative linguistics, which had begun treating the Bible "scientifically," as an historical document like any other. Hardy does locate a universal principle in nature, yet his Wessex is not the deified nature of poet William Wordsworth and many of the other English Romantics. At times, Hardy challenges Wordsworth directly, as when he says, "Some people would like to know whence the poet (Wordsworth) whose philosophy is in these days deemed as profound and trustworthy as his song is breezy and pure, gets his authority to speaking of 'Nature's holy plan.'" Nature for Hardy is instead an arena of conflict between "the two forces … at work … everywhere, the inherent will to enjoy, and the circumstantial will against enjoyment." In such an arena, "the call seldom produces the comer, the man to love rarely coincides with the hour for loving;" and we are constantly made to distinguish between the world as we perceive it and the world as it might be said to be in and of itself, and thus to acknowledge finally how relatively insignificant we are in the grand scheme of things.

Hardy himself objected to the charge of pessimism. While the bitterness or depression many readers feel after reading *Tess* may seem to make such an objection indefensible, audiences would do well to remember that there are many moments of joy in the novel. The "circumstantial will against enjoyment" is only half of the equation. And if in the end Tess is the victim of circumstance, the "sport" of the "President of the Immortals," those earlier moments of joy have not been without their value. Indeed, her final fugitive tromp through the countryside with Angel, a sort of extended moment,

a suspension of the last turning of the wheels of "Justice," is spiritually recuperative to such a degree that when she is captured, Tess says simply and quietly, "I am ready." Thus perhaps redemption is, in Hardy's view, available to us after all, though not in the places we might have expected (e.g., Christian faith). Rather, it is to be found in these moments—"moments of vision" (the title of his fifth volume of verse), "impressions," to be experienced and valued, in the words of Hardy's contemporary Walter Pater in *Hardy: A Biography,* "simply for those moments' sake."

Source: Stan Walker, in an essay for *Novels for Students,* Gale, 1998.

J. Hillis Miller

In the following excerpt, Yale University critic Miller discusses interpretations of the novel, focusing on its repetitive structure.

The episodes of *Tess of the d'Urbervilles* take place in a line, each following the last. Ultimately they form a row traced out in time, just as Tess's course is traced across the roads of southern England. Each episode in Tess's life, as it occurs, adds itself to previous ones, and, as they accumulate, behold!, they make a pattern. They make a design traced through time and on the landscape of England, like the prehistoric horses carved out on the chalk downs. Suddenly, to the retrospective eye of the narrator, of the reader, and ultimately even of the protagonist herself, the pattern is there. Each event, as it happens, is alienated from itself and swept up into the design. It ceases to be enclosed in itself and through its resonances with other events becomes a sign referring to previous and to later episodes which are signs in their turn. When an event becomes a sign it ceases to be present. It becomes other than itself, a reference to something else. For this reason Tess's violation and the murder must not be described directly. They do not happen as present events because they occur as repetitions of a pattern of violence which exists only in its recurrences and has always already occurred, however far back one goes.

In one way or another most analyses of prose fiction, including most interpretations of *Tess of the d'Urbervilles,* are based on the presupposition that a novel is a centered structure which may be interpreted if that center can be identified. This center will be outside the play of elements in the work and will explain and organize them into a fixed pattern of meaning deriving from this center. Hardy's insistent asking of the question "Why does Tess suffer so?" has led critics to assume that their main task is to find the explanatory cause. The reader tends to assume that Hardy's world is in one way or another deterministic. Readers have, moreover, tended to assume that this cause will be single. It will be some one force, original and originating. The various causes proposed have been social, psychological, genetic, material, mythical, metaphysical, or coincidental. Each such interpretation describes the text as a process of totalization from the point of departure of some central principle that makes things happen as they happen. Tess has been described as the victim of social changes in nineteenth-century England, or of her own personality, or of her inherited nature, or of physical or biological forces, or of Alec and Angel as different embodiments of man's inhumanity to woman. She has been explained in terms of mythical prototypes, as a Victorian fertility goddess, or as the helpless embodiment of the Immanent Will, or as a victim of unhappy coincidence, sheer hazard, or happenstance, or as the puppet of Hardy's deliberate or unconscious manipulations.

The novel provides evidence to support any or all of these interpretations. *Tess of the d'Urbervilles,* like Hardy's work in general, is overdetermined. The reader is faced with an embarrassment of riches. The problem is not that there are no explanations proposed in the text, but that there are too many. A large group of incompatible causes or explanations are present in the novel. It would seem that they cannot all be correct. My following through of some threads in the intricate web of Hardy's text has converged toward the conclusion that it is wrong in principle to assume that there must be some single accounting cause. For Hardy, the design has no source. It happens. It does not come into existence in any one version of the design which serves as a model for the others. There is no "original version," only an endless sequence of them, rows and rows written down as it were "in some old book," always recorded from some previously existing exemplar.

An emblem in the novel for this generation of meaning from a repetitive sequence is that red sign Tess sees painted by the itinerant preacher *THY, DAMNATION, SLUMBERETH, NOT.* Each episode of the novel, or each element in its chains of recurrent motifs, is like one of these words. Each is a configuration which draws its meaning from its spacing in relation to the others. In the strange notation of the sign-painter, this gap is designated by the comma. The comma is a mark of punctuation which signifies nothing in itself but punctuation, a pause. The comma indicates the spacing in the rhythm of articulation that makes meaning possible. Each episode of the novel is, like one of the words in the sign, separated from the others, but when all are there in a row the meaning emerges. This meaning is not outside the words but within them. Such is the coercive power of pre-established syntactic sequences, that a reader is able to complete an incomplete pattern of words. Tess completes in terror and shame the second sign the painter writes: *THOU, SHALT, NOT, COMMIT,* and the reader knows that the relation of 'Liza-Lu and Angel will repeat in some new way the universal pattern of suffering, betrayal, and unfulfilled desire which has been established through its previous versions in the book.

Tess wanders through her life like a sleepwalker, unaware of the meaning of what she is doing. She seeks a present satisfaction which always eludes her until her final happiness in the shadow of death. Her damnation, however, slumbereth not. This "damnation" lies in the fact that whatever she does becomes a sign, takes on a meaning alienated from her intention. Hardy affirms his sense of the meaning of Tess's story not by explaining its causes but by objectively tracing out her itinerary so that its pattern ultimately emerges for the reader to see.

Hardy's notion of fatality is the reflex of his notion of chance. Out of the "flux and reflux—the rhythm of change" which "alternate[s] and persist[s] in everything under the sky" … emerges as if by miracle the pattern of repetitions in difference forming the design of Tess's life. Such repetitions produce similarity out of difference and are controlled by no center, origin, or end outside the chain of recurrent elements. For *Tess of the d'Urbervilles* this alternative to the traditional metaphysical concept of repetition emerges as the way the text produces and affirms its meaning.

Tess of the d'Urbervilles, like Hardy's other novels, brilliantly explores the implications for an understanding of human life of a form of repetition which is immanent. Such a sequence is without a source outside the series.

On the basis of this definition of immanent repetition, it is possible to identify what Hardy means by the first half of his definition of *Tess of the d'Urbervilles* as "an attempt to give artistic form to a true sequence of things." The artistic form is the novelist's interpretation of the events. This interpretation does not falsify the events, but it imposes meaning on them by reading them in a certain way, as a sentence may have entirely different meanings depending on how it is articulated. The meaning is there and not there. It is a matter of position, of emphasis, of spacing, of punctuation.

Attention is insistently called to the act of reading, in the broad sense of deciphering, throughout *Tess*. One way is the many examples of false interpretation which are exposed by the narrator. These include the comic example of the bull who thought it was Christmas Eve because he heard the Nativity Hymn, or the more serious dramatization of Angel's infatuation with Tess and his interpretation of her as like Artemis or like Demeter..., or the description of Tess's "idolatry" of Angel..., or Tess's false reading of nature as reproaching her for her impurity. All interpretation is the imposition of a pattern by a certain way of making cross-connections between one sign and those which come before or after. Any interpretation is an artistic form given to the true sequence of things. Meaning in such a process emerges from a reciprocal act in which both the interpreter and what is interpreted contribute to the making or the finding of a pattern....

To add a new interpretation to the interpretation already proposed by the author is to attach another link to the chain of interpretations. The reader takes an impression in his turn. He represents to himself what already exists purely as a representation. To one purity the reader adds a subsequent purity of his own. This is Hardy's version of the notion of multiple valid but incompatible interpretations....

In *Tess of the d'Urbervilles,* in any case, the narrator always presents not only the event with its "objective" elements, but also his interpretation of the event. At the same time he shows his awareness that the interpretation is "purely" imposed not inherent, except as it is one possibility among a limited repertoire of others. An example would be the "objective" description of the sun casting its beams on Tess. This is first interpreted as like the act of a god, but that interpretation is then ironically undercut: "His present aspect ... explained the old time heliolatries in a moment."... The narrator's act in not only describing the true sequence of things but also giving it artistic form is shown as what it is by its doubling within the text in the interpretative acts of the characters. The narrator always sees clearly what is "subjective" in Tess's reading of her life, but this insight casts back to undermine his own readings. These multiple acts of interpretation are not misinterpretations in relation to some "true" interpretation. Each telling, even the

most clear-sighted one, is another reading in its turn. The bare "reality" Angel sees when he falls out of love with Tess is as much an interpretation as the transfiguration of the world he experiences when he sees her as a goddess and the world as irradiated by her presence.

The power of readings to go on multiplying means that Tess's wish to be "forgotten quite" cannot be fulfilled. The chain of interpretations will continue to add new links. Tess can die, but the traces of her life will remain, for example in the book which records the impression she has made on the narrator's imagination. Her life has a power of duplicating itself which cancels the ending her failure to have progeny might have brought. The life of her sister will be, beyond the end of the book, another repetition with a difference of the pattern of Tess's life. Beyond that, the reader comes to see, there will be another, and then another, ad infinitum. If the novel is the impression made on Hardy's candid mind by Tess's story, the candid reader is invited to receive the impression again in his turn, according to that power of a work of art to repeat itself indefinitely to which the novel calls attention in a curious passage concerning Tess's sensitivity to music. Here is a final bit of evidence that Hardy saw the principle of repetition, in life as in art, as impersonal, immanent, and self-proliferating rather than as controlled by any external power, at least once a given repeatable sequence gets recorded in some form of notation or "trace." The "simplest music" has "a power over" Tess which can "well-nigh drag her heart out of her bosom at times."... She reflects on the strange coercive effect church music has on her feelings: "She thought, without exactly wording the thought, how strange and god-like was a composer's power, who from the grave could lead through sequences of emotion, which he alone had felt at first, a girl like her who had never heard of his name, and never would have a clue to his personality."... In the same way, *Tess of the d'Urbervilles,* as long as a single copy exists, will have its strange and godlike power to lead its readers through some version of the sequences of emotion for which it provides the notation.

Source: J. Hillis Miller, "*Tess of the d'Urbervilles:* Repetition as Imminent Design," in his *Fiction and Repetition: Seven English Novels,* Harvard University Press, 1982, pp. 116–42.

Thomas Hinde

One of the "Angry Young Men" writers of the 1950s whose writings expressed bitterness and disillusionment with society, English novelist and critic Hinde examines the ways that Tess's fate mirrors the destruction of the agricultural class in England at the end of the nineteenth century.

The plot of *Tess of the D'Urbervilles* turns on a succession of accidents and coincidences. Again and again Tess's tragic fate depends on some disastrous mischance. One or two of these may seem possible—after all is full of mischance—but heaped on top of each other they produce a final effect of gross improbability. Does this matter? Are we to see them as blemishes on an otherwise fine novel ; or are they such a pervasive part of it that they must either condemn it or form part of its success?

At its face value the novel suggests not only that these accidents and misfortunes are included by intention but that it is the author's view that life does give human beings just such a succession of kicks downhill to disaster. The refrain 'where was Tess's guardian angel?' is more than an attack on the conventional Christian idea of a benevolent and protecting Almighty; it implies the exact opposite. Our problem, if we don't share this view, is that we see Tess as not so much the victim of Fate, nor as the victim of her own character and circumstances, but as Hardy's personal victim.

It is he who appears to make her suffer her improbable sequence of accidents. In criticizing this effect I do not imply that probability is a criterion by which we should universally or invariably judge. A novel sets its own standards, and no one, to take an obvious example, expects the same 'realism' from Kafka as from Tolstoy. The problem with Hardy's novels is that in most other ways they set up expectations of a quite conventional realism. It is against this self-established standard that the plot of *Tess,* as much as that of any of his novels which came before it and which it otherwise excels, at first sight appears equally to offend.

I say at first sight because my purpose is to suggest a way of looking at *Tess* which sees its many accidents and coincidences neither as blemishes, nor as valid samples of Hardy's neither credible nor particularly interesting view of the part played in life by a persecuting fate; if encouragement were needed to search for such a view it would be provided by *Tess*'s many admirers who seem undismayed by its improbabilities, though these begin on the very first page and feature regularly throughout the book.

Setting the scene, and necessary if there is to be any novel at all, is the coincidence of names: the rich north country manufacturer Stoke who buys his way into the southern landed gentry has arbitrarily chosen from a British Museum list of defunct families the name d'Urberville to add to his own, and this is the original name of the family from which Tess Durbeyfield is distantly descended. The story opens with Parson Tringham telling Tess's father about his aristocratic ancestors, which till now he has not known about. John Durbeyfield puts two and two together and makes five, concluding not only that he is related to the Stoke-d'Urbervilles but that he probably belongs to the senior branch.

Up to this point all could be said to be reasonable enough. If it is an accident it is one which sooner or later seems possible if not probable. In any case, even a realistic novelist may, without offending against his own criterion of probability, precipitate his story with such a single event, then stand back to demonstrate with no further interference the inevitable consequences.

There seems no such inevitability about the next kick downhill which Fate gives Tess. Driving her father's cart to market at night because he is too drunk to go, she is run down by the mail coach, and Prince, the horse on which his livelihood as a haggler depends, is pierced to the heart by the mail coach's shaft. Tess's guilt at what she has done persuades her to agree to her mother's plan that she should visit the *nouveaux riches* Stoke d'Urbervilles in the hope of making a prosperous marriage.

Here she meets the young and buckish Alec d'Urberville; once again a flavour of managed accident surrounds her seduction by him. Her quarrel, late at night in open country, with the drunken Trantridge village women provides her with just the motive which makes plausible her acceptance of Alec's offer of a pillion ride when he spurs up at a convenient moment. Criticism is only disarmed by the splendid dramatic quality of this scene, set as it is with sinister omen and diabolic detail.

At Talbothays, where Tess goes a few years later and after the death of her child to become a milkmaid, who should she meet but Angel Clare, the young man who, in a more insidious but surer way, is to lead her to her tragic end.

From this moment the plot turns on Angel's plan to marry Tess, and on whether or not Tess can bring herself to confess her sinful past with Alec d'Urberville before their wedding day. Though she can't tell Angel to his face she at last makes herself write to him and late at night pushes the letter under his door. Only on her wedding eve does she discover that Fate has struck again: she has accidently pushed it under the carpet as well as the door and Angel has never received it.

Her confession after her marriage leads to their separation, Angel to go to Brazil, Tess to return to Marlott. He has left her an allowance but a succession of minor misfortunes—in particular the neediness and imprudence of her parents—leaves Tess destitute by the time winter comes. Angel has told her that she should go to his parents if she is ever in need, but Fate, which has already put him personally beyond her reach, closes this escape too. She walks to Emminster and finds Angel's father, the vicar, out. Before she can try his door again Angel's brothers discover her walking boots which she has hidden on the outskirts of the village and Miss Mercy Chant bears them off for charity. Tess's courage fails her and she turns for home. 'It was somewhat unfortunate,' Hardy writes, 'that she had encountered the sons and not the father, who, despite his narrowness, was far less starched and ironed than they, and had to the full the gift of Christian charity.' Though we may read this as a confession of clumsy plotting, that is far from Hardy's intention. His tone is ironic. The world may consider that Tess here suffered an improbable and untypical stroke of ill luck, but Hardy, better informed about the working of Fate, knows that such accidents are in fact typical and probable.

Meanwhile Tess has taken on the humblest and most oppressive sort of agricultural labour: work on arable land. The description of her grubbing up swedes for cattle food, creeping across the icy uplands of Flintcomb Ash in drenching rain, is one of the most memorable in the book. And who should turn out to be her employer but a farmer who knows her past and whom Angel once struck on the jaw when he insultingly hinted at it during the last days before their marriage. Inevitably he takes his revenge on Tess.

Alec d'Urberville's conversion to evangelical Christianity—coincidentally performed by Angel Clare's father—now gives Alec the chance to harass Tess again and, more important, weakens her power to resist him. The scene is set for her final disastrous return to Alec. The various letters Angel ultimately receives from her and from others reach him at moments which time his return exactly too late to save her from the murder of Alec and ultimately the gallows.

Though this is only a brief selection of the blows which Fate strikes Tess, I hope it is suffi-

cient to show that the plot of the novel turns on a succession of disastrous accidents which far exceeds realistic probability. But as in all such abstracts, vital elements which seem unrelated to the book's plot have been left out, in particular one to which Hardy persistently returns even though his attention is overtly directed towards Tess and her personal tragedy. This is the equally sure and tragic destruction of the traditional society of the English village.

Twice he shows us mechanized agriculture at work; on the first occasion he describes how the reaping machine, with its red arms in the shape of a Maltese cross, gradually reduces the standing corn.

> Rabbits, hares, snakes, rats, mice, retreated into a fastness, unaware of the ephemeral nature of their refuge, and of the doom that awaited them later in the day when their covert shrinking to a more and more horrible narrowness, they were huddled together, friends and foes, till the last few yards of upright wheat fell also under the teeth of the unerring reaper, and they were every one put to death by the sticks and stones of the harvesters.

It needs little intuition to see that Hardy is here describing by parallel the fate of the human inhabitants of such a village as Marlott.

Humans themselves are the victims on the second occasion: Tess and her fellow workers who feed the monstrous itinerant threshing machine at Flintcombe Ash, with its diabolical master....

Apart from the implications of such incidents, Hardy as author continually comments on the changing and deteriorating condition of rural Wessex. The May Day dance, for example, where we first meet Tess, is 'a gay survival from Old Style days when cheerfulness and May were synonyms'. The refreshments which the rural labourers of Trantridge drink on Saturday nights are 'curious compounds sold to them as beer by the monopolizers of the once independent inns'. Still more important, it is the tenant farmers, deprived of their independence, who are 'the natural enemies of bush and brake', and to whom Tess falls victim at the lowest point of her decline at Flintcombe Ash.

And it is because Tess's family are victims of another aspect of this destruction of rural independence that she is finally exposed once more to Alec d'Urberville. As soon as her father dies her mother loses her right to their cottage, and the family must join all those other labourers' families which take to the road on Lady Day, their worldly goods loaded on to hired waggons, to hunt for new jobs and homes. Oppressed by responsibility for her family, she no longer feels she has the moral right to resist his advances when they could bring with them the financial help she so badly needs.

Indeed, a good many of Tess's misfortunes turn out, on closer inspection, to have economic causes which seem almost as important as the random vengefulness of Fate to which Hardy attributes them. It is only a short step from realizing this to wondering whether Hardy is not—consciously or unconsciously—concerned throughout the book not so much with Tess's personal fortune as with her fate as a personification of rural Wessex.

Just why Tess should be an appropriate figure to play this part is clearly explained in Chapter LI, in a passage which holds the clue to the book's social message....

At once much that appeared arbitrary becomes logical. The destruction of the haggler's daughter no longer seems a cruel mischance, but inevitable. And many more of the accidents she suffers, which on a personal level seem so excessive and gratuitous, become those which her class *must* suffer.

The mail coach which runs down the haggler's cart and kills his horse is the vehicle which will destroy the livelihood of all hagglers, whether they are drunkards like John Durbeyfield, or sober and hard-working. Deprived of their former independence, the children of this village middle class will be driven downwards into just the sort of menial labouring jobs that Tess is forced to take. Her downward progress from milkmaid to arable worker of the lowest sort is the path ahead for all of them.

Tess is of course many other things as well. She is, for example, the embodiment of 'nature' and in particular of natural womanhood. 'Women whose chief companions are the forms and forces of outdoor Nature retain in their souls far more of the Pagan fantasy of their remote forefathers than of the systematized religion taught their race at later date.' And however much she may stand for a principle or a passing society, she remains a lost and frightened human being in a world which misleads then persecutes her. Scenes such as the splendid but appalling one in which she baptizes her dying child in her bedroom wash basin may indeed seem to establish her tragedy too clearly as a personal one for the interpretation I am suggesting.

But such a view of Tess becomes less and less satisfactory as Hardy inflicts on her a less and less probable sequence of accidental and coincidental misfortune. It is only when she is seen to some extent also to be a daughter of the doomed rural England which Hardy loved, and in particular of that class in the rural community from which Hardy himself came and which was once 'the backbone of the village life' that her fate no longer seems arbitrary and author-imposed but inescapable.

Source: Thomas Hinde, "Accident and Coincidence in *Tess of the d'Urbervilles*," in *The Genius of Thomas Hardy,* edited by Margaret Drabble, Alfred A. Knopf, 1976, pp. 74–79.

Sources

Harold Bloom, "Introduction," in *Thomas Hardy: Modern Critical Views,* Chelsea House, 1987, pp. 1-22.

Donald Davidson, "The Traditional Basis of Thomas Hardy's Fiction," in *Hardy: A Collection of Critical Essays,* edited by Albert J. Guerard, Prentice-Hall, 1963. pp.

Albert J. Guerard, "Introduction," in his *Hardy: A Collection of Critical Essays,* Prentice-Hall, 1963, pp. 1-9.

Florence Emily Hardy, "Background: Hardy's Autobiography," in *Tess of the d'Urbervilles,* by Thomas Hardy, 2nd edition, edited by Scott Elledge, Norton, 1979, pp. 343-63.

Thomas Hardy, *Tess of the d'Urbervilles,* Norton Critical Edition, W.W. Norton, 1979.

John Holloway, "Hardy's Major Fiction," in *Hardy: A Collection of Critical Essays,* edited by Albert Guerard, Prentice-Hall, 1963, pp. 52-62.

Martin Seymour-Smith, *Hardy: A Biography,* St. Martin's Press, 1994.

Review of *Tess of the d'Urbervilles,* in *Anthenaeum,* January 9, 1892.

Review of *Tess of the d'Urbervilles* in *Times* (London), January 13, 1892.

Dorothy Van Ghent, "On *Tess of the D'Urbervilles,*" in *Hardy: A Collection of Critical Essays,* edited by Albert J. Guerard, Prentice-Hall, 1963, pp. 77-90.

For Further Study

Byron Caminero-Santangelo, "A Moral Dilemma: Ethics in *Tess of the d'Urbervilles,*" in *English Studies,* Vol. 75, No. 1, January, 1994, pp. 46-61.

Caminero-Santangelo begins by noting that the world of *Tess* is a post-Darwinian one in which ethics have no basis in nature. He then goes on to argue that the novel's "ethical center" can be located in a "community of careful readers" who will recognize the injustice in the novel and emulate Tess in challenging it.

Peter J. Casagrande, *Tess of the d'Urbervilles: Unorthodox Beauty,* Twayne's Masterwork Studies, 1992.

In this book-length study, Casagrande argues that Hardy, in exploring the question of why innocents suffer, finds beauty in Tess's suffering at the same time that he deplores that suffering.

Graham Handley, in *Thomas Hardy, Tess of the d'Urbervilles,* Penguin, 1991.

Handley analyzes *Tess* in terms of "narrative structures." He gives particular weight to the roles of the characters in the novel, and also examines the novel in terms of such things as its "figurative patterns" and "themes."

Irving Howe, *Thomas Hardy,* Macmillan, 1967.

Howe provides a lengthy discussion of *Tess,* including a comparison between Hardy's novel and Bunyan's *Pilgrim's Progress.*

Lionel Johnson, "The Argument," in *Tess of the d'Urbervilles,* by Thomas Hardy, 2nd edition, edited by Scott Elledge, Norton, 1979, pp. 389-400.

A portion of poet Lionel Johnson's acclaimed early analysis of Hardy's fiction in which he examines Hardy's attitude toward Nature, his depiction of the Wessex country folk, and his fatalistic view of life.

Hugh Kenner, "J. Hillis Miller, *Thomas Hardy: Distance and Desire,*" in *Nineteenth-Century Fiction,* Vol. 26, No. 2, September, 1971, pp. 230-34.

In the course of reviewing a book by scholar-critic J. Hillis Miller on Hardy, Kenner provides his own perspective on Hardy's merits and importance.

Andrew Lang, review of *Tess of the d'Urbervilles,* in *Longman's,* November, 1892.

An early review in which the critic finds little to praise in the novel.

Walter Pater, *The Renaissance: Studies in Art and Poetry,* University of California Press, 1980.

A landmark study focusing mainly on the visual arts in Renaissance Italy, and first published in 1873.

Elaine Showalter, *Sexual Anarchy: Gender and Culture at the Fin de Siecle,* Viking Penguin, 1990.

Showalter's study discusses gender issues in 1890s Britain and draws several parallels with the U.S. in the 1980s.

Peter Widdowson, editor *Tess of the d'Urbervilles,* Macmillan, 1993.

A collection of essays meant to represent a response to Hardy's novel from a range of critical positions, in particular Marxism, feminism, and poststructuralism.

Terence Wright, *Tess of the d'Urbervilles,* Macmillan, 1987.

This short book is divided into two parts. In the first, Wright surveys various critical approaches to the novel, which he divides into five basic categories. In the second, he attempts to synthesize what he considers to be the best elements of all these approaches into a single reading of the novel.

Their Eyes Were Watching God

Zora Neale Hurston
1937

When *Their Eyes Were Watching God* first appeared in 1937, it was well-received by white critics as an intimate portrait of southern blacks, but African-American reviewers rejected the novel as pandering to white audiences and perpetuating stereotypes of blacks as happy-go-lucky and ignorant. Unfortunately, the novel and its author, Zora Neale Hurston, were quickly forgotten. But within the last twenty years it has received renewed attention from scholars who praise its unique contribution to African-American literature, and it has become one of the newest and most original works to consistently appear in college courses across the country and to be included in updated versions of the American literary canon. The book has been admired by African-Americanists for its celebration of black culture and dialect and by feminists for its depiction of a woman's progress towards self-awareness and fulfillment. But the novel continues to receive criticism for what some see as its lack of engagement with racial prejudice and its ambivalent treatment of relations between the sexes. No one disputes, though, its impressive use of metaphor, dialect, and folklore of southern rural blacks, which Hurston studied as an anthropologist, to reflect the rich cultural heritage of African Americans.

Author Biography

Zora Neale Hurston's colorful life was a strange mixture of acclaim and censure, success

and poverty, pride and shame. But her varied life, insatiable curiosity, and profound wit made her one of the most fascinating writers America has known. Even her date of birth remains a mystery. She claimed in her autobiography to have been born on 7 January 1903, but family members swore she was born anywhere from 1891 to 1902. Nevertheless, it is known that she was born in Eatonville, Florida, which was to become the setting for most of her fiction and was the first all-black incorporated town in the nation. Growing up there, where her father was mayor, Hurston was largely sheltered from the racial prejudice African Americans experienced elsewhere in America.

At the age of fourteen, Hurston struck out on her own, working as a maid for white families, and was sent to Morgan Academy in Baltimore by one of her employers. Her educational opportunities continued to grow. She studied at Barnard College, where she worked under the eminent anthropologist Franz Boas. She also attended Howard University, and Columbia University, where she began work towards a Ph.D. in anthropology.

Hurston published her first story in 1921 and quickly gained recognition among the writers of the newly formed Harlem Renaissance, an outpouring of artistic innovation in the African-American community of Harlem. She moved there in 1925 with little money but much ambition, and became well-known as the most colorful member of the artistic and literary circles of the city. She also gained the attention of Mrs. Rufus Osgood Mason, a wealthy white patron who agreed to fund Hurston's trips to Florida where she gathered folklore. Although she married Herbert Sheen during this period, they lived together only eight months before her career came between them. While they split amicably, a later marriage to Albert Price III, which lasted from 1939 to 1943, ended bitterly.

Hurston's career as a novelist picked up in the 1930s. Her first novel, *Jonah's Gourd Vine,* appeared in 1934 and became a Book-of-the-Month Club selection. The following year, she published *Mules and Men,* a collection of folktales that mixed anthropology and fiction. This book gained her widespread recognition and helped her win a Guggenheim fellowship to study folklore in the West Indies. Before leaving for Haiti, she fell in love with a younger man. When he demanded that she give up her career, she ended the affair, but wrote the novel *Their Eyes Were Watching God* in seven weeks, translating their romance into the relationship between Janie and Tea Cake. The novel appeared in 1937 to some recognition and contro-

Zora Neale Hurston

versy, but it quickly receded from the limelight and was not a commercial success.

Although she published two more novels, another book of folklore, and dozens of stories, Hurston's literary reputation dwindled throughout the 1940s and '50s. In 1948 she was charged with committing an immoral act with a ten-year-old boy and was later absolved of the crime, but the damage to her public reputation had been done. Hurston felt that she was forever outcast from the African-American literary community of Harlem, so she spent the rest of her life in Florida, where she worked various jobs and tried to keep her head above water financially. When she suffered a stroke in 1959, she was committed to a welfare home where she died penniless and alone in 1960. She was buried in an unmarked grave in the segregated cemetery of Fort Pierce. The location remained unknown until 1973, when it was located by author Alice Walker.

Plot Summary

Chapter 1

Zora Neale Hurston's *Their Eyes Were Watching God* opens with a lyrical passage in which Janie Starks returns to her previous home, Eatonville.

The other townspeople observe her in judgment and speculate about what has brought her back. Through their dialogue, the characters of Pheoby, Janie's best friend, and Tea Cake, the young man she left with, are introduced. Eventually, Pheoby visits Janie, who tells her that Tea Cake is "gone." The rest of the novel will consist of the story Janie tells Pheoby about what has happened to her.

Chapters 2 through 4

Janie summarizes her childhood, when she lived with her maternal grandmother, Nanny, who also cared for several white children. At one point, a photographer takes a picture of all of the children. While examining the photograph, Janie realizes that she is black; until then she had thought she was like all of the white children. One spring afternoon years later, Janie is daydreaming under a pear tree when Johnny Taylor appears and kisses her. Nanny observes this and decides that Janie ought to get married soon. She has decided on Brother Logan Killicks as Janie's future husband; he is apparently a responsible man, but Janie does not find him attractive and cannot imagine loving him. But Janie and Logan are married, and shortly thereafter Nanny dies.

Sometime later, Logan decides that Janie should perform more manual labor and leaves to buy a mule so that Janie can help him with the plowing. While he is gone, another man appears, a stranger to the area who identifies himself as Joe Starks. He is on his way to a town populated entirely by black people, where he has large ambitions for himself. Although Joe invites Janie to accompany him, she hesitates because she imagines how her grandmother would disapprove. When Janie threatens to leave Logan, he scorns her background. The next morning she meets Joe Starks, and they travel to Green Cove Springs where they are married.

Chapters 5 through 9

Joe and Janie arrive in Eatonville, where Joe immediately asks to speak to the mayor and is informed that the town does not have one. Impressing the others, Joe pays cash for two hundred acres of land and begins advertising for additional people to move to Eatonville. After opening a store, Joe is soon appointed Mayor, but discord comes when he prevents Janie from making a speech some of the men have requested. Joe and Janie begin to grow apart emotionally.

Many of the men enjoy sitting on the store's porch and telling exaggerated stories. Although Janie longs to join in, Joe believes such activities and company are too low-class for her. Another man, Matt Bonner, owns a mule that he is working nearly to death. When Janie expresses dismay over the abuse of this mule, Joe forces Matt to sell the mule for five dollars. After the mule dies, Joe again forbids Janie to participate in the mock funeral with the rest of the town.

The tension between Joe and Janie continues to intensify, until one day Joe slaps her because his supper has been poorly cooked. Janie's image of Joe is destroyed at this moment, and although she appears to continue to be obedient, she begins separating her inner and outer lives. Then one day when Janie fails to cut a plug of tobacco properly, Joe humiliates her in front of the others, commenting on aspects of her body. This time Janie replies, ridiculing Joe for his own lack of masculinity in front of the other men. Joe is so angry that he can respond only by hitting her.

Joe subsequently becomes ill and believes Janie has cast a spell on him. Janie sends for a doctor, who reveals that Joe's condition is fatal. Although Janie attempts to have a final conversation with him, Joe refuses to listen and dies fighting death. His funeral is large and formal.

Chapters 10 through 13

After several months, another stranger appears. His name is Vergible Woods, but his nickname is Tea Cake. He teaches Janie to play checkers, and for the first time she feels that someone is truly treating her as an individual. They do many unconventional activities together, such as fishing at midnight, and Janie begins to fall in love with him. She hesitates to trust him, though, because she is several years older than he is and because, as Joe's heir, she is a comparatively wealthy woman. Janie decides to sell the store so that she can begin a new life with Tea Cake. He sends for her from Jacksonville, and she leaves on an early morning train. They get married immediately.

Janie has hidden two hundred dollars in a purse inside her clothes, but when she wakes up the next morning, Tea Cake is gone and so is the money. After another day, he returns with only twelve dollars; he had thrown a party but promises to win the money back gambling. When he does, Janie decides to trust him and tells him about additional money she has saved. Tea Cake suggests that they go down to the Everglades to work.

Chapters 14 through 17

Tea Cake teaches Janie to shoot, and she becomes quite skilled. Working in the Everglades is fun for both of them; they throw parties, and Janie participates in the playful atmosphere. Janie becomes jealous of another woman who is flirting with Tea Cake, but he assures Janie that she has nothing to worry about. They decide to stay in the Everglades during the off season. Another woman, Mrs. Turner, cultivates a friendship with Janie, hoping that she will leave Tea Cake and marry Mrs. Turner's brother. Mrs. Turner feels disdainful of other black people, especially if their complexion is particularly dark. At this point, Tea Cake becomes jealous and beats Janie in order to demonstrate to the Turners that he is boss in his household.

Chapters 18 through 20

A hurricane threatens the Everglades, and many of the residents leave, but Janie and Tea Cake decide to ride the storm out. When the storm becomes fierce, they sit in their cabin, appearing "to be staring at the dark, but their eyes were watching God." When the hurricane threatens to flood their house, they leave, attempting to walk toward Palm Beach. When Janie is nearly attacked by a dog, Tea Cake rescues her, but he is bitten. The wound appears superficial and begins to heal.

> The dog stood up and growled like a lion, stiff-standing hackles, stiff muscles, teeth uncovered as he lashed up his fury for the charge. Tea Cake split the water like an otter, opening his knife as he dived. The dog raced down the back-bone of the cow to the attack and Janie screamed and slipped far back on the tail of the cow, just out of reach of the dog's angry jaws. He wanted to plunge in after her but dreaded the water, somehow. Tea Cake rose out of the water at the cow's rump and seized the dog by the neck. But he was a powerful dog and Tea Cake was overtired. So he didn't kill the dog with one stroke as he had intended. But the dog couldn't free himself either. They fought and somehow he managed to bite Tea Cake high up on his cheek-bone once. Then Tea Cake finished him and sent him to the bottom to stay there. The cow relieved of a great weight was landing on the fill with Janie before Tea Cake stroked in and crawled weakly upon the fill again.

After the hurricane, black men are forced to act as grave diggers, but they must be careful to separate the white corpses from the black ones, because the white bodies will be placed in coffins while the black ones will be buried in a mass grave. After one day, Tea Cake decides they should return to the Everglades.

Three weeks later, Tea Cake falls ill. He has a headache and is unable to eat or drink. The doctor reveals that he has rabies and will likely die. He is concerned that Tea Cake will attack Janie and perhaps bite her also. Janie realizes that Tea Cake is becoming insane as his illness progresses. He eventually tries to shoot Janie, who shoots and kills him.

Janie must be tried for murder, but she is acquitted; the jury finds that she acted in self-defense. Janie provides an elaborate funeral for Tea Cake in Palm Beach. The novel concludes with a return to the conversation between Janie and Pheoby after Janie has returned to the house she lived in with Joe.

Characters

Janie Crawford

The heroine of the novel, Janie, is the first black woman character in African-American fiction to embark on a journey of self-discovery and achieve independence and self-understanding. But she does not do so until she is nearly forty years old. Many obstacles stand in her way, the first of which is her grandmother, who encourages her to marry Logan Killicks for material security. But Janie discovers that "marriage did not make love," and she decides to leave him. When Joe Starks enters her life, she believes she has found her ticket to the "horizon," so she marries him. But when they arrive in Eatonville, she discovers that she is going to be nothing but an ornament of his power and success. Stifled by Jody and cut off from the rest of the community by her status as the mayor's wife, she learns to hide her real self and wear a mask for Jody and the town that conforms to their expectations for her. But in the process she loses sight of the real self she has buried. The narrator tells us, "She had an inside and an outside now and suddenly she knew not how to mix them." After twenty years of marriage, an enmity has grown between Janie and her husband that results in her finally speaking up for herself. She tells him, in essence, that he is no longer a real man, and her outburst robs him of the will to live. As he lays on his deathbed, she sums up for him what their marriage has been like for her: "Mah own mind had tuh be squeezed and crowded out tuh make room for yours in me."

Having lost herself once, she vows not to do so again, and so she enjoys her freedom after his death. But when Tea Cake walks into her life, she finds a man who complements her search for self-

Media Adaptations

- *Their Eyes Were Watching God* has been recorded on cassette in an abridged version by Caedmon. This recording, which came out in 1991, was performed by Ruby Dee.

- In 1994, Recorded Books produced an unabridged recording of the novel on sound cassette, read by Michele-Denise Woods.

- The movie rights to the novel are owned by Quincy Jones and Oprah Winfrey, although as of 1997 no film had yet been made.

---

awareness rather than squelches it. Under the influence of his all-encompassing love, "her soul crawled out from its hiding place." With Tea Cake, she finds a spiritual sense of love that had been absent in her first two marriages. "Ah wuz fumblin' round and God opened the door," she tells him. But many critics have questioned Hurston's decision to make Janie discover her true self in the context of a relationship with a man. What has seemed like a feminist search for identity is undermined by Janie's apparent dependence on Tea Cake, some say. But Janie does eventually gain true independence when she is forced to kill Tea Cake, who has gone mad from being bitten by a rabid dog and has come after her with a gun. This final act, although it devastates Janie, also allows her to return home to Eatonville a fully self-sufficient woman who is finally at peace with herself. "Ah done been tuh de horizon and back and now Ah kin set heah in mah house and live by comparisons," she tells her friend Pheoby. Her journey of self-discovery is complete.

Hezekiah

After Jody's death, Hezekiah replaces him as the store's manager. Janie notices that Hezekiah also begins to take on many of Jody's characteristics.

Jody

See Joe Starks

Janie Killicks

See Janie Crawford

Logan Killicks

Janie's first husband. Her grandmother has encouraged her to marry him because he can give her a house and sixty acres of farmland, hence security. His ugly appearance and body odor prevent Janie from falling in love with him. When he tells her he is going to buy a mule for her to plow with, Janie decides that life with Logan is not what she bargained for. She leaves him when the more dashing Joe Starks comes along.

Motor Boat

A gambling friend of Tea Cake down on the muck. When the hurricane hits, Motor Boat flees with Janie and Tea Cake.

Nanny

Janie's grandmother, who raises her in the absence of her mother. A former slave who was raped by her master, Nanny teaches Janie that the "nigger woman is de mule uh de world." In her hopes that Janie will have a better life, she encourages her to marry Logan Killicks, a man who will offer her "protection." But not long after Janie marries him, Nanny dies. Later in life, after Jody has died, Janie reassesses the advice Nanny had given her. "Nanny had taken the biggest thing God ever made, the horizon … and pinched it in to such a little bit of a thing that she could tie it about her granddaughter's neck tight enough to choke her." Janie decides that she hates Nanny for teaching her to bury her own desires for the sake of security.

Nunkie

Young woman on the muck who attempts to lead Tea Cake away from Janie.

Sop-de-Bottom

A friend of Tea Cake on the muck. He applauds Tea Cake's beating of Janie and attempts to speak up at Janie's trial after she has killed Tea Cake. He wants to accuse Janie of murder but is silenced by a white lawyer.

Janie Starks

See Janie Crawford

Joe Starks

Jody rescues Janie from her first marriage, whisking her off to Eatonville, Florida, an all-black town where he intends to "be a big voice," something he has been denied in other towns where whites are in control. Although Janie is reluctant to go, Jody "spoke for far horizon," offering Janie a chance for adventure. But shortly after they arrive in Eatonville, Janie finds out that her life with Jody will be anything but exciting. When he becomes mayor and the most respectable citizen in town, she becomes a "pretty doll-baby," as he calls her, a token of his stature in the town. Jody defines himself by his position and possessions, the most valuable of which is Janie. So Jody stifles Janie's development as he silences her and keeps her from participating in the town's talk on the porch of their store. Jody's world becomes a kind of prison for Janie, who is isolated on a pedestal of bourgeois ideals. As Jody grows older and takes his fears of aging out on Janie, she realizes that her "image" of him has "tumbled down and shattered." When he ridicules her aging body in front of others at the store, something breaks in Janie, and she tells him, "When you pull down yo' britches, you look lak de change uh life." By belittling his manhood in front of the town, Janie figuratively kills him, as he begins a slow deterioration and dies of kidney failure. Janie attempts to come to terms with Jody on his death bed, and she tells him, "All dis bowin' down, all dis obedience under yo' voice—dat ain't whut Ah rushed off down de road tuh find out about you." But she comes to the conclusion that the only kind of change he was able to create in her life was an outward change in material conditions. Nothing has changed inside of him, and she has not been able to grow at all. When he dies, the only legacy he leaves Janie is his money. At the end of the book, it is the memories of Tea Cake that inhabit the house, not those of Jody.

Johnny Taylor

The boy who kisses Janie over the fence. This event signals Janie's sexual awakening and instigates Nanny's concerns that Janie will allow an unworthy man to lure her away.

Mr. Turner

Restaurant owner on the muck who has no control over his wife.

Mrs. Turner

A light-skinned mulatto woman who befriends Janie on the muck. Her prejudices against those who are blacker than herself reveal the racism within the black community. Her restaurant, which she owns with her husband, is destroyed by Tea

Upon her death in 1960, Zora Neale Hurston was buried in an unmarked grave in a segregated cemetery until novelist Alice Walker erected this headstone in 1973.

Cake and his friends, who resent her racist attitudes towards them.

Mrs. Annie Tyler

A woman from Eatonville who ran off with a younger man who was after her money. Her shameful return to the town after he has left her is a warning to Janie, who fears that Tea Cake will do the same to her.

Pheoby Watson

Janie's "bosom friend" who is her link to the Eatonville community. Pheoby's role in the book is an important one, as she is the audience for Janie's life story, which is the novel. After hearing the whole story, Pheoby tells her, "Ah done growed ten feet higher from jus' listenin' tuh you." Many critics see this statement as the feminist declaration that Janie's story will inspire other women to demand self-fulfillment.

Janie Woods

See Janie Crawford

Tea Cake Woods

See Vergible Woods

Vergible Woods

When Tea Cake, a young man of twenty-five, enters Janie's life, he changes it forever. He does not possess the outward manifestations of power, namely wealth and position, that Jody did. Instead, he possesses an inner power that comes with self-knowledge and being comfortable with himself. When Janie marries Tea Cake, they move to Jacksonville, and she is initiated into his world. At first he is afraid she will not want to be a part of his community. "You ain't usetuh folks lak dat," he tells her. But she assures him that she "aims tuh partake wid everything." When they move to the muck, then, to live amongst the migrant agricultural workers picking beans, Janie and Tea Cake's house becomes the center of the community, hosting dances and card games. Most importantly, Tea Cake allows Janie to feel like she belongs to this community in a way that Jody never let her belong to the Eatonville community. In fact, Tea Cake inspires two important developments in Janie's growth by encouraging her to accept herself and to feel at home in the black community. The space he creates for her that makes these two things possible is a loving relationship that satisfies Janie's spiritual needs, rather than focusing on the material wants that had defined her two previous marriages.

Their relationship is more equal as Tea Cake teaches her how to play checkers, hunt, and fish, activities from which Jody had excluded her because of her gender. Tea Cake almost becomes an idealized male figure in the book as he provides all of the support and love that has been lacking in Janie's life. However, he also falls back on attitudes of male dominance in his relationship with Janie. Many critics have seen his beating of Janie as an indication that Hurston believed all men possessed the need to overpower women and be the "boss." But Tea Cake is a part of Janie's life for only two years. As they try to escape the devastation of a hurricane in the Everglades, Tea Cake rescues Janie from a rabid dog, only to be bitten himself. By the time they discover Tea Cake's illness, it is too late. When he tries to kill Janie in his madness, she is forced to shoot him to protect herself.

Themes

Zora Neale Hurston's *Their Eyes Were Watching God* charts the development of an African-American woman living in the 1920s and 1930s as she searches for her true identity.

Search for Self

Although the novel follows Janie through three relationships with men, most critics see its main theme to be Janie's search for herself. She must fight off the influences of her grandmother, who encourages her to sacrifice self-fulfillment for security, and her first two husbands, who stifle her development. Her second husband, Jody, has an especially negative impact on Janie's growth as his bourgeois aspirations turn her into a symbol of his stature in the town. She is not allowed to be herself, but must conform to his notions of propriety, which means she cannot enjoy the talk of the townsfolk on the porch, let alone participate in it. After he is elected mayor, she is asked to give "a few words uh encouragement," but Jody interrupts the applause by telling the town, "mah wife don't know nothin' 'bout no speech-makin'. Ah never married her for her nothin' lak dat. She's uh woman and her place is in de home." After this, Janie feels "cold," realizing that by cutting her off, Jody has prevented her from deciding for herself whether or not she even wanted to give a speech. Throughout the rest of her marriage, Janie must bury her own desires to the point where she loses sight of them altogether. But after Jody's death she feels a freedom she has never known.

When the young Tea Cake enters her life, she decides that she has done what Jody and the town have wanted her to do long enough, so she rejects their ideas for her future and marries a younger man. Her relationship with Tea Cake allows her to find herself in a way that had not been possible before. But some critics see Tea Cake as another obstacle to Janie's development. In some ways, their relationship is conventional in the sense that Janie willingly defers to his judgment and follows him on his adventures. "Once upon uh time, Ah never 'spected nothin', Tea Cake, but being' dead from the standin' still and tryin' tuh laugh," she tells him. "But you come 'long and made somethin' out me." Statements like this have caused critics to question how successful Janie is at discovering her true self. Some see the ending as a reaffirmation that a woman must find herself on her own. By killing Tea Cake in self-defense, although she deeply regrets having to do so, Janie has come full circle in her development. She now knows who she is and has found "peace." In the closing lines the narrator tells us, "She pulled in her horizon like a great fish-net," indicating that she no longer has to seek for meaning outside of herself in the world; she has found it within herself.

Language and Meaning

Integral to Janie's search for self is her quest to become a speaking subject. Language is depicted in the novel as the means by which one becomes a full-fledged member of the community and, hence, a full human being. In Eatonville, the men engage in "eternal arguments, … a contest in hyperbole and carried on for no other reason." These contests in language are the central activities in the town, but only the men are allowed to participate. Janie especially regrets being excluded, but "gradually, she pressed her teeth together and learned to hush." But the dam of repressed language erupts when Jody ridicules her aging body in front of the men in the store. Her speech then becomes a weapon as she tells him (and everyone else), "When you pull down yo' britches, you look lak de change uh life." By comparing him to a woman going through menopause, she attacks his manhood in an irretrievable way. Janie has gained her voice, and in the process has metaphorically killed her husband, whose strength has resided in her silence and submission. Later, when Janie and Tea Cake are on the muck, Janie becomes a full member of the community, as signified by her ability as a speaking subject. "The men held big arguments here like they used to on the store porch. Only here, she could listen and laugh and even talk some herself if she wanted to. She got so she could tell big stories herself from listening to the rest." At the end of the book, Janie's return to tell her story to the town, through Pheoby, signals to some critics her reintegration in the community. Others, though, believe she is still excluded because she will not speak to them directly.

Race and Racism

Although there is very little discussion of relations between whites and blacks in the novel, racism and class differences are shown to have infected the African-American community. The supposed biological and cultural superiority of whiteness hovers over the lives of all the black characters in the book, as Janie witnesses the moral bankruptcy of those who value whiteness over their own black selves. Joe Starks is on his way to Eatonville when Janie meets him, because he is tired of being subservient to whites. He intends in an all-black town to have power over others, a kind of power that is modeled on that of white men. He possesses a "bow-down command in his face," and his large

Topics for Further Study

- Research the conditions under which southern blacks lived during the Great Depression and compare to the plight of migrant workers on the muck in *Their Eyes Were Watching God*.

- Research the feminist movement from the early twentieth century to today. Based on your understanding of what a feminist was then and is now, argue whether Janie can or should be considered a feminist by contemporary scholars.

- Study the relationships between wealthy white patrons and the writers of the Harlem Renaissance and argue whether *Their Eyes Were Watching God* is meant to appeal to white readers of the time or is directed only at black readers.

- Study the historic debates between Booker T. Washington and W. E. B. DuBois and, based on your reading of *Their Eyes Were Watching God*, create a response based on how you think Zora Neale Hurston would have responded to the fundamental issues of racial progress and race relations.

white house impresses the town because it makes the rest of the houses in town resemble "servants' quarters surrounding the 'big house,'" reflecting the housing arrangements of plantations during slavery. He also buys a desk like those owned by prominent white men in the neighboring town of Maitland and adopts behaviors which mimic the habits of middle-class whites. For Jody, success is measured by standards adopted from the white community, and as a result, he looks down on the townsfolk as "common" and even as his inferiors. One of the men comments, "You kin feel a switch in his hand when he's talking to yuh." Janie's rejection of Jody's feelings of superiority and his emphasis on attaining bourgeois respectability have led many critics to see the novel as a critique of middle-class blacks who had gained some prestige in the 1920s but had also lost their connection with the roots of the black community, the folk.

This critique becomes more explicit in Janie and Tea Cake's dismissal of Mrs. Turner's feelings of superiority over dark-skinned blacks. As a fair-skinned and financially well-off mulatto, Mrs. Turner desires to separate herself and Janie, who is also mulatto, from the "black folks." She tells Janie, "We oughta lighten up de race," and "Us oughta class off." But Janie responds, "Us can't *do* it. We'se uh mingled people and all of us got black kinfolks as well as yaller kinfolks." For Janie, there are no divisions in the black community. She has moved easily from her high-class position in Eatonville to her life amongst the folk with Tea Cake, and together they have welcomed the black workers from the Bahamas, who had previously been ostracized from the African-Americans on the muck. In addition, Mrs. Turner's racist ideas are ridiculed by the narrator, who writes, "Behind her crude words was a belief that somehow she and others through worship could attain her paradise—a heaven of straight-haired, thin-lipped, high-nose boned white seraphs. The physical impossibilities in no way injured faith." Racism and division within the African-American community are finally revealed as not only ridiculous but as tragic, as a woman like Mrs. Turner is consumed by self-hatred, the inherent by-product of her disdain of blackness. Only through a loving acceptance of all things black can one become a full, healthy human being, as Janie learns.

Style

Narration

Although the framing device of Janie telling Pheoby her story sets up the novel as Janie's story, it is not told in the first person. Instead, a narrative voice tells most of the story, and there has been much discussion of whose voice this is. Claire Crabtree, writing in *Southern Literary Journal,* argues that it is "always close to but not identical with Janie's consciousness," indicating that the omniscient narrator, who knows more about other characters' thoughts than Janie could know herself, is also closely aligned with the heroine. The narrator also uses free indirect speech at many points to convey Janie's thoughts, another indication that the narrator and Janie's consciousness are closely aligned. But Henry Louis Gates, Jr. in his *The Signifying Monkey,* argues that the narrative voice "echoes and aspires to the status of the impersonality, anonymity, and authority of the black vernacular tradition, a nameless, selfless tradition, at once col-

lective and compelling." The narrator, then, who speaks in standard English, while the characters speak in black dialect, becomes, according to Gates, more and more representative of the black community as it progressively adopts the patterns of black vernacular speech. The narrative voice takes on the aspect of oral speech, telling not only Janie's story, but many other stories as well. For example, Nanny's voice takes over as she tells the story of Janie's heritage, and the voices on the porch also take over for long stretches as their "arguments" tell the story of life in Eatonville. In essence, there are many storytellers within the larger story of Janie's life, and many voices inform the novel.

Folklore

One of the most unique features of *Their Eyes Were Watching God* is its integration of folklore with fiction. Hurston borrows literary devices from the black rural oral tradition, which she studied as an anthropologist, to further cement her privileging of that tradition over the Western literary tradition. For example, she borrows the technique of repetition in threes found commonly in folklore in her depiction of Janie's three marriages. Also, in the words of Claire Crabtree, "Janie follows a pattern familiar to folklorists of a young person's journey from home to face adventure and various dangers, followed by a triumphant homecoming." In addition, Janie returns "richer and wiser" than she left, and she is ready to share her story with Pheoby, intending that the story be repeated, as a kind of folktale to be passed on.

Harlem Renaissance

The Harlem Renaissance, which experienced its heyday in Harlem in the 1920s but also flourished well into the 1930s, was an outpouring of creative innovation among blacks that celebrated the achievements of black intellectuals and artists. The initial goal of the writers of the Harlem Renaissance was to overcome racism and convince the white public that African-Americans were more intelligent than the stereotypes of docile, ignorant blacks that pervaded the popular arena. In order to do so, then, most of the early writers associated with the movement imitated the themes and styles of mainstream, white literature. But later writers felt that African-American literature should depict the unique and debilitating circumstances in which blacks lived, confronting their white audiences with scenes of brutal racism. Zora Neale Hurston, considered the most important female member of the Harlem Renaissance, felt that the writings of

Harlem, 1927, the center of the African-American artistic and intellectual movement in the 1920s and '30s where Zora Neale Hurston wrote her novel, Their Eyes Were Watching God.

African-Americans should celebrate the speech and traditions of black people. The use of dialect in *Their Eyes Were Watching God* caused much controversy among other black writers of the day when it was first published because many felt that such language in the mouths of black characters perpetuated negative stereotypes about blacks as ignorant, but critics today agree that the novel's celebration of black language was the most important contribution Hurston made to African-American literature.

Historical Context

The Great Depression

For southern farmers, both black and white, who did not enjoy the prosperity of northern industrial centers, the Great Depression had begun in the 1920s, well before the stock market crash of 1929. Factors such as soil erosion, the attack of the boll weevil on cotton crops, and the increasing competition from foreign markets led to widespread poverty amongst southern farmers. The majority of African Americans were still farming in the South and they were much harder hit than the

white population, even after the advent of President Roosevelt's New Deal. The numbers of blacks on relief were three to four times higher than the number of whites, but relief organizations discriminated by race; some would not help blacks altogether, while others gave lower amounts of aid to blacks than they did to whites. Such practices led one NAACP leader to call the program "the same raw deal." Many critics have criticized *Their Eyes Were Watching God* for ignoring the plight of African-American farmers in the South during the 1920s and 30s, although Hurston does briefly describe the downtrodden migrant workers who come to pick beans on the muck. "Skillets, beds, patched up spare inner tubes all hanging and dangling from the ancient cars on the outside and hopeful humanity, herded and hovered on the inside, chugging on to the muck. People ugly from ignorance and broken from being poor."

The Great Migration and the Harlem Renaissance

A large number of African Americans fought in the First World War under the banner of freedom, only to return home to find how far they were from such a goal. By 1920, over one million blacks had fled the South, where they had little chance of

Compare & Contrast

- **1920s and '30s:** The numbers of unemployed African Americans during the Great Depression was as much as 25% in northern cities, and well over 50% in many southern cities, figures that were three to four times higher than the number of unemployed whites.

  Today: Unemployment among African-Americans averages between 10 and 11%, higher than the 4.5 to 5% among whites.

- **1920s and '30s:** Blues and jazz flourished from New Orleans to Harlem. Although these indigenous American music forms were the dominant mode of expression for the oppressed black culture, they also attracted a large audience of whites.

  Today: Rap and hip-hop are the major musical forms that express the unique experiences of black culture in America's ghettos, but they also have many non-black fans, not only in America, but all over the world.

- **1920s and '30s:** In the South, Jim Crow laws dictated that blacks and whites use separate drinking fountains, eat in separate restaurants, and learn in separate schools. In the North, although such laws did not exist, blacks were more subtly excluded from better jobs, schools, and neighborhoods, creating black ghettos in the major cities.

  Today: Affirmative action plans to end discrimination in hiring have been in place for fifteen years. Some people are now calling for their abolishment, claiming the goal has been achieved, while others believe there is still a long way to go.

- **1920s and '30s:** Although many women writers participated in the Harlem Renaissance, they experienced the prejudice of their male counterparts, who excluded all but a chosen few of them from the anthologies and prestigious periodicals.

  Today: African-American women writers are experiencing their own "Renaissance," as represented by Toni Morrison's receiving the Nobel Prize for Literature in 1993. Most contemporary critics agree that some of the most important literature being produced today is by African-American women, many of whom claim a direct heritage from Zora Neale Hurston.

rising out of poverty, and migrated to the industrial centers of the North where they obtained jobs in factories and packing houses, eventually making up as much as twenty percent of the industrial work force there. The migration of blacks to northern cities caused whites to fear that their jobs would be threatened, and increased racial tensions erupted in race riots in 1917. Nonetheless, many blacks began to vocally demand an end to discrimination. Out of this climate came calls for a "New Negro," who would be filled with racial pride and demand justice for his people. While earlier black leaders, represented by Booker T. Washington, had accepted segregation and preached co-operation and patience, new black leaders like W. E. B. DuBois insisted that concessions and appeasements were not the correct approach, and that complete equality could only be achieved by demanding it without compromise. DuBois also believed that the "Talented Tenth," his name for the small percentage of educated blacks, must lead the way for the masses of blacks who still lived in poverty and lacked educational opportunities. DuBois's ideas were reflected in the newly formed black middle class, which, although small, sought to exert an influence on behalf of all blacks. The new efforts of this black elite were centered in Harlem, where a large percentage of migrating blacks ended up, turning the area into a rich, thriving center of black culture. The new energy generated there by jazz musicians, writers, artists, actors, and intellectuals became known as the Harlem Renaissance. This artistic and intellectual movement confronted the racial prejudices of white America by demanding equal recognition for their talent and by depicting the injustices experienced by African-Americans. But ironically, although the artists of the Harlem Renaissance intended their works to promote better conditions for blacks less fortunate than themselves, few blacks around the country were even aware of the movement. In fact, it was more often whites who comprised the audiences and readerships of the products of the Harlem Renaissance. A cult of the primitive, which celebrated all things exotic and sensual, had become all the rage in New York and many wealthy whites flocked to Harlem to witness and participate in the revelry. But wealthy whites were essential to the livelihood of many black artists and writers who relied on their patronage, a fact regretted by many who felt that the artistic products of African Americans were muted to appeal to the tastes of the whites they depended on. Although the stock market crash of 1929 brought much of the activity in Harlem to an end, the creative energies of those involved had not abated, and many, like Zora Neale Hurston, produced their best work through the 1930s.

Race Colonies

After the Civil War, former slaves formed a number of all-black towns all over the South, in an effort to escape the segregation and discrimination they experienced amongst whites. By 1914, approximately thirty such towns were in existence. Eatonville, Florida, the town where Zora Neale Hurston grew up and the setting for much of *Their Eyes Were Watching God,* was the first such town to be incorporated and to win the right of self-governance. In Eatonville, the Jim Crow laws, that segregated public schools, housing, restaurants, theaters, and drinking fountains all over the South, did not exist.

Critical Overview

When *Their Eyes Were Watching God* first appeared, it was warmly received by white critics. Lucille Tompkins of the *New York Times Book Review* called it "a well nigh perfect story—a little sententious at the start, but the rest is simple and beautiful and shining with humor." But many of Hurston's fellow writers of the Harlem Renaissance criticized the novel for not addressing "serious" issues, namely strained race relations. Alain Locke, reviewing for *Opportunity,* recognized the author's "gift for poetic phrase, for rare dialect, and folk humor," but he asks, "when will the Negro novelist of maturity ... come to grips with motive fiction and social document fiction?" Richard Wright, in his review in *New Masses,* had even more scathing objections to the novel. According to Wright, "Miss Hurston *voluntarily* continues in her novel the tradition which was *forced* upon the Negro in the theater, that is, the minstrel technique that makes the 'white folks' laugh." Wright felt that instead of taking on "serious" subjects, she writes to entertain "a white audience whose chauvinistic tastes she knows how to satisfy." Many objected to the use of dialect in the novel, a difficult subject for Harlem Renaissance writers who felt that black speech had been exploited and ridiculed by mainstream theater and literature. As a result, many were reluctant to try to realistically depict the speech patterns of the black folk, and they saw in Hurston's use of dialect a degrading picture of rural blacks.

As a result of such criticisms, *Their Eyes Were Watching God* soon disappeared from print. But in the late 1960s, when interest in African-American and women's studies began to take hold, a number of African-American women across the country rediscovered the book and made it an underground sensation. Photocopies of the novel circulated at conferences, and Alice Walker's essay "Looking for Zora," published in *Ms.* magazine in 1975, galvanized efforts to get the novel back into print. Since 1978, it has been widely available, and the scholarly interest in it has been intense. In fact, previous judgements against the novel have been overturned by a number of respectable critics who have helped establish *Their Eyes Were Watching God* as a classic of African-American literature and helped procure it a prominent position in the American literary canon.

Most significantly, recent critics have recognized a celebration of black culture in the novel that belies any notion that Hurston is pandering to a white audience. As Cheryl Wall explains, in her article "Zora Neale Hurston: Changing Her Own Words," She asserted that black people, while living in a racist society that denied their humanity, had created an "alternative culture that validated their worth as human beings." And, she argues, by invoking this culture, Hurston shows us that black men and women "attained personal identity not by transcending the culture but by embracing it." One way that Hurston embraced the culture of rural, southern blacks, was to depict its folklore and language in a way that relished its creativity. Contemporary critics praise her for this above all else, for in her search for a suitable language for African-

American literature, she initiated an effort to free black language from domination by the white culture. Henry Louis Gates, Jr., explains the significance of this act: "For Hurston, the search for a telling form of language, indeed the search for a black literary language itself, defines the search for the self." In this way, critics have been able to show that Hurston, far from ignoring the serious social issues of her day, was engaged in a serious project of resuscitating a language and culture that was in danger of being corrupted by racist oppression. In fact, Gay Wilentz argues, in *Faith of a (Woman) Writer,* that the novel is one of "resistance" because it portrays "the pressure of the dominant culture on the thoughts and actions of the all-black community of Eatonville as well as blacks as a whole." In other words, although she largely ignored the overt racism that critics of the Harlem Renaissance wanted her to address, she explored the more subtle and perhaps more dangerous kind of racism that infects the black culture and makes it despise itself. The racial pride that Hurston preached, then, was as radical a statement as any of the Harlem Renaissance, contemporary critics argue.

Although scholars have been eager to embrace the novel's celebration of black culture, much more problematic has been understanding and accepting its perspective on gender. With the book's rediscovery in the 1960s, feminists lauded it as an expression of female self-development and empowerment. More recently, though, many scholars have begun to question such a reading. Jennifer Jordan argues, for example, in her article in *Tulsa Studies in Women's Literature,* that "Janie's struggle for identity and self-direction remains stymied. She never defines herself outside the scope of her marital or romantic involvements." Furthermore, as Mary Helen Washington insists in her article "'I Love the Way Janie Crawford Left Her Husbands': Emergent Female Hero," Janie never becomes a speaking subject, because "Hurston's strategy of having much of Janie's tale told by an omniscient third person rather than by a first person narrator undercuts the development of Janie's 'voice.'" But most troubling to critics has been the fact that Janie seems to discover herself in the context of a relationship with a man, Tea Cake, rather than on her own, a defect that many see as remedied by Janie's killing of Tea Cake. "[A]s a feminist," Claire Crabtree argues, Hurston "did not want Janie to find fulfillment in a man, but rather in her new-found self." But for others, the book does not end there, rather with her return to Eatonville, which seems to signal an end to her self-exploration, according to Washington, who claims that "left without a man, she (Janie) exists in a position of stasis." But Wall refuses to read the ending as "tragic." "For with Tea Cake as her guide, Jan[i]e has explored the soul of her culture and learned how to value herself."

Criticism

Lynn Domina

Domina, an author and instructor at Hofstra University, describes Hurston's novel in terms of Janie Stark's "voice" and how her ability to express herself evolves through the course of the story.

Their Eyes Were Watching God is generally considered Zora Neale Hurston's most important piece of fiction. Hurston, a major figure of the Harlem Renaissance, also published anthropological texts, including *Tell My Horse,* and an autobiography, *Dust Tracks on a Road. Their Eyes Were Watching God* was first published in 1937, and was quite popular, although some critics argued that she should have written a more aggressive protest similar to Richard Wright's *Native Son.* Although *Their Eyes Were Watching God* went out of print for several years, it came back into print during the late 1970s and has since remained a central text in many high school and college courses. In this novel, Hurston explores social and personal relations within black families and communities, while also examining issues of gender and class. One theme through which these issues of gender, race, and class are examined is voice. At several points in the text, Janie Starks, the protagonist, is prohibited from speaking, while at other points she chooses not to speak. Silence, then, is sometimes used as a tool of oppression and at other times as a tool of power.

During the course of the novel, Janie is married three times. The men differ from each other in significant ways, and each marriage helps Janie define her own desires and goals in life. Her first husband, Brother Logan Killicks, is chosen for her by her grandmother, Nanny, who recognizes that Janie is beginning to feel adult sexual desires, although Janie herself might not articulate her new longings this way. Because she has observed "shiftless Johnny Taylor" kissing Janie, Nanny believes Janie will soon act more dramatically on these desires and therefore urges her to marry a responsible and conventional man. Although Janie responds that

Logan Killicks "look like some ole skullhead in de grave yard," Nanny arranges the marriage because she worries about Janie's future. Realizing she is probably close to death, Nanny reminds Janie that she "ain't got nobody but me. And mah head is ole and tilted towards de grave. Neither can you stand alone by yo'self. De thought uh you bein' kicked around from pillar tuh post is uh hurtin' thing."

Janie's first marriage occurs, then, despite her resistance. Because of her youth and the lack of options available to her as a young and comparatively poor woman, Janie cannot act on her own desires; she marries Logan Killicks because she seems to have no other choice. Although she hopes love will follow marriage, Janie is soon disappointed, for Logan grows more rather than less distasteful to her. He refuses to bathe regularly and soon suggests that Janie should help him with the plowing. He leaves to buy another mule, one that would be "all gentled up so even uh woman kin handle 'im." This scene is reminiscent of a statement Nanny had made to Janie earlier, that "woman is de mule uh de world." Janie, however, decides that she will not be treated as a mule even if she has to reject the values her grandmother has taught her.

Janie meets Joe Starks, who invites her to accompany him to a town made "all outa colored folks." Because Logan begins to insult Janie's family history, she decides to leave him for Joe, who initially seems more considerate and companionable. Soon, however, Janie realizes that Joe perceives her simply as his trophy. He will be mayor of the new town, and she will be nothing more or less than the mayor's wife. Although the townspeople congregate on the porch of Joe's store, where Janie often works as a clerk, Joe forbids her to participate in their jokes or storytelling. Those conversations, Joe suggests, are not appropriate for a woman of her class. Because Janie is once again deprived of her voice, she can never be fully a member of this community and instead must live in emotional isolation.

During her marriage to Joe, the mule again appears as a symbol. A man in their town, Matt Bonner, owns a yellow mule which he seems to be working to death. When Joe overhears Janie quietly protesting, he forces Matt to sell the mule to him for $5.00, impressing his companions with his ability to satisfy his financial whims. Joe permits the mule to live the rest of his days in comparative ease, but when the mule dies, he forbids Janie to participate in the mock funeral the others hold. Similarly, although Joe doesn't want to work Janie like a mule in the manner of Logan Killicks, he has

What Do I Read Next?

- A classic feminist novel, *The Awakening* (1899) by Kate Chopin, follows a well-to-do white woman from Louisiana on a perilous path of self-discovery. The novel challenges the strict mores of a society that provides only one path of self-fulfillment for women, namely marriage and motherhood.

- *The Souls of Black Folk* (1903) by W. E. B. DuBois is a classic document of African-American cultural history. In this collection of essays, DuBois articulates, among other things, his influential theory of "double consciousness," which describes how African-Americans wrestle between two identities as black and American.

- *Mules and Men,* published in 1935, was Zora Neale Hurston's second book, and it was the first collection of black folklore published in America.

- David Levering Lewis' *When Harlem Was in Vogue* (1981) is a classic historical study of the Harlem Renaissance. Lewis surveys all the major writers, artists, and intellectuals associated with the movement.

- *The Bluest Eye* (1970) by Toni Morrison portrays a young black girl's obsession with blue eyes and blond hair. Having accepted society's definition of beauty as white, she has learned to despise her own black features, which leads to tragic consequences.

- Richard Wright's *Native Son* (1940) is a powerful depiction of how the oppressive environment of Chicago determines the fate of Bigger Thomas, a young black man who is doomed to act out the worst fears of racist whites.

metaphorically "bought" her as a demonstration of his own power.

Once again, Janie must choose either to accept what seems to be her fate or to actively oppose it. When Joe attempts to humiliate her publicly, "Janie took the middle of the floor to talk right into Jody's [Joe's] face, and that was something that hadn't been done before." She insults his masculinity, shaming him before the other men. After this, although Janie and Joe continue to live together, they live emotionally separate lives until Joe dies.

Janie's third husband's given name is Vergible Woods, although his nickname is Tea Cake. Most people cannot understand Janie's attraction to Tea Cake because he is neither conventional like Logan Killicks nor a middle-class businessman like Joe Starks. Rather, Tea Cake makes much of his money through gambling, and when he isn't gambling, he's often playing the guitar and planning a party. In addition, his complexion is very dark, at a time when some people (represented in this novel by the character of Mrs. Turner) believed that lighter skin was more attractive. Simultaneously, Tea Cake is several years younger than Janie, so some people suspect his motives. Yet Janie enjoys herself with Tea Cake more than she has with any other man. Tea Cake does not limit her to a particular role; he enjoys life and invites Janie to be simply herself. He invites her to play checkers on the porch as Joe never had, "and she found herself glowing inside. Somebody wanted her to play. Somebody thought it natural for her to play." Perhaps most significantly, "Look how she had been able to talk with him right off!"

The shift in Janie's character is demonstrated through several small changes. Although her luxurious hair is one of her most attractive characteristics, Joe had insisted she wear it bound up because he was jealous that other men might enjoy it. After Joe dies, she begins to wear her hair in a long braid. When she marries Tea Cake, she begins to dress in overalls rather than in middle-class dresses because she finds the pants more comfortable and convenient. She also begins to work in the fields after she and Tea Cake move to the Everglades, not because Tea Cake decides to treat her like a mule as Logan Killicks had or because Tea Cake fails to support her as a more "proper" husband would, but because she enjoys Tea Cake's company and the social interaction that occurs among the other workers. Janie hence achieves her greatest sense of fulfillment when she disregards conventional values and aspirations.

But the novel doesn't conclude with Janie and Tea Cake living happily ever after. During a hurricane, Tea Cake is bitten by a rabid dog while attempting to rescue Janie from drowning, and he himself contracts rabies. As his illness progresses,

he becomes increasingly paranoid and begins to distrust Janie's faithfulness. When he threatens to shoot her, Janie kills him in self-defense, though she had hoped he would die peacefully. Yet, even as Tea Cake dies, Janie desires to comfort him: "A minute before she was just a scared human being fighting for its life. Now she was her sacrificing self with Tea Cake's head in her lap. She had wanted him to live so much and he was dead. No hour is ever eternity, but it has its right to weep. Janie held his head tightly to her breast and wept and thanked him wordlessly for giving her the chance for loving service. She had to hug him tight for soon he would be gone, and she had to tell him for the last time." This hour is like eternity for Janie, however, because its effects will be permanent for her.

Janie is tried for Tea Cake's murder. Although many of her black acquaintances are angry that Tea Cake is dead, the all-white jury acquits her. Critics have debated the significance of the trial scene, for Janie's testimony is summarized rather than dramatized. While some critics have suggested that this scene indicates that Janie has once again lost (or been deprived of) her ability to speak, others suggest that she now can choose when and how to speak. During the trial, Janie is deprived of a community, since the black male and female witnesses oppose her, while the people who compose the jury and support her are all white men. Perhaps her voice is silent here not because she is unable to speak but because communication necessitates a receptive audience.

Readers must not forget, however, that the entire novel is in fact spoken in Janie's voice. The novel is framed by two chapters in which Janie is speaking to her best friend, Pheoby, and the action or plot of the novel is the story she tells Pheoby. So although the point of view frequently shifts in the novel, from one character's perspective to another's, *Their Eyes Were Watching God* is, finally, Janie's story.

Source: Lynn Domina, in an essay for *Novels for Students,* Gale, 1998.

Claire Crabtree

Crabtree maintains that the close connection between the themes of feminist/black self-determination and traditional or folk material needs to be further explored. She dwells, among other things, on the storytelling frame, on Hurston's use of language, and her incorporation of a folk consciousness in her narration.

Recent years have seen a renewal of interest in the work of Zora Neale Hurston marked by the publication of Robert Hemenway's 1977 biography and the anthology *I Love Myself When I Am Laughing.* Articles by Lloyd W. Brown, S. Jay Walker and Mary Helen Washington discuss Hurston's best novel, *Their Eyes Were Watching God,* in terms of its themes of feminism and black self-determination. An area that remains virtually untapped in Hurston criticism is the intimate connection between these themes and the folkloric themes and motifs which Hurston has embedded in her novel. Critics have largely neglected or misunderstood Hurston's conscious use of traditional or "folk" materials in the novel. Further, most readers find the ending of the novel dissonant and see it as weakening the work; while a recognition of the uses Hurston intended for traditional materials will not thoroughly justify her authorial decisions, it can help to explain the apparent weakness of the ending and to show that the novel presents a rhetoric of authenticity—an implicit assertion that it represents "real" black life—introduced initially by the storytelling frame and reinforced by various techniques throughout the novel.

It may be useful to delineate four aspects of the transformation of folk material into the body of the tale of Janie Crawford's journey through three marriages to a final position of self-realization. They are: Hurston's use of the storytelling "frame" of the story as well as of other conventions from oral tradition; her use of the language, metaphor and symbol of a specific rural community; her incorporation of certain kinds of gaming and other performances as incidents within the narrative; and her attempt to situate the narrative voice in a collective folk consciousness toward the end of the book. Folklore is, in fact, so thoroughly integrated into the fabric of the novel as to be inextricably bound to the themes of feminism and Black self-determination which Hurston is exploring. The value of the folk experience is itself as strong an assertion of the novel as the need of Blacks for self-determination and the right of women to be autonomous....

Hurston presents Janie's story within a storytelling frame, but equally significant, as a story that is designed to be repeated. In folkloristic terms, Janie's story is a memorate or true experience narrative placed within a fictional framework but nonetheless privileging itself and asserting its own authenticity. The form of a folktale is in part determined by its replicability; it must be developed through a series of events that can be recalled and reconstructed by various tellers....

Within the storytelling frame Janie's life is depicted as a spiritual journey, in Janie's words, a journey to the horizon and back as "a delegate to de big 'ssociation of life ... De Grand Lodge, de big convention of livin.'" Janie follows a pattern familiar to folklorists of a young person's journey from home to face adventure and various dangers, followed by a triumphant homecoming. Like the hero of a folktale, Janie Crawford leaves home behind her, meets strangers who become either allies or enemies, expresses the transformations she undergoes through costumes and disguises which are invested with special significance, experiences reversals in her perceptions of individual people and events, and returns cleansed, enlightened and alone. The folktale's repetition of events in a series of three is duplicated in Janie's three marriages, as well as by her movement out of the rural community of Nanny, her grandmother, and her first husband, to the town where she keeps a store with Joe Starks, and finally to the "muck" of the Everglades where she experiences joy and bereavement through Tea Cake, her third husband.

The three marriages and the three communities in which Janie moves represent increasingly wide circles of experience and opportunities for expression of personal choice. Nanny, Janie's grandmother, had in fact been a slave and had borne a child to her master. The marriage Nanny forces upon Janie represents a practical arrangement which brings with it another kind of servitude. Feminist themes fuse with themes of Black self-determination as Janie discards her apron, historically the badge of the slave woman as well as of the docile wife, and goes off with Joe Starks. Hurston justifies Janie's abandonment of her first marriage, not on the grounds that Janie feels no love for Killicks, who "look like some ole skullhead in de graveyard," but because Killicks decides to buy a mule for Janie to work the fields with—since she has borne him no heir. Janie needs freedom and an expansion of her horizons more than she needs love—a theme which will surface again, particularly when the novel's ending deflates the romanticism of the relationship with Tea Cake and excises the romantic hero from the heroine's life yet leaves her stronger rather than weaker. Here Hurston consciously rejects the happy ending of the traditional novel.

The second marriage to a man of higher ambitions puts Janie in touch with a larger world, that of the all-Black town which Joe founds, but leaves her stifled and controlled by Joe's white-inspired values. Like Killicks, Joe dictates Janie's work and prevents her from being a full participant in the social life of the town. Only after Joe's death does Janie find the freedom and spontaneity which she values and seeks, in her marriage to Tea Cake. Tea Cake expands Janie's horizons literally and figuratively by transplanting her to the Everglades to mingle with other itinerant workers as well as by simply encouraging her to determine her own work and to take part in the "play"—the music, dancing and gaming—of the workers in the "muck."

In recent years critics have been unanimous in praising the vitality of Hurston's language: Hurston is a master at transforming the language of a folk group, in this case the West Florida Blacks of the town in which she herself grew up, into convincing dialogue. The authenticity of the language, although documented, is much less important as a "slice of life" than as an implicit claim of authority about Black life. The success of Hurston's novel depends upon the melding of folkloric and fictional elements in such a way as to create characters whose speech is both reflective of the language of the folk and highly individualized. Hurston's novel asserts itself as a statement that goes beyond the limitations of the local color story because her characters and their speech are plausible, individualized and enduringly interesting....

Both the unselfconscious use of metaphoric language and the more performance oriented forms of expression found in the novel represent men's and women's use of imagination to enliven and elaborate upon the events of their lives. The very limitation and deprivation of life in rural areas and among poor people can produce, as Hurston knew from her work as a folklorist and anthropologist, a flowering of highly imaginative modes of thought and expression. If Hurston had sought simply to preserve the oral culture of this region of West Florida through her novel, she would not have produced a successful novel, but rather an ethnography. However, she instead has transformed folk materials into fiction. Specific performances in the novel symbolize for Janie the kind of active participation in life which has been denied to Blacks, women, and the poor by society and circumstance. The mock funeral of Matt Bonner's mule is linked in the reader's mind with Nanny's notion of woman as "de mule of the world," who carries the burdens laid on her by whites and by Black males. The political statements implicit in the courting rituals enacted in front of Joe Starks' store suggest the sexual politics operative in Janie's marriage to Joe, as

well as in her earlier marriage to Logan Killicks. In each of the instances, the woman is seen as valuable only as long as she hesitates; once she is won over and possessed in some way, she ceases to arouse interest or be perceived as valuable. The mule becomes a motif linked to Nanny, Killicks and Starks. It was, in fact, Killicks' decision to put Janie to work behind a mule which set the stage for her elopement with Starks.... Hurston's use of a narrative voice that parallels and reinforces Janie's expanding view of the world makes it clear that folklore is integrated into all levels of the text. In fact, the narrative voice, always close to but not identical with Janie's consciousness, becomes more prominent toward the end of the book, as if to suggest that the folkloric material is directly relevant to Janie's final achievement of harmony and peace. Folklore is a thematic element, as well as a component of the themes of Janie's search for identity and self-determination as a Black and as a woman.

If folklore is simply one way for men and women to order and interpret their lives and environments, then the title, whose relevance to the book as a whole is not transparent, becomes more accessible. The eyes of the folk watch God and the elements for signs of safety and indications of where and how each one fits into society and the world. *Their Eyes Were Watching God* is a book about a woman's journey of self-discovery, but also about a woman's exploration of the physical and social worlds available to her. If it were a simple tale of romantic love ... Janie's loss of Tea Cake at the end would be a tragedy, depriving her life of the meaning she had finally found. But this is not the case; Tea Cake represents something more to Janie than the presence of a single man. He is represented as a wanderer who shows Janie who she is and can be and who magically remains present to her even after his death.

Tea Cake combines a sense of his own identity as a Black and a concomitant ability to set his own standards for himself with a natural acceptance of and faith in Janie, which enables her to define her own standards for herself. The heart of the life that Janie so much enjoys in the Florida "muck" is folk expression in the form of playing and gaming in the fields or singing and tale-telling in the cabin and "jook."

The flood and Tea Cake's death toward the end of the novel are problematic from a traditional critical point of view. Janie's shooting of Tea Cake after he has been maddened by a bite from a rabid dog during the flood seems implausible. A traditional female protagonist would be happily placed in an appropriate marriage at the end of the book, or else would experience the loss of her man as a tragedy. Again Hurston challenges conventional norms by integrating the expectations of a folktale with the form of the novel, for Janie returns from her adventure into the big world with Tea Cake much as a young male character in a folktale returns home both richer and wiser than he left. Further, she has struggled with the giant—that is, with storms and death—and returned victorious. In the folk tale, the magical teacher is dispensed with as the hero triumphs, and so is Tea Cake left behind on Janie's journey. The flood serves to remove the characters from the life of social interaction in Eatonville and later in the Everglades and puts them into the elemental struggle of natural disaster. Here the narrative voice becomes strong and increasingly suggestive of a sort of collective, choric voice. Storm, flood and death are personified. The effect of this shift is an emphasis on the universal nature of Janie's experience.

When the narrator says of Janie, Tea Cake and their friends as they wait out the storm, "They seemed to be staring at the dark, but their eyes were watching God," Hurston is speaking of the universal human situation as well as of the specific plights of these characters. Aspects of performance and folk culture are portrayed by Hurston as an expression of courage and creativity in the face of everyday realities such as poverty and deprivation, as well as catastrophe and imminent death. The book's title suggests that men and women, confronting "dark" unknowns such as loss and death, create or recognize a force behind reality that makes sense out of it....

The apparent weakness of the ending of the novel is perhaps explained by the possibility that Hurston, as a feminist, did not want Janie to find fulfillment in a man, but rather in her new-found self, and thus tried to re-orient the form towards the traditional story of the young male. There is a suggestion of the literary theme of the birth of the artist, as well as of the folk theme of the triumphant young male.

Source: Claire Crabtree, "The Confluence of Folklore, Feminism, and Black Self-Determination in Zora Neale Hurston's *Their Eyes Were Watching God*," in *Southern Literacy Journal*, Spring, 1985, pp. 54–66.

Ellen Cantarow

Cantarow, a white feminist on a panel with a black feminist, speaks out on sex, race, and criticism, comparing Kate Chopin's The Awakening *to Zora Neale Hurston's* Their Eyes Were Watching God, *and contends that, of the two heroines, Janie, a slave's granddaughter, comes off the stronger compared to Edna, from an upper-class white family.*

I'd like to begin with a memory that came to my mind as I was re-reading the two books we're to discuss this morning. Two years ago, when I was teaching at SUNY/Old Westbury, my car broke down on my way to class. I found myself in one of those high-class, desolate neighborhoods. You know. Plush desolation. No stores. Beautifully manicured streets but not a soul in sight. Hundred thousand dollar houses surrounded by fences and exquisitely tended shrubbery. A woman let me in at one of these houses. She looked to be in her late fifties. It was noon, but she was still dressed in a robe. She let me use her phone. And then she begged me to have coffee with her. She told me her father had just died and that she was in mourning. She told me about her husband, a corporation lawyer who was away most of the time. And she told me about her children. "I've lived for them," she said.

The room we were sitting in was elegant. "The softest rugs and carpets covered the floors. Rich and tasteful draperies hung at doors and windows. There were paintings selected with judgment and discrimination, upon the walls." That description is lifted from *The Awakening*. It occurs when Edna and Leonce Pontellier have returned to their house in New Orleans from the vacation on Grand Isle that takes up the first half of the book. The description might just as well have been of the house in Long Island, or the houses in an upper-middle-class neighborhood I grew up in in Philadelphia. I knew women like the Long Island woman while I was growing up. One was a teacher married to a neurosurgeon. Mrs. Stevens was the aunt of a friend of mine. What always struck me as odd was that while she had her own profession she said her real life was her husband and children—much as Adele Ratignolle, Edna's friend in *The Awakening*, says her life revolves around her husband and children. In her fifties Mrs. Stevens tried to commit suicide. Later she became ill. Now, she's bedridden.

Women like Mrs. Stevens were sustained in their lives by black women's labor. Black women reared such white women's children—fed them, sang to them, nurtured them. It is a black woman—a licensed practical nurse who made it to that job from being a domestic for many years—who now nurses Mrs. Stevens. Mrs. Burden's life has been different from her employer's. While Mrs. Stevens tragedy is rooted in the dependency on her family, and the lack of self-confidence that's bound up with such dependency, Mrs. Burden's life problems have to do with continuous toil and with two unhappy marriages to men who might have been like Janie's first two husbands in *Their Eyes Were Watching God.*

Now, the reason I began with these sketches from my own experience is to point out that history has a long reach into our present lives, and to point out that the lives of white women and black women are intimately intertwined.

But let me come back to that and for the moment I'll turn to *The Awakening.* The reason I flashed on that morning in Long Island was because *The Awakening,* for all that it portrays Creole society and a round of group swims, parties, musicales, is a very solitary sort of book. It is about Edna's isolation, her imprisonment. She's imprisoned in her marriage. She's imprisoned in the house I described earlier. She's imprisoned as a possession, a display of her husband's wealth. But if *The Awakening* is about imprisonment, it's also about the possibilities of freedom. The foil for all the images of luxurious dalliance in the summer of Grand Isle, for all the images of household luxury, is one Chopin gives us at the beginning of the book. Edna describes a walk she took in her childhood in Kentucky through a meadow: "It seemed as big as an ocean to the very little girl walking through the grass, which was higher than her waist.... My sunbonnet obstructed the view. I could see only the stretch of green before me, and I felt as if I must walk on forever, without coming to the end of it." Edna can see only straight ahead, neither to right nor left. The sunbonnet obstructs breadth of vision. The stretch of green goes on forever. There are no landmarks in such undifferentiated loveliness, no certain goal. Which reminds us that clear visions of liberation even forty or fifty years after Seneca Falls were very difficult if not impossible for most white middle-and upper-class women. There were those female fetters—fetters not just of clothing but of ideology—which foreclosed a world in which men like Leonce Pontellier and Robert Lebrun were free to come and go as they pleased....

The lack of productive work is historically significant. By 1899, when *The Awakening* was published, remunerated labor was not readily available to white women of Edna's class. Before the Civil War, the home was still a center of production, and

upper-class white women really did have a role in that productivity. But by Edna's time the factory had taken over such production. Men like Leonce Pontellier were out in the world of industrial production, and captains of it. Women like Edna were the ornaments that proved a man's success in business and the professions. It's out of such history that the white women's movement of the late sixties and early seventies put such a stress on the phrase "meaningful work."

But let's think about that phrase. Meaningful work. For black women like Mrs. Burden, work has been meaningful historically, but the meaning is very different from what I've been talking about. While Edna was being shut up in the parlor, the great grandmother of Mrs. Burden, Mrs. Stevens' nurse, and Janie's grandmother in *Their Eyes Were Watching God,* were on the auction block. The black woman was colonized. The black woman had labor imposed on her. She was used for manual labor and house service. And there was that other kind of labor: she was "a breeder woman." And she was sexually exploited by the white men whose own wives were up there on the pedestal.

This is the background for what Janie's grandmother tells her at the beginning of the novel. She's caught Janie, in the midst of Janie's own sexual awakening, kissing Johnny Taylor over the fence. She slaps her, then she sits with Janie in her lap, and half-weeping tells Janie why she wants her to get married, in a decent marriage, quickly. "De nigger woman is de mule of de world ... Ah was born back due in slavery so it wasn't for me to fulfill my dreams of whut a woman oughta be and to do ... Ah didn't want to be used for a work-ox and a brood sow and ah didn't want mah daughter used dat way neither ... Ah wanted to preach a great sermon about colored women sittin on high but they wasn't no pulpit for me. Ah can't die easy thinkin maybe de men folks white or black is makin a spit cup outa you."

So Janie's nanny marries her off to the elderly Logan Killicks, who disgusts Janie sexually but who has a pedestal for her to stand on. To be precise, sixty acres of land and a nice house. When Joe Starks comes along down the road one day, Janie's attracted to his exuberance, his sweet talk, and a power she sees in him. So she goes off with him and marries him and for a while she lives vicariously off that power. But Joe, like Logan before him, considers Janie a possession. Like Logan, he wants her to work for, not with him. He loves what he calls her plentiful hair, but he makes her bind it up in a headrag while she minds his store. He's your complete male supremacist. At one point Janie says to him, "You sho loves to tell me whut tuh do, but Ah can't tell you nothin Ah see." "Dat's cause you need tellin," says Jody, "Somebody got to think for women and chillun and chickens and cows ... they sho don't think none theirselves."

This marriage is ready for the dust bin. Like Edna, Janie's an accessory to her husband's position and work. But there are deep differences. For one thing, Janie works in Jody's general store where she finds black folk who tell the tall tales, the "lies" Hurston loved and wrote about to reclaim the roots of a people. Janie gets sustenance from that company and that culture just as Hurston did in the Eatonville where she grew up, and in her travels collecting material for her book on black folklore, for her novels, and for her books on voodoo. It's in Jody's store, not in solitary confinement, in that society among those black folk, that Janie makes her break with Jody. Someone's said she hasn't cut a plug of tobacco right. Jody says, "I god amight! A woman stay around uh store till she get as old as Methusalem and still can't cut a little thing like a plug of tobacco! Dont stand dere rollin yo pop eyes at me wid yo rump hangin nearly to yo knees!" "Then, too," Hurston's narrator continues. "Janie took the middle of the floor ... 'Stop mixin up mah doins wid mah looks, Jody. When you git through tellin me how tuh cut uh plug uh tobacco, then you kin tell me whether mah behind is on straight or not ... Ah aint no young gal no mo but den Ah aint no old woman neither. Ah reckon Ah looks mah age too. But ahm a woman every inch of me and ah know it. Dats a whole lot more'n *you* kin say. You big-bellies round here and put out a lot of brag, but taint nothin to it but yo big voice. Humph! Talkin bout *me* lookin old! When you pull down you britches you look lak de change uh life.' 'Great God from Zion!' gasps a bystander, 'Y'll really playin the dozens tonight.'"

The dozens. A verbal artillery Edna doesn't have at her disposal. And there are other resources Edna doesn't have, which I'll return to in a moment. But for the minute I'll just say that between the two awakenings we're talking about today, I prefer Janie's. It's a lot better than suicide. Janie awakens to what the meaning of a white, upper-class style of marriage is, and she rejects it. She tells her friend Pheoby, "[My grandma] was borned in slavery ... sittin on porches lak de white madam looked lak uh mighty fine thing tuh her. Dat's whut she wanted for me ... Git up on uh high chair and sit dere. She

didn't have time to think whut tuh do after you got up on de stool uh do nothin. De object wuz tuh get dere. So ah got up on de high stool lak she told me, but Pheoby. Ah done nearly languished tuh death up dere. Ah felt like de world wuz cryin' extry and Ah aint read de common news yet."

Janie comes down off the pedestal when she stands up to Jody. And finally she's her own woman, on her own, after he dies. She meets Tea Cake, and with him she finds both companionship and sexual fulfillment. He's a gambler, a guitar player. Whites would call him shiftless. Hurston reclaims him, turns the stereotype against its creator. He should be a revelation to white readers. And so should Tea Cake and Janie's love, as opposed to all the stereotypes of black sexuality and marriage the Daniel Patrick Moynihans of this country have laid on us.

But if there's one thing that mars Janie and Tea Cake's relationship, it's Tea Cake's sometimes lingering feelings that he should be the boss. At one point he beats Janie. A friend says, "Lawd! wouldn't Ah love tuh whip uh tender woman lak Janie! Ah bet she don't even holler. She just cries, eh Tea Cake? ... mah woman would spread her lungs all over Palm Beach County, let alone knock out my jaw teeth ... git her good and mad, she'll wade through solid rock up to her hip pockets."

But Janie has that sort of strength, too. She fights Jody physically when she disovers he's playing around with Nunkie. Now I think Janie's psychological and physical strength come, ironically, out of precisely the experience her nanny wants to forget. It was W. E. B. Du Bois who captured the contradiction of black women's forced labor when he said: "Our women in black had freedom thrust contemptuously upon them. With that freedom they are buying an untrammeled independence and dear as is the price they pay for it, it will in the end be worth every taunt and groan." At one point Hurston describes Janie and Tea Cake working side by side on the muck, picking beans: "All day long the romping and playing they carried on behind the boss's back made Janie popular right away. It got the whole field to playing off and on. Then Tea Cake would help get supper afterwards."

I don't think it's accidental that the work, the sexuality, and the housework get all mixed together by Hurston here. It's a glimpse of real equality between a man and a woman in marriage. It's the kind of marriage that's impossible for Edna. And it's a glimpse on the meshing of work and marriage so much of the contemporary white women's movement has stressed. The deep partnership so many of us yearn for. It's a good possibility *Their Eyes,* in part autobiography, was wish-fulfillment. For Hurston herself, a woman on her own at home in the world, in Eatonville, in New Orleans, in Haiti, amongst the intelligentsia of Harlem, had deep conflicts between her life and her career.

There is another contradiction in what I've been saying this morning. Something else that nags at me. It's that in the comparison I've been making, Edna comes off the weaker of the two women. To contemplate Janie—her resourcefulness, her fulfillment in marriage, the power of language at her disposal—to contemplate all this, and her sexuality, is to have a vicarious experience of real strength. This poses difficulties, since finally my roots aren't in the tradition Hurston is writing out of.... For counterparts to Janie in white literature I must, then, turn perhaps not to Chopin's *The Awakening,* but to Colette's *The Vagabond,* or to Doris Lessing's *The Golden Notebook.*

Which is to raise a final question. What am I, a white feminist journalist and critic, doing talking about Hurston's work at all? Because she gives me not just vicarious strength, but also understanding. Never, for example, can I see women like Mrs. Stevens' nurse without thinking of women like Janie. Never can I speak with black women, working-or middle-class, without considering what I've learned of black life through writing like Hurston's.

Source: Ellen Cantarow, "Sex, Race, and Criticism: Thoughts of a White Feminist on Kate Chopin and Zora Neale Hurston," in *Radical Teacher,* September, 1978, pp. 30–33.

Sources

Claire Crabtree, "The Confluence of Folklore, Feminism and Black Self-Determination in Zora Neale Hurston's *Their Eyes Were Watching God,*" *Southern Literary Journal,* Vol. 17, no. 2, Spring, 1985, pp. 54-66.

Henry Louis Gates, Jr., *The Signifying Monkey,* Oxford, 1988.

Jennifer Jordon, "Feminist Fantasies: Zora Neale Hurston's *Their Eyes Were Watching God,*" *Tulsa Studies in Women's Literature,* Vol. 7, Spring, 1988, pp. 105-17.

Alain Locke, review in *Opportunity,* June 1, 1938, reprinted in *Zora Neale Hurston: Critical Perspectives Past and Present,* edited by Henry Louis Gates, Jr. and K. A. Appiah, Amistad, 1993, p. 18.

Lucille Tompkins, review in *New York Times Book Review,* September 26, 1937, reprinted in *Zora Neale Hurston: Crit-*

ical Perspectives Past and Present, edited by Henry Louis Gates, Jr. and K. A. Appiah, Amistad, 1993, pp. 18-19.

Alice Walker, "Looking for Zora," in *In Search of Our Mothers' Gardens,* Harcourt Brace Jovanovich, 1983, pp. 93-116.

Cheryl Wall, "Zora Neale Hurston: Changing Her Own Words," in *Zora Neale Hurston: Critical Perspectives Past and Present,* edited by Henry Louis Gates, Jr. and K. A. Appiah, Amistad, 1993, pp. 78-97.

Mary Helen Washington, " 'I Love the Way Janie Crawford Left Her Husbands': Emergent Female Hero," in *Zora Neale Hurston: Critical Perspectives Past and Present,* edited by Henry Louis Gates, Jr. and K. A. Appiah, Amistad, 1993, pp. 98-109.

Gay Wilentz, "Defeating the False God: Janie's Self-Determination in Zora Neale Hurston's *Their Eyes Were Watching God,*" in *Faith of a (Woman) Writer,* edited by Alice Kessler-Harris and William McBrien, Greenwood Press, 1988, pp. 285-91.

Richard Wright, review in *New Masses,* October 5, 1937, reprinted in *Zora Neale Hurston: Critical Perspectives Past and Present,* edited by Henry Louis Gates, Jr. and K. A. Appiah, Amistad, 1993, pp. 16-17.

For Further Study

Sharon Davie, "Free Mules, Talking Buzzards, and Cracked Plates: The Politics of Dislocation in *Their Eyes Were Watching God,*" in *PMLA,* May, 1993, pp. 446-459.
    Scholarly article which examines the relationships among control, reason, and language in the novel.

Robert E. Hemenway, *Zora Neale Hurston,* Illinois, 1977.
    A popular biography of the writer which includes a good discussion of her work and its relationship to her life.

Karla F. C. Holloway, *Moorings & Metaphors: Figures of Culture and Gender in Black Women's Literature,* Rutgers, 1992.
    A book-length study which considers the work of several black women writers and several of Hurston's works in addition to *Their Eyes Were Watching God.*

Pearlie Peters, "Women and Assertive Voice in Hurston's Fiction and Folklore," in *The Literary Griot,* Spring/Fall, 1992, pp. 100-10.
    An article which discusses the African-American oral tradition and its social significance.

Priscilla Wald, "Becoming 'Colored': The Self-Authorized Language of Difference in Zora Neale Hurston," in *American Literary History,* Spring, 1990, pp. 79-100.
    Scholarly article which discusses Hurston's ability to be both the observer and the observed and which compares her fiction to her studies of folklore.

Alice Walker, "Zora Neale Hurston: A Cautionary Tale and a Partisan View," in *In Search of Our Mothers' Gardens,* Harcourt Brace Jovanovich, 1983, pp. 83-92.
    An essay which discusses Walker's discovery of Hurston's work.

Wise Blood

Flannery O'Connor
1952

The story of a man named Hazel Motes, who denies his Christianity and takes desperate measures to prove his disbelief, Flannery O'Connor's *Wise Blood* made its debut in 1952. Harcourt Brace published the novel right after O'Connor spent a difficult winter suffering from symptoms that doctors later diagnosed as systemic lupus erythematosus. Critics concur that the disease greatly affected O'Connor's life and work, while they question the specific effects it had on her fiction. Many think that O'Connor's use of the grotesque arose from her own experiences with a disease-ravaged body, yet the general consensus is that O'Connor's religious southern upbringing was the most important influence on her writing.

When *Wise Blood* first appeared, critics gave it little attention and few accolades. O'Connor was not well known, and she was writing at the same time as famous writers William Faulkner and Daphne du Maurier. Critics viewed O'Connor as a minor writer, and put her in the same category as other Southern writers of the time, based on her use of violence and bizarre characters. The novel's religious meaning, later to become its strength, escaped recognition. Critic Isaac Rosenfeld, for example, stated in *New Republic* that Motes "is nothing more than the poor, sick, ugly, raving lunatic that he happens to be."

While most reviewers believed O'Connor's own testimony to the religious meaning in *Wise Blood,* novelist John Hawkes criticized O'Connor as being somewhat captivated by the Devil. Since

that time in 1962, however, critics have defended O'Connor's purpose. They applaud her ability to present her basic theme of Christ's redemption of mankind. In the final analysis, critics now view *Wise Blood* as an outstanding religious novel.

Author Biography

Flannery O'Connor wrote from her experiences as a Roman Catholic raised in the Protestant South. Her religion and regional upbringing greatly contributed to her themes and writing style. Yet critics agree that her father's death from lupus—as well as her own later suffering from the same disease—were also significant influences on her writing.

Born Mary Flannery O'Connor to Edward Francis and Regina Cline O'Connor on March 25, 1925, in Savannah, Georgia, O'Connor lived in that southern city until the Great Depression forced the family to seek job opportunities elsewhere. O'Connor and her parents moved to Milledgeville, Georgia, where her grandparents lived and where she attended high school and college. While the family was living in Milledgeville, O'Connor's father died of systemic lupus erythematosus ("lupus" or "SLE"), a disease that results when the body's immune system goes out of control. O'Connor was thirteen at the time.

During her high school and college years, O'Connor demonstrated a talent for cartooning and writing. The characters she drew and the writing she did provided an often sarcastic view of the difficulties of growing up. O'Connor graduated from Peabody High School in 1942 and continued to write. She completed an A.B. degree in 1945 at the Georgia State College for Women (now Georgia College at Milledgeville) and, in 1947, a Master of Fine Arts in creative writing at the prestigious University of Iowa Writers' Workshop.

O'Connor worked on her first novel, *Wise Blood,* during late 1948 and early 1949 while living in Connecticut and New York. She submitted it to Harcourt Brace for publication during the winter of 1950-51. At that same time, she began to show early symptoms of the disease that killed her father. Suffering from fatigue and aching joints, the twenty-five-year-old O'Connor moved back to the southern climate in Milledgeville, where she was living when she received her diagnosis of lupus.

While lupus attacked her body with greater force over the years, O'Connor continued to write,

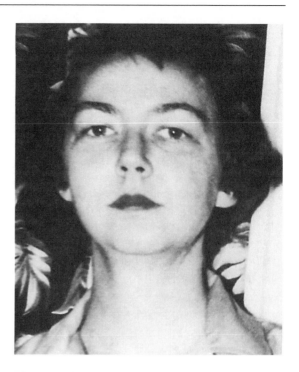

Flannery O'Connor

and always with spiritual undertones. She endured pain and disfigurement from the disease and its treatments without allowing them to shake her faith. She constantly believed that the human body was not the real body; the only true body was the body of the resurrected. Critics agree that her writing reflects this unwavering trust. For example, O'Connor's characters often exhibited grotesque appearances, actions, or personality traits—the imperfections resulting from a society that has lost its sense of spiritual purpose.

During the fourteen years after her diagnosis, O'Connor authored another novel and several short stories. She was the recipient of the a number of awards, including O. Henry Memorial Awards in 1957, 1963, and 1964; a Ford Foundation grant in 1959; a National Catholic Book award in 1966; and the National Book Award in 1972, which she won for her book *The Complete Short Stories.* O'Connor died of lupus-related renal failure on August 3, 1964, in Atlanta, Georgia.

Plot Summary

A New Church

Set in the fictional town of Taulkinham, Tennessee, Flannery O'Connor's first novel, *Wise*

Blood, tells the story of a confused and isolated young man who attempts to shed his obsessions with Jesus and Christian redemption. As a child, Hazel Motes—"Haze" for short—felt certain that he was destined to become a preacher like his grandfather. This certainty begins to fade when, at eighteen, he is drafted by the army and sent overseas. Haze spends four years away from home and, as a result, finds ample time to study his soul and assure himself "that it was not there." The novel explores the repercussions of that decision and chronicles Haze's life from the time he is released from the army until his death a short time later.

Upon leaving the army, Haze returns to his hometown of Eastrod only to find it run down and deserted. He takes a train to nearby Taulkinham, where, as he tells one of the passengers, he plans to do some of the things he has never done before. He spends his first night in town with a prostitute whose name he finds written on a bathroom wall. However, it is not long before his inner conflicts lead him elsewhere. The following night, he is handed a religious pamphlet by a young girl accompanying a blind preacher. Haze discards the leaflet but is drawn to the pair and follows them down the street. He is himself followed by Enoch Emery, a lonely eighteen-year-old boy who repeatedly informs Haze that Taulkinham is an unfriendly city.

When Haze and Enoch catch up to the preacher and the girl, the blind man tells Haze that he can "smell the sin on [his] breath" and "hear the urge for Jesus in his voice." Haze responds by saying that he does not believe in sin and that Jesus does not exist. He then announces that he, too, is a preacher, and that he is going to preach a new church: the church of truth without Jesus Christ Crucified. The name is eventually shortened to The Church Without Christ.

A New Jesus

The next morning, Haze suddenly decides to buy a car. He finds an old Essex on a used car lot and drives to the park where Enoch spends his afternoons. He has come to ask the boy for the preacher's address, but Enoch, who has long awaited the chance to share his "secret mystery," tells Haze that he must first show him something. Enoch leads Haze through a daily routine of pointless rituals until finally bringing him to a museum in the center of the park. The building is filled with glass cases and Enoch's "secret mystery"—the body of a small naked man shrunken by Arabs—is contained in one of them. Frustrated by the boy's

foolishness, Haze hits Enoch on the forehead with a rock and leaves.

Haze eventually finds the blind preacher and rents a room in the boarding house, where he and the girl live. Hawks, the preacher, shows Haze a newspaper clipping explaining how he promised to blind himself to prove that Jesus had redeemed him. Haze reads the clipping three times before leaving. He claims that nobody with a good car needs to be justified. After he is gone, the narrator reveals the existence of a second clipping telling how Hawks lost his nerve and did not actually blind himself.

Meanwhile, Enoch has decided that his life will never be the same. He believes that he has "wise blood" and is certain that something awful is expected of him. He tries to resist but eventually succumbs to the urgings of his blood. Led by his resignation, he happens across Haze preaching from his car. Enoch does not know about the Church Without Christ and is surprised to hear Haze talk of redemption and of the need for a new jesus. When Haze then asks to be shown where this new jesus can be found, Enoch, almost paralyzed in shock, whispers, "I got him, I can get him. You seen him yourself."

Despite Enoch's reaction, Haze does not have much luck attracting followers. Then, one night, an apparent disciple appears. As Haze's listeners begin to disperse, a man named Hoover Shoats steps up and tells how the prophet (Haze) changed his life. However, Shoats distorts Haze's words by telling the crowd that the new church is based on the Bible. He later threatens to put Haze out of business when he learns that the new jesus does not actually exist. The following night, while Haze is again preaching from the nose of his car, Shoats arrives with his own hired prophet: a man dressed exactly like Haze. Haze is shocked by the image he sees and leaves.

During this time, Enoch, thinking that he has found the new jesus, steals the shrunken figure from its glass case. He is on his way to deliver his discovery when he passes a crowd of kids waiting to meet Gonga the gorilla, a movie star. Enoch waits his turn to shake the ape's hand, but when his turn comes the ape-suited man tells Enoch to go to hell. Enoch runs off in humiliation and delivers his package to Haze. The latter is not impressed by the shrivelled body of the dust-filled figure and throws it out the door.

After an afternoon spent fidgeting in his room, Enoch experiences an "awakening" when he finds the schedule for Gonga's tour. He quickly travels to the star's next public appearance, where he attacks and strips the gorilla in the back of his truck. Enoch then runs into the woods, buries his clothes, and puts on the ape suit. He proceeds to mimic the gorilla's gestures of hand shaking, repeatedly extending his hand and shaking at nothing, but his efforts prove futile. After a few moments of practice, Enoch approaches a young couple, hand extended and still wearing the ape suit, but they run away.

On the night Hoover Shoats and his hired prophet, Solace Layfield, appear for a second time, Haze follows his twin home. He forces Solace to stop on the side of the road and runs him over with his car. Haze then tells the injured man that there are two things he cannot stand, "a man that ain't true and one that mocks what is." Solace dies and Haze, intending to leave town, drives off. Haze's plans change when his car is pushed over an embankment by a patrolman who initially pulled him over because, as he tells Haze, "I just don't like your face." Left without any means of transportation, Haze walks back to town and buys a bucket and some quicklime. He has decided to blind himself.

A New Hope?

In the final chapter, Haze, now referred to as the blind man, continues to live in the boarding house. His landlady, the complacent Mrs. Flood, thinks there may be some money to be made off the blind man and makes plans to marry him and have him committed. But she becomes accustomed to watching his face and soon decides that she would like to keep him. She suspects that he knows something and wishes she could penetrate the darkness and see for herself what was there. However, when she finally brings up marriage, the blind man gets up and leaves the house. Two days later, he is found lying in a ditch by two policemen; he dies moments later. The policemen bring him back to Mrs. Flood, who, upon looking into Haze's eyes to find out what has cheated her, feels that "she had finally got to the beginning of something she couldn't begin." She then sees the blind man moving "farther and farther into the darkness until he was [but a] pinpoint of light."

Characters

Enoch Emery

Enoch Emery meets Hazel Motes on Motes's second night in town. He becomes Motes's most dedicated follower, taking to heart Motes's call for a new jesus. A welfare woman who believed in the "old" Jesus had removed Emery from his father's care at the age of twelve. The woman had then sent him away to attend a Bible academy and threatened him with life in the penitentiary if he did not do what she demanded of him. After having successfully escaped the woman, Emery wants nothing to do with "the Jesus kind."

Emery returns to his father's home only to be thrown out at the age of eighteen. With a pimply face that resembles a fox's, Emery does not make friends easily. To pass the time, he maintains a daily routine that consists of work and a visit to the park at the end of his shift. It is at the park that he first climbs into bushes and spies on women at the pool. He then goes to a refreshment stand, where he orders a milkshake and makes lewd remarks to the waitress. Next, he views caged animals, hating and loving them at the same time. Finally, he visits a museum in the center of the park that houses a shriveled mummy. The mummy represents something important to him, something that he does not quite understand.

Emery feels compelled to show the mummy to someone, yet he does not know who that person is. He awakens one morning with a feeling in his blood, "wise blood like his daddy," that the person to whom he will show the mummy will appear. When Hazel Motes drives by the park that day, Emery realizes that his blood had been telling him the truth. After showing Motes the mummy, Emery again feels that his blood is telling him something—that he is going to be a part of something big that is only beginning.

Mrs. Flood

Mrs. Flood owns the boarding house in which Motes lives. After Motes blinds himself, she intends to marry and institutionalize him so that she can get the pension he receives from the government. She feels that the government owes her for the taxes she has paid over the years that were used to support people who did not deserve the help. Even though she raises Motes's room and board to get a larger share of his money, she still feels cheated. She believes Motes must have a plan for something more and that he is not sharing it with her.

Against her will, Mrs. Flood begins to enjoy her time spent with Motes. She tries to understand why he has blinded himself and why he has no interest in doing anything but sitting on her porch.

She puzzles over why he wears his shoes with rocks and glass in them and puts barbs of wire around his chest. When Motes becomes ill with the flu, Mrs. Flood decides to marry him and keep him. He dies, however, before she can complete her plan. She tries to look into his dead eyes to see how and by whom she was cheated, but she sees nothing. When she closes her own eyes, she sees a point of light far off in the distance that eventually becomes Motes. She has a feeling that she "finally got to the beginning of something she couldn't begin."

Asa Hawks

Scar-faced Asa Hawks pretends to be a preacher who has blinded himself for Jesus. Dressed in black, wearing dark glasses, and pale enough to look like a corpse, Hawks uses a white cane and carries a tin cup. He implores people to repent, but if they will not he asks them to help by putting coins in his cup. His daughter, Sabbath Lily, follows Hawks, handing out pamphlets that say "Jesus calls you."

While Hawks did have good spiritual intentions at one time, along with a congregation who believed in him, he has lost his sense of purpose. This loss of direction resulted from a failure in his own faith, when he lost his courage to blind himself to justify his belief in Jesus. He senses the true Jesus in Motes, while he himself has become nothing more than a beggar, competing with street "hawkers" for the buyers' money.

Sabbath Lily Hawks

Sabbath Lily Hawks imitates her father's false morality by handing out pamphlets that proclaim Jesus's desire for people to follow him. Fifteen-year-old Sabbath Lily's large red lips contrast vividly with skin that is almost as pale as her father's and the innocence that her homely appearance might imply.

Sabbath Lily tells her father "I never seen a boy that I liked the looks of any better," and wants her father to help her get Motes. She tries desperately to seduce Motes, telling him how she has written to the lovelorn column in the newspaper asking if she should go all the way or not. Nothing Sabbath Lily tries works to change Motes's mind, until she appears one night in his bed. She tells him that she knows he is "pure filthy right down to the guts" like her, and that she can teach him to like being that way.

Media Adaptations

- Director John Huston adapted *Wise Blood* to film in 1979. Brad Dourif starred as Hazel Motes. Other cast members included Ned Beatty, Harry Dean Stanton, Dan Shor, and Amy Wright. Rated PG, the film is distributed by Universal Studios Home Video.

While Sabbath Lily does succeed in seducing Motes, it does not result in the permanent relationship with Motes that she had hoped would free her from her father. Her father leaves her, and Motes ignores her. While she says that "she hadn't counted on no honest-to-Jesus blind man," she makes such a nuisance of herself at Motes's home that the landlady finally calls social services and has her put in a detention center.

Haze
See Hazel Motes

Mrs. Hitchcock
At the beginning of the novel, Motes finds himself seated on the train across from a fat woman who has pear-shaped legs that do not reach the floor. She identifies herself as Mrs. Hitchcock and tells Motes that she is traveling to Florida to visit her daughter. Dressed in pink with a flat, reddish face, Mrs. Hitchcock tries to get Motes to talk about himself. While she is drawn to Motes's eyes, she fears something in them and looks, instead, at the price tag still dangling from his coat. She represents the first of the characters who irritate Motes by trying to associate him with preaching.

Onnie Jay Holy
See Hoover Shoats

Solace Layfield
Shoats hires Solace Layfield to pose as the True Prophet because he drives a rat-colored car and wears a blue suit like Motes's. Suffering from tuberculosis, Layfield coughs continually from the

depths of his hollow-chested, gaunt body. Layfield only preaches for Shoats to earn money to support his wife and six children. Motes hates him for being "a man that ain't true and one that mocks what is." Motes follows Layfield one night, forces him to take off his suit, and runs over him with his car. Layfield's last words are "Jesus hep me."

Hazel Motes

O'Connor portrays Hazel Motes, the main character, as a man who takes everything at face value and wants to deny God's existence. People see Motes as a preacher, a label which he strongly protests. Even the taxi driver tells Motes that his hat and "a look in your face somewheres" make him look like a preacher.

Motes judges everyone by their appearances, yet he cannot help but search their faces for some indication of their worth. He yearns for proof that people have no connection to the divine. While he objects to his own spiritual connection, Motes feels a pull towards Christ, or "the wild ragged figure motioning him to turn around and come off into the dark."

Motes's name and appearance depict a man who peers into the beyond. Appropriately, the name "Hazel" comes from the Hebrew for "he who sees God." Motes's prominent forehead, hooked nose, creased mouth, and flattened hair prompt the landlady to note that his "face had a peculiar pushing look as if it were going forward after something it could just distinguish in the distance." In addition, Motes's deep-set, pecan-colored eyes beckon people to surrender their wills to one who is stronger. For example, when Mrs. Hitchcock meets Motes on the train, she feels drawn to his eyes, like they were "passages leading somewhere," but she senses danger in them, too.

In his efforts to deny God's existence, Motes attempts to establish the "Church Without Christ." He buys a car and uses it as his church, preaching from its hood. The car becomes a symbol of Motes's rejection of Christ. He claims that "Nobody with a good car needs to be justified." Motes preaches that since God does not exist, neither do sin or redemption. He offers people a new jesus that they can see, one who can save them in a way that their Jesus has not been able to. Ironically, it is the loss of his car that results in Motes's salvation.

Prophet

See Hazel Motes

Hoover Shoats

Hoover Shoats is a plump, curly-haired man who wears sideburns and a black suit with silver stripes. Shoats recognizes a way to make money when he sees one. When he hears Motes preaching his Church Without Christ message and losing his audience, he steps in and tries to sell himself as a man who has followed—and has absolute faith in—Motes and his church. Smiling, and with an honest look on his face, Shoats can convince people of almost anything.

Motes, however, does not appreciate Shoats's trying to take over. He especially dislikes his changing the church's name from the Church Without Christ to the Church of Christ Without Christ. Even though Shoats does his best to convince Motes that selling the public on the new jesus has great financial possibilities, Motes turns him down. In retaliation, Shoats hires Solace Layfield to pose as the "True Prophet" and preach the message of the Church of Christ Without Christ.

True Prophet

See Solace Layfield

Mrs. Watts

Mrs. Watts owns a house of ill repute in Taulkinham. When Motes arrives in town, he has the taxi driver take him there. He wants to prove to the driver, and to himself, that he is not a preacher and has no connection to Christ. Motes engages in illicit sex with Mrs. Watts to try to finalize this denial of religion in his life. To Motes, having sex with Mrs. Watts demonstrates that he believes in nothing.

Themes

God and Religion

Christ's redemption of humanity comprises the main theme of *Wise Blood*. The characters exhibit the qualities of people who have a misdirected sense of spiritual purpose, if they have any spiritual purpose at all. Motes, for example, endeavors to turn his back on his strict religious background by publicly denouncing Christ, engaging in illicit sex, and establishing the "Church Without Christ." Other characters, such as Shoats and Hawks, use religion as a means of making money. Yet as strongly as Motes denies Christ's presence in his life he cannot resist Christ's salvation in the end.

Topics For Further Study

- *Wise Blood* depicts a man who denies Christianity to the point of extremes. Like Hazel Motes, many people feel a pull towards holiness that can result in destructiveness when the impulse is carried too far. Psychologists often study this phenomenon in cult followers. Research one of the recent cult suicides/massacres (e.g., Jonestown, Branch Davidians, Heaven's Gate) to try to understand the "cult mentality." Explain cult members' actions in terms of Hazel Motes' actions in the novel and in terms of impulse carried too far.

- Form a panel of "specialists" who will come together to present their views on the characters' motives in *Wise Blood.* These "specialists" should include a psychologist, a member of the clergy, a business person, and a representative of the community at large. The "specialists" must speak as experts in their particular areas of

expertise and be prepared to cite examples of the characters' actions that will validate their views.

- Hazel Motes and Enoch Emery both see their obtaining material prosperity as a way for them to accomplish their goals. What do Hazel and Enoch acquire and accomplish, respectively, that symbolizes their prosperity and proves to them that they have "made it?" How do people today prove to others that they have "made it"? Be ready to defend your thoughts.

- Create a mask for one of the characters from *Wise Blood* that depicts the character's particular expression in a specific scene from the story. (For example, show Sabbath Lily Hawks at her most seductive.) Be prepared to explain the scene and the reasons for the expression you have chosen for your character.

Moral Corruption

Materialism corrupts mankind. If people focus on acquiring wealth and material goods, then they have little time for spiritual growth and awareness. They will engage in immoral acts because they must ignore the difference between right and wrong to prosper. For example, Motes and Emery see having a car and living the life of modern society, respectively, as ways to accomplish their goals. They kill without remorse, feeling justified in doing what is necessary to succeed. Additionally, Hawks lives a lie to make a living, and Shoats uses Layfield to con people out of their money. Other references to money throughout the novel emphasize the characters' preoccupation with it: Mrs. Hitchcock observes the price of Motes's coat; street vendors and car salesmen argue over prices; Shoats and Layfield reveal their salaries; and so on. Spiritual chaos reigns as a result of mankind's obsession with material prosperity.

Change and Transformation

Two characters in *Wise Blood* undergo changes that directly reflect the book's major themes. According to Erik Nielsen in *New Orleans Review,* Motes experiences several obvious transformations throughout the novel, while Mrs. Flood's single metamorphosis culminates the story. Motes's first transformation occurs when he decides in boot camp that he has no soul. He turns his back on his strict religious upbringing and becomes an atheist driven to immoral behavior. His second change results in his telling the taxi driver that he does not believe in anything; he becomes a nihilist. Motes's blinding himself represents his third transformation—a final effort at destroying his conscience. Living as a dutiful Christian in Mrs. Flood's house, Motes lives out his final stage in life. His ultimate transformation is from life to death. Mrs. Flood's transformation begins when Motes blinds himself. While she originally planned to marry him to acquire his money, she eventually grew fond of Motes and decided to care for him out of concern. According to M. J. Fitzgerald in *The Reference Guide to American Literature,* "There is only one person in the book who retains a human ambiguity in response to the call of religion and of Christianity and yet is transformed and converted by contact with Hazel."

Free Will

Hazel Motes tries desperately to find freedom from his conscience by choosing to ignore his belief in God. He believes that if he eliminates morality from his life, he can avoid Jesus. Once free of this hindrance, he will be able to do anything he wants without his conscience bothering him. He takes the opportunity to end his association with God when his boot camp buddies ask him if he is sure he has a soul. He decides at that point to exchange his soul for nothingness. Neither he nor any other of the characters, however, ever fully find the freedom they seek. While Motes endeavors to deny Christ, Motes's very association with the other characters forces them to momentarily realize Christ's presence.

Flesh vs. Spirit

The "Hazel Motes without a soul" can behave in any manner he wants. If he believes in nothing, then right and wrong do not exist. Thus, Motes tells the taxi driver he believes in nothing, then engages in sex with Mrs. Watts to prove to himself that he has eliminated his conscience, the religious upbringing that has always guided his recognition of right and wrong.

Conscience

Motes preaches that the conscience is a trick. He tells people that "if you think it does [exist], you had best get it out in the open and hunt it down and kill it, because it's no more than your face in the mirror is or your shadow behind you." Motes thinks that he has succeeded in eliminating his conscience. Yet Solace Layfield represents to Motes what is left of his conscience—his consciousness, or his remaining thoughts of his religious past. He hunts down and kills Layfield to try to rid himself of his consciousness once and for all.

Appearances and Reality

Often, appearance and reality oppose one another. In *Wise Blood,* however, appearance and reality both support and oppose one another. First, Motes looks like a preacher. Everyone thinks he is a preacher. In fact, while Motes hotly denies it, he actually is a preacher. On the other hand, even though Motes tries to act like someone who has no religion, the reality is that he can not escape it. From Motes's point of view, his appearance denies his reality. From everyone else's viewpoint, Motes's appearance reflects his true nature.

American Dream

Emery wants "to become something. He wants to better his condition until he is the best. He wants to be THE young man of the future, like the ones in the insurance ads. He wants, some day, to see a line of people waiting to shake his hand." To Emery, the city and its institutions represent the American Dream. They become his daily routine because he believes that being a part of the city's prosperous lifestyle will help him achieve his ambition. Motes, too, sees the American Dream as being a goal he can achieve through material prosperity. While he does not aspire to BE someone, he views car ownership as proof that he has accomplished his goal in life—to deny his relationship with God through the establishment of the Church Without Christ. Like people who are living the American Dream, Motes feels that his car is the mark of a person who has "made it."

Style

Point of View

Until Mrs. Flood enters the story at the end of the book, Flannery O'Connor writes *Wise Blood* from an "all-knowing" point of view, or, in other words, from a narrator's point of view. From this perspective, the author can enter the minds of all the characters and tell their thoughts. For example, O'Connor divulges that Emery secretly believes that the waitress at the Frosty Bottle is in love with him. At the end of the novel, however, O'Connor switches to the partially omniscient point of view, with Mrs. Flood telling the story. This switch comes in Chapter 14, where Mrs. Flood ponders her relationship with Motes. O'Connor has Motes act and speak, but she does not reveal his thoughts.

Setting

Taulkinham, a small town in Tennessee, sets the stage for the events that take place in *Wise Blood.* Although the author does not provide a particular time in history, critics believe that the book takes place in the mid-twentieth century.

Symbolism

Many symbolic images exist in *Wise Blood* to help portray Motes's denial of Christ. The reader first encounters the symbols of material prosperity that relate to Enoch Emery and Hazel Motes. Emery seeks to "become something." He views the zoo, park, pool, museum, and theater as conveniences that people who have achieved success can enjoy. Motes sees his car, a modern luxury, as proof that he has achieved his success in denying his religious upbringing: "Nobody with a good car needs to be justified," he declares.

In addition to the symbols of prosperity, literary experts have noted symbolic representation in characters' actions. First, both Motes's leaving Sabbath Lily and his throwing out the new jesus and his mother's glasses stand for his initial efforts to rid himself of his religious past. Second, killing his "twin," Layfield, represents Motes's destruction of another portion of his conscience. Motes's final symbolic attempt to deny his connection to Christ occurs when he blinds himself.

Grotesque

O'Connor portrays her characters as grotesque, or bizarre, in their appearances and natures. While many critics disagree over O'Connor's reasons for her use of grotesque characterization in *Wise Blood,* Marshall Bruce Gentry offers a unique view in a *Modern Fiction Studies* article. He suggests that while the characters' grotesqueness might be what critics view as a negative sign of their helplessness and individualism in an uncaring society, it might also present the positive traits that allow them to rejoin a community with whom they feel a kinship. In *Mystery and Manners,* O'Connor says of her own work that her characters "have an inner coherence, if not always a coherence to their social framework. Their fictional qualities lean away from typical social patterns, toward mystery and the unexpected." Gentry submits that while readers might interpret Motes's actions as basically evil, those actions actually stem from an inner adherence to a belief system that eventually leads him to salvation, or a rejoining with his religious past.

Imagery

Critics agree that the characters in *Wise Blood* exhibit animal-like tendencies. Not only do their names and appearances suggest beasts, but their actions also simulate those of animals. For example, Daniel Littlefield, Jr., says in *Mississippi Quarterly* that Hawks's name corresponds with the bird of prey, and that he turns his back on his daughter like a bird might throw its baby out of the nest. Littlefield also notes that several animal images relate to Emery, who resembles a hound dog with mange. Like a dog, he crawls on his belly and burrows under bushes to watch the woman at the pool. He even "becomes" a gorilla. Literary experts speculate that O'Connor uses animal images in this story to emphasize the characters' grotesqueness and their distorted spirituality.

Doppelganger

O'Connor uses Solace Layfield as Motes's doppelganger to represent part of Motes's consciousness. "Doppelganger" means spirit-like twin or counterpart. Layfield resembles Motes so much that one woman in the book asks, "Him and you twins?"

Flashback

Two flashbacks occur in *Wise Blood.* One happens when Motes is riding the train and dreaming about his grandfather. He pictures his grandfather preaching from the car hood and pointing Motes out as an example for sinners. Motes's night with Mrs. Watts prompts the second flashback. He remembers attending a carnival at age ten, seeing a naked woman, and his mother's punishing him for it. Both incidents depict Motes's strict upbringing and unhappy childhood.

Historical Context

According to Michael Kreyling in the introduction to *New Essays on Wise Blood,* O'Connor's attention to religious themes in her writing render her writing timeless. He also states that "the historical context of O'Connor's work has been the least-explored critical territory." O'Connor places the events of the story *Wise Blood* in Taulkinham, Tennessee, but does not specify exact dates. Given the events in the story and the time O'Connor wrote it, however, critics set the story sometime in the mid-twentieth century. One event that lends credence to critics' timeline for the story is Motes's reflection on his stint in the army and the war injury that sent him home. Given the fact that O'Connor wrote the book in the late '40s, and Harcourt published it in 1952, Motes probably served in World War II. The events of the story, then, most likely occur in the latter half of the 1940s.

Evangelist Tom Presnell draws a crowd in Chicago with the energetic, fire-and-brimstone style typical of so many preachers during the 1950s.

Post-World War II Growth and Prosperity

Immediately after World War II, Americans enjoyed a surge of population growth and prosperity. By 1950, the more than 151 million Americans could take advantage of many innovations that would make their lives easier and safer, and their leisure time more enjoyable. For example, technological advances created microwave ovens and fast foods, conveniences that helped provide Americans with more time. Medical researchers developed polio and measles vaccinations, as well as the birth-control pill, enabling children to live longer and couples to plan their families better. Since people had more time and were in better health, they found new ways to enjoy their free time. Commercial hotel chains and jet transport, modern turnpikes, and faster cars contributed to increased travel in America in the 1950s. Americans became passionate about automobiles and the conveniences cars allowed.

O'Connor uses America's obsession with prosperity and its love affair with cars to provide a basis for the spiritual chaos the characters in *Wise Blood* experience. O'Connor states in *The Living Novel: A Symposium* that she believes "unparalleled prosperity" results in a "distorted sense of

spiritual purpose." *Wise Blood* expands that theme more than any of her other works. Throughout the novel, O'Connor presents motifs and images portraying a prosperous society. Money reigns as king: Mrs. Hitchcock checks the price tag on Motes's coat; street vendors and used-car salesmen haggle over prices; and fake preachers brag about their salaries. In addition, commercial advertising takes over the landscape in the form of signs on buildings, billboards along the roadside, and the business establishments themselves. The novel's characters focus so intently on money-related issues and prosperity that their spirituality disappears and their morals disintegrate.

Religion

Religion attracted scores of Americans during the 1950s. Not only did church affiliation soar to 63.6 percent of the population, but also religious contributions, media attention, films, and books increased tremendously. For example, people's average yearly donations to the church peaked, and movies about biblical stories, such as *The Robe,* drew huge crowds. Ministers who brought modern, positive messages attracted the thousands who believed that having a religious identification was synonymous with being an American. Even polit-

Compare
&
Contrast

- **Late 1930s and 1940s:** Reeling from the effects of the Great Depression, Americans conserved their money.

  1950s: Americans became avid consumers, spending more and more money to buy the new products that technological advances provided them.

  Today: With the advent of shopping services on the Internet and television, as well as the proliferation of shopping malls (which first began in the 1950s), and a strong economy, consumerism defines much of American life.

- **Late 1930s and 1940s:** Population growth was at a virtual standstill. People did not want to have children for whom they could not provide.

  1950s: America experienced a baby boom related to the improved economy. The American people thought that having more Americans would better support the growing economy.

  Today: The Baby Boomers are aging, causing increased concerns about health care, while an increasing percentage of population growth is due to a new influx of immigrants from Asia, Mexico, and the Middle East.

- **Late 1930s and 1940s:** Americans viewed cars as workhorses; they took people where they wanted to go.

1950s: Americans began their love affair with automobiles. Faster, sleeker cars were available as well as better roads and services. Cars became symbols of prosperity and luxury.

Today: Cars are still a central part of American culture and a major status symbol; people are often defined by whether they drive a minivan, a sport utility vehicle, or a compact car. Cars become increasingly expensive due, in part, to safety regulations, spurring an increase in used car sales.

- **Late 1930s and 1940s:** People went to church as a matter of routine. The Protestant ethic dominated.

  1950s: A religious awakening began, with church affiliation at an all-time high. The Catholic Church became an American institution.

  Today: Increasing numbers of people are staying away from traditional churches, such as the Catholic Church, to the point that many religious leaders are concerned about shrinking memberships. More people who still wish to go to church are attending nondenominational congregations that stress social issues as much as—or even more than—religion.

---

ical advertising extolled the virtues of religion. Politicians allowed the addition of "under God" to the Pledge of Allegiance and adopted "In God We Trust" as the national motto. Some religious critics, however, wondered whether this wholesale acceptance of religion was sincere, or whether it was just another symbol adopted by people to demonstrate their status and prosperity.

Hazel Motes denies religion as vehemently as people of the 1950s embraced it. M. J. Fitzgerald states in the *Reference Guide to American Literature* that the "mystery of the impulse towards holiness ... and the destructiveness of that impulse when carried to extremes" is the basis of *Wise*

Blood. Motes's acts of violence suggest extremism, as does the seemingly blind adoption of religion by Americans living in the 1950s. O'Connor draws the parallel between the novel and real life with images of a prosperous society and of people who lack spiritual purpose as a result of it.

Critical Overview

While criticism of O'Connor's work varies from discussions of her ability to write short stories and novels to the question of her place among regional writers, the religious nature of her work reigns as the most important issue. Four theories have evolved over time.

First, O'Connor's earliest critics held that O'Connor's work had no connection to religion. Isaac Rosenfeld, one of O'Connor's primary critics, vehemently denied seeing any religious meaning in *Wise Blood*. This reflected the general consensus of other reviewers at the time. He said in a 1952 issue of *New Republic* that Hazel Motes "is nothing more than the poor, sick, ugly, raving lunatic that he happens to be." Some critics still hold this theory.

Other early critics spoke of O'Connor's writing with nearly as much hostility, yet they could not deny that her writing had to be taken seriously, if not admired. Influential magazines such as *Time* and the *Kenyon Review* published reviews of her work, giving it more attention than most beginning writers could even imagine. In 1955, there were twenty-seven articles published about her work; in 1960, the number doubled.

Skeptics still existed, however, and still do today. Critics adhering to the second school of thought related to O'Connor's work accept her religious intent, but they question whether her own religious vision was sufficiently positive to relay her intended message. They wonder if her views were too negative, represented by characters who are too grotesque to give her religious message credence. It is claimed by some that O'Connor's writing connects very little to real life or real problems. A few have felt that, though there may be some religious overtones in the book, the characters are more like creatures than people. Lewis Lawson writes in *Flannery O'Connor* that Haze is like a cartoon character, "unreal" and "a vehicle whose attitudes and actions would personify a spiritual view which [O'Connor] wished to reveal." Critics like Lawson place O'Connor's work in the School of Southern Gothic.

A third school of thought maintains that while religious themes do underlie O'Connor's writing, they appear to have a somewhat satanic influence. Andre Bleikasten, for example, writes in *The Heresy of Flannery O'Connor* "Even though O'Connor defended her use of the grotesque as a necessary strategy of her art, one is left with the impression that in her work it eventually became the means of a savage revilement of the whole of creation…. One may wonder whether her Catholicism was not, to some extent, an alibi for misanthropy. And one may also wonder whether so much black derision is compatible with Christian faith,

and ask what distinguished the extreme bleakness of her vision from plain nihilism."

The reviews published in 1960 reflect the trend towards positive criticism of O'Connor's work that began in 1958 with an article written by Caroline Gordon, O'Connor's friend and mentor. Gordon's views represent the final school of thought on O'Connor's writing. Adherents to this theory claim that O'Connor stands far above other writers in her ability to get to the heart of theological reasoning and to create characters that react realistically to their varying religious instincts. Gordon attacks several of O'Connor's most vocal critics in an issue of *Critique* that is devoted entirely to the work of O'Connor and J. F. Powers, a fellow Catholic. Gordon condemns O'Connor's contemporaries for their inability to create characters or plots that were true to religious doctrine. Gordon believed that O'Connor not only wrote with sincere religious intent, but proficiently portrayed that intent in her characters and plots.

Today, critics applaud O'Connor for her artistry. They recognize *Wise Blood* as a standard against which other writers should measure their work. They praise O'Connor's expert portrayal of the South, her concise and yet lively style, and her distinct ability to use grotesque characterization to emphasize the irony of life. Finally, critics honor her unwavering Christian faith, which underlies all of her writing. They understand that her unfailing belief offers hope for her characters as well as her readers.

Criticism

Jeffrey M. Lilburn

Jeffrey M. Lilburn is a writer and translator specializing in twentieth-century American and Canadian literature. In the following essay, he discusses the themes of faith and religion in Wise Blood.

The world of *Wise Blood* is a spiritually empty, morally blind, cold, and hostile place. Over the years, critics have often referred to Flannery O'Connor's first novel as dark and grotesque. They then use words such as repulsive, depraved, and unredeemable to describe its characters. There can be no denying that the inhabitants of *Wise Blood* are frequently deceptive, chronically unkind, and brutally violent. Both the principal character, Hazel

What Do I Read Next?

- Flannery O'Connor's "Everything that Rises Must Converge," first published in 1964, and included in the 1965 short story collection of the same title, comprises such themes as acculturation, aging, death and dying, disease and health, and the African-American experience. Set in the newly integrated South of the 1960s, it tells the story of Julian, a recent college graduate who is too attached to his mother. His prejudiced mother suffers a stroke during an incident with a black woman, and Julian feels the overwhelming effects of his dependency.

- "The Lame Shall Enter First," another short story included in the *Everything that Rises Must Converge* collection, weaves a disturbing story of a father's misdirected love, and his son's resulting suicide. The widowed father and grieving son seek solace beyond each other's embrace and are both influenced by a disturbed and disfigured young man who claims to be under Satan's power.

- *A Good Man is Hard to Find* is the title story of O'Connor's 1955 short-story collection by the same name. Originally published in 1953, the story is about a self-centered, smug grandmother and her family, who are traveling through the South, where a murderer is rumored to be hiding. When the family wrecks the car, three men confront them; Grandmother recognizes the murderer as "The Misfit." He kills the rest of the family first and then toys with Grandmother's emotions before killing her.

- William Faulkner's *As I Lay Dying,* published in 1930, influenced O'Connor's thinking and writing. Told in a stream-of-consciousness style using grotesque characterization, the story explores the nature of grieving, community, family, and society.

- Nathaniel West's writing also influenced Flannery O'Connor's thinking and style. She recommended *Miss Lonelyhearts,* in particular, to her friends. Published in 1933, the novel concerns a male newspaper columnist who tries desperately to give advice to the lovelorn. When he becomes involved with one of his correspondents, he is killed.

"Haze" Motes, and his young and simple follower, Enoch Emery, inflict and become the victims of acts of violence. Haze murders a man by running him over with his car, while Enoch beats and strips a man for his own personal gain. Yet despite the violence and seemingly unconscionable behavior exhibited by these and other characters, the cast of displaced wanderers who populate *Wise Blood* do have another trait in common: they are searching for something better.

In her Introduction to the second edition of *Wise Blood,* O'Connor describes Hazel Motes as a "Christian malgré lui" (a Christian in spite of himself). At twelve, Haze thought himself destined to become a preacher like his grandfather, but by the time he reaches early adulthood he convinces himself that he does not have a soul. Claiming that he does not "believe in anything," Motes embarks on a desperate mission to rid himself of his deeply rooted Christian beliefs. He founds the Church Without Christ and begins preaching a new jesus that is "all man, without blood to waste." According to Robert Brinkmeyer, Jr., Haze's preaching constitutes his attempt to "sunder forever the body and the spirit." It is also his way of negating the "nameless unplaced guilt" instilled in him during childhood by his mother and grandfather. However, Haze's attempt to eradicate the presence of Jesus from his life is ultimately unsuccessful. For O'Connor, a Christian writer who wrote about Christian concerns, it is Haze's inability to escape Christ and realize his conversion to nothing that raises him above the novel's other characters.

In addition to his religious struggles, Haze must also contend with solitude and homelessness. Upon his release from the army, he returns to his home town of Eastrod, Tennessee, only to find it run down and deserted. When he arrives in Taulkinham the following day, his situation does not improve: he is confronted with the realization that he has no place to go. This rootlessness and sense of displacement is, in fact, a condition shared by most of the novel's characters. Enoch Emery, for example, has only been in Taulkinham for two months and has spent much of his life moving and being moved. The same is true of Asa and Sabbath Hawks, who also move from place to place, begging for money and handing out religious pamphlets. Such widespread and long-lasting restlessness suggest that there is something seriously wrong with the world in which these characters live. It also suggests a common desire for something better.

The link between displacement and the striving for something other, or better, is made explicit when Haze purchases the rundown Essex. He tells the man who sells him the car that he wants it "mostly to be a house" because he "ain't got any place to be." But it becomes evident that Haze buys the car not to provide himself with a place to be, but for its ability to bring him someplace else. He brags that his car will get him anywhere he wants to go, and plans to make a new start in a new city. Such a plan is made possible by "the advantage of having a car," something that could move "to the place you wanted to be."

Significantly, it is also atop the nose of his Essex that Haze preaches his new jesus to a flow of exiting moviegoers. But the faith Haze places in both his car and his new savior is misguided. Instead of becoming the means through which he finds inner peace ("nobody with a good car needs to be justified," he tells Hawks), Haze uses his Essex to maim and kill another human being. The car leads Haze past signs that read "Jesus Saves," but he does not heed them. It is not until the car is destroyed that he recognizes his mistake and ceases to flee that which he knows he must accept. Similarly, it is only when Enoch delivers the manifestation of the new jesus to Haze's door that he recognizes its worthlessness. He realizes, as Margaret Peller Feeley suggests, that his false idol is "merely the incarnation of all people who reject the true God and make a god in their own image."

Like Hazel, Enoch follows a misguided path in an effort to find his reward. Hurt and dejected by the unfriendly reception he has received in Taulkinham, a city where everybody wants "to knock you down," Enoch longs to become a somebody. He wishes to better his condition and be like the young men he sees displayed in insurance ads. But instead of working towards that goal, Enoch buries himself in the rigidity of a daily routine. Even after he steals the "new jesus" from the museum, his brief moment of action is once again followed by passivity. He sits at home waiting for something to happen but, not surprisingly, the fake savior does nothing.

Enoch's final actions are even more pathetic and futile. Impressed by the line of people who wait to meet Gonga, a Hollywood movie star, he dreams of someday seeing a "line of people waiting to shake his hand." Unfortunately, he chooses to realize this dream by borrowing Gonga's persona and stripping the hired gorilla-man of his animal suit. Instead of becoming a somebody, Enoch loses himself completely and disappears into the suit. Such a strategy is doomed, Robert Donahoo argues, because the change is "superficial." According to his reading of the novel, Enoch's bestial transformation is representative of the "American tendency to address a problem by changing its appearance." Enoch's plan ultimately fails, and he is last seen alone and unchanged.

One of the major themes of the novel is faith and religious belief, but for most of the characters faith has become little more than an annoyance that is sold on city streets. It is not a relevant or meaningful part of their lives. Hoover Shoats, for instance, uses religion as a means for commercial profit, preying on the easily manipulated and the easily swayed. He is attracted to Haze's idea of a new jesus, not for any spiritual reasons, but because he thinks it is a lucrative opportunity that simply needs a little promotion. Conversely, Asa Hawks is made uncomfortable by Haze's religious preoccupations and refers to the young anti-preacher as a "Goddam Jesus-hog." Hawks, of course, has personal reasons for disliking Haze's activities—reasons that resurface when Sabbath reminds him that he too was once like Haze but eventually "got over it."

The idea that faith and religious belief are things one must get over, an obstacle to be overcome, is echoed by Mrs. Flood. She is unable to understand Haze's motives for blinding himself or for his walking with rocks in his shoes, much less for the more extreme act of wrapping himself in barbed wire. She tells him that these kinds of acts are no longer done, that they are something people have quit doing. Her attitudes and complacency reflect those of the society around her and provide an important clue as to why so many of the characters in *Wise Blood* are dissatisfied with their current situations. An oft-quoted passage from William Rodney Allen's reading of the novel explains what O'Connor seems to imply. Allen likens secular man living without God's grace to the many caged animals in the novel—both are hopelessly trapped. Stripped of its spiritual dimension, Allen argues that the world "is merely a prison for an odd collection of inmates—a zoo for the human animal."

Haze takes his first real steps away from that zoo after his car is rolled over the embankment. It is at this moment that Haze experiences what many critics agree is his moment of awakening. Staring into the "entire distance that extended from his eyes to the blank grey sky that went on, depth after depth, into space," Haze appears to perceive that which has eluded everyone else. The sky, complete with blinding white clouds with curls and a beard, is frequently described in *Wise Blood* but is never noticed by the people walking beneath it. Brinkmeyer has suggested that these celestial descriptions are the only hints of the divine in the novel. One might even read them as suggesting the presence of God. Whatever it is Haze sees, it is his recognition and appreciation of the depth before him that finally allows him to end his quest for some other place. It is also immediately after this revelation that he decides to blind himself. Allen has suggested that as Haze stares into the distance, his illusion of freedom destroyed, he perceives the dimension of spiritual freedom and blinds himself to see even deeper into that freedom.

But not every critic focusses on the religious aspects of O'Connor's novel. Jon Lance Bacon, for example, offers a reading of the novel that provides a different twist to some of the scenes already discussed. He argues that in *Wise Blood* O'Connor depicts a society pervaded by advertising and marketing techniques. In short, Bacon reads the novel as a critique of American consumer culture. Citing influential texts such as Marshall McLuhan's *The Mechanical Bride,* Bacon discusses the increasing influence that corporate capitalism exerts over individual identity. He observes that the citizens of Taulkinham are inundated with commercial appeals and that the boundaries of the urban setting are defined by electric signs. He offers Enoch as the character most identified with consumerism, describing him as "pathetically vulnerable to advertisers' messages." It is by appropriating the imagery of consumerism, Bacon argues, that Enoch hopes to become a new man; he anticipates a new and improved self, but the ape suit only leads to a loss of identity. Similarly, the value Haze attaches to his car is indicative of his susceptibility to the kind of thinking fostered by consumer society: the ownership of an automobile allows him to conceive himself as a totally free individual. It is only after the car is destroyed, Bacon notes, that he is forced to consider a reality other than the material world.

Still, a reading of O'Connor's fiction must take into account the author's religious concerns. In her introduction to *Three by Flannery O'Connor,* Sally Fitzgerald reminds readers that O'Connor herself thought the novel "a very hopeful book." It is true that Haze's act of self-mutilation does have a positive effect on the selfish and self-centered Mrs. Flood. Her attitudes change when, at the very end of the novel, she begins to feel that she has been cheated of something of a non-material nature. Initially, she felt cheated financially, but when Haze dies she thinks that he may have known something she did not. In the final scene, she stares deeply into the dead man's eyes, hoping to find the way into the pinpoint of light she sees before her. Brinkmeyer argues that this final chapter shows Mrs. Flood's faith slowly emerging; her selfish common sense "giving way to something closer to kindness and charity." Moreover, Feeley reads this as the most affirmative of O'Connor's endings: "That so limited and venal a creature can be moved signifies hope for all." Ultimately, it is up to each reader to decide whether or not hope and affirmation are to be found in O'Connor's twisted tale.

Source: Jeffrey M. Lilburn, in an essay for *Novels for Students,* Gale, 1998.

Gary M. Ciuba

In the following excerpt, Ciuba examines how most of the characters in Wise Blood *are unable to look beyond the surface of people and things. Only Hazel Motes, who himself begins by judging people at "face value," learns how to look beyond the literal and thus understand the divine nature of the universe.*

In *Wise Blood* Flannery O'Connor continually seems to stare at the faces of her characters. She does not just describe and constantly refer to the faces of Haze Motes and his fellow sinners with the hard, sharp eye that served her as a cartoonist in college and with the deep awareness that produced a haunting self-portrait with peacock in later life. She also focuses in vivid detail on the nameless faces of minor figures whose very existence in the novel depends on their description as they are suddenly caught by O'Connor in close-up. Enoch Emery remembers that the Welfare woman who cared for him was not old "'but she sho was ugly. She had theseyer brown glasses and her hair was so thin it looked like ham gravy trickling over her skull.'" A red-haired waitress at Walgreen's has "green eyes set in pink" so that she looks like a picture of a Lime Cherry Surprise, while another at the Paris Diner shows "a big yellow dental plate and the same color hair done up in a black hairnet." A woman with "a square red face and her hair … freshly set" carries a "cat-faced" baby as she listens to Haze preach.

All of these faces in O'Connor's portrait gallery of a novel lack both depth and completeness. As an artist, she flattens a three-dimensional world into two so that her characters resemble Haze's face at the moment it is pressed to the glass of his car watching Asa and his daughter: "a paper face pasted there." Moreover, O'Connor avoids portraying all the features of these faces, preferring to concentrate on striking and invariably ugly physical characteristics. Her extreme selectivity and exaggeration turn characters into spiritual cartoons. The unholy fools of *Wise Blood* exist not so much in the fullness of their flesh and blood but in the reduction to a set of yellow teeth, a pair of icy eyes, a patch of blotchy skin. Yet if O'Connor's gaze obliterates much, it leaves the essentials of the soul to be seen in the distorted outlines of the body.

O'Connor's caricatures illustrate her creed as novelist and believer. In her essays she repeatedly stresses that the writer must start where all human knowledge begins—the senses. Her art does not originate with philosophical questions, abstract problems or social issues but with whatever is near at hand and in front of her face. She quotes with approval Ford Madox Ford's injunction that the novelist cannot have a man appear long enough to sell a newspaper in a story without providing enough detail to make the reader see him. The starting point of literature is thus the literal. Because of her commitment to the surfaces of the world, O'Connor cannot do other than begin with the faces of her characters....

Since her characters so often live on this two-dimensional plane, far removed from their divine origins, she renders their faces in the most superficial terms. In *Wise Blood* O'Connor demonstrates that although literalism is a necessary approach to the world, it is unwise and sometimes even bloody as the final means of understanding it. The mistake that all of her comic caricatures make is that they only take the world at its face value and never really see the value in faces.

O'Connor dramatizes the limits of such literalism at the novel's beginning in the purblind sight of Mrs. Wally Bee Hitchcock. As she sits "facing Motes in the section" of the train, she is forced to look at his deep-set, pecan eyes and prominent skull. Haze's face invites the aspiring visionary to go beyond her sentimentalized faith that "yes, life was an inspiration." Captivated yet baffled by Haze's eyes, drawn continually to them yet irked because she can only try to see into them, Mrs. Hitchcock nearly confronts the tremendous and fascinating realm of the holy in the human world. Yet she never discovers the image and likeness of God in his creation, for she will not surrender herself to the depths beyond depths of Haze's face. Instead, she stubbornly defends herself against its challenge by concentrating only on face value. As she squints at the price tag on the sleeve of Haze's suit, she learns that it "had cost him $11.98. She felt that that placed him and looked at his face again as if she were fortified against it now."

Mrs. Hitchcock can only look at Haze if she abstracts him into a class and category. Having reduced a person to a price tag, she tries to protect herself against the summons from the mystery that she dimly senses by keeping her eye on the surface offered by Haze's face. O'Connor provides the first description of Motes from the viewpoint of Mrs. Hitchcock as if this lady were trying to steel herself against the invitation of his eyes by immersing herself in the superficial details of the rest of his features: shrike's nose, creased mouth and flattened hair. Mrs. Hitchcock prefers to see only the two-dimensional reality directly in front of her face rather than what O'Connor calls "the image at the heart of things." O'Connor represents Mrs. Hitchcock's failure to perceive the world in all its roundness by appropriately flattening her out. Glimpsed by Haze on her way to her berth, her hair a mass of knots and knobs that "framed her face like dark toadstools," she becomes nothing more than surfaces herself in O'Connor's mercilessly precise portraiture.

Mrs. Hitchcock is the first of O'Connor's literalists who, lacking their creator's profounder vision, view the world only on one level. Virtually every other character in the novel repeats her sin....

All of these foolish faces in *Wise Blood* seem blind to Paul's vision of how "we all, with open face beholding as in a glass the glory of the Lord, are changed into the same image from glory to glory, even as by the Spirit of the Lord" (2 Cor. 3:18). However, O'Connor with open face herself shows in Haze how one human image is made to conform to the divine model. Haze Motes develops from the literalism of Enoch Emery to the anagogical vision of Flannery O'Connor. Throughout much of the novel he consistently judges people by their face value. Although one mechanic already warned him that his dilapidated Essex could not be saved, he entrusts it to a huckster at a different garage, "certain that it was in honest hands." The scarred face and dark glasses of Asa Hawks, another salesman of salvation, convince Haze that this fraud once blinded himself for Jesus. The naif cannot understand how such a preacher could have fathered an illegitimate daughter like Sabbath Lily. When Haze looks at her homely face, he wisely reasons that the innocence of Sunday's child, normally full of grace, virtually beckons his blood to seduction. Actually, this paleface with her large, red lips hopes to seduce him because she has never seen a boy that she "'liked the looks of any better.'"

Each fails to lead the other into temptation on their trip into the country. Although Sabbath poses alluringly on the ground, Haze lies a few feet away and covers his face with his hat. His very literalism is a far greater lust, for in the dark this would-be Solomon tries to determine whether a bastard like Sabbath Hawks can be saved in his new religion. He finally concludes, "'There wouldn't be any sense to the word, bastard, in the Church Without Christ.'" His inclusiveness, however, does not result from discovering the Father's prodigal love which transcends all superficial distinctions but from deciding to take language merely at face value. Since Haze believes in the Church Without Christ, he must speak a language without any inherent Logos. The Word, indeed any word, even *bastard,* is just a sound devoid of sense. Hence, sin has no existence outside of speech. When Asa Hawks quite accurately charges Haze with "'Fornication and blasphemy and what else?'" Haze dismisses the accusation, "'They ain't nothing but words … I don't believe in sin.'"

Just as Haze separates word from concept until a name means nothing, he divorces Jesus' humanity from his divinity. His literalism drives him to seek a new jesus, "'one that's all man, without blood to waste.'" This jesus is purely human, for Haze's nihilism denies the plenitude of being which characterizes divinity. A jesus who cannot spend himself extravagantly is hardly God. The consequence of rejecting the incarnation is that there may be crucifixion but no resurrection, suffering but no redemption. Such a divorce destroys all significance, leaving behind merely emptied physical signs. "'Where in your time and your body has Je-

sus redeemed you?'" Haze asks the few faces who listen to him for proof in the flesh. "'Show me where because I don't see the place.'" Salvation becomes as meaningless as sin if the senses provide the sole guide to reality. When someone seems to suggest that the site of salvation may be in the conscience, Haze warns that conscience must be hunted and killed "'because it's no more than your face in the mirror is.'" Since Haze's face values exalt the letter over the spirit, Enoch brings him a literal version of his new jesus. A jesus without blood to waste is nothing more than an embalmed corpse. Haze's word for word reading of the world eliminates the divine Word so that only dead flesh and hollowed language remain.

Such blindness causes Haze constantly to overlook the visible features of the invisible God. He lives in the desert of Eliot's "Ash-Wednesday" where there is "No place of grace for those who avoid the face." Throughout his aborted idyll with Sabbath, he misses the significance of the brilliant white cloud "with curls and a beard" that follows his car. As Richard Giannone notes [in *Thought,* Vol. 59, 1984], the portrait in the heavens recalls the face of Moses, which glowed so brightly with divine glory that he had to veil it from the Israelites. Again God shows his presence by shining forth upon his creation, but *Hazel,* Hebrew for "he who sees God," puts on his own veil by covering his face with his hat.

Always in the dark, Haze misses another theophany when the car that he trusted to the supposedly honest mechanic breaks down. A one-armed attendant of a service station gives him a can of gas and his car a push—all gratis. These freely done services shine forth as rare and mysterious acts of goodness in a novel where so many prophets are profiteers. Like Haze but in a radically different sense, this good man so hard to find works for nothing. But his gratuitous kindness only provokes one more expression of Haze's nihilistic egotism. "'I don't need no favors from him,'" Haze boasts to save face. And when Sabbath praises his Essex, he completes the oneupsmanship of his lame triumph, "'It ain't been built by a bunch of foreigners or niggers or one-arm men.'" Haze can only respond to this stranger's generosity by labelling his appearance. Such reductionism removes the attendant's graciousness from the realm of amazing grace so that he becomes nothing more than what is observed, a man with one arm. By taking him at his face value Haze avoids an encounter with mystery which might expose his true dependency and demand that he bestow favor on others.

Despite his reduction of salvation to the superficial, Haze hears a call to see beyond the surface. He escapes being another of the novel's spiritual caricatures by becoming what Lewis A. Lawson calls [in his *Another Generation: Southern Fiction since World War II,* 1984] "an oxymoron as character." Haze searches for the value in faces *malgré lui.* As if the need for such wisdom were in his blood, he has the same face as his grandfather, a fiery fundamentalist preacher. The way he sits on the train in chapter one typifies his spiritual posture throughout the novel: he strains forward to see. He especially longs to look into the eyes of Asa Hawks that are hidden by dark glasses. And although he gives Asa's daughter the fast eye, he sends her a note that demonstrates a deeper understanding of language than Enoch's taking each word at its face value: "BABE, I NEVER SAW ANYBODY THAT LOOKED AS GOOD AS YOU BEFORE IS WHY I CAME HERE." When this rare good woman asks him whether he meant the adjective in its physical or moral sense, he answers, "'The both.'" A confirmed literalist like Enoch would not even perceive a possible pun.

Since Haze recognizes such double dimensions as well as constantly resists them, his literalism makes him half right rather than completely wrong. His attention to surfaces could become the starting point for a return to the divine source on which O'Connor always keeps her eye. When he criticizes a crowd so apathetic to the atonement that even if Jesus had saved them, "'You wouldn't do nothing about it. Your faces wouldn't move, neither this way nor that,'" he is as much insightful as overly insistent. He may emphasize appearance too much, but he recognizes that redemption should transform the stoney expressions of their spiritually stolid lives.

O'Connor forces Haze to face the limits of his literalism in two scenes that demonstrate the absurdity of taking the world at face value. After putting on his mother's glasses, Haze sees in the mirror "his mother's face in his." He hastens to take off the spectacles, for he recognizes his own sinfulness in the accusing image of his guilt-obsessed parent. Yet before he can remove them, "the door opened and two more faces floated into his line of vision." Sabbath enters the room like a mock-Madonna, cradling the pseudo-savior of Enoch Emery whom she shows Haze as his own child. O'Connor stages a horribly fitting Christmas tableau for Haze's new religion. In the Church Without Christ, the Virgin with Child becomes a whore with a dwarfed corpse, and Haze, the founder and father of lies, plays the role of daddy to a dead god.

Haze stares at this burlesque nativity with his head "thrust forward as if he had to use his whole face to see with" and then lunges at the "squinting face" of his shrivelled infant. The mommy and the mummy reflect the same image which Haze just spied in the looking glass. Glimpsing the depths of his own nothingness, he destroys the empty offspring of sin which his whole nihilistic faith has fathered. The iconoclast seems to brace himself for a blow of retribution, but it does not come immediately. He tries to flee in his car the truth of Sabbath's charge that he has never wanted anything except Jesus, but his flight ends in an about-face so that his way is God-ward (2 Cor. 3:4).

The violence which Haze expected as punishment is also a stroke of good fortune. Although O'Connor mentions that Haze was driving very fast, the patrolman offers neither speeding nor travelling on the wrong side of the road as reasons for stopping him. Rather, he simply says, "'I just don't like your face,'" and calmly pushes Haze's car over the cliff. Even if the officer's summary justice results from seeing "the ramshackle car and its unlicensed driver as a public threat" [Sr. Kathleen Feely notes in *Flannery O'Connor: Voice of the Peacock,* 1972], his method of law enforcement is so extreme that mere motives cannot adequately explain it. The very perverseness is O'Connor's point, for the scene dramatizes the consequences of living in a world where appearance has become the absolute law. When reality extends no farther than the surface, a person's face provides sufficient justification for pronouncing last judgment.

O'Connor could have planned no more appropriate climax for Haze's career. Having taken the world at face value, he is himself taken at face value. He suffers because of his own sin, but the effect of this chastisement is revelatory. As he gazes into the blank sky, he comes face to face with his own void. "His face didn't change and he didn't turn it toward the patrolman. It seemed to be concentrated on space." However, this vision is decidedly not superficial, for the empty heavens extend "depth after depth, into space." Haze "sees beyond the visage of evil," Jonathan Baumbach observes [in *The Landscape of Nightmare: Studies in the Contemporary American Novel,* 1965], "the ugly veil masking the real world, to the sight of limitless space—a manifestation of the infinite." In the face of such a sublime panorama, Haze discovers his profound nothingness. For the rest of his life he must submit himself to the consuming power of this same three-dimensional negation, converting physical deprivation into spiritual purification.

The superficial Mrs. Flood cannot understand such a paradoxical road to salvation. In words that might be applicable to virtually every literalist in the novel, O'Connor comments that Haze's landlady "was not a woman who felt more violence in one word than in another; she took every word at its face value but all the faces were the same." Mrs. Flood reads life word for word and understands each as a repetition of its predecessor. By turning God's word into just another linguistic face in the crowd, she denies the saving presence of the Logos which assumed a human image. Obsessed with Haze's face, she tries to take him at face value, yet she consistently fails to categorize or understand him. She notices that his "face had a peculiar pushing look, as if it were going forward after something it could just distinguish in the distance," but her own eyes prove that Haze surely cannot see: he has burned out his sight with lime. When he explains that he does penance because "'I'm not clean,'" Mrs. Flood, blind to the figurative dimension of language, replies, "'I know it … you got blood on that night shirt and on the bed. You ought to get you a washwoman.'"

Mrs. Flood recognizes sight but not insight, physical but not spiritual cleanliness. Haze has moved beyond such a literal view. He has turned the facial vision often developed by the blind into the gaze of a soul which has turned its face to God. His strange and violent actions force his landlady to search for the divine dimensions that she prefers to ignore. Holding his dead body, she struggles to go beyond face value. She peers into his face, now just a skull beneath the skin, and tries to penetrate the deep tunnels of his eyes. Although Mrs. Flood has not yet attained Haze's beatific vision, she has at least become dissatisfied with her former way of reading the world. If she could ever get beyond "the beginning of something she couldn't begin," Mrs. Flood might discover like Jacob (Gn. 33:10) the truth which O'Connor's own artistry incarnates: seeing the face of a man in all its graciousness could be like beholding the very countenance of God.

Source: Gary M. Ciuba, "From Face Value to the Value in Faces: *Wise Blood* and the Limits of Literalism," in *Modern Language Studies,* Vol. XIX, No. 3, Summer, 1989, pp. 72–80.

Daniel F. Littlefield

In the following excerpt, Littlefield explores how the materialism of modern society shown in Wise Blood *helps articulate O'Connor's major themes of Christian redemption and the grotesque.*

Much of the Criticism of Flannery O'Connor's *Wise Blood* (1952) has centered around her themes. For the most part, such criticism has illustrated and therefore confirmed, through analyses of her fiction, what Miss O'Connor had said about herself: that as a writer she is orthodox Christian (specifically Catholic), that her major theme in fiction is the redemption of man by Christ, and that she depicts the grotesque in society.

But the critics have ignored a significant point of her personal philosophy that appears as a motif in her fiction: that material prosperity has had ill effects on man's spiritual well-being. It is basic to the grotesqueness in modern society, it stunts man's spiritual growth, and it makes man's salvation more difficult, if not impossible. *Wise Blood* is her longest and most significant rendering of these ideas although they clearly appear in many of her other works.…

Wise Blood takes as its theme the redemption of man by Christ, a theme basic to most of O'Connor's work. It is the story of Hazel Motes, "a Christian *malgré lui*," who in his attempt to deny his belief in Christ establishes his Church Without Christ, but who cannot avoid the visitation of grace upon him and subsequently blinds himself to "justify" his belief in Christ. The reader sees in Hazel, as well as in the other characters, a grotesqueness, a distortion of spiritual purpose that O'Connor speaks of.…

The major characters—Hazel Motes, Enoch Emory, Asa Hawks, Sabbath Lily Hawks, Hoover Shoats, Mrs. Flood—all have one thing in common; they are all motivated by religion in one way or another. Melvin J. Friedman says [in "Flannery O'Connor: Another Legend in Southern Fiction," in *Flannery O'Connor,* ed. Robert E. Reiter] that "Hazel Motes meets a succession of false religionists and we are intended to measure the sincerity of his convictions against the hypocrisy of theirs." He includes Enoch among the hypocrites, but as will be shown later, Enoch is every bit as sincere as Haze (he was worshipping the new jesus, even though he did not know what it was, before he heard Haze preach). The significant thing here is that the division of characters into the sincere and hypocritical also separates the characters according to the way in which material prosperity affects their motives: the latter pursue it as an end while the former use it (though often symbolically) as a means to an end.

Prosperity does not mean wealth here, for as Miss O'Connor has said, most of her characters are poor. No character in this novel attains material prosperity, but a number of them *pursue* it. As a basis of that pursuit, most of them use religion—either a perversion or distortion of Christianity or religion in general. They adopt the tone and jargon of the high-pressure salesman and offer the people the "bargain" or the "something-for-nothing" routine.

Early in the novel the reader finds a man selling potato peelers on the street. He draws a crowd and offers his "bargain" to them. Then Asa Hawks and his daughter Sabbath Lily appear on the scene. She is handing out pamphlets that say "Jesus Calls You" (one is reminded here of the Uncle Sam posters), and he is begging, using religion as his persuader: "Help a blind preacher. If you won't repent, give up a nickel." The potato peeler salesman recognizes immediately that Hawks has a "gimmick" or a "racket," that he is hawking his wares, as his name implies, just as if they were potato peelers. The salesman says, "What the hell do you think you are doing?... I got these people together, how do you think you can horn in?" In other words, he recognizes Hawks for what he is—business competition. Hawks is an ex-evangelist of sorts who ten years before had promised his congregation to blind himself to justify his belief in Jesus. But his nerve had failed. Since that time he has faked blindness, which he uses to gain sympathy in begging. Here obviously is a man whose sense of spiritual purpose is distorted; yet, ironically, he has insight into Haze's problem. When Hawks first meets Haze, he says, "I can hear the urge for Jesus in his voice." Haze curses him and he says, "Listen boy, ... you can't run away from Jesus. Jesus is a fact."

Sabbath Lily Hawks helps her father beg by handing out pamphlets. She is a fifteen-year-old bastard who spouts perverted scriptures ("A bastard shall not enter the kingdom of heaven!") and tells gruesome tales about Jesus's visitation of horrible punishment on the sinful. She is "pure filthy right down to the guts...." She tells Haze, "I like being that way, and I can teach you how to like it. Don't you want to learn how to like it?" Through Sabbath, O'Connor makes significant commentary on one aspect of our prosperous society: the panacean approach to moral and spiritual problems. In this case, it takes the form of the love-lorn column in the newspaper. She writes Mary Brittle to find out if she should "neck" or not. Since she is a bastard and bastards do not enter the kingdom of heaven, she wants to know what difference it makes. Mary replies, "'Light necking is acceptable, but I think your real problem is one of adjustment to the modern world. Perhaps you ought to re-examine your religious values to see if they meet your needs in Life. A religious experience can be a beautiful addition to living if you put it in the proper perspective and do not let it warf you. Read some good books on Ethical Culture!'" As if this were not enough, O'Connor gives Sabbath's reply to it: "'What I really want to know is should I go the whole hog or not? That's my real problem. I'm adjusted okay to the modern world.'" Here we see the humorous and the serious, the normal and the abnormal—in short, the grotesque. But the ironic truth is that, for O'Connor, Sabbath *is* "adjusted okay to the modern world" to the extent that it has produced this spiritual chaos in which she and the other characters wander.

Hoover Shoats, alias Onnie J. Holy, sees this panacean approach to spiritual problems as a money-making "gimmick." He knows that Haze's Church Without Christ is an idea to capitalize upon, and he wants to form a business partnership with Haze. One night when Haze begins to lose his crowd, Shoats steps in and begins the pre-selling technique of selling himself: "I want to tell you all about me." Then he gives a testimonial about what the Prophet (Haze) has done for him. He follows that with the "something-for-nothing" technique: "I'm not selling a thing, I'm giving something away!" Shoats then preaches the value of the Church of Christ Without Christ (a change in title which Haze does not like). Like any good salesman, he tries to create faith in his product and make it appealing: "... you can absolutely trust this church—it's based on the Bible." Each member can "interpit" the Bible any way he chooses. The church is also up-to-date. Shoats then asks for the dollar it takes to become a member. And what is a dollar? "A few dimes! Not too much to pay to unlock that little rose of sweetness inside you!"

Shoats gives Haze his qualifications for the business partnership. He once had a radio program called "Soulsease," fifteen minutes of "Mood, Melody, and Mentality," the title of which sounds more like a commercial for a mattress manufacturer than a program of spiritual inspiration. He sees that the idea of a new jesus has possibilities: "All it would need is a little promotion." But Haze rejects the partnership and slams the car door on Shoats's thumb. Shoats threatens, "I'm going to run you out of business. I can get my own new jesus and I can get Prophets for peanuts...." He then hires Solace

Layfield, who looks like Haze and has a car like Haze's, to pose as the True Prophet. Thus, Miss O'Connor again reveals the distorted sense of spiritual purpose in the form of commercialized religion.

Mrs. Flood, Haze's landlady, also pursues material prosperity as an end. She plans to take advantage of Haze's blindness and asceticism. Since he has no use for money, she plans to marry him in order to get control of his government pension. When the policemen kill Haze, she feels that she has been cheated in some way, but in what way she is not sure.

The two characters who use material prosperity, though often symbolically, as a means to an end are Enoch Emory and Hazel Motes, the central character. Enoch's ambition is "to become something. He wanted to better his condition until he was the best. He wanted to be THE young man of the future, like the ones in the insurance ads. He wanted, some day, to see a line of people waiting to shake his hand." The achievement of this goal will be his reward from the new jesus. All of his actions are motivated by his religion.

The symbols most closely related to Enoch are those of the city and its institutions—the zoo, the park, the pool, the museum—and the movie theatre, all of which represent the leisure afforded by the prosperous society. When we first meet Emory, he tells Haze that he has been in Taulkinham only two months and that he already works for the city. We find that he works at the zoo and that his life has become the routine life of modern society.

This routine is best revealed in his worship of the new jesus, which he had discovered but did not recognize until he heard Haze preach. His religious ritual becomes a daily routine, all of which takes place in and involves those institutions maintained by the city: "Every day when he got off duty, he went into the park, and every day when he went in, he did the same things." He goes to the pool and hides in the bushes to watch women. This is among the things he must do to "build up to" visiting the center of the park. His next step is to go to the FROSTY BOTTLE, "a hotdog stand in the shape of an Orange Crush...." There he makes suggestive remarks to the waitress who he thinks secretly loves him. The FROSTY BOTTLE, a symbol of crass commercialism (and, therefore, material prosperity) intruding upon ground usually denied it, becomes a part of his religious ritual. His next stop is the zoo where he looks at the animals with awe and hate. He has to go by them before he can proceed with the ritual. He feels that they wait "evil-eyed for him, ready to throw him off time." One is reminded here of what was evidently one of Miss O'Connor's favorite quotations from St. Cyril of Jerusalem: "The dragon sits by the side of the road, watching those who pass. Beware lest he devour you. We go to the Father of Souls, but it is necessary to pass by the dragon." The animals are the dragon he has to pass to get to his new jesus. The temple of worship, in which dwells the new jesus (a mummified man, three feet long), is called M V S E V M, and Enoch shivers to pronounce it: "Muvseevum."

Enoch steals the new jesus for Haze, expecting a reward for his action to follow: "He pictured himself, after it was over, as an entirely new man, with an even better personality than he had now." Ironically, he is later transformed, and he finds his method of achieving that transformation on his way to deliver the new jesus to Haze. In front of a movie marquee he sees Gonga the gorilla, a great movie star. Enoch immediately recognizes Gonga as a symbol of success in the modern world. Here is someone who has "become something." Moreover, he has a long line of children waiting to shake hands with him. This product of the motion-picture industry becomes Enoch's motivating force. He usurps the position of the man in the gorilla suit by evidently killing him and stealing the suit in an effort to realize his ambitions.

With Hazel Motes, as with Enoch, material prosperity is basic to the achievement of his goal—to establish the Church Without Christ. The major symbol here is the automobile, perhaps *the* symbol (if there is such a thing) of the modern, mechanized, prosperous world. Haze's car is an old Essex with one door tied on, a horn that does not work, and windshield wipers that "clatter like two idiots clapping in church." In the car-buying scene, O'Connor sends the reader through the sales routines again. There is the haggling over prices; the salesman demonstrates how the car runs and stresses its quality. He wouldn't take a Chrysler for it, and it wasn't made by a "bunch of niggers" or, as Haze later says, Jews or one-armed men.

That Miss O'Connor devotes a chapter to this event is significant. The car becomes literally and figuratively the rock upon which Haze builds his church. Literally, it *is* his church. He climbs up on the hood and preaches his Church Without Christ, just as his grandfather had preached from the hood of his old Ford. Figuratively, it becomes the symbol of his disavowing the existence of Christ. When he finds that Asa Hawks has supposedly blinded himself to justify his belief in Jesus, he says, "Nobody with a good car needs to be justified." It becomes his escape, literally from Taulkinham and figuratively from Christ. It is what saves him from a visitation of grace. After the patrolman pushes the Essex over the hill and destroys it, Haze gives himself over to Christ, blinds himself to justify his belief, and mortifies his flesh by wearing barbed wire around his chest and putting rocks and glass in his shoes. He has no concern for money, and even throws it away. Material prosperity makes man's salvation more difficult or impossible. The only one saved is Haze, and that is possible only after a long struggle and after he loses his car—the symbol of material prosperity....

Miss O'Connor devotes very little space in *Wise Blood* to filling in the details of the setting within which these characters move. However, she quite often focuses our attention on certain details that relate to the motifs and images of the prosperous society. Throughout the novel is an emphasis on money. On the first page we find the lady on the train squinting to see the price tag on Haze's suit. There are the street venders and the used-car salesmen who haggle over prices. We are even told to the cent how much Shoats and Layfield make and what Layfield's salary is. The examples are endless. There is also an emphasis on commercialism in the form of advertising. One of the first things Haze sees in Taulkinham is signs: "PEANUTS, WESTERN UNION, AJAX, TAXI, HOTEL, CANDY." Several times O'Connor brings to our attention the CCC snuff and the 666 (a cure-all patent medicine) advertisements that appear on the roadsides. She also tells us of a cow dressed as a housewife and of calendars that advertise funeral homes and tire manufacturers. The FROSTY BOTTLE is itself an advertisement. Such details are used to purpose in a novel that contains so few details of setting. They support the motifs and images of material prosperity that underlie the themes of this novel.

In *Wise Blood,* Miss O'Connor presents her basic theme of the redemption of man by Christ. That redemption is difficult because of the distorted sense of moral purpose in the characters. They wander in moral and spiritual chaos, and only one of them is redeemed. The rest remain grotesque and bestial. In her presentation of these themes, as well as the characters and their motives, Miss O'Connor uses symbols, images, and details drawn from the society of "unparalleled prosperity," a society which provides little assurance of the joy of life. Thus, she produces in *Wise Blood* an underlying theme that material prosperity is basic to the spiritual chaos which she felt was rampant in our society.

Source: Daniel F. Littlefield, Jr., "Flannery O'Connor's *Wise Blood:* 'Unparalleled Prosperity' and Spiritual Chaos," in *The Mississippi Quarterly,* Vol. XXIII, No. 2, Spring, 1970, pp. 121–33.

Sources

William Rodney Allen, "The Cage of Matter: The World as Zoo in Flannery O'Connor's 'Wise Blood,'" in *American Literature,* Vol. 58, No. 2, May, 1986, pp. 256-70.

Jon Lance Bacon, "A Fondness for Supermarkets: 'Wise Blood' and Consumer Culture," in *New Essays on 'Wise Blood,'* edited by Michael Kreyling, Cambridge University Press, 1995, pp. 25-49.

Andre Bleikasten, "The Heresy of Flannery O'Connor," in *Critical Essays on Flannery O'Connor,* edited by Melvin J. Friedman and Beverly Lyon Clark, G. K. Hall, 1985, pp. 138-58.

Robert H. Brinkmeyer, Jr., "'Jesus, Stab Me in the Heart': Wise Blood, Wounding, and Sacramental Aesthetics," in *New Essays on "Wise Blood,"* edited by Michael Kreyling, Cambridge University Press, 1995, pp. 71-89.

Robert Donahoo, "The Problem with Peelers: 'Wise Blood' as Social Criticism," in *Flannery O'Connor Bulletin,* Vol. 21, 1992, pp. 43-57.

Margaret Peller Feeley, "Flannery O'Connor's 'Wise Blood': The Negative Way," in *Southern Quarterly,* Vol. 17, No. 2, 1979, pp. 104-22.

M. J. Fitzgerald, review in *Reference Guide to American Literature,* 3rd edition, St. James Press, 1994, p. 1058.

Sally Fitzgerald, "Introduction to 'Three by Flannery O'Connor,'" in *Three by Flannery O'Connor,* Signet Classic, 1983, pp. vii-xxxiv.

Marshall Gentry, "The Eye vs. the Body: Individual and Communal Grotesquerie in *Wise Blood,*" in *Modern Fiction Studies,* Vol. 28, No. 3, Autumn, 1982, pp. 487-93.

Caroline Gordon, "Flannery O'Connor's Wise Blood," in *Critique,* Vol. 2, 1958, pp. 3-10.

Michael Kreyling, "Introduction," in *New Essays on Wise Blood,* edited by Michael Kreyling, Cambridge University Press, 1995, p. 21.

Lewis Lawson, "Flannery O'Connor and the Grotesque: *Wise Blood,*" in *Flannery O'Connor,* edited by Robert Reiter, B. Herder Books, c. 1968, p. 52.

Daniel Littlefield, "Flannery O'Connor's Wise Blood: 'Unparalleled Prosperity' and Spiritual Chaos," in *Mississippi Quarterly,* Vol. 23, No. 2, Spring, 1970, p. 122.

Erik Nielsen, "The Hidden Structure of Wise Blood," in *New Orleans Review,* Vol. 19, Nos. 3 & 4, Fall & Winter, 1992, pp. 91-97.

Flannery O'Connor, "The Fiction Writer and His Country," in *The Living Novel: A Symposium,* edited by Granville Hicks, Macmillan, 1957, pp. 161-63.

Flannery O'Connor, *Mystery and Manners: Occasional Prose,* edited by Sally and Robert Fitzgerald, Farrar, Straus & Giroux, 1979, pp. 43-44.

Flannery O'Connor, *Wise Blood,* Noon Day Press, 1990.

Isaac Rosenfeld, "To Win by Default," in *New Republic,* July 7, 1952, pp. 19-20.

For Further Study

John Byars, "Notes and Discussion: Mimicry and Parody in *Wise Blood*," in *College Literature,* Vol. 11, No. 3, 1984, pp. 276-79.
    A review that describes ironies in the novel that O'Connor communicates through the use of twins: grandfather, Layfield, and Hawks. Byars also supports O'Connor's use of parody through various animal incidents.

Robert Fitzgerald, "Introduction" to *Everything That Rises Must Converge,* Farrar, Straus & Giroux, 1965.
    Fitzgerald shares his personal memories of O'Connor as a close family friend. He describes her difficult times with lupus and provides insight into some of her writing.

Robert Golden and Mary Sullivan, *Flannery O'Connor and Caroline Gordon: A Reference Guide,* G. K. Hall, 1977.
    This book provides a complete guide to reviews, articles, and books about Flannery O'Connor and her work. In addition, the introduction written by Golden explains criticism of O'Connor's works in terms of four schools of thought about the religious issues they raise.

Laura Kennedy, "Exhortation in *Wise Blood:* Rhetorical Theory as an Approach to Flannery O'Connor," in *Flannery O'Connor: New Perspectives,* edited by Sura Rath and Mary Shaw, University of Georgia Press, 1996, pp. 152-68.
    Kennedy explains the three distinguishable features of exhortative discourse and demonstrates how O'Connor's work meets the requirements.

Robert Phillips, *Coping with Lupus,* Avery, 1991.
    This book provides an explanation of lupus and the ways it can affect the body. Along with a straight-forward description of the function of the body's immune system, the book also addresses other effects on people—emotional, relational, and financial.

Jonathan Witt, "*Wise Blood* and the Irony of Redemption," in *The Flannery O'Connor Bulletin,* Vol. 22, 1993-94, pp. 12-24.
    This article presents evidence for the redemptive theme in the novel. The characters' names and their images take on new meaning through Witt's description.

A Yellow Raft in Blue Water

Michael Dorris

1987

Published in 1987, *A Yellow Raft in Blue Water* was Michael Dorris's first novel. Though the author went on to write six other works of fiction (including three young adult novels and a book of short stories) his first novel is generally considered his finest. *A Yellow Raft in Blue Water* is especially admired for his layered technique of telling the same story from multiple points of view. According to critic Louis Owens, Dorris borrowed that method from his wife, Louise Erdrich, a fellow writer and Native American who uses it in both *Love Medicine* and *The Beet Queen.* Dorris's novel, however, says Owens, "generates an impact sharper and stronger than either of [Erdrich's]." Although reviewers like Michiko Kakutani criticized Dorris for withholding key information from the plot in order to create a "false suspense," the critics' consensus is that what keeps readers involved is the vividly drawn characters rather than any formulaic mystery novel devices. A particular strength in the book is Dorris's portrayal of Indians who are neither stereotyped traditionalists nor mouthpieces for Red Power, but rather human beings in many ways like everyone else, trying to find their places in the world. As such they exemplify not just the clash between different cultures, but some of the great themes of fiction, whether it be the search for identity, the struggle within the self between strengths and weaknesses of character, or the clash of different cultures.

Author Biography

Michael Dorris was born on January 30, 1945, in either Louisville, Kentucky, or Dayton, Washington, the son of Jim and Mary Besy (Burkhardt) Dorris. Part Modoc on his father's side, he grew up on reservations in Montana and Kentucky. He graduated from Georgetown University with a B.A. cum laude in 1967. At Georgetown he studied theater, English, and the classics, and also developed a strong interest in cultural anthropology. Dorris received a M.Ph. from Yale University in 1970. Dorris began his academic career as an assistant professor of anthropology at the University of Redlands in California. Dorris then spent a year at Franconia College in New Hampshire before settling at Dartmouth College in Hanover, NH. He began there as an instructor in 1972 and rose to become chair of the Native American studies department (1979-1985); chair of the Master of Arts in Liberal Studies program (1982-1985); and professor of anthropology (1979-1988).

During this period, Dorris also received numerous fellowships, including a Danforth (1967); Woodrow Wilson (1967, 1980); National Institute of Mental Health (NIMH) (1970); Guggenheim (1978); and Rockefeller (1985-86). He also won an Indian Achievement Award and the *Choice* Magazine Award for Outstanding Academic Book of 1984-85 for *A Guide to Research on North American Indians. A Yellow Raft in Blue Water* won a best book citation from the American Library Association in 1988.

Dorris married writer Louis Erdrich in 1981, and they had six children, one of whom, his adopted son (called Adam in the book), was the subject of Dorris's nonfiction book *The Broken Cord: A Family's Ongoing Struggle with Fetal Alcohol Syndrome.* The book received the National Book Critics Circle Award in 1989 and was also made into an award-winning television film.

In practicality, through all of these efforts Dorris and Erdrich worked as a remarkably close editorial team. Under their system, whoever wrote the first draft received authorial credit, with the other spouse acting as editor. The dedication of *A Yellow Raft in Blue Water* is "For Louise: Companion through every page, Through every day, Compeer." Erdrich wrote the foreword to *The Broken Cord* and the two are listed as co-authors on two later books, *The Crown of Columbus,* (for which they received a $1.5 million advance, though the book did not live up to its advance publicity) and *Route Two and Back,* both published in 1991.

Michael Dorris

Beginning from his days as a single parent, Dorris's concern for children was evident in his life, his writing, and his charitable activities. In addition to being the adoptive father of many children, he wrote two young adult novels, *Morning Girl* (1992), which won the American Library Association Scott O'Dell Award and was named to five best books lists, and *Guests* (1995). Dorris also served as an advisory board member of Save the Children Foundation and on the U.S. Advisory Committee on Infant Mortality.

Despite these admirable achievements, Dorris's life was fraught with hardship. In 1991, his adopted son Reynold Abel died after being hit by a car. In 1995, another adopted son, Jeffrey, was tried for attempting to extort $15,000 from him. Adding to these strains, in 1997 he separated from his wife and was under investigation for child sexual abuse. Dorris committed suicide on April 11, 1997 in Concord, New Hampshire, by suffocating himself with a plastic bag in a motel room.

Plot Summary

Michael Dorris's *A Yellow Raft in Blue Water* describes the lives of three Native American women. Dorris complicates the novel, however, by having each woman narrate one section of the story from her own perspective with each woman's story adding new layers of meaning to their collective intergenerational saga. In addition, Dorris further complicates the plot by presenting the three stories in reverse order with Rayona, the "granddaughter," telling her story first, followed by her mother, Christine, and then her "grandmother," Aunt Ida. Consequently, Dorris's novel reads like a complex mystery, and the reader must carefully piece together its plot by continually uncovering new information and reassessing previous information as the story unfolds backwards in time.

Rayona's Story

Rayona begins her account by describing a typical fight between her Native American mother, Christine, and her African American father, Elgin, who is making one of his infrequent visits to see Christine while she is sick in the hospital. This fight, however, causes Christine to explode with anger because Elgin wants to divorce her and remarry a younger African American woman. Raging, Christine escapes from the hospital in a candy-striper's uniform and threatens to commit suicide by crashing her car to collect the insurance money. Fortunately, this attempted suicide is frustrated when her car runs out of gas, and Christine is forced to adopt a more rational plan: to leave Seattle, return to a reservation in Montana, and live with her "mother" Ida, who insists that she be called "Aunt Ida" instead of mother because Christine was born out of wedlock. In one of the novel's funniest sections, Rayona describes how the only attachment keeping Christine in Seattle is her lifetime membership at Village Video, which Christine bought because it was on sale even though she did not have a VCR. Christine reluctantly leaves the lifetime membership behind in Seattle but not without renting a couple of videos "for life" on the way out of town.

Christine and Rayona arrive at Aunt Ida's only to be greeted with another fight, which also ends in harsh words and Christine running away. Unable to catch her fleeing mom, Rayona ends up stranded with Ida who is a virtual stranger. For awhile, a young priest named Father Tom befriends Rayona and arranges for her to attend school and religious meetings with other youth on the reservation, but the priest ends up making sexual advances at Rayona en route to a religious revival. After they cool off, Rayona tells Father Tom that she does not want to return to the reservation, and he encourages her

and gives her money for a return ticket to Seattle. However, Rayona skips the train, pockets the cash, and stays in the area. She eventually meets Sky and Evelyn, who help her find a job at a state park and rent her a room in their trailer.

After a couple weeks, Evelyn and Sky help Rayona attempt to find her mother at a rodeo in a nearby town. The first person Rayona meets at the rodeo, however, is Foxy Cree, a boy who had ridiculed her back at the reservation school. After admitting that he is too drunk to perform his scheduled ride in the rodeo, Foxy asks Rayona to take his place, and Rayona agrees. Even though she rides poorly, she demonstrates enough determination that the judges award her a special consolation prize. When she goes to accept her award, however, everyone discovers that she is a woman, and she is quickly surrounded by all of her acquaintances: Evelyn, Sky, Foxy, Father Tom, and Dayton, the man who is now living with her mother. Dayton agrees to take Rayona back to his place to see her mother.

Christine's Story

After Rayona and Christine are reunited, Christine begins her story with an account of the night when she loses her faith in God because the mission nuns try to scare her into good behavior by convincing her that the world is going to end on New Year's Eve. Her devout faith is shattered, however, when the anticipated doomsday never arrives, and the nuns' only explanation is that a mystery prevented it. This memory leads Christine to other events from her childhood: the dangerous stunts that she performs to impress her brother Lee and his friends, and the rivalry that develops when Lee forms a new friendship with Dayton. Gradually, Dayton and Ida convince Lee to embrace his Native American identity while Christine assimilates mainstream America's values and fashions. When the Vietnam War breaks out, these differences cause Christine to support the war and Lee to oppose it, but Christine ultimately gets her way by convincing Dayton that Lee must enlist if he hopes to be respected as a tribal leader. Reluctantly, Lee enlists only to be killed in Vietnam, and meanwhile Christine uses an Indian relocation program to move to Seattle.

When news of Lee's death reaches Christine, she seeks solace in a bar where she meets an African American man named Elgin. Elgin initially consoles her, but solace quickly turns into sex and passionate romance. Eventually, Christine lets Elgin get her pregnant, and they decide to get married only to have the relationship turn sour. As Christine's pregnancy progresses, their passion becomes mixed up with various infidelities, accusations, lies, and hostilities. After Rayona is born, Christine raises her, but her relationship with Elgin and her personal stability continue to slide downhill. Her life in Seattle drifts further and further from her previous life on the reservation, and her periodic contact with the reservation only seems to accentuate her distance from it. She returns to the reservation for Lee's funeral only to feel blamed for causing his death, and Aunt Ida spends an uncomfortable week with her in Seattle while visiting a dying relative named Clara.

Ida's Story

In the final section, Ida reveals several surprises that not only fill in gaps in the story but also force the reader to reevaluate other aspects of the story in light of this new information. To begin with, Ida explains that she is not really Christine's mother after all. Christine's real mother is Clara, an aunt who came to take care of Ida's ill mother but ended up getting impregnated by Ida's father instead. To cover up the illicit pregnancy, Ida's father sent Clara and Ida to Denver where Clara could have the baby out of sight, and he instructed Ida to claim to be the baby's real mother when they returned. They planned for Clara to return with Ida and take primary responsibility for raising the child, but later Clara decided to remain in Denver and left Ida to raise Christine all by herself. Several years later, Clara did return to reclaim Christine in hopes of making money by putting her up for adoption, but Father Hurlburt helped Ida claim legal rights over Christine because she has raised Christine as her own daughter.

In addition, Ida also reveals the identity of Lee's father. After spending her youth as the sole parent of someone else's daughter, Ida courted one of the few men who would want her: a wounded veteran named Willard Pretty Dog. Providing each other with mutual solace from their troubled pasts, they became intimate friends, and Ida soon became pregnant with Willard's baby. A few weeks later, however, their relationship was shattered when Willard admitted that he loved her only because she showed compassion on him. They remained friends but never returned to the intimate relationship that they had previously, and Ida eventually gave birth to their son. Following tradition, she named him Lecon after her own father, but she called him Lee to distance him from the negative memories that she had of her father.

Putting a final ironic spin on the plot, the final page of Ida's story reveals how she seduced Father Hurlburt, the same priest who encouraged her both to raise Christine and to befriend Willard. Not only does this weave together several strands from Ida's own life, but it also ironically connects the three generations of women because Ida seduced the same priest who later supervised the priest who would attempt to seduce Rayona. Moreover, Ida does this on the same night that Christine's faith in God is shattered when the world does not come to an end. Nevertheless, many of these ironic connections are only recognized by the reader since the women themselves remain largely unaware of each others' deepest secrets.

Characters

Andy

One of Rayona's work colleagues on the maintenance crew at Bearpaw Lake State Park. Rayona thinks he probably lifts weights or plays football. He has a crush on Ellen.

Charlene

Charlene is Christine's "best friend," according to Rayona. She lives in Christine's apartment building and works in the pharmacy of the hospital where Christine is frequently a patient. Christine depends on Charlene to send her illegal refills of percocet to control the pain of her cancer, although we don't learn the nature of her disease until much later. Charlene reappears in Christine's story to warn her that she's killing herself by leaving the hospital, but she fulfills her promise to give Christine one more refill on her percocet prescription.

Buster Cree

Buster Cree, a "reformed mixed-blood from Wyoming who joined the church when he married Polly," is the father of Dale.

Dale Cree

Dale Cree, Polly and Buster's son, falls in love with Pauline when she comes to board at the Crees. He and Pauline marry, and they have a son, Foxy.

Kennedy Cree

Kennedy Cree (Foxy) is Pauline's son and Rayona's cousin whom Ray substitutes for at the rodeo when Foxy gets too drunk to ride. When Ray wins a prize, Foxy is humiliated.

Media Adaptations

- *A Yellow Raft in Blue Water* was recorded on an audiocassette by Colleen Dewhurst for Harper Audio in 1990.

Pauline Cree

Pauline is Clara and Ida's younger sister and Foxy Cree's mother. As Ida gradually becomes closer to Clara, Pauline is left out, though Ida concedes that "Pauline would have made a better mother [to Christine] than either Clara or me." Fed up with Lecon's unemployment and drinking and Annie's helpless condition, Pauline leaves home and gets a job with the Agency, boarding with Polly Cree's family. Pauline falls in love with Polly's son Dale, but when she marries him she asks none of her family to the wedding. Pauline is ashamed of her father's alcoholism and her sister Ida's single-mother status.

Polly Cree

Polly is Buster Cree's wife and the mother of twenty-year-old Dale Cree, who marries Pauline. She is also the midwife who delivers Lee.

Dad

See Elgin Taylor

Dave

Another of Rayona's work colleagues on the maintenance crew at Bearpaw Lake State Park. Of all her co-workers, Rayona likes him the best "because he's the only guy who pays attention to me."

Ellen DeMarco

A swimming teacher at Bear Lake, Ellen has all the things Rayona lacks: beauty, parents, and money. Ray is so entranced by Ellen's way of life that she fantasizes that a letter Ellen's parents wrote to their daughter is actually written to her.

Evelyn Dial

Evelyn, Sky's wife, is the cook at the Bearpaw Lake State Park who gives Rayona a place to live for a few weeks and acts as a surrogate mother.

Norman Dial

Sky, Evelyn Dial's husband, is the operator of the Conoco station. He introduces Ray to Bearpaw State Park and generously gives up his holiday pay to drive Ray to a rodeo where she hopes to see her mother.

Foxy

See Kennedy Cree

Annie George

Annie is Lecon's wife, Ida's mother, and Clara's sister, though the difference in ages meant that Clara and Annie were never close. Lecon calls on Clara to do the housekeeping chores when Annie develops heart trouble. Ida blames her mother for not anticipating that Lecon would be sexually interested in Clara. In her illness, however, there is not much that Annie can do to influence events. Her death, while sad, frees Ida at last to have more time for herself.

Clara George

Clara is Annie George's baby sister who comes to live with Ida when she is about twenty years old. Supposedly Christine's aunt, though actually her mother, Clara appears no more than five years older than Ida. Clara gets pregnant by her brother-in-law Lecon shortly after she arrives to help Lecon's wife Annie. To save the family's reputation, Clara makes up a cover story about being raped by a masked drifter. Clara's plan works, but four years later, when she shows up at Ida's to claim the child, Ida thwarts her by getting a birth certificate that says Ida is the birth mother. Christine meets Clara only once as an adult when Clara is in the hospital dying of cancer.

Aunt Ida George

Ida calls herself "a woman who's lived fifty-seven years and worn resentment like a medicine charm for forty…. If I were to live my life differently, I would start with the word No: first to him, my father; to Clara, then to Willard, before they left me; to Lee, to save his life. I was different with Christine, but it turned out no better." In her stubborn isolation, Ida distorts the truth that in the end it was she who rejected Clara and Willard Pretty Dog, not vice-versa. Yet Ida alone knows all the secrets that bind the main characters in the story.

Ida is Christine's ostensible mother, although everyone (even Christine) calls her Aunt Ida at her request, so that she can protect herself from disappointment if Christine's real mother, Clara, should ever come back to claim her child. When Clara returns four years later and calls herself Christine's mother, Ida is so shocked that she instinctively brings her fingers, which are carrying a hot teakettle, to her ears, thereby burning a plum-sized hole on her cheek that serves as a permanent reminder of her secret burden. Clara wants to give up Christine for adoption. To block her, Ida arranges for Father Hurlburt to get a birth certificate that declares Ida as Christine's legal mother. To seal Clara's fate, Ida threatens to reveal the truth about Clara's relationship to Lecon.

Ida dotes on Lee, her illegitimate son by Willard, and so Christine feels rejected. She decides to bring up Lee herself, just as she has brought up Christine, never revealing his true father. Ida has persuaded herself that when she was with a man she always "pretended to be stupid" and that she wanted Christine "to see me smart, to know she could be that way herself in front of any man." Ida's intelligence as she grows older is clear, for she successfully leases part of her land to make improvements in her own life. As the oldest of the three main characters, Ida has suffered the most; but by the same token she has perhaps earned the greatest portion of happiness, however small, having raised three children, to varying degrees, on her own and having achieved some financial stability in her life.

Lecon George

Lecon, Christine's real father, is a proud traditional Indian who, weakened by alcoholism, is not able to adapt to the present. When his wife Annie developed heart trouble, Lecon thought Ida's offer to drop out of school and help at home would be seen on the reservation as a sign of male weakness. Realizing this, Annie makes up the tale that Clara is coming to their house because she is homeless. When Lecon gets her pregnant, he readily accepts Clara's plan to pretend the child is Ida's by a stranger. But his remark when he first sees his new daughter—"It's in their family.... Nothing but girls"—shows his essential narrowness. Also disturbing is Lecon's delusion (especially when drunk) that it is Ida's behavior rather than his own that has brought shame on the family. When Lecon dies, Ida feels only relief that he will no longer be a burden to her.

Father Hurlburt

Hurlburt is the priest who recruits Rayona for the teen-age "God Squad" in his parish. Part Indian himself, he is a confidant and intermediary among

Dorris's first novel is also generally considered to be his finest work of fiction.

the various families in the parish. For example, outside of Lecon, Annie, and Clara, only Father Hurlburt knows that Christine is not Ida's child. It is Father Hurlburt who takes Ida and baby Christine home from the residence for unwed mothers and who later helps Ida obtain the birth certificate. As Pauline and others go along with Clara's fictional story that she was raped by an intruder, Father Hurlburt remains to Ida "the only honest one, tied to me by my secrets."

John

The third of Rayona's work colleagues on the maintenance crew at Bearpaw Lake State Park, he reminds her of "the chubby guy on 'Happy Days.'"

Lecon

Lee is Christine's half-brother and the illegitimate son of Ida and Willard. Raised by Ida, Lee never knows his real father. As a child, Lee is known for his good looks and his daredevil attitude. When Lee and Dayton become anti-Vietnam activists, Christine challenges Lee's patriotism, pointing out that Lee's political future as a reservation leader would be ruined if he evaded the draft. Lee enlists, but he dies in Vietnam, driving Christine into the faithless arms of Elgin and sowing new seeds of bitterness in Ida's heart.

Lee

See Lecon

Mama

See Annie George

Mom/Mama

See Christine Taylor

Mr. McCutcheon

Mr. McCutcheon is the maintenance supervisor at the Bear Paw Lake State Park who praises Rayona for her work.

Dayton Nickles

Dayton is a close friend of Lee and Christine and shelters her after she returns to the reservation. Later he shows up at the rodeo and takes Rayona back to her mother. Dayton is classified 4-A because his father was killed in World War II. A convicted child molester, Dayton turned his life around after getting out of prison and now has a good job as an accountant for the Tribal Council.

Tom Novak

Father Tom Novak is Father Hurlburt's assistant at the local reservation mission and the butt of Indian jokes because of his naivete. On a trip to a teen conference, he and Rayona have sex on the yellow raft in blue water after Ray saves him from drowning. Tom soon realizes his error and agrees to finance Ray's trip to Seattle.

Mrs. Pretty Dog

Willard's mother, concerned about her son's interest in Ida, finally visits her and sees that they have more than a nurse-patient relationship. At first disturbed because of Ida's low status on the reservation, Mrs. Pretty Dog is satisfied when Ida decides to reject him.

Willard Pretty Dog

Willard as a boy was handsome, but when he comes back from World War II with some of his face missing, he becomes bitter and reclusive. Only Ida goes to see him, hoping that in his present condition he will not find her so plain. She lays her life out before him in all its sadness, and he is moved to accept her love. When he gets Ida pregnant, however, Ida rejects him as a future husband, and he ends up marrying one of the nurses who looked after him in the hospital.

Ray

See Rayona Taylor

Sky

See Norman Dial

Annabelle Stiffarm

Annabelle is a fellow member of Father Hurlburt's God Squad and a friend of Foxy Cree who accompanies him to the rodeo where Ray substitutes for Foxy.

Christine Taylor

As a young adult, Christine describes herself as "the bastard daughter of a woman [Ida] who wouldn't even admit she was my mother." In fact, however, Christine is the illegitimate daughter of Ida's father Lecon and her sister Clara. Christine, however, is brought up as "Aunt" Ida's daughter and never learns the truth about her real parents. As a child, Christine "was never satisfied," but she develops a blind loyalty to her younger brother Lee and a strong faith in Catholicism, especially the martyred saints.

Christine's faith reaches a crisis when she takes too seriously the contents of the "Portugal letter" in which the end of the world is predicted unless Russia converts to Roman Catholicism. When nothing happens on the appointed night, Christine becomes disillusioned with the Church. Similarly, when Christine finds that Dayton Nickles doesn't want to be her boyfriend, her self-esteem takes such a plunge that "it took me years to forget." Christine's one true friend is her younger brother Lee. "He wasn't just my best friend, he was the only one I trusted, the only one who never let me down." When Lee switches his main allegiance from Christine to Dayton, an anti-Vietnam activist, Christine plots successfully to separate them by telling Lee that being considered unpatriotic would end his political future on the reservation.

Angry at Aunt Ida's disapproval of her promiscuous social life, Christine leaves home and moves in with Ida's sister Pauline's family. She takes a job at the Tribal Council, and continues her playgirl life, eventually leaving for Seattle. Distraught when Dayton writes that Lee is missing in action in Vietnam, Christine meets Elgin in a bar. They marry but it doesn't last, and by the time Ray is a teenager, Christine is dying from cirrhosis of the liver and pancreatic cancer. Angry because Elgin won't take responsibility for Ray, Christine decides to commit suicide. But Ray foils her plan, and Christine is forced to take her to her "Aunt"

Ida's, then hitch a ride to Dayton's, where she decides to spend her final days. With the financial and emotional stability that Dayton offers her in his new life after prison, Christine is able to get Ray back into her life for a brief period. She teaches Ray to drive and gives her daughter her prized silver turtle ring. But having learned from the secretive Ida not to reveal painful truths, she can never tell Ray that she is dying.

Elgin Taylor

Elgin is Rayona's black father, although he visits his daughter only occasionally. Though he is still officially married to Christine, he has not taken a consistent role in bringing up Ray. Christine was attracted to him because he gave her hope that Lee might still be alive. Elgin has a fairly steady job as a mailman, but his commitment to Christine and their child is never complete. For Christine, the final straw comes when Elgin borrows her car while she is in the hospital and returns it with a virtually empty gas tank.

Rayona Taylor

Rayona is the fifteen-year-old daughter of Christine and Elgin Taylor, a black serviceman Christine met soon after she learned that Lee was missing in action in Vietnam. Christine and Elgin marry but stop living together around the time Ray is born, and Christine raises her alone. Life has not been easy for Ray. When we first meet her, she is visiting her mother in the hospital. Elgin arrives, and her parents soon start to argue. Rayona doesn't believe that her mother is really sick, but Ray is soon left with the task of persuading Christine not to take a suicidal journey back to Seattle.

When the car breaks down, Christine flees to Dayton's and Ray ends up with Aunt Ida. With Ida to bring up Ray, Christine now hopes she can die without being a burden to her daughter. Ray joins Father Hurlburt and Father Tom's teenage "God Squad" but in her loneliness for a real family, she fantasizes about her real father. Father Tom is sexually attracted to Rayona, and after Rayona saves him from drowning, he experiences "an occasion of sin" with her on the yellow raft. In his guilt and naivete Father Tom gives her train fare back to Seattle to visit her father. Ray, however, decides to stay where she is, and is lucky enough to stumble into a surrogate family and a job at Bear Paw Lake State Park. She proves to be both a good park employee and an appealing boarder to Sky and Evelyn Dial. Ray has concealed the fact that she is a runaway, constructing a fictitious family out of her imagination and a scrap of a letter she found that turns out to have been a letter to Ellen, a swimming instructor at the park whom Ray admires.

When Ray's fantasy is exposed, however, Evelyn forgives her and offers to take her home. Hoping she will see her mother, Ray persuades the Dials to stop off at an Indian rodeo on the way back to the reservation and ends up winning an award for being the "roughest, toughest" broncobuster at the fair. At the rodeo Rayona finds her mother's childhood friend Dayton, who reluctantly takes her back to the reservation and her mother. But nothing has changed. Rayona still wants to believe that Christine is not really sick, and Christine is still caught in the mistakes of her past and overwhelmed with her own problems.

Tina Taylor
See Christine Taylor

Father Tom
See Tom Novak

Themes

Identity

In 1979, Michael Dorris wrote that "there is no such thing as 'Native American literature,' though it may yet, someday, come into being." Among the requirements for such a literature, Dorris continued, was a "shared consciousness, an inherently identifiable world-view." Expanding on this theme of identity in a 1992 essay, Owens notes that in *A Yellow Raft in Blue Water,* for the most part, "the individual who would 'be' Indian rather than 'play' Indian is faced with an overwhelming challenge." Only Aunt Ida "becomes … the bearer of the identity and order that are so fragile they may perish in a single generation if unarticulated." Although Ida, too, is unavoidably influenced by the bombardment of mainstream culture, Owens notes that "she can take off her earphones and wig, turn off the television soap operas, and become a story-teller, leaving her 'savings'—a recovered sense of self, identity, authenticity—to Rayona." The other characters in the story, on the other hand, are too enmeshed in sometimes conflicting, sometimes just unknown or unconscious forces of identity. Lee tries to become a Red Power representative but ends up bowing to the mainstream social forces that send him off to die in Vietnam. Lecon never rises above the stereotype of the traditional

Topics For Further Study

- As critic Paul Hadella has noted, Dorris's characters in the novel constantly refer to popular songs, movies, and TV programs "as a way of explaining their situations and defining their roles." Determine the lyrics, story, or subject matter and date of composition of as many song titles, TV shows, or movies referred to in the story as you can. By showing what light it casts on any of the characters in the novel, explain the significance, if any, of each reference.

- Describe the beliefs of the American Indian Movement as it expressed itself in the late 1960s and early 1970s, and compare the attitudes of Rayona, Christine, and Ida toward Lee and Dayton's brief attraction to these beliefs.

- Research the impact of the Catholic Church, or Christian missionaries in general, on Indian culture and education in the United States. Was there any historical basis for the "Portugal letter," which played an important role in Christine's losing her faith?

- Dorris's novel has been called a feminist work by Adalaide Morris. Compare the attitudes toward the opposite sex of the following characters—Ida, Lecon, Christine, and Rayona—to justify this view.

- Compulsive behavior, illness, and disability are important factors in the lives of several characters in the novel. Show how Lecon and Christine's alcoholism, Dayton's child molestation, Lecon's rape of Clara, Willard's disfiguration, and Annie's heart condition affect the course of the plot.

male, whether Indian or white, who sees women only as the servants of men. And though Christine struggles perhaps the hardest to establish herself as independent, she has only a vague sense of her real mother and not a clue about her real father. She goes from blind acceptance of Catholicism to total disillusionment and outright rejection of her faith. This ignorance and irrationality can be seen as coming partly from Ida's secretiveness but also, especially as she grows older, from Christine's own apparent lack of desire to explain why she is taking a given action, like dropping Rayona off at Ida's and then disappearing. As a result of this lack of communication between mother and daughter, Rayona must negotiate her sense of self and community in a cultural vacuum. As a mixed blood, however, Rayona is different from the other characters (except for Father Hurlburt, who serves as an important link between the white and Indian communities). The positive side of feeling left out that is so common to mixed bloods is that Rayona is willing to try new things. For example, she agrees to impersonate her male cousin at the rodeo

in which she wins a prize. (In fact, in an earlier version of the story, which appears in Bartlett, the narrator was Raymond, a male Rayona.) When we leave Rayona at the end of her section of the book, she is actively questioning her mother about the details of the mysterious letter from the Virgin Mary. In this curious, questioning attitude, there is hope that Rayona, like the resilient synthetic fabric whose name she bears, will forge a new identity, neither Indian nor white, male nor female, self- nor other-oriented, that will survive and even endure.

Strength and Weakness

Because Dorris's characters are developed by seeing them from several points of view, the reader gets a more rounded portrait in which different sides of the personality are revealed. This is evident when we examine each major character's strengths and weaknesses and the struggle within each figure to see which attributes will win out. As the youngest major character, Ramona has the least knowledge of what is going on, so ignorance is her main weakness. Thus she interprets Christine's leaving her at Ida's as abandonment, when it is in fact Christine's attempt, however cowardly, to protect her daughter from the truth about her mother's illness. Among Rayona's strengths, however, include courage, seen in her taking Foxy Cree's place in the rodeo. Rayona also shows great curiosity, which is evident in the many questions she is always asking, and her powerful imagination creates alternate identities that help her soothe the pain of not knowing the full truth about her mother and father. Christine's strengths include: her love for Rayona and Lee and her fierce desire to protect them; her fearlessness in taking up dares; and her perseverance and diligence when she is doing something she believes in, like helping the nuns (before her disillusionment). Never understanding the circumstances of her birth, however, and growing up without a father, Christine must constantly wrestle with feelings of isolation and dissatisfaction with her general lot. She also struggles with insecurity when males like Dayton seem to reject her. Ida is probably the most complex of the three major characters. She can count among her strengths her memory of important events in the past, which she thinks of as "savings." Ida also proves herself very practical in the way she outmaneuvers Clara to claim Christine as her legal daughter or manages her property to achieve some financial stability. Ida also shows perseverance in helping to raise three children, only one of whom is her own. She pays a price for her achievements, however. First, Ida is resentful toward her father and Willard, both of whom (like most men, she feels) make her feel stupid. Second, in her desire to cover up the sins of her father and Willard, as she sees them, Ida has isolated herself and left herself little room for any life of her own, literally branding herself (with the teakettle) as a misfit and recluse in the eyes of others.

Culture Clash

Though Dorris has been criticized for not emphasizing the importance of a distinct native American identity, *A Yellow Raft in Blue Water* shows that he is well aware of the factors that hamper its development. The book is a virtual catalogue of different forms of culture and the ways they rub against each other, sometimes creating barriers, and occasionally melding. There is Elgin's black culture and its conflict with Christine's upbringing on the reservation. "We're the wrong color for each other," Rayona has heard her mother tell Elgin. "That's what your friends think." There is the white

Catholic culture of Father Tom, who knows no Indian language and is the constant butt of Indian humor. There is the more traditional Indian culture in which Ida, who "wears resentment like a medicine charm," has been raised, despite her more recent exposure to Western media. Like the traditional Indian, Ida has an expanded awareness of the past—especially the truth about Christine's parentage and Lee's father. And finally, there is the mixed-blood heritage that exists in both Rayona (Indian-black) and Father Hurlburt (Indian-white). This heritage is both parodied, as in Father Tom's stilted reference to Rayona's "dual heritage," and respected, as seen in Father Hurlburt's important role in the story as a witness to and confidant of at least some of Ida's secrets.

Style

Point of View

Part of Dorris's genius in the book shows in his telling basically the same story from three different points of view. For example, we first interpret Christine's illness through Rayona's eyes (in critic Michiko Kakutani's words) as "a phony play for sympathy." Later, we see the same scene through Christine's own eyes and realize not only that her illness is real but also (again in Kakutani's words) that "her disappearance constitutes not an act of abandonment but a cowardly attempt to save her daughter from the knowledge of her imminent death." Similarly, at the beginning of the story Rayona believes that Aunt Ida is actually her grandmother but insists that she be called "Aunt" rather then be reminded that Christine was her own illegitimate offspring. In fact, as we learn only in the last section of the novel, Christine is the illegitimate offspring of Ida's father, Lecon, and her aunt, Clara, and Ida is therefore not Christine's mother but rather both her cousin and half-sister. As feminist critic Adalaide Morris has noted, one result of a story made up of similar examples involving this intertwined, intergenerational, multicultural family is a "new first-person plural storyteller" or, in the words of Adrienne Rich, "We who are not the same. We who are many and do not want to be the same." In short, the new "we, the plural" is a shifting coalition of different people, "a site where disparate subjectivities collide, converge, and continue to coexist." Thus, restless and unsatisfied Christine leaves Ida for Seattle, just as Rayona, restless to find her real family, later also leaves Ida, but Rayona and Christine are eventually reunited, despite their differences.

Symbolism and Imagery

Dorris's skill in providing concrete descriptions to suggest larger meanings is evident in the central symbols and recurring images of the book. The imagery in the title itself, for example, suggests the clarity and simplicity of a vision or dream that, for Rayona at least, is attainable only too briefly. Thus the yellow raft recalls not only Ray and Father Tom's sexual incident, which to Ray has the quality of a dream, but also Ellen DeMarco, who Ray first sees poised on the raft, representing "everything I'm not but ought to be." Another central image in the story is hair braiding, in which several separate strands are woven into one. Thus the story opens with Christine pulling Ray's hair into a braid and ends with the image of Ida braiding her own hair. In the same way, Dorris has woven the three separate angles of vision provided by Rayona, Christine, and Ida into one complex but unified tale. As Kakutani has noted, Dorris is also a master of the telling descriptive image: the broken taillight, "spilling a red at a funny angle," or the leaves on the trees, "heavy as tin" on a hot, breezeless day.

Allusion

Throughout the story, Dorris's constant allusions to songs, television shows, and movies from the 1960s-1980s pop scene emphasizes the degree to which all three major Indian characters have been molded by mainstream American culture rather than traditional Indian customs and beliefs. Rayona describes her mother's face as "like a stumped contestant on 'Jeopardy' with time running out." Christine, who grew up in the Sixties, remembers watching Vietnam protests on TV, listening to "Teen Beat" on the radio, and fantasizing that Dayton was her grieving lover in "Teen Angel." She considers it fitting to leave her daughter a lifetime membership in Video Village, and the two films she takes out on her first visit are significant for how they show the extent to which Christine has assimilated white American culture. "Christine" (1983) is a Stephen King horror movie featuring a car with demonic powers. In "Little Big Man" (1970), one of whose actors Christine claims to have dated, the main character is not a birthright Indian but a 121-year old white man adopted by Indians. Even Aunt Ida, at fifty-seven the oldest major Indian character and therefore one whose life would ostensibly be most traditional, is singing

along to a pop song on her Walkman when we first meet her. Ida turns out to be addicted to daytime soap operas on TV. In these examples, which are only some of many in the book, Dorris is suggesting that if there once was a conflict in the eyes of Indians between tribal heritage and mainstream culture or other cultures, it has long since been resolved in favor of mainstream culture. Only a naive European-American character like Father Tom can seriously speak of Rayona's "dual heritage."

Historical Context

The Status of Native Americans in the 1980s

The political situation of Native Americans in the United States is unique. Among many ethnic groups, Indians alone have land called reservations set aside by the government on which they can live without paying the usual land and property taxes. Indians who do not live on reservations pay the same taxes as other citizens. All Indians pay federal and state income taxes and have full voting rights, and receive some special job and health benefits, to which Christine refers. Usually the federal Bureau of Indian Affairs administers reservations. On some reservations, local tribal councils control some political and commercial activities. In 1983, President Reagan issued a policy statement promoting increased economic development on reservations. While many Indian leaders reacted skeptically to the announcement, some reservations have greatly profited from oil, gas, and uranium resources, while others have set up lucrative casinos. On other reservations, the tribal government is a major employer. Both Christine and Dayton hold jobs with the local tribal council, and Lee is being groomed for a political future in the tribal government when he goes off to Vietnam. Courts have generally supported Indian land claims, either by granting repossession (usually of only a portion of the lands claimed) or by payments in exchange for relinquishing of claims. Many reservations, however, remain economically underdeveloped. On one small reservation in Wyoming with an unemployment rate of 80 percent, the suicide rate of 233 per 100,000 is almost twenty times the national average. The rate of alcoholism, an important factor in the characterization of both Lecon and Christine, is a serious problem among Indians. Indians are four times more likely to die from alcoholism than the general population. Dorris explores Indian al-

A group of American Indians march to mark the 100th anniversary of the battle of Little Big Horn, where American troops were defeated by the Sioux in 1876.

coholism at length in his prize-winning book, *The Broken Cord: A Family's Ongoing Struggle with Fetal Alcohol Syndrome.*

The Indian Power Movement, 1969-1973

During the 1960s, some Indian groups began to press for more economic and political rights. In 1972, the American Indian Movement (AIM) occupied the Bureau of Indian Affairs building in Washington; in 1973 AIM members seized Wounded Knee, South Dakota, demanding the return of all lands taken from Indians in violation of treaty agreements. After nine years as a fugitive from prosecution for assault and rioting charges in connection with the seizure, AIM leader Dennis Banks (who received protection in various forms from the governors of both California and New York), finally surrendered in 1983. He served one year of a three-year term before being released in 1985. Like Lee and Dayton, many Indians were inspired by AIM or similar groups to take a stand against the U.S. government in other areas as well, notably in protesting the war in Vietnam. Other pro-Indian activities mentioned in *A Yellow Raft in Blue Water* include protests over limitation or abrogation of fishing rights and participation in in-

tertribal activities designed to stress Indian unity. Like Christine, however, most Indians rejected these militant tactics. The majority of American Indians during the Vietnam War were patriotic, as is seen in the favorable way Lee is treated by the tribal elders after he decides to enlist. In 1986 the Grandfather Plaque or Amerind Vietnam Plaque was dedicated at Arlington National Cemetery. Roughly 43,000 Native American combatants served in Vietnam, or one out of every four eligible Indian males.

Critical Overview

A Yellow Raft in Blue Water was both a popular and critical success when it was first published in 1987, although some critics (notably Michiko Kakutani) found fault with the way the author withholds crucial information about the secret of Christine's birth, while others (like Robert Narveson) thought he put uncharacteristic words in characters' mouths to make a thematic point. Yet even these critics admitted that the "meticulously delineated world" (Kakutani) and the "drenched ... particularity of motive, of action, of perception" (Narveson) in the story moved the reader happily along and created a series of strikingly unique yet interconnnected lives. Reviewer Penelope Moffet also found the major characters in the novel irresistible and Dorris's writing "energetic, understated and seductive." Reiterating the positive reception to the book, Roger Sale called it a "fine novel" with "clearly drawn and clearly felt characters." Writing in 1988, Sale predicted (sadly, in view of Dorris's suicide almost nine years later) that "Michael Dorris works with an impersonality that gives promise that his list of achievements can grow long." *A Yellow Raft in Blue Water* also found a special place in the writings of feminist critics like Adalaide Morris, who categorized this book, along with two others, as "feminist in their focus on gender but 'postfeminist' in their … return to that antagonist of 'room of one's own' feminism: the greedy, sticky-fingered, endlessly complicated family." Morris noted that "despite its conservative force … the family is the one force in our culture that regularly binds together people of different ages, genders, interests, skills, and sexual preferences and sometimes also people of different ethnic traditions, racial or religious backgrounds, and economic classes." At the "source" and center of *A Yellow Raft in Blue Water,* as Morris sees it, is Ida, "a figure who embodies the overdetermined, ambiguous multiplicity behind 'we the plural,' a multiplicity Dorris's narrative extends outward from Christine's 'birth' family to the 'family' she finally constructs, a temporary but tenacious alliance between individuals of different genders, ages, races, economic classes, and sexual preferences." Christine's family thus comes to include not only the pureblooded Indian Ida, who is relatively well off because of her land rentals. It also numbers Christine's childhood friend, the half-white (and probable homosexual) Dayton (also relatively well off after a period in prison), who takes in not only Christine, who is genuinely impoverished, but also Christine's Indian-black daughter Rayona. That such a family is unstable in traditional terms goes without saying. In fact, according to Morris, "these coalitions can be effective and lasting only if they are also contested and dialogic, subject to the unending splits, shifts, and struggles that characterize any genuine plurality." For Morris, Dorris's book is part of a "project of constructing a subject position from which such a politics could operate, a first-person plural in which the words 'first,' 'person,' and 'plural' would keep both their separate meanings and their collective force." Whether Dorris's critical reputation will

survive the disturbing facts surrounding his suicide in 1997 remains to be seen. But for those who believe that a writer's personal life should be considered completely separate from the works of fiction that he or she creates, there is little question that Dorris's body of work as a whole, and certainly *A Yellow Raft in Blue Water,* occupy a distinguished place in Native American literature of the late twentieth century.

Criticism

Robert Bennett

Bennett is a doctoral candidate at the University of California at Santa Barbara and has published essays on various postcolonial and Native American authors in academic journals. In the following essay, he analyzes how Michael Dorris's A Yellow Raft in Blue Water *demonstrates the complexity of history by interweaving the stories of three Native American women.*

Michael Dorris's *A Yellow Raft in Blue Water* develops an intricate plot structure that weaves together the lives of three Native American women. Instead of using an all-knowing narrator to tell their stories from a single, consistent perspective, however, Dorris has each character narrate one section of the story from her own biased perspective. Consequently, the novel's three main characters all assume dual functions as combined character-narrators. While this multiplication of character-narrators may initially seem to be a minor part of the plot, a careful reader will recognize that it radically alters the entire experience of reading the novel because the three narrators frequently offer different interpretations of the same event.

When this happens, the reader cannot simply continue reading passively while waiting for the "true" narrator to finally explain what happened because none of the character-narrators has access to all of the facts, and all of the characters are biased by their own experiences and emotions. Instead, the reader must play a more active role in interpreting the novel either by deciding which narrator's story seems most believable or by combining the most reliable pieces from each narrator's story into a coherent whole. This task is made more difficult, however, because Dorris reverses the order of the story. Instead of beginning with the oldest character, Aunt Ida, he begins with the youngest character, Rayona, and works backwards through time.

What Do I Read Next?

- In *Cloud Chamber* (1997), Dorris returns to Ida, Christine, and Rayona, focusing this time on their ancestors, including a shipwrecked Spaniard who washed up on the shores of Ireland and his descendant, Rose Mannion. Rose is the central character in this five-generation epic that covers more than one hundred years.

- *Paper Trail* (1994) is a collection of essays by Dorris written during the 1980s and 1990s on topics ranging from family and Indians to fetal alcohol syndrome and libraries. Of special interest to readers of *A Yellow Raft in Blue Water* are the articles describing the important adults in Dorris's own life when he was growing up.

- Dorris's *Morning Girl* (1992) is a young adult novel that explores the lives of young Bahamians living in 1492, on the eve of Columbus's discovery of their island. The Book was awarded the 1992 American Library Association (ALA) Scott O'Dell Award for Best Historical Fiction for Young Readers and was named a notable book of the year by *Horn Book, School Library Journal,* ALA *Booklist,* and the *New York Times Book Review.*

- *Tracks* (1988), by Michael Dorris's wife Louise Erdrich, is part of a projected quartet of novels by the part-Chippewa novelist that also includes *Love Medicine* (1984) and *The Beet Queen* (1986). As a prequel to *Love Medicine, Tracks* focuses on the crucial moment in the early twentieth century when the Chippewa saw the last part of their centuries-old traditional life vanish. The novel is divided into nine chapters, one for each of the Chippewa seasonal cycles, and uses the same technique of interwoven tales about a complex family group that Dorris employs in *A Yellow Raft in Blue Water*

Since important information about the characters' past is not revealed until the end of the novel, the reader must continually reinterpret everything as each narrator reveals new information about the past. In this sense, *A Yellow Raft in Blue Water* is not simply a story about three Native American women, but at a deeper level it is also a story about the process of interpretation itself: it explores how people's experiences, biases, and preconceptions influence their explanations of events. This makes the experience of reading the novel more exciting because the reader must constantly reevaluate both the events described in the novel and the narrators who are telling the story.

While William Faulkner, Gertrude Stein, and many other modernist writers have also created novels with multiple narrators, Dorris's use of multiple narrators in *A Yellow Raft in Blue Water* is particularly interesting because all of his narrators are Native American women. Consequently, Dorris's novel is not just generally about how the world is seen differently by different people, but it is specifically about how gender and ethnicity influence our experiences and understanding. While one might assume that it would be easier for Dorris to represent Native Americans than women because he is part Modoc but not a woman, the critical response to Dorris's work seems to suggest the opposite. Some critics actually argue that Dorris's representations of Native Americans are not strong enough, and Dorris himself has frequently stated that his fiction does not seek to promote any particular Native American agenda. On the other hand, most critics and readers generally agree that Dorris's representations of women are quite convincing.

As Dorris has explained in various interviews, his ability to understand women comes partly from his own experiences living with many strong women: his mother, grandmothers, aunts, and wife. In addition, his wife, Louise Erdrich, is a famous Native American novelist herself, and their close collaboration has also helped Dorris write about women from a woman's perspective. While reading the novel, therefore, it is important to pay particular attention to how both gender and ethnicity influence the characters' lives. The most significant events in these women's lives, such as bearing and/or raising children or being sexually assaulted, are often specifically connected to their experiences as women. In addition, these women also draw on both their experiences as women and their relationships with other women in order to find strategies for dealing with these challenging events. At the same time, however, one must not lose sight of these women's ethnic identity as Native Americans because they frequently experience even "female" events differently than many white Anglo-American women.

To say that Dorris's writing represents how gender influences experience, however, is not to suggest either that his novel is limited to women's experiences or that it has a narrow interpretation of what it means to be a woman. On the contrary, Dorris's novel also emphasizes traditionally "male" experiences such as going to war. Moreover, both Rayona's rodeo riding and Aunt Ida's seduction of Father Hurlburt demonstrate that Dorris's female characters do not conform to predictable gender stereotypes, and the unconventionality of Dorris's characters is even more evident when he represents their ethnic identity as Native Americans. Aunt Ida's addiction to soap operas and Christine's marriage to a black man are only two examples of the numerous ways in which Dorris's characters seem to mix cultural and ethnic identities instead of remaining rigidly confined by them. In fact, the characters' lives continually and unexpectedly move across cultural boundaries throughout the novel.

After spending their whole lives on the reservation, both Aunt Ida and Christine suddenly find themselves relocated to cities, and for Rayona this process of relocation happens just as abruptly only in reverse. Similarly, at one moment Lee is a Native American activist agitating for tribal sovereignty and pacifism, but the next moment he finds himself enlisted to fight for the United States military itself. Consequently, Dorris's fiction explores both ethnicity and gender but not in any simplistic or deterministic sense. In fact, sometimes there is as much cultural difference between different Native American characters as there is between Native American and non-Native American characters in his novel, and the same can be said for gender identity as well.

By interweaving three generations of Native American women, Dorris's novel also develops a historical dimension that chronicles the evolution of Native American life during most of the twentieth century. The vast differences between Aunt Ida's life and Rayona's demonstrate how Native

Americans continue to change and continue to be influenced by history. Like all people, they evolve and adapt to historical changes, and even reservations cannot isolate them from the political and cultural changes influencing the rest of the United States. Consequently, Dorris situates his unnamed Native American reservation against the backdrop of broader forces in U. S. history, which are external to Native American life but still influence it: Catholic missionary work, American popular culture, and the Vietnam War.

In many ways, these external historical forces actually influence the lives of Dorris's characters as powerfully if not more powerfully than any historical forces internal to Native American culture, since these external historical forces either directly or indirectly cause many turning points in the characters' lives: Christine's loss of faith, Lee's death, and Father Tom's sexual advances toward Rayona. When the reader connects these turning points, Dorris's novel suggests that the external forces of American culture not only exert a powerful influence on Native American life but their influence generally destroys Native American culture or forces it to assimilate toward mainstream American culture. In the end, Aunt Ida divides her time between the television or listening to her walkman, Christine grows up on American culture, Lee dies for American politics, and Rayona's urban childhood makes reservation almost a foreign country. It is as if Dorris's characters are almost incapable of resisting the attraction of the dominant culture, even when they attempt to resist it like Lee and Ida.

In closing, however, one must constantly resist the temptation to oversimplify Dorris's novel. Clearly, Dorris does not intend for his novel to be a simplistic denunciation of the evils of Anglo-American history or the impossibility of resisting it, but instead he wants to depict cultural tensions that are more subtle, complex, and multi-dimensional. The world that he represents cannot be reduced into black and white divisions between good and evil. After all, Ida's Native American father is more sexually promiscuous than Father Tom, and he is more directly culpable than Father Hurlburt for deciding Ida's fate. Also, the Catholic missionaries bring as much good to the reservation as they do harm: Father Hurlburt helps raise Christine more than her real Native American mother does, and the missionaries do provide an educational system even if it has some serious problems.

Moreover, there are mutual exchanges between mainstream and Native American cultures, even if those exchanges are not always equal. After all, Father Tom's attempts to assimilate Native American culture resemble Christine's attempts to assimilate American popular culture, and Rayona's return to the reservation suggests that cultural change can run in either direction. What Dorris's novel represents, therefore, is the complexity of history and cultural interactions. In this sense, its historical dimensions parallel its personal ones: both individual lives and cultural histories are constantly retold from many perspectives. Just as the three character-narrators have their own interpretations of their personal, family history, each historian has his or her own interpretation of history itself, so there are as many interpretations of history as there are historians. Additionally, Dorris seems to suggest that no one version of history is completely accurate because a historian cannot take into account all of the facts or overcome all personal bias any more than an individual can. Thus, Dorris suggests that there is value in listening to many versions of history because only by synthesizing their competing claims can we come to understand history's true complexity. Coming to terms with the complexity of Dorris's narrative, therefore, can help us become more aware of the complexity of history itself.

Source: Robert Bennett, in an essay for *Novels for Students*, Gale, 1998.

Louis Owens

In the following excerpt, Owens discusses the significance of identity in the lives of three generations of Native American women.

At the end of Michael Dorris's novel *A Yellow Raft in Blue Water* (1987), one of the book's three narrators and protagonists, Aunt Ida, is braiding her hair as a priest watches: "As a man with cut hair, he did not identify the rhythm of three strands, the whispers of coming and going, of twisting and tying and blending, of catching and of letting go, of braiding." The metaphor of braiding—tying and blending—illuminates the substance of this novel, for it is, like [Louise] Erdrich's works, a tale of intertwined lives caught up in one another the way distinct narrative threads are woven to make a single story. Like Erdrich, Dorris—part Modoc and for many years a professor of Native American studies at Dartmouth College—constructs his novel out of multiple narratives so that the reader must triangulate to find the "truth" of the fiction. And like Erdrich and other Indian writers, Dorris makes the subject of his fiction the quest for identity through a re-membering of the past.

Yellow Raft is told in three parts by three narrators—daughter, mother, grandmother, beginning with the youngest generation—so that as we move through the novel, stories are peeled off one another like layers of the proverbial onion as blanks are gradually filled in and we circle in both time and space from an unnamed Montana reservation to Seattle and back, and from the present to the past and back again. As in so many other fictions by Indian writers, the women in this novel live oddly isolated and self-sufficient lives, raising their children and keeping their stories intact without the aid of the alienated males whose lives intersect briefly with theirs. These intersecting lives are caught up in pathos rather than tragedy, and though most of the events of the novel take place on a reservation and involve characters who identify primarily as Indian, Dorris succeeds in highlighting the universality of tangled and fragile relationships.... Though this book may not be about "real people," these characters suffer through many of the same confusions and conflicts, pleasures and pains that we might find in a Los Angeles barrio or a Chicago suburb. Like Erdrich, Dorris has succeeded in *Yellow Raft* in allowing his Indian characters to be human to escape from the deadly limitations of stereotyping.

The first narrator of *Yellow Raft* is Rayona, a young half-Indian, half-African American teenager with all the resiliency of the synthetic fabric for which she is named. Like most mixedbloods in fiction by Indian writers, Rayona is trying to comprehend her life, particularly her abandonment by her Black father and her strangely tenuous connections to her Indian mother, Christine.... *Yellow Raft* opens with the singular *I* as Rayona describes her position in her mother's hospital room. Though Rayona does not realize it at the time, her mother, Christine, is dying, having destroyed her internal organs through drinking and hard living. With an intensely undependable mother and a mostly absentee father, of whom she ironically says, "Dad was a temp," Rayona is cast back upon the *I* that is the novel's first word and the dangerous antithesis of the communal identity central to Native American cultures. Relying mostly upon her self, Rayona has achieved a precariously balanced sense of self that straddles what the lecherous Father Tom calls her "dual heritage."

The closest thing to a secure community Christine can offer her daughter is a lifetime membership at Village Video. "It's like something I'd leave you," Christine says in a statement that offers a brilliant contrast to the legacies of tribal identity left to other characters in [other] novels.... [Video] permeates *Yellow Raft,* to the extent that the old idea of an Indian "village" could be said to have given way to a more modern—and culturally bankrupt— "Video Village." Christine emphasizes this disturbing transformation when she looks at a videotape of *Little Big Man* and says, "I dated a guy who played an Indian in that movie." We are left to wonder if the guy was an Indian "playing" what Hollywood defines as Indian or if he was a white man playing an Indian. Either way, there is an unmistakable suggestion that "Indian" is a role to be played and identity something conferred by script and camera. Dorris will reinforce this video omnipresence throughout the novel, with characters constantly referring to movies and television to reaffirm their shifting senses of reality....

Even Aunt Ida, a character with a strong sense of self, seems an MTV caricature when we first encounter her wearing overalls, a "black bouffant wig" tacked on by shiny bobby pins, a dark blue bra, sunglasses, and Walkman speakers. Pushing a lawn mower that has no effect upon the grass, Aunt Ida is belting out, like a Stevie Wonder imitation in the wrong tune, the words to what should be considered the novel's theme song: "I've been looking for love in all the wrong places." For the rest of the novel, Ida will seldom be far from a television set, involving herself in the twisted lives of scripted characters of soap operas while living in virtual isolation from the rest of her family and tribe. And when Christine and Aunt Ida confront one another for the first time after many years, Rayona can only say, "I ... watch as though I'm seeing this scene on an old movie and a commercial could come along any time." Christine, in turn, says, "I couldn't guess what Ray had in mind for a grandmother. Probably somebody from TV, Grandma Walton or even Granny from 'The Beverly Hillbillies,' but they were a far cry from Aunt Ida." These mixed-blood characters suffer from a loss of authenticity intensified by an inability to selectively assimilate the words and images besieging them from the ubiquitous media....

The characters in Dorris's novel, seemingly trapped in a dialectic that never moves toward *telos,* or resolution, incapable of dialogue and without significant community to aid them in developing a coherent sense of self, become comic reflectors for the monologic discourse of the privileged center beamed to them in their isolation. The result is poignantly funny, pathos pointing—like the narrator's frozen father in *Winter in the Blood*— toward cultural tragedy.

Despite her resiliency, Rayona is as lost between cultures and identities as any character in Indian fiction, truly a stranger in a very bizarre land. Father Tom, who is trying to convince Rayona to go back to Seattle and far from the reservation where she might tell about his sexual advances, says, "And you won't feel so alone, so out of place.... There'll be others in a community of that size who share your dual heritage." In a nicely ironic testimony to her dilemma, the lascivious priest offers Rayona a cheap, pseudo-Indian medallion he has been wearing, saying, "Wear this. Then people will know you're an Indian." Identity is all surface. The center is lost. With a medallion, Rayona may become Native American rather than African American. Rayona's predicament is underscored even more ironically when she stops beneath a sign that reads, "IF LOST, STAY WHERE YOU ARE. DON'T PANIC. YOU WILL BE FOUND." Rayona takes this advice and stays at Bearpaw Lake State Park, where the ladies' restroom "has a cartoon picture of an Indian squaw on the door." She doesn't panic, though she does attempt halfheartedly to appropriate the identity— rich family and all—of a popular, spoiled white girl, and she is found by Sky, a good-hearted draft-dodger who doesn't notice trivial details like skin color, and his tough-as-nails wife, Evelyn. Appropriately, Sky and Evelyn—Father Sky, Mother Earth—subsist in the "video village" of contemporary America on TV dinners; and lying on their couch, Rayona muses upon her fragmented self: "It's as though I'm dreaming a lot of lives and I can mix and match the parts into something new each time." Indian identity is further undercut when the wealthy white parents of Rayona's coworker talk of their "adopted" Indian son who lives on a "mission": "When he writes to us now he calls us Mother and Pops just like one of our own kids." Such an image suggests the distantly marginalized voice, ... writing back to the metropolitan center— "Pops," the white father—in a poignant imitation of the expected discourse.

Rayona returns to the reservation and her mother via an Indian rodeo, where she achieves a totally unconvincing bronc-busting triumph that reminds everyone of Lee, Christine's brother killed in Vietnam. And once she is back, the three strands of family begin to be woven into one thread. Rayona's mother, Christine, begins the second book of the novel by declaring, "I had to find my own way and I started out in the hole, the bastard daughter of a woman who wouldn't even admit she was my mother." In a novel in which identity is obscure at best, Christine is actually the daughter of Ida's father and Ida's mother's sister, Clara; she is the half-sister of the woman she thinks of as her mother. It is ironic that among many tribes, … it was once common for a man to take his wife's sisters as additional wives, especially if his first wife was in need of assistance and one of her sisters, like Clara, needed a home. According to traditional tribal values, at one time there might have been nothing at all improper about Clara bearing the child of her sister's husband had the situation been handled correctly. But that world is long gone, and Clara's pregnancy is a potentially damning scandal. In spite of the fact that Christine has taught Rayona to speak "Indian" and Ida still knows how to dance traditionally, most values have been lost in the confusion of a reservation where young girls mouth the lyrics to "Poor Little Fool" … while awaiting Armageddon, grandmothers wear black wigs and Walkmans, and a talented boy is labeled "the Indian JFK" and ridiculed by his sister when he speaks of "Mother Earth and Father Sky."

Christine's "brother," Lee, is the son of Ida and Willard Pretty Dog. A warrior, Willard has come home … with hideous scars and no hero's welcome, taken in like a refugee by Ida. Out of pride, Ida has ultimately rejected Willard and never acknowledged him as her son's father. Thus while Christine mistakenly believes Ida to be her mother and Lee her brother, neither Christine nor Lee can claim a father. Noting her differences from Lee, Christine says, "We were so different I wondered if we had the same father…. I studied middle-aged men on the reservation for a clue in their faces." At Lee's funeral, Christine observes, "A woman who was somehow related to us wailed softly," and of the crowd of men she says, "One of them was probably Lee's father, my father, but that was an old question that would never be answered." When Ida finally takes Christine to visit Clara as Clara lies dying in a hospital, Ida drags Christine away quickly, obviously afraid that Clara will confess that she, not Ida, is Christine's mother. Christine, with little time left to live, will never learn the truth of her biological mother, but she will by the end of the novel be accepted once again as a daughter by Ida.

In the third book of the novel, Ida tells her story, and the threads of relationships in the novel become more clear. It is in this book that relationships are also reforged. Christine, who jealously hounded Lee into the military and toward his death, is forgiven by Ida and forgives the bitter old lady in return. Dayton, Lee's best friend, both forgives

Christine and is in turn forgiven. Rayona is reunited with Christine and taken in as a daughter by Dayton, the mixedblood with whom Christine lives out her final days. Father Hurlburt, silent witness and participant in all—who is vaguely part Indian and has learned to speak Ida's language—is there in the end to watch and approve. And most significantly, Ida becomes the novel's supreme storyteller, as befits the Indian grandmother. "I tell my story the way I remember, the way I want," she says, adding:

> I have to tell this story every day, add to it, revise, invent the parts I forget or never knew. No one but me carries it all and no one will—unless I tell Rayona, who might understand. She's heard her mother's side, and she's got eyes. But she doesn't guess what happened before. She doesn't know my true importance. She doesn't realize that I am the story, and that is my savings, to leave her or not….

Within Ida resides the power to abrogate the authority of that "other" discourse assaulting Indians from the media of Euramerica: she can take off her earphones and wig, turn off the television soap operas, and become a story-teller, leaving her "savings"—a recovered sense of self, identity, authenticity—to Rayona.

Though resolution and closure come with a somewhat unpersuasive rapidity and ease in this novel, *A Yellow Raft in Blue Water* moves energetically into Welch's Montana terrain to illuminate the lives of Indians who live on vestiges of tribal identities and reservation fringes, bombarded by video and the American Dream. In choosing to write of a nameless tribe on a nameless reservation, Dorris deliberately emphasizes the ordinariness of these experiences…. Writing in a prose style that inundates the reader with an occasionally annoying plethora of incidental detail, Dorris forces his reader to share his characters' experience of incessant strafing by the foreign and the trivial. The world of permanence and signficance, where every detail must count and be counted … has given way to an Indian Video Village in which alien discourses assert a prior authority and resist, with their privileged cacophony, easy assimilation. The individual who would "be" Indian rather than "play" Indian is faced with an overwhelming challenge.

Source: Louis Owens, "Erdrich and Dorris's Mixedbloods and Multiple Narratives," in *Other Destinies: Understanding the American Indian Novel,* University of Oklahoma Press, 1992, pp. 192–224.

Robert D. Narveson

In the following excerpt, Narveson contends that the narratives given by the three characters are just as perplexing to them as to the reader. Each character is carefully sorting out the over-lapping conflicts in their lives.

It used to be said … that there were few memorable women characters in American fiction. I haven't heard that said lately, but I am reminded of it because Michael Dorris's novel has three memorable women characters as narrators.

This three-generational story unfolds backward. Its narrators, each telling one large chunk of the story, are what we have been persuaded to call Native American, but what they themselves call Indian. The first to narrate is fifteen-year-old Rayona whose father is black but who is raised by her Indian mother, about whom she knows much and doesn't know more; the second is Rayona's wayward mother Christine, who doesn't know anything at all about *her* mother; the third is the woman whom both call Aunt Ida, who raised Christine and keeps the secret of her motherhood.

Who is she really, this non-grandmother who insists on being called Aunt Ida? The question is introduced early by Rayona and answered late by Ida herself. Much of the suspense of the novel comes from waiting to get this and other things straightened out. In a novel, we can be interested in what has happened already, what is happening now, and what will happen. Here, beyond our pleasure in the sharp particularity of what is happening now, the question is less what will happen than what has already happened long before.

Rayona, the fifteen-year-old who narrates first, suffers from feelings of rejection and neglect. Her father comes home rarely; her mother, sick, wrapped up in her own affairs (lots of them), takes her from Seattle to Aunt Ida's on a reservation in Montana and there deserts her. Aunt Ida takes her in, after a fashion. Rayona finds the friendliest refuge of her life while working at a state park where she lives with a warm-hearted middle-aged hippie couple—it's difficult to describe this briefly—who take her to a rodeo where she rides a wild mare for her Indian cousin, who is too drunk to take his turn. Once back together, she and her mother achieve a fragile reconciliation. But her mother's behavior is still a mystery waiting to be cleared up.

At the end of Rayona's section, Christine tells her about the schoolgirl experience because of which she "lost her faith." One New Year's night, she had waited for the world to end, a termination predicted by her imaginative Catholic nun teachers. Next day she had asked why it hadn't happened and was told "It's a *mystery*." Her disillusionment had been extreme: "A *mystery*. The old three-in-one answer. I never went to church again." Christine refers to the experience in her own narration, and Aunt Ida tells it again in hers. Mystery, as I say, is important to the story. Christine goes on to tell us much more that we are entertained to learn and glad to know, but more knowledge can mean not less but more mystery.

"Tell all the truth but tell it slant." So said Emily Dickinson. I do not suppose that these characters could say directly what they think or feel, or that it would be better if they could. Michael Dorris displays confidence in what his fiction can do and how it should do it. The understated scene of reconciliation with which Christine ends her story gets its emotional power (at least for me) from eloquent details ostensibly about other things: "It was a shock to see the dark glasses on my face. The light was so bright and gold I had forgotten I had them on." This example is representative.

This fiction, however, more than most, makes difficult the question of how the story gets told. Each of the women narrates in the first person, but when, and to whom, and why, and in what relation to the narrations of the other two? The narratives hang suspended in space and time. Why and how do Rayona and Christine tell their stories? Is it for their own sakes? Is it because of things about their mothers, and consequently about themselves, they don't feel that they know or understand and want to puzzle out? Not that that's the whole story, but it's central to the mystery that absorbs them. It's why, after meeting Rayona and hearing her story, I want to hear Christine, and after hearing Christine, I wait for Aunt Ida to clear things up, as to an extent she does.

In Aunt Ida's section, the question of narrative stance rises even more insistently. Aunt Ida says, rather too self-consciously, "I have to tell this story every day, add to it, revise, invent the parts I forget or never knew. No one but me carries it all and no one will—unless I tell Rayona, who might understand." We don't observe Aunt Ida telling her story every day, and she's not revising it while we watch (some storytellers, after all, do that). If she's inventing parts she has forgotten or never knew, I, as reader, will never know it. "My recollections are not tied to white paper," she says. "They have the depth of time." So I'm to imagine I'm overhearing her thoughts? The problem with so thinking is that what she says is not tailored to the needs of any audience *she* could imagine. Instead it is tailored to the needs of the audience imagined by the author who has contrived all three narrators. It isn't Aunt Ida's imagined need to tell that makes her story end with this recollection from when Christine was in school:

> "What are you doing?" Father Hurlburt asked.
>
> As a man, he did not identify the rhythm of three strands, the whispering of coming and going, of twisting and tying and blending, of catching and of letting go, of braiding.

The image is lovely, suggesting the intricate intertwining of the lives of the three women. Note also the echo of the "three-in-one" from a passage quoted earlier. The image comments aptly on the three narratives as a whole. Too aptly. The author could hardly be more intrusive if he returned to pre-Jamesian omniscience. The image too evidently serves the narrator's desire to make his thematic point.

I do not suggest that transparent contrivances of this sort obtruded themselves on my consciousness with great frequency as I read. Mostly I read along happily, noting and enjoying the solid particularity of narration. The book is drenched in particularity of motive, of action, of perception. Each character is distinct, each sharply drawn, each living a convincingly human life. Dorris does not focus insistently on the Indian identity of his characters, but makes what is Indian in them contribute to their identities as individuals in a way that seems perfectly natural and taken for granted. It becomes clear before the book's end that what braids together these life stories is place, family, gender, tribe, nation—all those geographical, cultural, and biological determinants that combine with individual passion and will to form unique yet interconnected human lives.

Source: Robert D. Narveson, in a review of *Yellow Raft in Blue Water,* in *Prairie Schooner,* Vol. 63, No. 3, Fall, 1989, pp.126–28.

Sources

Michael Dorris, "A Yellow Raft in Blue Water," in *The New Native American Novel,* Mary Bartlett, ed., University of New Mexico Press, 1986, pp. 93-107. Cited in Hadella (1994) and Owens (1992).

Michael Dorris, "Native American Literature in an Ethnohistorical Context," in *College English,* Vol. 41 October, 1979, pp. 147-62. Cited in Owens (1987).

Paul Hadella, "Michael Anthony Dorris," in *Reference Guide to American Literature,* St. James Press, 1994, pp. 263-65.

Michiko Kakutani, "Multiple Perspectives," *New York Times,* May 9, 1987, p. 17.

Penelope Moffet, review of *A Yellow Raft in Blue Water,* in *Los Angeles Times Book Review,* June 21, 1987, p. 2.

Adalaide Morris, "First Persons Plural in Contemporary Feminist Fiction," *Tulsa Studies in Women's Literature,* Vol. 11, No. 1, Spring, 1992, pp. 11-30.

Robert D. Narveson, review of *A Yellow Raft in Blue Water,* Prairie Schooner, Vol. 63, No. 3, Fall, 1989, pp. 126-28.

Louis Owens, "Acts of Recovery: The American Indian Novel in the '80s," *Western American Literature,* Vol. 23, No.1, Spring, 1987, pp. 55-7.

Louis Owens, "Erdrich and Dorris's Mixedbloods and Multiple Narratives," in *Other Destinies: Understanding the American Indian Novel,* University of Oklahoma Press, 1992, pp. 218-24.

Adrienne Rich, "Notes toward a Politics of Location," in *Blood, Bread, and Poetry: Selected Prose 1979-1985,* Norton, 1986, p. 25. Cited in Morris.

Roger Sale, "American Novels, 1987," a review of nine novels, including *A Yellow Raft in Blue Water,* in *The Massachusetts Review,* Vol. 29, No. 1, Spring, 1988, pp. 71-86.

For Further Study

Hans Bak, "The Kaleidoscope of History: Michael Dorris and Louise Erdrich's *The Crown of Columbus* (with a coda on Gerald Vizenor's *The Heirs of Columbus,*" in *Deferring a Dream: Literary Sub-versions of the American Columbiad,* edited by Gert Buelens and Ernst Rudin, Birkhauser Verlag, 1994, pp. 99-119.

> An analysis of how Dorris's novels rewrite history by including the previously marginalized perspectives of Native Americans.

Anatole Broyard, "Eccentricity Was All They Could Afford," review in *The New York Times Book Review,* June 7, 1987, p.7.

> This review argues that Dorris's excellent writing and complex plot give significance to the otherwise uneventful lives of his characters.

Allan Chavkin and Nancy Feyl Chavkin, editors, *Conversations with Louise Erdrich and Michael Dorris,* University Press of Mississippi, 1994.

> These interviews with Michael Dorris and/or Louise Erdrich, his wife, help explain how Dorris sees his own fiction.

David Cowart, "'The Rhythm of Three Strands': Cultural Braiding in Dorris's *A Yellow Raft in Blue Water,*" in *Studies in American Indian Literatures: The Journal of the Association for the Study of American Indian Literatures,* Vol. 8, No. 1, Spring, 1996, pp. 1-12.

> An analysis of how Dorris's three narrators weave diverse experiences and perspectives into a complex plot.

Louise Erdrich, *Conversations with Louise Erdrich and Michael Dorris,* University Press of Mississippi, 1994.
A more detailed examination of the nature of the unusually close collaboration between these two Native American writers who were also husband and wife.

Louis Owens, "Acts of Recovery: The American Indian Novel in the '80s," in *Western American Literature,* Vol. 22, No. 1, Spring, 1987, pp. 53-57.
This review argues that Dorris's novel contributes to a recent renaissance of excellent, sophisticated Native American fiction.

Ann Rayson, "Shifting Identity in the Work of Louise Erdrich and Michael Dorris," in *Studies in American Indian Literatures: The Journal of the Association for the Study of American Indian Literatures,* Vol. 3, No. 4, Winter, 1991, pp. 27-36.

An analysis of how Dorris's collaboration with his wife, Louise Erdrich, enables him to write about situations from diverse racial and gender perspectives.

Barbara K. Robins, "Michael (Anthony) Dorris," *Dictionary of Native American Literature,,* Garland, 1994, pp. 417-22.
A brief summary of Michael Dorris's life and a general introduction to the themes developed in both his literary and non-literary writings.

Hertha D. Wong, "An Interview with Louise Erdrich and Michael Dorris," in *North Dakota Quarterly,* Vol. 55, No. 1, Winter, 1987, pp. 196-218.
An interview with Michael Dorris and Louise Erdrich, his wife, which describes their collaboration in writing *A Yellow Raft in Blue Water* and explains how some of the material for the novel derives from their personal experiences.

Glossary of Literary Terms

A

Abstract: As an adjective applied to writing or literary works, abstract refers to words or phrases that name things not knowable through the five senses.

Aestheticism: A literary and artistic movement of the nineteenth century. Followers of the movement believed that art should not be mixed with social, political, or moral teaching. The statement "art for art's sake" is a good summary of aestheticism. The movement had its roots in France, but it gained widespread importance in England in the last half of the nineteenth century, where it helped change the Victorian practice of including moral lessons in literature.

Allegory: A narrative technique in which characters representing things or abstract ideas are used to convey a message or teach a lesson. Allegory is typically used to teach moral, ethical, or religious lessons but is sometimes used for satiric or political purposes.

Allusion: A reference to a familiar literary or historical person or event, used to make an idea more easily understood.

Analogy: A comparison of two things made to explain something unfamiliar through its similarities to something familiar, or to prove one point based on the acceptedness of another. Similes and metaphors are types of analogies.

Antagonist: The major character in a narrative or drama who works against the hero or protagonist.

Anthropomorphism: The presentation of animals or objects in human shape or with human characteristics. The term is derived from the Greek word for "human form."

Antihero: A central character in a work of literature who lacks traditional heroic qualities such as courage, physical prowess, and fortitude. Antiheroes typically distrust conventional values and are unable to commit themselves to any ideals. They generally feel helpless in a world over which they have no control. Antiheroes usually accept, and often celebrate, their positions as social outcasts.

Apprenticeship Novel: See *Bildungsroman*

Archetype: The word archetype is commonly used to describe an original pattern or model from which all other things of the same kind are made. This term was introduced to literary criticism from the psychology of Carl Jung. It expresses Jung's theory that behind every person's "unconscious," or repressed memories of the past, lies the "collective unconscious" of the human race: memories of the countless typical experiences of our ancestors. These memories are said to prompt illogical associations that trigger powerful emotions in the reader. Often, the emotional process is primitive, even primordial. Archetypes are the literary images that grow out of the "collective unconscious." They appear in literature as incidents and plots that repeat basic patterns of life. They may also appear as stereotyped characters.

Avant-garde: French term meaning "vanguard." It is used in literary criticism to describe new writing that rejects traditional approaches to literature in favor of innovations in style or content.

B

Beat Movement: A period featuring a group of American poets and novelists of the 1950s and 1960s—including Jack Kerouac, Allen Ginsberg, Gregory Corso, William S. Burroughs, and Lawrence Ferlinghetti—who rejected established social and literary values. Using such techniques as stream of consciousness writing and jazz-influenced free verse and focusing on unusual or abnormal states of mind—generated by religious ecstasy or the use of drugs—the Beat writers aimed to create works that were unconventional in both form and subject matter.

Bildungsroman: A German word meaning "novel of development." The *bildungsroman* is a study of the maturation of a youthful character, typically brought about through a series of social or sexual encounters that lead to self-awareness. *Bildungsroman* is used interchangeably with *erziehungsroman*, a novel of initiation and education. When a *bildungsroman* is concerned with the development of an artist (as in James Joyce's *A Portrait of the Artist as a Young Man*), it is often termed a *kunstlerroman*. Also known as Apprenticeship Novel, Coming of Age Novel, *Erziehungsroman,* or *Kunstlerroman.*

Black Aesthetic Movement: A period of artistic and literary development among African Americans in the 1960s and early 1970s. This was the first major African-American artistic movement since the Harlem Renaissance and was closely paralleled by the civil rights and black power movements. The black aesthetic writers attempted to produce works of art that would be meaningful to the black masses. Key figures in black aesthetics included one of its founders, poet and playwright Amiri Baraka, formerly known as LeRoi Jones; poet and essayist Haki R. Madhubuti, formerly Don L. Lee; poet and playwright Sonia Sanchez; and dramatist Ed Bullins. Also known as Black Arts Movement.

Black Humor: Writing that places grotesque elements side by side with humorous ones in an attempt to shock the reader, forcing him or her to laugh at the horrifying reality of a disordered world. Also known as Black Comedy.

Burlesque: Any literary work that uses exaggeration to make its subject appear ridiculous, either by treating a trivial subject with profound seriousness or by treating a dignified subject frivolously. The word "burlesque" may also be used as an adjective, as in "burlesque show," to mean "striptease act."

C

Character: Broadly speaking, a person in a literary work. The actions of characters are what constitute the plot of a story, novel, or poem. There are numerous types of characters, ranging from simple, stereotypical figures to intricate, multifaceted ones. In the techniques of anthropomorphism and personification, animals—and even places or things—can assume aspects of character. "Characterization" is the process by which an author creates vivid, believable characters in a work of art. This may be done in a variety of ways, including (1) direct description of the character by the narrator; (2) the direct presentation of the speech, thoughts, or actions of the character; and (3) the responses of other characters to the character. The term "character" also refers to a form originated by the ancient Greek writer Theophrastus that later became popular in the seventeenth and eighteenth centuries. It is a short essay or sketch of a person who prominently displays a specific attribute or quality, such as miserliness or ambition.

Climax: The turning point in a narrative, the moment when the conflict is at its most intense. Typically, the structure of stories, novels, and plays is one of rising action, in which tension builds to the climax, followed by falling action, in which tension lessens as the story moves to its conclusion.

Colloquialism: A word, phrase, or form of pronunciation that is acceptable in casual conversation but not in formal, written communication. It is considered more acceptable than slang.

Coming of Age Novel: See *Bildungsroman*

Concrete: Concrete is the opposite of abstract, and refers to a thing that actually exists or a description that allows the reader to experience an object or concept with the senses.

Connotation: The impression that a word gives beyond its defined meaning. Connotations may be universally understood or may be significant only to a certain group.

Convention: Any widely accepted literary device, style, or form.

D

Denotation: The definition of a word, apart from the impressions or feelings it creates (connotations) in the reader.

Denouement: A French word meaning "the unknotting." In literary criticism, it denotes the resolution of conflict in fiction or drama. The *denouement* follows the climax and provides an outcome to the primary plot situation as well as an explanation of secondary plot complications. The *denouement* often involves a character's recognition of his or her state of mind or moral condition. Also known as Falling Action.

Description: Descriptive writing is intended to allow a reader to picture the scene or setting in which the action of a story takes place. The form this description takes often evokes an intended emotional response—a dark, spooky graveyard will evoke fear, and a peaceful, sunny meadow will evoke calmness.

Dialogue: In its widest sense, dialogue is simply conversation between people in a literary work; in its most restricted sense, it refers specifically to the speech of characters in a drama. As a specific literary genre, a "dialogue" is a composition in which characters debate an issue or idea.

Diction: The selection and arrangement of words in a literary work. Either or both may vary depending on the desired effect. There are four general types of diction: "formal," used in scholarly or lofty writing; "informal," used in relaxed but educated conversation; "colloquial," used in everyday speech; and "slang," containing newly coined words and other terms not accepted in formal usage.

Didactic: A term used to describe works of literature that aim to teach some moral, religious, political, or practical lesson. Although didactic elements are often found in artistically pleasing works, the term "didactic" usually refers to literature in which the message is more important than the form. The term may also be used to criticize a work that the critic finds "overly didactic," that is, heavy-handed in its delivery of a lesson.

Doppelganger: A literary technique by which a character is duplicated (usually in the form of an alter ego, though sometimes as a ghostly counterpart) or divided into two distinct, usually opposite personalities. The use of this character device is widespread in nineteenth- and twentieth-century literature, and indicates a growing awareness among authors that the "self" is really a composite of many "selves." Also known as The Double.

Double Entendre: A corruption of a French phrase meaning "double meaning." The term is used to indicate a word or phrase that is deliberately ambiguous, especially when one of the meanings is risqué or improper.

Dramatic Irony: Occurs when the audience of a play or the reader of a work of literature knows something that a character in the work itself does not know. The irony is in the contrast between the intended meaning of the statements or actions of a character and the additional information understood by the audience.

Dystopia: An imaginary place in a work of fiction where the characters lead dehumanized, fearful lives.

E

Edwardian: Describes cultural conventions identified with the period of the reign of Edward VII of England (1901-1910). Writers of the Edwardian Age typically displayed a strong reaction against the propriety and conservatism of the Victorian Age. Their work often exhibits distrust of authority in religion, politics, and art and expresses strong doubts about the soundness of conventional values.

Empathy: A sense of shared experience, including emotional and physical feelings, with someone or something other than oneself. Empathy is often used to describe the response of a reader to a literary character.

Enlightenment, The: An eighteenth-century philosophical movement. It began in France but had a wide impact throughout Europe and America. Thinkers of the Enlightenment valued reason and believed that both the individual and society could achieve a state of perfection. Corresponding to this essentially humanist vision was a resistance to religious authority.

Epigram: A saying that makes the speaker's point quickly and concisely. Often used to preface a novel.

Epilogue: A concluding statement or section of a literary work. In dramas, particularly those of the seventeenth and eighteenth centuries, the epilogue is a closing speech, often in verse, delivered by an actor at the end of a play and spoken directly to the audience.

Epiphany: A sudden revelation of truth inspired by a seemingly trivial incident.

Episode: An incident that forms part of a story and is significantly related to it. Episodes may be either self-contained narratives or events that depend on a larger context for their sense and importance.

Epistolary Novel: A novel in the form of letters. The form was particularly popular in the eighteenth century.

Epithet: A word or phrase, often disparaging or abusive, that expresses a character trait of someone or something.

Existentialism: A predominantly twentieth-century philosophy concerned with the nature and perception of human existence. There are two major strains of existentialist thought: atheistic and Christian. Followers of atheistic existentialism believe that the individual is alone in a godless universe and that the basic human condition is one of suffering and loneliness. Nevertheless, because there are no fixed values, individuals can create their own characters—indeed, they can shape themselves—through the exercise of free will. The atheistic strain culminates in and is popularly associated with the works of Jean-Paul Sartre. The Christian existentialists, on the other hand, believe that only in God may people find freedom from life's anguish. The two strains hold certain beliefs in common: that existence cannot be fully understood or described through empirical effort; that anguish is a universal element of life; that individuals must bear responsibility for their actions; and that there is no common standard of behavior or perception for religious and ethical matters.

Expatriates: See *Expatriatism*

Expatriatism: The practice of leaving one's country to live for an extended period in another country.

Exposition: Writing intended to explain the nature of an idea, thing, or theme. Expository writing is often combined with description, narration, or argument. In dramatic writing, the exposition is the introductory material which presents the characters, setting, and tone of the play.

Expressionism: An indistinct literary term, originally used to describe an early twentieth-century school of German painting. The term applies to almost any mode of unconventional, highly subjective writing that distorts reality in some way.

F

Fable: A prose or verse narrative intended to convey a moral. Animals or inanimate objects with human characteristics often serve as characters in fables.

Falling Action: See *Denouement*

Fantasy: A literary form related to mythology and folklore. Fantasy literature is typically set in non-existent realms and features supernatural beings.

Farce: A type of comedy characterized by broad humor, outlandish incidents, and often vulgar subject matter.

Femme fatale: A French phrase with the literal translation "fatal woman." A *femme fatale* is a sensuous, alluring woman who often leads men into danger or trouble.

Fiction: Any story that is the product of imagination rather than a documentation of fact. Characters and events in such narratives may be based in real life but their ultimate form and configuration is a creation of the author.

Figurative Language: A technique in writing in which the author temporarily interrupts the order, construction, or meaning of the writing for a particular effect. This interruption takes the form of one or more figures of speech such as hyperbole, irony, or simile. Figurative language is the opposite of literal language, in which every word is truthful, accurate, and free of exaggeration or embellishment.

Figures of Speech: Writing that differs from customary conventions for construction, meaning, order, or significance for the purpose of a special meaning or effect. There are two major types of figures of speech: rhetorical figures, which do not make changes in the meaning of the words, and tropes, which do.

Fin de siecle: A French term meaning "end of the century." The term is used to denote the last decade of the nineteenth century, a transition period when writers and other artists abandoned old conventions and looked for new techniques and objectives.

First Person: See *Point of View*

Flashback: A device used in literature to present action that occurred before the beginning of the story. Flashbacks are often introduced as the dreams or recollections of one or more characters.

Foil: A character in a work of literature whose physical or psychological qualities contrast strongly with, and therefore highlight, the corresponding qualities of another character.

Folklore: Traditions and myths preserved in a culture or group of people. Typically, these are passed on by word of mouth in various forms—such as legends, songs, and proverbs—or preserved in customs and ceremonies. This term was first used by W. J. Thoms in 1846.

Folktale: A story originating in oral tradition. Folktales fall into a variety of categories, including legends, ghost stories, fairy tales, fables, and anecdotes based on historical figures and events.

Foreshadowing: A device used in literature to create expectation or to set up an explanation of later developments.

Form: The pattern or construction of a work which identifies its genre and distinguishes it from other genres.

G

Genre: A category of literary work. In critical theory, genre may refer to both the content of a given work—tragedy, comedy, pastoral—and to its form, such as poetry, novel, or drama.

Gilded Age: A period in American history during the 1870s characterized by political corruption and materialism. A number of important novels of social and political criticism were written during this time.

Gothicism: In literary criticism, works characterized by a taste for the medieval or morbidly attractive. A gothic novel prominently features elements of horror, the supernatural, gloom, and violence: clanking chains, terror, charnel houses, ghosts, medieval castles, and mysteriously slamming doors. The term "gothic novel" is also applied to novels that lack elements of the traditional Gothic setting but that create a similar atmosphere of terror or dread.

Grotesque: In literary criticism, the subject matter of a work or a style of expression characterized by exaggeration, deformity, freakishness, and disorder. The grotesque often includes an element of comic absurdity.

H

Harlem Renaissance: The Harlem Renaissance of the 1920s is generally considered the first significant movement of black writers and artists in the United States. During this period, new and established black writers published more fiction and poetry than ever before, the first influential black literary journals were established, and black authors and artists received their first widespread recognition and serious critical appraisal. Among the major writers associated with this period are Claude McKay, Jean Toomer, Countee Cullen, Langston Hughes, Arna Bontemps, Nella Larsen, and Zora Neale Hurston. Also known as Negro Renaissance and New Negro Movement.

Hero/Heroine: The principal sympathetic character (male or female) in a literary work. Heroes and heroines typically exhibit admirable traits: idealism, courage, and integrity, for example.

Holocaust Literature: Literature influenced by or written about the Holocaust of World War II. Such literature includes true stories of survival in concentration camps, escape, and life after the war, as well as fictional works and poetry.

Humanism: A philosophy that places faith in the dignity of humankind and rejects the medieval perception of the individual as a weak, fallen creature. "Humanists" typically believe in the perfectibility of human nature and view reason and education as the means to that end.

Hyperbole: In literary criticism, deliberate exaggeration used to achieve an effect.

I

Idiom: A word construction or verbal expression closely associated with a given language.

Image: A concrete representation of an object or sensory experience. Typically, such a representation helps evoke the feelings associated with the object or experience itself. Images are either "literal" or "figurative." Literal images are especially concrete and involve little or no extension of the obvious meaning of the words used to express them. Figurative images do not follow the literal meaning of the words exactly. Images in literature are usually visual, but the term "image" can also refer to the representation of any sensory experience.

Imagery: The array of images in a literary work. Also, figurative language.

In medias res: A Latin term meaning "in the middle of things." It refers to the technique of beginning a story at its midpoint and then using various flashback devices to reveal previous action.

Interior Monologue: A narrative technique in which characters' thoughts are revealed in a way that appears to be uncontrolled by the author. The interior monologue typically aims to reveal the inner self of a character. It portrays emotional experiences as they occur at both a conscious and unconscious level. Images are often used to represent sensations or emotions.

Irony: In literary criticism, the effect of language in which the intended meaning is the opposite of what is stated.

J

Jargon: Language that is used or understood only by a select group of people. Jargon may refer to terminology used in a certain profession, such as computer jargon, or it may refer to any nonsensical language that is not understood by most people.

L

Leitmotiv: See *Motif*

Literal Language: An author uses literal language when he or she writes without exaggerating or embellishing the subject matter and without any tools of figurative language.

Lost Generation: A term first used by Gertrude Stein to describe the post-World War I generation of American writers: men and women haunted by a sense of betrayal and emptiness brought about by the destructiveness of the war.

M

Mannerism: Exaggerated, artificial adherence to a literary manner or style. Also, a popular style of the visual arts of late sixteenth-century Europe that was marked by elongation of the human form and by intentional spatial distortion. Literary works that are self-consciously high-toned and artistic are often said to be "mannered."

Metaphor: A figure of speech that expresses an idea through the image of another object. Metaphors suggest the essence of the first object by identifying it with certain qualities of the second object.

Modernism: Modern literary practices. Also, the principles of a literary school that lasted from roughly the beginning of the twentieth century until the end of World War II. Modernism is defined by its rejection of the literary conventions of the nineteenth century and by its opposition to conventional morality, taste, traditions, and economic values.

Mood: The prevailing emotions of a work or of the author in his or her creation of the work. The mood of a work is not always what might be expected based on its subject matter.

Motif: A theme, character type, image, metaphor, or other verbal element that recurs throughout a single work of literature or occurs in a number of different works over a period of time. Also known as *Motiv* or *Leitmotiv.*

Myth: An anonymous tale emerging from the traditional beliefs of a culture or social unit. Myths use supernatural explanations for natural phenomena. They may also explain cosmic issues like creation and death. Collections of myths, known as mythologies, are common to all cultures and nations, but the best-known myths belong to the Norse, Roman, and Greek mythologies.

N

Narration: The telling of a series of events, real or invented. A narration may be either a simple narrative, in which the events are recounted chronologically, or a narrative with a plot, in which the account is given in a style reflecting the author's artistic concept of the story. Narration is sometimes used as a synonym for "storyline."

Narrative: A verse or prose accounting of an event or sequence of events, real or invented. The term is also used as an adjective in the sense "method of narration." For example, in literary criticism, the expression "narrative technique" usually refers to the way the author structures and presents his or her story.

Narrator: The teller of a story. The narrator may be the author or a character in the story through whom the author speaks.

Naturalism: A literary movement of the late nineteenth and early twentieth centuries. The movement's major theorist, French novelist Emile Zola, envisioned a type of fiction that would examine human life with the objectivity of scientific inquiry. The Naturalists typically viewed human beings as either the products of "biological determinism," ruled by hereditary instincts and engaged in an endless struggle for survival, or as the products of "socioeconomic determinism," ruled by social and economic forces beyond their control. In their works, the Naturalists generally ignored the highest levels of society and focused on degradation: poverty, alcoholism, prostitution, insanity, and disease.

Noble Savage: The idea that primitive man is noble and good but becomes evil and corrupted as he becomes civilized. The concept of the noble savage originated in the Renaissance period but is more closely identified with such later writers as

Jean-Jacques Rousseau and Aphra Behn. See also Primitivism.

Novel of Ideas: A novel in which the examination of intellectual issues and concepts takes precedence over characterization or a traditional storyline.

Novel of Manners: A novel that examines the customs and mores of a cultural group.

Novel: A long fictional narrative written in prose, which developed from the novella and other early forms of narrative. A novel is usually organized under a plot or theme with a focus on character development and action.

Novella: An Italian term meaning "story." This term has been especially used to describe fourteenth-century Italian tales, but it also refers to modern short novels.

O

Objective Correlative: An outward set of objects, a situation, or a chain of events corresponding to an inward experience and evoking this experience in the reader. The term frequently appears in modern criticism in discussions of authors' intended effects on the emotional responses of readers.

Objectivity: A quality in writing characterized by the absence of the author's opinion or feeling about the subject matter. Objectivity is an important factor in criticism.

Oedipus Complex: A son's amorous obsession with his mother. The phrase is derived from the story of the ancient Theban hero Oedipus, who unknowingly killed his father and married his mother.

Omniscience: See *Point of View*

Onomatopoeia: The use of words whose sounds express or suggest their meaning. In its simplest sense, onomatopoeia may be represented by words that mimic the sounds they denote such as "hiss" or "meow." At a more subtle level, the pattern and rhythm of sounds and rhymes of a line or poem may be onomatopoeic.

Oxymoron: A phrase combining two contradictory terms. Oxymorons may be intentional or unintentional.

P

Parable: A story intended to teach a moral lesson or answer an ethical question.

Paradox: A statement that appears illogical or contradictory at first, but may actually point to an underlying truth.

Parallelism: A method of comparison of two ideas in which each is developed in the same grammatical structure.

Parody: In literary criticism, this term refers to an imitation of a serious literary work or the signature style of a particular author in a ridiculous manner. A typical parody adopts the style of the original and applies it to an inappropriate subject for humorous effect. Parody is a form of satire and could be considered the literary equivalent of a caricature or cartoon.

Pastoral: A term derived from the Latin word "pastor," meaning shepherd. A pastoral is a literary composition on a rural theme. The conventions of the pastoral were originated by the third-century Greek poet Theocritus, who wrote about the experiences, love affairs, and pastimes of Sicilian shepherds. In a pastoral, characters and language of a courtly nature are often placed in a simple setting. The term pastoral is also used to classify dramas, elegies, and lyrics that exhibit the use of country settings and shepherd characters.

Pen Name: See *Pseudonym*

Persona: A Latin term meaning "mask." *Personae* are the characters in a fictional work of literature. The *persona* generally functions as a mask through which the author tells a story in a voice other than his or her own. A *persona* is usually either a character in a story who acts as a narrator or an "implied author," a voice created by the author to act as the narrator for himself or herself.

Personification: A figure of speech that gives human qualities to abstract ideas, animals, and inanimate objects. Also known as *Prosopopoeia*.

Picaresque Novel: Episodic fiction depicting the adventures of a roguish central character ("picaro" is Spanish for "rogue"). The picaresque hero is commonly a low-born but clever individual who wanders into and out of various affairs of love, danger, and farcical intrigue. These involvements may take place at all social levels and typically present a humorous and wide-ranging satire of a given society.

Plagiarism: Claiming another person's written material as one's own. Plagiarism can take the form of direct, word-for-word copying or the theft of the substance or idea of the work.

Plot: In literary criticism, this term refers to the pattern of events in a narrative or drama. In its simplest sense, the plot guides the author in composing the work and helps the reader follow the work. Typically, plots exhibit causality and unity and have a beginning, a middle, and an end. Sometimes, however, a plot may consist of a series of disconnected events, in which case it is known as an "episodic plot."

Poetic Justice: An outcome in a literary work, not necessarily a poem, in which the good are rewarded and the evil are punished, especially in ways that particularly fit their virtues or crimes.

Poetic License: Distortions of fact and literary convention made by a writer—not always a poet—for the sake of the effect gained. Poetic license is closely related to the concept of "artistic freedom."

Poetics: This term has two closely related meanings. It denotes (1) an aesthetic theory in literary criticism about the essence of poetry or (2) rules prescribing the proper methods, content, style, or diction of poetry. The term poetics may also refer to theories about literature in general, not just poetry.

Point of View: The narrative perspective from which a literary work is presented to the reader. There are four traditional points of view. The "third person omniscient" gives the reader a "godlike" perspective, unrestricted by time or place, from which to see actions and look into the minds of characters. This allows the author to comment openly on characters and events in the work. The "third person" point of view presents the events of the story from outside of any single character's perception, much like the omniscient point of view, but the reader must understand the action as it takes place and without any special insight into characters' minds or motivations. The "first person" or "personal" point of view relates events as they are perceived by a single character. The main character "tells" the story and may offer opinions about the action and characters which differ from those of the author. Much less common than omniscient, third person, and first person is the "second person" point of view, wherein the author tells the story as if it is happening to the reader.

Polemic: A work in which the author takes a stand on a controversial subject, such as abortion or religion. Such works are often extremely argumentative or provocative.

Pornography: Writing intended to provoke feelings of lust in the reader. Such works are often condemned by critics and teachers, but those which can be shown to have literary value are viewed less harshly.

Post-Aesthetic Movement: An artistic response made by African Americans to the black aesthetic

movement of the 1960s and early '70s. Writers since that time have adopted a somewhat different tone in their work, with less emphasis placed on the disparity between black and white in the United States. In the words of post-aesthetic authors such as Toni Morrison, John Edgar Wideman, and Kristin Hunter, African Americans are portrayed as looking inward for answers to their own questions, rather than always looking to the outside world.

Postmodernism: Writing from the 1960s forward characterized by experimentation and continuing to apply some of the fundamentals of modernism, which included existentialism and alienation. Postmodernists have gone a step further in the rejection of tradition begun with the modernists by also rejecting traditional forms, preferring the anti-novel over the novel and the antihero over the hero.

Primitivism: The belief that primitive peoples were nobler and less flawed than civilized peoples because they had not been subjected to the tainting influence of society. See also Noble Savage.

Prologue: An introductory section of a literary work. It often contains information establishing the situation of the characters or presents information about the setting, time period, or action. In drama, the prologue is spoken by a chorus or by one of the principal characters.

Prose: A literary medium that attempts to mirror the language of everyday speech. It is distinguished from poetry by its use of unmetered, unrhymed language consisting of logically related sentences. Prose is usually grouped into paragraphs that form a cohesive whole such as an essay or a novel.

Prosopopoeia: See *Personification*

Protagonist: The central character of a story who serves as a focus for its themes and incidents and as the principal rationale for its development. The protagonist is sometimes referred to in discussions of modern literature as the hero or antihero.

Protest Fiction: Protest fiction has as its primary purpose the protesting of some social injustice, such as racism or discrimination.

Proverb: A brief, sage saying that expresses a truth about life in a striking manner.

Pseudonym: A name assumed by a writer, most often intended to prevent his or her identification as the author of a work. Two or more authors may work together under one pseudonym, or an author may use a different name for each genre he or she publishes in. Some publishing companies maintain "house pseudonyms," under which any number of authors may write installations in a series. Some authors also choose a pseudonym over their real names the way an actor may use a stage name.

Pun: A play on words that have similar sounds but different meanings.

R

Realism: A nineteenth-century European literary movement that sought to portray familiar characters, situations, and settings in a realistic manner. This was done primarily by using an objective narrative point of view and through the buildup of accurate detail. The standard for success of any realistic work depends on how faithfully it transfers common experience into fictional forms. The realistic method may be altered or extended, as in stream of consciousness writing, to record highly subjective experience.

Repartee: Conversation featuring snappy retorts and witticisms.

Resolution: The portion of a story following the climax, in which the conflict is resolved. See also *Denouement.*

Rhetoric: In literary criticism, this term denotes the art of ethical persuasion. In its strictest sense, rhetoric adheres to various principles developed since classical times for arranging facts and ideas in a clear, persuasive, appealing manner. The term is also used to refer to effective prose in general and theories of or methods for composing effective prose.

Rhetorical Question: A question intended to provoke thought, but not an expressed answer, in the reader. It is most commonly used in oratory and other persuasive genres.

Rising Action: The part of a drama where the plot becomes increasingly complicated. Rising action leads up to the climax, or turning point, of a drama.

Roman a clef: A French phrase meaning "novel with a key." It refers to a narrative in which real persons are portrayed under fictitious names.

Romance: A broad term, usually denoting a narrative with exotic, exaggerated, often idealized characters, scenes, and themes.

Romanticism: This term has two widely accepted meanings. In historical criticism, it refers to a European intellectual and artistic movement of the late eighteenth and early nineteenth centuries that sought greater freedom of personal expression than that allowed by the strict rules of literary form and logic of the eighteenth-century neoclassicists. The Romantics preferred emotional and imaginative expression to rational analysis. They considered the individual to be at the center of all experience and so placed him or her at the center of their art. The Romantics believed that the creative imagination reveals nobler truths—unique feelings and attitudes—than those that could be discovered by logic or by scientific examination. Both the natural world and the state of childhood were important sources for revelations of "eternal truths." "Romanticism" is also used as a general term to refer to a type of sensibility found in all periods of literary history and usually considered to be in opposition to the principles of classicism. In this sense, Romanticism signifies any work or philosophy in which the exotic or dreamlike figure strongly, or that is devoted to individualistic expression, self-analysis, or a pursuit of a higher realm of knowledge than can be discovered by human reason.

Romantics: See *Romanticism*

S

Satire: A work that uses ridicule, humor, and wit to criticize and provoke change in human nature and institutions. There are two major types of satire: "formal" or "direct" satire speaks directly to the reader or to a character in the work; "indirect" satire relies upon the ridiculous behavior of its characters to make its point. Formal satire is further divided into two manners: the "Horatian," which ridicules gently, and the "Juvenalian," which derides its subjects harshly and bitterly.

Science Fiction: A type of narrative about or based upon real or imagined scientific theories and technology. Science fiction is often peopled with alien creatures and set on other planets or in different dimensions.

Second Person: See *Point of View*

Setting: The time, place, and culture in which the action of a narrative takes place. The elements of setting may include geographic location, characters' physical and mental environments, prevailing cultural attitudes, or the historical time in which the action takes place.

Simile: A comparison, usually using "like" or "as", of two essentially dissimilar things, as in "coffee as cold as ice" or "He sounded like a broken record."

Slang: A type of informal verbal communication that is generally unacceptable for formal writing. Slang words and phrases are often colorful exaggerations used to emphasize the speaker's point; they may also be shortened versions of an often-used word or phrase.

Slave Narrative: Autobiographical accounts of American slave life as told by escaped slaves. These works first appeared during the abolition movement of the 1830s through the 1850s.

Socialist Realism: The Socialist Realism school of literary theory was proposed by Maxim Gorky and established as a dogma by the first Soviet Congress of Writers. It demanded adherence to a communist worldview in works of literature. Its doctrines required an objective viewpoint comprehensible to the working classes and themes of social struggle featuring strong proletarian heroes. Also known as Social Realism.

Stereotype: A stereotype was originally the name for a duplication made during the printing process; this led to its modern definition as a person or thing that is (or is assumed to be) the same as all others of its type.

Stream of Consciousness: A narrative technique for rendering the inward experience of a character. This technique is designed to give the impression of an ever-changing series of thoughts, emotions, images, and memories in the spontaneous and seemingly illogical order that they occur in life.

Structure: The form taken by a piece of literature. The structure may be made obvious for ease of understanding, as in nonfiction works, or may obscured for artistic purposes, as in some poetry or seemingly "unstructured" prose.

Sturm und Drang: A German term meaning "storm and stress." It refers to a German literary movement of the 1770s and 1780s that reacted against the order and rationalism of the enlightenment, focusing instead on the intense experience of extraordinary individuals.

Style: A writer's distinctive manner of arranging words to suit his or her ideas and purpose in writing. The unique imprint of the author's personality upon his or her writing, style is the product of an author's way of arranging ideas and his or her use of diction, different sentence structures, rhythm, figures of speech, rhetorical principles, and other elements of composition.

Subjectivity: Writing that expresses the author's personal feelings about his subject, and which may or may not include factual information about the subject.

Subplot: A secondary story in a narrative. A subplot may serve as a motivating or complicating force for the main plot of the work, or it may provide emphasis for, or relief from, the main plot.

Surrealism: A term introduced to criticism by Guillaume Apollinaire and later adopted by Andre Breton. It refers to a French literary and artistic movement founded in the 1920s. The Surrealists sought to express unconscious thoughts and feelings in their works. The best-known technique used for achieving this aim was automatic writing—transcriptions of spontaneous outpourings from the unconscious. The Surrealists proposed to unify the contrary levels of conscious and unconscious, dream and reality, objectivity and subjectivity into a new level of "super-realism."

Suspense: A literary device in which the author maintains the audience's attention through the buildup of events, the outcome of which will soon be revealed.

Symbol: Something that suggests or stands for something else without losing its original identity. In literature, symbols combine their literal meaning with the suggestion of an abstract concept. Literary symbols are of two types: those that carry complex associations of meaning no matter what their contexts, and those that derive their suggestive meaning from their functions in specific literary works.

Symbolism: This term has two widely accepted meanings. In historical criticism, it denotes an early modernist literary movement initiated in France during the nineteenth century that reacted against the prevailing standards of realism. Writers in this movement aimed to evoke, indirectly and symbolically, an order of being beyond the material world of the five senses. Poetic expression of personal emotion figured strongly in the movement, typically by means of a private set of symbols uniquely identifiable with the individual poet. The principal aim of the Symbolists was to express in words the highly complex feelings that grew out of everyday contact with the world. In a broader sense, the term "symbolism" refers to the use of one object to represent another.

T

Tall Tale: A humorous tale told in a straightforward, credible tone but relating absolutely impossible events or feats of the characters. Such tales were commonly told of frontier adventures during the settlement of the west in the United States.

Theme: The main point of a work of literature. The term is used interchangeably with thesis.

Thesis: A thesis is both an essay and the point argued in the essay. Thesis novels and thesis plays share the quality of containing a thesis which is supported through the action of the story.

Third Person: See *Point of View*

Tone: The author's attitude toward his or her audience may be deduced from the tone of the work. A formal tone may create distance or convey politeness, while an informal tone may encourage a friendly, intimate, or intrusive feeling in the reader. The author's attitude toward his or her subject matter may also be deduced from the tone of the words he or she uses in discussing it.

Transcendentalism: An American philosophical and religious movement, based in New England from around 1835 until the Civil War. Transcendentalism was a form of American romanticism that had its roots abroad in the works of Thomas Carlyle, Samuel Coleridge, and Johann Wolfgang von Goethe. The Transcendentalists stressed the importance of intuition and subjective experience in communication with God. They rejected religious dogma and texts in favor of mysticism and scientific naturalism. They pursued truths that lie beyond the "colorless" realms perceived by reason and the senses and were active social reformers in public education, women's rights, and the abolition of slavery.

U

Urban Realism: A branch of realist writing that attempts to accurately reflect the often harsh facts of modern urban existence.

Utopia: A fictional perfect place, such as "paradise" or "heaven."

V

Verisimilitude: Literally, the appearance of truth. In literary criticism, the term refers to aspects of a work of literature that seem true to the reader.

Victorian: Refers broadly to the reign of Queen Victoria of England (1837-1901) and to anything with qualities typical of that era. For example, the qualities of smug narrowmindedness, bourgeois materialism, faith in social progress, and priggish morality are often considered Victorian. This stereotype is contradicted by such dramatic intellectual developments as the theories of Charles Darwin, Karl Marx, and Sigmund Freud (which stirred strong debates in England) and the critical attitudes of serious Victorian writers like Charles Dickens and George Eliot. In literature, the Victorian Period was the great age of the English novel, and the latter part of the era saw the rise of movements such as decadence and symbolism. Also known as Victorian Age and Victorian Period.

W

Weltanschauung: A German term referring to a person's worldview or philosophy.

Weltschmerz: A German term meaning "world pain." It describes a sense of anguish about the nature of existence, usually associated with a melancholy, pessimistic attitude.

Z

Zeitgeist: A German term meaning "spirit of the time." It refers to the moral and intellectual trends of a given era.

Cumulative Author/Title Index

Cumulative
Nationality/Ethnicity Index

Blair, Eric Arthur
   Animal Farm: V3
Brontë, Emily
   Wuthering Heights: V2
Conrad, Joseph
   Heart of Darkness: V2
Forster, E. M.
   A Passage to India: V3
Golding, William
   Lord of the Flies: V2
Hardy, Thomas
   Tess of the d'Urbervilles: V3
Orwell, George
   Animal Farm: V3
Shelley, Mary
   Frankenstein: V1

Canadian

Kogawa, Joy
   Obasan: V3

Colombian

García Márquez, Gabriel
   Love in the Time of Cholera: V1

Hispanic American

Cisneros, Sandra
   The House on Mango Street: V2

Native American

Dorris, Michael
   A Yellow Raft in Blue Water: V3

Nigerian

Achebe, Chinua
   Things Fall Apart: V3

Russian

Dostoyevsky, Fyodor
   Crime and Punishment: V3

South African

Paton, Alan
   Cry, the Beloved Country: V3

West Indian

Kincaid, Jamaica
   Annie John: V3

Subject/Theme Index

Subject/Theme Index